BY
THE
PEOPLE

BY THE PEOPLE

DEBATING AMERICAN GOVERNMENT

Brief Second Edition

JAMES A. MORONE
Brown University

ROGAN KERSH
Wake Forest University

NEW YORK OXFORD
OXFORD UNIVERSITY PRESS

Oxford University Press is a department of the University of Oxford.
It furthers the University's objective of excellence in research, scholarship,
and education by publishing worldwide.

Oxford   New York
Auckland   Cape Town   Dar es Salaam   Hong Kong   Karachi
Kuala Lumpur   Madrid   Melbourne   Mexico City   Nairobi
New Delhi   Shanghai   Taipei   Toronto

With offices in
Argentina   Austria   Brazil   Chile   Czech Republic   France   Greece
Guatemala   Hungary   Italy   Japan   Poland   Portugal   Singapore
South Korea   Switzerland   Thailand   Turkey   Ukraine   Vietnam
Copyright © 2016, 2014 by Oxford University Press.

For titles covered by Section 112 of the US Higher Education
Opportunity Act, please visit www.oup.com/us/he for the
latest information about pricing and alternate formats.

Published in the United States of America by
Oxford University Press
198 Madison Avenue, New York, NY 10016
http://www.oup.com

Oxford is a registered trade mark of Oxford University Press.

Cataloging-in-Publication Data is on file with the Library of Congress

ISBN 978-0-19-021673-3

Printing number: 9 8 7 6 5 4 3 2 1

Printed in the United States of America
on acid-free paper

Many teachers and colleagues inspired us. We dedicate this book to four who changed our lives. Their passion for learning and teaching set the standard we aim for every day—and on every page that follows.

Richard O'Donnell
Murray Dry
Jim Barefield
Rogers Smith

The title of the book comes from the Gettysburg Address. Standing on the battle-field at Gettysburg, President Abraham Lincoln delivered what may be the most beautiful presidential address in American history—defining American government as a government "of the people, by the people, for the people." Here is the full address.

Four score and seven years ago our fathers brought forth on this continent, a new nation, conceived in Liberty, and dedicated to the proposition that all men are created equal.

Now we are engaged in a great civil war, testing whether that nation, or any nation so conceived and so dedicated, can long endure. We are met on a great battle-field of that war. We have come to dedicate a portion of that field, as a final resting place for those who here gave their lives that that nation might live. It is altogether fitting and proper that we should do this.

But, in a larger sense, we can not dedicate—we can not consecrate—we can not hallow—this ground. The brave men, living and dead, who struggled here, have consecrated it, far above our poor power to add or detract. The world will little note, nor long remember what we say here, but it can never forget what they did here. It is for us the living, rather, to be dedicated here to the unfinished work which they who fought here have thus far so nobly advanced. It is rather for us to be here dedicated to the great task remaining before us—that from these honored dead we take increased devotion to that cause for which they gave the last full measure of devotion—that we here highly resolve that these dead shall not have died in vain—that this nation, under God, shall have a new birth of freedom—and that government of the people, by the people, for the people, shall not perish from the earth.

Brief Contents

Contents

About the Authors

JAMES MORONE (BA, Middlebury College, and MA and PhD, University of Chicago) is the John Hazen White Professor of Political Science and Public Policy at Brown University and five-time winner of the Hazeltine Citation for outstanding teacher of the year. Dr. Morone, an award-winning author, has published ten books, including *The Devils We Know* (2014), *The Heart of Power* (2009, a New York Times Notable Book), *Hellfire Nation* (2003, nominated for a Pulitzer Prize), and *The Democratic Wish* (1990, winner of the American Political Science Association's Kammerer Award as the best book on American politics and a New York Times Notable Book of the Year). Dr. Morone served as president of the politics and history section of the American Political Science Association and the New England Political Science Association. He has been on the board of editors for eight scholarly journals, has written more than 150 articles and essays, and comments on politics in the *New York Times*, the *London Review of Books*, and the *American Prospect*. He is currently the chair of the Brown University faculty and serves as director of the Brown Public Policy Center.

ROGAN KERSH (BA, Wake Forest University, and MA and PhD, Yale) is Provost and Professor of Political Science at Wake Forest University. A leading scholar in American political science, Dr. Kersh is best known for his work on health reform, obesity politics, and interest groups and lobbying. As a political science faculty member at Syracuse University from 1996 to 2006, he won three different teaching awards; from 2006 to 2012, as Associate Dean of New York University's Wagner School of Public Service, he won both Wagner and NYU-wide teaching awards, as well as the Martin Luther King Jr. Award for scholarship, teaching, and university service. Dr. Kersh has published two books and more than fifty academic articles and has provided commentary on U.S. politics for dozens of different media outlets including CNN, *Newsweek*, and the *New York Times*. He was president of the American Political Science Association's organized section on health politics and policy in 2011–2012 and is an elected fellow of the National Academy of Public Administration.

Preface

At first, they came in small numbers: one child, two children, a few huddled together. Then a surge: In the spring and summer of 2014, tens of thousands of unaccompanied minors crossed the Mexican border into the United States. The exhausted children—mostly from Honduras, Guatemala, and El Salvador—faced poverty and violence at home. Together, this was a humanitarian tragedy. But it was also a political problem.

Conservative critics of the Barack Obama administration slammed the White House for not acting sooner to stem the tide and for being "soft on immigration." From the left, another set of voices condemned the president for not providing services to children whose families were so desperate they would send them alone across dangerous ground to an uncertain destiny. Whatever course the administration took, it faced angry rebukes.

As partisans traded insults and pundits criticized the government's mistakes, something remarkable happened. Americans of all backgrounds came together to help the children. College students and local residents joined to hand out medical kits and food packets. Lawyers flew in to offer free legal assistance in securing asylum. Church leaders created makeshift shelters and organized short-term housing among the congregants. One bishop in San Antonio, Texas, said the crisis had deepened his prayer life. This is a classic story that runs right through American history: People pull together in the face of troubled times.

Help or Clash?

That's the United States in a nutshell. People pitch in. This is a nation of joiners and helpers and activists. It always has been. Visitors in the nineteenth century were astonished by the nation's civic spirit. To this day Americans form book groups, organize car washes to raise money for good causes, stack sandbags during floods, send checks to the Red Cross, support the military, and insist that the government help those who need help. "We are inevitably our brother's keeper because we are our brother's brother," wrote Martin Luther King. "Whatever affects one directly affects all indirectly."[1]

But that's only one side of the story. Stream a news show and what do you see? Fights! A few years ago, one of us (Jim) was about to go on a news show to discuss the fallout after singer Janet Jackson inadvertently (and very briefly) went X-rated during the Super Bowl halftime show. Jim was scheduled alongside another commentator who was very agitated about Jackson's behavior and believed that it signaled the decline of America. Jim told the producer that, after exploring our different views, it would be great if we could find some common ground. No way, retorted the producer, who explained her ideal closing shot: You'll be shouting over each other on a split screen while the host coolly ends the segment by saying, "We'll have to leave it there for now, but feelings run high and we'll be hearing a lot more on this topic." Unfortunately, searching for common ground does not draw an audience like people screaming onscreen.

The producer was demonstrating another side of America: rugged individualists push their own views and self-interests. Individualism is also an all-American story. Its origins lie in a frontier culture that expected everyone to watch out for him or herself. This is the America that resents anyone—especially the government—telling people what to do.

Which is the real America? They both are. Sometimes this is a land of cooperation, sometimes a nation of competition. American politics, as you'll see, reflects both views.

By the People?

This brief edition of *By the People* was created for those who want a shorter, streamlined, and less expensive version of the more comprehensive edition. While we have condensed the longer book's story of American government—there is less history and policy here—we think we have preserved the book's essential features, engagements, insights, and tone.

We picked the book's title—*By the People*—because Lincoln's phrase raises the deepest question in American politics: Who has the power? Or to put it more pointedly, do the people rule in this day and age? Democracy is

---

[1] *Where Do We Go from Here: Chaos or Community?* (New York: Harper & Row, 1967) 181.

a constant struggle; it is an aspiration, a wish, a quest. In every chapter we'll ask how well Americans are living up to Lincoln's ideal. Does the new media (Chapter 7) or the contemporary Congress (Chapter 10) or the bureaucracy (Chapter 12) or state government (Chapter 3) support or subvert government by the people? We'll present the details—and let you decide whether we should press for reform or leave things alone.

We'll be straight with you: we won't pretend there was a golden age in some imaginary past. After all, the United States has been home to political machines that enthusiastically stole votes, maintains an Electoral College designed to distort the people's vote for president, and governs through an elaborate system of checks and balances that blunts the popular will. (Again, you'll soon see two sides to each of these features of American government.) At the same time, you'll read about bold popular movements and unexpected electoral surges that changed the face of the nation. In many ways, these are the most exciting moments in American history. They spring up at unexpected times, inspiring ordinary people to achieve great things.

Who Are We?

Here's Jim's very first political memory: My parents were watching TV, and as soon as I walked into the room I could see that my mother was trying hard not to cry. "What's going on?" I asked my parents nervously. My dad—a proud Republican who had fought in World War II—said, "Well, the U.S. had a racial problem, but that man there, he's going to get us past it." "That man there" was Martin Luther King Jr., giving one of the most famous speeches in American history: "I have a dream," said King, that "my four little children will one day live in a country where they will not be judged by the color of their skin but by the content of their character." My mother had been born in Poland and her near tears reflected pride in her new nation—and the uplifting aspirations of that August day.

Both of us authors grew up thinking about the dream—and about the nation that dreams it. America is constantly changing, constantly new. In every chapter we'll ask the same question: Who are we? We'll explore a lot of different answers.

Four themes are especially important in this book. **Race** touches everything in the United States, from the Constitution (Chapter 2) to the political parties (Chapter 9). The nation rose up out of both freedom and slavery; race quickly became one of the great crucibles of American liberty. Similarly, **immigration** includes some of history's saddest passages involving the mistreatment of recent arrivals. And yet we are a nation of immigrants that continues to welcome the world's "huddled masses yearning to breathe free"— the famous words long associated with the Statue of Liberty. More than a fifth of all the emigrants around the globe come to the United States every year. Race and immigration are tied up in another powerful topic: **gender and sexuality**. From women in Congress to same-sex marriage, from teen pregnancy to abortion, we'll show how negotiating an answer to "Who are we?" always puts an emphasis on questions of gender and sexuality. Finally, we're especially interested in **American generations**, and more specifically the attitudes and contributions of today's young people, the millennial generation. If you're one of them, the future belongs to you. This book is an owner's manual for the government that you're going to inherit. We'll have much to say about you as we go along.

The most important thing about all these categories is not their history, or the ways they've influenced voting behavior, or how the courts treat them—although we'll cover all those topics. Rather, what matters most about American politics are the opportunities for getting involved. As you'll see, groups and individuals can and do make a difference in a nation that is always evolving. We hope our book inspires you to actively participate in making the American future.

How Government Works

We won't oversell the role of individuals. People's ability to advance political change is always shaped by the way the government is organized and operates. From the very start, this book emphasizes the unusual structure of American government.

Begin with a Constitution full of checks and balances, add a multilayered federalism, develop a chaotic public administration (President Franklin Roosevelt cheerfully called the uproar a three-ring circus), spin off functions to the private sector (especially during wars), complexify Congress (thirty-one different committees and subcommittees tried to claim jurisdiction over just one national health insurance proposal), and inject state and federal courts into every cranny of the system. Then throw the entire apparatus open to any interest group that shows up. The twenty-first century adds a 24/7 news cycle with commentary all the time and from every angle.

Turn to foreign policy, where high principles contend with tough-minded realism in a fractious world. When the most formidable military in human history is mustered into action, watch presidential power expand so rapidly that it sets off international debates about whether the great republic is morphing into an empire.

In Short

As you read this book, you'll repeatedly encounter four questions:

- *Who governs?* This is the question of democracy and power—or, as we put it above: Is this government by the people? And if and where it falls short, how might we refresh our democracy?

- *How does American politics work?* Our job is to make you think like a political scientist. What does that involve? You'll learn in the next chapter—and throughout the book.

- *What does government do?* You can't answer the first two questions if you don't know what the courts or the White House or Congress or interest groups actually do—and how they do it.

- *Who are we?* Americans endlessly debate America's identity. We are students, businesspeople, Hispanics, seniors, Texans, environmentalists, gays, Republicans, Democrats, Christians, Muslims, military families—and the list goes on. Sometimes it adds up to one united people; at other times we're left to wonder how to get along. Either way, American politics rises up from—and shapes—a cacophony of identities and interests.

Changes to the Brief Second Edition

In this new edition, we have:

- Added more than forty specific national policy events of 2013–2014, from wider acceptance of same-sex marriage to Edward Snowden's revelations about the National Security Agency.

- Introduced numerous new state-level policy changes, such as legalization of marijuana in Colorado and the aftermath of a major oil spill on West Virginia's Elk River.

- Reported extensively on the opening year and a half of President Obama's second term.

- Covered the details of the 113th Congress's first session and part of its second session (through June 2014).

- Provided highlights of the 2014 midterm elections, such as the landmark primary loss of House Majority Leader Eric Cantor (R-Virginia).

- Reflected on recent Supreme Court and other federal decisions, such as *U.S. v. Windsor*, 133 S. Ct. 2675 (2013).

- As appropriate, included updated references to political events in other countries, such as India's landmark 2014 elections and Russia's seizing of the Crimean Peninsula.

- Included recent important political-science, economics, law, and sociology scholarship, often as cited in revised/expanded endnotes.

- Featured current cultural examples that help shape our politics, including films and events like President Obama's interview with comedian Zach Galifianakis.

- Updated photographs, illustrating vital points in the book, often substituted for older images in the first edition.

- Tightened and streamlined writing throughout; text is roughly 10% shorter overall.

- Updated every chapter's By the Numbers feature to reflect political/governmental reality in 2013–2014.
- Similarly, updated opinion-polling information to extend to 2014 or 2013 (depending on poll availability) throughout the book.

Getting Involved

By the People is a new approach to courses in American government. The book displays U.S. politics and government in all its glory, messiness, and power. Like every textbook, this one informs our readers. But, as we hope you can already see, we don't describe government (or ideas about government) as inert and fixed. What's exciting about American politics, like the nation itself, is how fast it changes. And the constant, endless arguments about what it is and what it should be next. Our aim is to get you engaged—whether you already love politics, are a complete newcomer to government, or whether you are a newcomer to the United States itself. In the pages that follow, we'll bring American government to life. Get ready to start a great debate . . . about your future.

One final word: We've been working out the story line for this book throughout our teaching careers. We've taught everything from very large lectures to small seminars. Like all teachers, we've learned through trial and error. We've worked hard to pack this book with the stories, questions, and features that our own students have found effective. That spirit—the lessons we've learned in the classroom—animates everything that follows.

Ensuring Student Success

Oxford University Press offers instructors and students a comprehensive ancillary package for qualified adopters of *By the People*.

- **Dashboard**

  Online homework made easy! Tired of learning management systems that promise the world but are too difficult to use? OUP offers you Dashboard, a simple, nationally hosted, online learning course—including study, review, interactive, and assessment materials—in an easy-to-use system that requires less than fifteen minutes to master. Assignment and assessment results flow into a straightforward, color-coded gradebook, allowing you a clear view into your students' progress. The system works on every major platform and device, including mobile devices. Dashboard offers quizzes, exams, and essay questions, all correlated to chapter learning objectives; CNN videos with corresponding test items; and web links for additional resources. New to this edition, five interactive media activities integrate learning across chapters, with results and quizzes that report to the gradebook. These simulations include: *Comprehensive Immigration Reform, Managing a Congressional Election, Advocating for a New Warship, Playing President on Foreign Policy,* and *All the Way to the Supreme Court.*

Only $5 with the price of a new book! Also available for sale on its own. Contact your local OUP representative to order *By the People,* Brief Second Edition, and the Access Code Card for Dashboard. Please use package ISBN 978-0-19-023377-8 to order.

- **Ancillary Resource Center**

  This convenient, instructor-focused website provides access to all of the up-to-date teaching resources for this text—at any time—while guaranteeing the security of grade-significant resources. In addition, it allows OUP to keep instructors informed when new content becomes available. Register for access and create your individual user account by clicking on the Instructor's Resources link at www.oup.com/us/morone. Available on the ARC:

  - **Instructor's Manual:** The Instructor's Resource Manual includes chapter objectives, a detailed chapter outline, lecture suggestions and activities, discussion questions, video resources, and web resources.

  - **Test Item File:** This resource includes nearly 2,100 test items, including multiple choice, short answer, and essay questions. Questions are identified as factual, conceptual, or applied, and correct answers are keyed to the text pages where the concepts are presented.

  - **Computerized Test Bank:** Using the test authoring and management tool Diploma, the computerized test bank that accompanies this text is designed for both novice and advanced users. Diploma enables instructors to create and edit questions, create randomized quizzes and tests with an easy-to-use drag-and-drop tool, publish quizzes and tests to online courses, and print quizzes and tests for paper-based assessments.

  - **PowerPoint presentations:** Each chapter's slide deck includes a succinct chapter outline and incorporates relevant chapter graphics.

- **Companion website at www.oup.com/us/morone**

  This open access companion website includes a number of learning tools to help students study and review key concepts presented in the text including learning objectives, key-concept summaries, quizzes, essay questions, web activities, and web links.

- *Now Playing: Learning American Government Through Film*

  Through documentaries, feature films, and YouTube videos, *Now Playing: Learning American Government Through Film* provides variety of suggested video examples that illustrate concepts covered in the text. Each video is accompanied by a brief summary and discussion questions. It is available in both a student and an instructor version and can be packaged with *By The People* for free.

- **CNN Videos**

  Offering recent clips on timely topics, this DVD provides 15 films tied to the chapter topics in the text. Each clip is approximately 5-10 minutes in length, offering a great way to launch your lectures. Contact your local OUP sale representative for details.

- **E-Book**

  Available through CourseSmart.

- **Course Cartridges**

  To order course cartridges, please contact your local OUP sales representative.

Packaging Options

Adopters of *By the People* can package *any* Oxford University Press book with the text for a twenty percent savings off the total package price. See our many trade and scholarly offerings at www.oup.com, **then contact your local OUP sales representative to request a package ISBN.** In addition, the following items can be packaged with the text for free:

- *Now Playing: Learning American Government Through Film*: ISBN 9780190233358
- Williams, *Research and Writing Guide for Political Science*: ISBN 9780190243548
- Dashboard: ISBN 9780190237677

We also encourage the following texts for packaging:

- Very Short Introduction Series:
  - Valelly, *American Politics*
  - Crick, *Democracy*
  - Boyer, *American History*
- Lindsay, *Investigating American Democracy: Readings on Core Questions*
- Miethe/Gauthier, *Simple Statistics: Applications in Social Research*
- Niven, *Barack Obama: A Pocket Biography of Our 44th President*
- Wilkins, *Questioning Numbers: How to Read and Critique Research*

Acknowledgments

When he signed us up to write this book, publisher John Challice looked us each in the eye and said, "You know, this is going to be so much work—you're going to be married to us." He was right. Yes, it was lot of work. And yes, the Oxford team has been like a family that carried us through the process.

There would be no book without Jennifer Carpenter, our extraordinary editor. She guided us through the process with enormous skill. Along the way, Jen earned the highest praise authors can give their editor: she cared about the book as much as we did. Our development editor, Naomi Friedman, helped us so much she ought to be considered a coauthor—she suggested, edited, cut, and cheered. Development manager Thom Holmes gracefully turned our messy manuscript into a tight narrative bursting with special features. Editorial assistant Brianna Provenzano guided the art program and tracked down every picture in the following pages. Production manager Lisa Grzan and senior production editor Theresa Stockton coordinated an amazing production process; we broke the publishing record for the number of times two authors wrote, "Good point!" in the margins of an edited manuscript. Susan Brown did a fine copyedit on an impossible schedule. Art director Michele Laseau did the beautiful design. We are especially grateful to Tony Mathias for getting this book into your hands. To all of you in our immediate Oxford family: Thank you! Thank you!

We had an even more important team at our side—our families and our friends. Over the course of this book's initial conception and subsequent writing, Rogan moved from Syracuse University's Maxwell School to New York University's Wagner School, with a sabbatical leave at Yale along the way—and then, just as we were finishing the manuscript, to Wake Forest University. Colleagues in all four places were unfailingly generous with ideas and comments; thanks especially to Suzanne Mettler, Jeff Stonecash, David Mayhew, Ellen Schall, Shanna Rose, and Shankar Prasad. Because we strive throughout to get both the political science and the practical politics right, a group of experienced and reflective inside-the-Beltway friends cheerfully and patiently provided insight into their world: Bill Antholis, Matt Bennett, Laura Schiller, Erik Fatemi, Tom Dobbins, Dan Maffei, Bob Shrum, Marylouise Oates, and Don and Darrel Jodrey. Grateful thanks to them as well as a wonderful set of current and former students, many now working in government and politics.

By the People's long journey to completion grew infinitely more enjoyable once Sara Pesek joined me for the trip—through this book and everywhere else, from Australia to Ze Café in midtown NYC. Sara's insights into public policy made for the liveliest newlyweds' conversations (if you're a politics junkie) imaginable; my biggest bouquet of thanks to her for that rarest of gifts: loving, fully joined partnership.

Jim offers warm thanks to my colleagues at Brown who form a wonderful community of scholars and teachers—always ready for coffee, lunch, or wine and a conversation about political science. Extra thanks to Peter Andreas, Mark Blyth, Corey Brettschneider, Ross Cheit, Elisabeth Fauquert, Alex Gourevitch, Rebecca Henderson, Bonnie Honig, Sharon Krause, Rick Locke, Susan Moffitt, Rich Snyder, Wendy Schiller, and Ashu Varshney. And my wonderful students sampled every idea in this book. They are my constant teachers. Special thanks Dan Ehlke, Jeremy Johnson, Kevin McGravey, Aarron Weinstein, and Liza Williams. I'm grateful, too, to Puneet Bhasin, David Blanding, Kelly Branham, Aimee Bourassa, Dan Carigg, Nick Coburn-Palo, Ryan Emenaker, Pat Endres, Oddny Helgadottir, Matt Hodgetts, Dan Kushner, Ferris Lupino, Matt Lyddon, Rachel Meade, Aytug Sasmaz, Kaitlin Sidorsky, Meghan Wilson, and Cadence Willse.

My brothers, Joe and Peter Morone—and their families—are lifelong companions always ready with a cheerful take on the state of politics and the world. Special thanks to Lindsay, Ann, Joe, James (now a rising political scientist at Penn), Noreen, and Maegan Morone. My mother, Stasia, kept reminding me to enjoy the journey—and that there might be more to life than *By the People*. And the memory of my dad was a constant visitor as I read, and thought, and wrote.

Manuscript Reviewers

We have greatly benefited from the perceptive comments and suggestions of the many talented scholars and instructors who reviewed the manuscript of *By the People*. They went far beyond the call of duty in sharing thoughts and making corrections. Their insight and suggestions contributed immensely to the work.

Second Edition

Nathan Blank
Casper College, University of Wyoming, Kentucky Community & Technical College System

Nichole Boutte-Heiniluoma
Jarvis Christian College

Blake Farrar
Texas State University

Jennifer Felmley
Santa Fe Community College

Paul Foote
Eastern Kentucky University

Jeneen Hobby
Cleveland State University

Gary Johnson
Weber State University

Steven Nawara
Valdosta State University

Geoffrey Peterson
University of Wisconsin-Eau Claire

Ronald C. Schurin
University of Connecticut

John Shively
Longview Community College

Toni-Michelle C. Travis
George Mason University

First Edition

Brian A. Bearry
University of Texas at Dallas

Emily Bentley
Savannah State University

R. M. Bittick
Sam Houston State University

Wendell S. Broadwell Jr.
Georgia Perimeter College

Allison Bunnell
Fitchburg State University

Frank P. Cannatelli
Southern Connecticut State University

Jason P. Casellas
University of Texas at Austin

Stefanie Chambers
Trinity College, Hartford, Connecticut

Suzanne Chod
Pennsylvania State University

Michael Cobb
North Carolina State University

McKinzie Craig
Texas A&M University

Michael Crespin
University of Georgia

Amanda DiPaolo
Middle Tennessee State University

Stewart Dippel
University of the Ozarks

Jasmine Farrier
University of Louisville

Michaela Fazecas
University of Central Florida

Joseph J. Foy
University of Wisconsin–Parkside

Megan Francis
Pepperdine University

Rodd Freitag
University of Wisconsin–Eau Claire

Joseph Gardner
Northern Arizona University

David Goldberg
College of DuPage

Frederick Gordon
Columbus State University

Jeff Harmon
University of Texas at San Antonio

Jeneen Hobby
Cleveland State University

Mark S. Jendrysik
University of North Dakota

Brian Kessel
Columbia College

Christopher L. Kukk
Western Connecticut State University

Sujith Kumar
University of Central Arkansas

Lisa Langenbach
Middle Tennessee State University

William W. Laverty
University of Michigan–Flint

Jeffrey Lazarus
Georgia State University

Angela K. Lewis
University of Alabama at Birmingham

Gregg Lindskog
Temple University

Brent A. Lucas
North Carolina State University

Thomas R. Marshall
University of Texas at Arlington

A. Lanethea Mathews
Muhlenberg College

Vaughn May
Belmont University

Lauri McNown
University of Colorado at Boulder

Christina A. Medina
New Mexico State University

Patrick R. Miller
University of Cincinnati

Michael K. Moore
University of Texas at Arlington

Roger Morton
California State University, Long Beach

Yamini Munipalli
Florida State College at Jacksonville

Gary Mucciaroni
Temple University

Jason Mycoff
University of Delaware

Steven Nawara
Valdosta State University

Anthony Neal
Buffalo State College

Mark Nicol
Saginaw Valley State University

Stephen A. Nuño
Northern Arizona University

Michael Parkin
Oberlin College

Richard Pious
Barnard College

Elizabeth A. Prough
Eastern Michigan University

Wesley B. Renfro
St. John Fisher College

John F. Roche, III
Palomar College

Amanda M. Rosen
Webster University

Anjali Sahay
Gannon University

Joanna Vecchiarelli Scott
Eastern Michigan University

Samuel Shelton
Troy University

Majid Shirali
University of Nevada–Las Vegas

Joyce Stickney Smith
Hillsborough Community College–Ybor Campus

Mitchel A. Sollenberger
University of Michigan–Dearborn

Chris Soper
Pepperdine University

Barry L. Tadlock
Ohio University

Edwin A. Taylor III
Missouri Western State University

Delaina Toothman
Texas State University

Jan P. Vermeer
Nebraska Wesleyan University

Jennifer E. Walsh
Azusa Pacific University

Donn Worgs
Towson University

Larry L. Wright
Florida A&M University

Shoua Yang
St. Cloud State University

Mike Yawn
Sam Houston State University

Melanie C. Young
University of Nevada–Las Vegas

Khodr M. Zaarour
Shaw University

Marketing Reviewers

Oxford University Press would also like to acknowledge the contribution of additional scholars and instructors who class tested and provided their assessment of the completed manuscript, using this work with hundreds of students in classrooms across the nation.

Second Edition

Ted Anagnoson
University of California–Santa Barbara

Steven Bayne
Century College

Joshua Berkenpas
Western Michigan University

Jeff Bloodworth
Gannon University

Theodore C. Brown
Virginia State University

Kim Casey
Northwest Missouri State University

Jay Cerrato
Bronx Community College

Ericka Christensen
Washington State University

Kevin Davis
North Central Texas College–Corinth

Dennis Driggers
California State University–Fresno

Paul Gottemoller
Del Mar College

Sara Gubala
Lamar University

Dan Guerrant
Middle Georgia College

Timothy Kersey
Kennesaw State University

Michael Latner
California Polytechnic State University

Maurice Mangum
Texas Southern University

Donna Merrell
Kennesaw State University

Patrick Moore
Richland College

Martha Musgrove
Tarrant County College–Southeast Campus

Michael Petersen
Utah State University

Mikhail Rybalko
Texas Tech University

Joanna Sabo
Monroe County Community College

Hayden Smith
Washington State University

First Edition

Gayle Alberda
Owens Community College

Herrick Arnold
Orange Coast College

Alex L. Avila
Mesa Community College

John Barnes
University of Southern California

Charles Barrilleaux
Florida State University

Ronald Bee
Cuyamaca College

Michael Berkman
Pennsylvania State University

Angelina M. Cavallo
San Jacinto College

Paul M. Collins
University of North Texas

Adam Chamberlain
Coastal Carolina University

Matt Childers
University of Georgia

Benjamin Christ
Harrisburg Area Community College

Diana Cohen
Central Connecticut State University

William Corbett
New Mexico State University

Mark Ellickson
Missouri State University

Deborah Ferrell-Lynn
University of Central Oklahoma

Paul Foote
Eastern Kentucky University

Peter L. Francia
East Carolina University

Rodd Freitag
University of Wisconsin–Eau Claire

Fred Gordon
Columbus State University

John I. Hanley
Syracuse University

Jeff Hilmer
Northern Arizona University

Jeneen Hobby
Cleveland State University

Ronald J. Hrebenar
University of Utah

Mark Jendrysik
University of North Dakota

Aubrey Jewett
University of Central Florida

Gary Johnson
Weber State University

Michelle Keck
The University of Texas at Brownsville

William Kelly
Auburn University

John Klemanski
Oakland University

Richard Krupa
Harper College

Christine Lipsmeyer
Texas A&M University

Brent Lucas
North Carolina State University

Margaret MacKenzie
San Jacinto College

Jason McDaniel
San Francisco State University

John Mercurio
San Diego State University

Melissa Merry
University of Louisville

Roger Morton
California State University–Long Beach

Gary Mucciaroni
Temple University

Adam J. Newmark
Appalachian State University

Randall Newnham
Pennsylvania State University

Roger Nichols
Southwestern College

Anthony J. Nownes
University of Tennessee–Knoxville

Anthony O'Regan
Los Angeles Valley College

Kenneth O'Reilly
Milwaukee Area Technical College

Sunday P. Obazuaye
Cerritos College

Amanda M. Olejarski
Shippensburg University

Kevin Parsneau
Minnesota State University

Michelle Pautz
University of Dayton

Martin J. Plax
Cleveland State University

Sherri Replogle
Illinois State University

Kim Rice
Western Illinois University

Ray Sandoval
Dallas County Community College District

Laura Schneider
Grand Valley State University

Scot Schraufnagel
Northern Illinois University

Ronnee Schreiber
San Diego State University

Ronald Schurin
University of Connecticut

Jeffrey M. Stonecash
Syracuse University

Katrina Taylor
Northern Arizona University

Ryan Lee Teten
University of Louisiana

John P. Todsen
Drake University

Delaina Toothman
University of Maine

Dan Urman
Northeastern University

Ronald W. Vardy
University of Houston

Adam L. Warber
Clemson University

Gerald Watkins
Kentucky Community & Technical College System

Patrick Wohlfarth
University of Maryland–College Park

Wayne L. Wolf
South Suburban College

Jeff Worsham
West Virginia University

Finally, thanks to you for picking up this book. We hope you enjoy reading it as much as we did writing.

Jim Morone and Rogan Kersh

BY THE PEOPLE

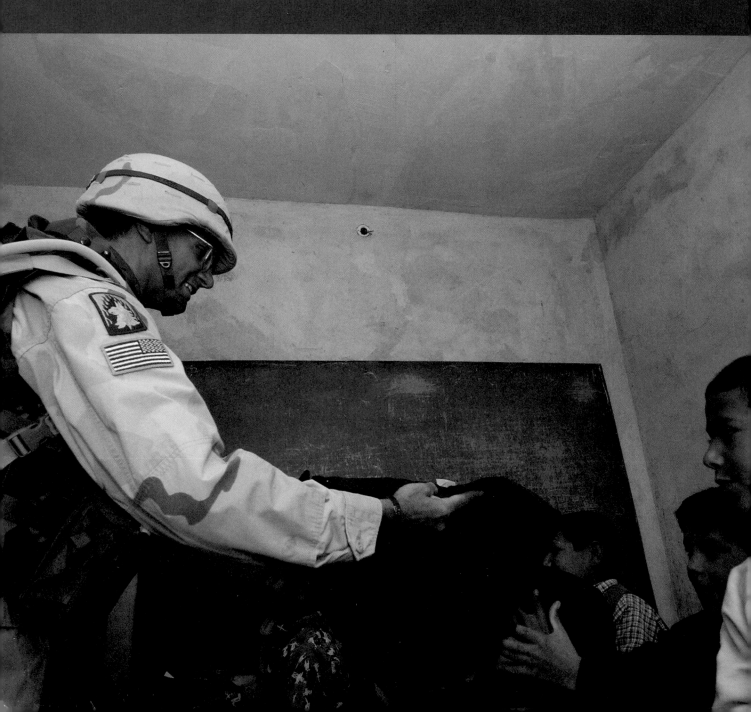

1

Ideas That Shape American Politics

ARMY CAPTAIN RUSSELL BURGOS hunkered down in his bunker as mortars ripped through the night. A year ago he had been a political science professor; now he was fighting in Iraq. Burgos's unit was operating in the Sunni Triangle, where the fighting was fiercest. "A mortar attack in the middle of the night," he mused, "is an odd place to reconsider a course syllabus." But that is exactly what he found himself doing. Experiencing war made him see politics and societies in new ways.

As shells fell on the American base, Burgos thought about something that his classes had been missing: the study of ideas. The United States entered the war because of what key decision makers believed. American leaders spent enormous energy insisting that the United States was in Iraq as a liberator rather than as a conqueror or occupier; explaining American ideas seemed crucial to both civilian and military leaders. In the war zone, Burgos saw the same thing. All around him, men and women were fighting and dying over ideas—ideas like freedom, democracy, equality, power, and faith in God.

Strangely enough, Burgos wrote later, ideas—and especially how ideas affect politics—had barely come up in his own political science classes. Yet ideas helped explain why the United States launched the war, how it fought the war, and why everyone up and down the chain of command acted as they did. Burgos ended up rethinking his approach to politics.[1]

Who are we? Our ideas tell us—and they tell the world. The United States is a nation built on ideas. You will see ideas at work in every chapter of this book, for they touch every feature of government and politics. They affect the way Americans define their national ideals, their political goals, and their nation itself. As you read about these ideas—and as you continue through this book—think about other important ideas that should be added to the list alongside the seven we discuss in this chapter. If you come up with a compelling example, we may quote you in the next edition.

IN THIS CHAPTER, YOU WILL:

● Learn about four key questions: Who governs? How does American politics work? What does government do? and Who are we?

● Learn about the seven key American ideas: liberty, self-rule, limited government, individualism, the American dream, equality, and faith in God.

● Explore the essential question: How do ideas affect politics?

● *Army Captain Russell Burgos hands out supplies to Iraqi children in 2004.*

BY THE NUMBERS
American Ideas

- The Declaration of Independence talks about protecting *life, liberty, and the pursuit of happiness.* Rank order of American citizens in self-reported happiness compared to citizens of more than 100 other nations, according to three recent studies: **15, 19, 23**
- Number of times the word "rights" appears in the Declaration of Independence: **10**
- Number of times the word "rights" appears in the original Constitution: **0**
- Number of times the word "rights" appears in amendments to the Constitution: **15**
- Percentage increase in inequality in the United States since 1970: **30**
- Percentage increase in inequality in Canada since 1970: **5**
- Percentage *decrease* in inequality in Germany since 1970: **10**
- Percentage of Americans who say it is "more important to be free to pursue my own goals rather than making sure that no one is in need": **58**
- Percentage of Spaniards and French, respectively, who say this: **30, 36**
- Percentage of Italians, Poles, and Americans, respectively, who agree that "it is the role of the government to take care of people who cannot care for themselves": **66, 56, 23**
- Percentage of Americans who belong to a church or religious organization: **57**
- Percentage of British, Swedes, and French who belong to a church: **22, 9, 4**
- Percentage of Americans who agree that "everyone who works hard will get ahead" in 2005: **86**
- Percentage of Americans agreeing in 2013: **65**
- Percentage of young people who say it is very important for them to achieve the American dream: **55**
- Percentage of baby boomers who say this: **33**

 The Spirit of American Politics

Throughout this book we make sense of American politics by exploring four questions: Who governs? How does American politics work? What does government do? And who are we? By the time you finish reading, you will understand the debates each question has generated—and be ready to participate knowledgeably yourself.

Who Governs?

As Benjamin Franklin left the Constitutional Convention in 1787, a woman stopped him. "What kind of government have you given us?" she asked. According to legend, the wise old Franklin responded, "A republic, madam—if you can keep it." The United States organized itself around a ringing declaration of popular rule: governments derive "their just power from the consent of the governed." In a **republic**, the people are in charge. Franklin knew, however, that popular governments are extremely difficult to "keep." All previous republics—like Athens, Rome, and Florence—had collapsed. His point was that the people must be vigilant and active if they are to maintain control.

Who governs? Do the people rule? Some of us would answer "yes—and today more than ever." Others are not so sure. What if the people are not in charge—then who is?

Over the years, political scientists have developed four theories to answer the question of where power really lies in American politics. *Pluralism* suggests that people can influence government through the many interest groups that spring up to champion everything from fighting global warming to banning abortions. *Elite theory* counters that power actually rests in the hands of a small number of wealthy and powerful people. As American society has grown more unequal, vast wealth leads to growing influence. *Bureaucratic theory* argues that the real control of government lies with the millions of men and women who carry out the day-to-day operations of modern government and business. Finally, *social movement theory* answers that mass popular uprisings have the potential to introduce great changes regardless of who is in control of ordinary, day-to-day politics.

We will return to this question in every chapter. Who rules? How well have we, the people, kept the republic? It is one of the most important questions in America today.

How Does American Politics Work?

Consider a classic definition of politics: who gets what, when, and how.[2] Every society has scarce things like money, prestige, and power. Politics helps determine how those resources are distributed—to which people, in what amounts, under which rules. A second definition is even simpler: politics is how a society makes its collective decisions. Every nation has its own way of deciding. This book explains how collective decisions are made in the United States. The key to understanding our political decision making lies in four "I's": ideas, interests, individuals, and institutions such as Congress, the Supreme Court, and the media.

Ideas.   Powerful ideas shape American politics. As you'll see later in this chapter, we stress seven essential ideas: liberty, democracy (or self-rule), individualism, limited government, the American dream, equality, and faith in God. At first glance, they may all look simple; as you will quickly learn, however, each has at least two very different sides. Each idea provokes long, loud controversies about what values and policies Americans should pursue.

Institutions.   When most people talk about politics, they think about individuals: politicians like President Barack Obama and Senator Ted Cruz,

Republic: A government in which citizens rule indirectly and make government decisions through their elected representatives.

The U.S. Capitol, Washington, D.C. Tourists see an impressive monument to democracy. Political scientists see an institution with complicated rules that advantage some individuals and groups in the nation's political debates.

Institutions: The organizations, norms, and rules that structure government and public actions.

commentators such as Jon Stewart or Rush Limbaugh. Political scientists, on the other hand, stress **institutions**—the organizations, norms, and rules that structure political action. Congress, the Supreme Court, and the Department of Homeland Security are all institutions.

Think about how institutions influence your own behavior. Students may compete in a classroom by making arguments. If the debate gets heated and you shove someone, however, you are in trouble. But on the basketball court, after class, things are quite the opposite. There, a little shoving is fine, but no one wants to play hoops with someone who is always arguing. Different institutions—the classroom, the gym—have different rules, and most people adopt them without a second thought. Note how the different institutional rules give some people advantages over others. Smart students who think quickly have an advantage in one institution (the classroom), while athletic students who move fast have an advantage in another (the gym). Political institutions work in the same way. The Supreme Court, the House of Representatives, the city council in Chicago, the Texas legislature, the state courts in Colorado, the governor's office in Wisconsin, the Marine Corps, the Department of Agriculture, and thousands of others all have their own rules and procedures. Each institution organizes behavior. Each gives an advantage to some interests over others. By the time you finish this book, you will know to ask the same question every time you encounter a political issue. Which institutions are involved, and how do they influence politics?

Interests.   For many social scientists, interests are the center of the story. Political action often springs from individuals, groups, and nations pursuing their own self-interest. In the chapters that follow, we explore three types of interests: we examine whether rational self-interest motivates people's political actions and opinions (known as **rational choice theory**); we trace the political influence of interests and groups; and we consider the ideal of a public interest shared by everyone in society.

Individuals.   Finally, individuals make politics. This book puts special emphasis on how ordinary people change their world. Our hope is simple: we want to inspire you, the reader, to get involved. Civic engagement in any community and at any level can be profoundly rewarding. It can change the world—as you will see, again and again.

Rational choice theory:
An approach to political behavior that views individuals as rational, decisive actors who know their political interests and seek to act on them.

What Does Government Do?

Back in 1787, the Constitution's creators set out the basic functions of the U.S. government, as they imagined them then: "establish justice, ensure domestic tranquility, provide for the common defense, promote the general welfare, and secure the blessings of liberty." Their list is still remarkably accurate, even as the size of our government has expanded dramatically.

Americans have a very active civil society. People come together voluntarily to achieve a goal through groups, such as a Bible study circle, a group of recycling volunteers, a business association, or a student government. In the abstract, at least, they prefer voluntary groups to government action. Polls consistently reflect public disapproval for all aspects of government: bureaucrats, the mainstream media, lobbyists, and Congress. Today, only about 13 percent of Americans trust the national government "to do the right thing most of the time."[3]

You can get a good idea of the federal government's priorities by looking at its major budget categories. Figure 1.1 shows you how the federal government

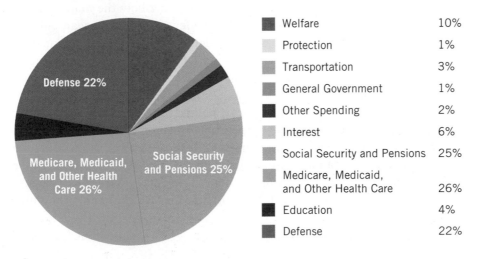

Federal Spending for United States - FY 2014

Category	%
Welfare	10%
Protection	1%
Transportation	3%
General Government	1%
Other Spending	2%
Interest	6%
Social Security and Pensions	25%
Medicare, Medicaid, and Other Health Care	26%
Education	4%
Defense	22%

● **FIGURE 1.1** *The U.S. federal budget (Christopher Chantrill, http://www.usgovernmentspending.com/).*

spends its $3.5 trillion annual budget. Many people are surprised when they see the federal budget for the first time. More than 65 percent of all federal government spending goes to just four programs: the military, Social Security (which provides a steady income for people over the age of sixty-five, as well as for people with disabilities and other groups), Medicare (which provides health care for people over sixty-five), and Medicaid (which provides health care for some poor people; about half of Medicaid spending also goes to people over sixty-five). America's national government devotes most of its resources to the military and to seniors.

All four of these big-ticket items are immensely popular programs. Although every politician is for smaller government, very few have the courage to take on any of these four programs—no matter how much they cost. In short, Americans dislike government in the abstract. However, by and large, they support many of the things that government actually does.

The government also sets the rules for society. Drive on the right side of the street. Stop at red lights. No tobacco for children. No rat hairs or bug parts in restaurant food. No discrimination against women when hiring. Sometimes the rules make sense to most people; at other times they trigger fierce debates. In either case, governments affect what we do almost every minute of every day. By the time you finish this book, we think you'll have strong feelings about what government should do, what it should stay out of, and why.

Who Are We?

In a rapidly changing, diverse, immigrant nation, this is the deepest question of all. If the people aspire to rule, we must understand who the people are. The United States is a nation of immigrants, a country where individuals come to reinvent themselves. The nation is always changing as well (see Figure 1.2). American politics constantly addresses the most fundamental question about a people: Who are we?

We begin every chapter of this book by showing how the major topics in the chapter help explain who we are. All the features of American politics— foundational ideas, the Constitution, presidents, justices, media personalities, bureaucrats, interest groups, and more—are part of the struggle to define and redefine the nation.

The most important answer to that question is you. As part of the next generation, you are the future of American politics. To us, that is a comforting thought. Studies of the millennial generation (or Generation Y) show that you are, on average, more responsible, harder working, and more law-abiding than the generations that came before (including ours). You tend to volunteer more, donate a higher share of your income to charity, and start more entrepreneurial organizations with social impact. You might just be the generation that finally

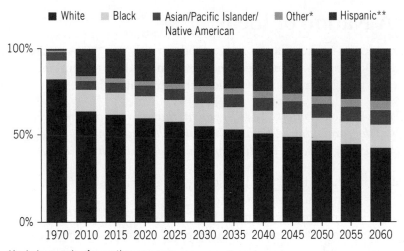

■ White   ■ Black   ■ Asian/Pacific Islander/ Native American   ■ Other*   ■ Hispanic**

*Includes people of more than one race
**Considered an ethnicity; Hispanics may be any race

● **FIGURE 1.2** *Race and ethnicity in America—yesterday, today, and tomorrow (U.S. Census Bureau).*

redeems the endless American quest for racial harmony and gender equality. You are also a generation at home in a rapidly changing and diverse world.

We have one worry, however. Will this generation take up the challenge of American politics and government? Compared to previous generations, millennials show less interest in government service, trust national leaders less, and follow political news at a lower rate. If a whole generation is reluctant to get involved, American democracy will suffer.

THE BOTTOM LINE

● We explore American government by asking four questions: Who governs? How does American politics work? What does government do? And who are we?

● In a republic, power rests with the people. However, this is a difficult form of government to maintain.

● American political decisions are shaped by four "I" factors: ideas, institutions, interests, and individuals.

● Americans tend to dislike their national government—but like the benefits that government programs provide.

● Because the nation is so diverse—and so rapidly changing—the answer to the question of who we are is constantly being rewritten.

● Every feature of American politics influences this constant debate over defining the nation and its people.

🔴 A Nation of Ideas

As the colonies broke away from England, on July 4, 1776, American leaders issued a Declaration of Independence explaining their revolutionary actions. Its second paragraph describes the idea that animated them:

We hold these truths to be self-evident, that all men are created equal, that they are endowed by their Creator with certain unalienable rights, that among these are life, liberty and the pursuit of happiness.

Most of us have heard that line so often that it has lost its force, but it is one of the most powerful ideas in history. It explains the role of government—securing each individual's rights to life, liberty, and the pursuit of happiness. The Declaration states that this is why people form governments—"*to secure those rights.*" And, although the men and women who fought the revolution would fall far short of this ideal, they left the nation an inspiring goal. Every American generation argues about how it can best achieve the Declaration's shimmering ideal and "secure" the rights of every citizen.

Many people, including some political scientists, often describe the United States as a unique nation, different from every other. That view is known as **American exceptionalism**. Of course, every nation is distinctive in some way. The United States is exceptional, in large part, because of seven key ideas that guide our politics. Most of them can be traced back to the Declaration of Independence.

What are the seven big ideas? Liberty, self-rule (which is often called democracy), limited government, individualism, the American dream, equality, and faith in God. These ideas touch almost everything we do as a nation. They are the foundation of U.S. national government and lie at the core of what makes America unique.

There is an unusual twist to these ideas. Americans rarely agree on what they mean. Instead, we constantly argue about them. All our foundational ideas have (at least) two sides and spark ardent disputes. To reveal the real truth about American politics, we should post signs at all the airports that say: "*Welcome to the great argument that is the USA.*"

Now let's consider the first key idea.

American exceptionalism: The view that the United States is unique because it is motivated by a set of ideas such as equality, democracy, and limited government.

JOHN HANCOCK'S DEFIANCE.

🔴 *Ideas have consequences. John Hancock of Massachusetts defiantly signs the Declaration. According to legend, he signed it in big, bold letters so King George could read Hancock's name without his spectacles—and "double the reward for my head."*

🔴 Liberty

As the Revolutionary War broke out, the royal governor of Virginia promised freedom to any slave who joined the British. Eighty thousand slaves ran for the

British lines. Some of them fought in black units, with their motto—"liberty for the slaves"—sewn onto their uniforms.[4]

The enslaved men and women who fought for the British saw their hopes dashed when their side surrendered at the Battle of Yorktown in 1781—effectively ending the Revolutionary War. After the battle, the Redcoats, as the English soldiers were known, began to withdraw, rowing out to the warships bobbing in the harbor for their long retreat. One desperate group of slaves raced past the sentries on the wharf, dove into the sea, and swam toward the long rowboats that were ferrying the defeated British troops out to their naval vessels.

As the black men tried to clamber aboard the small boats, British troops pushed them away. Fearful that the swimmers would swamp the craft, the troops pulled out axes and hacked off the slaves' hands and fingers. And *still* they kept coming, trying to surge aboard, thrashing after their fading dream of liberty. The image is unforgettable: These men were so desperate for freedom that even as the Redcoats swung their bloody hatchets, they kept clutching for the boats that might carry them to freedom.

"The Land of the Free"

No idea comes up more often in American history than freedom or liberty (we use the words interchangeably in this book). The national anthem declares America "the land of the free." During the civil rights movement of the 1950s and 1960s, young high school students spilled out of Baptist churches and marched toward dogs and high-pressure fire hoses, singing "everyone shout freedom, freedom, freedom!" The Statue of Liberty is inscribed "Give me . . . your huddled masses yearning to breathe free." Americans have tried to spread their faith in freedom to countries across the globe; as President George W. Bush put it in his second inaugural address, "The best hope for peace in our world is the expansion of freedom in all the world."

What is **freedom**? *It means that the government will protect your life, your liberty, and your property from the coercion of others (including public officials) in order to permit you to pursue the goals you define for yourself.*

> **Freedom:** The ability to pursue one's own desires without interference from others.

The Two Sides of Liberty

Everyone agrees that freedom is a basic American value. But, in practice, Americans disagree about what it means—and what governments should do to ensure it. There are two different views: negative liberty and positive liberty.[5]

The more familiar view is **negative liberty**: *freedom is the absence of constraints*. Society's responsibility, from this perspective, is to make sure that others (especially government officials) do not interfere with individuals pursuing their own goals. Negative liberty firmly limits government action. Public officials violate your freedom when they collect taxes from you to feed the hungry or punish you for smoking tobacco or marijuana. Negative freedom is the right to act as you want.

> **Negative liberty:** Freedom from constraints or the interference of others.

The alternative is **positive liberty**: *the freedom to pursue one's goals*. From this perspective, individuals cannot really be free—they cannot pursue their

> **Positive liberty:** The freedom and ability to pursue one's goals.

desires—if they lack the basic necessities of life. Protecting liberty means ensuring that every citizen has education, food, shelter, and health care. After all, how can people truly be free if they are hungry or homeless? This view justifies government action as a way to give all people a legitimate chance to achieve their desires.

President Franklin D. Roosevelt forcefully expressed this view in 1941. As the United States prepared for World War II, he proclaimed that the nation was fighting for four freedoms: freedom of speech, freedom of worship, freedom from want, and freedom from fear. The first two—freedom of speech and religion—were traditional negative liberties: no one could infringe on these individual rights. However, "freedom from want" was something new, a positive update of the original American idea of freedom. Freedom from want means helping needy people who have fallen on hard times. Roosevelt was suggesting that social welfare policies like unemployment insurance and Social Security were part of the all-American idea of freedom. Contemporary ideas of positive freedom include efforts to ensure that all people are well educated or to stop them from smoking. The guiding notion is that a lack of education, or the weight of addiction or disease, will make it difficult for them to pursue their goals.

Which side is correct? That depends on your values. Beneath these two visions of liberty lie different approaches to the good society. The negative view emphasizes personal autonomy: taxing me so that needy people can get food or decent health care violates my freedom of property. Strong proponents of negative liberty are known as **libertarians** and oppose most forms of government action. Libertarians call for a small government that simply leaves people alone as long as they are not interfering in the rights of others. The positive view follows Roosevelt: membership in a free society means sharing enough wealth so

see for yourself 1.1

Go online to hear President Roosevelt deliver his speech on the Four Freedoms.

Libertarians: People who believe in minimal government: specifically, that public officials' only role should be defending borders, prosecuting crime, and protecting private property.

COUNTERTHINK

ART - DAN BERGER   CONCEPT - MIKE ADAMS   WWW.NATURALNEWS.COM

● *A conservative cartoonist celebrates negative freedom (no one interferes with freedom of speech or religion) but mocks positive freedom (the idea that society should provide everyone with basic needs like health care). Beginning with Franklin Roosevelt in 1933, liberals disagreed with this cartoon's perspective and embraced "freedom from want."*

that everyone enjoys freedom from want. The two perspectives reflect different values, different visions of society, and different definitions of liberty.

The Idea of Freedom Is Always Changing

Once upon a time, Americans permitted slavery. And racial segregation. Women lost all their legal rights the day they were married; their possessions—even their very bodies—passed into the custody of their husbands. Chinese immigrants were denied any hope of becoming Americans no matter how long they lived in the country. And gay couples could be prosecuted as sexual criminals. The ideal of freedom moved Americans to reverse each of these prejudices.

Scholars disagree about how to interpret the results. Some see American history as a steady march toward greater liberty. Yes, they admit, American history is full of oppression. However, our faith in freedom leads oppressed groups to fight for their rights. Other political thinkers warn that the outcome in the fight is never inevitable. Instead, freedom is won and lost... and won and lost again. Americans fought their bloody civil war to end slavery, only to watch new forms of racial segregation and oppression take hold and last almost for another century. We should never take liberty for granted.[6]

What Do You Think?

NEGATIVE VERSUS POSITIVE LIBERTY

Americans often disagree about the meaning of "freedom." Is freedom the absence of constraints (negative liberty) or the freedom to pursue one's goals with equal opportunity (positive liberty)?

Do you believe in negative liberty? Government should not interfere with individuals. Freedom means leaving every person alone to do what he or she wishes—without interference.

Or do you believe in positive liberty? Freedom simply is not a meaningful concept if you or your family are chronically hungry. A decent society must lift everyone to a basic minimum. That's what living in a democracy should be about.

Do your beliefs fall somewhere in between? The truth is that few people would build a society around a pure form of negative or positive liberty. Think about how you might combine these two concepts. You might find it easier to answer this question after reading about the other major ideas. If you are not ready to choose, read on—and then return to this question.

- Liberty—or the freedom to pursue your goals—is the most often praised American value.

- There are two different views of what liberty means. *Negative liberty* emphasizes a lack of constraints on individuals, even if those constraints are intended to help others. *Positive liberty* requires the community to help everyone satisfy their basic needs.

- Guarantees of individual liberty have developed over time. Some scholars see the rise of freedom as inevitable, reflecting American ideals; others see it as a constant battle that can always go either way.

● Self-Rule

As the American Revolution began, mobs gathered in the towns and cities. The people, they declared, would seize authority from royal governors (appointed by the tyrannical king) and exercise power themselves. "The mob has begun to think for itself," lamented one wealthy New Yorker. "Poor reptiles, before noon they will bite" (meaning *revolt*).[7]

Patriotic crowds ignored the skeptics. At mass meetings, the people voted for laws, enforced decrees, and even issued wedding licenses. They dispatched boisterous pro-American toughs, who used sticks and stones to discourage individuals from acknowledging British institutions. Here is a powerful image of democracy: American people bypassing government officials and running the country themselves from the town commons. The people ruled.

That principle sounds simple. The United States is the world's longest-running democracy—of course, the people rule. But from the beginning, a great debate arose about how to achieve **self-rule**. The Constitution was meant to settle the issue—but we are still arguing about its meaning, 225 years later.

How do we achieve self-rule? Americans have long vacillated between two very different paths—a *democracy* and a *republic*.

Self-rule: The idea that legitimate government flows from the people.

One Side of Self-Rule: Democracy

Democracy means that citizens participate directly in making government decisions. (*Demos* is the Greek word for "the people.") In early New England, citizens governed directly in town meetings—without relying on elected officials.

Thomas Jefferson, who drafted the Declaration of Independence and served as the third U.S. president, was the most vocal proponent of maximizing democracy. "The will of the majority," wrote Jefferson, is a "sacred principle" and "the only sure guardian of the rights of man." If the people cannot govern themselves, asked Jefferson, how can they possibly be trusted with the government of others?[8]

Democracy: A government in which citizens rule directly and make government decisions for themselves.

● *Direct democracy in action: A town meeting mixes people from all walks of life.*

The result is a rich American legacy of taking to the streets to demonstrate, rally, and protest. Recent examples include the summer 2014 protests in Ferguson, Missouri, following the shooting by a police officer of unarmed local resident Michael Brown; "Occupy Wall Street" demonstrations against income inequality in many U.S. cities; widespread rallies, especially attracting Latinos, in recent years to protest immigration policies; and Tea Party protests against taxes and big government that helped fuel Republican Party enthusiasm in the 2014 midterm elections.

Thomas Jefferson's dream of direct democracy lives on. Idealists through American history return to the democrat's first principle: the people should exercise power as much as possible.

Another Side of Self-Rule: A Republic

Most of the men who drafted the Constitution did not agree with Jefferson about democracy. The states had tried to create direct democracy right after the American Revolution. George Washington thought the result was chaos. "We have probably had too good an opinion of human nature," he grumbled. James Madison put it most famously: "Democracies have [always] been spectacles of turbulence and contention . . . as short in their lives as violent in their deaths." The problem, said Madison, was that in direct democracy, the majority often gets carried away. They push their self-interest without paying attention to the rights of the minority. Direct democracy, he concluded, offers no barrier to lynch mobs crying for blood.[9]

The alternative is a republic. In this form of government, the people rule indirectly through their elected representatives. The constitutional framers made an important contribution to the theory of self-rule: classical democratic theory was wrong in expecting that popular government would only work if the people were virtuous. In fact the people are often not virtuous at all. "If men were angels," wrote Madison in *Federalist* No. 51, "no government would be necessary." The great challenge, he argued, was to devise government institutions that would protect individual rights even if a majority of the people were selfish and corrupt.

A Mixed System

Which view of self-rule holds in the United States? Both do. We can say that the United States is a democratic republic because it includes elements of a democracy *and* a republic. There are plenty of opportunities for direct participation. At the same time, American government is organized to check the majority. The House, the Senate, the president, and the Supreme Court all put the brakes on one another. And all of them face fifty different state governments, each with its own politics, powers, and programs. American government operates through elected and unelected officials who answer (sometimes indirectly) to the public.

The sheer number of elected officials—more than five hundred thousand—reveals our hybrid form of government. That's one elected government official for every six hundred people in the country. Few other nations come close to this ratio. We elect representatives, reflecting our origins as a republic, but the enormous number of opportunities to serve in elective office moves us closer to a democracy.

While our government combines elements of both democracy and republic, the debate continues about which way we should tilt. Which stance do you prefer?

THE BOTTOM LINE

- Self-rule is a powerful and enduring idea guiding American government. Lincoln put it best: "government of the people, by the people, for the people."

- There are two chief pathways to government by the people: a *democracy* and a *republic*. Americans have always sought to balance these two ideals.

⬤ Limited Government

Back in 1691, while America was still part of Britain, the king appointed Benjamin Fletcher to be governor of New York and gave him control over the New England colonies (which had been independent until then). The Connecticut legislature did not want to cede its power to Governor Fletcher and immediately selected a new commander for the local militia—a direct challenge to the new governor's authority. Fletcher sailed to Hartford, the capital of Connecticut, with a small detachment of troops. He assembled the Connecticut militia and had an officer read the royal proclamation declaring his authority over the state—and its militia.

As the officer read aloud, the Connecticut militiamen began to beat their drums in defiance. Fletcher tried to restore order by commanding his soldiers to fire their muskets in the air. In response, the commander of the Connecticut militia stepped forward, put his hand on the hilt of his sword, and issued his own warning: "If my drummers are again interrupted, I'll make sunlight shine through you. We deny and defy your authority." Outnumbered and in no mood for bloodshed, Fletcher beat a quick retreat to his vessel and sailed ignominiously back to New York City. Since the king and his ministers were more than three thousand miles away, they never even heard about this little rebellion against their authority.[10]

The Origins of Limited Government

The tale of Governor Fletcher illustrates an enduring idea: Americans distrust centralized leadership and have consistently sought to limit its power. Eighty years before the Revolutionary War, Connecticut had grown used to electing its own leaders and going its own way. The people saw the king as a distant figure with no right to interfere in their affairs. That image runs through American history: central government as a remote, unfeeling, untrustworthy authority that threatens our freedoms.

Why did Americans develop this distrust? The answer lies in how the people secured their rights in the first place. In most nations, the central government—made up of kings or aristocrats or both—grudgingly granted the people rights like the vote or jury trials. Sometimes the people rebelled (as in France), sometimes they negotiated with kings (England), and sometimes monarchs expanded rights to modernize their nations (Thailand). All these countries share a common experience: kings or the central governments that replaced them were the source of rights and liberties. No wonder people in these nations instinctively look to the government for help in solving their problems. The United States was dramatically different. Experience taught Americans to see the central government not as a potential source of rights, but as a threat to their life, liberty, and happiness.

And Yet . . . the United States Has a Big Government

Here is the paradox lying at the heart of the limited-government idea. People across the political spectrum demand government action. Many **conservatives** seek to use federal authority to crack down on drugs, root out obscenity, limit marriage to heterosexual couples, get tougher on crime, forbid abortions, or enhance homeland security.

Most **liberals** reject the idea that public officials should interfere in people's private lives. But they are all for active government when it comes to economic policy or corporate regulation. They call on the government to sponsor fast

Conservatives: Americans who believe in reduced government spending, personal responsibility, traditional moral values, and a strong national defense. Also known as *right* or *right-wing*.

Liberals: Americans who value cultural diversity, government programs for the needy, public intervention in the economy, and individuals' right to a lifestyle based on their own social and moral positions. Also known as *left* or *left-wing*.

trains, bank regulations, environmental protections, and school lunch programs (there's the freedom from want again).

Limits on Government Action

In short, Americans often say they do not like government and then demand government action for causes they care about. Their calls for action generally face two hurdles: the desire to limit government and the Constitution.

When the framers designed our political system, they organized suspicion of government right into the system. The federal Constitution includes an intricate system of checks and balances on power, which we will explore in the next chapter. The Constitution carefully limits what Congress may do—although Americans vigorously debate exactly where those boundaries actually are.

Although it is difficult for government officials to undertake new tasks, the barriers are not insurmountable. During times of crisis, people turn to the government and demand action. Skilled leadership can also negotiate sweeping changes. And once programs go into effect, they often prove popular.

Ironically, the limits on change make it difficult to repeal new programs once they make it past all the hurdles and are up and running. For example, Social Security was passed in 1935 during the economic crisis of the Great Depression; Medicare passed in part because of a great electoral landslide (in 1964). Both are now extremely popular policies; in fact, they are so popular that they are known in Washington as "the third rails" of American politics—touch them and die (politically, of course).

● *New Jersey Governor Chris Christie comforts victims of Hurricane Sandy, a massive 2012 storm. During crises like this one, even staunch antigovernment critics set their views aside to demand action.*

When Ideas Clash: Self-Rule and Limited Government

When Barack Obama ran for re-election in 2012, he vowed to raise taxes on wealthy people—those making $250,000 or more. His Republican opponent, Mitt Romney, denounced this idea and instead claimed that reducing taxes for everyone would boost economic performance.

Democrats and Republicans offered very different economic policies. And in the 2012 election, the people made a clear choice: Obama over Romney. Did this mean that the winning Democrats could swiftly act on this signature issue? No! There were too many barriers in Congress. Even after his big re-election victory, Obama had to compromise with the Republicans who controlled the House of Representatives.

Note the clash between two ideas that we have discussed: self-rule and limited government. Self-rule says that since the Democrats won the election, they should put their policies into place. Jefferson expressed this point plainly: "The will of the majority," he wrote, is a "sacred principle" and "the only sure guardian of the rights of man."[11] So President Obama should be able to do what

see for yourself 1.2

Go online and listen to the 2012 Republican National Convention chant.

What Do You Think?

SELF-RULE VERSUS LIMITED GOVERNMENT

Many observers think we no longer have government by the people because it is too difficult for elected officials to get things done. These reformers seek an easier path to government action. However, that prospect raises fears of a more active government. Which should we emphasize, self-rule or limited government? It's time to make your own choice.

I'm with Thomas Jefferson. It should be easier for elected officials to enact the programs they promised. If they cannot do so, elections become less meaningful. When the people vote for something and their representatives fail to deliver, it fosters cynicism about the entire political process. Self-rule requires us to follow the people's mandate. If the majority does not like the results, it can express its displeasure in the next election.

I'm with James Madison. The checks and balances that make large-scale reforms difficult protect the United States from overbearing government and from sudden changes—whether rapidly expanding or cutting programs. The barriers to government action *should* be high. If the public really wants something, it will probably happen over time. Limited government is more important. Don't change the process.

Not sure? This is a formidable question. You may very well change your mind— maybe more than once—as you continue to read this book.

he promised. Most democratic nations more faithfully follow this path to government by the people.

But another value, limited government, says: Not so fast. We don't like government meddling in our lives, so we make it very difficult for elected officials to follow through on their promises. Even a president who wins a national election by a large margin must still convince the majority in the House of Representatives and 60 percent of the Senate to vote his way.

The result is an important question for political scientists—and for all Americans: How should we balance self-rule and limited government? Erecting too many boundaries means that we undermine government of the majority. But if voters get everything the winning candidates promise them, the result could be a host of new programs and policies.

THE BOTTOM LINE

- Americans *distrust their government* far more than people in most other democracies. The Constitution builds that distrust into our governing rules by providing for *limited government.* The result is a durable status quo.

- In other countries, when politicians are elected promising a program, they can usually deliver. In the United States, winners confront multiple barriers to fulfilling their campaign promises. That's the antigovernmental strain in American thinking.

- However, once programs do go into effect, they often prove popular and difficult to change.

Individualism

Political scientist John Kingdon was visiting his niece in Norway. She was expecting a baby and Professor Kingdon asked what she planned to do about her job. Casually, she replied that she would receive a full year's leave at 80 percent of her normal pay and that her company was required to give her job back after the leave. "Who pays for all this?" asked Professor Kingdon. "The government, of course," his niece replied. She was surprised the question had even come up. "Is it any different in the United States?" she asked innocently.[12]

As Kingdon explained, it is completely different in the United States: advocates fought for years to pass the Family and Medical Leave Act (1993), which requires employers with more than fifty workers to allow up to twelve weeks of *unpaid* leave for pregnancy, adoption, illness, or military service. In 2012, the Supreme Court struck down part of the law by ruling that a state government employee who had been denied leave could not sue the state for cash.

Norwegians, through their government, take care of new parents. In fact, they take pretty good care of all their citizens. To pay for an array of public services, tax rates are much higher than ours. Almost half of a Norwegian's income goes to taxes.

Americans generally value **individualism**: *the idea that individuals, not the society or the community or the government, are responsible for their own well-being*. We, as a society, do not pay for maternity leave. Instead, we expect private individuals and families to handle birth, or adoption, or caregiving.

> **Individualism:** The idea that individuals, not the society, are responsible for their own well-being.

Community versus Individualism

The idea of individualism is a source of controversy in every nation. There are two ways to see any society: as a single *community* or as a collection of *individuals*. Clearly every nation is both, but government policies can be designed to emphasize the community or to focus on individuals. Let's take a closer look at these two principles.

Countries that emphasize the community are called **social democracies**. Social democrats believe that members of a society are responsible for one another. They use government as a source of mutual assistance. The government provides citizens with the basics: good health insurance, retirement benefits, generous unemployment packages, and—as we saw in the Norwegian case—maternity benefits.

> **Social democracy:** A government in which citizens are responsible for one another's well-being and use government policy to ensure that all are comfortably cared for.

In exchange, people pay high taxes. One effect of high taxation is to make it difficult for most citizens to get very rich. At the same time, the extensive welfare state makes it far less likely that people will live in poverty. Communal societies are far more equal than individualist ones—not in opportunity, but in outcome. Most Western European nations are social democracies.

Social democracies are based on *solidarity*, the idea that people have a tight bond and are responsible for one another. Some societies exhibit a strong sense of solidarity; in general, this sense increases during wars, economic depressions, or other crises that get everyone to pull together. Scholars have found that more homogeneous societies—where people look alike, share the same values, and practice the same religion—exhibit higher rates of solidarity than very diverse societies.

American politics includes a streak of solidarity. Martin Luther King put it eloquently: "I am inevitably my brother's keeper because I am my brother's brother."[13] The commitment to solidarity rises and falls in the United States; today it appears weaker than it has often been in the past.

● *Solidarity in Columbus, Ohio: Students from Central State University give the black power salute during a meeting on the Statehouse steps.*

Some groups in the United States are more likely to express high levels of solidarity within their group. Immigrants often feel this way. From Irish arrivals in the nineteenth century to Latino immigrants today, historians have chronicled a sense of shared fate among first- and second-generation Americans. African Americans, too, have traditionally displayed high levels of solidarity.

Now let us turn to individualism. In this view, people and their families are responsible for their own welfare. The economist Milton Friedman famously wrote that "the world runs on individuals pursuing their separate interests." Leave people free to choose their interests, Friedman continued, and the public interest of the whole society will emerge.[14] Rather than taxing people and using funds to aid the less well-off, proponents of this perspective opt for low taxes. People who work hard will get ahead, and society will grow and prosper.

Individualists value the chance to get ahead more than they value a society where everyone is equal. In social democracies, government regulations aim to protect workers. In contrast, individualists oppose government controls and believe that private companies should be able to expand or contract their workforce as they see fit (as long as they hire and fire without discriminating). Individualism points toward limited government, faith in economic markets, and a strong emphasis on *negative liberty*.

Opinion polls confirm what political theorists have long suspected: Americans tend to lean more to individualism than to social democracy—much more so than most other nations. In one prominent cross-national study, for example, people in many nations were asked whether "it is the responsibility of the government to take care of very poor people who cannot take care of themselves." More than 60 percent of the public strongly agreed in England, France, and Italy; 70 percent agreed in Spain. In contrast, only 23 percent of Americans agreed.[15]

The Roots of American Individualism: Opportunity and Discord

Americans lean toward individualism and away from social democracy. Why? Two famous explanations look to the past. One finds the answer in golden opportunities. A second emphasizes social and racial discord.

Golden Opportunity.   For centuries, most Europeans and Asians lived as serfs or peasants working small plots of land. Powerful rulers kept them firmly in their place—there was no chance for individuals to get ahead by working hard. In early America, by contrast, there appeared to be endless land and opportunity. With hard work and a little luck, anyone (at least any white male) could earn a decent living and perhaps even a fortune. Stories about early settlers clearing their own land were later reinforced by images of rugged individuals on the western frontier. Hard workers relied on themselves—not the government.

There is a lot of myth in these stories. Frontier life was less about brave individualism and more about people helping one another out. Settlers couldn't build a barn, a church, or a meetinghouse without their neighbors' help. But the image of hardy individuals on the frontier remains a powerful ideal in American political culture. And there was an important truth at its core: few

● *Individualism in historical memory: At high noon on April 22, 1889, bugles sounded and a great mob—lined up impatiently outside the territory—surged across the border and snatched up as much land as they could stake out. Although the government sponsored the land giveaway, the image that sticks is of the people grabbing their land for themselves. Oklahoma still honors the scalawags that snuck in early (or sooner) and staked the best land ahead of time—that's where the motto "The Sooner State" comes from.*

societies have ever offered so many individuals as much opportunity to rise and prosper as early America did.[16]

Social Conflict.   An entirely different explanation for American individualism emphasizes the enormous differences within our society: the country is too big and the population too diverse to develop a sense of solidarity. What, after all, did Calvinist Yankees in New England have in common with Roman Catholics in Baltimore or Anglican planters in Virginia—much less Spanish speakers in Florida or Texas? Moreover, a nation that included 4 million black slaves by 1860 had a terrible divide running through its heart.

By the 1830s there was still another source of division. Immigrants were arriving by the tens (and later hundreds) of thousands—speaking different languages and practicing what seemed like strange customs. Each generation of immigrants added to the American cacophony. For example, Irish Catholics (who arrived in the 1830s and 1840s) appeared strange and threatening to the English Protestants who had immigrated a century earlier. Could Catholics, with their allegiance to a foreign pope, really understand or uphold American values? All these divisions made solidarity far more difficult to feel than in more stable, homogeneous populations.

Which explanation is correct? Both are on target. Unprecedented economic opportunity and vast social divisions have reinforced individualism.

Who We Are: Individualism and Solidarity?

Americans are not individualists pure and simple. Rather, the two themes always compete in American politics. Individualism is more robust and more often in evidence, but a sense of solidarity also unites the American population. We often pull together as a nation. We often take care of our neighbors and pass government programs to improve the lives of people we do not know. The United States may have deep divisions, but it is remarkable how quickly they

INDIVIDUALISM VERSUS SOLIDARITY

Please score yourself on the following ten statements:
0 = Disagree strongly
1 = Disagree
2 = Agree
3 = Agree strongly

1. It is the responsibility of the government to take care of poor people who cannot take care of themselves.	0 1 2 3
2. Everyone should have health insurance in case they become ill.	0 1 2 3
3. In fact, everyone should have the *same* health insurance. It doesn't make sense for some people to get better care than others just because they can afford it.	0 1 2 3
4. I'd be willing to pay *a little more* in taxes so no person in America goes hungry or homeless.	0 1 2 3
5. I'd be willing to pay *a lot more* in taxes so that everyone in America has a pretty decent life.	0 1 2 3
6. I agree with Dr. Martin Luther King: "I am inevitably my brother's keeper because I am my brother's brother [and my sister's sister] . . . the betterment of the poor enriches the rich."	0 1 2 3
7. I don't believe big companies should be permitted to fire people without providing two months' salary and some retraining.	0 1 2 3
8. Most Americans want the same things out of life.	0 1 2 3
9. We should think about others as much as we think about ourselves.	0 1 2 3
10. It is wrong to step over others to get ahead in life.	0 1 2 3

Scoring

0–5 You are truly a rugged individualist!
5–14 You are largely an individualist.
15–20 You are a moderate who sees both sides of the issue.
20–24 You are a social democrat.
25–30 You are a true-blue believer in solidarity!

Now, speak with someone who scored very differently from you. Try to explain how and why you came to hold your views.

can disappear. A substantial majority of Americans today are children, grandchildren, or great-grandchildren of immigrants—many of whom were once regarded as strange and different.

All this raises another question to ponder: Where would you draw the line between solidarity and individualism? The answer directly relates to one of this book's central questions: *Who are we?* Take the test in "What Do You Think? Individualism versus Solidarity" to learn where you stand on the continuum between rugged individualism and strong solidarity.

THE BOTTOM LINE

- American politics includes both individualism and solidarity.

- Different leaders, parties, groups, and individuals weigh the two values in different ways. However, compared to other nations, the United States is very much at the individualist end of the spectrum.

The American Dream

Benjamin Franklin perfected a classic American literary form—tips for getting rich. Anyone, he assured his readers, could be successful by following a formula: be frugal ("A penny saved is a penny earned"), hardworking ("No gains without pains"), steady ("Little strokes fell great oaks"), bold ("God helps those who help themselves"), and—most important—morally upright ("Leave your vices, though ever so dear").[17]

Franklin was summarizing what later became known as the American dream: *if you are talented and work hard, you can achieve financial success.* A popular historian, James Truslow Adams, was the first to actually call this doctrine an American dream: "a land in which life should be better and richer and fuller for everyone, with opportunity for each according to ability or achievement."[18] The idea scarcely changes across generations. "The American dream that we were all raised on is a simple but powerful one," averred President Bill Clinton, more than two centuries after Ben Franklin. "If you work hard and play by the rules, you should be given a chance to go as far as your God-given abilities will take you."[19]

Spreading the Dream

The legacy of the Revolutionary War, according to historian Gordon Wood, was the spread of the American dream to all classes. National leaders originally imagined that they were establishing a classical republic, like Athens, in which a few outstanding men would govern the people. Instead, the Revolution established the common people as the basis of government and gave them an unprecedented chance to make their fortunes. What did the mass of people care about? "Making money and getting ahead," writes Wood. Yes, the goal was vulgar, material, crass, and even anti-intellectual. But opportunity had never been available on such a broad scale before.[20]

Enabling the dream of success remains an important part of any policy debate. Will a proposal help small business? Will it create jobs? Will it stifle entrepreneurs? Immigrants still come to the U.S. in large numbers—far more than to any other country—partly to pursue the dreams of success. Politicians from both parties eagerly try to spread the idea to other nations (which are not always enthusiastic because it can threaten the solidarity principle).

Challenging the Dream

Like every important idea, the American dream generates conflict. Critics raise two questions: Has the system become rigged to favor some (usually the wealthy) over others? And is the pursuit of wealth an undesirable value, either on its own merits or because it crowds out other important values?

Is the System Tilted Toward the Wealthy?   Some critics question whether the American dream is still open to everyone or whether it has grown biased toward the rich and powerful. For much of U.S. history, including the boom years after World War II, middle-class incomes rose faster than incomes at the top. Then, starting at the end of the 1970s, this trend changed. Money began to flow to the wealthiest more than to the other classes. Figures 1.3 and 1.4 compare the two periods.

Today, the top 1 percent of Americans hold more wealth than the bottom 90 percent combined. Three million people enjoy more wealth than do

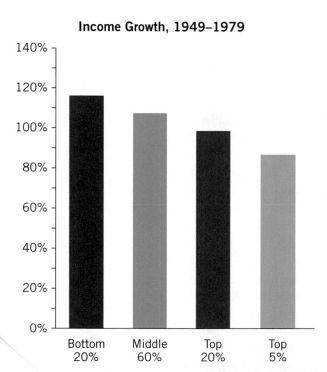

Income Growth, 1949–1979

IRE 1.3 *Between 1949 and 1979, those on the bottom saw their ⌐w faster than those on the top. . . . (Robert Frank,* Falling

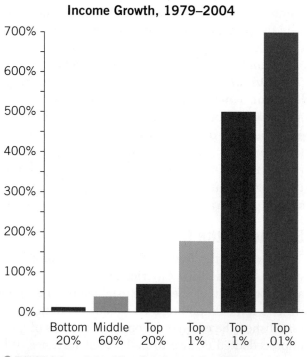

Income Growth, 1979–2004

● **FIGURE 1.4** *. . . but look how that changed after 1979. Now those on the bottom have little income growth whereas the wealthy have rapid growth. Is this a bad thing? Americans disagree. (Sawhill and Morton,* Economic Mobility)

270 million others. Sixty million Americans at the bottom of the charts own almost nothing—one-tenth of 1 percent of the national wealth. Many social scientists now argue that the chance of moving up—from poverty to wealth—is fading in the United States. Critics—both liberal and conservative—increasingly challenge the system for not offering real equality of opportunity.[21]

Does the American Dream Promote the Wrong Values? A second critique of the American dream questions the chase for wealth as a human value. Environmentalists criticize the damage caused by big houses, sprawling suburbs, gas-guzzling cars, and opulent lifestyles. Others cite the harm to old-fashioned communal ideals. "These dark days will be worth all they cost us," said President Franklin Roosevelt during the depths of the Great Depression, "if they teach us that our true destiny is . . . to minister . . . to our fellow man." Repeatedly, he urged Americans to rethink their basic values before an upturn in the stock market "dulled their moral sense." Voices like these have questioned the pursuit of economic success to the exclusion of community and social justice.[22]

The capitalists who celebrate wealth often have to wrestle with economic populists who would rather share it. During difficult economic times—like those accompanying the "Great Recession," which began in the fall of 2008—faith in the American dream lags.

Despite critics and challenges, Americans usually celebrate the gospel of success. The nation's politics, economics, and culture accommodate the dreams of wealth. In comparison with other wealthy nations, our taxes are relatively low, we regulate business less, we take fewer vacations, and we place more emphasis on getting ahead. As Figure 1.5 shows, younger people are far more likely than their parents or grandparents to believe they can achieve the American dream in their lifetime. They also believe they work harder than their parents did.

THE BOTTOM LINE

- The American dream is the belief that anyone who works hard can get ahead and grow wealthy.

- Critics argue that hard work is no longer enough to achieve the dream. They make two criticisms: the poor and middle class are falling farther behind the wealthy because of bias in the political economy, and other values are more important than wealth.

- Despite the critics, the dream remains a powerful American idea.

● Equality

When Tocqueville arrived in the United States in 1831, he was amazed by the widespread degree of equality. In one of his first letters home, he reported watching servers in a tavern sit down at the next table to eat and drink

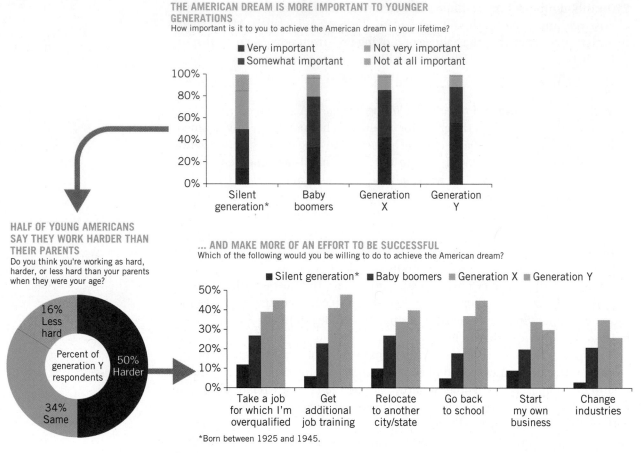

THE AMERICAN DREAM IS MORE IMPORTANT TO YOUNGER GENERATIONS
How important is it to you to achieve the American dream in your lifetime?

■ Very important   ■ Not very important
■ Somewhat important   ■ Not at all important

HALF OF YOUNG AMERICANS SAY THEY WORK HARDER THAN THEIR PARENTS
Do you think you're working as hard, harder, or less hard than your parents when they were your age?

16% Less hard
Percent of generation Y respondents
50% Harder
34% Same

... AND MAKE MORE OF AN EFFORT TO BE SUCCESSFUL
Which of the following would you be willing to do to achieve the American dream?

■ Silent generation*   ■ Baby boomers   ■ Generation X   ■ Generation Y

*Born between 1925 and 1945.

● **FIGURE 1.5** *The evolving American dream. Younger people are far more likely than their parents or grandparents to believe they can achieve the American dream in their lifetime.* (Good Magazine)

alongside the guests. People who declared bankruptcy were not shunned, as they would have been in France, but were treated the same as any other businessperson who had suffered a temporary setback. Here was a society where people from all ranks shook hands, discussed politics, and chased money. Everyone seemed to be equals.

Tocqueville distilled this thought into the first sentence of his great book *Democracy in America*: "No novelty in the United States struck me more vividly . . . than the equality of condition." In a world that was still full of aristocrats and inherited privilege, American society embodied the great idea at the heart of the Declaration of Independence: "All men [and women] are created equal."[23]

Equality means that *every citizen enjoys the same privileges, status, and rights before the laws.* There are three different kinds of equality to consider when analyzing the concept: *social, political,* and *economic.*

ality: All citizens enjoy ne privileges, status, before the laws.

Three Kinds of Equality

Social equality means that all individuals enjoy the same status in society. There are no American barons or archdukes who inherit special benefits when they are born. Except for slavery, there have never been fixed social classes. Few American politicians boast of noble origins or good family lineage. On the contrary, for the past 150 years candidates have flaunted (or invented) their working-class roots. Even very wealthy politicians often claim to have risen up from humble origins (for many years, they boasted about the log cabins they supposedly grew up in). An old cliché in American politics, one with a lot of truth to it, is the saying that any little boy or girl could grow up to be the president—or a millionaire. You don't have to be born into the "right" family or attend one specific school.

> **Social equality:** All individuals enjoy the same status in society.

Political equality means that every citizen has the same political rights and opportunities. Americans enjoyed universal white, male *suffrage*—or the right to vote—much earlier than did citizens of most nations. Over time the opportunity to vote spread. Today there are lively debates about whether we still ensure everyone an equal opportunity to affect the political process.

> **Political equality:** All citizens have the same political rights and opportunities.

Some reformers suggest, for example, that if everyone is to have the same chance to influence the political process, we should remove money from elections. Otherwise, the wealthy will have outsized influence. The quest for political equality raises a range of other issues: Does everyone enjoy an equal right to a fair trial—or have the costs of going to court elevated this basic right beyond the reach of many people? Does the voting system make it too difficult for some people to register and cast their ballots? All these questions reflect the fundamental issue of political equality: Does every citizen have an *equal opportunity* to influence the political process and are they all treated the same way before the law?

Economic equality focuses on differences in wealth. When President Washington toured the country in 1790, there were few very wealthy individuals and little poverty. For more than a century and a half, the nation truly was exceptional in its economic equality.[24] Today the United States has changed dramatically—toward inequality.

> **Economic equality:** A situation where there are only small differences in wealth between citizens.

How Much Economic Inequality Is Too Much?

Inequality in America by 2014 had reached levels not seen for a century or more. One illustration of national differences in economic inequality arises from the "salary gap." In 1965, the **median** (or typical) American chief executive officer (CEO) made twenty-six times more than a typical worker in his or her company. In Japan today the figure is roughly the same. But in the contemporary United States, the median CEO makes between three hundred and five hundred times the salary of the average employee (depending on the study). Is this a problem for the idea that "all men are created equal"? People in many countries would answer "yes." Too much inequality, they say, divides society.

> **Median:** A statistical term for the number in the middle or the case that has an equal number of examples above and below it.

As we have seen in our discussion of the American dream, our public policies (and public opinion) often endorse the race to wealth. Why not let the

● *Should we worry about economic inequality? LeBron James makes more than $60 million in salary and sponsorships for playing basketball. Is that too much for a superstar—even one as good as James? Should we change the rules so that the wealthy get less and poor people get more? Where you stand on these hotly debated questions depends on different ideas about equality.*

winners—basketball stars, successful musicians, bank executives, and break-through entrepreneurs—enjoy fabulous success? Some activists charge that the richest 1 percent take advantage of everyone else; critics on the other side dismiss such talk as un-American and as fostering "class warfare." In fact, this is an old debate stretching back through time.

Opportunity or Outcome?

Many Americans accept high levels of economic inequality, contending that these are not fatal to our hopes for an egalitarian society. That's because of an important distinction between *equal opportunity* and *equal outcome*.

Equal opportunity: The idea that every American has an equal chance to win economic success.

Equal opportunity is the idea that every American has an equal chance in life. Politically, this means each person gets one vote and the process is transparent and open to all. In economics, it means that every individual gets a fair shot at achieving the American dream. Whether you're white or black, Anglo or Latino, male or female, rich or poor, you have a similar opportunity to influence the political process and to win economic success.

Equal outcome: The idea that citizens should have roughly equal economic circumstances.

Equal outcome, in contrast, is the idea that a society guarantees not only opportunity but also results. Some nations reserve a minimum number of seats in the national legislature for women or members of specific ethnic groups. And, as we have already seen, others keep their taxes high and offer extensive social benefits, knowing that this arrangement will keep successful people from getting too far ahead of everyone else.

Today, the United States aims for equal opportunity. The winners fly in private jets; the losers may end up with nothing. Still, questions—and hard political choices—about equal opportunity remain. How do we give people a real chance to affect the governing process? How much education is enough to help ensure that a graduate can make it in the marketplace? Do we need to provide early childhood reading programs? Offer English-language programs for everyone who is not fluent? Guarantee basic nutrition? Remove lead paint that might leave children mentally impaired? And what should we do about past injustice? Does the long legacy of slavery, segregation, and repressive policies toward American Indians require our society to offer special forms of compensation to groups that suffered generation after generation of mistreatment?

These questions return us to the same policy debates we introduced during the discussion of positive and negative liberty. Should we guarantee the basics—or simply protect individual rights and let every person run the great race alone? As you can see, debates about equality lead back to debates about freedom (positive or negative) and individualism.

Might the gap between rich and poor grow so large that it undermines equality of opportunity? By 2014, middle-class Canadians, and people in many other wealthy nations, had incomes higher than middle-class Americans—who had long led the world in average incomes.[25] As the gap continues to widen, liberals warn that growing disparities are creating a land of billionaires and hungry children with grim future prospects. Conservatives respond that the effort to redistribute wealth from rich to poor violates American ideas.

Over time, the United States has gone from the most equal society in the world to one that is considerably less equal than other wealthy nations (see Figure 1.6). The past thirty-five years, in particular, have seen a sharp spike

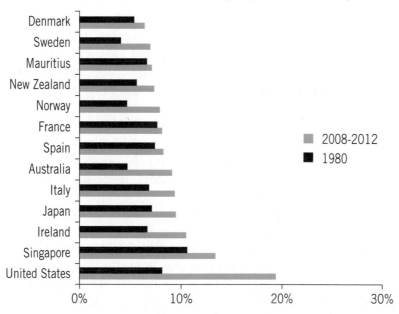

The share of national income going to the richest one percent

■ 2008-2012
■ 1980

● **FIGURE 1.6** *The gap between rich and poor: comparing 1980 to 2008–2012. Note how much more unequal the United States has become. ("Working for the Few," Oxfam, 2014)*

in inequality. American politics has come to emphasize other ideas—negative liberty, individualism, the American dream of getting ahead—over equality. Still, we live in a dynamic and fluid society. Today, many Americans, both conservatives and liberals, have begun to call for renewed efforts to increase equality of opportunity.

THE BOTTOM LINE

- Equality means that every citizen enjoys the same privileges, status, and rights before the law.

- Equality applies to social status, political rights, and economic conditions.

- Today, America generally aims for *equal opportunity* rather than *equal outcome*, although heated discussions rage over what society must provide to ensure equal opportunity.

Religion

In the 1630s, a large contingent of Puritans sailed to New England with an ambitious aim: to establish a biblical commonwealth that would serve as a Christian model for the rest of the world. Governor John Winthrop, in his shipboard sermon, called their settlement "a city upon a hill" and expected "the eyes of all people on us." How did they fare? If anyone really was watching, they soon saw unexpected complications.

For example, Quakers from Pennsylvania—whom the New England Puritans despised for lacking discipline—began sailing north to convert the New Englanders. If the Quakers succeeded, they would subvert the whole idea of a model Puritan society. New England's women, the ministers worried, might be especially vulnerable to Quaker heresies. The authorities banned Quakers from Massachussetts under threat of having an ear cut off (one each for the first and second offenses), their tongues pierced by hot pokers (third offense), and finally death. Quaker martyrs piously and joyfully challenged the Puritan authorities. Four were hanged before English authorities ordered an end to the punishment.

This story reflects several enduring American themes: the importance of religion, the intense competition between sects, and a missionary fervor about saving the world. Even today, politicians of every stripe repeat the idea of a "city on a hill" (although few realize that Winthrop was quoting the Sermon on the Mount in the New Testament).

Still a Religious Country

Religion plays an enduring role in American politics and society. The centrality of religion may not surprise you. But it is a powerful example of American exceptionalism, helping inspire a sense that this nation is unlike any other.

As most nations grow wealthier, their religious fervor wanes. Citizens in developed countries, from Britain and France to Japan and South Korea, tell pollsters that God is not very important in their lives. In contrast, Americans maintain high (and by some measures, rising) levels of religiosity. Some 95 percent of Americans say they believe in God, almost 60 percent belong to a church, and nearly 40 percent attend church regularly (see Figures 1.7 and 1.8). To find higher levels you have to go to poorer nations such as India, Egypt, and Indonesia.[26]

So Many Religions

Americans have a lot of religions to choose from. One recent survey found sixteen different Christian denominations with more than a million members each.[27] That is just the beginning. Jews number over 6.7 million, Muslims some 3 million, and seven other non-Christian groups have over one hundred thousand adherents each (two of the fastest growing are Wiccans and Pagans).[28] In contrast, many other nations have a single major faith, often supported by the government through tax dollars.

Why so many religions? From the start, different colonies began with distinct religious affiliations. By forbidding the federal government from boosting any official faith, the Constitution kept the field open for any new preacher with a religious idea that might attract a following. Since none can win official recognition, each religious institution is only as strong as the congregation it can muster.

Percentage of the Population That Belongs to a Church or Religious Organization

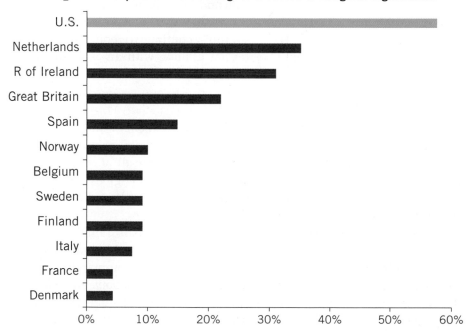

● **FIGURE 1.7** *Look how American religiosity stands out. As nations grow wealthy, religion nearly always loses its importance. The United States is the great exception.* (*Pew Research Center*)

What Do You Consider Yourself First?

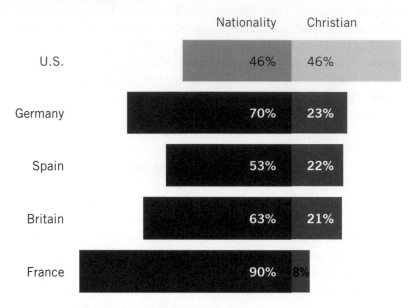

● **FIGURE 1.8** *For many Americans, religion is as important as national identity. This chart shows that American Christians take their faith as seriously as being American—in contrast to European Christians, who emphasize their country over their religion. (Pew Research Center)*

This open market explains why new religions spring up all the time. It does not explain why Americans respond. One of the great mysteries of our political culture is why Americans continue to worship, whereas citizens in other wealthy nations show a declining interest in religion.

Religious observance is not the same throughout the United States. Texas and Georgia (proud members of the "Bible Belt") have high religiosity, Florida and Missouri are in the middle, Colorado and Wisconsin are not especially religious, and Maine is the least religious of all. Generational change is also at work: while Americans under the age of thirty continue to report high rates of religious faith, an unusual number do not affiliate with any denomination. Most believe in God but not organized religions.[29]

The Politics of Religion

How is religion relevant to politics? The First Amendment declares, "Congress shall make no law respecting an establishment of religion or prohibiting the free exercise thereof." Thomas Jefferson described "a wall of separation between church and state." And yet America's energetic religious life—marked through our history by great evangelical revivals—injects three different kinds of political issues into American politics.

First, there is the question of what exactly the Constitution forbids. May teachers lead prayers in public schools? May students in the bleachers organize prayers before football games? May judges post the Ten Commandments in a courthouse? Questions like these spark intense debates about just where to draw the line between church and state.

Second, religious faith often inspires people to throw themselves into political issues. A religious revival sparked the abolitionist fight against slavery, beginning in the 1830s, with abolitionists condemning slavery as a sin. More than a century later, the civil rights movement spilled out from Baptist and Methodist churches across the South, brimming with religious rhetoric, religious symbols, and religious zeal. The opponents of racial equality—arguing

● *What constitutes religious teaching?*

for slavery and segregation—also framed their response in religious terms. In American politics, both sides often invoke God. The controversies swirling around the politics of peace, abortion, the environment, gay marriage, and many other issues have all, to varying extents, made the same leap from pulpit to politics. Today, conservatives are more likely to take their faith into the political arena, but this has not always been true. Over time religion has inspired people across the political spectrum to take action.

Third, religious fervor sometimes fosters a missionary sense in American politics. As the nation expanded westward, Americans declared their "manifest destiny"—God had given an entire continent to his chosen people. Many foreign policies also express a special American mission in the world. During the Cold War, American leaders constantly invoked God as a way of contrasting the United States with communist nations. Congress added "under God" to the Pledge of Allegiance (in 1954) and "In God We Trust" to paper money (1955). John Winthrop's idea—America as a model for the world—echoes from one generation to the next.

THE BOTTOM LINE

- Religion plays an enduring role in American politics and society. This is unusual—almost unique—among wealthy countries.

- Americans have an unusually large number of faiths to choose from, although younger people are less likely to affiliate with an organized religion.

- Religious politics raise questions about the role and the extent of religion in our national public life. They inspire political participation on a host of issues—from civil rights to abortion. And they foster a missionary sense in American foreign policy.

● How Do Ideas Affect Politics?

Most political scientists agree that the seven ideas of this chapter are central to U.S. society. But how do these ideas influence our politics? There are two familiar answers. Either ideas influence our culture or they operate through our institutions. There is still another possibility to bear in mind, however: perhaps they have a life all their own.

Ideas in American Culture

Political culture: The orientation of citizens of a state toward politics.

Each nation has a unique **political culture**, constructed over the years by a people and its leaders. Anthropologist Clifford Geertz, in his classic work *The Interpretation of Cultures*, described culture as the stories a group tells about itself. Ideas such as liberty, the fear of government, individualism, and the American dream together are the foundation of American political culture. They are the stories we tell about ourselves.

A culture shapes the way people think about politics and government. When Tea Party activists rallied against President Obama's health plan, they drew on a shared set of traditions, references, and values (like direct democracy, negative liberty, and the American dream) that would make no sense to people in, say, Denmark or Mexico. Critics of the growing "wealth gap" in the United States seize on overlapping parts of the American legacy—direct democracy, equality, and positive liberty—to promote a different set of political aims.

Culture develops slowly over time, shaped by history and experience. Colonial Americans' shared beliefs, stories, and mental habits—their culture—inspired the founding generation to develop a Constitution that limits the power of government. Why did the framers add a Bill of Rights to the Constitution? Their abiding faith in individualism. Why are there so many checks and balances in our national government? The old American fear of too much government. Why do we regulate and tax less than other nations? The American dream's gospel of success. This shared culture leads men and women to fight for policies that reflect freedom or democracy; policies that reflect social-democratic solidarity are more difficult to win because they resonate more faintly through American culture. American hopes and fears often seem peculiar to people in other nations—just as their hopes and fears may not make sense to us.

Cultures change slowly. To be sure, the American dream has expanded to include African Americans, Asians, Latinos, and women—all excluded from basic rights a century ago. But they pursue a vision of success that looks quite similar to the one that a much smaller circle of Americans found alluring a century or two ago.

The Ideas in Political Institutions

A different perspective suggests that political institutions, more than political culture, drive events. According to this view, the Constitution's drafters were guided less by cultural values; rather, they were looking for organizational arrangements that would regulate political behavior.

James Madison explained the *institutional perspective*. Past political theory expected republican citizens to virtuously seek the public interest. But, Madison continued sardonically in the *Federalist Papers*, "enlightened statesmen will not always be at the helm."[30] The Constitution did not ask people to be virtuous; instead, it developed a government that would operate smoothly even if citizens were greedy and their leaders corrupt. The institution—the rules and organizations built into the government—would shape popular behavior.

Many political scientists follow Madison's argument. It is our governing institutions, starting with the Constitution, that shape American political behavior. Institutions, they say, even influence our values. Government organizations and programs create their own self-reinforcing political dynamics. Each new organization and public policy readjusts the political world.

From an institutional perspective, the barriers to enacting new programs emerge not from a dislike of government but from the way the government is organized in the first place. A look at Congress reveals checks, balances, fragmented power, and multiple barriers to getting anything done. Similar limits affect government in the states and cities. The U.S. government is slow to act, according to this view, because we have *designed* it to be slow to act. When Americans criticize their policy makers for inaction, perhaps they miss the point: gridlock is a consequence of the institutions we have inherited.

Culture or Institutions?

Although historians and sociologists tend to emphasize political culture, many political scientists are skeptical about its explanatory power. How, they ask, can something as static as national culture explain the fluid, fast-changing American political scene?

For example, the cultural perspective suggests that the United States has never passed national health insurance, supplied and paid for by the federal government, because Americans don't trust government. The institutional perspective counters that it is less a matter of popular belief and more the way we've designed the government. After all, they continue, Harry Truman won the presidential election of 1948 in part by promising national health insurance. But Congress—using the checks and balances central to our national government's institutions—buried the proposal.

In fact, continue institutionalists, when government actually manages to create universal programs—such as Social Security or Medicare—they generally turn out to be extremely popular. If Americans are habitually suspicious of government, why are programs like Social Security so cherished?[31]

Proponents of culture respond that cultural values are not meant to explain every possible political action. Events, leaders, movements, and government agencies all introduce change. But culture forms the boundary of those changes. It limits the possibilities, shapes our perceptions, and influences our reactions. When terrorists launch an attack, for example, the American response—and the debate about that response—is deeply influenced by the values and ideas we share.

THE BOTTOM LINE

- How do the foundational ideas influence politics? Political scientists point to three different ways.

- First, ideas shape American culture, which in turn affects our politics.

- Second—and most popular among political scientists—ideas operate through political institutions. We must study those institutions to appreciate how ideas shape politics and policies.

- Third, ideas may have their own independent power.

● Conclusion: Culture and Institutions, Together

Do the ideas described in this chapter add up to a political culture that shapes the attitudes of American men and women? That cultural argument seems intuitive to many people. On balance, however, most political scientists underscore the importance of institutions.

As a political science student, you can decide for yourself on the relative power of ideas and institutions as you read this book. But you don't have to choose one or the other. We believe that culture and institutions together play a role in American politics. They reinforce each other. Yes, national institutions make it difficult to pass big national programs like universal health insurance; and yes again, opponents invoke powerful cultural norms—like individualism and liberty—to persuade Americans that such legislation threatens their values. For us, the most interesting question is how ideas, culture, and institutions (along with interests and individuals—the four I's introduced earlier in this chapter) all interact to shape American politics.

Finally, ideas have a power of their own—above and beyond the culture and institutions they have helped to shape. Ideas of liberty, democracy, or the American dream can move people to act. That's exactly what Captain (and Professor) Russell Burgos was thinking as the mortars came flying into his post in northern Iraq.

As you read through this book, you will constantly encounter the seven ideas we have described in this chapter. Think about which seem most important and powerful to you. And pay attention to how they appear to operate—through the culture, through institutions, with a life of their own, or (as we believe) in all these ways at different times and in different circumstances.

CHAPTER SUMMARY

● This book examines four key questions: Who governs, how does American politics work, what does government do, and who are we?

● Seven important ideas influence American politics. Each idea has at least two different interpretations—differences that spur intense political debates.

● *Freedom* means that the government will protect your life, liberty, and property from the coercion of others (including government) so that you can pursue the goals you define for yourself. In one view, freedom requires *positive government* action to make sure that everyone has the basics to permit them to pursue their goals. In another view, the government guarantees only *negative freedom*—the freedom to pursue your goals. You are free to succeed or to fail on your own, but there are no guarantees about food, or homes, or health care.

● *Self-rule* means that people govern themselves through clearly defined procedures like elections. In a democracy, citizens participate directly in making government decisions. In a republic, the people rule indirectly through their elected representatives. The American system is a combination of the two, a democratic republic.

● Americans value *limited government*: they distrust government and place limits on the authority it can exercise.

● *Individualism* means that individuals—not society or the government—are responsible for their own well-being. For those who favor community or social democracy, the public interest is best served when members of a society use government to take care of one another. Americans take both an individual and a communal view, but in contrast to many other nations, the individualistic view is more powerful.

● The *American dream* holds that if you are talented and work hard, you will succeed and grow

wealthy. Critics argue that the system is rigged or that the dream promotes the wrong values. However, the dream remains a powerful force in American politics.

● *Equality* allows each citizen to enjoy the same privileges, status, and rights before the law. Some define equality as a matter of *opportunity*—the idea that every American has an equal chance. Others promote equal *outcome*—a guarantee of results. There are three kinds of equality to consider: Social equality means that all individuals enjoy the same status in society. Political equality guarantees every citizen the same rights and opportunities to participate in politics. Economic equality minimizes the gap between citizens' wealth and earnings.

● *Religion* plays an enduring role in American politics and society. The great question is how we limit government interference without limiting religion itself.

● These seven ideas mark Americans' beliefs as a people. They can shape politics through national culture, through political institutions, and through their own influence on Americans.

KEY TERMS

American exceptionalism, 10
Conservatives, 17
Democracy, 14
Economic equality, 29
Equality, 28
Equal opportunity, 30
Equal outcome, 30
Freedom, 11

Individualism, 21
Institutions, 6
Liberals, 17
Libertarians, 12
Median, 29
Negative liberty, 11
Political culture, 36
Political equality, 29

Positive liberty, 11
Rational choice theory, 7
Republic, 5
Self-rule, 14
Social democracy, 21
Social equality, 29

STUDY QUESTIONS

1. The second paragraph of the Declaration of Independence boldly explains why "governments are instituted among men." Why? Why are governments formed? Do you agree with that assertion about government's most basic function?

2. Liberty is often described as the most important American idea. Describe the two different views of liberty. Which do you think is more accurate?

3. Review the seven principal "American ideas" we have identified in this chapter. Are *new* foundational ideas bubbling up in American politics today? What examples can you imagine?

4. The Declaration of Independence asserts that all men are endowed by their creator with the inalienable rights to life, liberty, and the pursuit of happiness. Over time, Americans have extended that idea to more and more people, such as former slaves and women. Are there groups in our society today who are *not* getting the full benefits of this ideal?

5. What is the difference between a democracy and a republic? Which principle does contemporary American government reflect, or does it reflect both? If you were a Founder, which of these principles would you emphasize?

6. Think of the various groups that you belong to. How would you describe each group? And in what ways is each group part of larger American society?

7. There are three forms of equality—social, political, and economic. Define each.

8. Describe the two approaches to economic equality: opportunity and outcome.

9. When it comes to religion, the United States is different from most wealthy societies. How? How do young people differ from previous generations in their approach to religion?

10. Ideas operate through both culture and institutions. Explain.

2

The Constitution

THE R. R. MOTON HIGH SCHOOL in Farmville, Virginia,

was a mess. The roof leaked, the heat worked poorly, the classrooms were over-crowded, and the school bus kept breaking down. When it rained, students sat under umbrellas and shivered in their coats. Moton was a black school; across town, the white students were warm and dry. On April 23, 1951, a Moton junior named Barbara Johns decided to take action. She fooled the principal into leaving the school for the day and forged notes to the teachers calling an assembly. When the students had all filed into the auditorium, the sixteen-year-old stood on stage, called for a strike, and led a student march to the Prince Edward County Courthouse to protest the shabby state of the school.

The students and their families called a leading civil rights group, the National Association for the Advancement of Colored People (NAACP), which dispatched a team of lawyers. The lawyers explained that local governments run American schools, and there was not much the NAACP could do about the conditions at Moton High School. However, continued the lawyers, they could challenge the entire policy of racial segregation. If the black students went to the same school as the white students, they would probably have a nicer school-house. The NAACP sued the school district, arguing that forcing African Americans into a separate school violated the U.S. Constitution. The Supreme Court took the case, *Davis v. School Board of Prince Edward County*, bundled it together with four similar cases, and three years after the student strike, delivered one of the most famous court decisions in American history, a ruling known as *Brown v. Board of Education*.

A sixteen-year-old took a bold risk, the Supreme Court unanimously ruled that she was right, and hundreds of laws across many states were struck down for violating the Constitution. The Court ruled that segregated education facilities are inherently unequal and violate the Fourteenth Amendment of the U.S. Constitution, which declares: "No state shall . . . deny to any person . . . the equal protection of the laws."[1]

Stop and think about the power Americans invest in this document written more than 225 years ago. The Constitution is the owner's manual and rulebook

IN THIS CHAPTER, YOU WILL:

● Discover the roots of the Constitution in colonial and revolutionary America.

● See why Americans declared independence from England and learn about their first constitution, the Articles of Confederation.

● Follow the arguments that shaped the Constitution and get an overview of the final document.

● Read about the great national debate over whether to adopt the Constitution.

● Learn how Americans have changed the Constitution—and how the Constitution has changed America.

● *The student strikers at Moton High School, led by Barbara Johns. They had an enormous impact because civil rights lawyers found a way to place their grievance in the context of the U.S. Constitution.*

for American government. It specifies how the government operates, setting out what the government may do and how to do it. If you want to learn about any feature of American politics, always check the Constitution first.

Who are we? The answer to that question is always changing, but the Constitution provides the ground rules for those changes, today as always. It organizes our political life. The Declaration of Independence sets out the ideas behind America. The Constitution creates an institution that can put the ideas into effect. It *institutionalizes* American ideas.

This sounds simple: the Constitution guides the government. But there is a wrinkle. It is often unclear how the Constitution applies to modern questions. After all, it is just 4,400 words written on four pages of parchment more than 225 years ago. Many provisions can be read two (or more) different ways; and

---

BY THE NUMBERS

The Constitution

- Number of articles (or sections) in the U.S. Constitution: **7**
- Number of articles in the constitution of India (1950) and the constitution of South Africa (1996), respectively: **395; 244**
- Number of times the word *power* or *powers* appears in the U.S. Constitution: **16**
- Number of times the word *liberty* appears in the Constitution: **1**
- Number of times the word *equality* appears in the Constitution: **0**
- Years after the Constitution was written that the Fourteenth Amendment added the idea of equality to the document: **81**
- Number of *proposed* amendments to the Constitution introduced in Congress since 1791: **more than 100,000**
- Number of *successful* amendments since 1791: **17**
- Number of amendments to the California state constitution: **more than 520**
- Percentage of the U.S. population that can block a constitutional amendment: **3**
- Number of the 13 states that ratified (voted for) the Constitution within 6 months: **6**
- Number of states that initially voted against the Constitution: **2**
- Number of delegates in New York, Virginia, and Massachusetts who could have defeated the entire Constitution by switching their votes: **18 (3% of total delegates)**
- Number of words that the Constitution uses to describe and empower Congress: **2,243**
- Number of words that the Constitution uses to describe and empower the president: **1,015**
- Number of words that the Constitution uses to describe and empower the courts: **364**

the document is silent on many topics. As a result, we always have to *interpret* how the Constitution applies to a case today.

Segregation is a prime example. The Constitution does not say anything about racial segregation. Back in 1896, the Supreme Court ruled that segregation did not violate the "equal protection" clause of the Fourteenth Amendment. In 1954, the Court ruled that it did. Different justices in different eras read the same words differently. We constantly debate exactly how to read the words in the Constitution and how to apply them to the questions we face.

● The Colonial Roots of the Constitution

No nation in the eighteenth century had anything like the American Constitution. Most nations wrote their governing documents much later; some countries, like England and Israel, never wrote one at all. However, the American Constitution did not spring up from nowhere. Many features of colonial politics propelled the new nation toward its constitution.

- First, the colonies were three thousand miles away from the king and his armies. The authorities back in England debated policies and issued orders; the American colonists frequently ignored them and did what they wished. No one back in London paid much attention. The English policy of ignoring colonies was known as *salutary neglect*; it permitted the colonies to develop their own political institutions. When England started interfering in colonial affairs, the Americans revolted.

- Second, beginning with the Virginia House of Burgesses in 1620, every colony elected its own legislature. As a result, the colonists had a great deal of experience with representation. New settlements demanded seats in the assemblies. New immigrants wanted the right to vote (for example, Polish men went on strike in Virginia over the issue). In some places, like New Jersey, women with property could vote. America grew up arguing about representation—and that prepared them for the debate over the Constitution.

- Third, plentiful land created opportunities for ordinary people. Early America was not an equal society by any means: there were aristocratic families and slaves, prosperous merchants and **indentured servants**. However, by the standards of the time, the New World was a land of extraordinary social mobility. When North Carolina tried to set up a system of titles and social classes, the effort collapsed as ordinary people made their fortunes and soon were wealthier than the would-be lords and dukes. Economic conditions helped foster a republic.

Indentured servant:
A colonial American settler contracted to work for a fixed period (usually three to seven years) in exchange for food, shelter, and transportation to the New World.

Compact: A mutual agreement that provides for joint action to achieve defined goals.

Covenant: A compact invoking religious or moral authority.

- Fourth, some colonies began with mutual agreements between the settlers, known as **compacts** or **covenants**. The Pilgrims, who landed in Massachusetts in 1620, introduced the idea; before they went ashore all forty-one adult males signed a mutual agreement known as the Mayflower Compact (named after their vessel, the *Mayflower*). In most nations, the right to rule stretched back through history and was based on tradition and military force. In contrast, the individuals on the *Mayflower* deliberately formed a new society, based on their mutual agreement and consent. Many New England communities began with such compacts or covenants—rough, often religiously inspired forerunners of a constitution. In fact, the preamble to the U.S. Constitution took the same form as the New England covenants.

- Fifth, many colonists came to the New World to practice their religion in peace. Beginning in Rhode Island in 1636, a revolutionary idea began to emerge: the individual's freedom to practice religion without government interference. In some colonies, it was followed by other rights, like freedom of speech and freedom of the press. The rights of citizens would become the single greatest issue in the debate over whether to accept (ratify) the new constitution.

- Sixth, border areas in early America were violent and insecure. Brutal wars with the Native Americans marked many of the colonies. The French claimed land to the north and west, the Spanish to the south and

● *The Mayflower Compact. The settlers agree among themselves to enter into a "civic body politic"— a government. The authority of their government rose from their own agreement—signed only by the men.*

west. Colonists also constantly fought one another over their own boundaries. After the break with England, insecure borders helped inspire the colonists to adopt a strong central government.

Each colony governed itself in its own way. However, the six features described here—distance from English authority, representation, social mobility, covenants, individual rights, and violent borders—all propelled Americans toward the Constitution of 1787.

Why the Colonists Revolted

The roots of the American Revolution lie in a great English victory. Centuries of rivalry between England and France burst into war in 1754. Known as the French and Indian War, the conflict spread through the colonies from Virginia all the way to Canada. Colonial American militias fought side by side with the British army and defeated the French in 1763. Thirteen years later the colonists declared independence and turned their muskets on the English.

Why did the Americans suddenly revolt? Because the victory over France introduced two fateful changes. First, ten thousand English troops remained in the colonies to protect the newly won land. The existence of those "Redcoats" meant that England could now enforce its policies: the days of salutary neglect were over. Second, the English had run up a crushing debt during the ten years of war and decided that their colonists should help pay it. Americans' reaction was explosive.

The Colonial Complaint: Representation

It was not just Britain's demand for money that provoked the colonists. Americans had grown used to making their own decisions through their elected assemblies. When the English imposed new taxes, without the approval of the colonial assemblies in the thirteen colonies, they violated the colonial idea of self-rule. The result was an unusual revolution. Most revolutionaries rise up against regimes that have long repressed them. In contrast, the Americans fought to preserve rights that they had been exercising during the many years of happy neglect.

Beneath the conflict lay a deep philosophical difference about representative democracy. The colonists considered their assemblies the legitimate voice of the people; if taxes had to be raised, they were the ones to do it. Colonial assemblies were very responsive to the voters and their daily concerns—they worried about things like building roads and surveying new lands. Political theorists call the colonial view of governance **delegate representation**.

The British never understood this view of representation because they operated with an entirely different one. Unlike the colonists, the English did not change their electoral districts every time the population shifted. English elected

Delegate representation: When representatives follow expressed wishes of the voters.

officials were expected to pursue the good of the whole nation. Your representative is not an "agent" or an "advocate," argued English statesman Edmund Burke, but a member of Parliament who must be guided by "the general good." This English view of representation is known as **trustee representation**.

Trustee representation: Representatives do what they regard as the best interest of the voters—independent of what the voters want.

The Conflict Begins with Blood on the Frontier

After the French and Indian War, settlers poured westward (Figures 2.1 and 2.2). Native Americans fought back; they rallied around Chief Pontiac and overran colonial settlements and English forts in Virginia, Maryland, and Pennsylvania. To end the fighting, England closed the western border and prohibited settlers from moving westward, past the crests of the lengthy Appalachian mountain chain. The colonists were stunned. The arbitrary boundary, announced in the Proclamation of 1763, had been drawn amid lobbying by land speculators, who could make or lose fortunes depending on whether their own land was open to settlement. The proclamation threatened the westward thrust that spelled opportunity to the restless colonists. American settlers did not care about Native American rights to the land. As they saw it, a corrupt English monarchy was blocking American pioneers from settling the wide-open spaces that they had helped win from France.

The colonists responded in their traditional way—they ignored regulations that did not suit them. But now there was a British army in America, enabling the English to enforce their policies. The Proclamation of 1763 was followed by the Quartering Act (1765), which required colonial assemblies to billet British troops in empty barns and warehouses. Suddenly, the Redcoats began to feel like an occupying army.

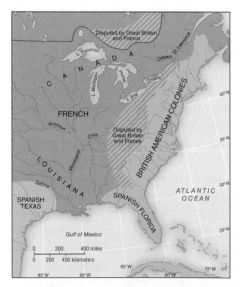 

● **FIGURES 2.1 and 2.2** *The colonies before (left) and after (right) the French and Indian War. Spain lost Florida but gained the land west of the Mississippi in compensation for having supported France. Napoleon would grab it back from Spain and then, in 1803, sell it to the United States. Note the line formed by the Proclamation of 1763 on the map on the right. England tried to forbid settlers from crossing that line.*

Britain also began to enforce its **mercantilist** trade policies, which meant American ships had to bypass their traditional (and lucrative) partners and do business only with English colonies at higher prices. Colonists who ignored the decree were charged with smuggling: wealthy merchants suddenly faced imprisonment or large fines for trading with French colonies. To make matters even worse, the English introduced taxes to help support their army of Redcoats. These widely reviled duties culminated in the Stamp Act of 1765.

Mercantilism: An economic theory according to which government controls foreign trade to maintain prosperity and security.

The Stamp Tax and the First Hints of Independence

Stamp taxes were a common way to raise money in England, but the effort to impose one on the colonies set off a firestorm. Parliament ignored the colonial assemblies (violating colonial ideas of representation) and simply declared the tax. Colonists responded by convening a Stamp Act Congress that met in October 1765. Delegates from nine colonies sent a protest to the king and to Parliament. The English policies were pushing the colonists into working together. In fact, the name *Stamp Act Congress* may have been more alarming to the English authorities than the petition the body drafted. In the eighteenth century, the word *congress* meant a diplomatic assembly of representatives from independent nations. The very name of this meeting intimated independence.

Protests against the stamp tax spread through the colonies. Mobs hung, burned, and beheaded tax collectors in effigy. They attacked tax collectors' offices and homes. Across the sea, the English authorities were incredulous about the violence. All they could see were ungrateful colonists who refused to pay for their own protection.[2]

The Townshend Acts Worsen the Conflict

After an alarmed Parliament reluctantly lifted the stamp taxes, colonists celebrated the repeal and tensions eased—until Parliament followed up with the Townshend Acts in 1767. These acts instituted another round of new taxes; revenues were earmarked to pay a new colonial authority, the American Board of Customs, which would collect taxes independently of the colonial assemblies. Now an imperial bureaucracy was explicitly pushing aside the colonial assemblies. The Townshend Acts also suspended the New York State Assembly for refusing to house and supply British troops.

Once again, American colonists responded with meetings, petitions, and mobs. New Yorkers and, later, Bostonians seethed with anger over having their legislatures dissolved. Mobs harassed the customs officials, who found it impossible to carry out their duties and called for help. A British warship arrived and officials seized a vessel owned by John Hancock, one of the resistance leaders, and charged him with smuggling. That move set off riots, bringing British troops into the city to restore order. Before long, there were almost four thousand Redcoats in a city of fifteen thousand people. The mobs harassed the soldiers with taunts, rocks, and snowballs until on March 5, 1770, one detachment of Redcoats panicked and fired point-blank on the crowd.

● An engraving of the Boston Massacre done by Paul Revere. This version of the event makes the British look like cold-blooded killers—not historically accurate but powerful propaganda for independence.

The Boston Massacre, as the event quickly became known, left five civilians dead. The first to fall was a sailor named Crispus Attucks, the son of an African slave and a Natick Indian. Attucks himself is thought to have escaped slavery some twenty years earlier. Ironically, the son of two groups who would not be liberated by the revolution—an African slave and an American Indian—was the first to bleed for the cause. Paul Revere memorialized the massacre with an engraving that transformed the panicky soldiers threatened by a mob into a line of killers firing into a heroic cluster of civilians. A leading U.S. history textbook calls the engraving "perhaps the most famous piece of anti-military propaganda in American history."[3]

English policy was in shambles; colonists' anger approached a fever pitch. At the start of the crisis, six years earlier, colonial leaders were respectfully petitioning the king to rescind imperial policies. Now, blood had been shed and the colonists began to talk about rebellion.

The Boston Tea Party

The British repealed all the Townshend duties except a tariff on tea. Tea was a global industry in 1773; think of it as the must-have tablet product of the eighteenth century. But the East India Tea Company, which had a monopoly in England, was on the verge of bankruptcy. In 1773, Parliament tried to rescue the Company by granting it a monopoly over the tea trade in the New World. The colonial shippers who had long been trading tea would be shut out by this rival trading network.

When ships with East India tea arrived, mobs in Philadelphia and New York forced them to sail away without unloading their cargo. In Boston, however, Governor Thomas Hutchinson would not permit such nonsense. He insisted that the three ships in Boston Harbor not leave until their tea was safely delivered. On a dark December night, about fifty men, some "dressed in the Indian manner," blackened their faces and boarded one of the ships. They hefted 342 chests of tea onto the deck, bashed them open with hatchets, and dumped the contents—worth a fortune of about £90,000 (between $1 million and $3 million today)—into Boston Harbor.[4]

Revolution!

British leaders were furious. Past insubordination paled next to this direct economic hit on a struggling British company. They first demanded compensation; when a Boston town meeting voted that down, the English introduced what colonists dubbed the Intolerable Acts. The laws closed Boston Harbor until the tea was paid for, abolished town meetings, authorized the quartering of troops in any home in Massachusetts, and essentially put the state under military control. King George himself put it bluntly: "The colonists must either triumph or submit."

Americans were not going to submit. Instead, twelve colonies sent representatives to the **First Continental Congress** in September 1774. The Congress petitioned for an end to the Intolerable Acts, called for a boycott on British goods, and asserted colonial rights to "life, liberty, and property." They agreed to meet again in May 1775.

Before the Continental Congress reconvened, fighting had begun. In April 1775, the British commander in Boston, General Thomas Gage, sent one thousand troops out from Boston to seize guns and ammunition stored at Concord, Massachusetts. Armed colonists who called themselves "minutemen" blocked the way and came under British fire at Lexington and Concord. Eight were shot dead. The British found and destroyed the weapons, but their march back to Boston was horrific. Minutemen hid behind rocks and trees and sniped at them all along the way. By the time the English army limped back into the city, they had lost three hundred men.

First Continental Congress: A convention of delegates, from twelve of the thirteen colonies, that met in 1774.

A Long Legacy

Revolutionary images and slogans still resonate in American politics today. The "Tea Party" holds rallies around the nation. Civilians anxious about immigration call themselves minutemen and patrol the border with Mexico. "Militias" organize and train to defend their personal rights. The Revolution left the new United States with symbols, slogans, and an enduring political concern: arbitrary government that threatens the people's liberties.

THE BOTTOM LINE

- For more than a century England ignored its American colonies which elected assemblies governed the colonists. After the French and Indian War, the English bypassed the colonial legislatures and imposed new rules and taxes.

- These actions violated traditional colonial rights and exposed two different ideas of representation—the American concept of *delegate representation* (representatives respond to their constituents' desires) and *trustee representation* in England (representatives do what they consider best for all, regardless of constituent demands).

- English action also harmed colonial economic interests. The conflict very quickly escalated.

- Americans fought an unusual revolution: rather than demanding new rights, they were trying to preserve rights and economic interests they had long been exercising.

The Declaration of Independence

The **Second Continental Congress**, which met in May 1775, faced the job of declaring independence, mobilizing an army, organizing a government, and rallying thirteen very different colonies around a single cause. A year later, on July 4, 1776, the Congress voted to adopt a Declaration of Independence as a statement to the world of America's purpose. The document has two parts: a statement of principles and a list of grievances. (The full Declaration is reprinted in this book's Appendix I.)

Second Continental Congress: A convention of delegates from the thirteen colonies that became the acting national government for the duration of the Revolutionary War.

The Principle: "We Hold These Truths . . ."

In one elegant paragraph, the Declaration of Independence distills America's political philosophy into five towering ideals:

- All people are equal.
- They are endowed with rights that cannot be taken away.
- These rights include life, liberty, and the pursuit of happiness.
- People form governments to protect those rights.
- Governments derive their just powers from the consent of the governed.

These ideas were not new. Political philosophers, especially the English thinker John Locke, had used similar language. In his *Two Treatises on Government*, published more than a century earlier, Locke had argued that in a natural state, there are no rules. Life is ruled by force and violence. To secure a measure of safety and freedom, people contract with one another, enter into civil society, and form governments that can protect one another's life, liberty, and property.

As a statement of governing ideals, the Declaration of Independence was—and to this day, still is—breathtaking. In 1776, it was also a far cry from reality. Thomas Jefferson, who drafted much of the document, was a slave-owner. The Declaration essentially invites future cruelty when it refers to "merciless Indian savages." Its authors did not live up to their noble sentiments. We do not fully live up to them today. Even so, this document stands as the great statement of American idealism—something every generation can fight for.

Grievances

The second part of the Declaration lists twenty-seven grievances against King George III. These tell us what the American colonists cared about as they began the Revolution. Three complaints dominate the list:

- *Violations of the right of representation.* This complaint comes up in ten of the twenty-seven charges against England. It is by far the most intensely felt grievance described in the Declaration.

- *Maintenance of a standing army not under civilian control.* In particular, British soldiers acted in peacetime without the consent of American legislatures. Five complaints are about the British military.

- *Loss of an independent court.* This violation of traditional justice comes up six times.

Today the Revolution is often boiled down to the colonists' slogan "No taxation without representation." The Declaration emphasized *representation* much more than taxation; taxes did not show up until way down the list, as grievance number 17 ("Imposing taxes on us without our consent").

THE BOTTOM LINE

- The Declaration of Independence asserted philosophical ideals as the basis of the new American government.

- The first part of the Declaration features five ideals that sum up the nation's political principles.

- The second part of the Declaration lists twenty-seven grievances that led to the break.

● The First American Government: The Articles of Confederation

When the United States declared its independence, it linked the thirteen former colonies—now states—into a **confederation**, or *alliance of independent states.* Although this first American government lasted only a little more than a decade, it taught the new nation valuable lessons about effective government.

The National Government

The Continental Congress approved its first constitution, called the Articles of Confederation, in November 1777. The document, which reflected Americans' recent experience with England, kept the national government weak and dependent on the states.

Central government power was placed in a Congress whose members were selected and paid for by the states. There was no chief executive (the states would implement the laws), no central authority to tax (all revenues would come from state governments), and no central power to muster an army (the states supplied the troops). Each state had a single vote in Congress. Important matters required the vote of nine states. Any changes to the Articles of Confederation required the agreement of all thirteen states. It was a very weak central government.[5]

Confederation: A group of independent states or nations that yield some of their powers to a national government, although each state retains a degree of sovereign authority.

A series of legends have grown up around Molly Pitcher, whose real name was Mary Ludwig Hays McCauley. The most famous has her stepping up to the cannon to take the place of her fallen husband during the Battle of Monmouth. The stories are most likely a composite of descriptions of many women who fought with the American army.

Some Success . . .

Americans had good reason to be proud of their new government. Power remained close to the people. The new government overcame incredible odds and, by April 1783, had defeated the most powerful military force in the world. The population grew rapidly in the 1780s—the fastest rise of any decade in American history. After a brief postwar recession, the economy also expanded. Americans were democratic.[6]

The Continental Congress also won a major policy success when it stopped the squabbling among states claiming western land. Instead, the Northwest Ordinance of 1787 established a process by which individuals could buy western lands: when an area attracted a minimum number of settlers, it could apply to be a state with all the same powers and privileges as the existing states. With this act, the United States established its mechanism for western expansion.

. . . And Some Problems

But four major problems plagued the new American government.

First, Congress could not raise taxes and had no money of its own. The states were reluctant to provide funds. The Continental Congress had trouble supplying (much less paying) the army throughout the Revolutionary War. George Washington himself drew a lesson that would always guide his politics: *The new republic needed a vigorous national government if it was to survive.*[7]

Second, requiring unanimity made it impossible to amend the Articles. When Congress tried to fix its financial problems by levying a 5 percent tax on imported goods, twelve of the states agreed. However, Rhode Island's legislature denounced the proposal as "the yoke of tyranny fixed on all the states."[8] When loans from France and Holland came due, there was no way to pay them. Again, many leaders drew a lesson: *A vigorous national government needed a stable source of revenue.*

Third, state governments were dominated by their legislatures, which operated without any checks and balances. The result was too often bias and even chaos. Legislatures wrote (and repealed) laws to benefit individuals. They forgave debts. They seized private property. Yet another important lesson: *Different sources of government power should balance one another; governors should balance legislatures; and the central government should balance the states.*

Fourth, the weak national government had a difficult time standing up to foreign powers. Spain closed the Mississippi to American vessels. Britain's trade policy played the states off against one another. Pirates brazenly seized American ships in North Africa. National-minded Americans reached an obvious conclusion: *A weak central government left the nation vulnerable.*

YOUR ADVICE IS NEEDED

If you could go back and offer advice to American leaders in 1787, what would you tell them? Should they stick with the Articles of Confederation or write a new constitution?

Yes, stick with the Articles of Confederation and give the current system more time. It is weak and at times chaotic. But this balanced arrangement is also very democratic and reflects popular wishes for self-government. It does not rely on a distant national government to make and impose policies. America is best off with small, local, democratic governments. That means it will not be a world power—but preserving democracy makes this a good trade-off.

No, build a new central government. Leaders will be less responsive to the public on day-to-day matters. However, the nation will be more stable, more powerful, and more secure. The government, although less democratic, will be more efficient.

I am divided about this. Of course, at the time, the colonists voted no—but it was a close call, as you will see. Since Americans were quite evenly divided, it is useful to think about where you would have stood. It helps clarify the political values you care about most.

One event, Shays' Rebellion, dramatized the problems of government under the Articles. Captain Daniel Shays, a veteran of the Revolutionary War, led a rebellion that broke out in western Massachusetts in August 1786 and spread across the state. Thousands of farmers, protesting high taxes and interest rates, took up their muskets and shut down courthouses to stop foreclosures on their farms. When Governor James Bowdoin summoned the local militia to defend the Worcester courthouse, members refused; some joined the rebellion. Finally, Bowdoin hired an army and broke the rebellion. Shays's sympathizers shifted strategy: they won several seats in the legislature the following year and legislated the debt relief that the farmers had been fighting for.[9]

For many national leaders, Shays' Rebellion was the last straw. Under the Articles of Confederation, neither the national government nor an individual state was strong enough to protect public property (like courthouses) or private property (the repayment of loans). The Rebellion pushed the most influential men in the colonies to write a new constitution. Not everyone agreed. Many Americans thought that problems like Shays' Rebellion were the growing pains of a more democratic government that reflected the people and their desires.

The First Step: Annapolis Convention

Alarmed by spreading chaos, the Continental Congress called for a national meeting in Annapolis to impose order on commerce among the states. Only twelve delegates from five states showed up—not enough to do official business.

● Captain Daniel Shays led a
rebellion in protest of farm
foreclosures in 1786.

With Shays' Rebellion raging, the delegates requested each state to appoint representatives to meet in Philadelphia the following May, in 1787, to devise such "provisions as should appear to them necessary to render the constitution of the federal government adequate to the exigencies of the union." That may not sound earthshaking, but the twelve delegates in Annapolis had quietly authorized a convention that would write an entirely new constitution.

Secrecy

Spring 1787 arrived cold and blustery, delaying many of the delegates on their way to Philadelphia. James Madison from Virginia got there first, with a plan for a new constitution. Madison was short, shy, and balding; today, we recognize him as one of America's greatest political thinkers. The next delegate from Virginia arrived with more fanfare. As George Washington approached, church bells pealed, cannons thundered, army officers donned their old uniforms to ride escort, and the citizens lined the streets and cheered. The presence of the great American hero made the convention's success more likely.

On the first day, the delegates unanimously elected George Washington to chair the convention. Then they agreed on a controversial rule: the deliberations would be completely secret. Guards were placed at the doors. Windows were shut and remained closed, even after the Philadelphia summer turned stifling.

Was it a good idea to impose secrecy? The young republic had only recently opened up its political process to the people. Thomas Jefferson called the decision to close the convention "an abominable precedent." In a republic, he argued, the people should always know what their leaders are doing.[10]

However, the delegates wanted to speak their minds freely without worrying about how their words would appear in the newspapers. Many also believed that powerful politicians in their home states would withdraw their delegation as soon as they heard that the convention was debating an entirely new constitution. Without secrecy, they might have to abandon their bold plan and simply amend the Articles of Confederation—which was, after all, what they had been asked to do.

THE BOTTOM LINE

- Under the Articles of Confederation, thirteen independent states bound themselves into a confederation with a weak central government that had to rely on the states to implement its decisions.

- Although feeble, this first U.S. government was, by the standards of the time, a very democratic one.

- Delegates to the Constitutional Convention convened to fix the problems with the Articles of Confederation but chose to go much further and propose a new American government.

The Constitutional Convention

As they thought about reorganizing their new government, American leaders balanced the two political dangers they had recently encountered.

- British officials' behavior warned them that a powerful central government could strip the people of their rights.

- Experience with the Articles of Confederation warned them that a weak government could fail to protect their rights.

The delegates debated from May into September. They touched on almost every aspect of government, ranging from how to elect the legislature to what to do about slavery. Throughout the discussions, six major themes dominated their attention.

How Much Power to the People?

The delegates faced a dilemma. They wanted their government to answer to the public; that was why they had fought the Revolution. Recent experience, however, also made them fear a system that responded too readily to the people (or, more precisely, white men with property). The delegates wished to represent the public through better-educated, wealthier, and more experienced leaders—men like themselves.

Over the course of the convention, the delegates developed a view of representation that Madison called *filtration*, or *indirect elections*: the public would

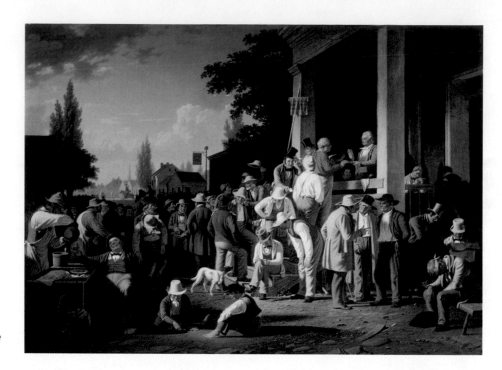

● Over time, common men began voting in American elections. This painting shows the raucous results. Note the heavy drinking—and how this election was a completely male event.

vote for men (and later women) who would, in turn, vote for public officials. The speeches during the convention's first days are a bit shocking to the contemporary reader. The delegates were making the public *less* involved in government than they had been in the eleven years since the United States declared its independence. The new Constitution would permit the public to vote for only one federal office—members of the House of Representatives.

The debate about public involvement did not end with the Constitution. Over time, Americans would get a more active role in their governance. Citizens would win more control over electing presidents and choose their senators directly. The "public" would also expand to include all women, African Americans, and younger Americans (eighteen- to twenty-year-olds), as we will see in future chapters.

The debate that began at the Constitutional Convention continues to this day. It animates one of the key ideas we discussed in Chapter 1: self-rule, balanced between direct democracy and indirect representation. At a still more fundamental level, the debate speaks to one of the great questions of American politics: *Who governs?* Public involvement in government has grown dramatically over the centuries, but Madison's principle of filtration still keeps the people at arm's length from their government in many areas.

National Government versus State Government

The Articles of Confederation left most power with the states. Madison's plan for the new government took that power and vested it in a strong national government. The very first motion that the delegates debated called for "a national government . . . consisting of a *supreme* legislature, executive, and judiciary." In fact, Madison's original plan would have shifted most governing authority to the national level.[11]

Many delegates disagreed with this dramatic change. They believed that state and local governments were closer to the people and could more accurately reflect public sentiments—precisely what Madison was trying to avoid. Some pro–states' rights delegates charged Madison and his allies with trying to "abolish the State Governments altogether." Ultimately, delegates from New York walked out of the convention and Rhode Island refused to send any delegates in the first place. The convention was now down to eleven of the thirteen states.[12]

In the end, the delegates compromised on a system that included both national and state power. The federal government took over many functions—but far fewer than Madison had originally proposed. The states kept many duties—but far fewer than states' rights advocates would have liked. This mixed system, with a stronger national government that nevertheless leaves considerable power with the state governments, is called **federalism** (and we'll discuss it in Chapter 3). The debate about how to balance national government power and state power continues to the present day.

Big States versus Small States

Another intense dispute at the Constitutional Convention revolved around a division we rarely think about today: the large states (led by Virginia and Pennsylvania) versus the small states (led by New Jersey and Delaware). Debate turned on how to apportion power in the national government. Large states argued that representation should be based on population; small states wanted each state to have an equal voice. That debate led to two different plans, one put forward by Virginia (a big state) and the other by New Jersey (on behalf of the small states).

The Virginia Plan. Large and small states squared off early in the convention, when Governor Edmund Randolph of Virginia presented Madison's original plan for the Constitution. A powerful speaker, Randolph addressed the delegates for four hours. The plan, which became known as the **Virginia Plan**, had five key points.

1. Congress would have two chambers, a form known as a **bicameral** legislature, with representation in both chambers based on state population.

2. Citizens would vote for members of the House of Representatives. The House of Representatives would, in turn, vote for senators from a list of candidates provided by the state legislatures. This limited the states' role and is an example of filtration, or indirect elections.

3. Congress would elect the president. Here the Virginia Plan suddenly turned vague and did not specify whether the president would

Federalism: Power divided between national and state government. Each has its own independent authority and its own duties.

Virginia Plan: Madison's plan, embraced by Constitutional Convention delegates from larger states; strengthened the national government relative to state governments.

Bicameral: Having two legislative houses or chambers—like the House and the Senate.

be one man or a committee; nor did it say how long the executive would serve.

4. A national judiciary with one or more supreme courts would be established and the judges would have life tenure.

5. Congress would have broad powers to legislate in all cases where the states were "incompetent." A "council of revision" made up of the president and the Supreme Court would have the authority to review and nullify any state law.

The Virginia Plan empowered Congress to "call forth the force of the union" against any state "failing to fulfill its duties" under the new constitution. The federal government could strike down state laws. Early votes indicated that the Virginia Plan enjoyed a small majority at the convention.

Delegates from small states were especially critical of Madison's blueprint. Small states like New Jersey lamented that they would soon "be swallowed up." Each state had "its peculiar habits, usages, and manners," small-state advocates insisted, and these must be protected. Under Madison's plan, three states (Virginia, Pennsylvania, and Massachusetts) would have enough members in Congress to form a majority all by themselves. Representatives from the smaller states repeatedly threatened to walk out of the convention.[13]

The New Jersey Plan.   The small states pushed back with their own plan, introduced by William Paterson of New Jersey and known as the **New Jersey Plan**. Rather than construct a new national government, this plan focused on strengthening the Articles of Confederation. It had four key points:

New Jersey Plan: Put forward at the convention by the small states, it left most government authority with the state governments.

Unicameral: Having a single legislative house or chamber.

1. Congress would have only one chamber, a form known as a **unicameral** legislature. Each state would have one vote in Congress, regardless of its size—exactly the same as in the Articles. However, congressional acts would be the supreme law of the land, making the new constitution stronger than the Articles of Confederation.

2. Congress would elect a committee to serve as the federal executive for one term only.

3. The executive committee would select a supreme court, which would be responsible for foreign policy, economic policy, and the impeachment of federal officials.

4. The national government could tax the states and would have the exclusive right to tax imports.

The New Jersey Plan left the states at the center of American government but took a step toward union by building a stronger national government, one that could raise its own taxes and exercise more authority over interstate commerce. When the vote was called, only three states supported the New Jersey Plan.

● *Louis Glanzman's recent painting of the Constitutional Convention. Washington towers over everyone at the center in a black frock coat. To his right stands James Madison. Alexander Hamilton is the red-haired man standing sixth from the right. Aged Benjamin Franklin, now eighty-one, sits at the center of the room, chatting with Hugh Williamson, a delegate from North Carolina.*

The Connecticut Compromise.   Convention delegates decisively approved the Virginia Plan's bicameral Congress with a House and a Senate. They voted for a House of Representatives based on population. Then debate turned to the Senate. If the delegates voted with the Virginia Plan—that is, the House of Representatives would vote for senators—the big states would essentially win the debate. Tempers grew short. Luther Martin, a garrulous delegate from Maryland, wrote home that the convention was on the verge of breaking up over this issue.[14]

Big states seemed to have the votes to carry seven states and win the Virginia Plan's version of Senate elections. But when the roll was called, on July 2, one big-state supporter from Maryland and two from Georgia slipped out of the convention hall. With their exits, both states shifted and the vote came out a tie: five states for the Virginia Plan, five against, and one evenly split.

To break the deadlock, the delegates formed a committee, which was tilted toward the small states. It came up with a compromise, brokered by Roger Sherman of Connecticut and therefore known as the Connecticut Compromise. The House would be based on population; the Senate would have two representatives for each state, chosen by the state legislature. (Americans did not vote directly for their senators in all states until 1913.) Since legislation had to pass through both houses, the public and the states would each have a say. Because the delegates wanted power over taxes and spending to be in the people's hands, they required that all finance-related bills had to be introduced first in the House.

The compromise squeaked through—five states voted "yes," four "no," and one split. The big states won the House of Representatives; the small states got their way in the Senate. The compromise continues to confer on rural states a great deal of clout in the Senate—and, since all legislation requires approval from both houses, in Congress.

More immediately, the Constitution had its legislature. Two difficult issues, however, remained—the power of the president and the agonizing question of slavery.

The President

Even the master planner James Madison arrived at the convention without a clear design for the presidency—also known as the *executive authority* since it *executes* (or puts into effect) the laws. The delegates even wavered about whether executive authority should be placed in one individual or a committee.

Committee or Individual?   Many delegates worried that a single executive would grow powerful and become, as Governor Randolph put it, "the fetus of monarchy." Madison and his allies, however, feared that the Connecticut Compromise opened the Senate door to the same petty state politics that had wrecked the Articles of Confederation. They therefore decided that the president should be one individual, independent of Congress, who could represent the public. After much back and forth, they settled on a four-year term and permitted reelections. (In 1951, the Twenty-Second Amendment limited the president to two terms.)

Electoral College: The system established by the Constitution to elect the president; each state has a group of electors (equal in size to that of its congressional delegation in the House and the Senate); the public in each state votes for electors who then vote for the president.

The Electoral College.   How would the United States choose the president? The Constitution's framers saw a problem with every option. They did not think the people had enough information or wisdom. They did not trust state legislators to put aside their own narrow concerns and think about the national interest. What could they do? In response, they came up with the most complicated rigmarole in the Constitution: the **Electoral College**. Each state would select individuals known as *electors*—whom the delegates hoped would be well-known individuals with sound judgment, who would then choose the president.

How many electors would each state have? Another compromise: each state would have the same number of electors as it had members of Congress. That meant a state's population would matter (given proportional representation in the House) but also that every state was assured of two more votes (reflecting their representation in the Senate). If no individual received a majority of electoral votes—which last happened in 1824—the House of Representatives would choose from among the five candidates with the most votes. They would vote by state, and each state would get just one vote—again, a concession to small states.

Who would elect the electors? The convention simply left this question to the states. At first, the state legislatures got the job of voting for the electors. But by the late 1820s the states ceded this right to the people (again, white men, although now they did not need to own any property). The people voted state by state for their electors—as we still do.

Today, all the electors in a state generally cast their votes for the candidate who won the state (although only twenty-six states require them to do so) (Figure 2.3).

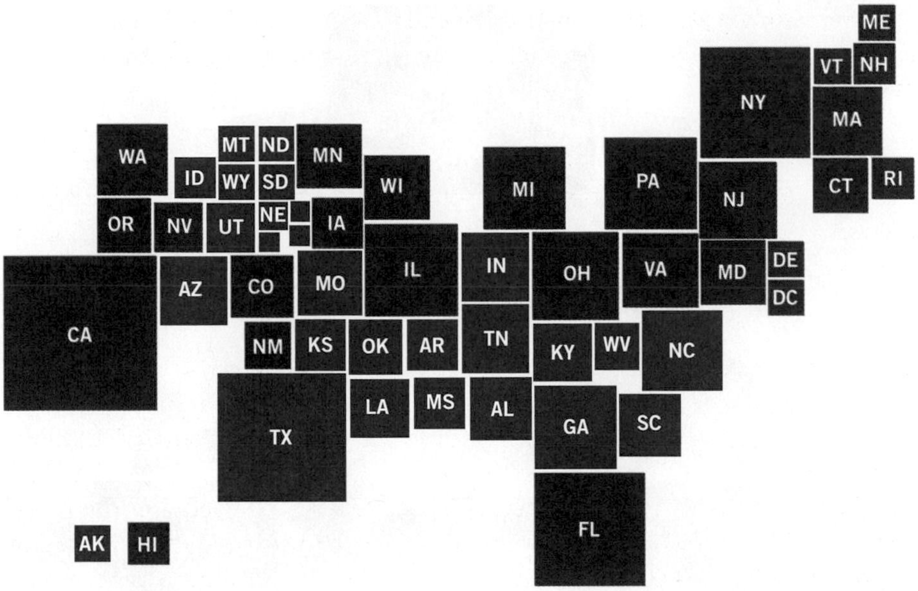

● **FIGURE 2.3** *Electoral College map for the 2012 presidential election. The size of each state is distorted to emphasize its share of electoral votes.*

Separation of Powers

One idea that evolved during the convention was the separation of powers. Each branch of government—the president, Congress, and the judiciary—has its job to do: the delegates vested "all legislative powers" in Congress, the executive power in the president, and the judicial power (to try cases) in the courts. The Articles of Confederation had created only a national legislature; in Britain power was also concentrated in Parliament, their national legislature. Now, the United States would have three independent branches.

The framers added a crucial twist: checks and balances. *Each power the Constitution grants to Congress, the presidency, or the courts is balanced by a "countervailing" or checking power assigned to another branch.* Each branch is involved in the others' business. In this way, as Madison later put it, one branch's ambition for power would always check the other branches' ambitions (see Figure 2.4).

For example, Congress passes legislation but needs the president to sign a bill into law. The president can veto (reject) the bill (checking Congress); Congress can override the veto by a two-thirds vote of both chambers (balancing the president).

The president is commander in chief, but the Constitution gives Congress the power to declare war and set the military's budget. The president negotiates treaties, but the Senate must ratify them by two-thirds vote. The president appoints ministers and Supreme Court justices, but the Senate must approve (or confirm) them. Congress holds the ultimate power over all federal officers. The House can impeach (or formally accuse) the president or any other officer in the executive or judicial branch of "Treason, Bribery or other high Crimes and Misdemeanors"; the Senate looks into the accusation and decides whether to actually remove the person from office. What is a "high crime and misdemeanor"? Well, because they have never been fully defined, Congress must use its judgment.

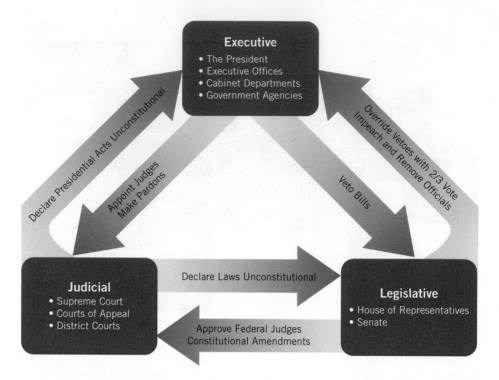

Executive
- The President
- Executive Offices
- Cabinet Departments
- Government Agencies

Declare Presidential Acts Unconstitutional

Override Vetoes with 2/3 Vote
Impeach and Remove Officials

Appoint Judges
Make Pardons

Veto Bills

Judicial
- Supreme Court
- Courts of Appeal
- District Courts

Declare Laws Unconstitutional

Approve Federal Judges
Constitutional Amendments

Legislative
- House of Representatives
- Senate

● **FIGURE 2.4** *Separation of powers—the checks on the federal level. Multiply them across all three levels and a vital question of American politics arises: Is this chaotic and fragmented state ready to take on the world? We've been posing the question since 1787.*

These checks and balances are one of the most distinctive features of the American Constitution. The French political philosopher Montesquieu wrote an influential treatise, *The Spirit of the Laws* (published in 1748), which argued that to avoid tyranny, the executive, legislative, and judicial functions of government must be separated from one another—and never placed in a single individual or body. However, few governments have ever developed this principle as fully as the U.S. Constitution did.

Checks and balances continue to spark disagreement in the present: Has the U.S. government developed too many checks and balances to meet the challenges of the twenty-first century? Has the executive power slipped its constitutional leash, especially in controlling military and foreign policy? Or do the Constitution's checks and balances remain in good working order, controlling power and preserving self-rule—just as James Madison predicted they would?

"A Principle of Which We Were Ashamed"

The convention rethought almost every aspect of government—except slavery. Why? For some delegates, the answer came down to self-interest. Of the fifty-five delegates, twenty-five were slave owners. George Washington brought three slaves with him to Philadelphia. In three states—Georgia, South Carolina, and Virginia—slaves made up more than one-third of the population. And the men and women in bondage were a source of wealth and power. Each time the subject of slavery came up, delegates from South Carolina and Georgia offered the convention a stark choice—protect slavery or form a union without us.

In the end, the delegates wanted a strong union more than they hated slavery. The Constitution includes three major references to slavery. Each time, the slaveholding states pretty much got what they wanted.

The Three-Fifths Compromise.   Slavery was first thrust on the convention's agenda with the question of how to count slaves when allocating seats in the House of Representatives. As Table 2.1 shows, nearly four in ten of Virginia's residents were slaves. If slaves were counted as part of the population, southern states would have as many members in the House of Representatives as the northern states.

As soon as the issue came up, James Wilson of Pennsylvania sprang to his feet and offered a compromise. For the purpose of apportioning representation, Wilson proposed, let the total number of slaves count as three-fifths of the free people of a state. The strange fraction came from the Continental Congress. When it was trying to raise revenue from the states, Congress calculated each state's wealth on the basis of population. It then arbitrarily estimated that slaves would generate three-fifths as much wealth as free people.

This crude calculation now came back to haunt the Constitution. The delegates immediately accepted the Three-Fifths Compromise. Its actual wording is as peculiar as the rule itself.

> *Representatives . . . shall be apportioned among the several states according to their respective numbers, which shall be determined by adding the whole number of free persons, including those bound to service for a term of years [indentured servants] and excluding Indians not taxed, three fifths of all other persons.*

TABLE 2.1 Population in 1790

STATE	TOTAL POPULATION	SLAVES	PERCENT ENSLAVED
Connecticut	237,655	2,648	1.1
Delaware	59,096	8,887	15.0
Georgia	82,548	29,264	34.5
Maryland	319,728	103,036	32.2
Massachusetts	378,556	0	0.0
New Hampshire	141,899	157	0.1
New Jersey	184,139	11,423	6.2
New York	340,241	21,193	6.2
North Carolina	395,005	100,783	25.5
Pennsylvania	433,611	3,707	0.9
Rhode Island	69,112	958	1.4
South Carolina	249,073	107,094	43.0
Virginia	747,550	292,627	39.1

The Constitution never says "slave," but simply "three fifths of all other persons." In fact, a reader who did not know that the passage refers to slavery would have a hard time understanding it. Why did the Constitution's framers—who were usually so precise—write such a convoluted sentence? They did not want the word *slavery* to appear in the Constitution. John Dickinson, a thoughtful delegate from Delaware, put it best: the awkward wording was, he said, "an endeavor to conceal a principle of which we were ashamed."[15]

The Slave Trade.   A second question involved the slave trade. Could the federal government regulate or abolish it? Many delegates were repulsed by the idea of stealing human beings from Africa, chaining them into the hulls of ships, dragging them to America, and selling the survivors to the highest bidder. George Mason from Virginia rose and gave the most prophetic speech of the convention: "Every master of slaves is born a petty tyrant. They bring the judgment of heaven on a country. As nations cannot be rewarded or punished in the next world they must be in this. Providence punishes national sins, by national calamities. I lament that our eastern brethren [Georgia and South Carolina] had from a lust of gain embarked on this nefarious traffic." It was a powerful speech. However, Mason himself owned more than three hundred slaves. Their worth would rise if the slave trade were abolished.

No one else at the convention was willing to follow Mason's attack. In the end, backers of a strong Constitution struck a bargain and permitted the slave trade for another 20 years, in exchange for more national power over interstate commerce and the authority to tax imports. Historian William Beeman calculates that extending the slave trade condemned 200,000 Africans to slavery—almost equaling the total (250,000) from the preceding 170 years.[16]

Fugitive Slaves.   Finally, in August, as the convention was winding down, delegates from the slave states proposed a fugitive slave clause—requiring the rest of the nation to assist in returning runaway slaves. This time there were no deals and barely any debate. The northern delegates simply accepted the proposal.

"The National Calamity."   Many Americans revere the document that has guided the nation for 225 years. However, George Mason was right when he predicted a "national calamity." Seventy-two years later, Abraham Lincoln would echo Mason as he reflected in his second inaugural address on the carnage of the Civil War: "God . . . gives to both North and South this terrible war as the woe due to those by whom the offense [of slavery] came."

The Constitution's slavery passages—like the Civil War that led to their repeal—remind us that the convention was the beginning of an American journey. Each generation must face up to the same challenge that confronted the founders. Who are we? Can we try to make the United States more just, more democratic, and more inclusive? The Declaration of Independence gives America its ideals: all people are created equal. The Constitution, in turn, provides the rules. Americans have struggled over the meaning of the ideals and the implementation of the rules ever since these documents were written.

LEAP OF THE FUGITIVE SLAVE.

● *This print illustrates a terrified slave running for her freedom. As the print suggests, slavery would provoke a powerful national debate in the decades ahead. Fifty years after the Constitutional Convention, abolitionists rose up and denounced the Constitution as a "covenant with death and an agreement with hell" because of its slavery compromises.*

THE BOTTOM LINE

● The constitutional framers balanced two dangers: government that was too strong (the king of England) versus government that was too weak (the Articles of Confederation).

● The debates focused on five great issues:

1) Should the people be directly involved in government? Most delegates believed in filtration, or indirect elections.

2) National versus state power, which came down to a standoff between larger and smaller states. Led by Madison, the big states introduced the Virginia Plan. Small states countered with the New Jersey Plan. The Connecticut Compromise offered a solution: House members were elected on the basis of population, but every state had two Senate seats.

3) The nature of the presidency.

4) How best to separate powers, answered through a system of checks and balances. For the most part, these limits on concentrated authority would continue to develop long after ratification.

5) Slavery. Pragmatic compromise in the name of union overcame moral concerns. Delegates took care to not use the word *slavery* in the Constitution, but several clauses enabling the institution to grow and expand would lead to the greatest conflict in the nation's future.

An Overview of the Constitution

By September 17, after four months of deliberation, the Constitutional Convention had done its work. Thirty-nine of the original fifty-five delegates lined up to sign the document. There are only seven articles in the Constitution, each broken down into multiple sections. (Their full text appears in Appendix II.) These passages remain the institutional foundation of the American political system.

Preamble

The Constitution begins with a preamble, the most elegant sentence in the document:

> *We the people of the United States, in order to form a more perfect union, establish justice, insure domestic tranquility, provide for the common defense, promote the general welfare, and secure the blessings of liberty to ourselves and our posterity, do ordain and establish this Constitution for the United States of America.*

The Constitution's authority rests, not on the states, but on "we the people." As we have seen, the Constitutional Convention produced a weak version of the people—one that permitted slavery, excluded women, and permitted "we the people" to vote for exactly one branch of Congress. The next phrase—"in order to form a more perfect union"—addresses these limitations. Americans always struggle toward that more perfect union.

The preamble also offers six goals for a successful government. Ask yourself how you would rate the U.S. government on each of them today.

Article 1: Congress

Article 1, the longest in the Constitution, describes the new Congress. Section 2 of the article establishes a House of Representatives whose members are elected every two years to represent a district of 30,000 voters. (Today, average district size has grown to nearly 710,000 voters.) Representatives must be twenty-five years old and have been citizens for seven years. Section 3 establishes a Senate with two members from every state, elected every six years; they must be at least thirty years old and have been a citizen for nine years.

Section 8 is the most important passage in Article 1—and perhaps the entire Constitution. Its seventeen short paragraphs tell Congress what it may do, including the "power to lay and collect taxes," declare war, regulate interstate commerce, coin money, and raise an army.

Think about the reach of congressional authority. The largest and most expensive program that Congress oversees is Social Security, which pays monthly pensions to retired people over sixty-five. If you read all of Section 8, you may be puzzled—nothing in it remotely justifies paying for retirement pensions. How, then, could Congress pass and run the Social Security program? Because the very last paragraph of Section 8 empowers Congress

[T]o make all laws which shall be necessary and proper for carrying into execution the foregoing powers, and all other powers vested by this Constitution in the government of the United States.

That phrase, known as the *necessary and proper clause*, gives Congress—and the government—a great deal of creative leeway. What are the limits of the power granted to Congress by this clause? This is another point on which the delegates in Philadelphia disagreed. Not surprisingly, scholars argue still about how far the necessary and proper clause stretches congressional authority.

Section 9 of Article 1 lists the things Congress may *not* do. Its second prohibition is especially important today: "the privilege of the writ of Habeas Corpus shall not be suspended unless when in cases of rebellion or invasion the public safety may require it." *Habeas corpus* means that government cannot hold prisoners without formally charging them with a crime. The U.S. government may not simply throw someone in jail without a charge. What about terrorist suspects held without charges? Again, experts disagree. Advocates of the Obama administration's policy argue that "public safety" requires indefinite detention. Others argue that this practice undermines liberty, one of the basic rights that the Constitution was established to protect.

Article 2: The President

The Constitution's second article shifts focus from the legislature to the executive branch. The president, Article 2 specifies, must be a natural-born American at least thirty-five years old and is chosen by electors for a four-year term. As we saw, each state originally decided who elects the electors—today the people in every state make this choice. Our process for selecting the head of state is still very different from that followed by other nations.

Whereas Article 1 lists congressional dos and don'ts in detail, Article 2 says very little about presidential powers and duties. The president is commander in

What Do You Think?

HAVE WE ACHIEVED THE CONSTITUTION'S GOALS TODAY?

Think about the goals listed in the preamble. Then give a grade to each: an "A" if you think the United States has lived up to its goals, and a . . . well, we're sure you know all about grades!

Goal:	Grade Today:
Form a strong union	_____
Establish equal justice for all	_____
Insure domestic tranquility (that is, peace at home)	_____
Provide for the common defense (today, we might say homeland security)	_____
Promote the general welfare	_____
Secure liberty for ourselves and posterity	_____

chief of the army and the navy. Presidents make treaties if two-thirds of the Senate approve; they appoint ambassadors, Supreme Court justices, and all other officials—again with the advice and consent of the Senate. Although that seems like a limited set of powers, the Constitution includes another clause that has permitted an enormous expansion of presidential powers: "The executive power shall be vested in a President of the United States." What that "executive power" is, and how far it can stretch, has been debated throughout American history.

Section 4 allows for removing a president "on impeachment for, and conviction of, treason, bribery, or other high crimes and misdemeanors." What constitutes a high crime or misdemeanor? Again, the Constitution does not say, which makes any impeachment effort highly charged on all sides. Three presidents have faced formal impeachment proceedings, although only one, Richard Nixon, has been forced to resign his office.[17]

Article 3: The Courts

Article 3 creates the Supreme Court and authorizes Congress to organize additional courts. Alexander Hamilton later called the Supreme Court "the least dangerous" branch of government, and the Constitution describes it only briefly. The justices are selected by the president, approved by the Senate, and have tenure for life—still another buffer against democratic politics. Article 3 grants the Supreme Court power over all cases "arising under this Constitution, the laws of the United States and treaties made."

The Constitution is silent on the Court's most formidable power: May it overrule an act of Congress? Sixteen years after the Constitutional Convention, Chief Justice John Marshall, in deciding a case called *Marbury v. Madison*, ruled that the Court could strike down an act of Congress. (We'll review this case in detail in Chapter 13.)

Article 4: Relations Between the States

Article 4 defines the relationship between the states that had so plagued the Articles of Confederation. A state may not discriminate against citizens of other states, and each must give "full faith and credit" to the official acts of other states. Article 4 also describes the process for adding new states to the union and requires the United States to guarantee every state a republican form of government.

The full faith and credit clause raises some controversial questions today. When same-sex couples marry in states like Massachusetts, does the full faith and credit clause bind other states to recognize those marriages? Many states have refused, adopting rules that define marriage as a heterosexual union. The Supreme Court has not yet ruled on the matter. Stay tuned.

Article 5: Amendments

Article 5 authorizes amendments to the Constitution. Creating an amendment is an extremely difficult process. Two-thirds of both the House and Senate must approve. Then three-fourths of the states must ratify—either through the state legislature or through state conventions. (The only amendment to be ratified the second way was the Twenty-First, which in 1933 repealed the prohibition on alcohol, fourteen years after the Eighteenth Amendment prohibited its "manufacture, transportation or sale.") More than one hundred thousand amendments have been proposed since 1791 (when the first ten amendments, or Bill of Rights, went through); only seventeen have passed. When citizens or companies disagree with a Supreme Court ruling, occasionally they try for a constitutional amendment. As you can see from the numbers, it is a very difficult thing to actually win.

The Constitution forbids amendments on two matters: no amendment could stop the slave trade before 1808, and no state can be denied equal suffrage in the Senate (two seats) without its approval. In this way, the two fiercest debates at the convention were placed beyond the reach of future generations.

Article 6: The Law of the Land

Article 6 makes the Constitution the supreme law of the land. It also specifies that there must be no religious test for holding any federal office. Some states, however, had religious tests for holding office and even voting until the 1830s.

Article 7: Ratification

Article 7 announced that the Constitution would go into effect after nine states had ratified—a controversial move because the United States was still operating under the Articles of Confederation, which could be amended only by all thirteen states.

The Missing Articles

Many Americans thought that the original Constitution was missing something important. Only a handful of individual rights were mentioned in the document. It said nothing about free speech, free press, freedom of religion, jury trials, or the right to bear arms. The debate over ratifying the Constitution would quickly expose this weakness. As we will see, ratification helped introduce an important addition: the ten amendments known as the Bill of Rights.

⬥ Ratification

The new Constitution now went to the states, where ratifying conventions would vote it up or down. Most states were closely divided over whether to ratify, but the Constitution had two big advantages. First, it offered a clear plan in a time of trouble; opponents could only say "no" and force the nation to start all over again. Second, the convention had attracted many of the most prestigious men in America, beginning with Washington and Franklin, who were the most widely admired figures in two of the nation's largest states. Supporters of the Constitution were known as *Federalists*—making their opponents the *Anti-Federalists*.

The Anti-Federalists

Classical republicanism: A democratic ideal, rooted in ancient Greece and Rome, that requires citizens to participate directly in public affairs, seek the public interest, shun private gains, and defer to natural leaders.

The Anti-Federalists rooted their argument against ratification in **classical republicanism**. Popular government, in this view, ought to model itself on ancient republics like Athens and Rome. Republics should be small and local, permitting maximum popular participation in public affairs. When we discussed the idea of self-rule in Chapter 1, we introduced the idea of direct democracy (celebrated by Thomas Jefferson); classical republicanism is the original version of that idea.

The Anti-Federalists were not interested in a muscular nation-state like the European empires. They had four major criticisms of the new Constitution:

- First, it stripped political control from citizens and placed it in a powerful national government over which the people would not have much influence.
- Second, the president looked too much like a king.
- Third, standing armies and navies were a threat to peace and liberty. Republics relied on citizen militias—which could be mustered during wartime—to protect the people.
- Fourth, and most important, the Anti-Federalists hammered away at the Constitution's missing piece, a bill of rights.[18]

Politics also played a role in the Anti-Federalist argument. Many of the men who opposed the Constitution were powerful political figures in their own states. A national government would diminish their influence.

Aspects of the Anti-Federalist (and civic-republican) argument remain alive and well in the United States. Americans often criticize the federal government and cheer the idea of restoring power to state and local officials, who are closer to the people. The Anti-Federalists may have lost the debate in 1788, but their fear of federal power and their yearning to return authority to the people endures—and shapes one answer to our great question, Who are we?

The Federalists

The arguments in favor of the new Constitution were summarized by an editorial dream team. James Madison and Alexander Hamilton (with a little help from John Jay, who would become the first chief justice of the United States) wrote eighty-five short essays that appeared in newspapers to explain and defend the Constitution to the voters of New York. Known as the Federalist Papers, these essays achieve three very different purposes. First, they are

● *The ratification of the Constitution was a close call. Patrick Henry, a powerful orator, led the opponents (known as Anti-Federalists) in Virginia. Virginia was one of seven states where the vote was close.*

pro-Constitution editorials, even propaganda; the authors were fighting to get New York to approve the new Constitution and they did not pretend to be neutral. Second, they are the single best guide to the thinking that guided the Constitution. However, we must read them carefully, always weighing the Papers as persuasive rhetoric on the one hand and as explanations of constitutional logic on the other. Finally, the Federalist Papers are brilliant theoretical essays about politics and government.

The two most famous Federalist Papers, no. 10 and no. 51, are reprinted in Appendix III to this book. The eighteenth-century language may sound strange to our ears, but the argument is brilliant. Federalist no. 10 argues, surprisingly, that a large national government can protect liberty more effectively than small local governments. Madison, the essay's author, begins by introducing the "mortal disease" that always destroys popular government. You might imagine that he was referring to tyrants like George III. Instead, he points to *factions*—groups that pursue their self-interest at the expense of others.

How can we control the effects of factions? Not through local governments, argued Madison. In each local area, one economic interest is likely to predominate—farmers, merchants, big manufacturers, or even poor people eager to tax the rich. Since the same local group will always be in the majority, it is difficult to stop that group from taking advantage of the minority.

Madison's realistic assessment was a breakthrough in political theory. The classical view assumed that for popular government to survive, the people—that is, the voters—had to be virtuous and respect one another. Madison introduced a more modern view: expect people to pursue their own self-interest. As he wrote in Federalist no. 51, "if men were angels, no government would be necessary." If popular government is to survive, it must be organized to protect minorities from majorities who are going to pursue their own self-interest.

How can we do this? Move the debate to the national level, said Madison. A larger political sphere—a bigger government—will always have a great many diverse interests, arising from all the states. With so many different factions, no one interest will be able to dominate. Each faction will form a small minority of the whole and will therefore need to form alliances. As the issues change, so will the groups that are in the majority and the minority. As a result, no one faction will be able to impose its will on the minority for very long.

Two Strong Arguments

To this day, both sides—Anti-Federalist and Federalist—sound persuasive. The Anti-Federalists tapped into a deep American yearning for local governments that respond directly to popular concerns. The Federalists argued that only a national government could really protect the people's rights and turn the new nation into a great power.

A Very Close Vote

The small states got their way at the Constitutional Convention and, not surprisingly, they ratified quickly and unanimously—Delaware, New Jersey, and Georgia all signed by January 2, 1788. In Pennsylvania, some members of the assembly hid to slow down the process. Enthusiastic mobs found the reluctant members and marched them to the very hall where the Constitution was written. The public crammed into the hall and gathered outside the building. After a month, Pennsylvania ratified the Constitution 46–23. (See Table 2.2 for a summary of the voting.)

In Massachusetts, Governor John Hancock, who had been the first delegate to sign the Declaration of Independence, dramatically switched from the

TABLE 2.2 The Final Vote for the Constitution

STATE	DATE OF RATIFICATION	VOTE IN STATE CONVENTION
1. Delaware	December 7, 1787	Unanimous [30–0]
2. Pennsylvania	December 12, 1787	46–23
3. New Jersey	December 18, 1787	Unanimous [38–0]
4. Georgia	January 2, 1788	Unanimous [26–0]
5. Connecticut	January 9, 1788	128–40
6. Massachusetts	February 7, 1788	187–168
7. Maryland	April 28, 1788	63–11
8. South Carolina	May 23, 1788	149–73
9. New Hampshire	June 21, 1788	57–47; required two meetings
10. Virginia	June 25, 1788	89–79
11. New York	July 25, 1788	30–27
12. North Carolina	July 21, 1789 [after election of Washington]	194–77
13. Rhode Island	May 29, 1790 [first Congress in session]	34–32
Key: Easy ratification Tough fight Originally refused		

Anti-Federalist side—on one crucial condition. He asked that amendments protecting individual rights be introduced to the new Constitution. It was the first prominent insistence on a bill of rights. Even with the switch, Massachusetts delegates approved only narrowly, 187–168. Other states followed the two Massachusetts precedents: request a bill of rights and unite after the debate.

After Maryland and South Carolina voted for the Constitution, the action moved to Virginia—the largest state and the most intense contest to date. Governor William Randolph, who had presented the Virginia Plan at the convention, and George Mason, who had scorched the slave trade, both refused to sign the Constitution. Yet Virginia voted for the Constitution 89–79.

In New York, the new Constitution squeaked through by a 30–27 vote.

Not every state voted in favor. Rhode Island town meetings rejected even holding a convention to debate the Constitution. Rhode Island would reluctantly join the union after George Washington had been president for two months. North Carolina initially rejected the Constitution by a lopsided vote of

● New York City celebrates ratification with a model ship called the Hamilton after Alexander Hamilton, one of the authors of the Federalist Papers.

184–83. In New Hampshire a convention met, refused to ratify, and adjourned; four months later the delegates reconvened and voted yes, and on June 21, 1788, New Hampshire became the ninth state to ratify. The Constitution would now be the law of the land.

Ratification was a very close contest. If a total of just 3 percent of the delegates across Virginia, Massachusetts, and New York had changed their vote, the Constitution would have gone down to defeat. Americans came within a whisker of rejecting the Constitution that now defines the nation and its government.

THE BOTTOM LINE

- The Constitution's seven Articles address a wide range of features of American government. But as ratification discussions began in each state, critics noted only scant mention of individual rights.

- The debate over ratifying the Constitution featured two visions of American government.

- The *Federalists* argued that only an energetic national government could protect the nation and secure liberty. The *Anti-Federalists* called instead for a modest government that left power in state and local hands.

- The state-by-state voting on ratification was very close; it took well over a year before the Constitution was approved.

- More than 225 years later, Americans are still debating the same question—how strong should the federal government be?

Changing the Constitution

Although most Anti-Federalist leaders eventually rallied to the new Constitution, they insisted on and won a crucial promise: A bill of rights would be added to the Constitution.

The Bill of Rights

Today, the first ten amendments to the Constitution, known as the **Bill of Rights**, form a crucial feature of the Constitution and of American government. *These set out the rights—the protections from government—that every citizen is owed.* Freedom of speech, freedom of the press, freedom of religion, the right to bear arms, and the long list of additional rights are an essential part of America's identity. Table 2.3 summarizes the amendments that make up the Bill of Rights.

Originally, the Bill of Rights applied only to the federal government. The First Amendment reads, *"Congress shall make no law . . .* abridging the freedom of speech." At the time, states that wanted to limit speech or set up an official religion were free to do so.

The Fourteenth Amendment, ratified after the Civil War in 1868 to protect the former slaves, commands that no *state* may deny "any person . . . the equal

The Bill of Rights: The first ten amendments to the Constitution, listing the rights guaranteed to every citizen.

TABLE 2.3 Summarizing the Bill of Rights

1. Congress may not establish a religion or prohibit the free exercise of religion; it may not abridge freedom of speech or of the press or of the people's right to assemble and to petition government.
2. Citizens have the right to bear arms.
3. No soldier may be quartered in any house without the consent of the owner.
4. There must be no unreasonable search or seizures. Government authorities may not break into your house without a search warrant.
5. No one may be forced to testify against him- or herself (declining to do so is now known as "taking the Fifth"); no one may be deprived of life, liberty, or property without due process of law. The government may not take private property (if, for example, it wants to build a highway) without just compensation.
6. Certain rights are guaranteed in criminal trials.
7. Accused persons are guaranteed the right to trial by jury.
8. The government may not force citizens to pay excessive bails and may not impose cruel and unusual punishments.
9. Enumerating these rights does not diminish the other rights retained by the people.
10. Any powers not given to the federal government are reserved for the states and the people.

Incorporation: The process by which the Supreme Court declares that a right in the Bill of Rights also applies to state governments.

protection of the laws." In theory, this amendment extended the Bill of Rights to the states—meaning state governments must honor each right just as the national government must do. However, the Fourteenth Amendment only began a long process, known as **incorporation**, of applying the Bill of Rights to the state governments, one right at a time. That process continues down to the present day: the Supreme Court "incorporated" the right to bear arms in 2010. Ratifying the Constitution and the Bill of Rights was just the start of a long debate.

The Seventeen Amendments

After the Bill of Rights was passed, constitutional amendments became rare events. Only four more were ratified in the next 115 years. Successful amendments—remember, only seventeen have passed since 1791—all do at least one of four things: They extend rights—for example, guaranteeing the right to vote to eighteen-year-olds (seven amendments extend rights). They adjust election rules—for example, limiting the president to two terms (eleven amendments focus on elections). They change the operations of government—for example, switching Inauguration Day from March to January (four amendments focus on government rules). Or they adjust governmental powers over individuals—for example, prohibiting alcohol and then (fourteen years later) permitting alcohol again. Table 2.4 summarizes the seventeen amendments that have been ratified since 1791.

Apart from formal amendments, American government—and how we interpret the Constitution—has changed over time. We constantly debate how to apply the Constitution and its amendments to current issues. May Congress limit the money corporations give political candidates? May the CIA waterboard suspected terrorists? May the City of Chicago stop people from carrying guns? May businesses be exempted from providing health insurance to employees because of religious objections to "Obamacare," as in the Supreme Court's *Hobby Lobby* decision of 2014? The wording of the Constitution permits different interpretations. These questions—and many more—require Americans to read the Constitution and reflect on what it tells us, more than two and a quarter centuries after it was ratified.

The Constitution Today

The political life of the American colonies prepared the way for something no nation had done before: the United States organized a new government around a Constitution, written in the people's name and voted on by the people's representatives in every state. The document still guides American politics today. Who are we? Reading the U.S. Constitution is one important way to find out.

But there is a catch. Americans disagree about how to read the Constitution. One view, called **originalism**, or *strict construction*, insists that *Americans are bound to the literal meaning of the Constitution and its amendments, as their original authors and debaters understood them.* From this perspective, the Constitution's meaning does not change with the times.

Originalism: A principle of legal interpretation that relies on the original meaning of those who wrote the Constitution.

TABLE 2.4 Amendments to the U.S. Constitution

AMENDMENT	DESCRIPTION	YEAR RATIFIED	RESULT
11	Required state consent for individuals suing a state in federal court	1795	Modified government operations
12	Separated votes within the Electoral College for president and vice president	1804	Shifted election rules
13	Prohibited slavery	1865	Expanded individual rights
14	Provided citizenship to former slaves and declared that states could not deny civil rights, civil liberties, or equal protection of the laws	1868	Expanded individual rights
15	Granted voting rights to members of all races	1870	Expanded individual rights
16	Permitted national income tax	1913	Expanded government powers over individuals
17	Provided direct election of senators	1913	Shifted election rules
18	Prohibited alcohol	1919	Expanded government powers over individuals
19	Extended the vote to women	1920	Expanded individual rights
20	Changed Inauguration Day from March to January	1933	Modified government operations
21	Repealed Prohibition	1933	Adjusted government powers over individuals
22	Limited president to two terms	1951	Shifted election rules
23	Extended the vote for president to citizens in Washington, D.C.	1961	Expanded individual rights
24	Prohibited a poll tax [one way to keep black people from voting]	1964	Expanded individual rights
25	Established succession plan in case of president's death or disability	1967	Modified government operations
26	Extended the vote to eighteen- to twenty-year-olds	1971	Expanded individual rights
27	Established that congressional pay raise couldn't go into effect until the next election	1992	Modified government operations

Seventeen amendments in 215 years, ten of which are about elections and individual rights:
   Expanded individual rights
   Shifted election rules
   Modified government operations
   Expanded or adjusted government powers over individuals

● *What does the Constitution say about praying in schools? Americans disagree. In 2012, Florida governor Rick Scott signed legislation permitting prayers in public schools, over vociferous objections that the legislation was unconstitutional. So far, school districts have avoided introducing prayer for fear of lawsuits. The legislation stipulates that the school districts, not the state of Florida, will be responsible for any legal or court fees that result from introducing prayer in the schools.*

see for yourself 2.1

Go online to view *The 10-Minute Guide to the Constitution* from Cornell University.

Pragmatism: A principle of legal interpretation based on the idea that the Constitution evolves and that it must be put in the context of contemporary realities.

Another view was first articulated by Thomas Jefferson, who warned Americans not to view the Constitution with "sanctimonious reverence," as if it were "too sacred to be touched." The nation's founders were not superhuman in their wisdom, he insisted. He knew their limits, he said, because he was one of them. "I know also," concluded Jefferson, "that laws and institutions must go hand in hand with the progress of the human mind."[19] Many scholars and politicians have followed Jefferson's advice. They see a living, breathing, changing Constitution—one that speaks to each generation a little differently. This view of an evolving Constitution is known as **pragmatism**. *We cannot help bringing our own background, ideas, and judgments to bear as we think about the meaning of the document.*

As we will see throughout this book, it is often hard to tell exactly how the Constitution applies to our times. Different people reading the document come to very different conclusions—even if they're searching for the original meaning. In the end, the difference between originalism and pragmatism may not be as large as their proponents think.

THE BOTTOM LINE

- The Bill of Rights comprises the first ten amendments to the Constitution, which define the rights of American citizens.

- Seventeen more amendments (of more than one hundred thousand proposals) followed over the next 215 years.

- American politics is always changing, but the Constitution still stands as the American political rulebook. However, the Constitution must be interpreted for it is often unclear what the document means and how it applies to contemporary cases.

● Conclusion: Does the Constitution Still Work?

Every chapter that follows will focus on a different feature of the Constitution as it operates today—federalism, civil liberties, civil rights, Congress, the presidency, the courts, and so on. As you explore these institutions, keep a major question in mind: Does the world's oldest constitution still work? Almost all politicians—and most Americans—would surely say that it does. That's why it has lasted so long. But some disagree. Robert Dahl, a leading political scientist, argues that the Constitution is not democratic enough.[20] It does not include modern rights. The checks and balances are sometimes too cumbersome, making it difficult to pass needed laws. Congress no longer checks the president when it comes to war.

The debate takes us back to the very first question we asked in Chapter 1. Who governs? Do "we the people" still rule? Or has real power slipped away to the rich and powerful? These are questions that, directly or indirectly, every chapter will address.

Regardless of whether you're an *originalist*, a *pragmatist*, or somewhere in between, you should check to see what the Constitution says every time you study another feature of American politics. Start with the Constitution and you'll know the basic rules of American politics.

What Do You Think?

●●● HOW STRICTLY SHOULD WE INTERPRET THE CONSTITUTION?

After considering the two approaches to interpreting the Constitution known as originalism and pragmatism, choose a position.

I'm an originalist. Contemporary justices should not try to substitute their judgment for that of the Constitution's framers. We cannot avoid the arbitrary use of power if we allow everyone to read the Constitution as they like. Before long, the Constitution will not mean anything at all.

I'm a pragmatist. Times change and conditions evolve. The modern world imposes challenges that the framers could not have imagined. Failing to permit the text to evolve would turn the document into an eighteenth-century straitjacket.

I'm in the middle. I believe the difference between these positions is far less stark than it appears at first glance. Even if we try very hard to get back to the document's original meaning, we always read the Constitution in light of the present. Every effort to interpret the Constitution will be guided by our own ideas and our own times.

CHAPTER SUMMARY

● The Constitution provides the ground rules for American politics. However, it is often unclear exactly how the Constitution applies to contemporary issues. We have to interpret its meaning.

● The colonial experience prepared America for thinking about a constitution. The English practice of *salutary neglect* permitted the colonies to develop their own political institutions, centered on their legislatures. Americans got used to *delegated representation* (reflecting voter sentiment), which contrasted with the British view of *trustee representation* (representing the whole nation regardless of public opinion).

● The Declaration of Independence has two parts. First, it states the American ideal: All people "are created equal" and "endowed by their creator with certain unalienable rights" including "life, liberty, and the pursuit of happiness." Second, it lists colonial grievances, emphasizing the rights of free people to elect their legislatures.

● The first American government, under the Articles of Confederation, was an alliance of independent states that maximized popular participation. This government had some great successes, but many leaders felt that it was too weak and left the United States vulnerable to foreign powers.

● The Constitutional Convention, convened to fix the problems with the first American government, focused on six broad issues: popular involvement, national versus state power, big versus small states, checks and balances, the presidency, and slavery.

● Ratification of the Constitution involved an extremely close battle between Anti-Federalists, who opposed the Constitution, and Federalists, who supported it. The first ten amendments, known as the Bill of Rights, came out of the ratification debates and were approved by the First Congress. Seventeen more amendments followed in the next 215 years. American politics has changed enormously, but the Constitution continues to stand as the basic blueprint for American political life.

KEY TERMS

Bicameral, 59
Bill of Rights, 77
Classical republicanism, 72
Compact, 46
Confederation, 53
Covenant, 46
Delegate representation, 47

Electoral College, 62
Federalism, 59
First Continental Congress, 51
Incorporation, 78
Indentured servant, 45
Mercantilism, 49
New Jersey Plan, 60

Originalism, 78
Pragmatism, 80
Second Continental Congress, 52
Trustee representation, 48
Unicameral, 60
Virginia Plan, 59

STUDY QUESTIONS

1. Describe five ways that the colonial experience prepared the United States for a constitution.
2. Winning the French and Indian War drove two wedges between England and the colonies. What were they?
3. What is the difference between delegate representation and trustee representation? How did the difference lead to the American Revolution?

4. What are the five overarching ideas introduced by the Declaration of Independence? In your opinion, how close are we to achieving those aspirations today?
5. Describe the first government that Americans organized after they broke away from England. Where was most of the power located? What problems arose under this government? What was successful about it?

6. When it came to writing the Constitution, the delegates had to balance two fears. One emerged from the battle with England and the other from American experience under the Articles of Confederation. Describe these two fears.

7. What did Madison mean by "filtration of representatives"? List two examples of filtration in the original Constitution.

> *What do you think?* Would you support filtration or the direct election of representatives?

8. Describe the differences between the Virginia Plan and the New Jersey Plan. If you had to choose between them, which would you choose and why?

9. Describe what the Constitution says about the following:

> How the House of Representatives is elected
> How the president is elected
> How the Supreme Court is chosen
> How amendments can be added to the Constitution

10. Describe the differences between the Federalists and the Anti-Federalists. Which side would you be on? Why?

> Optional assignment: Choose one of the thirteen original states. Now, write a speech to be presented before its ratifying convention arguing for or against the new constitution.

3

Federalism and Nationalism

IN APRIL 2010, Arizona passed a tough immigration law that required police to check the immigration status of anyone they stop for any reason. In addition to this "show me your papers" policy, the Arizona law had other features: fines for employers who hire individuals without papers, penalties for "sheltering" undocumented aliens, and efforts to ensure that no state services go to the undocumented.

Arizona's new legislation raised a ticklish issue: Immigration enforcement is a *national* government responsibility. However, state officials justified their involvement by charging that the federal government had failed to perform its duty and secure the borders. Arizona officials argued that waves of undocumented aliens were illegally entering the state, straining public services, increasing drug traffic, and driving down wages for working-class Arizonans (including legal immigrants). So they had no choice, these officials said, but to take matters into their own hands.

National controversy erupted in the wake of Arizona's restrictive policies. Latino advocacy groups and their allies led marches calling for fair treatment of all immigrants. They launched an economic boycott that alarmed Arizona business owners. The Obama administration denounced Arizona's crackdown on immigration: It sued the state, claiming that it had encroached on national government's authority.

Among many conservatives, however, Governor Jan Brewer—who signed the Arizona restrictions—became a hero. In 2012 the Supreme Court struck down much of Arizona's law for infringing on federal authority; however, it unanimously permitted the mandatory immigration check—the most controversial feature of the Arizona policy.

After the court ruled, forty-three other states passed immigration measures between 2012 and 2014. Some states followed Arizona and piled on restrictions and "show me your papers" laws. Others went out of their way to assist undocumented residents—permitting immigrants to qualify for driver's licenses, in-state college tuition, and scholarships to public universities.

The tug of war between different levels of government spread to issue after issue. For example, on August 9, 2014, an 18-year-old black man named Michael Brown was shot dead by a white police officer in Ferguson, Missouri.

IN THIS CHAPTER, YOU WILL:

● Learn what federalism is.

● Explore the strengths of federal and state governments.

● Examine how federalism works— and how it has evolved.

● Review the contemporary conflicts that surround federalism.

● Explore American nationalism, the force that binds and shapes our federalist polity.

The contentious relationship between state and federal government: Arizona governor Jan Brewer publicly scolds President Barack Obama over immigration control.

His body lay in the street, uncovered and bleeding from six gunshot wounds; instead of assisting, the Ferguson police were waiting for county officials responsible for investigating homicides.

The following night, vigils turned to riots; black residents were especially angered by what they perceived as police department efforts to justify Brown's shooting by smearing the victim. As the protest grew, local police donned sophisticated combat gear that made them look, to many observers across the nation, like an occupying army. Where did they get such expensive equipment? From the U.S. Defense Department, which had given local police forces 500 million dollars' worth of surplus military gear in the previous year alone. Video images showed the heavily-armed, mainly white police firing tear gas and rubber bullets at the mostly African American protesters.

Missouri Governor Jay Nixon, fearing a worsening of the situation, ordered the Missouri State Highway Patrol to manage security. Four days later, as the protests grew, the governor called in Missouri's National Guard. Meanwhile, the attorney general in Washington D.C., traveled to Ferguson and instructed the Justice Department to monitor the situation. The Federal Bureau of Investigation separately opened its own civil-rights investigation.

As in the immigration case, the lines of authority in Ferguson were all tangled up. Local police were responsible for public safety. The county government was responsible for investigating the murder. Missouri state government became involved when Governor Nixon deployed highway police and the National Guard. The federal government armed the local police, dispatched Justice Department monitors and launched FBI investigations. Who was in charge? They all were: local, country, state and federal authorities . . . which also seemed to mean that no one was really in charge.

Welcome to the politics of federalism. In the United States, most problems and many government programs fall under both national and state jurisdiction. To complicate matters still further, counties, towns and cities also play a vital role. The lines of responsibility between the levels of government are often blurred. The federal government controls immigration policy, but state and local police enforce those rules. The local government is responsible for public safety, but the county, state and federal governments are enmeshed throughout the crisis in Ferguson. Public officials from Washington, D.C., to Phoenix (the Arizona state capital) to Jefferson City (the Missouri capital) to Ferguson are all partners in American government. The line between their jurisdictions—between federal, local, and state responsibility—is endlessly negotiated and renegotiated.

● *Opponents of the Affordable Care Act ("Obamacare") found supporters for their efforts to repeal, defund, or otherwise cripple the law in many state legislatures as well as Congress, but it remains on the books.*

In the last chapter, we saw the constitutional checks and balances among Congress, the executive, and the courts. Now we add the most intricate balancing act of them all: federalism. The term denotes the relationship between different levels of government, sharing and squabbling over power. This complex interplay stretches all the way back to the debates between Federalists (who wanted a strong national government) and Anti-Federalists (who sought more power for the states). The division of power among national, state, and local officials reflects longstanding American debates about democracy, equality, and effective government.

Who are we? A nation of divided loyalties and governments. We are Americans *and* Coloradans *and* residents of Boulder; Americans *and* Texans *and* Houstonians. The results facilitate innovation, protect liberty, and sow confusion. A hurricane in Louisiana, an oil spill off Alaska's coast, or a pipe bomb in Boston bring out local authorities, state officials, and national agencies, all scrambling to get on the same wavelength. The same goes for education policies, environmental protection, food-assistance programs, and the definition of marriage. Federalism is permanently ingrained in our Constitution, our institutions, and our national culture. This chapter looks at its remarkable persistence—and how it changes over time.

BY THE NUMBERS
Federalism

- Estimated number of governments in the United States: **87,576**
- Number of national governments: **1 (0.0011%)**
- Number of state governments: **50 (0.057%)**
- Number of county or parish governments: **3,034 (3.46%)**
- Number of town or city governments: **84,451 (96.4%)**
- Number of counties in Texas, each with its own government: **254**
- Number of counties in Hawaii, each with its own government: **4**
- Number of U.S. states whose capital is located in the state's largest city: **19**
- Number of nonmilitary personnel who work for the federal government: **2.7 million**
- Number who work for state governments: **4.4 million**
- Number who work for local governments: **12.2 million**
- Number of Americans who move to a different county each year: **17 million**
- Percentage of Americans who say they trust the federal government to do what is right most of the time: **19**
- Percentage who said this in 1958: **73**
- Percentage who trust the state government to do what is right: **57**
- Percentage who trust the local government: **63**
- Percentage of Americans over age 65 who believe the United States is "the greatest country in the world," 2013: **64**
- Percentage of Americans under age 30 who believe this: **32**
- Percentage of Americans who are "extremely" or "very" proud to be American: **83**
- Percentage of whites expressing this sentiment: **86**
- Percentage of African Americans expressing this sentiment: **81**
- Percentage of Latvians who are "extremely" or "very" proud to be Latvian: **38**

Unitary government:
A national polity governed as a single unit, with the central government exercising all or most political authority.

Confederation: A group of independent states or nations that yield some of their powers to a national government, although each state retains a degree of sovereign authority.

 ## Forging Federalism

Most nations in the 1780s had **unitary governments**. The national government—the king and Parliament in England, for example—made policy for the nation. Local governments simply carried out their decrees. To this day, most nations are organized this way. Local government is an administrative extension of national government. Americans rebelled against Britain's unitary government and were certainly not going to reintroduce the same system all over again.

A second, less-used traditional form, **confederation**, leaves most power in the states or provinces while a weak central authority provides common defense or economic benefits. Today, the European Union is struggling to make a confederation work. Americans tried this system under the Articles of Confederation. As we saw in the previous chapter, it proved too weak.

At the Constitutional Convention, the delegates devised an innovative hybrid: a *federal system* in which power is divided and shared between national and state governments. The Constitution reserves some decisions for the national government (declaring war, coining money), others reside with the states (establishing schools), and some are held at both levels (taxing, spending, establishing courts, regulating business). Since each level is independent and their powers overlap, conflict is built into the system—as we can see in the clash among authorities in Ferguson.

On the surface, the states might seem to have a built-in advantage in any conflict with the national government. As Figure 3.1 shows, the more local the government, the more the people trust it.[1] Yet Americans also express an unusually strong *nationalist* outlook: few people in other countries are quite as patriotic. As we'll see, that unusual mixture of patriotism and mistrust of public officials directly affects our politics and government.

Further complicating matters, the United States also has independent local governments, at the town, city, and county level. These add still more layers of elected officials, government employees, services to provide, and taxes to be paid. However, local governments are *not* sovereign units of the federal system. Rather, they are, in legal terms, "creatures of the state." All local powers come from the state government. Some states grant their local governments broad powers, known as *home rule*; others jealously hold onto authority and approve or reject every major action a local government wishes to take. When Detroit mayor Dennis Archer (a Democrat) wanted to take control of the failing Detroit school system, he needed more than a "yes" vote in the city. He needed approval from the Michigan governor (a Republican) as well as the state legislature (which originally said no, then relented). All the

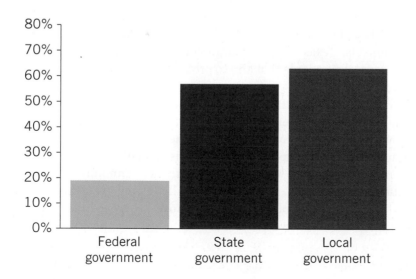

● **FIGURE 3.1** *Trust in government gets stronger as government gets closer to the public. (Pew Research Center for People and the Press)*

overlap and conflict we have described between federal and state governments gets replicated—sometimes with even more intensity—between state and local governments.

THE BOTTOM LINE

- The United States rebelled against a *unitary* system and rejected a *confederation* after trying one for a decade.

- The Constitutional Convention created a new hybrid form of government: a federal system of shared and overlapping powers. Power is divided and shared between national and state governments.

- American federalism is further complicated by local governments, which are reliant on state government for their authority.

● Who Holds Government Authority?

A federal system constantly poses the same question: Where should we locate authority? Let's start with two recent cases.

In January 2014, three hundred thousand people in West Virginia were warned to stay away from their water faucets. Old liquid storage tanks (built in the 1940s and 1950s) had leaked MCHM, a toxic chemical, into the Elk River and contaminated the region's water supply. People were frightened and angry. Someone should have been examining the rusty tanks. But who? Some residents charged that state officials were only concerned with protecting the local coal and chemical industries and called for national regulation and oversight. Others noted that West Virginians were proud of their state's independence and antiregulatory stance; it would be "political suicide," they concluded, for any politician to call for more federal regulation. Different states have very different attitudes toward regulating industry. Vermont and New York offer strong controls; Texas and West Virginia tend to limit regulation. Should we insist on federal standards that aim to protect all citizens? Or leave regulatory policies to the states?

Starting January 1, 2014, adults in Colorado could legally buy up to an ounce of marijuana in licensed stores. This initiative, approved by the state's voters, violated federal laws that outlaw the possession, manufacture, and sale of marijuana (with up to lifetime imprisonment for growing more than ninety-nine plants). The Obama administration announced it would not prosecute legal users in Colorado—essentially setting aside the federal laws. Meanwhile, cities like Colorado Springs moved to forbid marijuana stores in their areas. Should we leave marijuana use to the states? Or insist on a national criminal law? How about other illegal drugs—should they be controlled by national or state/local laws?

Each of these cases raises federalism's most important question: Who holds authority—the federal government or the states? And where responsibility is shared, where do we draw the line between the roles played by different governments? Political scientists generally see advantages to each level of government.[2]

Advantages of State-Level Policy

First, proponents of state action argue that state officials are *more responsive* to citizen needs and desires. The vast United States spans states with very different problems and cultures. Maine and Minnesota do not need to regulate water in the same way as desert states like Arizona and Nevada. Large cities try to curb gang violence with curfews and gun buy-back programs that would not make much sense in rural areas. In short, state and local government can match policies to local conditions and values without a "one size fits all" national policy.

Second, states sometimes offer more *protection for individual rights.* Same-sex couples found success on the state level long before federal officials were willing to support their right to marry. On the other hand, states vehemently denied African Americans the right to vote, forcing supporters of racial equality to take the fight to the national level (we'll explore all these cases in Chapters 4 and 5).

Third, federalism fosters *political innovation*. Different states can experiment with different programs. Supreme Court Justice Louis Brandeis put it famously: "One of the happy incidents of the federal system [is] that a single courageous State may . . . serve as a laboratory; and try novel social and economic experiments without risk to the rest of the country."[3] Ever since, states in a federal system have been called "laboratories of democracy"— allowing us to test and learn what policy options work best. Throughout American history, innovations have bubbled up from the states before going national. The list includes Social Security pensions for retirees, environmental protection, worker safety rules, direct election of senators, welfare reform, child nutrition programs, and even alcohol prohibition. This process of testing and spreading ideas is known as **diffusion.**[4]

Finally, some argue that federalism gives people more *choices*. Each state offers a different bundle of costs and services.

Diffusion: The spreading of policy ideas from one city or state to others; a process typical of U.S. federalism.

● *Environmental regulations differ dramatically across the United States. Here, West Virginians line up for bottled water after a 2014 chemical spill threatened the state's water supply—the third chemical accident in the lightly regulated state over the past five years.*

People who want or need many government services can move to Connecticut or New Jersey. Those who want a more limited government can choose the South or the "red states" west of the Rocky Mountains.[5]

This last point is controversial with advocates who point out that many Americans are not free to simply move. If a policy is a good one, they argue, all Americans deserve to enjoy it—which brings us to the advantages of national policies.

The Advantages of National Policy

First, national policy is often more *fair*. A single mother working full time for eight dollars an hour can be treated for breast cancer under New York's Medicaid program but is not eligible for any treatment at all in Texas. Additionally, America's racial experience suggests that, at least sometimes, national decisions are required to overcome local prejudices.

This desire for fairness leads critics to worry that competition between states and localities leads to a *race to the bottom*. Leave social welfare policy to the states, argue defenders of national standards, and the result is a bidding war in which each state tries to cut programs (and taxes) more than neighboring states—to attract middle-class people and new business. Political scientists have found some evidence that states do copy one another as programs are cut and benefits are reduced.[6]

Second, national policies can *equalize resources across the nation*. Every time there is a crisis—a hurricane, an oil spill, or an earthquake—all eyes turn to the U.S. government, which can bring more resources and expertise to bear on the problem than individual states. Those resources can also make day-to-day policies work across all fifty states. That way, even poorer states can have the resources they need.

Third, national policies can *standardize best practices* across the nation. After we've tested new policies in the state "laboratories of democracy," a national policy can ensure that the lessons are spread to everyone. Minimum standards ensure that no state chooses inadequate health or education policies for its children.

Finally, leaving authority in state hands introduces *problems of coordination* among federal, state, and local agencies. With many different agencies responding to multiple layers of authorities, using different procedures, and trying to achieve slightly different goals, the result can be chaos. A patchwork of rules and regulations across the states

● Concern over personal health and the environment has led to anger about fracking—a method of extracting oil and natural gas from far below the earth. Different states and communities regulate fracking in different ways.

PRESERVING LOCAL VALUES OR CONTINUING A TERRIBLE INJUSTICE?

Law-and-order issues are largely in the hands of local and state governments. One result: California has 731 people waiting on death row; Ohio has 147. Meanwhile, New York, Minnesota, and many other states have no one waiting to be executed because they ban the death penalty altogether. Should we leave the question of executions to the states? What do you think?

Yes.
Law enforcement ought to reflect local values. This is just the way it should be, because conditions such as crime rates and public attitudes vary from state to state. Let the local population decide.

No.
Executions are too important to leave up to such a patchwork of local laws. This should be a question we decide collectively as a nation, so that a death sentence does not depend on the state you live in. We might decide as a nation to *abolish* the death penalty altogether. Or we might choose to permit executions, while seeking to ensure that no innocent person is executed, perhaps by mandating DNA testing of the accused.

Not sure where you stand?
In the next chapter we'll explore whether the death penalty violates the Constitution—if so, it would not be permitted anywhere regardless of what the people in a particular locality think.

leaves many citizens and national companies bewildered about what rules apply where.

In sum, the ambiguity in federalism sets up a constant dispute about where to place authority. Do we leave decisions with the states because they are "closer to the people"? Or do we place them on the national level to try to promote equality and high standards across the country, even if local people resent them? For many Americans, the answer shifts with the issue.

Should federal laws criminalizing marijuana possession trump state efforts to decriminalize it? Liberals generally say no and support local choice. Should national clean-air standards override state pollution regulations and national health care standards override state insurance regulations? Now most liberals switch sides and say yes, whereas conservatives disagree. These debates began at the Constitutional Convention and rage around every problem and every policy. They are built right into our federal institutions. They are an integral part of our federalist system. Yet, at the same time, we should recognize one key institutional point: *Federalism gives advocates on both sides many different political venues in which to face problems, challenge policies, and assert rights.*

THE BOTTOM LINE

- The central question in federalism is where to place responsibility—on the state or national levels.

- State-level policy has at least four advantages: It responds to local needs, enables innovations in the laboratories of democracy, protects individual rights, and enhances choice.

- National-level policy also has four main advantages: it enhances fairness (avoiding a race to the bottom), equalizes resources, promotes national standards and best practices, and facilitates coordination.

- Understanding the pros and cons of federalism is important as we decide whether to create national standards and programs or whether to leave judgments to local populations. This question is generally decided issue by issue and program by program.

How Federalism Works

So far this chapter's message is clear: federalism offers endless opportunities for confusion and discord, as different layers of government tussle over who has responsibility for what. However, there are well-defined patterns to this contest. Americans have hammered out rules that enable our federalist system to function pretty well—most of the time. These rules evolve, and they are not always clear and straightforward. Even the terminology can be elusive: Americans routinely call the national government the "federal government," a practice we follow in this chapter, although that term formally refers to the whole system of shared powers stretching across national, state, and local units.

The Constitution Sets the Ground Rules

The Constitution can be read two ways: at times it restricts the national government in favor of the states; in other ways, it empowers it.

The Constitution Empowers National Authority.   Article 1, Section 8, lists nineteen powers vested in the national government: Congress has the authority to pay debts, raise an army, punish pirates, establish a post office, handle U.S. foreign policy, and so forth. Because they are laid out in black and white, scholars call these **granted powers**—also known as *express* or *enumerated powers*

Granted powers: National government powers set out explicitly in the Constitution.

(you can read them in the Constitution in Appendix II). This section of the Constitution is crisp and clear about the limited list of national government powers.

The final clause of the section, however, complicates matters by authorizing Congress to make all laws *necessary and proper* for carrying out the enumerated powers—*or any other power the Constitution vests in the national government*. This **necessary and proper clause** is also known as the *elastic clause*, because it stretches national government authority to include anything implied in the Constitution's text. Across two centuries, the elastic clause has been used to justify expanded national authority over everything from creating banks to regulating airlines to overseeing zoos. These new areas of jurisdiction are **inherent powers**—powers that are implied by, but not specifically named in, the Constitution's text.

The **supremacy clause**, found near the end of the Constitution in Article 6, buttresses these granted (or explicit) and inherent (or implicit) powers. The clause declares that the national government's laws and treaties are the "supreme law of the land" and are superior to state laws whenever the two clash. The supremacy clause formed the basis of the Obama administration's legal challenge to the Arizona immigration law, introduced at the start of this chapter.

The Constitution Protects State Authority. At the same time, the states have their own authority guaranteed by the Tenth Amendment—the final amendment in the Bill of Rights. This "reserves" to the states all powers not expressly granted to the national branches in Washington. The Tenth Amendment seems to bolster the argument of small-government advocates. After the Republican Party won control of both chambers of Congress in 1994, its leaders distributed cards imprinted with the Tenth Amendment to House and Senate Republican members, reminding them to limit federal government actions whenever possible.

The states' **reserved powers** include public education, public health, commerce within the state, and organizing state elections. Police, prisons, and courts are also in each state's hands. State and local officials carry out most investigations, arrests, trials, and incarcerations—unless a federal law has been violated. State prisons and local jails hold 89 percent of the inmates in the United States.

The Constitution Authorizes Shared Power. It is a mistake to think of federalism simply as conflict between government levels. State and national authorities share many responsibilities, termed **concurrent powers**. Both national and state governments have the power to raise taxes, build roads, construct bridges, build railways, update telecommunications networks, borrow money, and regulate business. The next time you're stuck in traffic inching past a sign announcing new transportation construction, look it over carefully: you'll usually see a combination of national, state, and local funds listed in support.

Federalism also involves relations among the states. The Constitution directs each state to give **full faith and credit** to the actions of other states. This requirement becomes controversial, however, when states disagree with policies

Necessary and proper clause: The constitutional declaration (in Article 1, Section 8) that defines Congress's authority to exercise the "necessary and proper" powers to carry out its designated functions.

Inherent powers: National government powers implied by, but not specifically named in, the Constitution.

Supremacy clause: The constitutional declaration (in Article 6, Section 2) that the national government's authority prevails over any conflicting state or local government's claims.

Reserved powers: The constitutional guarantee (in the Tenth Amendment) that the states retain government authority not explicitly granted to the national government.

Concurrent powers: Governmental authority shared by national and state governments, such as the power to tax residents.

Full faith and credit clause: The constitutional requirement (in Article 4, Section 1) that each state recognize and uphold laws passed by any other state.

enacted by others. Take gun control laws, which vary widely from state to state. Washington, D.C., restricts people from carrying guns in public. Virginia, which surrounds Washington's southern half, allows gun owners to bring legally registered weapons into restaurants and other public places. In 2012, the state went further, eliminating local Virginia communities' ability to fingerprint those applying for a concealed carry permit. Should D.C. officials grant "full faith and credit" to Virginia's generous policy? Constitutional law is unclear and must be sorted out case by case. In 2014, some Virginia legislators proposed a law to deny the legitimacy of *all* new national laws restricting gun rights: federalism in action once more.

The Constitution also sets up some definite barriers. A state may not launch its own navy, conclude treaties with another country, or coin its own money. The Bill of Rights—although it originally applied only to the federal government—imposes a long list of limits on government in the name of individual rights and freedoms. In short, the Constitution both empowers and limits the national and state governments alike.

Emphasizing some parts of the Constitution—such as inherent powers, the necessary and proper clause, the supremacy clause—justifies a robust national government. This reading of the Constitution enables a national government that regulates toxic spills, enforces airport security, and prosecutes the war on drugs. Emphasizing other clauses, like the Tenth Amendment, yields a more modest national government that defers to the people of each state. That's the reading that leaves West Virginia alone to regulate its own water supply, enables Colorado to decide on marijuana, and limits the federal government's role in fighting discrimination in private clubs or restaurants.

Again we return to a vital point: American government is a perpetual argument, a work in progress. The Constitution's ground rules for federalism are open to interpretation and reinterpretation. They have guided a long, often creative debate about which level of government should be doing what.

In different eras, Americans have organized the federal system in different ways. The next sections introduce the most important shifts over the years.

Dual Federalism (1789–1933)

Dual (or layer cake) federalism: Clear division of governing authority between national and state governments.

For its first 150 years or so, the United States practiced a form of **dual federalism**, in which state and national governments had relatively clear responsibilities. The state governments wielded at least as much authority as the federal governments. American historians with an eye for metaphor describe this arrangement as "layer cake" federalism: the different levels of government—national, state, and local—fell more or less into separate layers. Each level of government was supreme within its own band of influence (see Figure 3.2).

This division of labor left the national government in charge of three major areas. One was international relations—trade, war, diplomacy, and immigration. This was a significant role, as the United States deployed troops overseas 165 times in its first 150 years—and that count does not include a long and bloody series of conflicts with Native American tribes.

American Federalism
Layer Cake or Marble Cake?

Layer Cake Federalism
has a clear division of
governing authority between
national and state governments.

Marble Cake Federalism
mingles governing authority with
functions overlapping across
national and state governments.

● **FIGURE 3.2** *Different federalist styles across American history.*

Second, the national government was responsible for "internal improvements" like transportation and a single currency. In early America, it was cheaper to ship iron from London to Philadelphia than it was to move it fifty miles inland from Philadelphia. Transportation networks like roads, canals, and railroads solved the problem of moving freight (and people). For the first eighty years, Americans did not even share a currency. The Banking Acts of 1863 and 1864 finally set a uniform currency.

Finally, the federal government regulated relations and commerce between the states. This became an explosive issue when slave states demanded assistance in capturing men and women running for their freedom.

States retained control over almost everything having to do with individual citizens (and corporations, which were granted the same rights as individual citizens). The states oversaw education, marriage, divorce, professional regulation, business contracts, driving, drinking, burials, and so on. To this day, state governments wield primary responsibility over individual behavior—although the federal government now touches most of these matters directly or indirectly.

The layer cake was never quite as clear-cut as the metaphor suggests. The national government distributed land in unsettled territories. Before the Civil War, it wrestled endlessly with the slavery issue. In the 1870s it used control of interstate commerce to crack down on pornography, restrict contraception, and fight abortion. In 1920, the Nineteenth Amendment forbade the transportation and sale of intoxicating liquors. State and national authorities had overlapping jurisdiction in enforcing the act[7]—and when states like New York decided to ignore the ban on liquor, federal officials stepped in to enforce it (a 1920s version of the

● *Constructing canals, bridges, roads—and, later, railroads—was a major national government responsibility in the nineteenth century.*

marijuana debate—with all the violence and corruption of the late-twentieth-century drug wars). Still, despite many exceptions, government activity remained, very roughly, separated into layers.

Cooperative Federalism (1933–1981)

During the New Deal of the 1930s, the dual arrangement finally collapsed. President Franklin Roosevelt and large Democratic majorities in Congress vigorously responded to the Great Depression by passing policies that decisively strengthened the national government's role. Roosevelt presided over a shift toward **cooperative federalism**, characterized by blurred lines of authority and a much more active national government (Table 3.1). A new bakery metaphor emerged: a *marble cake*, in which the various ingredients—different government functions—all swirled together. In one program after another, the responsibilities of federal, state, and local governments were increasingly mingled: funding, rules, administration, implementation, and execution cut across the different layers of federalism (Figure 3.2).

Officials in Washington provided federal funds through **grants-in-aid**—national funds accompanied by specific instructions to state and local officials about how the money could be spent. Governors and other state leaders, desperate for resources during the Depression, accepted these national grants for roads, bridges, hospitals, health care clinics, Social Security support for

Cooperative (or marble cake) federalism: Mingled governing authority, with functions overlapping across national and state governments.

Grants-in-aid: National government funding provided to state and local governments, along with specific instructions about how the funds may be used.

TABLE 3.1 Comparing Dual and Cooperative Federalism

DUAL FEDERALISM	COOPERATIVE FEDERALISM
NATIONAL POWERS	
Enumerated: The national government may only utilize powers specifically listed in the Constitution.	**Elastic:** The national government may wield powers "necessary and proper" to support its function.
LOCATION OF SUPREME AUTHORITY	
Separate sovereignty: National and state governments each have authority within their own spheres.	**National supremacy:** States retain important powers but are subordinate to the national government except where the Constitution strictly forbids.
KEY PRINCIPLE	
States' rights: Each state is largely free to govern its own affairs.	**Power sharing:** National and state officials work together wherever possible—also with local officials, who became more prominent after the 1930s.
NATIONAL–STATE RELATIONS	
Competitive: Relationship characterized by tension, not cooperation.	**Cooperative:** Relationship considered joint, not competitive.

seniors, welfare payments for poor people—the list goes on. Most of the funds were accompanied by Washington rules and oversight.

After the long Depression and World War II, a new era of economic prosperity emerged. Many state and local officials began expressing resentment at the national meddling in their affairs. Federal funds continued to flow, however, and even the most ardent states' rights advocates were not going to deny their constituents this national bounty.

Cooperative federalism, with Washington dominating many policy areas, lasted from the New Deal through the 1970s. Senator Everett Dirksen (R-IL) quipped in 1964 that if the trend toward increasing national power continued, "the only people still interested in state boundaries would be Rand-McNally," the noted U.S. mapmaker.[8]

New Federalism

Ronald Reagan's presidency (1981–1989) ushered in another significant change in American federalism, enthusiastically termed **New Federalism** by its advocates. Reagan and fellow conservatives tipped the pendulum of power away from national officials, promoting more decision-making authority by state and local officials. In place of grants-in-aid, with national officials carefully specifying the rules and regulations that accompanied the funds, the Reagan administration relied more heavily on **block grants**. Block grants also channel federal dollars to a specific policy area, like education or transportation or health, but leave the program's details to state and local bureaucrats. Block grants had been developed and expanded through the 1970s. Reagan used them to rethink federalism.

One feature of block grants has made them controversial. The grants-in-aid that marked cooperative federalism often provide unlimited funding for a specific purpose; for example, everyone who qualifies for Medicaid receives hospital coverage, and anyone eligible for food stamps gets food stamps. In contrast, block grants provide a fixed amount of funds for health care or nutrition. State and local officials get to do what they think best with the funds; however, the federal government limits its contribution, forcing state officials to make hard choices about who qualifies and who doesn't. As a result, every effort to shift an existing grant-in-aid program to a block grant creates controversy.

Note that New Federalism does not restore the neat layers of dual federalism—if anything, the lines of authority are even more swirled together than ever. Now, federal, state, and local authorities all compete for influence over programs. Imagine this situation as a multiflavored marble cake.

New Federalism: A version of cooperative federalism, but with stronger emphasis on state and local government activity, versus national government.

Block grants: National government funding provided to state and local governments, with relatively few restrictions or requirements on spending.

"In Two Words, Yes And No"

● *Struggles over the extent of cooperative federalism, captured in 1949—and still an issue, more than 60 years later.*

- The Constitution grants the national government both enumerated (or explicit) powers and inherent (or implicit) powers. You can read it to emphasize broad national powers (using the elastic clause) or state dominance (emphasizing the Tenth Amendment).

- There have been three important eras of federalism: dual federalism included clearly demarcated authority (the layer cake); cooperative federalism, arising with FDR's New Deal, introduced federal dominance and blurred lines of authority (the marble cake); President Reagan's New Federalism still relies on federal funds, but shifts more decision making about spending those monies back to the states.

Battles over Federalism Today

Throughout American history, people have debated the balance of power between federal authority (embodied in the supremacy clause) and states' rights (enshrined in the Tenth Amendment). This question exploded over the spread of slavery, and was settled only by the Civil War. Today disagreements over federalism are generally fought with words and regulations rather than swords and cannonballs, but they remain heated.

Drowned in the Bathtub?

Devolution: The transfer of authority from national to state or local government level.

The debate over federalism often reflects a particular American passion (especially strong among conservatives): The desire to reduce the size and scope of government. One pillar of the New Federalism movement was **devolution**, or the transferring of responsibility for government programs from national to state and local authorities—and then to the private sector. Devolutionists have fought to reduce the influence of government at every level. "I don't want to abolish government," declared conservative activist Grover Norquist. "I simply want to reduce it down to the size where I can . . . drown it in the bathtub."[9]

The strategy raises a major question: Will moving policies to the state level guarantee a less active government response? Even when it does, serious problems often lead to a greater national government role. For example, many states' rights advocates have pushed hard to limit federal endangered species regulation. Yet after the national government cut back Environmental Protection Agency and Forest Service supervision of wildlife management, invasive species like zebra mussels and milfoil (a plant native to Asia that has choked the life out of many American ponds and lakes) overwhelmed local wildlife agencies and caused billions of dollars in damage. Harmful plants and creatures are oblivious to local and state boundaries; a federal government response, coordinating eradication efforts across multiple jurisdictions, was needed.

Unfunded Mandates

Other voices in federalism debates accept that the national government has legitimate authority in some areas, but they argue that when responsibility is passed to state or local officials, there must be resources to match. Otherwise, they claim, Washington saddles state and localities with an **unfunded mandate**— a law or regulation that imposes a duty that must be paid for primarily by state or local officials. For example, when federal regulations impose new safety requirements on commuter trains, state and local governments are left to buy and install the new technology—regardless of what shape their budget is in. In 1995, Congress passed the Unfunded Mandates Act, designed to rein in the practice—but many federal laws, rules, regulations, and even grants still require states and local governments to put up their own funds.

Unfunded mandate:
An obligation imposed on state or local government officials by federal legislation, without sufficient federal funding support to cover the costs.

Federalism and the Parties

Dual, cooperative, and New: These successive versions of federalism point to perpetual negotiations about government power and accountability. Republicans continue to urge state and local control on most issues, whereas Democrats are more likely to seek Washington-based solutions.

This rule of thumb is often violated in practice. President George W. Bush campaigned as a small-government conservative but strenuously promoted a national education policy. His administration's No Child Left Behind (NCLB) education program required strict (and frequent) student testing to evaluate schools. It led to widespread criticism from parents, teachers, and principals about "meddling Washington bureaucrats." Many of those critics also pointed out that NCLB programs also amounted to an unfunded mandate, since federal funds were rarely sufficient to cover the cost of preparing students and administering the tests. This Republican policy sure looked Democratic.

Conversely, Bill Clinton's Democratic administration rewrote welfare policy to shift authority and discretion to state and local governments. Clinton ended a program with roots in the Social Security Act of 1935, Aid to Families with Dependent Children (AFDC, often known simply as "welfare"). AFDC provided funds (under strict federal regulations) to support roughly one in six American children. In its place, the administration (working with Republicans in Congress), substituted a block grant program called Temporary Assistance for Needy Families (TANF). By the 1990s, AFDC was providing unlimited state funds accompanied by strict regulations about eligibility for assistance and many other program details. TANF, in contrast, sends block grant funds and leaves most details up to the states. This Democratic program sure looked Republican.

Democratic and Republican administrations regularly stray from their parties' images. Why? The context matters: Abstract debates about national and state power run into policy reality as public officials struggle to make troubled programs more effective. Both the Bush and Clinton administrations also had an eye on politics, for each was trying to quiet criticism. Republicans

INTERGOVERNMENTAL LOBBYING, AMERICAN STYLE

Although the title sounds deceptively plain, intergovernmental affairs liaison offices keep the wheels of American federalism turning. No other country's chief executive has established a formal office to *lobby* (and be lobbied by) its own different levels of government: This is a hallmark of U.S. federalism. Imagine that you're invited to become the president's deputy assistant for governmental affairs. You'll spend your time smoothing the White House's relations with governors from all fifty states: sometimes one or more governors will seek you out to secure a favor from the president, and other times you will be tasked with winning a governor's backing for something the White House wants to achieve. If you were in this job, how would you characterize your role in government?

It would feel like a valuable public service. I would help build bridges across the different layers of federalist government.

I would just be another lobbyist. My role would rely on winning favors for my client—who happens, in this case, to be the president of the United States.

wanted to show they cared about social policy; Democrats were trying to remove the stigma of being "pro-welfare."

Today, relations between national, state, and local levels take a dizzying array of forms. Sometimes officials work in partnership; sometimes they are locked in combat. To keep all the tangled relationships clear, intergovernmental liaison officers work across national, state, city, and even town governments.

The Obama administration's stamp on federalism has been to emphasize *competition* among states or cities for federal funds. The administration seeks to nudge states toward desired policy goals without relying on overbearing national regulations. The Department of Education's "Race to the Top" program, for example, encourages states to compete for pools of national dollars by devising creative education policies. Winning proposals have included promoting charter schools, basing teacher pay on performance rather than the number of years served, and developing new measures to track student progress.

● *Children from public schools in Chatfield, Minnesota, seen with President Barack Obama. They are publicizing the Race to the Top program. The initiative makes federal funds available and invites states and localities to compete for the money—a novel wrinkle in America's federalist varieties.*

Like the administrations that preceded it, the Obama administration is not always consistent in its approach. Faced with the Bush administration's testing requirements, the Obama administration permitted many states to waive national rules and design their own procedures. This was a step in the direction of reduced Washington regulations. On the issue of health reform, in contrast, the administration was far more eager to promulgate national requirements for insurance companies and health providers.

Federalism in the Courts

Most federalism disputes are about drawing a line where national power ends and states' authority begins—and how best to ensure that the division of power is honored in practice. One explanation for the major shifts in federalism is simple: the party in power. The Roosevelt administration initiated a new (Democratic) era in Washington and soon introduced cooperative federalism. The Reagan administration brought Republicans to the center of power and introduced New Federalism. Republicans took control of Congress in 1995 and immediately passed limits on unfunded mandates.

Another key to the tides of federalism lies in the judicial branch. U.S. courts early on became a key source of allocating powers between the states and nation. Judges have typically played a balancing role when it comes to federalism. Supreme Court decisions favored national prerogatives during the early republic, when many individual states had more power and prestige than the federal government in Washington. During the country's first decades, it was often unclear whether the national government could sustain its strength compared to the power enjoyed by long-established states. In a series of landmark decisions, the Supreme Court—led by Chief Justice John Marshall—protected national government powers from state incursions.

The first such case was *McCulloch v. Maryland*, decided in 1819.[10] A year before, Maryland's legislature had sought to impose a tax on the Baltimore branch of the first U.S. national bank. The bank refused to pay and was sued by the state. The Maryland Supreme Court ruled that the Constitution is silent about the federal power to establish a bank, and that the bank was therefore unconstitutional. Maryland was perfectly free to tax it. Marshall overruled the Maryland court and struck down the tax. Invoking the necessary and proper (or elastic) clause, he ruled that Congress could draw on "implied powers" required to operate a functional national government and that states blocking such actions—in this case, by levying a tax on the bank—violated the Constitution. In these and later decisions, Marshall and many other officials in the early republic were anxious to keep dual federalism in balance. At the time, doing so meant expanding national power.

We will follow the way that subsequent U.S. courts interpreted federalism in Chapter 13. As we'll see, in some eras—such as the period between the 1880s and the 1930s, the judiciary tilted away from federal authority—to states and private corporations. Conversely, the rise of activist government during the 1930s probably would not have been possible if the Supreme Court had not, quite dramatically, reversed its course and accepted New Deal legislation beginning in 1937.

In recent years—beginning under Chief Justice Rehnquist in the mid-1990s and gaining strength with a consistently conservative majority under Chief Justice Roberts since 2005—the Supreme Court has emphasized local and state power. A series of prominent cases has shifted power away from the national government toward states (see Table 3.2). Recent examples include the Court's ruling striking down the Obamacare requirement that states must expand their Medicaid program, as well as its overruling the Defense of Marriage Act. If history is a reliable guide, the current judicial trend will fade over time, as the pendulum of state and national power swings again.

TABLE 3.2 Recent Supreme Court Decisions on Federalism

- *U.S. v. Lopez* (1995). Struck down a law prohibiting handguns near schools, claiming Congress had overreached its authority.

- *Seminole Tribe v. Florida* (1996). Reversed Congress's decision allowing Indian tribes to sue a state in federal court; limited individuals' right to sue a state for failing to uphold national laws.

- *Printz v. U.S.* (1997). Struck down portions of the Congress-passed Brady bill requiring background checks before gun sales.

- *U.S. v. Morrison* (2000). Struck down portion of the Violence Against Women Act as "an unconstitutional exercise . . . of Congressional power."

- *Board of Trustees of the University of Alabama v. Garrett* (2001). One of a series of cases that upheld "state sovereign immunity" by expanding state rights under the Eleventh Amendment (which stipulates that states may not be sued in federal court by citizens of another state).

- *Gonzales v. Oregon* (2006). Ruled that national government power to regulate drugs was limited by a state's right to exercise authority over drug laws within its jurisdiction.

- *Medellin v. Texas* (2008). Permitted states to file a type of legal petition repeatedly, overturning national government rules declaring otherwise.

- *Bond v. United States* (2011). Extended to individuals the right to challenge federal statutes on the grounds that the statutes interfere with powers reserved to the states.

- *National Federation of Independent Business v. Sebelius* (2012). This decision on the Affordable Care Act, aka "Obamacare," struck down the national government's power to set standards for expanded Medicaid eligibility across the states.

- *United States v. Windsor* (2013). The Court struck down a section of the federal Defense of Marriage Act and declared that same-sex couples who are legally married deserve equal rights to all federal benefits that other married couples enjoy.

- Americans have always debated the proper balance between national and state authority.

- Devolution transfers responsibility back to state and local governments; unfunded mandates refer to congressional requirements that the states perform tasks without sufficient national funding. Both strategies are controversial.

- Administrations trying to improve programs often take a pragmatic approach that belies the simple expectation that Democrats seek national programs while Republicans try to devolve power to state and local authorities.

- The judicial system, especially the Supreme Court, has trended toward returning power to state and local government in recent years.

Nationalism, American Style

Federalism trains our focus on the Constitution (the elastic clause versus the Tenth Amendment); on how institutions evolve (dual federalism vs. cooperative federalism, layer cake versus marble cake); and on the clash between national vs. state (seeking equity vs. "drown it in the bathtub!"). However, something deeper holds the entire complicated apparatus in place. It is the elusive cultural sentiment known as *nationalism*, or the U.S. public's sense of identity as Americans.

Without a sense of nationalism, the entire federal experiment might have collapsed long ago. Tested by regional divides, Southern secession during the Civil War, economic strains in every era, and partisan conflict between red and blue states today, it might seem a wonder the states remain united at all.

More than one analyst has suggested that the New England towns, the southern Bible Belt, the midwestern plains, and the liberal "Left Coast" belong in different countries. Each region has fundamentally different social cultures and attitudes about politics.

One secret to American nationhood lies in its unusual version of national identity. Nationalism helps maintain the federal balance by instilling loyalty to nation, state, and locality. In this section, we explore the development of American nationalism.

The Imagined Community

Time was running out on the U.S. national soccer team at the 2014 World Cup. Stuck in a 1-1 tie, with barely four minutes left in the opening-round match, the U.S. substitute John Brooks knocked the ball past Ghana's goalkeeper. The result was an instant YouTube sensation: Crowds of Americans, watching the match in city plazas, restaurants, and sports bars across the country (and around the world), exploded in delirium as the winning goal flew into the net. Wild cheers broke out: "U-S-A! U-S-A!"

Stop and ponder what these crowds were celebrating. The patriotic fervor was about something more than a goal scored by mostly unknown players in a sport that many Americans ignore. What did the cheering represent? Put simply, the joy of fellow-feeling among members of the same country. That feeling, known as *nationalism*, can be difficult to explain. Yet it runs powerfully through most societies and even leads people to sacrifice their lives for their nation. One famous description of this feeling comes from political scientist Benedict Anderson: Nationalism is membership in an "imagined community," a sense of connectedness across millions of people who will, for the most part, never see or meet one another. A nation exists, Anderson concludes, because people believe that it does.[11]

Such a strong nationalist outlook presents a puzzle: The United States ranks very high—often first—in polls that ask about patriotism. Yet Americans are also suspicious of "Big Government" in Washington, D.C. In contrast to most other nations, the United States features a robust self-conscious national community (strong nationalism) and also a weak central government, split into multiple levels by federalism and then further divided on each level by checks and balances. The juxtaposition—strong nation, weak national government— shapes American politics, governing practices, and policy making.

The Rise of American Nationalism

In the excitement of the Revolution, former colonists from New Hampshire to Georgia celebrated the defeat of the British army. Yet the loose federation of states, weakly bound together under the Articles, featured a waning sense of "Americanhood." By the mid-1780s, founders like John Adams worried that "we are finished as a united nation, before we are properly begun."[12]

Restored national sentiment came from an unlikely source—a piece of parchment. The Constitution became a touchstone for Americans' shared sense of belonging. Following ratification in 1789, celebrations broke out across the new nation. In Boston, a three-day festival featured a town feast for twelve thousand and a grand parade with more marchers than today's Macy's Thanksgiving Day Parade—at a time when Boston held barely one-hundredth the population of modern New York City. Despite North Carolina's delay in ratification, its capital Raleigh greeted the Constitution with so many twenty-one-gun salutes (using cannons) that elderly residents feared the Revolutionary War had started again.

In sum, Americans exhibit a passionate sense of nationalism linked to a relatively weak set of governing institutions. Today, we measure the strength of central governments by looking at an updated version of the same principles: size, authority, and independence.

Size.   American national government was traditionally smaller than those in other nations. It grew, in leaps, during World War I, the Great Depression,

● *The Constitution's passage inspired passionate public celebrations in towns and cities across the new nation. Over time, the nationalist spirit grew to include rich and poor.*

World War II, the Cold War, and the Great Society of the 1960s. Each growth spurt brought protests and efforts to cut the government back to size. Opponents of the growing New Deal bureaucracy in the 1930s called President Franklin Roosevelt a communist, a socialist, and worse. Critics blasted presidents George W. Bush and Barack Obama for adding thousands more federal employees. Despite all the fears—or perhaps because of them—the U.S. government still spends less than do most other wealthy nations.

Authority. By the mid-nineteenth century, most developed nations—from France and Germany to China and the British colonies in India—had powerful and efficient national bureaucracies, known as the civil service. In sharp contrast, nineteenth-century American government engaged its citizens (that is, its white males) without a strong central administration or bureaucracy.

Communal activity stretched well beyond the government. American **civic voluntarism** presented a virtually unprecedented spectacle in the nineteenth and early twentieth centuries: robust nationalist feeling, stimulating widespread individual effort in cooperation with other community members. The spirit of voluntary participation has lived on for generations, inspiring mass public involvement in everything from bowling leagues to civil rights organizations.[13]

Civic voluntarism: Citizen participation in public life without government incentives or coercion (speaking at a town meeting versus paying taxes, for example).

Independence. In a powerful centralized system, government officials can act forcefully—as long as their superiors approve. In contrast, Americans separate and divide governing power more extensively than any other modern country. Federalism operates along a vertical dimension, as power is shared among different levels of government—national, state, and local. At every level and within every branch and institution there are further internal checks. All but

● *Civic voluntarism in action—a source of wonder for nineteenth-century European visitors like Tocqueville and a key feature of American-style federalism and nationalism.*

one American state legislature, like Congress, has two chambers (Nebraska is the lone exception); all have multiple committees and subcommittees within each chamber. Each legislature faces an executive and an independent judiciary. In short, checks and balances at every level multiply federalism's horizontal division of power. No public official can act independently. Each needs cooperation from others.

THE BOTTOM LINE

- Americans have long felt a strong sense of nationalism. This helps bind together a large and diverse nation with a fragmented government.

- "Strong nation, weak national government" is a longstanding American paradox. A weak government means that American institutions (and officials) rank relatively low on three dimensions: size, authority, and independence.

- The political results of this paradox include an emphasis on citizen participation, the importance of building alliances, and a reliance on power and money.

● Conclusion: Who Are We?

Federalism seems, on the surface, like a simple matter of government engineering: How do we decide who does what on the federal, state, and local levels? In reality, federalism reflects an intense philosophical debate, carved into institutional stone.

That debate—about power and democracy, fairness and liberty—pervades politics across American history. Successive eras allocated power differently.

Dual federalism (the layer cake) largely kept the state and national spheres separate. The era of cooperative federalism saw the national government expand its role and mix with state and local functions (the marble cake). Today, conservatives and courts promote a New Federalism that devolves more decisions to state and local governments. These efforts involve more government bureaucrats and make more ambiguous than ever who is responsible for what.

Issue after issue returns us to this question of where to locate government authority: federal, state, or local. Who should decide whether to decriminalize marijuana? Oversee hydraulic fracturing or fracking? Mete out the death penalty? Promote educational standards? Regulate insurance companies? Protect the homeland?

Federalism generally marks a more feeble national government. However, the paradox of American politics is that weak government is balanced by a powerful nation with a robust, patriotic sense of national identity. That force helps bind together all the centrifugal institutions of a federal system shot through with checks and balances on every level of government.

Many critics suggest that the weak central government diminishes American capacity for the challenges of the twenty-first century. Others fear the opposite: An inexorably growing state marks the decline of American liberty. We'll revisit these fears throughout this book. For now, simply recognize that this debate echoes those that Federalists and Anti-Federalists were expressing in the 1780s. The conflict involves balancing the most important American values, never an easy task.

● This cheering throng celebrates its hard-won victory to legalize marijuana in Colorado, which took effect in 2014.

In summary, Chapter 1 examined seven enduring American ideas. Chapter 2 showed how those ideas were institutionalized in the American Constitution. Here, in Chapter 3, federalism raised the question of how government institutions evolved, constantly balancing power and liberty, the fear of government, and the quest for equality. Federalism offers us the institutional framework—and philosophical arguments about the institutional framework—for everything that follows in this book. In the next two chapters, we will address the important role federalism plays in the great American quest for civil liberties and civil rights.

CHAPTER SUMMARY

● Americans are a people of multiple loyalties—to their nation, state, and home city or town. These divides are mirrored in our federalist politics. The United States separates power in multiple ways, both horizontally (across branches of government) and vertically (across national, state, and local levels).

● Only two dozen nations worldwide share America's federalist-style political organization; most have more centralized unitary governments. The American founders adopted a federalist system, in part to protect against concentrating too much power in one person or branch, but also to expand protections for individual rights, increase government's flexibility, and enable more political innovations to flourish. Federalism has drawbacks, but it has never seriously been questioned as the American governing style.

● Different versions of federalism are evident in U.S. history, from dual federalism (states and nation performing largely separate functions) to cooperative and new versions that involve closer partnership across government levels. Issues like devolution and unfunded mandates mark ongoing negotiations over the terms of the elaborate arrangement of local, state, and national governing power.

● Given this divided authority, we might wonder what has held the United States together, especially given regional differences that culminated in civil war. An uncommonly strong sense of national identity is a large part of the answer. Born during the Revolution and powerfully evident after the Constitution's ratification, Americans' devotion to national unity was instrumental in building a robust nation—although nationalism has its ugly, xenophobic sides as well.

● Alongside the concept of a strong nation is an anomaly among most countries with a similarly robust national spirit: a relatively weak American national government. This less powerful set of government institutions is found across American history, in both the limited size of our federal bureaucracy and Washington's constrained capacity to act.

● An abiding commitment to separated powers, evident in the Constitution, helps explain the persistence of this weak-government phenomenon alongside our strong nation. Debates have also persisted about how to reform the U.S. federalist, separated-powers polity. We invite you to join the conversation in the months and years to come.

KEY TERMS

Block grants, 99
Civic voluntarism, 107
Concurrent powers, 95
Confederation, 88
Cooperative (or marble cake)
    federalism, 98
Devolution, 100

Diffusion, 91
Dual (or layer cake)
    federalism, 96
Full faith and credit clause, 95
Granted powers, 94
Grants-in-aid, 98
Inherent powers, 95

Necessary and proper clause, 95
New Federalism, 99
Reserved powers, 95
Supremacy clause, 95
Unfunded mandate, 101
Unitary government, 88

STUDY QUESTIONS

1. Can you imagine the United States without federalism? Suppose that a central national authority ran the country, and governors and mayors—and other subnational officials—were entirely subordinate to the national government. Describe some of the changes that would likely result. Would this shift toward a unitary state be an improvement, in your view? Why or why not?

2. The current Supreme Court has tended to side with state and local governments in federalist clashes, limiting the national government's power in case after case. Why has the Court adopted this approach? Do you find it desirable?

3. Think about your own political loyalties. Are they most strongly felt for your hometown or home city, the state where you grew up (or where you live now), or the nation as a whole? What do you think accounts for your outlook? If you are not from the United States, reflect on your own sense of political identity: Is it primarily to a nation, a region, or a local place?

4. If you feel a strong sense of national pride, do you think it comes with any undesirable aspects? If you are not an especially avid American nationalist, why not? What would it be like if most citizens exhibited a skeptical outlook toward the country?

Civil Liberties

STORMS OF PROTEST GREETED a proposed Islamic community center near the site of the 9/11 terrorist attacks in New York. Opponents lined up at a public hearing. "I do have a problem with having a mosque on top of the site where [terrorists] can gloat about what they did," said Al Santora, a fire department chief who had lost his son in the attack. In Florida, Pastor Terry Jones announced plans to burn a Quran, the Muslim holy book. Kathleen McFarland, a security analyst for Fox News, summarized the opposition: Many New Yorkers consider the proposed center "an abomination" and "a recruiting station for terrorists."[1]

Imam Feisal Abdul Rauf, who had proposed the center, tried to win people over with a plea for tolerance—and for his rights. "We are Americans, we are Muslim Americans . . . We have no higher aspirations than to bring up our children in peace and harmony in this country." The crowd blew up when he added, "Freedom of assembly is the right of all Americans." One woman shouted, "Not at the World Trade Center!" According to a CNN poll, 68 percent of New Yorkers and 61 percent of all Americans agreed: not at Ground Zero![2]

Was Imam Rauf correct? The First Amendment to the Constitution *does* protect "the right of the people peaceably to assemble," as well as their right to the "free exercise . . . of religion." This is bedrock of American liberty: protecting individuals when they want to speak out, practice their religion, or assemble in peace—even if what they say or believe is very unpopular.

However, every right has limits. Individual protections are always counterbalanced by community needs. As Supreme Court Justice Oliver Wendell Holmes put it back in 1919, every action "depends upon the circumstances in which it is done. . . . The most stringent protection of free speech would not protect a man from falsely shouting "fire" in a crowded theater and causing a panic."[3]

Who are we? We are a nation always wrestling with a great trade-off—individual rights versus majority rule. On the one hand, we are the home of rugged individualism, which tilts us toward protecting individual rights. On the other hand, we believe in self-rule—which means the majority should get its way. The tension is exacerbated because we are (and always have been) a nation of

● *Protests greet the so-called Ground Zero mosque.*

minority groups—black, Latino, Hmong, Muslim, same-sex partners—the list goes on. When the majority feels threatened or offended—as they did at Ground Zero—it sometimes moves to limit the minority's rights, making civil liberties all the *more* important.

What are **civil liberties**? They are the limits we put on governing bodies (and the majorities that elect them) so that individuals can exercise their rights and freedom. The Islamic center is a classic case. A minority claims its rights. The majority is offended, even angry. It calls on government to forbid the construction. The Constitution protects the minority's right to build the center unless it

Civil liberties: The limits on government so that people can freely exercise their rights.

BY THE NUMBERS
Civil Liberties

- Number of rights listed in the Bill of Rights: **31**
- Number of rights protecting freedom of religion: **2**
- Number of rights protecting people accused of crimes: **19**
- Number of times the Supreme Court has permitted the government to block publication of sensitive material: **0**
- Number of years after the Bill of Rights was ratified before the Supreme Court ruled that state governments could not interfere with freedom of speech: **134**
- Number of years before it ruled that states could not interfere with the right to bear arms: **219**
- Number of new rights secured by constitutional amendment in the past 50 years: **1** (the 26th Amendment extended the right to vote to 18- to 20-year-olds)
- Percentage of Americans who favor a constitutional amendment to ban flag burning (according to a Gallup poll in 2006): **56**
- Number of votes by which a flag-burning amendment failed to clear Congress: **1**
- Rank of the United States among all nations for number (and percentage) of citizens in jail: **1**
- Ranks of Russia, Rwanda, Iran, and England: **2, 3, 40, 83**
- Percentage of Americans who supported the death penalty in 1990 and today: **78, 62**
- Percentage support for the death penalty:
  - Among white evangelicals: **74**
  - Among the nonreligious: **61**
  - Among Hispanic Catholics: **43**
  - Among black Protestants: **37**
- Number of states that have not executed anyone since 1976: **16**
- Total number executed in Texas, Virginia, Oklahoma, and Florida since 1976: **758**
- Total number executed by the federal government in that period: **3**

really is, or could become, "a recruiting station for terrorists." This brings us to the eternal complication of civil liberties—deciding who deserves which rights.

The Islamic center did open, fifteen months after the protests. The first exhibition in its gallery featured portraits of children from 160 countries taken by Danny Goldfield, a Jewish photographer. The new director of the center acknowledged that there would have been a better way to balance majority fears and minority rights. "We made an incredible mistake," he said, not to "include 9/11 families."[4]

The Rise of Civil Liberties

May a racist burn a cross as a symbol of white supremacy? May a skinhead stand on a street corner and urge people to attack Latinos, Sikhs, or Jews? Is pornography legal? The answer to all three questions is "sometimes." We always weigh the rights of individuals against the concerns and safety of the community. Who decides? Usually, the courts do. And there is often more than one reasonable answer when the courts take up a question.

Civil rights: The freedom to participate in the full life of the community—to vote, use public facilities, and exercise equal economic opportunity.

Civil Rights and Civil Liberties

Civil rights and liberties demand opposite things from government. Civil rights require government action to help secure individual rights; civil liberties restrict government action to protect individual rights. Until people have won their rights, the idea of protecting them is meaningless. When governments enforce civil rights for some people, they often limit the liberty of others. For example, as we will see in Chapter 5 the Civil Rights Act of 1964 outlawed segregated restaurants. That legal action freed blacks and Latinos to eat where they wished but limited the liberty of racist restaurant owners to serve whomever they wanted to serve.

In practice, the two concepts are not opposites. The long battle for civil rights led to more robust civil liberties for everyone. The fight against slavery eventually led to the Fourteenth Amendment, which—as we'll soon see—is the cornerstone of modern civil liberties. Without the long American struggle for civil rights, "we the people" would have many fewer civil liberties.

Both civil liberties and civil rights became increasingly important to American politics through the twentieth century.

see for yourself 4.1

Go online to view the outcome of the Ground Zero Islamic Center.

● *Legal? Sometimes!*

The Slow Rise of Rights

The Bill of Rights barely touched American life in the nineteenth century because it only applied to the federal government. The First Amendment begins, "*Congress* shall make no law" prohibiting the exercise of religion or restricting speech. Well, what about the states? Were they also bound by the individual protections in the Bill of Rights?

In 1833, John Barron found out. Barron owned a thriving wharf in Baltimore Harbor until the city diverted the water and left his wharf high and dry. Barron sued, arguing that the city had violated the Fifth Amendment by taking his property for public use "without just compensation." The Supreme Court ruled (in *Barron v. Baltimore*) that the Fifth Amendment applied only to the federal government. The Anti-Federalists, reasoned the justices, had demanded the Bill of Rights to protect them from the national government. Washington could not strip Barron of his property rights—but Maryland or Baltimore could.[5]

The Bill of Rights eventually reached the states thanks to the quest for civil rights. After the Civil War, Congress passed the Fourteenth Amendment (ratified in 1868) to protect the newly freed slaves. Every discussion of civil liberties turns the spotlight on one passage in the Fourteenth Amendment:

> No state shall . . . deprive any person of life, liberty, or property, without due process of law; nor deny any person within its jurisdiction the equal protection of the laws. [emphasis added]

Look again at the first two words. Obviously, the amendment is addressed directly to the states. States may not deprive any person of life, liberty, or property, which are exactly what the Bill of Rights protects. The amendment *seems* to apply the Bill of Rights to the states. In 1873, the Supreme Court disagreed: The Fourteenth Amendment applied only to freed slaves and to no one else.[6]

Over time, the Court changed its mind. In 1897 the Court returned to the issue in *Barron v. Baltimore* and ruled that state governments could not seize property without compensation. One phrase of the Fifth Amendment now applied to state and local government. The Supreme Court had incorporated the right into the Fourteenth Amendment. The Supreme Court decides, case by case, which rights applied to state governments—a process called **selective incorporation**.

Selective incorporation: Extending protections from the Bill of Rights to the state governments, one right at a time.

The Court was very slow to force constitutional rights on the states. In 1937, it formally declared its principle for deciding which rights to incorporate: Is the right in question essential to our idea of liberty? If so, the Fourteenth Amendment's due process clause—quoted above—required states to respect that right and the Court then incorporated, or applied, it to the states.[7] In time, the Court incorporated almost every phrase of the Bill of Rights, beginning with freedom of speech (in 1925), continuing with the practice of religion (1940), and moving recently to the right to own guns (in 2010). (Table 4.1 provides an overview of what rights the Court applied and when.)[8]

In the rest of the chapter, we examine the most important civil liberties and the issues they raise.

TABLE 4.1 Incorporation of the Bill of Rights into the Fourteenth Amendment

THE BILL OF RIGHTS	YEAR	KEY CASE
I.* Free exercise of religion	1940	*Cantwell v. Connecticut*
No establishment of religion	1947	*Everson v. Board of Ed*
Free press	1931	***Near v. Minnesota****
Free speech	1925	***Gitlow v. New York***
Right to peaceful assembly	1937	*De Jonge v. Oregon*
Right to petition government	1963	*NAACP v. Button*
II. Right to keep and bear arms	2010	***McDonald v. Chicago***
III. No quartering of soldiers		*Not incorporated*
IV. No unreasonable search and seizure	1949	*Wolf v. Colorado*
No search and seizure without warrant	1961	***Mapp v. Ohio***
V. Right to grand jury indictment		*Not incorporated*
No double jeopardy	1969	*Benton v. Maryland*
No forced confession	1964	*Escobedo v. Illinois*
Right to remain silent	1966	***Miranda v. Illinois***
No seizure of property w/out compensation	1887	*Chicago Burlington and Quincy RR v. Chicago*
VI. Right to public trial	1948	*In re Oliver*
Right to speedy trial	1967	*Klopfer v. North Carolina*
Right to trial by impartial jury	1966	*Parker v. Gladden*
Right to confront witnesses	1965	*Pointer v. Texas*
Right to compel supportive witnesses to appear	1967	*Washington v. Texas*
Right to counsel in capital punishment cases	1932	***Powell v. Alabama***
Right to counsel in felony cases	1963	***Gideon v. Wainright***
VII. Right of jury trial in civil cases		*Not incorporated*
VIII. No excessive bail		*Not incorporated*
No cruel and unusual punishment	1962	*Robinson v. California*
IX. Rights not limited to rights listed in the first eight amendments		*Not relevant to incorporation*
X. Powers not delegated to the national government are reserved to the states and the people		*Not relevant to incorporation*

* Note how the First Amendment rights were incorporated early in the process. Most protections for those accused of crimes were applied between 1962 and 1968.
** Boldfaced cases are discussed in this chapter.

THE BOTTOM LINE

- The Supreme Court neatly defined civil liberties in 1943: The Bill of Rights withdraws certain subjects from political controversy and places them beyond the reach of majorities and officials.

- The Bill of Rights did not apply to the states until the Fourteenth Amendment required that *no state* could deprive any citizen of life, liberty, or property.

- The Court applied the Bill of Rights to the states one right at a time between 1897 (no taking of property without compensation) and 2010 (the right to bear arms).

Privacy

We begin with an especially controversial right that, unlike all the others we will examine, is never directly mentioned in the Constitution. Instead, the majority on the Supreme Court ruled that it is implied by the First, Third, Fourth, Fifth, and Ninth Amendments.

Penumbras and Emanations

In the mid-nineteenth century, contraceptives were widely available. Then, in the 1870s, every state, encouraged by the national government, banned them—partly because of fears that immigrants would have more children than native-born Americans. Almost a century later, the director of Planned Parenthood of Connecticut defied that state's ban and dispensed condoms at a birth control clinic in New Haven. The Supreme Court heard the case (*Griswold v. Connecticut*, 1965), struck down the law, and declared a dramatic new right: the right to privacy.

How could the Court protect privacy if the Constitution does not even mention it? Justice William O. Douglas explained: The rights that are specifically mentioned in the Bill of Rights "have penumbras . . . that give them life and substance." The *penumbras*—literally, the shadows—of the First Amendment create "zones of privacy" in which people have a right to make their own choices free from government interference. So do the "emanations" from other amendments, like the Third Amendment's ban on quartering soldiers in private homes—which, he pointed out, was designed to protect privacy. In addition, the Ninth Amendment declares that other rights exist besides the ones mentioned in the Constitution and they are also "retained by the people." Privacy is one of those rights.

In 1787, when the Constitution was written, no one was thinking about condoms. But if you apply the logic of the Constitution to modern times, the right to privacy—and to contraceptives—emerges. They reflect the spirit of the Constitution.

IS THERE A RIGHT TO PRIVACY?

Are you ready to try your first case? How would you rule in *Griswold v. Connecticut*? Do you agree that there is "a right to privacy" in the Constitution that permitted the Court to strike down the Connecticut ban on contraceptives?

Yes.
Although the Constitution does not specifically mention privacy, a modern reading of the document would conclude that privacy is a basic right that the courts ought to protect.

No.
We have to stick to the simple language of the Constitution itself. We disrespect and even damage the document by reading things into it. Anyone who opposes Connecticut's ban on contraceptives can go to the legislature and lobby them to change it.

What it means.
No matter how you voted, you're part of a long intellectual tradition. If you said yes, you agree with a school of thought (which we call *pragmatist*) that says the courts must be guided by the *general ideas* that underpin the Constitution to try and determine the best outcome in a particular case. If you voted no, you're voting with *originalism*, the school of thought that limits judges to considering the original intent as explicitly stated in the Constitution's text.

The *Griswold* case itself did not stir much controversy. After all, most people thought married couples had every right to use condoms. In 1973, however, the right to privacy led to one of the most controversial Court decisions ever.

Roe v. Wade

In *Roe v. Wade* (1973) the Supreme Court drew on the right to privacy and struck down a Texas law banning abortion. The Court ruled that the right to privacy is "broad enough to encompass a woman's decision whether or not to terminate her pregnancy." *Roe v. Wade* changed American politics. People who support the decision—known as "pro-choice"—view the decision as essential to gender equality because it enables women to control when (and whether) they have children. From this perspective, *Roe* opens the door to vocations and careers for women. It protects women's health by doing away with the dangerous "back alley" abortions that desperate women sought out before *Roe* made abortions safe and legal. Democrats, for the most part, are pro-choice.

Pro-choice versus pro-life—one of the great conflicts in modern American politics.

Those who oppose the decision—known as "pro-life"—believe that life begins at conception and that abortion is murder. Many religious activists took *Roe v. Wade* as a call to enter politics. The grassroots campaign to overturn the decision became a powerful force in modern conservativism. Within a decade, the Republican Party had committed itself to overturning *Roe*.

The debate added new intensity to American politics, since activists on each side felt they were fighting for the soul of the nation: on the one side, equality for women; on the other side, the most basic rights of the unborn. The intensity has helped politicize Supreme Court appointments. Each new nomination raises the same questions. What is his or her attitude toward abortion? Will it swing the Court?

Challenges to *Roe v. Wade* led to a string of Supreme Court decisions. In 1980, the Court accepted a congressional ban on federal funding for abortions. In 1989, it upheld a Missouri prohibition on abortions in public hospitals. In 1992, the Court took up a Pennsylvania law that seemed to directly challenge *Roe* by imposing regulations on women seeking abortions, even in the first trimester. Pennsylvania required a twenty-four-hour waiting period, parental notification for minors, and prior notification of spouses. Many observers, on both sides of the issue, predicted that the Court would overturn *Roe v. Wade* and permit states to outlaw abortions.

Instead, in *Planned Parenthood v. Casey* (1992), the Court voted (5–4) to take a middle ground. The court upheld a woman's right to terminate her pregnancy, as a "component of liberty." However, it rejected *Roe v. Wade*'s trimester framework, which forbade any state limitations in the first trimester. In short, the right to choose an abortion could be balanced—but not overruled—by the state's desire to protect potential life so long as state regulations did not impose "an undue burden" on the woman's choice.

The original *Roe* decision had propounded a judicial rule. Rules set clear boundaries between what is lawful and what is not: the states may not interfere in the first trimester. Now, *Casey* replaced the rule with a judicial standard. A standard establishes a more general guiding principle rather than a hard-and-fast rule. What is an "undue burden"? That's a judgment call. Meanwhile, twenty-two states passed abortion restrictions in 2013 alone—many of them headed straight to the courts for rulings on constitutionality. The controversy continues.[9]

Sexuality Between Consenting Adults

Does the right to privacy extend to same-sex couples? In 1986, the Supreme Court ruled it did not, upholding Georgia's antisodomy law. In 2003, the Supreme Court reversed itself (in *Lawrence v. Texas*) and extended the right of privacy to same-sex couples. In striking down the Texas antisodomy law the majority echoed the original *Griswold* decision: "Liberty protects the person from unwarranted government intrusion into . . . private places."

The privacy cases reflect public opinion. By 1965, most Americans believed that couples should be permitted to use birth control. Although with *Roe v. Wade* the Court did not reflect popular views, later decisions have balanced a right to abortion with state restrictions—roughly in line with majority views. It may seem a good idea that courts reflect majority opinion. But the Constitution and the Court are designed to stand up to the majority. They are supposed to protect the rights of unpopular minorities like Jehovah's Witnesses in the 1940s and gay Americans in the 1980s.

Of course, as we will see throughout this chapter, applying the Constitution is never simple. The United States is founded on two ideas that often clash. We believe in government by the people. Yet at the same time, we believe that all individuals are endowed with inalienable rights. The story of civil liberties is the story of managing the collisions between the two great principles—the needs and desires of the community versus the rights of the individual.

● *John Geddes Lawrence (left) and Tyron Garner (right). The police, investigating a gun disturbance complaint, broke into Lawrence's apartment—which had gay posters prominently displayed on the walls. When Lawrence began to argue, the police arrested both him and Garner for "deviate sexual intercourse." In* Lawrence v. Texas *the Supreme Court struck down the Texas antisodomy law for violating the Constitution's privacy protections.*

THE BOTTOM LINE

- The Court discovered a right to privacy implicit in the shadows of the First, Third, Fourth, Fifth, and Ninth Amendments.

- The Court applied the right to privacy to strike down laws banning abortion. In *Roe v. Wade*, the court issued a *rule* prohibiting states from interfering during the first trimester. In *Planned Parenthood v. Casey*, the Court replaced the rule with a *standard* forbidding laws that put "an undue burden" on the right to privacy.

- The Court extended privacy rights to same-sex couples by striking down antisodomy laws in 2003. It forbade the federal government from rejecting same-sex marriages, but has not yet ruled on whether states are violating the rights of same-sex couples by forbidding them to marry.

● Freedom of Religion

The Bill of Rights begins with religion.

> *Congress shall make no law respecting an establishment of religion, or prohibiting the free exercise thereof.*

The First Amendment gives two succinct commands regulating religion. The federal government may not establish an official religion—known as the

Establishment clause: In the First Amendment, the principle that government may not establish an official religion.

Free exercise clause: In the First Amendment, the principle that government may not interfere in religious practice.

establishment clause. And it may not interfere in religious practice—the **free exercise clause**.

The Establishment Clause

By the time the Constitution was written, Americans already practiced many faiths: Puritans (or Congregationalists) in Massachusetts, Quakers in Philadelphia, Baptists in Rhode Island, Anglicans in Virginia, Catholics in Maryland, and Jews in Newport, Rhode Island. The Constitution posed a threat. What if the federal government imposed a national religion? The First Amendment's establishment clause is designed to prohibit that. But what exactly did it forbid the government from doing? The debate began immediately.

President George Washington (1789–1797) called for a national day of prayer each year. Was that encouraging religion? President Thomas Jefferson (1801–1809) thought so and rejected the practice. The First Amendment, wrote Jefferson, builds "a wall of separation between church and state."[10] When the Supreme Court extended the establishment clause to the state governments in 1947, Justice Hugo Black quoted Jefferson's "wall of separation."[11] Until recently, Jefferson's metaphor guided the court's efforts.

Jefferson's principle is a difficult guide because there has never been a true wall of separation. The cash in American pockets is inscribed "In God We Trust"; children pledge allegiance to "one nation, under God"; Moses, holding the Ten Commandments, is carved into the Supreme Court building. Congress opens each session with a prayer; and presidents end their speeches with "God bless America"—a sentiment no leader would invoke in England, France, or Japan. Despite these and other interconnections, the courts have tried to separate church and state. The question is how?

The establishment clause is clearly designed to keep government officials from favoring one religion—or religion over nonreligion. In a blockbuster case, *Engel v. Vitale* (1962), the Supreme Court ruled that New York's practice of starting the school day with a prayer violated the establishment clause.[12]

A long string of controversial decisions followed. Each returns to the vexing question about exactly where to construct Jefferson's wall. May public schools introduce a minute of silent prayer or meditation? (No.) May graduation include a prayer? (No.) May students lead prayers at football games? (No.) May children recite "under God" during the Pledge of Allegiance? (No definitive ruling

● *The Truro synagogue in Newport, Rhode Island, inspired George Washington's beautiful letter on American religious pluralism.*

has yet taken place.) May a city put up a Christmas display? (Yes, if it includes secular as well as religious symbols—known sarcastically as the "two-reindeer" rule.)

In 1971, the Court established a test to guide decisions about separating church and state. In *Lemon v. Kurtzman* the Court ruled on a Pennsylvania law that paid teachers who taught nonreligious subjects in church-affiliated (mainly Catholic) schools. The Court forbade the practice and promulgated what became known as the *Lemon test* for judging what government actions are permissible. First, the law must have a *secular* purpose. Second, its principal effect must *neither advance nor inhibit religion*. Finally, it must not *excessively entangle* government in religion. Paying the teachers in religious schools was, the Court ruled, an "excessive entanglement," and Pennsylvania could not do it.

As the Court grew more conservative, the Lemon test came under fire. Today, two different perspectives have emerged. **Strict separation** still tries to separate church and state using the Lemon test. An alternative view is known as **accommodation**: government does not violate the establishment clause so long as it does not confer an advantage on some religions over others. Accommodation is gathering momentum; until the Court settles on a definitive set of guidelines, establishment clause cases can be unpredictable and even erratic.

Free Exercise of Religion

The First Amendment also prohibits government from interfering with the "free exercise" of religion. Once again, the Court's view has evolved.

The first landmark case was decided in 1963. Adell Sherbert was a Seventh-Day Adventist who refused to work on Saturday because it violated her faith. She was fired. South Carolina rejected her claim for unemployment benefits because she refused other jobs that also required work on Saturday. Claiming that the state was infringing on her free exercise of religion, Sherbert sued the state for her unemployment benefits. In deciding the case, Justice Brennan introduced a two-part test, known as the *Sherbert* or *balancing test*. First, was the government imposing a "significant burden" on her ability to exercise her faith? Second, did the government have a "compelling interest" for imposing the burden? In this case, the Court ruled that there was a real burden on Adell Sherbert and no compelling state interest for denying her unemployment benefits.

The Sherbert test lasted until 1990, when the Court took a completely different approach. Two Oregon men participated in a Native American ritual that included taking peyote—a hallucinogen. The men were fired from their jobs at a private drug rehab center and then were denied unemployment benefits for violating Oregon drug laws. The men sued, arguing that they should be exempted from the peyote ban because it was essential to their religious practice. Under the Sherbert test they might have won. However, the Supreme Court ruled (6–3) against the two men and, in the process, made it much more difficult to sue the government for interfering with religious expression. In *Employment Division v. Smith*, the Court asked simply if the Oregon drug law was a neutral

Strict separation: The strict principles articulated in the Lemon test for judging whether a law establishes a religion. (See "accommodation.")

Accommodation: The principle that government does not violate the establishment clause as long as it does not confer an advantage to some religions over others. (See "strict separation.")

MAY THE CHRISTIAN YOUTH CLUB MEET IN SCHOOL?

The Good News is a Christian youth club that wanted to meet in school after class hours. The school district said that this was religious worship and would amount to a public school's endorsement of Christianity. The case went to the Supreme Court. Justices Stevens (who argued against Good News) and Scalia (who supported Good News) each wrote opinions. Which opinion would you sign on to?

Justice Stevens: "Evangelical meetings designed to convert children to a particular faith . . . may introduce divisiveness and tend to separate young children into cliques that undermine the school's educational mission." The school district is right to stop the practice.

Justice Scalia: Religious expression cannot violate the establishment clause where it is (1) purely private and (2) open to all on equal terms. Milford [the school district] is discriminating against a religious group since it lets other groups meet.

Testing these views. As you consider whose side to take, consider how one would decide this case using the Lemon test (with Stevens) or the accommodation view (with Scalia). How did the court actually rule? The answer is in the endnotes.[13]

law applied in a neutral way. Yes, the law was neutral. It was not aimed at Native American religious practice, because it forbids *everyone* from smoking peyote.

The *Employment Division* case replaced the Sherbert balancing test with a *neutrality test*. The new test does not ask whether a law interferes with religious practice or whether a compelling government interest is at stake (the two questions of the Sherbert test). It asks only whether the same law applies to everyone. So long as the law does not target a religious group, the Court will permit it. Obviously, this makes it much more difficult to sue on the basis of "free exercise" of religion.[14]

Religious groups—from the Catholic Church to the *Witches' Voice*—mobilized against the Court's decision. Congress passed the Religious Freedom Restoration Act of 1993, which required federal and state governments to use the old Sherbert balancing test. In 1997, the Court stepped in again. It ruled that Congress lacked the constitutional authority to order the states to use the balancing test.

A major test of Religious Freedom Restoration Act came in a landmark case, *Burwell v. Hobby Lobby* (June, 2014). The owners of a private, for-profit chain store charged that the Affordable Care Act's requirement that they provide contraceptive coverage for their employees violated their religious beliefs. The Supreme Court agreed (5–4) and, for the first time, exempted a business

● *Using the neutrality test, the courts struck down a Florida law for specifically targeting the Cuban Santeria religion when it forbade the use of animal sacrifices.*

from a law that applies to everyone. The Court majority, citing Religious Freedom Restoration Act, ruled that the federal government's contraception mandate interfered with the company owners' free exercise of religion. National policy would once again have to balance between a compelling government interest and the right—in this case, the corporate owners' right—to the free exercise of religion.

THE BOTTOM LINE

- The First Amendment has two religious clauses: The government may not *establish* a religion and it may not interfere with the free *exercise* of religions.

- The courts have ruled on establishment cases by trying to approximate Jefferson's wall separating church and state. The Court requires three things of government action: It must *have a secular purpose, neither advance nor inhibit religion*, and *not excessively entangle* government in religion (the three requirements are known as the Lemon test). A more recent view (known as accommodation) simply requires that government not promote one religious view over another.

- In protecting the free exercise of religion, the courts traditionally asked if the government had a compelling interest for imposing a burden. In 1990, the Supreme Court simply required that government action be neutral and apply to everyone. Congress and some state governments responded with the Religious Freedom Restoration Act, a return to the traditional balancing view, which the Supreme Court applied in upholding Hobby Lobby's suit against the contraception mandate in the Affordable Care Act.

Hate crime: Crime stemming from prejudice based on someone's personal characteristics, such as race, ethnicity, religion, or sexual orientation.

Hate speech: Hostile statements based on someone's personal characteristics, such as race, ethnicity, religion, or sexual orientation.

 # Freedom of Speech

Now, we turn to the most important civil liberty of all, freedom of speech. After its religious clauses, the First Amendment states:

> *Congress shall make no law . . . abridging the freedom of speech or of the press.*

A Preferred Position

Today, the Supreme Court gives the First Amendment a "preferred position" among all the amendments to the Constitution; free speech holds preferred position among the rights in the First Amendment (free speech, religion, press, assembly, and the right to petition government). Indeed, when freedom of speech conflicts with any other right, the Court generally will "prefer" or protect speech.[15]

 What Do You Think?

DAVID'S LAW

In April 2006, two men attacked David Rae Ritcheson, a Mexican American high school student. They beat him, burned him, sodomized him with a patio umbrella, poured bleach on his face, and left him for dead. One of the assailants, a self-proclaimed racist skinhead, screamed ethnic slurs during the torture. David spent months in the hospital, undergoing one operation after another. He struggled to regain a normal life, slid into depression, and committed suicide. Some members of Congress proposed what they called David's Law. This legislation would target **hate crimes** and **hate speech** by enhancing law enforcement and penalties. The sponsors' goal is to provide special protection for members of groups that sometimes face intense discrimination— African Americans, Latinos, gays, and others. These groups, proponents argued, need protection because too many people are ready to harm them. David's Law encountered fierce opposition. Of course, the two men must be punished for their crime. However, opponents argued, hate crime legislation would create taboo subjects. Anyone condemning or even criticizing immigrants or homosexuals could be prosecuted. Once again, we face the civil liberties balancing act. How would you vote?

Yes. Vote for David's Law.	We must protect Mexican Americans, gay people, people of color, and other groups who face hatred and violence. Hate speech fractures communities and hurts people. It is frightening and painful to the targeted groups.
No. Vote against David's Law.	Everyone has the right to an opinion—even if it is a horrible opinion. We can punish criminal behavior. We should never punish people for simply expressing their views.
Not sure?	In the next sections we'll examine freedom of speech and you'll learn how the Court has ruled on such cases.

Why do contemporary courts put so much emphasis on the right to express opinions? Because democracy requires vigorous debate. As a result, the courts will be skeptical of any effort to curb speech, however hurtful. (See how you would vote on David's Law.) However, if you voted for David's Law, you'll find an argument to support your position later in this section.

Of course, every right has limits. Much of the debate that surrounds the right to speech is about identifying the boundaries—the limits—of protected speech.

Political Speech

The forceful defense of free speech took a long time to develop. In every generation, political leaders are tempted to stop subversive talk—or harsh criticism. Under the John Adams administration, just ten years after the Constitution was ratified, Congress drafted the Alien and Sedition Acts. Tensions with France were running high, and the acts made it illegal to "print, utter, or publish . . . any false, scandalous, and malicious writing" against the government. The meaning of the acts was brutally simple: criticize the government and face prosecution.

The first modern free speech cases arose during World War I. President Woodrow Wilson had signed the Espionage Act. Charles Schenck, general secretary of the Socialist Party of Philadelphia, was found guilty of violating the act by printing and distributing a document that urged men to resist military recruitment for a war designed, he claimed, to pour profits into greedy Wall

Test Yourself: The Simpsons versus the First Amendment— Which Do You Know Better?

Five rights are listed in the First Amendment, and there are five Simpsons. Thirty-four percent of Americans can name four of the five Simpsons. Only 1 percent of Americans can name four of the five rights.

How about you? How many First Amendment rights can you name? How many Simpsons? (Answers below.)

Source: McCormick Tribune Freedom Museum (Chicago).

Answers:

The Simpsons from left to right: Homer, Bart, Lisa, Marge, and Maggie.
First Amendment rights: Freedom of religion, speech, press, and assembly, and the right to petition government.

Clear and present danger: Court doctrine that permits restrictions of free speech if officials believe that the speech will lead to prohibited action like violence or terrorism.

Street. Was his freedom of speech abrogated? Under normal circumstances it might be, wrote Justice Oliver Wendell Holmes for a unanimous court, but this was wartime. Distributing these documents, he wrote, was like falsely shouting "fire" in a crowded theater. Holmes then formulated the most famous test for free speech: speech is not protected if it poses "*a **clear and present danger*** that it will lead to 'substantive evils'" (*Schenck v. United States*, 1919).

In the early 1920s, many Americans were anxious about foreigners, immigrants, socialists, communists, and anarchists. The Supreme Court hardened the "clear and present danger" test by ruling that judges did not have to "weigh each and every utterance." They could simply determine whether the "natural tendency and probable effect" of the speech was to "bring about something bad or evil"—even if that danger lay in the distant future.[16]

The clear and present danger test stood for decades. After fifty years, in 1969, the Court complained that "puny" threats, which no one took seriously except "nervous judges," were being declared a clear and present danger. The issue arose when a Ku Klux Klan leader, Clarence Brandenburg, organized a rally where the Klan members burned crosses, waved guns, and called for "revengence" against Jews and African Americans. The Supreme Court struck down Brandenburg's conviction and rewrote the clear and present dangers test. The state may not interfere with speech unless the speech "incites imminent lawless action" *and* is likely to actually "produce such action."

Symbolic expression: An act, rather than actual speech, used to demonstrate a point of view.

The result makes it very difficult to curtail political speech for clear and present danger. The government may limit the speech only if the bad effects— the lynching, the overthrow of American government, or the terrorist attack— are likely to happen immediately. During this case, *Brandenburg v. Ohio* (1969), the Supreme Court formally declared the "preferred position" of free speech.[17]

● *Members of the Westboro Baptist Church picket military funerals to protest homosexuality with signs that read "Fag sin = 9/11" and "You're going to hell." Albert Snyder, the father of a marine killed in Iraq, sued the church. Forty-eight states and veterans groups supported the suit. The Supreme Court did not. It acknowledged that the protests were hurtful but protected them as an exercise of free speech.*

Symbolic Speech

When Clarence Brandenburg burned his cross, he engaged in a form of speech known as **symbolic expression**. He was demonstrating a point of view with an act rather than as a speech. The First Amendment protects symbolic speech—again, within limits.

In 2003, the Supreme Court identified those limits when it took two cross-burning cases on the same day. The Ku Klux Klan burned crosses to terrorize black neighbors. In Klan lore, the original cross burnings, after the Civil War, signaled the execution of a former slave. The Court drew a fine distinction. Individuals may burn crosses to express their views, but not

● *Is this symbolic speech protected? The Supreme Court ruled that it was.*

to intimidate others.[18] On the same day, however, the Court upheld the conviction of another cross burner. In this second case, two men came home after a night of drinking and burned a cross on a black neighbor's lawn. Their act went beyond speech, ruled the Court. It was intimidation. Even if there is no immediate (or clear and present) danger, intimidating people is not protected by the First Amendment.

Burning the American flag is another unpopular symbolic expression. Gregory Lee Johnson lit up a flag during the Republican National Convention in 1984 and was arrested for violating a Texas law against flag desecration. Forty-eight states and the federal government banned flag burning. The Supreme Court narrowly struck down the law (by a 5–4 vote).[19] The minority argued that the national flag deserved special protection. Congress responded by passing legislation defending the flag. The Court overturned that, too. Congress then debated an amendment to the Constitution protecting the flag. It passed in the House (286–130) but fell one vote short of the two-thirds vote required in the Senate.

Limits to Free Speech: Fighting Words

Is there any way to rein in cross burning, gay bashing, and other forms of hateful speech? Other democracies are much tougher on hurtful speech; so are many colleges and universities. Their logic is simple: How can you build a good community if some members feel singled out, threatened, or diminished?

Fighting words: Expression inherently likely to provoke violent reaction and not necessarily protected by the First Amendment.

One legal doctrine offers a limit to hate speech by restricting **fighting words**. The Supreme Court defined these as "personally abusive epithets which, when addressed to the ordinary citizen, are, as a matter of common knowledge, inherently likely to provoke violent reaction."[20] The Court states the principle but has been reluctant to apply it. If the words are political, they must be protected. If hate crime legislation singles out some fighting words (like racial epithets) but not others, the Court will reject it. However, even while the Court keeps striking down the efforts, it reaffirms that there *are* "fighting words" not protected by the Constitution. The key test is that the language does not advance any specific political position. Reformers trying to create codes of decent language, like David's Law, generally rely on the logic of fighting words.

Limited Protections: Student Speech

Student speech has sparked controversy and litigation. In the landmark *Tinker* decision, the Court announced that students "do not shed their constitutional right to freedom of speech or expression at the schoolhouse gate." That decision, however, has been qualified in a series of cases that balance student rights with the schools' educational mission.

In 1965, John (fifteen years old) and Mary Beth Tinker (thirteen) violated school rules by wearing a black armband to protest the Vietnam War. They were suspended and told to return when they were ready to abide by the rules. The Supreme Court overturned the suspension and established what became known as the Tinker rule: The students' right to free speech could be curtailed only if it "materially and substantially interferes with the requirements of appropriate discipline in the operation of the school."[21]

In subsequent cases, the Court found that teachers and school officials had an obligation to teach students proper conduct and could regulate speech that was vulgar, indecent, offensive (1986), or inconsistent with the educational mission of the school (1988).[22] The most celebrated recent case arose from an incident at Juneau-Douglas High School in Alaska. The school permitted students to leave class and watch the Olympic torch pass through town. One student, Joseph Frederick, unfurled a big banner reading "Bong Hits 4 Jesus," to the merriment of his schoolmates. The principal suspended Frederick for ten days. The Supreme Court upheld the suspension for advocating drugs in violation of the school's antidrug policy.

In short, the First Amendment offers students less protection than adults. School officials may regulate speech as long as they do not do so arbitrarily. The reasons that the Court has accepted include disruption, violations of prevailing standards of good behavior, and behavior that contradicts the educational mission of the school. However, as the Frederick case shows, the justices disagree about how much latitude to grant high school students. What do you think? Should Frederick have been permitted his free speech? Or was he appropriately disciplined?

THE BOTTOM LINE

- Free speech is crucial to democracy, and the Court gives it a privileged position—even against angry public opposition to flag burning, cross burning, or homophobic displays at military funerals.

- Free speech can be curtailed if it poses a "clear and present danger." Today, the court requires the danger to be both imminent and likely to occur.

- There are limits to free speech, including fighting words and student speech. In the next section, we'll discuss additional limits on obscenity and libel.

Freedom of the Press

Freedom of the press follows most of the same rules as freedom of speech. The written word has always been essential to politics. The form changes—pamphlets during the revolutionary period, newspapers in the mid-twentieth century, and new media today. Written words share the "preferred position." Broadcast media are slightly different and subject to federal regulation (as we will explore in Chapter 7).

Prior Restraint

The effort to stop speech before it occurs is known as **prior restraint**. Although the Supreme Court has permitted government officials to punish people for what they have said or printed, it has never allowed federal government agents to gag citizens before they have had their say. In this view, prior restraint is nothing more than a technical term for *censorship*—the practice of dictators who close down newspapers or suppress stories they do not like. Some historians have argued that the real intent of the First Amendment was to forbid censorship.

The Supreme Court announced restrictions on prior restraint in 1931 after public officials in Minneapolis shut down a newspaper named the *Saturday Press*, published by an avowed racist who claimed that Jewish gangs were running the city. The Court ruled that the state could not suppress the paper, no matter how obnoxious, but it left the door open to prior restraint for national security reasons. The government would be justified for stopping someone from publishing information about "the number and location of troops in the field," it said, but not for publishing anti-Semitic harangues (*Near v. Minnesota*, 1931).

In one famous case of prior restraint, a State Department official leaked a rich archive of classified material, the Pentagon Papers, that exposed the mistakes and deceptions that led the United States into the Vietnam War. The Richard Nixon administration, claiming a threat to national security, went to court to block the *New York Times* from publishing the papers. Within days, the Supreme Court heard the arguments and, by a 6–3 vote, lifted the ban and

Prior restraint: Legal effort to stop speech before it occurs—in effect, censorship.

● The courts have been reluctant to stop publication of information—a process known as prior restraint. New media and sites like WikiLeaks make it very difficult for them to do so even when they try.

permitted publication. The majority opinion emphasized the "heavy presumption" against prior restraint.[23]

The shift from print media to the web has profoundly changed the logic of prior restraint. In 2008, WikiLeaks, a web-based venue for anonymous whistle-blowers, published internal documents from a Swiss bank that appeared to show tax evasion and money laundering at the bank's Cayman Islands branch. The bank went to court and won a restraining order against publication of the leaked documents. Stopping a newspaper from publishing is straightforward: the court enjoins the publisher. However, since WikiLeaks operates anonymously and globally, it is almost impossible for a court to suppress the information. In the WikiLeaks case the court tried to seal the site's American address. The documents simply appeared on mirror sites. After two weeks, Judge Jerry White dissolved the injunction and acknowledged that the court's effort had only publicized the documents.[24]

The most dramatic illustration of press freedom and new media erupted when Edward Snowden, a contractor working for the National Security Agency (NSA), leaked a huge cache of documents detailing the NSA's extensive data collection. The reports, published in the *Washington Post* and the British newspaper, *The Guardian,* revealed one controversial secret after another: The United States had listened in on foreign allies like Chancellor Angela Merkel of Germany; the NSA was collecting metadata on millions of cell phone calls; the PRISM program tapped data from Apple, Google, Facebook, You-Tube, and others (with the cooperation of those companies). The story went public—there was no prior restraint—and created an enormous public debate. But the leaker still faced criminal charges for leaking classified documents.

Obscenity

The First Amendment does not protect obscenity. However, the courts always face the same problem: What is obscene? Justice Potter Stewart put it famously when he said simply, "I know it when I see it." Of course, different people see it in different things. The Court's emphasis on free speech leads it to reject aggressive regulation of obscenity.

In *Miller v. California* (1973), the Supreme Court created a three-part test for judging a work to be obscene. The Miller test holds that speech is not protected by the First Amendment if it has all three of these characteristics:

1. "The average person, applying contemporary community standards, would find that the work, taken as a whole, appeals to the prurient interest" (meaning that it is meant to be sexually stimulating).
2. It depicts sexual conduct in a "patently offensive way."
3. The work lacks "serious literary, artistic, political or scientific value."

The Miller test only created new questions. What does it mean to be patently offensive? Offensive to whom? How do we rely on community standards of decency when the Internet and the new media flow across borders?

In recent years, the Court has been hostile to most efforts at banning material. The Court flatly forbids child pornography, however. Abusing minors is criminal. In 2008, it upheld a law that forbade efforts to "provide or obtain child pornography." The case involved a man who boasted online, "Dad of toddler has 'good' pics of her and me for swap of your toddler pics, or live cam." He followed up with hard-core images of minors engaged in sexual behavior. Even in this case, two members of the Court disagreed. They argued that the posting violated the laws only if it could be proven that the pictures were really of minors. Simply having the defendant say so was not enough. Feminist scholars have tried to change the framework. Pornography, they argue, is a form of hate speech because it subordinates women the same way that hate speech demeans minorities. To date, the court has refused to accept this position.

Libel

There are limits to the false things one can write or say about someone. (Written falsehoods are known as *libel*, spoken falsehoods are known as *slander*.) The courts have made it very difficult for public officials or celebrities to win a libel (or slander) judgment. To do so, they must prove not just that a statement was false and that it caused them harm but also that it was made with malice or a "a reckless disregard for the truth."

Today, the Court allows even outrageous claims, cartoons, spoofs, and criticism directed at public officials and celebrities. By contrast, English law is just the opposite and puts the burden of proof on the writers to prove the truth of what they have written.

The Right to Bear Arms

The Second Amendment is a uniquely American right: No other national constitution includes it. The text in the Constitution is ambiguous:

A well regulated militia, being necessary to the security of a free state, the right of the people to keep and bear arms shall not be infringed.

On one reading, it simply protects colonial-era militias. On the other, it guarantees the right to own weapons. Recently, the Supreme Court has rendered a decisive ruling—again by a 5–4 vote—guaranteeing the right to arms.

A Relic of the Revolution?

Skeptics question whether there is any right to bear arms at all. The Second Amendment, they say, protected state militias. Early Americans believed that only kings and tyrants kept permanent armies. In a republic, the citizens volunteered for service in local militias that defended their communities and their nation. The Second Amendment, in this reading, is a "relic of the American Revolution" and simply forbids the government from disarming the local militias that were so important in the eighteenth century. It does not involve a constitutional right to tote weapons.

Those who favor this view generally emphasize public safety and gun control. America's high homicide rate reflects the easy availability (and the rising caliber) of American weapons. Many cities and some states regulate or limit gun ownership.

The Palladium of All Liberties?

Proponents of gun rights read the same constitutional sentence very differently. As Justice Scalia explained, the Second Amendment has two parts—a preface about militias and a clause that really matters, declaring that "the right . . . to . . . bear arms shall not be infringed." Many see the right to bear arms as the most important right of all—"the palladium of the liberties of the republic," as

Justice Story put it. "When all else fails," declared Charlton Heston, actor and longtime honorary president of the National Rifle Association, "it is the one right that prevails. . . . It is the one right that allows rights to exist at all."[25]

The Supreme Court has been moving firmly to defend gun rights. In 2008, the Court struck down a District of Columbia rule that restricted guns in people's homes.[26] In 2010, the Court finally *incorporated* the Second Amendment. For the first time, the constitutional right to bear arms applied to state and local governments (*McDonald v. Chicago*).[27] The *McDonald* decision is likely to make it far more difficult for cities and states to regulate weapons.

Few rights issues have split Americans like the Second Amendment. Conservative and rural Americans generally defend gun rights, which they view as deeply rooted in American culture and essential to personal protection. Where conservatives find safety, liberals fear carnage: domestic disputes turn deadly, children kill their friends, and urban neighborhoods become combat zones. Horrific shootings—like the murder of twenty children and six adults in Newtown, Connecticut—constantly keep this difficult debate on the political agenda.

THE BOTTOM LINE

- Some critics see the Second Amendment as an outmoded defense of citizen militias.

- Others see it as an important individual right—perhaps even the most important right in the entire Constitution.

- In 2010, the Supreme Court incorporated the right to bear arms as an essential individual right.

● The Rights of the Accused

The Bill of Rights places special emphasis on protecting people accused of crimes. Four amendments (Four, Five, Six, and Eight) list thirty-one different rights for those who face criminal charges. No other issue gets as much attention. Protecting the accused involves another careful balancing act. On the one hand, the courts must restrain law enforcement and defend the constitutional freedoms that define America. On the other hand, too many curbs on law enforcement might lead to more crime. The challenge of civil liberties is finding the right balance between protecting the accused and keeping the society safe.

Americans Behind Bars

The Supreme Court has recently been strengthening free speech and gun rights. When it comes to the rights of the accused, however, the courts are

END THE DEATH PENALTY?

In a recent case, Justice Stevens called for ending the death penalty. Is capital punishment a form of "cruel and unusual punishment"?

No.	Yes.
Some crimes are so terrible they require this punishment. Justice demands it. It brings closure to the victims' families. American public opinion supports it. If there is a deterrent effect, executing criminals might save innocent lives. Some criminals are so hardened that they pose a safety threat to other prisoners, to prison officials, and to the public. Finally, multiple safeguards are in place to guarantee that innocent people are not executed.	It is time for the United States to join the other industrial democracies. Executions are unfair and fall almost entirely on poor and black defendants. No government should have this power. Killing is morally wrong, and two wrongs do not make a right. Furthermore, it is impossible to ensure that no innocent people will be killed. The deterrent effect is not proven. Even the American Medical Association refuses to let physicians participate.

moving away from individual protections and toward enhanced government powers. Again, this reflects a conservative trend. After vastly expanding the rights of the accused in the 1960s, the courts—in step with Congress, presidents of both parties, and most states—now tilt firmly toward law enforcement.

Today, 2.3 million Americans are behind bars—more than in any other nation (see Figure 4.1). The number of Americans in jail has risen about fivefold in the past forty years. Do these numbers mean that we might have gone too far in dismantling the rights of the accused? Those who favor tough law enforcement respond by pointing to the low crime rates. Locking up criminals, they argue, has reduced crime. Skeptics, however, fear that American rights are eroding. Even many "crime hawks" (people who are tough on crime) worry that incarcerating too many people—especially for nonviolent crimes—might eventually make crime worse by destroying communities and leaving children without their parents. Many point as well to an alarming racial dimension.

In this section, we examine the most important (and controversial) protections one at a time. As you read, think about the trade-offs between safe streets and civil liberties. As always, there are solid arguments on both sides of the issue.

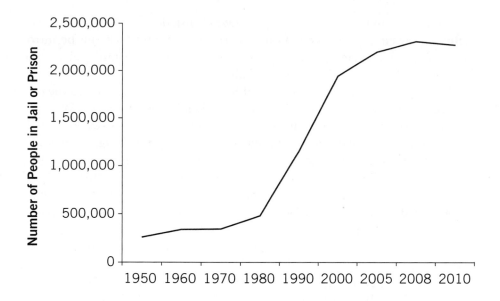

● **FIGURE 4.1** *Incarceration rates in the United States began to soar in the 1980s and now stand at five times their traditional levels. (Justice Policy Institute and U.S. Bureau of Justice).*

The Fourth Amendment: Search and Seizure

The Fourth Amendment protects people from government officials bursting into their houses:

> *The right of the people to be secure in their persons, houses, papers, and effects, against unreasonable searches and seizures, shall not be violated, and no Warrants shall issue, but upon probable cause, supported by Oath or affirmation, and particularly describing the place to be searched, and the persons or things to be seized.*

British officials in the 1770s ransacked people's homes, searching for weapons or smuggled goods. The Fourth Amendment prevents that from happening again. Justice Lewis Brandeis described it "as the right to be left alone—the . . . right most valued by civilized men."[28] The police may not enter a home unless they go before a judge and explain why they suspect that evidence of a crime can be found in a specific place. The judge determines whether there is "probable cause" to issue the warrant. It sounds simple, but there are large gray areas.

The landmark search and seizure case began in 1957 with a tip that Dollree (Dolly) Mapp was hiding a bombing suspect in her apartment. In addition, the police suspected she had illegal gambling paraphernalia in her apartment. The police knocked at her door, but she refused to let them in. They eventually broke the door down, and when she demanded to see a warrant they waved a piece of paper—not a warrant—in the air. The police searched the apartment and the basement. They never found the bombing suspect or the gambling material, but they did discover a suitcase of pornographic material—which was then illegal. Mapp was convicted on obscenity charges. The Supreme Court

Exclusionary rule: The ruling that evidence obtained in an illegal search may not be introduced in a trial.

threw out the conviction and, in *Mapp v. Ohio* (1961, decided 6–3), devised the **exclusionary rule**: Evidence obtained in an illegal search may not be introduced in a trial. Even evidence that clearly proves someone is guilty of a crime may not be used if it was improperly obtained.

Twenty years later, President Ronald Reagan (1981–1989) attacked the rule and urged both Congress and the courts to abolish it. John Roberts, the young Justice Department attorney who wrote the memos supporting Reagan's criticism, is now chief justice of the United States. During the Reagan years, the courts began making exceptions to the exclusionary rule. For example, in 1984 police arrested Alberto Leon when they discovered a large quantity of illegal drugs in his possession. Their warrant had expired but the Supreme Court made a "good faith" exception and permitted the drugs to be introduced as evidence.[29] By 2009, Justice Roberts wrote (in a 5–4 opinion) that there was no need to exclude evidence if the police violated a suspect's Fourth Amendment rights because of "isolated negligence."

A long list of cases explores when officers need a warrant.[30] May they use wiretaps to eavesdrop without a warrant? (Yes, said the courts, in 1928; no, in 1967; sometimes, in 2001.)[31] May they search garbage put out on the curb, without a warrant? (Yes, 1988.) May they search students? (School officials may, but law enforcement officers need to show a cause.) May they search a dorm room? (Yes, 1982.) May they pat down suspicious people on the street? (Yes, 1968 and 1993.) May they search cars? (Yes, 1968.)

In 2011 the Supreme Court crossed an important threshold. It permitted officers to break into a house without a warrant. The officers in the case knocked, identified themselves, and heard movements that sounded like the destruction of evidence of drug use. Only one justice dissented. This ruling would, wrote Justice Ruth Bader Ginsburg, seriously curtail the use of warrants by police. Writing for the majority, Justice Samuel Alito took a hard line. Residents who "attempt to destroy evidence have only themselves to blame."[32]

The Fifth Amendment: Rights at Trials

The Fifth Amendment lists a long series of rights focused largely on criminal trials. Consider them one clause at a time.

> *No person shall be held to answer for a capital, or otherwise infamous crime, unless on . . . indictment of a Grand Jury.*

Grand jury: A jury that does not decide on guilt or innocence but only on whether there is enough evidence for the case to go to trial.

Before the government can prosecute, it must persuade a jury. A **grand jury** does not decide on guilt or innocence, only on whether there is enough evidence for the case to go to trial. The grand jury meets secretly and hears only from the prosecutor, so, as one New York judge once quipped, a decent prosecutor should be able to get a grand jury to "indict a ham sandwich."[33]

> *Nor shall any person be subject for the same offense to be twice put in jeopardy of life or limb.*

An individual cannot face **double jeopardy**, or be tried twice for the same offense. ("Jeopardy of life and limb" refers to the old colonial practice of punishing people by lopping off an ear or damaging other limbs.) Without this provision, the government could simply keep trying people over and over.

Despite this prohibition, individuals sometimes face multiple trials. They can be tried on different charges, tried in federal court after being acquitted in state court, and—if they are acquitted on criminal charges—they can be sued for damages. Rodney King, a black motorist, was brutally beaten by four Los Angeles police officers. The officers were all acquitted in a state court (shocking observers and setting off riots). However, two of the officers were subsequently convicted on federal charges. In another famous case, former football star O. J. Simpson was acquitted of murdering his wife and her companion, only to lose a civil judgment for damages to the victims' families.

> *Nor shall be compelled in any criminal case to be a witness against himself.*

The Constitution aimed to protect citizens from torture and coerced confessions. The liberal Warren Court tried to put teeth into this right by requiring police officers to inform suspects that they have the right to remain silent, now known as the **Miranda warnings** (*Miranda v. Arizona*, 1966). The Court ruled that any evidence acquired before the warning could not be admissible in court. The ruling created an enormous outcry. Richard Nixon used *Miranda* in the 1968 presidential campaign as evidence that the United States had grown "soft on crime." Congress tried to pass a law to get around the ruling.

Over the past forty years, the courts have limited the *Miranda* rights—permitting confessions made to a police officer posing as another inmate (1990), carving out an exception for public safety (1984), and limiting the rules when defendants take the stand in their own defense (1970).[34]

The Sixth Amendment: The Right to Counsel

The Sixth Amendment guarantees a speedy and public trial decided by an impartial jury. It includes another important provision, the right to counsel:

> *In all criminal prosecutions, the accused shall . . . have the assistance of counsel for his defense.*

The Supreme Court weighed in on the issue in an explosive case, known as the trial of the Scottsboro Boys. In 1931 nine young African American men, riding a freight train in Alabama, were accused of raping two white women. Despite evidence that the charges were false (one woman immediately recanted), angry mobs gathered, and eight of the young men were rushed through trials and condemned to death. In *Powell v. Alabama* (1932), the Court ruled that, at least in a capital case (a case that could end in the death penalty), the defendants are entitled to lawyers and that the lawyers must be given enough time to meet with their clients

Double jeopardy: The principle that an individual cannot be tried twice for the same offense.

Miranda warnings: A set of rights that police officers are required to inform suspects of, including the right to remain silent.

● The Scottsboro Boys, with their attorney Samuel Leibowitz, under guard by the state.

and prepare their case. This Scottsboro case was a civil rights breakthrough for another reason: None of the African Americans unfairly accused of raping a white woman was executed.

In 1963, the Court expanded the right to counsel to all felony cases. Clarence Gideon, a Florida drifter, was allegedly caught breaking into a poolroom where he had stolen beer, soft drinks, and the change out of the jukebox. When he came to trial, he demanded a lawyer, but the Florida court denied the request. Gideon was convicted and sentenced to five years, but from his jail cell, working with legal texts, he scrawled an appeal. "Something astonishing . . . happened," wrote Anthony Lewis in a book on the case. "This loser's plea made it all the way to the Supreme Court." In *Gideon v. Wainwright* (1963), the Supreme Court ruled that the Sixth Amendment supported his claim and that the state must provide a lawyer to defend those who cannot afford one. With a competent lawyer, Gideon was acquitted.[35] Attorney General Robert Kennedy commented, "An obscure Florida convict had . . . changed . . . the whole course of American legal history." A network of public defenders spread across the country.

In 2012, the Court dramatically increased the scope of the right to competent counsel by ruling that defendants have a constitutional right to effective attorneys during plea bargain negotiations (in a 5–4 ruling). Today, almost all federal cases (97 percent) involve a plea bargain, in which the defendant pleads guilty in exchange for a lighter sentence without actually going through a formal trial. The Court ruled that defendants can appeal if the negotiations were not competently handled.[36]

In practice, the right to counsel has grown increasingly difficult to maintain. The public is reluctant to spend tax revenues on lawyers who defend poor men and women accused of crimes. Public defenders face huge caseloads with small salaries—the average legal aid attorney in New York handles 592 cases a year and about 103 at any one time. Other cities and counties report similar ratios.[37] The attorneys' own clients often disparage them. For all the problems, however, publicly funded criminal defense remains an essential part of civil liberty and American justice.

The Eighth Amendment: The Death Penalty

The Eighth Amendment introduces the question of capital punishment.

Cruel and unusual punishment . . . shall not be . . . inflicted.

Is execution cruel and unusual punishment? Around the world, ninety-seven nations have abolished the death penalty—including all of Western Europe, where it is considered a violation of human rights. In contrast, the United States executed thirty-eight people in 2013. The number has been falling steadily, although more than 3,250 men and women have been sentenced to capital punishment and are waiting on death row. Some 60 percent of the

American public supports executions, although the number has been slipping over the past fifteen years (see Figure 4.2).

Proponents argue that some crimes are so terrible that justice demands capital punishment. It brings closure to grieving families. It may deter future murders (although there is no definitive evidence one way or the other). Moreover, some criminals are so dangerous they should be executed to protect other prisoners, prison officials, and the general public.

Opponents respond that killing people is immoral and that no government should be given the power to "play God." Because social systems are imperfect, some—perhaps many—innocent people will be executed. The system is tilted against African Americans; blacks make up 12 percent of the population but, from year to year, between 25 and 50 percent of those executed.

In 1972, the Supreme Court halted all executions, arguing that state laws were so vague that similar cases produced different outcomes. "The death standards are cruel and unusual," wrote Justice Potter Stewart in *Furman v. Georgia*, "the same way that being struck by lightning is cruel and unusual"—meaning that death sentences seemed to be meted out randomly. Thirty-five states drafted new capital punishment laws using *Furman* as a guide. In 1976, the Court permitted executions to go forward where state statutes included clear criteria to guide judge and jury in weighing death sentences.

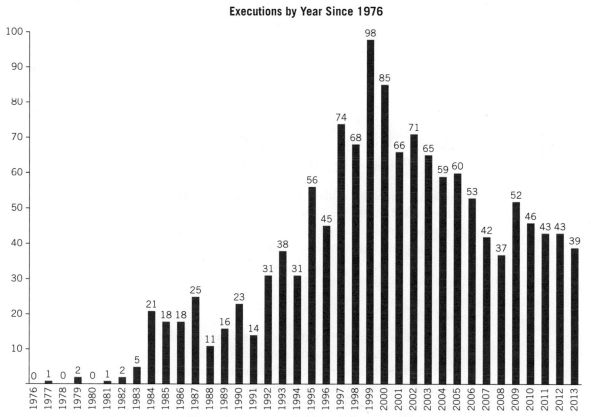

Executions by Year Since 1976

● **FIGURE 4.2** *Annual number of executions in the United States (Death Penalty Information Center).*

Beginning in 1992, a network of law students and their professors began to use DNA evidence to review capital cases. Known as the "Innocence Project," they documented false convictions of more than 120 death row inmates (all of them now released).[38]

The Court has imposed some additional limits. It has ruled that it is "cruel and unusual" to execute people convicted of crimes other than murder, striking down five state laws that allowed execution for child rape (2008). It has forbidden the execution of mentally ill individuals (2002) and of juvenile offenders (2005). In a much-discussed case, however, the Court ruled that lethal injections did not constitute cruel and unusual punishment despite the claim that they caused "an intolerable risk of pain" (2007).[39]

THE BOTTOM LINE

- The Bill of Rights places special emphasis on the rights of those accused of crimes. Even so, American incarceration rates are the highest in the world.

- The police may not search or seize without a warrant; they must inform suspects of their right to remain silent; the accused have a right to legal counsel. The courts have widened the legal right but it is often limited by underfunded public defenders.

- Under current interpretation, capital punishment is not considered "cruel and unusual punishment." However, the number of executions has been falling.

- Between 1962 and 1968, the Supreme Court vastly expanded the rights of the accused. Recent Court decisions have tilted the balance back toward law enforcement.

● Fighting Terrorism and Protecting Liberty

USA Patriot Act: Legislation that sought to enhance national security, passed in the aftermath of the September 11, 2001, attacks.

After the terrorist attacks on September 11, 2001, Congress passed the **USA Patriot Act**. In the fear and emotion of the terrible moment, few criticized the legislation, which passed in the Senate 98–1. The act tried to enhance security by removing restrictions on law enforcement. Removing restrictions, however, means limiting rights. The Patriot Act and the broader campaign against terrorism has provoked debate about the balance between civil liberties and public safety.

Surveillance

Domestic surveillance requires a warrant. As part of the war on terror, the Bush administration issued a secret executive order permitting the NSA to conduct international surveillance without a search warrant. Although the order targeted foreign parties outside the United States, it applied to communications with American citizens in the United States. News of the program leaked and was published by the *New York Times* in 2005. (To sidestep government efforts to seek a prior restraint, once the editors decided to publish, the *Times* posted the story on its website.) Congress approved the warrantless wiretap program in 2007 and the Obama administration continued the program.

Major controversy erupted in 2013 when leaks by former NSA contractor Edward Snowden revealed the scale of the data collection. The NSA has been collecting bulk data—more than a trillion pieces of information—on phone calls, computer searches, texts, and more. The phone data, for example, includes the caller, the receiver, the date and time of the call, the length of the call—but not a transcript of the conversation itself.

Some public officials defended the NSA. Senator Dianne Feinstein (D-CA) put it this way: "New bombs are being devised. New terrorists are emerging. . . . We need to be prepared." Senator Rand Paul (R-KY) responded by announcing that he was filing a suit to preserve his privacy against data collection—and invited citizens to join him. Once again, public safety must be balanced with the right to privacy. President Obama tried to cut a middle ground; he proposed putting the metadata in private hands and placing tighter restrictions on how it could be accessed by security agencies. Opinion polls reflected a divided public. The debate will engage Americans—and the courts—for a long time.

Critics of the surveillance programs charge that the United States is now so focused on fighting terrorists that it is trampling on the Constitution. Supporters argue that the United States faces peril and that the Constitution itself permits exceptions to basic rights when "public safety may require it" (Article 1). The debate remains heated on both sides because the stakes are high. Americans are trying to balance the long legacy of rights with the security needs of the twenty-first century.

THE BOTTOM LINE

- The response to the terrorist attacks in 2001 created a new debate about the balance between civil liberties and public safety.

- The most controversial issue today is the NSA data collection of phone records and Internet surveillance. The debate centers on whether the practice is constitutional and what controls might be necessary to safeguard privacy rights.

Conclusion: The Dilemma of Civil Liberties

How should the government balance its duty to keep the public safe with its responsibility to protect private rights? It is the eternal dilemma of civil liberties and one of the most important issues facing American democracy. If we tilt too far toward combating terrorism, Americans lose the liberties that have defined the nation since 1776. If we tilt too far the other way, the nation may be vulnerable to attacks. Getting the balance right is a major challenge facing Americans today. The courts take the lead in protecting rights, but elected public officials define the policies that the courts are weighing. Ultimately, the balance between communal needs and individual rights is in the hands of the voters.

Isn't that exactly where it belongs? Not necessarily. The Supreme Court put it well in 1943: "The very purpose of a Bill of Rights was to withdraw certain subjects from the vicissitudes of political controversy, to place them beyond the reach of majorities and officials and to establish them as legal principles to be applied by the courts."

The point of civil liberties is to protect the rights of individuals—even if it means stopping the majority of the country. We saw the birth of American liberty in Chapter 2 with the Declaration of Independence and the Constitution. In this chapter we have examined how American rights are interpreted and protected. In the next chapter, we'll see how they grew and spread.

CHAPTER SUMMARY

● Civil liberties are the limits we put on governing bodies (and the majorities that elect them) so that individuals can exercise their rights and freedom. Disputes are usually resolved by the courts and guided by the Bill of Rights.

● The Bill of Rights did not apply to the states until the Fourteenth Amendment required that *no state* could deprive any citizen of life, liberty, or property.

● The Supreme Court applied the Bill of Rights to the states one right at a time between 1897 (no taking property without compensation) and 2010 (the right to bear arms). The process is known as incorporation.

● The Court discovered a right to privacy implicit (in the shadows) in the First, Third, Fourth, Fifth, and Ninth amendments. The Court applied the right to privacy to strike down laws banning abortion. In *Roe v. Wade* the Court issued a rule prohibiting states from interfering during the first trimester. In *Planned Parenthood v. Casey*, the Court replaced the rule with a standard forbidding laws that put "an

undue burden" on the right to privacy. The Court extended privacy rights to same-sex couples by striking down antisodomy laws in 2003.

● The Constitution bans government from establishing religion. In one view, this means separating church and state. The Lemon test guided judicial decisions. A more recent view requires simply that government not promote one religious view over another. The Constitution also forbids government from interfering with religious practice. The courts traditionally asked if the government had a compelling interest for imposing a burden. Today, they require only that the government action be neutral and apply to everyone. Congress and some state governments have tried to return to the original rule.

● Free speech is crucial to democracy, and the Court gives it a privileged position—even against angry public opposition to flag burning, cross burning, or homophobic displays at military funerals. Free speech can be curtailed if it poses a "clear and present danger." Today, the Court requires the danger to be both imminent and likely to occur. There are limits to free speech involving fighting words, student speech, commercial speech, and obscenity.

● Some critics see the Second Amendment as an outmoded defense of citizen militias. Others see the right to bear arms as an important individual right—perhaps the most important right in the Constitution. In 2010, the Supreme Court ruled it an essential constitutional right.

● The Bill of Rights places special emphasis on the rights of those accused of crimes. Even so, American incarceration rates are the highest in the world. The police may not search or seize without a warrant, they must inform suspects of their right to remain silent, and the accused have a right to legal counsel. Under current interpretation, capital punishment is not considered "cruel and unusual punishment."

KEY TERMS

Accommodation, 123	Exclusionary rule, 138	Miranda warnings, 139
Civil liberties, 114	Fighting words, 130	Prior restraint, 131
Civil rights, 115	Free exercise clause, 122	Selective incorporation, 116
Clear and present danger, 128	Grand jury, 138	Strict separation, 123
Double jeopardy, 139	Hate crime, 126	Symbolic expression, 128
Establishment clause, 122	Hate speech, 126	USA Patriot Act, 142

STUDY QUESTIONS

1. What are civil liberties? How are they different from civil rights?

2. In *Barron v. Baltimore*, the Supreme Court ruled that the Fifth Amendment did not protect a landowner if the state took his property. Why?

3. Describe how the Bill of Rights was applied to the state governments.

   First, describe the constitutional amendment that directly addressed the states.
   Then, describe the process of incorporation by which the Supreme Court applied the Bill of Rights to the states.

4. Describe how the Supreme Court declared the right to privacy.

   Discuss the case from a pragmatist's and an originalist's perspective.
   Would you vote to maintain the right to privacy? Or to overrule the precedent? Explain your reasoning.

5. Describe the three-part Lemon test for determining whether a state action violates the establishment clause.

Justice Scalia has been highly critical of the Lemon test. What is his view?
Do you agree with it or not? Explain why.

6. Sometimes the Court permits a racist to burn a cross. Sometimes it forbids it. Explain the reasoning in each case. Do you agree with the Court's distinction or would you rule differently?

7. There are two interpretations of the Second Amendment right to bear arms. Describe each. Which do you support? Why?

8. The Supreme Court gives free speech a "privileged position" among the rights in the Bill of Rights.

   What does that mean?
   How does the Court justify that position?

9. How does the USA Patriot Act raise questions about the balance between public safety and civil liberties? How do you think about balancing civil liberties with protection against terrorism? If you had to emphasize one goal more than the other, which would you emphasize? Why?

5

The Struggle for Civil Rights

"WHAT DO YOU WANT TO BE when you grow up?" asked the eighth-grade teacher. Malcolm Little, the class president, responded. "I've been thinking I'd like to be a lawyer." "Malcolm," snapped the teacher, "you've got to be realistic about being a n——[he used a racial epithet]. A lawyer—that's no realistic goal for a n——." The student would later change his name to Malcolm X and redefine black nationalism. But when Malcolm was in eighth grade, black kids could not even dream of professional careers. The same year, novelist Richard Wright imagined a black teen in Chicago "playing white" by pretending to be an army general, a corporate executive, or an airline pilot. These professions were all out of reach for most African Americans—and for women.

When Congress unexpectedly outlawed sex discrimination in the Civil Rights Act of 1964, the *Wall Street Journal* quoted a flummoxed airline executive: "What are we going to do now when a gal walks into our office, demands a job as an airline pilot, and has the credentials to qualify?" The idea of a woman piloting a commercial airline was no more sensible than Malcolm becoming a lawyer or a black kid on the South Side of Chicago selling stocks. At least they all had an advantage over Chinese children, who were forbidden from becoming American citizens. Things we now take completely for granted—black professionals, women pilots, Chinese Americans—were either rare or illegal in the past.[1]

Who are we? We are a profoundly diverse nation, founded on the idea that all people are "created equal" and "endowed" with "unalienable rights" including "life, liberty and the pursuit of happiness." We are also a nation that often does not live up to its noble founding vision.

Civil rights are the freedom to participate in the life of the community—to vote in elections, to enjoy public facilities like parks, and to take full advantage of economic opportunities like good jobs. People face discrimination when they are denied rights and opportunities because of their race, gender, ethnicity, religion, disabilities, age, or other personal characteristics. Once citizens have won their rights, the attention shifts to protecting them. We covered that topic—known as civil liberties—in the last chapter. The long battle to win civil rights is perhaps the most powerful story in American history. It reveals the deepest truths about the United States and its values. It tells us who we are.

Civil rights: The freedom to participate in the full life of the community—to vote, use public facilities, and exercise equal economic opportunity.

● *These athletes don't realize how the Civil Rights Act changed their world.*

We can view the history of civil rights in two different ways. Some observers see a steady march toward a deeper and richer American equality. If you reread the opening paragraph of this chapter, it's hard not to see enormous progress. An African American lawyer? One has been elected to the Oval Office. Women pilots? Women began flying combat missions twenty years ago. Asian Americans? There are thirteen in Congress. The American promise marches relentlessly on.[2]

Other observers, however, believe that there is nothing inevitable about civil rights. Sometimes rights expand, sometimes they contract. Yes, Asians won full rights, but Native Americans did not. African Americans scaled the old barriers, but only three served in the Senate in the entire twentieth century. African Americans are almost three times as likely to be poor as the rest of the population. They have a life expectancy five years shorter than whites—and nearly eight years shorter than Latinos. There is nothing inevitable about

BY THE NUMBERS
Civil Rights

- Number of black mayors in 1965: **0**
- Number of black mayors in 2014: **more than 500**
- Percentage of southern students who attended integrated schools 8 years after *Brown v. Board of Education* ruled against desegregated schools in 1954: **1**
- Percentage of southern students who attended integrated schools 8 years after the passage of the Civil Rights Act of 1964: **91**
- Percentage of white and black Americans who were poor in 1959: **18, 55**
- Percentage of white Americans who are poor today: **8.6**
- Percentage of Hispanic Americans who are poor: **21.5**
- Percentage of black Americans who are poor: **24.7**
- Percentage of Native Americans who are poor: **32.2**
- Number of Hispanic members of Congress in 1990, 2000, 2014: **10, 18, 38**
- Number of women elected to full Senate terms between 1920 and 1970: **3**
- Number of women serving in the Senate today: **20**
- Nations with a higher percentage of women serving in their national legislature than the U.S. has (as of November 2013): **78**
- Year the Supreme Court struck down laws forbidding marriage between blacks and whites: **1968**
- Percentages of whites, blacks, Hispanics, and Asians married to a member of a different race today: **9, 17, 26, 28**
- Percentage of whites, Latinos, and blacks who report "a great deal" or "a fair amount" of confidence in the police: **78, 61, 53**

American equality, say proponents of this perspective, and citizens should never take it for granted.[3]

As you read this chapter, ask which view seems most accurate to you: Has the United States marched toward greater civil rights for all? Or has the progress been unsteady?

Winning Rights: The Political Process

How does a group win political rights? Each civil rights campaign has its own unique history. However, the efforts usually involve the following stages—not necessarily in order.

Seven Steps to Political Equality

1. *A group defines itself.* Discrimination usually stretches back through time: whites ruled blacks, men took responsibility for "the weaker sex," Indians were "savages," society pitied the disabled, and psychiatrists defined homosexuality as an illness. In the first step toward civil rights, a group embraces its shared identity and redefines itself as a victim of discrimination. Groups usually reject their old, often demeaning label and find a new name: Negroes, Miss, queers, and cripples became African Americans, Ms., LGBTQ individuals, and persons with disabilities.

2. *The group challenges society.* The next step involves entering the political arena and demanding rights. Civil rights campaigns often go beyond normal politics and include marches, demonstrations, creative protests (like kneel-ins before segregated churches), and even riots.

3. *The stories change.* Civil rights always involve a contest over the stories that a society tells about a group. Why does the United States discriminate against people in the first place? Because the majority portrays a group as dangerous, inferior, or helpless. Winning rights requires changing the story. As you read about efforts to secure rights—past and present—be alert to the many different stories we tell about the groups in our society.

4. *Federalism comes into play.* Civil rights politics splashes across local, state, and federal governments. Because many minority groups are concentrated in certain states and regions, discrimination often begins on the local level. Furthermore, state and local officials control many of the policies that impact civil rights: education, law enforcement, and voting rules.

   In other cases, states and localities first introduce reforms: before the Nineteenth Amendment established woman's suffrage nationally, women won voting rights in western states.

● *Lucretia Mott, who helped organized the Seneca Falls convention for women's rights, is attacked by a mob of angry men. Women who challenged their own subordination faced violence in the nineteenth century.*

5. *The executive branch often breaks the ice.* Presidents can issue executive orders (rules that have the force of law but do not require congressional approval); these can create opportunities and momentum for a civil rights campaign. President Truman desegregated the U.S. military in 1948.

6. *Congress legislates a blockbuster.* Typically, it is Congress that passes great changes, which finally secure civil rights and echo through history. The Fourteenth Amendment to the Constitution, ratified in 1868, still dominates every effort to win rights. The Civil Rights Act of 1964 profoundly changed civil rights in the United States.

7. *It all ends up in court.* The courts are the ultimate arbiters of civil rights. They rule on what the Constitution requires of Americans.

Notice how many moving parts there are in the reform process. We've already seen why this is so: American government is unusually fragmented, marked by overlapping actors and institutions all balancing one another. That makes it difficult to change deep social norms—like racial or gender discrimination. Reformers have to win over many different power centers—state legislatures, Congress, governors, the judiciary, the media, and the public.

How the Courts Review Cases

Since civil rights generally end up in court, the judicial framework is important. The courts use three categories for determining whether acts violate "the equal protection of the laws" guaranteed by the Fourteenth Amendment.

Strict scrutiny: The tendency to strike down as unconstitutional any legislation that singles out race or ethnicity, unless the government has a compelling interest in such legislation.

Suspect Categories.   Any legislation involving *race*, *ethnicity*, or *legal aliens* faces **strict scrutiny**. The Supreme Court is primed to strike down any law that singles out a race or ethnicity unless there is a strong reason for doing so. The Court will ask: Does the government have a *compelling government interest* in singling out a race or an ethnicity? In *Brown v. Board of Education*, for example, the Court decided that the state governments had no *compelling interest* in segregating schools.

Quasi-suspect Categories.   In 1976, women's advocates won a special category for gender cases. Any legislation—federal, state, or local—that introduces sex-based categories has to rest on an *important state purpose*. This is not as strong a test as a *compelling* interest. But it is still a powerful requirement, one that can touch many aspects of politics, economics, and society. For example, in 1996 the Court ruled that excluding women from the Virginia Military

 Latinos demonstrating for immigration reform waving American flags. Observers were amazed at the size, scope, and fervor of the rallies.

Institute did not serve an important state purpose. VMI had to open its doors to women cadets or forgo state funding.

Nonsuspect Categories.   Other categories do not face special scrutiny—at least not yet. Legislation based on age, sexual orientation, or physical handicaps simply has to have some rational connection between the legislation and a legitimate government purpose. This is the weakest test, but it can still bar discrimination. Using this test, for example, the Court struck down an Oregon law that banned Catholic schools from the state (in 1925) and a Colorado constitutional amendment that forbade all legislation designed to protect people based on their sexual orientation (1996). The Court ruled that there was no rational government interest in forbidding Catholic education or ruling out all protections of gay people.[4]

This threefold division is the framework for civil rights law. Like almost everything else in American government, politics produced these categories. Groups argued, lobbied, demonstrated, and sued to win stricter scrutiny.

THE BOTTOM LINE

- The battle for civil rights generally includes seven stages. The group seeking rights must define itself, challenge society, and change the way it is viewed. The contest for rights spills across federalism and all three branches of government.

- Courts interpret charges of discrimination using three standards: suspect, quasi-suspect, and nonsuspect.

● Race and Civil Rights: Revolt Against Slavery

Few groups in American history have suffered worse treatment than African Americans. By now, the painful images are familiar: men and women chained in the holds of slave ships, sold at auction, raped at will, separated from families, and murdered for challenging their oppression. Even after liberation, black Americans faced another century of repression. In fighting back, African Americans developed the tactics that other groups would use in their battles for civil rights; black movements forged the laws, amendments, and judicial doctrine that opened the door to civil rights reforms across society. The black quest for freedom included two powerful crusades, one in the nineteenth century and one in the twentieth.

Abolition: A nineteenth-century movement demanding an immediate and unconditional end to slavery.

The Clash over Slavery

Slaves were permitted to have churches, and in the early nineteenth century, religion offered leadership, organization, and a powerful message. Black leaders drew on the Christian Bible to compare Africans to the Israelites, bound in slavery but waiting for deliverance to freedom. By the middle of the nineteenth century, the dream of freedom had become a kind of religious faith in the slave quarters.[5] Three additional forces precipitated a national crisis over slavery: a moral crusade for abolition, economic interests, and political calculations.

Abolition. An **abolition** movement rose up, branded slavery sinful, and demanded its immediate end. The movement was small and radical, but its newspapers and pamphlets created a furious reaction. Many Americans—in the south and the north—feared the abolitionists would incite the slaves to rebellion. Most people preferred to ignore the issue.

Economics. It was impossible to avoid the slavery question for a fundamental economic reason. As the United States spread west, every new settlement prompted the same question—would it be slave or free? Northerners opposed slavery on the frontier because it robbed them of the opportunity to claim new lands. Southerners, however, insisted that slavery needed to spread into new states to survive. Because the federal government controlled territories until they became states, the question—slave or free?—constantly haunted Congress.

BRANDING SLAVES,
ON THE COAST OF AFRICA PREVIOUS TO EMBARKATION.

● *The cruel institution.*

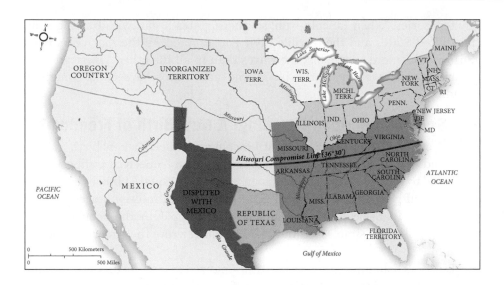

● **FIGURE 5.1** *The Missouri Compromise—all new American territory below the line would permit slavery, all above (except Missouri) would be free.*

Politics.   Every time a territory applied for statehood it called into question the political balance between slave states and free states in the Senate. Since every state has two senators, an equal number of free and slave states permitted the South to defend its peculiar institution.

The Senate managed to negotiate the tensions with a series of artful compromises. The **Missouri Compromise**, in 1820, drew a line through the Louisiana Territory (see Figure 5.1). All new states and territories north of the line except Missouri would be free; everything south of the line would be open to slavery. In 1845, as Americans moved west, Congress extended the line to include Texas. In 1850, California wanted to enter the Union, but extending the old line to the coast would split the new state—half slave and half free. The solution was another compromise, the **Compromise of 1850**, which turned the decision over to residents of the territories.

Dred Scott v. Sandford

In 1857, the Supreme Court stepped in with a shattering decision that upset all the careful compromises. A slave named Dred Scott sued for freedom. He argued that he had been taken to live in a free territory before returning to Missouri and that, as a result, he should be free. Chief Justice Roger Taney ruled that he was not free because neither the territories nor the federal government had the power to limit slavery or give a black man rights. What about the Missouri Compromise? Unconstitutional, ruled Taney. The ***Dred Scott v. Sandford*** decision ruled that no territory could restrict slavery, much less elevate blacks to citizenship.

The Dred Scott decision created an uproar. The Republican Party rose to national prominence by explicitly rejecting it. In 1860, Abraham Lincoln won the presidency on a platform that flatly opposed the extension of slavery into

Missouri Compromise: An agreement to open southern territories west of the Mississippi to slavery while closing northern territories to slavery.

Compromise of 1850: A complicated compromise over slavery that permitted territories to vote on whether they would be slave or free. It also included a fugitive slave law forcing northerners to return black men and women into bondage and permitted California to enter the Union as a free state.

Dred Scott v. Sandford: A landmark Supreme Court decision holding that black men could not be citizens under the Constitution of the United States. It created a national uproar.

any territories. When Lincoln won, southern states began withdrawing from the United States and the terrible Civil War erupted. In the four years from 1861 to 1865, more people lost their lives than in all the other American wars combined. However, from the blood and ashes arose a second American founding.

The Second American Founding: A New Birth of Freedom?

In his Gettysburg Address, President Lincoln announced "a new birth of freedom" and declared that the United States had been "conceived in liberty and dedicated to the proposition that all men are created equal." Lincoln expressed a view of self-government that the Declaration had not fully embraced and the Constitution had rejected: "government of the people, by the people, for the people."[6] With this simple declaration, Lincoln rewrote the American idea of freedom.

Lincoln's bold innovation was institutionalized in four documents. In 1863, Lincoln's **Emancipation Proclamation** freed the slaves—but only in areas that were still rebelling. Ironically, Lincoln freed the slaves in the states where he had no power to enforce his decree. The slaves themselves, however, bolted by the thousands toward the Union army and transformed it, as one historian wrote, into "a reluctant dragon of emancipation." When the Civil War was finally over, Congress wrote three "Civil War amendments" that gave full legal force to Lincoln's new birth of freedom.

The *Thirteenth Amendment* (ratified in 1865) abolished slavery.

The *Fourteenth Amendment* (1868) made anyone born in the United States, crucially including former slaves, a U.S. citizen. Today, this provision is at the heart of the immigration debate; even the children of undocumented immigrants, born on American soil, are American citizens.

The most crucial passage of the Fourteenth Amendment, however, comes in the sentence: *No state shall "deprive any person of life, liberty or property without due process of law; nor deny to any person . . . the equal protection of the laws."* By directing the language at the states—"no *state* shall deprive any person"—the Fourteenth Amendment applied the federal Constitution and the Bill of Rights to the states. The key phrase—the **equal protection of the laws**—would become the legal weapon in the battle for civil rights. It might be the single most important addition to the Constitution in the past two hundred years. It forbids any law designed to harm a group.

The *Fifteenth Amendment* (ratified in 1870) guarantees the right to vote. "The right of citizens . . . to vote . . . shall not be denied . . . on account of race, color, or previous condition of servitude." Can you see what is not mentioned? Gender. Women had reasoned that since they were citizens, their right to vote should not be "denied or abridged," but the Supreme Court rejected this interpretation in 1875.

Like the original Constitution, all these amendments were inspired by political calculation. For example, Republicans in the North, who controlled

Emancipation Proclamation: An executive order issued by President Abraham Lincoln that declared the slaves in all rebel states free.

Equal protection of the laws: The landmark phrase in the Fourteenth Amendment that requires equal treatment for all citizens.

Congress, knew that the South would return to the Union with more seats in Congress than they had before the Civil War—the slave had counted for three-fifths of a vote; the freedman counted for a whole vote. Since the former slaves were very likely to vote for the party of Lincoln (and their former masters were not), the Republicans in Congress had a very good reason to protect their right to vote.

Freedom Fails

What happened to the former slaves? The era after the Civil War began with soaring hopes—and ended bitterly. Black families—torn apart during slavery—joyously reunited. African Americans formed communities, organized churches, voted, entered politics, and demanded respect from their former owners. Two African Americans were elected to the U.S. Senate and twenty-one to the House of Representatives. However, black empowerment met fierce resistance. Many whites found it difficult to treat the former slaves as equals. Some were outraged when the freedmen no longer stepped aside on the sidewalks; many whites faced economic hardship, even ruin, now that their labor force had disappeared.

Southern state and local governments reacted by passing *black codes*. These regulations tied blacks to the land, restricted their movements, established curfews, and stripped them of rights like voting, or owning guns and property. Legal restrictions were backed up by the violent Ku Klux Klan (KKK), which sprang up to intimidate former slaves and prevent them from exercising their new rights.

For a time, Congress supported the former slaves. In an effort known as **Reconstruction**, it tried to rebuild the South around a vision of racial justice. Congress organized a *Freedmen's Bureau* to assist the former slaves. The Civil Rights Act of 1866 guaranteed African Americans the same property rights as white Americans; the Civil Rights Act of 1875 limited private racial discrimination in hotels, restaurants, and theaters.

However, dreams of racial equality began to slip away. The North, weary of the conflict, withdrew the army from the South in 1877. Congress repealed the laws that implemented (or put into effect) the Civil War amendments; no national mechanism was left to enforce "the equal protection of the laws." In the Civil Rights Cases of 1883, the Supreme Court struck down the Civil Rights Act of 1875, ruling that Congress did not have the authority to stop private discrimination. It took eighty-nine years before the Civil Rights Act of 1964 would find a way around this barrier.[7]

By the 1890s, the state governments had gutted the Fifteenth Amendment right to vote. The *grandfather clause* forbade people from voting if their grandfathers hadn't voted; obviously, if your grandfather was a slave, he did not vote. Poll taxes required paying a fee that most black people could not afford. **Literacy tests** required voters to read and interpret any passage in the state constitution. These new rules did what violence and intimidation had

Reconstruction: The failed effort, pursued by Northerners and Southerners, to rebuild the South and establish racial equality after the Civil War.

Literacy test: A requirement that voters be literate; in reality, a way to restrict black suffrage.

Jim Crow: The system of racial segregation in the U.S. South that lasted from 1890 to 1965.

Plessy v. Ferguson: An 1896 Supreme Court case that permitted racial segregation.

see for yourself 5.1

Go online to see clips from *The Birth of a Nation.*

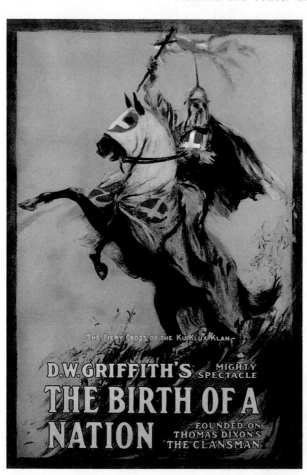

● *Terrorism as chivalry.*

failed to accomplish—they drove blacks out of politics. The white majority built a system of segregation known as **Jim Crow** (named after minstrel shows in which white singers and dancers blackened their faces and pretended to be Africans). Jim Crow laws segregated—or separated—the races. African Americans could not go to white schools, play in the park, visit the zoo (Thursday eventually became "black day" at many zoos), drink from the same fountain, eat at a white restaurant, stay in a white hotel, go to a white hospital, pray in a white church, or vote.

In 1896, the Supreme Court ruled in *Plessy v. Ferguson* that there was nothing inherently discriminatory in requiring separate but equal facilities for black and white races. "If one race be inferior to the other socially," wrote the majority, "the Constitution of the United States cannot put them upon the same plane."[8]

The entire system of segregation was held in place by the raw brutality of lynching—ritualized murders of black men (and occasionally women) who had violated the codes. The murders—hanging, mutilation, burning—were not crimes of mob passion but organized events with police directing traffic around the scene and white families posing for pictures around the victim's charred body. They served as a horrific way to enforce racial separation. The *Negro Year Book* recorded 1,799 blacks lynched between 1882 and 1920 alone.

The white majority directed extraordinary fury at men and women who fell in love across the racial divide because they threatened the entire structure of segregation. Thirty states passed laws forbidding interracial marriage, and sixteen still had them in 1968 when the Supreme Court finally ruled that they violated "the equal protection of the laws" guaranteed by the Fourteenth Amendment.[9]

How could the majority accept such repression? Once again, the white majority told a false story about black men's supposed sexual lust for white women. Black men were dangerous. The story in its most blatant form provided the plot for one of the seminal works in cinematic history. *The Birth of a Nation* (1915) features lust-filled black men, backed by federal troops, menacing white women until the KKK saves the day. In one of the last triumphant scenes, the KKK disarms the skulking black men and stops them from voting. Woodrow Wilson screened the film in the White House and it became one of the top grossing films of all time.[10]

THE BOTTOM LINE

- The clash over slavery eventually led Lincoln to redefine the American idea of self-rule: "government of the people, by the people, for the people."

- *Institutional changes* marked the rise and the fall of civil rights. The president issued the Emancipation Proclamation, Congress passed the Civil Rights Acts, and the states ratified the Thirteenth, Fourteenth, and Fifteenth Amendments.

- The Fourteenth Amendment contains the crucial legal rule for civil rights: "No state shall . . . deprive any person of . . . the equal protection of the laws."

- Later, courts struck down some civil rights laws, Congress repealed laws implementing the Civil War amendments, and the states introduced segregation, which the Supreme Court accepted.

- However, it was *culture*—the terrible stories that white Americans told about their fellow citizens—that fixed the new legal chains in place by inducing the majority to ignore the violations of black rights.

The Fight for Racial Equality

World War II revolutionized the race line by changing American attitudes. The United States fought a bitter war against a Nazi enemy that held horrific theories of racial superiority; all ideas of racial superiority became suspect. Over one hundred thousand black troops fought in the war and returned home with new ideas of freedom and dignity.

Beginning in the 1920s, many African Americans left the South and moved to more lucrative factory jobs in the northern cities—a journey known as the **Great Migration**. By the 1950s, 40 percent of the black population lived in the North, where they faced a completely different kind of racial discrimination.

Two Kinds of Discrimination

There are two kinds of discrimination. Legal discrimination—known as **de jure discrimination**—involves laws that explicitly deny civil rights. By the time the civil rights movement ended, around 1970, Americans had ended de jure discrimination—an enormous achievement.

A second kind of discrimination—known as "in fact" or **de facto discrimination**—exists without explicit laws and is more subtly embedded in society. De facto discrimination is much harder to address. An essential civil rights question is whether de facto restrictions still exist today—and, if so, how much.

Great Migration: The vast movement of African Americans from the rural South to the urban North between 1920 and 1950.

De jure discrimination: Discrimination established by laws.

De facto discrimination: More subtle forms of discrimination that exist without a legal basis.

The Civil Rights Campaign Begins

In 1909, black leaders formed the **National Association for the Advancement of Colored People, or NAACP,** and began fighting segregation. In 1941 they finally won the first executive order on race since Reconstruction. President Franklin Roosevelt signed an order barring racial discrimination by defense contractors and created the Fair Employment Practices Committee to ensure compliance. What pushed Roosevelt to act? Black leaders, led by A. Philip Randolph, threatened a massive protest march on Washington just as the United States was gearing up to fight the racist Nazi regime in World War II. In 1948, Harry Truman desegregated the armed forces, making the military the first racially integrated institution in the United States.

The Courts

The NAACP also went to court and chipped away at Jim Crow laws enforcing segregation. In 1944 the Supreme Court struck down the all-white Democratic primary; the Court rejected the idea that a political party could discriminate.[11] Just nine years earlier, the Court had unanimously upheld an all-white primary. Between the two decisions, President Franklin Roosevelt appointed eight new justices to the nine-person Supreme Court, changing the outlook of the Court toward race (and many other matters). The Court struck down various forms of segregation—on interstate buses, law schools, graduate schools—and then took a monumental step.[12]

In May 1954, in ***Brown v. Board of Education***, the Court ruled that segregated schools violated the equal protection clause of the Fourteenth Amendment.

National Association for the Advancement of Colored People, or NAACP: A civil rights organization formed in 1906 and dedicated to racial equality.

Brown v. Board of Education: The landmark Supreme Court case that struck down segregated schools as unconstitutional.

● *"Separate but equal" for George McLaurin meant a desk in the hallway. McLaurin, who was pursuing his PhD at the University of Oklahoma, sued, and the Supreme Court ruled against segregated classes in graduate school.*

In public education, ruled the court, "the doctrine of separate but equal has no place." Separate facilities were inherently unequal.

The media presented *Brown* as a momentous decision. The follow-up to the ruling, however, was less dramatic: almost nothing changed. The Court did not impose a strong timetable or implementation plan. National officials did little to support *Brown*, and state and local leaders did much to oppose it. A decade after *Brown*, less than 1 percent of the schools in the South had been desegregated.

Where desegregation did occur, as in Little Rock, Arkansas, the results could be explosive. The day before schools opened in 1957, Governor Orville Faubus came out against the desegregation of Little Rock's Central High School. The Arkansas National Guard turned away the nine high school students who tried to enter the school the next day.

The governor backed off in the face of a court order. When the students came back two weeks later, the National Guard had been replaced by what the *New York Times* called "a mob of belligerent, shrieking hysterical demonstrators" shouting racial epithets. President Dwight Eisenhower, a Republican, reluctantly dispatched the 101st Airborne to enforce the court order and desegregate Central High.

Elected officials throughout the South could not help but notice that Governor Faubus had become a local white hero and was returned to office for an unprecedented third term. Many white politicians reacted by staunchly supporting segregation. Without political support, even a major court decision like *Brown v. Board of Education* would neither crack segregation nor integrate the schools.

● *Elizabeth Eckford, one of nine black teens who integrated Little Rock High School in 1957, had to brave a gauntlet of screaming whites.*

The Civil Rights Movement

What defeated segregation was not the Supreme Court or the paratroopers from the 101st Airborne, but ordinary American people who rose up and seized the moment in an organized movement that began in Montgomery, Alabama, on a December afternoon in 1955.

Rosa Parks was riding the bus home. The white section filled up and, when a white man got on board, the driver called out that he needed another row. Everyone in the first black row was expected to get up and move so the white man could sit down—segregation meant that people from different races could not sit in the same row. Parks refused and was arrested. The local NAACP called a boycott of the Montgomery bus lines and put twenty-six-year-old Martin Luther King Jr. in charge.

It took a more than a year and direct intervention by the Supreme Court to desegregate the buses in Montgomery. But the pattern was set: the Court had opened the legal door. More and more people began to protest in more and more ways. In February 1960, four black college students from North Carolina A&T University sat at a white lunch counter and inspired a tactic that spread throughout the South. Within a year, seventy thousand people—black and white—had sat at segregated counters while onlookers jeered, poured ketchup and mustard on the sitters, and held cigarette lighters to the women's hair. From lunch counters, the sit-ins spread to movie theaters, parks, pools, art galleries, libraries, and churches.

Freedom Riders: Black and white activists who rode buses together to protest segregation on interstate bus lines.

In 1961, activists came up with a new tactic. Groups of young people rented Greyhound buses as **Freedom Riders** to protest segregated interstate bus lines and terminals. The first bus was pursued by a "citizens' posse" and set ablaze. Angry men tried to hold the doors of the burning bus shut, and the students narrowly escaped—only to get a vicious beating with bats and pipes.

Despite the protests, segregation *still* did not yield. The stalemate was finally broken by a civil rights campaign in Birmingham, Alabama. Marchers, including schoolchildren, tumbled out of churches and walked, singing and clapping, into appalling police violence. Fire hoses sent marchers sprawling, police dogs snapped and bit. Television flashed the images around the world.

● *The civil rights movement took courage. Here, protesters sitting at a whites-only lunch counter have been taunted and doused with ketchup . . .*

● *. . . and Freedom Riders escaped the burning bus, although some were beaten bloody.*

WOULD YOU HAVE PROTESTED?

Look at the images on these pages—young people at a sit-in are humiliated, those on a Freedom Bus almost burned and then beaten. College students carried out the early sit-ins and Freedom Rides like those depicted here. The question for you to think about—one we often ask ourselves—is simple: *If you were in college between 1960 and 1962, would you have taken part?* It would have taken conviction, courage, and (for most students) a willingness to ignore parents horrified by the risks.

What would you have done? Explain why.

The police overreaction appalled the nation. Americans who had mildly supported civil rights became incensed.

The Democratic Party was divided between northern liberals and southern segregationists, and the Kennedy administration did not want to lose southern support. The images from Birmingham forced the issue, and the administration finally submitted strong civil rights legislation to Congress.

Congress and the Civil Rights Act

Despite the protests, Congress blocked civil rights legislation—as it had done many times in the past. This time, however, activists prevailed. In May and June 1963, a great wave of protests followed Birmingham. Media stories about demonstrations, violence, and arrests fostered a sense of crisis. The **1963 March on Washington** marked the high point of the peaceful protest movement; the entire nation watched Martin Luther King Jr. put aside his prepared text and declare, "I have a dream." Hope filtered through the crisis and the result was enough to move a civil rights bill through the House of Representatives.

In November 1963, President Kennedy was assassinated, and the Civil Rights Act became, as President Lyndon Johnson would put it, a martyr's cause. The **Civil Rights Act of 1964** was powerful legislation. It forbade state and local governments from denying access to public facilities on the basis of race, color, or national origin. The law prohibited employers from discriminating on the basis of race, color, religion, sex, or national origin. It barred discrimination in private motels, hotels, theaters, and other public accommodations. There would be no more black Thursdays at city zoos. Congress slipped past the limits imposed by the 1883 Civil Rights Cases (Congress could not force private businesses to desegregate) by relying on its constitutional authority over interstate commerce.

Opponents sued, claiming that private businesses like motels should be free to choose their own patrons; the Supreme Court ruled that since motels served people from other states, Congress could use its power over interstate commerce to stop the owners from discriminating. Ollie's Barbecue did not have patrons from other states. However, the Court ruled that because it

see for yourself 5.2

Go online to see Martin Luther King's "I Have a Dream" speech.

1963 March on Washington: A massive rally for civil rights highlighted by Martin Luther King's "I Have a Dream" speech.

Civil Rights Act of 1964: Landmark legislation that forbade discrimination on the basis of race, sex, religion, or national origin.

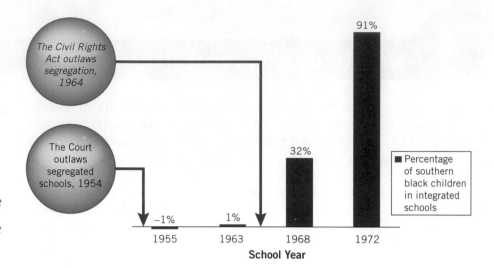

● **FIGURE 5.2** *The Civil Rights Act of 1964—rather than the* Brown v. Board of Education *Supreme Court decision in 1954—led to rapid integration of southern schools.*

received supplies through interstate commerce, it too fell under congressional jurisdiction. The era when traveling African Americans had to sleep in their cars was finally over.[13]

The Civil Rights Act also empowered the federal government to withhold funds from segregated schools. In less than a decade the number of southern schoolchildren in integrated schools jumped from almost none to more than 90 percent (see Figure 5.2). Today, court decisions on civil rights continue to cite this blockbuster legislation.

The following year Congress passed the Voting Rights Act of 1965. This law protected the right to vote, struck down voter-suppression tactics like the literacy test, and empowered the attorney general and the U.S. District Court of Washington, D.C., to weigh any voting change in suspect areas for its potentially discriminatory effect. The legislation effectively secured the Fifteenth Amendment guaranteeing the right to vote. African Americans surged to the ballot boxes, and following behind black voters came black elected officials (see Table 5.1). Over time, the number of elected black officials skyrocketed—increasing 129-fold in forty years. However, African Americans, who comprise more than 12 percent of the American population, still make up only about 2 percent of all elected officials.

TABLE 5.1 Total Number of Black Elected Officials

	1964	1970	1980	1990	2008
Mayors	0	81	205	314	641
Members of Congress	5	9	19	19	42
Total black elected officials in the United States	70	1,469	4,914	7,370	9,040

- The NAACP won a series of cases against segregation, culminating in *Brown v. Board of Education*; however, implementation proved difficult.

- In the early 1960s, ordinary men, women, and children—black and white—organized in mass movements to turn the legal promise of the *Brown* decision into a practical reality. As the images from marches became more dramatic, surging public opinion pushed Congress to pass the Civil Rights Act of 1964 and the Voting Rights Act of 1965.

- Taken together, these institutional changes ended de jure segregation in the United States.

- The black movement set the model for future civil rights campaigns by many other groups.

Affirmative action: Direct, positive steps to recruit members of previously underrepresented groups into schools, colleges, and jobs; sometimes involves setting aside positions (known as quotas).

● The Achievements of the Civil Rights Era

After the successful challenge to de jure segregation, civil rights reformers faced the perplexing problems of subtle, de facto discrimination. Protesters can kneel in front of a segregated church, but how do they challenge dead-end jobs and shabby neighborhoods? Several policies have attempted to address de facto discrimination.

Affirmative Action in the Workplace

In the 1960s and 1970s, a new approach emerged to assist groups that had faced discrimination. **Affirmative action** means taking direct, positive steps to increase the representation (especially in schools and workplaces) of groups that have faced discrimination in the past.

The American ideal of *equality of opportunity* involves giving every individual a fair chance at achieving success if they are talented and hardworking. What should the nation do to give African Americans a fair chance to achieve the American dream after three hundred years of poverty, political exclusion, and poor education? Affirmative action and other remedies for past discrimination appeared to guarantee *equality of outcome*: reserving jobs or opportunities for individuals based on their race or gender. Is this necessary to right past wrongs? If so, for how long? And are these remedies—extended to minorities and women—unfair to white men?

Affirmative action eventually created a backlash from people who failed to get jobs despite being qualified, and the

● *Years of resistance to basic civil rights eventually radicalized many African Americans. The frustration burst into urban riots—also known as urban insurrections—between 1965 and 1968.*

Supreme Court began to narrow its use. In 1986, the Court warned that such programs could be used only in cases of "severe discrimination" and should not "trammel the interests of white employees."[14] By 1995, after almost twenty-five years of affirmative action programs, a more conservative Court rejected the entire idea of explicitly setting aside places for racial groups.[15]

In 2009, the New Haven, Connecticut, fire department offered a written exam for promotions. The top scorers on the test were all white. If the city accepted the test results, black and Hispanic firefighters could sue under **disproportionate impact**—arguing that the test created "headwinds" unrelated to fighting fires. When New Haven threw out the results, white firefighters who had scored well on the test sued for the promotions and the Court agreed. The case is so difficult because both sides have a good argument: The New Haven fire department needs diverse leadership, but ignoring the test results seems unfair to the individuals who did well.

Disproportionate impact: The effect some policies have of discriminating, even if discrimination is not consciously intended.

Affirmative Action in Education

Civil rights advocates believed that if children from different races and ethnicities went to school together, they would shed the prejudices that marked their parents and grandparents. The problem, however, was that since many children lived in single-race neighborhoods, local schools would inevitably be segregated. One solution, known as **school busing**, aimed to achieve racial integration by driving students to other neighborhoods. The policy became especially controversial when courts applied it to cities that had never experienced Jim Crow segregation—like Denver and Boston. Busing declined after the 1980s, but observers still disagree about whether the busing effort was a noble and often successful experiment or whether it was a disastrous mistake that whipped up racial animosity.

School busing: An effort to integrate public schools by mixing students from different neighborhoods.

Another controversy arose over affirmative action programs that reserved places in universities for members of minority groups. Many schools sought to make up for past discrimination and, at the same time, enhance diversity across their student body. These quotas, too, created a backlash.

One of the defining education cases focused on the medical school at the University of California at Davis, which held sixteen places in its entering class of one hundred for members of minority or economically disadvantaged groups. Allan Bakke, a white man who had been rejected by the medical school, sued, arguing that his academic scores were higher than the scores of minority applicants who had been accepted. In a 5–4 decision, *University of California v. Bakke* (1978), the Supreme Court ruled in favor of Bakke; setting a quota, as the university had done, violated the equal protection guarantee of the Fourteenth Amendment. Although the Court barred racial quotas, it accepted the use of race as a "plus" factor in the admissions process.[16] But how should the plus factor work? The Court has not yet resolved the issue.

The Court has painfully picked its way through the minefield of equal opportunity. Crucial questions abound: How does a nation make up for past discrimination? How much is owed to people who have been terribly mistreated for generations? How long should preferential programs last? And what about people who feel they are losing out today because of efforts to address past injustice?

HIGHER EDUCATION AND AFFIRMATIVE ACTION

One of the most difficult problems in politics is how to make up for past injustice. What do we, as a society, owe to groups who have faced violence and discrimination for many generations? Consider the topic of higher education—the path to success in contemporary society. Which of the following positions would you support?

I favor affirmative action *for as long as it takes*. People who have faced many years of discrimination deserve affirmative action in education for as long as it takes them to catch up to the rest of society.

I favor affirmative action *with an end in sight*. People who have faced discrimination should get affirmative action in higher education for a fixed period. But, how long should that period run? *In Grutter v. Bollinger* (2003), the Supreme Court implied the correct period should last, roughly, three generations, or sixty years (1965–2025). Do you agree? If not, how much time you would allow?

I favor affirmative action only *if it doesn't set back others*. People who have faced discrimination should get special educational opportunities if and only if it does not harm other people's chances. Can you think of some ways to do this?

I am against affirmative action if discrimination has ended. People who have faced discrimination should not get any special treatment. Once the discrimination ends, they must compete like everyone else. But: How do you measure the end of discrimination? By the passage of a law or by practice in society?

Voting Rights Today

Protesters march for voting rights. Lawsuits charge racial discrimination at the polls. Protesters gather outside the Supreme Court as the justices weigh key provisions of the Voting Rights Act of 1965. The 1960s? No, 2013.

Widespread accusations of new voting restrictions surfaced in the wake of Barack Obama's election in 2008. By 2012, when Obama ran for re-election, minority groups' right to vote was a prominent story. Officials in several states, warning against voter fraud, passed laws requiring more elaborate forms of voter ID, eliminating same-day voter registration and early voting, and other restrictions that disproportionately affect black, Latino, and young voters—all groups that tend to vote Democratic. Then in 2013, the Court struck down the act's central requirement—that southern states where Jim Crow restrictions had effectively denied African Americans the vote were required to clear voting-rights changes with the federal Justice Department.

In short, the civil rights movement set off an extraordinary effort to overcome three hundred years of racial injustice. The United States developed programs in workplaces, in unions, and on every level of the education system.

The effort, as we shall see in the next sections, went beyond race and aided many other groups as well. But did the nation do enough to give every member of society a genuine opportunity to succeed? Is America, as Justice Roberts has declared, truly "changed?" The debate continues.

Where Are We Now?

How close has the United States come to achieving racial equality? A few key indicators measure how the civil rights movement changed America—and how far we still have to go.

The progress is undeniable. African Americans once faced violence, segregation, poverty, and exclusion at every turn. Fifty years ago there were no black mayors in the United States. There were only five black members of Congress. Most professions were closed to blacks. It was an enormous cultural milestone when the Brooklyn Dodgers signed Jackie Robinson to play major league baseball (to the taunts and curses of both fans and players). Shops, parks, pools, restaurants, and hotels were all segregated. Many states forbade blacks and whites to marry. Today, these are all just painful memories from long ago. There are more than five hundred black mayors. A black man became president with a larger percentage of the vote than any Democratic candidate in forty-four years; then he became the first Democrat to win reelection with a majority of the vote since 1936. The progress toward racial justice in America has been astonishing. In many ways, the United States has lived up to its founding principles.

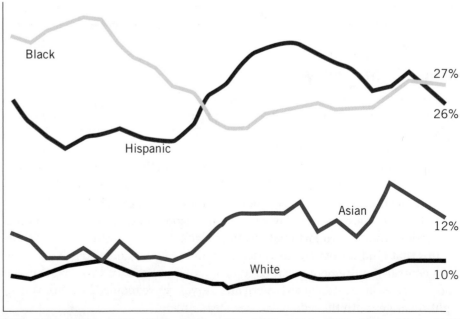

● FIGURE 5.3 *Percentage of people in poverty, by race. (U.S. Census)*

TABLE 5.2 Amazing Progress or Shocking Disparity?

YEAR	LIFE EXPECTANCY (YEARS) AT BIRTH, BY RACE			
	TOTAL	WHITE	BLACK	DIFFERENCE
1935	61.7	62.9	53.1	9.8
1970	70.8	71.7	64.1	7.6
1980	73.7	74.4	68.1	6.3
1990	75.4	76.1	69.1	7
2000	76.8	77.3	71.8	5.5
2010	78.7	79	75.1	3.9

Source: U.S. National Center for Health Statistics, "Deaths: Final Data for 2006," National Vital Statistics Reports (NVSR), April 17, 2009.

Major issues remain, however. Health is the most basic indicator of social equality. In 1935, large differences separated black and white life expectancy: whites lived 9.8 years, or 15 percent, longer than African Americans. The most recent numbers reduce the gap to 3.9 years, or 5 percent. What do you think? Is this enormous progress? Still a distressing disparity? Or perhaps both?

Income is another important metric of equality. In 1959, just before the sit-ins began, 55 percent of African Americans lived in poverty. By 1979, the poverty rate among blacks was 31 percent, and today it is 27.4 percent (see Figure 5.3). Few groups anywhere in history have experienced such a rapid rise out of poverty as African Americans did between 1959 and 1980. Yet, for the entire half-century, the black poverty rate has remained at three times the white poverty rate. Again, we can read the numbers as extraordinary progress or a need for greater action (see Table 5.2).

THE BOTTOM LINE

- To make up for past discrimination, legislatures and courts turned to affirmative action in the 1960s and 1970s. Employers and schools that had previously excluded African Americans now set aside places for them.

- The courts initially sponsored affirmative action programs but are increasingly skeptical of any race-based categories, including those designed to ameliorate past injustice.

- Did the nation do enough to give every member of society a genuine opportunity to succeed? By many measures, the United States has made extraordinary progress toward racial justice. By other measures, the United States still has a long way to go.

● Gender

In the early nineteenth century, an American woman had no political rights. She could not vote, serve on a jury, or enter into a contract after marriage. The **laws of coverture**, adopted from English common law, meant that her political rights and duties all operated through her husband. He controlled her property, her wages, and even her body. Husband and wife are one, mused Justice Hugo Black, and "that one is the husband."[17]

Laws of coverture: An outmoded legal tradition holding that a woman's rights and duties all operate through her husband.

Suffrage

The struggle for gender rights in the United States goes back as far as the fight for racial equality, and the two battles have often been interconnected. The first American gathering for woman suffrage, the 1848 **Seneca Falls Convention**, grew directly from the abolition movement. When women joined the abolition movement they quickly grew frustrated by the barriers that confronted them. They could lecture to women but not men (because that would be "promiscuous") and they could join abolition societies but not be elected officers.[18]

In the 1870s, the women's movement gained momentum. The Women's Christian Temperance Union enrolled almost two hundred thousand women, most in small towns across America. The movement attacked alcohol as a cause of male violence against women. It championed voluntary motherhood (no more marital rape), suffrage for women, and decent wages. Two other groups focused on winning the vote. Success came first in the West, beginning with the Wyoming (1869) and Utah (1870) territories. By 1916 an effective political campaign had won full suffrage in fifteen states and partial suffrage in twenty-three others. Women voted in every state of the West and Midwest except New Mexico. The issue remained contentious, however. Four states in the North voted to reject suffrage during the 1916 presidential election, and the South remained strongly opposed for fear that women would oppose segregation (see Figure 5.4).

During World War I, women took on new roles while men went overseas. Led by Alice Paul and the National American Woman Suffrage Association, women stepped up political pressure for a national suffrage amendment. The group continued agitating during World War I—Paul herself was jailed—and eventually, President Woodrow Wilson put aside his condescension and supported suffrage as a "wartime measure." The Nineteenth Amendment cleared Congress, over stiff opposition in the Senate, in 1919 and was ratified by the states in 1920.

Although they had secured suffrage, women were slow to win political office, especially higher offices (see Figure 5.5).

Seneca Falls Convention: A convention dedicated to women's rights held in July 1848.

The Civil Rights Act of 1964

The breakthrough in the struggle for gender rights slipped into the Civil Rights Act of 1964. This landmark law, as we have seen, was designed to bar racial discrimination. Congressman Howard Smith, a segregationist from Virginia,

● **FIGURE 5.4** *Before the Nineteenth Amendment, women had full voting rights in the West, limited rights in the Midwest, and none in the South and East. For women, winning the vote took a difficult political campaign that lasted more than 80 years.*

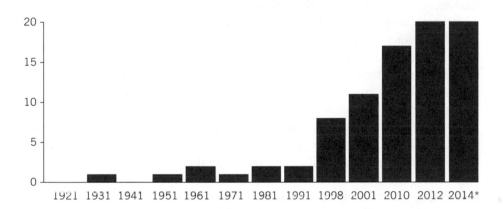

● **FIGURE 5.5** *Number of women in the U.S. Senate (*Projected as of November 6, 2014).*

proposed adding a single word—"sex"—to the legislation with the hopes of making a mockery of the entire legislation and killing the bill. The tactic did not work and the Civil Rights Act passed, barring discrimination based on "race, color, religion, *sex* and national origin."

At the time, no one predicted that the gender provision in the Civil Rights Act would have the same far-reaching consequences for gender rights as *Brown v. Board of Education* had for African Americans—but it did. Like the Supreme Court decisions on race, the Civil Rights Act merely opened the door to gender change. The women's movement had to seize the opportunity.

At first, officials ignored the gender provision. The **Equal Employment Opportunity Commission** (**EEOC**), charged with monitoring compliance to the Civil Rights Act, considered it a "mischievous joke perpetrated on the floor of the House of Representatives." In response, a network of women organized the **National Organization for Women** (**NOW**), drawing directly on the tactics of the civil rights campaign—demonstrations, rallies, lobbying, and litigation.

Equal Employment Opportunity Commission (EEOC): Federal law enforcement agency charged with monitoring compliance to the Civil Rights Act.

National Organization for Women (NOW): An organization formed to take action for women's equality.

Congress and the EEOC began to pay attention. For example, in 1972, Congress passed Federal Education Amendments that denied federal funds for programs that discriminated against women (Title VI) and that required equal athletic opportunities for men and women (Title IX). Next time you watch a women's basketball championship, thank the Civil Rights Act for making the sport what it is today.

The Courts

The women's movement also echoed black civil rights leaders in targeting the courts. Led by Ruth Bader Ginsburg (now a Supreme Court justice), advocates challenged discriminatory state laws, case by case. Because gender was a *nonsuspect category*, the courts upheld any state law as long as it had some "rational connection to a legitimate state purpose." In a series of cases, culminating in *Craig v. Boren* in 1976, the Court lifted gender into a new category of *heightened scrutiny*—not as rigorous a test as the scrutiny the courts give racial classifications, but a more rigorous test than that applied to other social groups. Ironically, the Court created the category—a major victory for women's rights—when men challenged an Oklahoma statute that set the drinking age for beer at eighteen for women and twenty-one for men.

The courts also applied the prohibition on gender discrimination in the Civil Rights Act to sexual harassment. In 1998, the Supreme Court expanded the protection by ruling that an employee did not have to prove a specific instance of sexual harassment if there was a hostile workplace environment—this might include sexual advances, lewd comments, or general attitudes. The Court ruled that even if employers were not aware of specific instances of harassment, they remained liable for the general culture of the workplace.

Women's advocates raised the issue of differential pay more than a century ago. Today, women working full time earn, on average, three-fourths as much as men—although the exact amount of the disparity is hotly disputed and varies from 75 percent to 95 percent, depending on the methodology and assumptions. In a famous case, Lilly Ledbetter sued after a nineteen-year career as a supervisor with Goodyear Tire Company because she had been paid less than men in the same position. A jury found Goodyear guilty of pay discrimination, but the Supreme Court reversed the judgment by a 5–4 vote. The majority ruled that Ledbetter should have sued within 180 days after Goodyear set her pay—long before she knew about the salary differential. In 2009, President Obama signed equal-pay legislation—the Lily Ledbetter Act—that permits an employee to sue 180 days from her last paycheck (resetting the clock each time she gets a lower paycheck). It was the first act that Obama signed into law.[19]

Recent Supreme Court decisions, however, have made it more difficult to sue businesses for discrimination. In a major case, decided in 2011, the court turned down a **class action** suit brought against Walmart. The suit alleged that the company systematically discriminated against women by offering them less pay and fewer promotions. The Supreme Court ruled against the plaintiffs (the women who were suing). The Court argued that simply showing that women received less pay was not enough to prove discrimination. Rather,

Class action: A lawsuit filed on behalf of an entire category of individuals, such as all people in public housing in a state, or all the female managers of a large company.

TABLE 5.3 Women CEOs of Fortune 500 Companies: Steady Progress or a Long Way to Go?

YEAR	2000	2001	2002	2003	2004	2005	2006	2008	2010	2012	2014
Women CEOs	3	5	10	8	6	9	11	12	15	18	23

Source: Knowledge Center, "Women CEO's of the Fortune 1000" (January 15, 2014).

the plaintiffs needed to demonstrate a specific company-wide policy that set lower wages for all the women involved in the class action.

Progress—But How Much?

There had never been a woman Supreme Court justice until Ronald Reagan named Sandra Day O'Connor in 1981; today, three of the nine justices are women. There had never been a female president of an Ivy League university before 1990; twenty years later, four of the eight schools had women at the helm. There had never been a woman CEO of a Fortune 500 company until 1972. In 2000, the number of women CEOs at Fortune 500 companies had inched to three; by 2014, it had risen to twenty-three—the highest number of female CEOs in American history but a still not very inspiring 4.6 percent of America's largest companies (see Table 5.3). Once again, American society has witnessed extraordinary progress, but still has a long way to go to reach gender equality.

Reproductive Politics

Reproductive control may have introduced the greatest change in gender rights—and gender politics. When birth control pills went on the market in 1960, they seemed revolutionary. Controlling pregnancy made professional careers easier to manage. Reproductive rights became far more controversial when the Supreme Court ruled, in *Roe v. Wade* (1973), that laws banning abortion violated a woman's right to privacy.

The fierce politics of abortion spilled into other areas of gender politics. Feminists had introduced an **Equal Rights Amendment (ERA)** in Congress every year between 1924 and 1972. The amendment was simple: "Equality of rights under the law shall not be denied . . . on account of sex." By 1972 it had become uncontroversial and Congress passed it by lopsided margins (354–23 in the House, 84–8 in the Senate). Five years later, the ERA was just three states short of ratification (thirty-eight states were needed to ratify an amendment). Then, a Republican activist from Florida named Phyllis Schlafly organized the STOP ERA movement. Schlafly argued that American women would lose their special rights and privileges—like the right to alimony and their exemption from the military draft. More important, she argued, the ERA threatened traditional family life. By **reframing the issue**, Schlafly stopped the Equal Rights Amendment in its tracks.

Equal Rights Amendment: An amendment, originally drafted by Alice Paul in 1923, passed by Congress in 1972, and ratified by thirty-five states, that declared: "Equality of rights . . . shall not be denied or abridged . . . on account of sex."

Reframe the issue: To redefine the popular perception of an issue; to show it in a new light with a new set of costs or benefits.

THE BOTTOM LINE

- In nineteenth-century law, women's political rights operated through their husbands. When women organized to win rights, they met with ridicule and violence.

- Women first won voting rights in states—especially in the West and Midwest—before finally securing the Nineteenth Amendment, guaranteeing the right to vote regardless of gender.

- The Civil Rights Act of 1964 bars gender discrimination. Like the civil rights movement of the 1950s and 1960s, the women's movement organized to take advantage of legal changes. The law transformed American gender roles in political and professional life.

- Following *Roe v. Wade* (in 1973) and the Equal Rights Amendment (in the mid-1970s), gender politics became especially controversial, spilling into many other issues.

● Hispanics

Hispanics, or Latinos (we will use the words interchangeably), play a powerful and growing role in American politics and culture. Today, Hispanics are the largest and fastest-growing minority group, making up 16.5 percent of the American population.

Latinos have long faced discrimination. Latinos were already living in the Southwest—in Arizona, California, New Mexico, and parts of Colorado, Nevada, Utah, and Texas—before the United States took those lands from Mexico in 1848. As white settlers poured into the new territory, they often displaced Latino residents from their homes and farms. As the nation urbanized, Latinos were pushed into segregated schools, excluded from jobs, and barred from housing in white neighborhoods. They also faced hostility and violence. For example, after sensational newspaper headlines reported that Mexicans had beaten up a sailor (during World War II), thousands of soldiers and sailors poured through Los Angeles attacking Mexican men. The police did not intervene.

Challenging Discrimination

Latinos adapted many of the tactics of the black civil rights movement. They organized the League of United

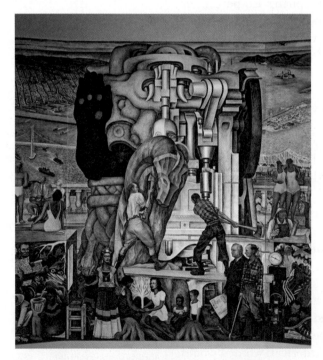

● *A detail of Diego Rivera's magical mural, Pan-American Unity. Mexican gods, dancers, revolutionaries, and workers mix with George Washington, Abraham Lincoln, Henry Ford, and Charlie Chaplin in a vibrant celebration of an America without borders.*

Latin American Citizens (LULAC) in 1929. Like the NAACP, the organization fought segregation through lawsuits. In *Mendez v. Westminster*, decided in 1947, the court struck down Latino school segregation in Orange County, California; the case was an important precursor to *Brown v. Board of Education* and involved some of the same lawyers.

During the 1960s, young Latinos launched more active protests. In 1968, high school and college students called a massive student strike that reverberated through the Southwest. They pushed LULAC and other mainstream organizations to fight more aggressively against discrimination and they challenged immigration policies that restricted movement across the Mexican border. Many young people took a slur against Mexicans, *Chicano*, and turned it into a movement they labeled **Chicanismo**—a defiant pride in their heritage and culture.

At the same time, the **United Farm Workers** (**UFW**) organized the most vulnerable population—migrant workers who picked crops up and down the West Coast. The UFW became a symbol of Latino mobilization. Throughout the 1960s and 1970s traditional organizations like LULAC, activist students, and farm workers all challenged discrimination. Their efforts prepared the entry of Latino elected officials at every level of government. Today, the central questions for Latino politics turn on immigration, language, and just how the very diverse Hispanic population might mobilize for political action.

Chicanismo: A defiant movement expressing pride in Latino origins and culture in the face of discrimination.

United Farm Workers: An influential union representing migrant farm workers in the West.

The Politics of Immigration

Despite Hispanics' long heritage in the land, Hispanic politics is very much wrapped up with immigration. Although the United States is an immigrant nation, the door to foreigners has historically swung from wide open to shut tight. Since 1965, the United States has experienced an era of high immigration—today one in eight American residents was born abroad.

Immigrants always trigger the same fears: They will undermine American values and culture; they will remain loyal to their own languages, their home countries, and their supposedly un-American ideas; they will take away jobs. As long ago as 1752, Benjamin Franklin worried that there were so many Germans in Philadelphia, "instead of them learning our language, we must learn theirs or live as in a foreign country." Today, some observers have grown alarmed about the *disuniting* of the United States. The issue has focused especially on Hispanic Americans because they are, by far, the largest immigrant group.

Immigration groups fall into three different categories with very different legal claims on civil rights.

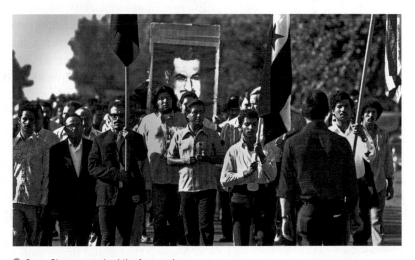

● *Cesar Chavez organized the farm workers.*

1. Those who were born in the United States or have become American citizens (roughly 60 percent of the Latino population) claim the same rights as any citizen. They are in the same protected legal category as African Americans. Any law that singles them out is "suspect" and subject to strict scrutiny by the courts.

2. Foreigners who have not become citizens fall into a second category known as resident aliens. They may work in the United States, they pay taxes, but they cannot enjoy the benefits of citizenship. Aliens may not vote, and many government programs explicitly exclude them. Legislation in 1996, for example, barred aliens from receiving a range of welfare benefits.

3. Some immigrants are unregistered—they are not legal residents of the United States. Many arrived on a temporary visa, got a job, settled down, and simply remained when their legal time in the country expired. Others crossed the borders illegally (more than 350,000 people were caught doing so in 2013, down from 1.64 million in 1999). Undocumented aliens have no constitutional rights and, when caught, are liable to immediate deportation. Those who marry an American become eligible for a green card—that is, they can become resident aliens; and anyone born in the United States, even if their parents are undocumented, is a citizen.

The debate over the rights of illegal aliens is intense and often angry. Some argue that undocumented immigrants are part of the American economy and society. They live in fear of jail and deportation. As a result, they are wary of going to a hospital, visiting their children's school, or reporting crimes against them. American policy, they argue, should offer undocumented people a path to legal status. Opponents of this idea respond that the undocumented are breaking the law and should not be rewarded for unlawful behavior. They urge vigorous prosecution of undocumented aliens and all those who hire or help them.

Even Hispanic citizens whose families have lived on American soil for many generations consider immigration a defining political issue. It has thrust their community into controversy. It leads police to single out Latinos, a practice known as **racial profiling**. Hispanic immigration is a major contributor to the fundamental American question, *Who are we?*

In 2012, President Obama signed an executive order—bypassing a deadlocked Congress—that gave young undocumented aliens temporary work permits and removed the threat of deportation. Tens of thousands lined up to apply for the program the day it went into effect. In 2014, the Senate passed immigration reform but the issue of undocumented aliens sunk the effort in the House. The debate—and the stalemate—continues.

The Controversy over Language

Spanish language is another major issue. In 1974, the Supreme Court ruled in *Lau v. Nichols* that equal protection required schools to assist students whose

Racial profiling: A law enforcement practice of singling out people on the basis of physical features such as race or ethnicity.

primary language was not English. The Court did not specify a remedy, but many school districts established bilingual education programs—eventually generating a backlash. Opponents argue that bilingual education divides the community, undermines traditional American culture, and disadvantages students who fail to learn English.

Many Latinos support English-language education—they are eager to boost their children toward achieving the American dream. At the same time, they worry that behind the English-only movement lies prejudice against the Spanish-speaking population. Won't their children be disadvantaged if no Spanish at all is allowed in the schools? Won't Spanish speakers face problems if all ballots must be printed only in English?

Political Mobilization

Hispanic Americans face many other issues and challenges. More than one in five live below the poverty line—two and a half times the rate for non-Hispanic whites. They are less likely to have health insurance than any major population group.[20]

One way to address these concerns is through politics. Latinos face both barriers and advantages in the political arena. The biggest barrier lies in the nature of the Hispanic community itself. In fact, *Hispanic* is a misnomer. Hispanic people come from many different places, each with its own interests and concerns. Figure 5.6 shows the diversity of the Latino community.

● The owner of Geno's Steaks in Philadelphia announces that people should speak English. This is a hot issue and always has been. More than 250 years earlier, Benjamin Franklin complained that all he heard on the streets of Philadelphia was German. Franklin later changed his mind and cheered the immigrants. No word about whether the people at Geno's have changed their minds too.

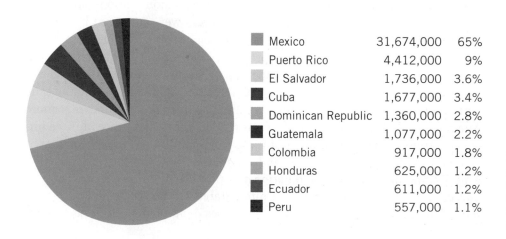

■	Mexico	31,674,000	65%
▫	Puerto Rico	4,412,000	9%
▫	El Salvador	1,736,000	3.6%
■	Cuba	1,677,000	3.4%
▪	Dominican Republic	1,360,000	2.8%
■	Guatemala	1,077,000	2.2%
▫	Colombia	917,000	1.8%
▪	Honduras	625,000	1.2%
▪	Ecuador	611,000	1.2%
■	Peru	557,000	1.1%

● **FIGURE 5.6** *Countries of origin—Latinos in America. Most of the Latinos who live in the United States were born here. This figure shows their national heritage. (U.S. Census)*

For Mexican Americans, concentrated in the Southwest, the politics of immigration looms large. In contrast, Puerto Ricans, the second-largest Hispanic population, are American citizens by birth; immigration is less relevant to them. Their focus is on economics and, especially in the Northeast, on politics. Cuban Americans offer still another contrast. They have high average incomes and generally do not share the same political concerns as Mexican Americans or Puerto Ricans. In fact, Cuban Americans traditionally stand apart from most Hispanic groups by voting Republican. Salvadorans, now the third-largest Latino group, face the problems of more recent immigrants—poverty, social integration, and community building. Dominicans, in turn, introduce a slightly different spectrum of political concerns. When we talk of Hispanics we are using shorthand that, although sometimes useful, obscures a great many differences.

Is there a common political denominator across this diverse population? Today, a pan-Latino movement seeks to find common ground and mobilize voters around issues that transcend any one country or group. Popular DJs on Spanish radio champion unity. The Hispanic caucus in Congress aims to speak for Hispanic voters; in 2014, the caucus stood at a record number, with twenty-eight in the House (5.4 percent of the total membership) and three in the Senate. Some Hispanics worry that a pan-Latino construction may lead to the loss of national identity and pride—they point out that you don't see Irish and Italian Americans talking about pan-European heritage. Others respond that finding common cause is an important step to political influence.

Shared political influence, if Latinos seek to exercise it, figures to be formidable: The Hispanic population has grown three times faster than the general population in the past two decades. Latino leaders note that Mexican American voters moved California decisively into the Democratic column in the past fifteen years. They may very well do the same for swing states from Colorado to Florida if the Republican Party does not find a way to reach out and include them.

In 2006, when the Republican-led Congress proposed tough new legislation focused on undocumented aliens, massive demonstrations sprang up around the United States. Even veteran observers were surprised by the size and energy of the gatherings, which echoed the energy and optimism of the civil rights era. In the past, Latino protesters had waved Mexican flags and symbols. This time, they marched under a sea of American flags. Researchers, who were undertaking a major survey of Hispanic Americans during the time period, discovered that the protests made Hispanics feel significantly more American.[21] The surge in demonstrations reflects the convergence of three important trends: the rapid growth of the Latino population, a sense of shared identity within that population, and an increasing identification with the American homeland. This combination may prove to be one of the most important political developments for the United States. In the 2012 election, 71 percent of the growing Hispanic vote went to President Obama. Both parties are scrambling to appeal to Hispanic voters. The politics of immigration has helped to define American history. It may define its future as well, given Hispanics' potential to reshape American politics.

THE BOTTOM LINE

- Latinos are the largest immigrant group and one of the fastest-growing populations in the United States today.

- Latinos are a diverse people with many different national identities, histories, cultures, and concerns.

- A key political question is whether Latinos will mobilize around shared interests and concerns. If they do, they will become an even more formidable political force.

Asian Americans

Asian Americans are the third-largest minority in the United States—after blacks and Hispanics. Unlike Latinos, they do not share a common language; unlike African Americans, they do not share a common historical experience. As you can see from Figure 5.7, Asian Americans range from Indians to Vietnamese, from Koreans to Laotians.

As a group, Asian Americans have the highest education level and the highest median personal income among American population groups. Members of this group run seven Fortune 500 companies (see Figure 5.8). However, the statistics mask as much as they reveal because Asian Americans range from Indian Americans

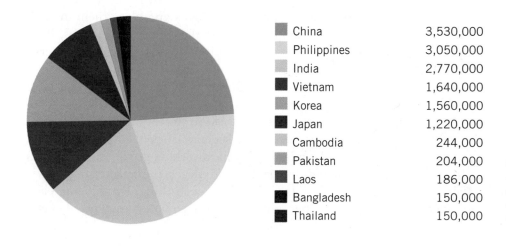

China	3,530,000
Philippines	3,050,000
India	2,770,000
Vietnam	1,640,000
Korea	1,560,000
Japan	1,220,000
Cambodia	244,000
Pakistan	204,000
Laos	186,000
Bangladesh	150,000
Thailand	150,000

● **FIGURE 5.7** *Countries of origin—Asians in America. 14.9 million residents of the United States have an Asian heritage. (U.S. Census)*

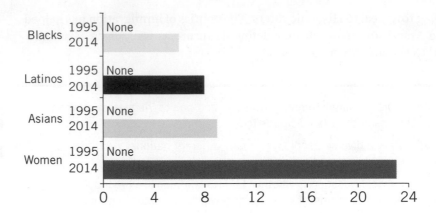

● **FIGURE 5.8** *Fortune 500 CEOs (Richard L. Zweigenhaft and G. William Domhoff,* The New CEOs; *Rowman & Littlefield Publishers, 2014, p. xiii).*

with high income and education levels to the Hmong from the mountains of Laos with income levels about one-third the U.S. average.

Asian Stereotypes

Asians have a long history of negotiating the complicated American lines between "us and them." The first Asians to arrive were Chinese railway workers in the nineteenth century. When the economy deteriorated in the 1880s, American-born workers turned against these immigrants. Congress passed the Chinese Exclusion Act (1882) barring Chinese immigrants and declaring Chinese people ineligible for citizenship. By 1917, Congress had extended the ban to "all natives of Asia including the whole of India." The California Alien Land Law of 1913 forbade "aliens ineligible for citizenship"—that is, Asian immigrants—from owning land. Each restriction came with painful stereotypes. The Chinese were excluded because, as one California congressman put it, "His ancestors have bequeathed to him the most hideous immoralities. They . . . are so shocking and horrible that their character cannot even be hinted."[22]

After the Japanese attack on Pearl Harbor in 1941, President Roosevelt ordered the army to round up Japanese Americans and place them in cold, flimsy, miserable internment camps. They lost their liberty, their jobs, their property, and their bank accounts. The Supreme Court upheld the internments. In 1968, Congress finally awarded restitution, a payment of twenty thousand dollars to the sixty thousand former inmates who were still alive (about 5 percent of the total).

Perhaps the oddest cultural twist of all is the stereotype that emerged in the 1960s. Many Asian groups—once despised and singled out for exclusion—were perceived as the "model minority": a hardworking group that makes its own way without any demands for rights or privileges. It may seem that this is a "good" stereotype, but of course there is no such thing. By reducing each individual to nothing more than a member of a group, stereotypes demean individuals and stoke social tensions.

- Asian Americans are the third-largest minority group in the United States and now comprise 5 percent of the population.

- Like other minority groups, Asian Americans have faced stereotypes and discrimination—including, today, the image of a "model minority" that, like any stereotype, is simplistic and hurtful.

- Asian Americans are a tremendously diverse group that, on the surface, appear to have little in common with one another. The key to their political effectiveness as Asian Americans lies in finding (and acting on) common interests as well as forging ties to other groups.

Native Americans

The original natives of the United States own the saddest story about rights denied. Before the Europeans arrived, 10 million American Indians lived on the land that would become the United States. The colonists brought diseases, war, and expulsion.

The Lost Way of Life

The dark side of American expansion was the policy of "Indian removal." Again and again, Indian tribes were forced from their homelands as European settlers moved in. Alexis de Tocqueville watched along the banks of the Mississippi as an immense tribe of Choctaws—tired, cold, and hungry—were forced westward. He described their journey, in the middle of winter, in the most moving passages of *Democracy in America*: "It is impossible to imagine the terrible afflictions of those forced migrations. . . . There is famine behind them, war ahead, and misery everywhere." He described the Indians' dogs who suddenly realized they were being left behind and, with a mournful howl, plunged into the icy river and struggled to swim after their masters.[23] By the time the United States stretched from coast to coast, only about 1 million of the 10 million natives remained.

Recent historians have warned us against simply seeing Native Americans as the passive victims of American westward expansion. The Indians built their own empires and, at times and in places, forced the white settlers to retreat. During King Philip's War (1675–1678), natives sorely tested the New England colonists, destroying all or parts of one in five Massachusetts villages. (The war is named after the Native American leader, Metacomet, known to the English as "King Philip.") Between 1750 and 1850, the Comanches dominated economic and military life in the Southwest and pulled white settlers, Spanish colonies, and other tribes into what amounted to an imperial system. Still, despite these victories and achievements, the final result was the eventual destruction of their way of life as they were forced to live on reservations.[24]

Indians and the Federal Government

Domestic dependent nation: Special status that grants local sovereignty to tribal nations but does not grant them full sovereignty equivalent to independent nations.

Native Americans have had an ambiguous legal relationship with the United States. In 1831, the Supreme Court ruled that Indian tribes were "**domestic dependent nations**"—essentially, a separate people but without the rights of an independent nation. Native Americans were not considered citizens, protected by the Constitution, until Congress passed the Indian Citizenship Act in 1924. Even today, their legal status remains ambiguous. Of a total population of 2 million, about 1 million Native Americans live on tribal reservations, which are independent jurisdictions not subject to state governments. These Indians are both American citizens and members of self-governing independent lands, subject to federal regulation and oversight.

The primary connection to American government is bureaucratic rather than electoral. The Bureau of Indian Affairs is responsible for Native American issues. The early placement of the bureau offered a telling symbol of the long and tortured relationship between Indians and the federal government: it was part of the Department of War. Later, Congress moved it to the Department of the Interior, whose chief purpose is to promote and protect natural resources and public lands.

Social Problems and Politics

Indians face social problems similar to many other minority groups. Indian poverty rates are approximately three times as high as the national rates and stand at 32.2 percent—well above any other American group. Life on the reservations is especially difficult, as most are in rural areas with few jobs or resources. Native American life expectancy is about 2.4 years lower than the national average—although it is considerably higher than that for blacks (see Figure 5.9). Native Americans also suffer from low education levels and high infant mortality rates—again, faring worse than whites, Hispanics, and other ethnic groups but somewhat better than African Americans.

Native Americans politics divide, roughly, into two camps. The *ethnic minority* perspective argues that Indians should mobilize for rights and equality precisely like other minority groups in the United States. Members of this perspective urge fellow Indians to engage American democracy. The alternative is the separatist *tribal movement*, which advocates

● *Red Cloud, Chief of the Oglala Sioux Tribe.*

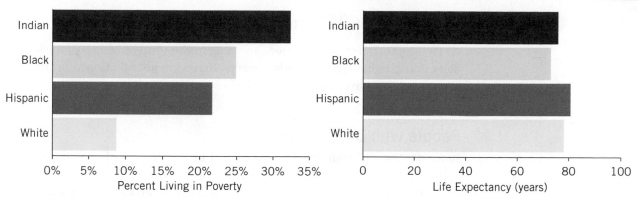

● **FIGURE 5.9** *American Indians have the highest poverty rate . . . but have life expectancy almost three years longer than black Americans. Note that Hispanics have the highest life expectancy of any group. (U.S. Census/ Pew Research)*

withdrawing from American politics and society and emphasizing Native American traditions.

Led, in some cases, by the American Indian Movement (or AIM), tribes occupied the Bureau of Indian Affairs in Washington, D.C., during the Civil Rights Era. They "captured" Alcatraz Island in San Francisco Bay. They seized control of the Village of Wounded Knee, the site of a massacre of Indians in 1890, and exchanged gunfire with federal marshals. The goal of the protests was to dramatize the plight of Native Americans—robbed of their ancestral lands, forced onto reservations, relegated to poverty.

In recent years, some tribes have used their exemption from state laws to create highly profitable gambling businesses and resorts. The Supreme Court ruled, in 1987, that because tribes are considered sovereign entities, they are free from state prohibitions on gaming. According to the gaming industry, 233 of the nation's 565 tribes run casinos. However, whether this is a positive thing—for the tribes, for the communities around them, and for the United States—is a matter of hot debate.

THE BOTTOM LINE

- Native Americans lost their way of life in the face of disease, armies, and settlers.

- The Supreme Court gave American Indians a special status: a separate people without rights. Although they retain the special status, they became U.S. citizens in 1924.

- Indians support two different strategies to the problems they face: The ethnic minority approach argues for winning political rights and benefits. The tribal movement approach prefers to withdraw and to emphasize a separate Indian society and culture.

● Groups Without Special Protection

As civil rights burst on the American scene in the 1960s and 1970s, the idea of demanding rights spread to other groups that were not mentioned in the Civil Rights Act and have never drawn special scrutiny from the courts.

People with Disabilities

Section 504: An obscure provision in an obscure rehabilitation act that required all institutions that received federal funds to accommodate people with disabilities.

Before 1970, children in wheelchairs did not go to school, and most blind children never learned how to read. People with disabilities lived outside mainstream society. The great political breakthrough came in an unnoticed provision, which liberal congressional staff slipped into an obscure bill. **Section 504** of the 1973 Rehabilitation Act borrowed language directly from the Civil Rights Act of 1964 and applied it to the disabled: "No . . . handicapped individual . . . shall, solely by reason of his handicap, be excluded from participation in, or be denied the benefits of . . . any program or activity conducted by an executive agency." Suddenly, any university receiving federal funds and all government agencies had to accommodate the handicapped. The implementation rules that put the law into effect might normally have been assigned to the obscure rehabilitation bureaucracy that traditionally dealt with handicapped issues; instead, Congress gave the task to the more powerful Office of Civil Rights in the Department of Health, Education, and Welfare.

Section 504 gave activists a political focus and they immediately made the most of it. When the department was slow to issue regulations, for example, sit-ins at the regional office pushed the matter forward. Note the dynamic: Congressional staffers dreamed up a change, giving advocates a focus for action. People with handicaps and their advocates soon mobilized for widespread change on every level of government. Local health boards, planning agencies, and school officials all began hearing from the advocates. As the groups participated in politics, they exerted more influence. The political pattern resembles African Americans after *Brown v. Board of Education* and feminists after the Civil Rights Act: Government action provided new legal rights; the group then organized and demanded further change.

Advocates went from requesting welfare benefits to demanding civil rights. The process culminated in 1990, when Congress passed the Americans with Disabilities Act (ADA). The ADA forbade companies of twenty-five or more employees from discriminating against handicapped people. It also required companies to make "reasonable accommodations" for handicapped people. Unlike racial discrimination, however, a business can avoid making accommodations if it would be expensive or inconvenient to do so. Courts constantly weigh the costs and benefits of making accommodations in specific places. What is reasonable to ask a firm or a store or a university to do to accommodate special needs? Even with this delicate balancing of costs and access, the ADA created what amounts to a massive affirmative action program for people with disabilities. Public transportation, schools, shops, and businesses all must help facilitate a normal, mainstream life for people with special needs.

Sexual Orientation

The movement for same-sex rights began with a riot. In 1969, police raided a New York City gay bar named the Stonewall Inn. Traditionally, gay people responded to such raids with shame. This time, the gay community broke the unwritten rules and erupted into violent protest. The Stonewall riot marks the moment that members of the LGBT community stopped apologizing and announced their identity. Four years later, in 1973, the American Psychiatric Association removed homosexuality from its list of mental disorders.

When activists turned to politics, their first targets were state antisodomy laws, which criminalized gay sex. Chapter 4 discussed the evolution of Court thinking that led, eventually, to *Lawrence v. Texas*, which struck down such laws.[25]

In the early 1980s, gay communities were devastated by a mysterious and deadly plague. At the time, no one knew exactly what the illness was or how it was transmitted—only that it was invariably deadly. In every city, gays organized to confront AIDS; they established links to the medical community, local governments, and social service networks. Some, under the banner of Act Up, took more radical action to prod politicians and drug companies into action. Around the country, a network of gay groups mobilized and developed political skills. The terrible disease pushed them into local politics.

American politics and culture have begun to accept same-sex civil rights. In 1993, the newly elected Bill Clinton ran into a firestorm in Congress when he promised to open the military to gay men and women. The compromise policy, known as "don't ask, don't tell," permitted gay individuals to serve as long as they kept their sexual orientation hidden. Eighteen years later, the Obama administration ended the policy—the relatively quiet reaction in Congress is a mark of changing cultural norms.

The central controversy today is same-sex marriage. As we will discuss in Chapter 6, Vermont created shock waves in 2000 by permitting civil unions—giving same-sex couples the same benefits, protections, and responsibilities as married couples. Three years later, Massachusetts became the first state to permit same-sex marriage. Other states followed. At the start of 2014, thirty-one states had amended their constitutions or passed laws to bar gay marriage. The courts, in turn, began to strike down the limits. By the end of 2014, thirty-two states and the District of Columbia were performing same-sex marriages. The barriers are falling quickly, in one state after another.

The U.S. Constitution requires states to recognize official acts of other states (under the privileges and immunities clause); however, most states refused to recognize same-sex marriages performed in other states. Congress protected the reluctant states with the Defense of Marriage Act (DOMA, passed in 1996), which defines marriage as a union between a man and a woman and permits states to reject same-sex marriages performed in other states. The Supreme Court overturned DOMA in June 2013—returning debates to the state level. What is the current rule on recognizing same-sex marriages in your state?

The past twenty years has seen a profound change in the legal status and rights of gay Americans. With each passing year they move closer to attaining full civil rights.

THE BOTTOM LINE

- People with disabilities leveraged an obscure bureaucratic rule, used it to mobilize, and eventually won the sweeping rights of the Americans with Disabilities Act. The goal is to mainstream disabled people as much as possible.

- The gay (and lesbian) movements were born in a burst of pride and anger in 1969. Gays were the first to confront AIDS—a harrowing plague (in its early years) that pushed them into politics, health provision, and community building.

- Gay, lesbian, bisexual, and transgender communities have moved from taboo to mainstream. Barriers to military service, civil unions, and marriage have eroded. Nevertheless, the conflict over marriage and childrearing remains a flash point of contemporary culture wars. Few other issues demonstrate as large an age gap.

Conclusion: By the People

The United States is a land of ideas—and arguments about ideas. No American idea is more powerful than the idea of inalienable rights; and none generates more arguments—which is clear from the many 5–4 Supreme Court votes on rulings described in this chapter.

Government actions are crucial in settling the arguments about rights. Perhaps the most important lesson to draw from this chapter is the far-reaching consequences of laws and court cases. The 1964 Civil Rights Act, for example, ended de jure segregation, focused the women's movement, changed gender relations in schools and workplaces, inspired the disabilities rights movement—and its influence goes on.

Ultimately, however, the quest for rights lies with the public. The *Brown* decision became an enormous force for change only after the civil rights movement sprang into action. Throughout this chapter, we have seen people rise up to transform the politics of rights—marching into violence in Birmingham, asserting pride in **black power**, prodding a reluctant government to implement the gender provisions in the Civil Rights Act of 1964, waving American flags over immigrant rights in Chicago, taking over a bureaucrat's office to hurry implementation of disability rules in Washington, or fighting back when the police raided a gay bar in New York City. It was the people who helped shape the meaning of the legislation and court decisions. Through their passion and their activism, the people are constantly pushing the United States to live up to its founding ideals.

Black power: A slogan that emphasized pride in black heritage and the construction of black institutions to nurture black interests. It often implied racial separation in reaction to white racism.

CHAPTER SUMMARY

● The battle for civil rights generally includes seven stages. A group seeking rights must define itself, challenge society, and change the cultural story. The contest for rights spills across federalism; the executive branch can break the ice; Congress is the key to deep social change; the courts are the final arbiters of civil rights.

● The Fourteenth Amendment contains the crucial legal rule for civil rights: "No state shall . . . deprive any person of . . . the equal protection of the laws."

● A great mass movement rose up in which ordinary men, women, and children turned the legal promise of the *Brown v. Board of Education* decision into a practical reality. Protests eventually led to the Civil Rights Act of 1964 and the Voting Rights Act of 1965. The black civil rights movement set the model for future civil rights campaigns by many other groups.

● To make up for past discrimination, legislatures and courts turned to affirmative action in the 1960s and 1970s. The courts, and the public, have become increasingly skeptical of these programs.

● Women first won voting rights in the states—across the West—before finally securing the Nineteenth Amendment, guaranteeing the right to vote regardless of gender.

● The Civil Rights Act of 1964 bars gender discrimination. The women's movement organized to take advantage of the legal changes. The results transformed American gender roles in political and professional life.

● Following *Roe v. Wade* (in 1973) and the Equal Rights Amendment (in the mid-1970s), gender politics became especially controversial.

● Latinos are the largest immigrant group and one of the fastest-growing populations in the United States today. Latinos are a diverse people with many different national identities, histories, cultures, and concerns. The great political question is whether they will mobilize around shared interests and concerns. If they do, they will become a formidable political force.

● Asian Americans are the third-largest minority group in the United States and now comprise 5 percent of the population. They are also a tremendously diverse group.

● Native Americans lost their way of life in the face of disease, armies, and settlers. The Supreme Court gave them a special status: a separate people without rights. Although they retain the special status, they became U.S. citizens in 1924.

● People with disabilities leveraged an obscure bureaucratic rule, used it to mobilize, and eventually won the sweeping rights of the Americans with Disabilities Act.

● The gay (and lesbian) movements were born in a burst of pride and anger in 1969. Gays were the first to confront AIDS—a harrowing plague (in its early years) that pushed them into politics, health provision, and community building.

● Gay, lesbian, bisexual, and transgender communities have moved from taboo to mainstream. Nevertheless, the conflict over marriage and child-drearing remains a flash point of contemporary culture wars.

KEY TERMS

1963 March on Washington, 161
Abolition, 152
Affirmative action, 163
Black power, 185
Brown v. Board of Education, 158
Chicanismo, 173
Civil rights, 147
Civil Rights Act of 1964, 161
Class action, 170
Compromise of 1850, 153
De facto discrimination, 157
De jure discrimination, 157
Disproportionate impact, 164

Domestic dependent nation, 180
Dred Scott v. Sandford, 153
Emancipation Proclamation, 154
Equal Employment Opportunity Commission (EEOC), 169
Equal protection of the laws, 154
Equal Rights Amendment, 171
Freedom Riders, 160
Great Migration, 157
Jim Crow, 156
Laws of coverture, 168
Literacy test, 155
Missouri Compromise, 153

National Association for the Advancement of Colored People (NAACP), 158
National Organization for Women (NOW), 169
Plessy v. Ferguson, 156
Racial profiling, 174
Reconstruction, 155
Reframe the issue, 171
School busing, 164
Section 504, 182
Seneca Falls Convention, 168
Strict scrutiny, 150
United Farm Workers, 173

STUDY QUESTIONS

1. Name the seven steps involved in civil rights campaigns. Give examples of three, drawing on historical material in this chapter.
2. Describe the Civil War Amendments. Why was the Fourteenth Amendment so important?

3. What was Jim Crow legislation? What happened to Jim Crow practices?
4. Describe the sit-ins and Freedom Rides of the civil rights movement. What was the point?

5. Describe three effects of the Civil Rights Act of 1964.

6. What is affirmative action?

For further reflection: Write your own Supreme Court decision. Would you accept affirmative action in your college or university? Why or why not?

7. What are undocumented aliens?

For further reflection: What should the United States do about undocumented aliens?

8. What is the Lilly Ledbetter Law?

For further reflection: Why do you think President Obama chose that as the first law to sign as president?

Public Opinion and Political Participation

IN 2000 VERMONT became the first state to recognize same-sex civil unions. Although the legislation did not permit marriage, it did give same-sex couples the same rights and duties as married couples. The state erupted in protests. Signs sprang up across the state urging local people to *"Take Back Vermont."* The major issue in the next election, held later that year, was whether to repeal the law. Opponents managed to win the Vermont House (which promptly voted to repeal), but the Vermont Senate preserved the reform. At the time, only one in three Americans approved of same-sex marriage. No state permitted it.

While Vermonters were battling it out, a friend called us and asked whether the law was going to survive. Would the law still be there, she asked, in a year? Neither of us, back in 2000, could even dream of what would happen in the next decade.

What happened was a revolution in public opinion. The change began with the millennials (born after 1981), a generation that grew up as the gay rights movement swept across the United States. When pollsters began to ask their opinion, they surprised most observers: 51 percent approved of same-sex marriage in 2003. It took older people some time to shift their views. However, by 2010 overall approval broke the 40 percent barrier and by 2014, 54 percent of the public approved of same-sex marriage—an enormous increase over the course of the decade (see Figures 6.1 and 6.2). Age still matters—now millennials' approval is up to 68 percent while only 38 percent of the people born before 1945 approve.

With public approval rapidly rising, state legislatures began passing same-sex marriage laws. And the courts, which had been slow to move in the past, now began to strike down bans on same-sex marriage. In one courtroom after another, the justices ruled that the bans violated the Fourteenth Amendment guarantee of "equal protection under the laws" (which we discussed in Chapters 4 and 5). By 2014, thirty-two states permitted same-sex marriage and in five additional states, the courts have struck down bans on same-sex marriage—but appeals are still in progress. By the time you read this, the number is likely to be higher.

What happened? Legislatures reflected the shift in public opinion and began to introduce new laws. The courts also followed the shifting popular views. Although we expect legislatures to weigh public opinion, courts are

IN THIS CHAPTER, YOU WILL:

● Identify the sources of our opinions.

● Explore how public opinion is measured.

● Reflect on the role of public opinion in a democracy.

● Explore different forms of political participation across U.S. history.

● Identify the benefits and drawbacks of an emerging "clickocracy" as political engagement moves online.

● *A revolution in public opinion: same-sex marriage.*

BY THE NUMBERS
Public Opinion and Political Participation

- Percentage of the American public unable to name their House member, 1960, 2010: **47, 59**
- Percentage of Millenials and Silent generation (69 and over) who approve of marijuana legalization: **69, 30**
- Percentage who believe abortions should be legal in all or most cases: **56, 42**
- Percent who would rather have a smaller government providing fewer services: **38, 64**
- Percentage of U.S. college students expressing trust in U.S. government, 1961 and in 2011: **74, 38**
- Highest approval rating recorded by Gallup for any president throughout term (John F. Kennedy): **70.1**
- Lowest average approval rating (Harry Truman): **45.4**
- President Obama approval rating, February 2010, 2011, 2012, 2014: **49, 52, 51, 45**
- U.S. Congress (split-party control) approval rating, after one month in office (February 2011, Gallup): **23**
- U.S. Congress (split-party control) approval rating, February 2014 (Gallup): **12**
- Proportion of Americans expecting another terrorist attack in the next 5 years, October 2011: **32**
- Proportion of Americans expecting another terrorist attack in the next 5 years, February 2014 (CNN): **57**
- Percentage of U.S. college students who volunteer for public service, 2013: **53**
- Percentage of 'Baby Boomers' (ages 50–68, roughly) who volunteer, 2013: **34**
- Percentage turnout of voting-age population, U.S. presidential election, 1840: **80**
- Percentage turnout of voting-age population, U.S. presidential election, 1940: **63**
- Percentage turnout of voting-age population, U.S. presidential election, 2012: **57**
- Proportion of eligible black residents registered to vote, Lowndes County, Alabama, 1965: **0**
- Proportion of eligible black residents registered to vote, Lowndes County, Alabama, 2012: **79**
- Amount donated to U.S. state election campaigns by the 10 richest Americans, 2010: **$22.6 million**
- Estimated amount donated to state campaigns by the bottom 50% of U.S. wage earners, 2010: **$3 million**
- Estimated number of political-themed blogs, 2001: **500**
- Estimated number of political-themed blogs, 2014: **98,800**

supposed to protect rights regardless of how people feel about them (that's why federal justices are appointed for life). But in this case, public opinion combined with organized political action by the gay rights movement also seemed to drive the courts forward.

Who are we? The world's oldest democracy. The issue of public opinion—what the public says it wants—and political engagement lies at the heart of self-rule. Somehow, the government must reflect popular views—but how? Government officials constantly balance public opinion and their own best judgment. Yet their responsiveness to popular views is linked to who among the populous is actively participating in our political system. So, who we are rests, to a large extent, on who is willing to join in, express their views, and become part of our political system.

● *Vermont's fight over same-sex marriage has largely ended, because increasing majorities of Vermonters—like most parts of America—view the issue positively.*

● Sources of Public Opinion

Public opinion is simply the sum of individual beliefs and opinions. Your views about same-sex marriage, the right to carry firearms, global warming, and whether *Game of Thrones* is too violent for television—along with the views of everyone else in the country—make up public opinion. One central question for this chapter is what role your views ought to play when public officials make policy. But before we ponder that, let's turn to a more basic question: Where do your opinions come from? Let's take a look at some classic sources.

Self-Interest: Voting Our Pocketbooks

Some experts believe that economic self-interest matters most. Whether you are rich or poor, you will try to increase your wealth. According to this perspective, people with more money will vote for lower taxes, and people with less will vote for more social programs.

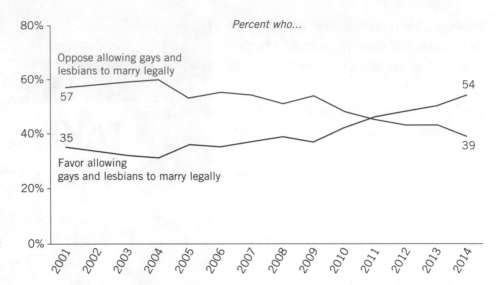

FIGURE 6.1 *Support for same-sex marriage has risen dramatically . . . (Pew Research Center)*

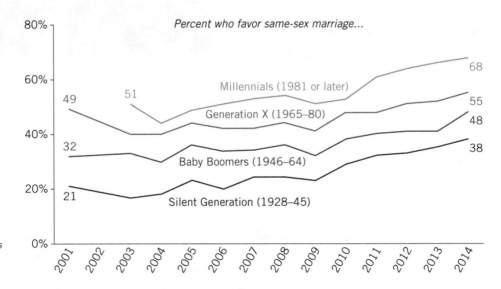

FIGURE 6.2 *. . . with millennials setting the pace (Pew Research Center).*

In practice, economic interests are important—but they are only one factor among many. Many wealthy liberals, especially in cities like New York and San Francisco, call for more social programs and higher taxes. One of the richest Americans, Warren Buffett, says that it is just not right that he pays a lower tax rate than his secretary. On the other hand, many lower-income Americans disagree with Buffett and oppose raising taxes on the rich; they criticize government efforts to redistribute wealth—even in their own direction. In a book entitled *What's the Matter with Kansas?*, economist Thomas Frank points out that Kansas has some of the lowest average incomes in the country but votes for a Congressional delegation made up exclusively of Republicans, who support cutting taxes and social programs. If they focused on their economic interest, argues Frank, they would be more likely to vote for Democrats. As he discovered, public opinion does not simply spring out of people's wallets.

Despite these caveats, wealthier people do, on average, tend to vote Republican. Poorer Americans generally vote for Democrats. But there are enough exceptions that we have to look further if we want to fully understand the roots of public opinion.

Demography—Race, Gender, Age, and More

President Lyndon Johnson once remarked, "Tell me where a man comes from, how long he went to school, and where he worships on Sundays, and I'll tell you his political opinions." LBJ, a big-talking Texan, may have overstated the case, but political scientists confirm his point. Basic demographic details—such as race, age, gender, ethnicity, and level of education—are strong predictors of people's political outlook.

Do you have confidence in the police? Whites say yes at a higher rate (78 percent) than blacks (53 percent) or Latinos (61 percent). Should the United States use drones to assassinate terrorists? Men tend to say yes (73 percent) while women are more evenly divided (53 percent yes). Do you support legalizing marijuana? Most millennials say yes (69 percent), boomers are divided (52 percent yes), and people sixty-nine and older generally say no (only 30 percent approval). (See Figure 6.3.)

Demographic differences look even more dramatic when we turn to elections. If only whites voted for the president, Republicans would have clobbered

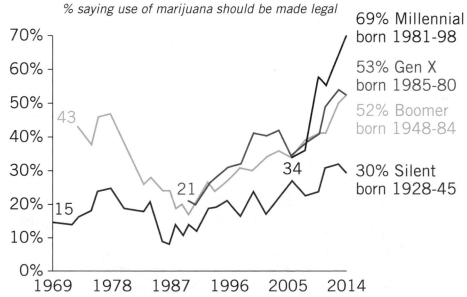

Growing Support for Marijuana Legalization
% saying use of marijuana should be made legal

69% Millennial born 1981-98

53% Gen X born 1985-80

52% Boomer born 1948-84

30% Silent born 1928-45

● **FIGURE 6.3** *Support for marijuana legalization is growing, but look at the age differences— millennials strongly support, the middle generations are divided, and older people strongly oppose (Pew Research Center).*

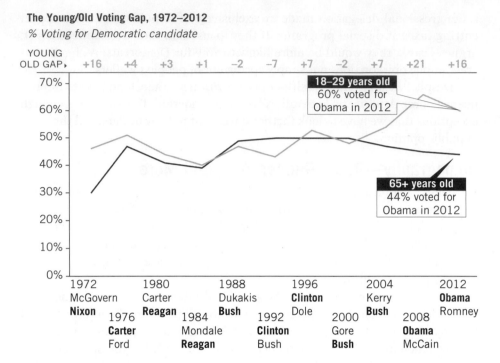

The Young/Old Voting Gap, 1972–2012

% Voting for Democratic candidate

FIGURE 6.4 *Voter turnout by age. In the past 15 years, a major gap has opened up between the youngest and the oldest voters (Pew Research Center).*

the Democrats in every election in the past forty years (see Figure 6.4). If only Hispanics or blacks voted, Democrats would have won by a landslide every time. There is also a pronounced **gender gap**. Women prefer Democratic presidential candidates, by an average of five percentage points. That may not sound like much, but if only women were allowed to vote in American presidential elections, the only Republican candidate who would have won in the past forty-five years is Ronald Reagan in 1984—although he would have lost in 1980. (Thanks to white, male voters, the Republicans actually won six of eleven elections.)

Demography is not destiny. However, tell us your race, your gender, your age, your religion, and where you live, and we'll be able to make some pretty good guesses about your opinions.

Gender gap: Patterned differences in political opinions between women and men.

Party

Party preference is an even stronger predictor of individual opinions than factors like race and religion. Most politically active Americans register as either Democrats or Republicans and generally stay committed to that party. In recent years the differences between the parties has grown—on almost every issue. "From immigration reform to food stamps to student loans," commented one respected pollster, "Republicans and Democrats inhabit different worlds."[1] Your party tells us more about your opinions than even strong demographic factors, like race and religion.

For a time, political scientists believed that elected officials were far more partisan than the public at large. Political Scientist Morris Fiorina and his colleagues argued that, at least on cultural issues like abortion, most Americans are moderates. More recent polling suggests a major surge in partisan difference within the public. As Figure 6.5 shows, the effect of party identification has shot up in the past twenty years. Today the difference between Democratic and Republican voters, across a host of issues, is a whopping eighteen points—more than race (twelve points), education (eleven), income (ten), or gender (six).[2] We will examine political parties in Chapter 9.

Elite Influence

Stop for a moment and think about whom you listen to when you make up your mind about an issue. Most people turn to friends and family. A series of studies, most notably by the political scientist John Zaller, suggests that people also look to **political elites.** People receive signals from political leaders and embrace those that are consistent with their prior beliefs.[3]

The greatest influence is wielded by figures who have the most credibility. Such "experts" on issues may include academics and think tank analysts, news anchors and other familiar sources of commentary, and popular political leaders—especially presidents. Unpopular presidents are much less likely to influence public opinion. That's another reason smart politicians watch presidents' approval ratings—and why presidents pay close attention as well.

When elites compete to shape members of the public's views on issues, they are trying to *frame* the issue—to give the issue a particular slant. For example, when obesity became a source of widespread popular concern, policy makers and advocates pushed hard to influence public opinion. What, if anything, should government do in response to sharp increases in Americans' obesity rate? Many leaders—and the food industry—framed the issue as one of personal responsibility: Obesity was, they said, a problem of self-control. The solution was simple: eat less, exercise more. Others framed the problem as a toxic food environment—too much high-fat, low-nutrition food is available at low cost—from fast-food drive-throughs to pharmacies to convenience stores to school cafeterias. As the public health consequences of obesity became clearer, the toxic-food-environment perspective gained traction. The framing battle reached a fever pitch when New York mayor Michael Bloomberg proposed banning sugary drinks larger than sixteen ounces—prompting cheers from public health advocates and a long rant from Jon Stewart sounding off against the nanny state.

Wars and Other Focusing Events

Americans pull together during crises. Tragedy, terrorist attacks, and the start of wars generally produce consensus—and a spike in the government's approval ratings. Franklin D. Roosevelt faced plenty of opposition when he tried to arm

Partisan Gap Grows While Other Divides Are Stable

Average difference on 48 values questions by key demographics

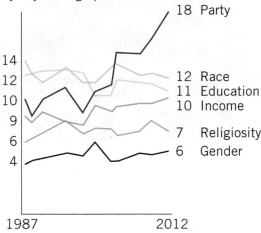

● **FIGURE 6.5** *The largest divide in American politics today: what party you identify with (Pew Research Center).*

Political elites: Individuals who control significant wealth, status, power, or visibility and who, consequently, have significant influence over public debates.

see for yourself 6.1

Go online to see Jon Stewart resisting Mayor Bloomberg's call to restrict soda sizes. (Flash required)

● *Mayor Rudolph Giuliani shaped reactions to the 9/11 attacks—in New York and around the nation—with his dramatic "walking press conferences."*

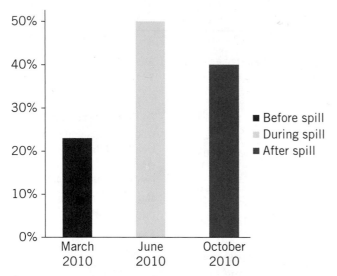

● **FIGURE 6.6** *Deepwater Horizon explosion, April 2010. Public opinion turned sharply against offshore oil drilling in the wake of the Gulf of Mexico oil-spill disaster . . . then shifted again a few months later (CNN Opinion Research Poll, April 19, 2011, pp. 3–4).*

Britain against Germany after World War II broke out—until December 7, 1941. On that day, the Japanese bombed Pearl Harbor, galvanizing public support for the war effort. Six decades later, nearly 90 percent of Americans backed the decision to invade Afghanistan a few weeks after the September 11, 2001, terrorist attacks on the World Trade Center and the Pentagon.

Wars inspire a strong sense of "We're all in this together," a nationalist sentiment that has characterized public response to wars in almost every country. But that sentiment typically fades over time. Consider the U.S. conflict in Iraq. When President Bush launched the war, in March 2003, almost 80 percent of the public approved. Four years later, approval for American involvement in Iraq had fallen to barely 30 percent in some polls.

Most dramatic events have a similar, if smaller, effect on public opinion. When the Deep Water Horizon drilling rig exploded and sent oil gushing into the Gulf of Mexico, the public turned sharply against offshore drilling. A few months later, as the crisis began to fade, so did the opposition to the drilling (see Figure 6.6). Savvy political scientists discount the spikes in public opinion—knowing the poll numbers generally come back down again.

THE BOTTOM LINE

● Our political opinions are influenced by a wide range of factors: financial interest, family, friends, demographics, party identification, and political elites.

● Party identification has become the most reliable predictor of public opinion in recent years.

● How issues are framed can shift individual and collective views.

● Dramatic events, especially wars, also have a powerful role in shaping our opinions.

Measuring Public Opinion

How do we know what the people are thinking? Professional polling firms like Gallup, major media organizations, partisan outfits, and academic research centers all jostle to provide the most up-to-date polls. Candidates for office commission private polls to tell them how they're performing; presidents and governors retain pollsters to gauge public opinion on various policy items. Let's take a look at why good polling techniques are important and how good polls are designed, where not-so-good polls cut corners, and—most important—how to recognize each kind.

Early Polling Bloopers

Well thought-out, scientific polling techniques might have averted polling's first major embarrassment. Back in 1920 a magazine named the *Literary Digest* helped introduce the idea that polls could predict presidential elections. The magazine relied on postcards sent in by subscribers to predict the elections. Until 1936, it could brag that it had never failed to predict the winner. Then, in October of that year, the *Digest* forecast a big lopsided defeat for incumbent President Franklin D. Roosevelt—who went on to win the biggest landslide in a century (he took every state but two). Why was *The Literary Digest* so far off base? Because its readers tended to be wealthy people who did not like President Roosevelt or his policies. The Literary Digest learned the hard way about one of the great challenges in polling: find a way to accurately reflect everyone's views—not just a segment of the population—like the readers of a literary magazine.

Since that famous mistake, polling professionals have worked hard to make the polling process as accurate, reliable, and scientific as possible.

Polling 101

Imagine that you are hired to conduct a public survey about preferences in the next mayoral election. Where do you start? You could ask a few friends in your American government class whom they plan to vote for, but that would probably not help you predict the winner. Professional pollsters are very careful to define their **sampling frame**—the types of people they plan to survey. If the poll is to accurately reflect public views, your survey respondents must reflect the population: that means they must vary in *age, education, income, race* or *ethnic group, gender,* and many other factors, such as where they live. Asking only your classmates would bias the poll toward college-educated and, probably, young people. A good representative survey includes **demographic groups** in rough proportion to their presence in the city's population.

You will also have to make a related sampling decision. Do you want your poll to represent *all* city residents or only those who will probably turn out and vote? Survey researchers tend to prefer polls of **likely voters**, which more accurately predict the outcome of most elections. Pollsters also often survey likely voters on policy questions, not just election polls.

see for yourself 6.2

Go online and listen to excerpts from Roosevelt's fiery campaign speech.

Sampling frame: A designated group of people from whom a set of poll respondents is randomly selected.

Demographic group: People sharing specific factors: for example, age, ethnicity/ race, religion, or country of origin.

Likely voters: Persons identified as probable voters in an upcoming election. Often preferred by polling organizations, but difficult to specify with great accuracy.

Before you start knocking on doors or dialing numbers, consider the *timing* of your survey. When do you conduct the poll? If you do it during the day, people with jobs will be away from home or unable to talk; if you conduct a telephone poll on a Friday evening, you're unlikely to find many younger residents at home—skewing your results to older people's opinions.

Once you have chosen your sampling frame and decided when to ask questions, you face an even more important question: What exactly will you ask? If this were a chat with your classmates, you might ask simply, "Whom do you support in the 2015 mayoral election?" But surveys must take into account **framing effects**: the *way* pollsters ask a question often influences the response.

For example, researchers from Pew polling asked people to choose between a tax cut and "funding new government programs." The public overwhelmingly picked the tax cut (60 percent to 25 percent). Then the pollsters adjusted the question and asked people to choose between a tax cut and funding for "programs on education, the environment, health care, crime fighting and military defense." Now, 69 percent opted for the government programs and only 22 percent for the tax cut. The wording made all the difference. Just avoiding a single word can also make a difference: 51 percent of the respondents favored "making it legal for doctors to assist terminally ill patients to end their lives" but only 44 percent favored "making it legal for doctor to assist terminally ill patients to commit suicide."[4] What's the difference between helping someone end his or her life and helping someone to commit suicide? Well, to the pollster it's six points—and majority approval of a controversial policy. Pollsters get a different response if they mention "poor people" rather than "African Americans or "Latinos." Likewise, "the economic effects of free trade" polls higher than "the effects of free trade on American jobs."

Sometimes these biases can be subtle. In polls on more obscure political races (other than president, governor, or big-city mayor), many respondents prefer the candidate who is named *first*, no matter what party or other identifying details are included in the question. A really good poll will pretest the questions to sniff out the subtle biases that creep in with different wordings.

Frequently, campaign or advocacy groups *want* to skew their survey results—and use framing effects to their advantage. Some polls go even further and actually try to influence respondents' views. These efforts—which do not even pretend to be legitimate efforts to measure opinions—are termed **push polls**. These "polls" are essentially a form of negative telemarketing; they have more impact on unsuspecting respondents because they are campaign advertisements masquerading as scientific surveys.

One notorious push poll was used during the 2000 Republican presidential primary. George W. Bush was losing his lead in the polls to a surging John McCain, and South Carolina loomed as a decisive primary contest. An anonymous political operative—the Bush campaign denied any involvement—conducted a push poll that asked hundreds of South Carolina voters: "Would you be more likely or less likely to vote for John McCain for president if you knew he had fathered an illegitimate black child?" The question itself was

---

Framing effects: The influence, on the respondent, of how a polling question is asked; changes in wording can significantly alter many people's answers.

Push poll: A form of negative campaigning that masquerades as a regular opinion survey. Usually conducted by a campaign or allied group; features strongly critical or unflattering information about an opponent.

Margin of sampling error: The degree of inaccuracy in any poll, arising from the fact that surveys involve a *sample* of respondents from a population, rather than every member.

Response bias: The tendency of poll respondents to misstate their views, frequently to avoid "shameful" opinions like sexism or racism.

Bandwagon effect: When people join a cause because it seems popular or support a candidate who is leading in the polls.

damning because it implied sexual misconduct and stirred up the complex brew of American racial politics; it contributed to Bush's decisive victory in South Carolina. (Senator McCain and his wife had adopted a daughter from Bangladesh, who was accompanying them on the campaign trail.)

A related trap for the unwary is the spread of online "polls," such as those you may have seen at your favorite websites. Internet "insta-polls" like these may be harmless enough—but their host sites (and even some media organizations) report them as representative of the entire U.S. public, when they are usually quite skewed. Different websites attract different kinds of people—precisely the mistake *The Literary Digest* made in 1936. As a result, online polls violate the polling gold standard: The answer comes from a self-selected group, not from a random sample.

Younger Americans are especially hard to reach and survey. Can you guess why? Many young people use mobile phones rather than land lines. Today, more than 40 percent of Americans of all ages have no land line, a number that continues to increase. Survey researchers must adapt.

Finally, you have collected the raw data from all your surveying. Time to tell the world about the details of your poll? Not so fast. You still need to determine your poll's **margin of sampling error**, a statistical calculation for how accurate your results are. By carefully designing their polls, national surveys are able to achieve small errors with as few as 1000–1500 respondents.

Pollsters also must consider **response bias** in publicizing their findings. Studies show that some respondents purposely mislead pollsters. A classic example of response bias arose when Tom Bradley, the first African American mayor of Los Angeles, ran against a white candidate, George Deukmejian, for governor of California in 1982. Bradley had a comfortable double-digit lead in opinion surveys as Election Day approached—but lost the race. Since then, other high-profile campaigns have similarly featured black candidates who had large leads in the polls but lost the election, a result that confounded survey researchers. The apparent inclination of some survey respondents to avoid appearing racist or racially motivated has become known as the "Bradley effect."

Sample size, framing effects, and margin of error: Account for all these, and you're well on your way to conducting a truly scientific public opinion survey. One important reason to understand the design of polls is so that you can distinguish the good from the bad. Table 6.1 summarizes some of the tips in this section.

Do Opinion Surveys Influence Us?

Might the profusion of polls also affect the decisions we citizens make—including how to vote? Evidence suggests that they do. Candidates who are leading in the polls tend to pick up support from voters who were undecided—or who weakly supported the opponent. The **bandwagon effect** in polling varies considerably from place to place and election to election. It can be exaggerated by media coverage.

TYPES OF POLLS

Benchmark polls. Conducted by a campaign as the race begins, these surveys provide a basis for comparison, or "benchmark," for later polls. With a benchmark number, candidates can tell if their likelihood of winning is rising or falling.

Straw polls. Informal polls carried out by local party organizations or news outlets; they often involve actual (nonbinding) votes cast by party members. Media organizations (and the straw poll winners) report results, especially during presidential primaries.

Brushfire polls. Internal surveys conducted by a campaign once election season begins. They provide details about how a candidate is performing; if things are going poorly, the campaign can work to put out the "brushfire" (burning swiftly, potentially spreading fast) of opposition.

Exit polls. Performed on Election Day, both by campaigns and news organizations, these surveys intercept voters as they exit the voting location. Media reporters often rely on exit polls to call results for one or the other candidate, even if ballots haven't been officially counted.

TABLE 6.1 Five Tips on Reading Polls

1. *Check out the margin of error.* Then reread the poll that figures it in. A 3 percent margin of error means plus or minus 3 percent—turning a 50 percent approval rating into one of 47–53 percent.
2. *What is the timing?* The further away from Election Day, the less meaningful the results.
3. *The random sample is the gold standard.* If the respondents chose themselves (by deciding to take the survey), then it may be fun to read . . . but it is probably not an accurate picture of the public.
4. *What is the sample size?* Be wary of polls that interview a small number of people.
5. *Compare across polls.* Since every poll has biases, read a range of polls, toss out the extreme findings, and take an average of the rest.

Boomerang effect: The discrepancy between candidates' high poll ratings and election performance, caused by supporters' assumption that an easy win means they need not turn out.

Underdog effect: Sympathy for a candidate behind in the polls, contributing to a higher-than-predicted vote total—and sometimes a surprise election victory.

A close cousin of polling's bandwagon effect is the **boomerang effect**. Here, a candidate who has been consistently ahead in opinion surveys performs more poorly than expected on Election Day. The logic is that supporters see a big lead for their candidate, figure that she will win without any difficulty, and so don't bother to vote. Scrambling the issue further, some voters also appear to follow the *opposite* of the bandwagon effect. The **underdog effect** is invoked when a candidate losing in the polls performs better than expected in the election, sometimes even surprising pollsters with a victory.

● *Even the best-designed surveys cannot avoid response bias— including some respondents who misrepresent their views on purpose.*

THE BOTTOM LINE

- Scientific surveys have come a long way since their origins in 1936. Professionals now design well-specified polls that capture popular views with a high degree of accuracy.

- Poll results can affect public opinion.

- Sampling errors, response bias, and other potential flaws inevitably confer a measure of uncertainty on any survey.

Public Opinion in a Democracy

Americans care about public opinion because of the direct connection to democracy—a word that comes from the Greek *demokratia* and means "rule by the people." For the public to have any meaningful say in ruling, political leaders must listen to their views. Do the people know enough to shape government? Is the public rational and capable of self-government? Or are we ignorant masses? Let's look at two different views.

Ignorant Masses

"The masses are asses!" insisted Walter Lippmann in his pathbreaking book *Public Opinion* (published in 1922). Lippmann, a well-known political journalist and cultural critic, believed the typical American was distracted by celebrities and minor scandals, rarely followed policy issues closely enough to understand the details, and yet readily offered up personal views on any topic. Paying attention to uninformed masses was no way to run a country. Lippman, along with many others, believed that governing involved technical decisions that were best left to well-trained experts.[5]

In 1960, four University of Michigan professors published a book that hit America like a thunderclap. Most citizens interviewed and surveyed in *The American Voter* did not know much about what either political party stood for, or about the main policy issues at the time. "Most people don't have real opinions at all," concluded the authors. When interviewers came to the door or called on the phone, people gave "doorstep opinions"—whatever happened to pop into their head at the time. The results—American public opinion—were meaningless.

Recently, another quartet of political scientists set out to investigate the same territory as that of *The American Voter*; in *The American Voter Revisited*, they drew very similar conclusions: Americans remain politically ignorant. One of the best-selling political books of the past few years, by popular historian Rick Shenkman, has a title that sums up this gloomy perspective: *Just How Stupid Are We? Facing the Truth About the American Voter.*[6]

The Rational Public

The alternative view arose in the 1980s, most prominently captured in a book-length response to *The American Voter* called *The Rational Public*. The authors, Benjamin Page and Robert Shapiro, staunchly defended public opinion's legitimate role in policymaking. Yes, most voters were generally inattentive to policy issues and uninformed about many political details. However, measured across large groups of people, public opinion moves in coherent, stable ways that signal shared views about policy issues. Although a single voter or poll respondent may hold inconsistent or even self-contradictory notions, these are submerged in the collective outlook of tens of millions of voters (or a carefully specified representative sample).

The journalist James Surowiecki summarized this perspective in the title of his book: *The Wisdom of Crowds*. Even if any one individual does not have clear views, argues Surowiecki, a large crowd, taken together, does add up to a rational public. In fact, a random collection of people, he continues, is actually wiser than a group of experts when it comes to devising the best solution to a policy dilemma.

Overall, however, if the group is of sufficient size—at least a few dozen—and members feel free to speak their minds, they will zero in on a good collective decision. Often these are innovative, outside-the-box solutions. Experts, on the other hand, are typically trained in similar ways and are subject to **groupthink**: they tend to reinforce one another's existing prejudices.

Surowiecki offers an example that neatly summarizes his point. At a county fair in England, a prize was offered to whoever could guess the correct weight of a giant ox on display. Cattle experts weighed in with their own well-founded opinions, but all were considerably off the mark. More than eight hundred locals offered up guesses as well. Although no one hit the correct weight (1,198 pounds), averaging the crowd's collective estimate came out at 1,197—just one pound below the correct total, and much closer than that offered by any agricultural or farming expert.[7]

Groupthink: The tendency among a small group of decision makers to converge on a shared set of views; can limit creative thinking or solutions to policy problems.

What Do You Think?

CAN WE TRUST THE PUBLIC?

Which side makes more sense to you: *The American Voter*, which concludes that the public is clueless? Or *The Rational Public*, which insists, on the contrary, that the people are the wisest political actors? The answer to this question is crucial for the practice of democracy.

I believe the public is thoughtful and informed. Are you and your friends contributors to a thoughtful American viewpoint, based on your interest in politics or your daily experience?

I believe the public is clueless. Or are you more likely to offer clueless "doorstep opinions" that change in unpredictable ways depending on your mood at the time?

Both. You believe that both positions contain valuable insight. When we add up all our friends and neighbors, what emerges is the "wisdom of crowds."

The optimistic view about the wisdom of the crowd restores traditional hopes about self-rule. However, if public opinion is to guide government, three conditions must be met.

1. The people know what they want and guide government decisions.
2. The public can clearly communicate its desires to political leaders.
3. Political leaders pay attention to public views—and respond.

That three-step process reflects the argument for public opinion's vital role in democratic governance.

Do the People Know What They Want?   Public officials in a democracy aim to reflect majority opinion—while taking the rights and needs of the minority into account. However, public views often fail to provide a guide for policy makers. For example, after the economic collapse between 2008 and 2010, polls showed a majority of Americans were angry with Wall Street banks. But when Congress and Obama administration economic advisers tried to translate this public discontent into concrete legislative solutions, popular consensus evaporated. Should we regulate derivatives as we do stocks and bonds so that their trading is transparent? Half the public said yes, half said no. Limit CEOs' pay or the multimillion-dollar bonuses the financial wizards receive each year? Maybe, or maybe not, Americans told surveyors. Does the public know what it wants? In a general way, it probably does. But political leaders have to supply the policy specifics.

How Do the People Communicate Their Desires?   It is difficult for the people—even a clear majority—to convey their views to policy makers. None of our instruments for adding up and transmitting millions of people's views are particularly effective. As we have seen, **survey research**, or scientific measure of popular opinion, is now everywhere in American politics and government. It is a crucial part of the political process and can offer solid impressions of public policy. Of course, democracies also rely on elections. Candidates who win often claim they have a **mandate:** The people have spoken. But it is difficult to translate an election into support for any single policy. Barack Obama thought the 2012 election gave him a mandate to overhaul immigration, but that effort was derailed in Congress. In short, it is difficult to translate electoral victory into instructions for any policy area.

Do Leaders Respond to Public Opinion?   On the surface, the answer seems to be unambiguous: yes! Polls are everywhere, and politicians seem

Survey research: Systematic study of a defined population, analyzing a representative sample's views to draw inferences about the larger public's views. Also termed *opinion poll*.

Mandate: Political authority claimed by an election winner as reflecting the approval of the people.

● *The uninformed American voter. Political humorists have long found an easy target in the "ignorant voter." Should public leaders take seriously the views of an often disengaged public?*

hooked on them. Our national campaigns collectively spend upward of $1 billion annually on polling. All members of every institution you will read about in this book—senators, presidents, lobbyists, even judges—avidly consume polls about their performance, as well as about the hot issues of the day. **Approval ratings**, which are routinely reported for top U.S. political figures and national institutions, can boost a leader's power when ratings rise and weaken his or her standing when they fall.

Franklin D. Roosevelt initiated the practice of private presidential polling, using multiple pollsters to assess public opinion on both election and policy matters. John F. Kennedy was the first president to poll-test specific phrases to describe major policy initiatives. Three decades later, Clinton administration presidential pollsters like Mark Penn were described as having "close to veto power" on some policy decisions.[8] However, attention to public views doesn't necessarily mean that politicians always slavishly follow the poll results. Let's return to President Bill Clinton. Despite his poll-happy reputation, he often broke with the findings. For example, in 1994, Mexico faced a major financial crisis. Clinton's economic advisers recommended a multi-billion-dollar loan to the Mexican government—which Americans overwhelmingly opposed. One top Clinton aide warned that the public would blame the president for "pissing billions of dollars down a Mexican rat hole."[9] In the face of strong popular opposition, with no support from Congress, Clinton signed an **executive order** directing the loan to go through—as it turned out, helping to stabilize Mexico's economy.

Recent work on public opinion has discovered that Clinton's veto was typical. Political leaders—and presidents in particular—use polling to find the arguments that will resonate with the public. These polls do not redefine the president's positions; rather, they guide political leaders in their efforts to persuade the public of their own views—and criticize the opposition and its ideas.[10]

Polls clearly matter in setting the **policy agenda**. Public opinion helps shape what topics governing officials pay attention to in the first place. If the public (and the media, as we will see in the next chapter) thinks something is important, political leaders will usually respond.

Spikes in public opinion have an especially significant effect on Congress. Members are often reluctant to legislate in the face of strong popular opposition. As we'll see in Chapter 14 public views weigh significantly in deciding which items get a hearing. Americans may ignore many topics; but when large numbers of us pay attention to something, politicians generally respond. That's exactly what we saw at the start of this chapter with same-sex marriage.

Although collective public opinion holds sway, the opinions of some groups matter more than others. As we have seen, pollsters target the opinions of likely voters—individuals they expect to participate in elections. Social movements, interest groups, and political parties work to collect and transmit their views and can have a more direct influence on public policies. By participating in the political system, your voice is more likely to be heard.

Approval rating: A measure of public support for a political figure or institution.

Executive order: A presidential declaration, with the force of law, that issues instructions to the executive branch without any requirement for congressional action or approval.

Policy agenda: The issues that the media covers, the public considers important, and politicians address. Setting the agenda is the first step in political action.

THE BOTTOM LINE

- Some Americans have viewed public opinion as an unreliable, even dangerous, guide to government policy making, based in part on voter ignorance.

- Others argue that, in practice, a "rational public" is the best source of democratic decision making.

- One way to combine these clashing views is to focus not on what individuals know about politics but on how the many different popular views add up to a "wisdom of crowds."

- If public opinion is to guide politics, three conditions must be met: The public must know what it wants; its views must be effectively communicated; and leaders must pay attention.

- Even strong public opinion may not be specific enough to offer policy guidance.

- United States government officials devote more resources to polling operations than top officials in other nations.

- All government officials constantly have to weigh doing what they think is best against doing what the public desires. Popular views can help set governing agendas.

 Getting Involved

When we do get involved, what are the main avenues to doing so? Unless they are checked out entirely from politics, U.S. residents engage in a variety of participatory practices. Political scientists divide these into three categories: *electoral activities*, of which the most familiar is voting; *civic voluntarism*, ranging from group membership to raising funds for your favorite charity; and *political voice*, which encompasses such expressive acts as sending an e-mail to your local newspaper editor or engaging in protests.

Electoral Activities

If you have voted in any U.S. election, you know the basic drill. First, register to vote, which you can do using your driver's license as ID. Second, arrive on Election Day at your assigned polling place (hopefully you know who's running and what the issues are). Some states, most notably Oregon and Washington, conduct elections by mail to make it easier to vote.

Next comes the act of voting. In some locations, you wait in line for a while. Depending on state law, you may have to provide your identification to the polling

SHOULD EVERYONE PARTICIPATE IN POLITICS?

Americans vote at relatively low rates. Is this a danger to democracy?

Yes! A vibrant republic requires active participation by the people. American history is full of examples of common people who stood up for social change. Apathetic people soon lose their rights and liberties. We should facilitate public participation in every way possible.

No! Participation—even voting—is a privilege as well as a right. People ought to inform themselves. We shouldn't make voting too easy—it's probably a good thing if uninformed people stay home. It makes politics and governing more efficient.

Not sure? Today, political observers make arguments on both sides. Democrats are usually in the Yes! Column; Republicans have increasingly been voting No! on this issue. You'll probably have a stronger opinion by the time you've finished this book.

workers, who are usually volunteers and not paid for their time—another form of electoral involvement. They will direct you to a voting booth, often adorned with distinctive blue curtains. Inside, you encounter one of many different American voting mechanisms. Some jurisdictions use touch screens, others have you mark paper ballots much as the first U.S. voters did in 1789 (usually in public, back then), and some states use voting machines with levers. If many different offices are listed on the ballot, perhaps along with an issue referendum or two (which we discuss later in this book), it might take you several minutes to work your way down the ballot and make all your choices. In local elections featuring just a handful of races, you may finish voting in thirty seconds or so.

Compared to other countries, the United States holds more frequent national elections—every two years for House members—and requires elections for a wider range of offices, including many judgeships. This difference helps explain why our **voter turnout**, the percentage of eligible citizens who actually make it to the polls, is among the lowest for the world's developed democratic nations.

Beyond the sheer number of elections, another reason for lower American voter turnout is the difficulty that working people may have in finding time to make it to their polling place on a Tuesday. To overcome this problem, thirty-two states and the District of Columbia now permit early voting—more than a third of the ballots are now cast before Election Day. Despite the changes, voter turnout has not changed much in the past half century (see Figure 6.7).

Voting is the most widely recognized form of civic participation. More than 120 million people turned out for the 2012 presidential election. Voting usually

Voter turnout: A measure of what proportion of eligible voters actually cast a legitimate ballot in a given election.

● *Americans vote almost anywhere: in schools, churches, mosques—and pool rooms.*

Turnout of U.S. Voting Eligible Population, 1948-2014

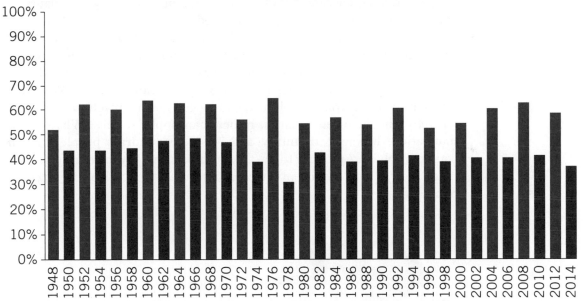

● **FIGURE 6.7** *Voter turnout for presidential elections (red) is much higher than for midterm elections (blue). Neither rate has changed much in the past half century. (Michael McDonald and Samuel Popkin, "The Myth of the Vanishing Voter" (2001); United States Elections Project).*

takes only a few minutes—it is a limited form of political participation. Beyond voting, Americans engage in other **electoral activities.** They go to meetings and rallies. They post signs on their lawns and bumper stickers on their cars featuring the candidates they support. They donate money to candidates, causes, or a political party. In the 2012 presidential election, more than

Electoral activities: Public engagement in the form of voting, running for office, volunteering on a campaign, or otherwise participating in elections.

5 million Americans donated funds (some as little as five dollars, others millions) to the Obama and Romney campaigns.

Civic Voluntarism

Many Americans—young, middle-aged, and seniors alike—volunteer for causes. Others donate money. Such **civic voluntarism** has a long pedigree. When the young French visitor Alexis de Tocqueville, whom we met earlier in this book, traveled through the United States in 1831–1832, he was struck by Americans' propensity to get involved. In *Democracy in America*, Tocqueville repeatedly remarks on the way Americans join voluntarily to build public institutions like roads, schools, and hospitals; in France, he notes, such projects would require elaborate layers of government approval—and in England, would need the patronage of a lord.[11]

Americans still volunteer for causes at higher rates than citizens of other democratic countries. And Generation Y—a group currently in their teens and twenties, including many of your college peers—is the most active in modern U.S. history when it comes to volunteering their time for worthy causes. Over the past decade, the proportion of teenagers who volunteer has more than doubled. Resume padding for career advancement? Recent studies say no—Figure 6.8 shows the major reasons Gen Y gets involved.

Voluntary engagement comes in dozens of different forms. Many people of all ages generously help out in their local communities: They serve in a food bank, teach English as a Second Language, join a volunteer fire department, or help raise money for high school basketball uniforms. Volunteers may not see their work as political, and indeed getting involved is often related to a hobby or enthusiasm, rather than public service. Whatever the motivation, however, voluntary activity tends to draw people into the common sphere. And once there, the payoff is clear. If you volunteer, you're more likely to vote, pay attention to political affairs, and otherwise engage in public life.

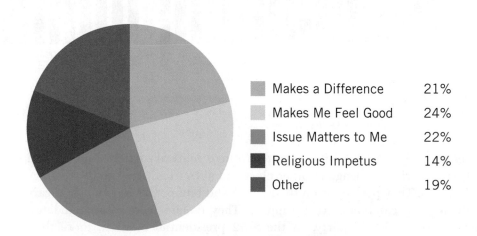

Makes a Difference	21%
Makes Me Feel Good	24%
Issue Matters to Me	22%
Religious Impetus	14%
Other	19%

● **FIGURE 6.8** *Americans aged 15–25: Reasons for volunteering.* (Brookings Institution)

Political Voice

When you praise or critique a public official or weigh in on an issue (on a blog or in person at a public forum), you are expressing your **political voice**. This type of participation in civic life can be as simple as following the news headlines or discussing politics—at meals with friends, or on Skype with your parents.

Such activity may not sound like much, but in nondemocratic systems people can be imprisoned—or worse—for speaking their mind on political matters. And by engaging in these ordinary activities, you are moving up the scale from uninvolved to scorekeeper—and perhaps eventually to passionate. On average, Americans tend to exercise their political voice more often and more openly than citizens of many other advanced democracies.

Some participants register their political voice in dramatic fashion. Martin Luther King Jr., for example, led civil rights marches in Birmingham, Alabama, on behalf of black Americans. After King was arrested for "agitation," he wrote *Letter from Birmingham Jail* to defend his acts of civil disobedience, an especially inspiring example of political voice. Today, Chinese Americans protest the Jimmy Kimmel Show (for an alleged anti-Chinese skit), students demonstrate against products made in sweat shops, and small business owners march to challenge Obamacare.

Sometimes it can be difficult to tell the difference between passionate expressions of political voice and illegal activity. When unidentified opponents of the Affordable Care Act, or "Obamacare," defaced a House member's district office in Georgia after he indicated support for the bill or threw rocks

Political voice: Exercising one's public rights, often through speaking out in protest or in favor of some policy change.

● *Political voice or lawlessness? The office of former Representative Gabrielle Giffords (D-AZ) was vandalized after she defended health care reform in 2009.*

● *The Boston Tea Party as imagined by an eighteenth-century American artist (December 1773).*

through a Colorado member's office window, were they taking political action, destroying property—or both? What about the patriots who dumped three valuable shiploads of tea into Boston Harbor in 1773, helping to spark the American Revolution? Today we see them as courageous revolutionaries, but at the time they were mere lawbreakers in the eyes of many British Americans.

Whatever counts as legitimate political voice, exercising this form of participation serves multiple purposes. Government officials are more likely to pay attention when a constituent speaks up—and they really notice when large numbers of people gather to express their views in a focused way. Environmental advocates were active in the United States throughout the 1960s. But when millions of Americans gathered to promote cleaner air and water at the first Earth Day in April 1970, Congress had passed major clean-air legislation within a month, and a Clean Water Act followed. That kind of political-voice activity is the lifeblood of democracy.

Now that you have a handle on what public participation looks like, let's move on to *why* many people get involved in public life. As you read, keep in mind that far more Americans are content to stay on the sidelines.

THE BOTTOM LINE

- Political participation can be categorized in three main ways: electoral activities, civic voluntarism, and political voice.

- Compared to people in other countries, Americans tend to engage less widely in electoral activities, volunteer at higher rates, and express political voice more freely and frequently.

- Each of these raises vital questions: Why don't more Americans vote? Does volunteer activity in needy communities serve a valuable purpose, or is it better described as short-lived "voluntourism"? And how can we tell legitimate expressions of political voice from destructive mischief? Political scientists and public officials are still debating the answers.

Paradox of voting: For most individuals, the cost of voting (acquiring necessary information, traveling to polling site, and waiting in line) outweighs the apparent benefits. Economic theory would predict very low voter turnout, given this analysis.

 ## What Inspires Political Participation?

Economist Anthony Downs famously asked, why should anyone vote? His theory, the **paradox of voting,** suggests that voting is irrational. One person is not going to change an election. Yet, millions of Americans troop to the polls. Why? Whether we are voting, volunteering, or expressing our political voice, something or someone—and often both—generally helped inspire us to do so. What makes Americans more or less likely to engage in political activity?

Spurs to Individual Participation

Four factors spur individuals to participate: their personal background (especially age, wealth, and education); the influence of *family members* or close friends, especially in communities with high levels of **social capital**, or civic engagement and mutual trust; *mobilization efforts* by advocacy groups and political parties; and—perhaps surprising—*receiving benefits* from government. Let us look at each in turn.

Background: Age, Wealth, and Education. One strong predictor of political engagement is *age*: Older people vote more often. Figure 6.9 displays voting rates for different American generations. Note that *young* adults vote less, in election after election.

Another strong predictor of political participation is related to wealth. Top earners tend to be much more involved in public life than those farther down the ladder in income and wealth. The wealthiest 5 percent of Americans, for example, provide a very high proportion of the dollars contributed by individuals to political campaigns. And the higher the income, the more likely individuals are to vote or get involved in politics in other ways.[12]

Wealthy Americans (those making more than $150,000) do tend to vote Republican—but as Figure 6.10 illustrates, not by a very large margin (no more than 5 to 10 percent in the last four presidential elections).[13]

Education also predicts political involvement—and education level closely tracks income. As Figure 6.11 shows, the more education the higher the voting levels. Less than 30 percent of the people who did not finish high school normally vote in presidential elections; citizens with a college degree are more than twice as likely to vote.

Social capital: Relations between people that build closer ties of trust and civic engagement, yielding productive benefits for the larger society.

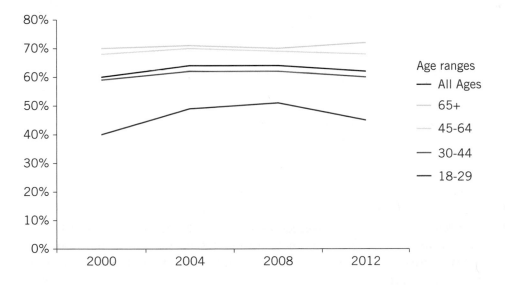

● **FIGURE 6.9** *Voter turnout in presidential election by age (The Center for Information and Research on Civic Learning and Engagement).*

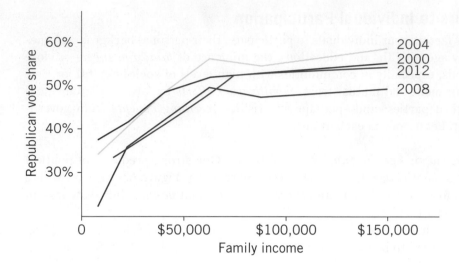

● **FIGURE 6.10** *Rich voters continue to lean Republican (data from exit polls).*

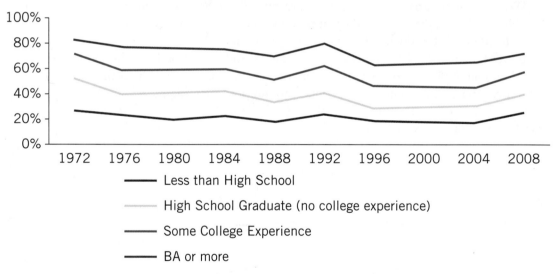

● **FIGURE 6.11** *Youth voter turnout in presidential elections by educational attainment (The Center for Information and Research on Civic Learning and Engagement).*

People with a college degree are far likelier to be politically involved in other ways than those who did not finish high school. Because many political acts require advanced social, managerial, and bureaucratic abilities—including information processing and English-language mastery—they tend to correlate with higher levels of education.

Like most countries around the world, the United States features civic education in elementary and secondary grades. Students are introduced to ideas like the desirability of democracy, a free-enterprise system, and individual liberty. They often learn about the Constitution and the American presidents. Still, the United States is less intensive in its national civic instruction than many other nations.

If we were writing this book fifteen years ago, we would have to add another major category: race. Traditionally, African Americans voted in lower numbers than white Americans. Gradually, however, the gap began to close and, in 2012, for the first time in American history, black Americans voted at a slightly higher rate than white Americans (see Figure 6.12). Latino and Asian Americans, however, vote at a lower rate. Just under 50 percent of eligible voters in these communities cast ballots. This has to do with the many barriers that they face. However, as their numbers grow, they are becoming an increasingly important political force.

● *Social capital on the big screen. Characters from* It's a Wonderful Life, *a 1946 film that portrays the power of social networks and civic engagement.*

Friends, Family, and Social Capital.   Another way to predict whether someone will vote or volunteer is to find out whether their parents and closest friends do. On average, someone whose family or peers vote regularly is likely to do so as well. An even more powerful inspiration is being *asked* to vote, volunteer, or otherwise exercise political voice by people close to you. Political science studies

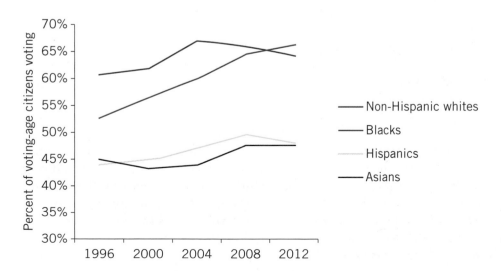

● **FIGURE 6.12** *Voter turnout by ethnicity (U.S. Census Bureau).*

HOW MOBILIZERS SEE US
Political strategists and
mobilizers have a language
of their own. Below are
some of the terms you'll
hear if you work in advocacy
or campaign politics long
enough.

Grassroots: A movement for
political reform that is sparked
at the local level, "from the
ground up": figuratively
speaking, from the grassroots.

Astroturf: A movement for
reform that *appears* to be
from the grassroots but is
actually mobilized by
political professionals.

Dog whistling: Using insider,
"coded" language to rouse
constituents or interest-
group members who care
strongly about an issue.
(The rather rude analogy is
from training dogs, which
hear high-frequency
whistles that other

find that face-to-face encouragement is the most reliable route to political activity. Encouragement to vote even by a stranger, as long as it is in person, tends to get results.[14]

Your type of community also seems to make a difference. In areas where neighbors are more trusting and civic participation is strong, people are more likely to get involved—both in local activities, like block watches or school fundraisers, and in voting for national office. Such communities, organized around a commitment to building social capital, tend to house happier, healthier residents. Through active communication and a strong foundation of trust among citizens, Americans can realize the benefits of engagement on a wide scale.

People who live in areas high in social capital are more deeply involved in activities like book clubs or community gardens or bowling leagues and spend more time connecting informally with one another than in places where people live more anonymously and watch a lot of television. It may sound simple: A key to political participation is to live in a highly participatory community. But transforming a neighborhood into one with strong social capital—or sustaining civic connections once they exist—is no easy task. Think about ways that you might cultivate a spirit of engagement around you.

The connection between family and participation may run deeper than our tendency to imitate the behavior of those closest to us. Recent studies suggest that we may *inherit* a tendency to political participation. In other words, your desire to vote or volunteer is determined by your genes—but only partly.[15] Political involvement is shaped by several influences simultaneously, so genetic inheritance, like level of social capital in a community, is one factor among many.

Political Mobilization.   The work of **political mobilization** has traditionally been carried out by party organizations. Both major parties remain powerful sources of encouraging millions of people to get involved—especially at election time. On **issue advocacy** campaigns, however, when professional and amateur organizations seek to attract public involvement in a specific cause, interest groups have become our mobilizers in chief.

In the eyes of professional political mobilizers—advocacy groups, campaign strategists, and other members of the enormous "political industry" based in Washington, D.C.—each of us is a potential resource. If we can be inspired to sign a petition, write our congressional representatives, get out and vote, or otherwise engage politically, we are part of democracy in action.

Government Beneficiaries.   A fourth factor encouraging participation in public life may strike you as odd at first glance: receiving government benefits. If your grandparents get a monthly Social Security check, your older brother or sister was covered by your parents' health insurance past age twenty-one, or you receive a federally guaranteed student loan (which keeps the interest rates low), you are a beneficiary. Receiving such support can boost active participation later in life. Researchers have shown that when the government rewards service—as when returning soldiers receive free or discounted college tuition through the GI Bill—recipients are considerably more likely to get involved as volunteers and to exercise their public voice.[16]

These spurs to participation all focus on individual factors. Being asked, imitating your parents and friends, responding to incentives, or receiving government benefits influences your own inclination to engage in the public sphere. But there is a larger backdrop to participation as well.

Context

Major shifts in the economy and in politics affect both the intensity and the favored types of participation. In the rural South during the 1950s, for example, an infestation of boll weevils (tiny insects that feed on cotton plants) devastated the cotton crop. Many African American subsistence farm workers, their livelihood gone, moved to southern cities—where they became recruits for the civil rights movement. In part because of the boll weevil, they became deeply involved in politics.

Context deeply influences opportunities for political engagement.[17] During certain historical periods, Americans have been more likely to engage in public life than at other times. In fact, these periods of heightened participation seem to occur in regular cycles across U.S. history, with highest-involvement periods separated by intervals of around thirty years.

Talking POLITICS

CONTINUED

animals—including humans—cannot.)

Actorvist: A professional actor involved in political issue campaigns, increasingly valuable in winning attention for one's cause. Leonardo DiCaprio on environmental issues and George Clooney on expanding aid to Africa are just two of the many "actorvists" engaged in American policy mobilization efforts today. Also sometimes heard is "raptivist," a term describing rappers who get involved in political causes.

THE BOTTOM LINE

- Participating in politics and government is influenced both by personal factors: background characteristics such as income and education; family and friends; political mobilization; and receiving government benefits.

- Political mobilization is also influence by the larger social and historical context.

◆ What Discourages Political Participation?

Analysts have identified four broad reasons to explain further why many people of all ages, income levels, and educational backgrounds drop out or never join political life in America: alienation, barriers to participation, complacency, and shifting mobilization patterns.

Alienation

Alienation from public life may be described as a feeling of powerlessness or inability to control one's own political fate. The result is usually abstention

Congressman Joe Wilson (R-SC) became an instant celebrity when he shouted "You lie!" during President Obama's speech to Congress in September 2009.

from public involvement, although alienation can also lead to intense and even violent protest. A sense of alienation is reported more often in the United States among members of historically excluded groups, especially African Americans.[18] Alienation is also higher among younger people and recent immigrants.

These findings raise a basic question: Do some groups feel alienated because they lack a history of participation? Remember, one predictor of whether a person will get involved in politics is whether his or her parents or peer group are actively engaged. Or is the desire to participate high among immigrants, minorities, or young people, but many become alienated because they are systematically excluded from politics? Researchers have not fully untangled this puzzle; in a moment we will look further at institutional barriers that discourage participation.

A sense of alienation from politics and government can also come in less extreme forms. The sheer number of elected offices and the high frequency of U.S. elections can result in public exhaustion and eventually disengagement, especially when campaigns feature seemingly endless negative advertisements. Sharp partisan differences also play a role. In *Why Americans Hate Politics*, political analyst E. J. Dionne notes a widening gulf between liberals and conservatives in U.S. political debates. The angry debates accompanying this polarization have led many Americans to "hate politics and politicians."[19] Alienated citizens charge the political establishment with focusing on matters that do not solve real problems facing the people. Government officials seem more interested in winning arguments and elections.

In countries with totalitarian or oligarchic rather than democratic political systems, alienation can become pervasive. Large majorities of the population are turned off completely from government or politics. Compared to such places, a relatively small portion of the U.S. citizenry exhibits a weaker form of alienation, but the phenomenon is demonstrably present in America.

Institutional Barriers

When Will Walker, a young black farmer, arrived to cast his vote in Tuscaloosa, Alabama, in 1964, he was first required by state law to pass a literacy test, one supposedly designed to prove that he was capable of exercising political judgment. None of the white voters streaming past Will to the voting booths had to take such a test. Will shrugged and turned to the paper before him, brandished by an unfriendly poll worker. He had brushed up on his basic U.S. government facts, and he knew plenty about the various candidates running for election. Yet no amount of studying could have prepared Will for questions like these:

- The electoral vote for president is counted in the presence of two governmental bodies. Name them: _____ and

  _____.

- The president is forbidden to exercise his or her authority of pardon in cases of _____.

- If the president does not wish to sign a bill, how many days is he or she allowed in which to return it to Congress for reconsideration? _____ days.

- At what time of day on January 2 each four years does the term of the president of the United States end? _____

Will filled out as many of the twenty questions as he could; he did better than most political science majors might today. But he was turned away from the polls. Alabama allowed only black voters with a perfect score to vote. Owing to this and other deliberate efforts to block participation, like the "poll tax" you read about in Chapter 5, many counties across the Jim Crow South featured voting-registration rates among African Americans that approached zero.

Most of these overtly racist obstacles to participation were eliminated during the 1960s, although some critics continue to point out structural barriers to participation in American public life—such as the disenfranchisement of individuals convicted of a crime, even after they have served their sentence. Young Americans who long found it difficult to sign up as new voters, for example, are able to register when applying for a driver's license, thanks to the National Voter Registration Act of 1993, usually referred to as the **motor voter law**. Another longtime limit on public participation involves the difficulty of accessing information. This obstacle is greatly diminished, thanks to the massive amounts of political detail available on the Internet. National, state, and local governments also make information, including ballots, available in multiple languages.

Even so, the battle over institutional barriers goes on. Many states have introduced new voting regulations: tougher identification requirements, limits on same day registration (that permits voters to register and vote at the same time), reductions in the voting periods, and other limits. Opponents (mainly Democrats) call this voter suppression and charge that it is an effort to limit young people, minorities, and others from voting. Proponents (mostly Republicans) counter that they are fighting to preserve the integrity of the ballot.

Motor voter law: Passed in 1993, this act enables prospective voters to register when they receive their driver's license.

Complacency

A further perspective on nonparticipation grows out of surveys showing that many people find their lives going reasonably well. Without nagging

● African Americans protesting for voting rights at the Supreme Court in 2013.

problems or issues they want solved, why bother to get involved? Research shows, for example, that large membership-based interest groups tend to attract more new members and receive a boost in financial contributions when the group's core issues are threatened. After a big oil spill or new warning about global warming, environmental groups attract more public interest. Conversely, when concerns are lessened, citizen groups find it hard to mobilize their followers.

A different view of political apathy comes from the economist John Kenneth Galbraith, who coined the phrase "culture of contentment" to describe America. His view was that the upper-middle class, and those at the top of wealth distributions, will fight hard to sustain their "contented" way of life. Those less well-off are increasingly discouraged from political participation.[20]

Shifting Mobilization Patterns

Before the 1960s, when political parties were Americans' main source of political mobilization, wealthy and poor people were organized to participate in roughly similar proportions. The main focus was on getting people out to vote in elections, so intensive door-by-door canvassing at election time was the norm. A surge in advocacy-group organizing since the 1960s has boosted the public's collective voice in politics. Movements on behalf of consumer rights, the environment, and many other causes represent a major gain in public leverage. These gains, however, have primarily benefited the relatively well-off, who can devote resources of time and money to public involvement.

THE BOTTOM LINE

- Participation in civic life tends to vary by age, income level, and education.

- Several other factors have fueled a decline in Americans' political participation in recent years. These include alienation, barriers to participation, complacency, and shifting mobilization patterns.

● The Internet, Social Media, and Gen Y Participation

Younger Americans, like eighteen- to twenty-four-year-olds in many countries, have lower rates of political participation than do older age groups. The exception is in volunteering for organizations that serve the public. From "candy stripers" at hospitals to programs for at-risk kids, young Americans in Generation Y, also termed millennials (born between the early 1980s and 2001), volunteer at unusually high rates.

Rates of participation in electoral or "voice" political activities are much lower among Generation Y members, however, as we saw in Figure 6.9.

Beyond voting rates, Gen Y members are less likely than previous groups of eighteen- to twenty-four-year-olds to get involved in political campaigns, join or organize advocacy groups dedicated to policy issues, or express interest in politics and government.[21] These findings are worrisome, given that generational trends in participation tend to persist over time. Millennials' relatively low participation rates can seem puzzling, given their high engagement as volunteers. But volunteering is generally an individual activity. Although you may sign up to volunteer with a friend, you often carry out service work on your own schedule, donating your personal time. Other types of public engagement are more *collective*, and here Generation Y members begin to shrink away from involvement. Late teens and twenty-somethings display relatively low levels of trust in their fellow citizens—a strong marker of inclination to engage in political activities. Responding to a Pew Charitable Trusts poll, 70 percent of Generation Y members agreed with the statement "Most people look out for themselves," compared to only 40 percent of "matures," or Americans over sixty-five, who agreed. A similar gap was present for the statement "Most people would take advantage of you" (56 percent of Gen Y compared to 29 percent of matures).

At the same time, Generation Y's members report a desire to participate in political life (Figure 6.13). Has this been your experience or that of your friends? Would you be more likely to engage in political and social questions if the chance arose?

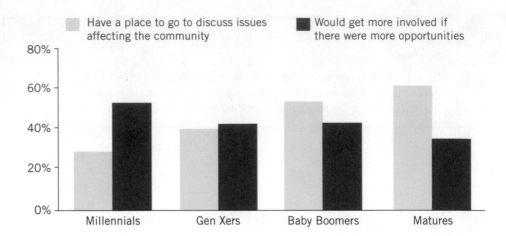

Have a place to go to discuss issues affecting the community

Would get more involved if there were more opportunities

● **FIGURE 6.13** *Opportunities/ demand for participation, by generation. (National Conference on Citizenship)*

● **FIGURE 6.13** *Opportunities/ demand for participation, by generation. (National Conference on Citizenship)*

Another distinguishing feature of Generation Y: its members are the most wired group of Americans in history. They are connected to one another and the wider world through smartphones, social media, and the Internet. What influence have these massive shifts in personal technology had on political participation? Once again, there are two sides to the story.

Some observers predict a new era of citizen participation.[22] Others take a much less sunny view and warn about fragmented communities, central government control of emerging outlets, and viral malice.

Scenario 1: Rebooting Democracy

First, optimists begin by pointing out how *active* Internet users are. People seek out news, follow links, and access a world of information. Advocates have a term for this new style of participation: **clicktivism**—democracy enhanced through the click of a mouse.

Clicktivism: Democracy enhanced through the click of a mouse.

Second, people can easily respond. The web offers multiple opportunities for talking back: tick the "Like" icon, fire off an irate e-mail, launch a blog, or communicate with a network of like-minded people. Democracies, when they're working well, *hear* their people. New technologies give individuals many opportunities to exercise their political voice.

Third and relatedly, the web vastly expands the range of commentary. Traditionally political pundits were limited to a small circle of well-known personalities and authors. Today if you have something to say you can launch a blog, send a tweet to dozens or hundreds (or millions) of followers, or post opinions on Facebook.

Fourth, the web offers new ways for politicians and parties to reach out. Barack Obama refined the technique and turned his 2008 and 2012 campaigns into a kind of movement. By the 2014 midterms, Republicans—and especially Tea Party conservatives—had developed ways to use the web to launch a movement of their own.

In sum, optimists argue that social media and other Net-based sources promote active users, link people to one another, permit citizens to bypass the

● *The Arab Spring and social media.*

talking heads and make their own comments, and offer politicians a powerful tool to mobilize, connect, and collect. None of these factors ensures that the new media will help refresh American democracy. But they suggest a great deal of promise.

Scenario 2: More Hype and Danger Than Democratic Renaissance

All this potential, however, might be squandered. Technological change might not enhance democracy and, according to some skeptics, is already harming it. Critics level four main charges against the Internet and social media as keys to political participation.[23]

First is the sustained power of central control, usually by government sources, over even the sprawling chaos of the Internet. In the United States, former National Security Agency employee Edward Snowden revealed in 2013 that federal officials were screening virtually all traffic over Google, texts on all major phone carriers, and other supposedly private social-media connections. Hackers are also able to disrupt systems, slowing interaction and endangering users' privacy. Shifting more forms of political participation online could result in severe disruptions of public activity.

Second, skeptics dismiss the web's promise for elevating new voices. Individuals can write all they want, but few will actually be read—limiting their political voice. There is no denying the reach of *Buzz Feed* or *Daily Kos*. But they are rare exceptions. Look again at the measure of Nate Silver's success: His posts moved to the *New York Times*, the essential old media.

Din: Shorthand for the sheer volume of information and noise generated by online sources; can be a disincentive to participate politically.

Third, with more than 250 million websites on the web, the sheer volume and variety of available information are mind-boggling. The resulting chaos can also be mind-numbing. Researching or following a specific topic often involves wading through a forest of anonymous posts, partial information, and deliberate misinformation. One term for this is **din**.

Try Googling this chapter's topic, political participation, for example. As of 2014, we found some 4.5 million relevant web sources. Which ones provide valuable or even useable details about participation in the public sphere? Merely to scan each site for one minute would take more than eight and a half years.

Fourth, the web incubates lies, malice, and falsehood. Rumors start and spread. Racism, anti-Semitism, misogyny, and character assassination all flourish in the hyperconnected, often anonymous new media. The democratic promise of the web comes with a dark side.[24]

In sum, critics worry that the Internet and social media will have a corrosive effect on American democratic participation. They point out that government control is evident in many countries, including the United States. Yes, people can post and blog, but not many develop an audience. Finally, the speed and connectivity of the web can lead to misinformation and malice as easily as communication and community—and also to users feeling overwhelmed by the sheer amount of information.

THE BOTTOM LINE

- The tendency to disengage is most pronounced among Generation Y, which includes most college students today.

- The Internet, and especially social media, have launched a revolution that is changing the way Americans participate politically.

- An emerging age of activism and connection may refresh American democracy. Or troubling developments may diminish it. Both effects are in play; ultimately, the public will determine whether new technologies can enhance our communal life.

● Conclusion: Government by the People

The Declaration of Independence states a powerful American ideal: the consent of the governed. The Constitution begins "We the People." Lincoln memorably reaffirmed this national commitment in his Gettysburg Address: "government . . . by the people." Self-rule appears to demand that public opinion guides—or at least influences—the government and that the people maintain an active involvement in government affairs.

Public opinion surveys are the most widely used effort to understand the popular mind. Scientific techniques have refined polling to a point of remarkable accuracy—especially as an election approaches.

However, public opinion often seems whimsical or uninformed. The framers of the Constitution were skeptical of public opinion, and their view is now echoed by many political scientists who conclude that the people just do not know enough. Good policy must rely on experts and political leaders. Other scholars argue that collective decisions—the wisdom of crowds—are better decisions than even those made by well-trained experts. Public officials have a major effect in setting the agenda, framing issues, and signaling popular views. They can take the lead in encouraging us to be better stewards of democracy. Keep in mind, at the same time, that public opinion can easily be manipulated. U.S. history is colored by officials' appeals to popular fears or other strong emotions to advance a particular policy aim—or the leader's own personal agenda. The best democratic officials instead emphasize civic education: provide the public with the tools to determine its own political path.

A politically active and informed public serves as a check on those officials who would manipulate public attitudes. The twenty-first-century has experienced lower electoral participation rates among Americans, especially the less educated and economically worse off—yet a simultaneous rise in civic voluntarism, particularly among "millennials."

Concrete evidence indicates that political involvement both enhances the collective whole and enhances each participant's personal prosperity, happiness, and health. Perhaps social media will encourage more engagement, especially among the superwired millennial generation. Possibly an expanded roster of government "nudges" will subtly incentivize people to get involved. Whatever the source, expanded participation in politics and government is at the heart of America's democratic aspiration: enhancing the ability to govern ourselves as a free people.

CHAPTER SUMMARY

● In a democracy, public opinion ought to guide the government. But are the people capable of self-rule? From the Constitutional Convention to contemporary social scientists, many experts consider public opinion uninformed and unreliable—and therefore a dangerous guide to decision making.

● Others respond that the public, taken as a whole, is a rational, reliable source of government decision making. Even if individuals do not know much, there is wisdom in crowds.

● Public officials generally balance public opinion with their own beliefs about the best decisions.

● Popular views can be especially important in setting the agenda: if something seems important to the public (and the media), politicians respond.

Congress, in particular, pays attention to spikes in public opinion. Presidents find it easier to get their policies passed when public opinion is strongly in favor of those policies.

● Scientific surveys have come a long way since the *Literary Digest* in 1936. Professionals now design well-specified polls that capture popular views with a high degree of accuracy. However, be cautious when reading polls, such as those without a well-defined sample (for example, online surveys). Always pay attention to the margin of error when interpreting results.

● Many different sources shape public opinion. The most important are family and friends, economic interests, demographics, party affiliation, the view of political elites, and defining events like war.

● Participation in civic and political life is a long-standing American tradition—helping, in the view of nineteenth-century visitors like Tocqueville, to distinguish the United States as a rising nation. Today, although Americans still exhibit higher levels of voluntarism than citizens of other countries, our rates of participation in politics and government have fallen to disturbing levels.

● People participate in public life in different ways: some through voting or otherwise engaging in campaigns, some through volunteer activities, and others by exercising their political voice—getting involved in issues that matter to them.

● Whether someone engages in civic life depends on both personal factors—those with politically active family members and close friends, or with higher education levels, are more inclined to participate—and political context.

● Mass engagement in politics and other civic activities is the lifeblood of American democracy, helping explain why analysts are so anxious to expand participation.

KEY TERMS

Approval rating, 204
Bandwagon effect, 198
Boomerang effect, 200
Civic voluntarism, 208
Clicktivism, 220
Demographic group, 197
Din, 222
Electoral activities, 207
Executive order, 204
Framing effects, 198
Gender gap, 194
Groupthink, 202
Issue advocacy, 214
Likely voters, 197
Mandate, 203
Margin of sampling error, 198
Motor voter law, 217
Paradox of voting, 210
Policy agenda, 204
Political elites, 195
Political mobilization, 214
Political voice, 209
Push poll, 198
Response bias, 198
Sampling frame, 197
Social capital, 211
Survey research, 203
Underdog effect, 200
Voter turnout, 206

STUDY QUESTIONS

1. "The masses are asses," wrote one observer. He was summarizing a perspective that public opinion is not a reliable guide to government. Why, exactly, is public opinion unreliable?

2. *Public officials must always balance public opinion with their own beliefs.*

a) Explain why.
b) What problems face political leaders who *always* follow the polls in deciding what to do?
c) What problems face political leaders who *never* follow the polls in deciding what to do?

d) How can polls help leaders who already know what they want to do?

3. Define the following terms: A push poll. A sampling frame. The margin of error. The Bradley effect.

4. What does it mean to "frame an issue"? Illustrate using the issue of obesity.

5. What are the different categories of involvement in civic or political life? Do any appeal more or less to you?

6. What features distinguish "Generation Y" when it comes to participation in civic and political activities?

7

The Media

IN 1961, the American Medical Association enlisted Ronald Reagan, then an actor, to help fight President John F. Kennedy's health care plan. Reagan cut a record (on vinyl) that the medical association sent (by snail mail) to every physician's home. "If this program passes," warned Reagan, "one day we will awake to find that we have socialism. . . . We will spend our sunset years telling our children and our children's children what it was like in America when men were free." The record asked doctors' wives to invite their friends, serve coffee, play Reagan's message, and then write letters to Congress opposing government health insurance. Congress voted down the program, although another version passed four years later and is now known as Medicare.

In 1993, the Health Insurance Association of America aired television ads opposing President Bill Clinton's health plan. The ads featured "Harry and Louise," a pleasant middle-aged couple, concerned that national health insurance would create a bureaucratic monster and wreck their health care. "They [the Washington bureaucrats] choose," intones a voice at the end of the ad. "You lose." Congress soon buried the Clinton health proposal.

In 2009, Sarah Palin posted a Facebook entry attacking President Barack Obama's health care plan, then being debated in Congress. "The America I know and love is not one in which my parents or my baby with Down Syndrome will have to stand in front of Obama's 'death panel' so his bureaucrats can decide . . . whether they are worthy of health care. Such a system is downright evil." Palin's "death panel" charge went viral. Talking heads, bloggers, tweeters, radio shock jocks, editorial writers, members of Congress, and citizens all repeated the phrase. Although health reform eventually won a narrow victory in Congress, the Palin post helped galvanize opponents who kept right on fighting to repeal the law—as some still are in 2015.

Each snapshot captures the media technology of a different era—and the politics they have channeled. In 1961, a recording reached an elite audience, which responded by mailing letters to Congress. In 1993, a TV ad ran in select markets and then spread via talking television heads. In 2009, a posting instantly reached millions of Facebook friends and followers, generating reaction in both new formats (blogs, tweets, texts) and traditional ones (newspapers,

● *Media reporters swarm a politician.*

IN THIS CHAPTER, YOU WILL:

● Learn how media coverage of politics is changing.

● Consider the democratic promises and pitfalls of social media.

● Explore how the media is (and is not) biased.

● Understand the rules that channel the media into its current forms.

● Discover how U.S. media is unique.

● Assess how media coverage influences politics, campaigns and elections.

see for yourself 7.1

Go online to hear Reagan's "Operation Coffee Cup" recording.

see for yourself 7.2

Go online to see the Harry and Louise ad.

radio, TV). Three major changes mark the evolution of issue campaigns across more than fifty years:

First, *the media keeps delivering information faster and faster.*

Second, *today's media includes many more voices and formats.*

Third, *the new media permits the public to be much more active.* You can comment on a Facebook posting more easily (and in more ways) than you could respond to a record in 1961 or a TV commercial in 1993.

What is the media?* It is all the ways people get information about politics and the wider world: television, Twitter, radio, newspapers, Internet searches,

---

BY THE NUMBERS
The Media

- Number of daily newspapers in print in the United States in 1850: **254**
- Number in 1900: **2,226**
- Approximate number in 2014: **1,380**
- Expected number in 2020, according to the Congressional Research Service: **700**
- Estimated number of African American–owned newspapers: **200**
- Number of African American–owned newspapers that print daily editions: **0**
- Percentage of Republicans and Democrats who called the media "biased" in 1989: **25**
- Percentage of Republicans who say so in 2013: **74**
- Percentage of Democrats who say so in 2013: **19**
- Number of channels in most homes outside of major cities in 1960: **3**
- Number of television channels received by the average home today: **118.6**
- Number of households reached by NBC: **112,770,700**
- Number reached by the largest Spanish-language network: **57,950,000**
- Number reached by the largest Christian network: **68,940,000**
- Rank of Comcast, Time Warner, and Walt Disney among all the media companies of the world: **1, 2, 3**
- Percentages of African Americans, Hispanics, and whites who report being active on social network sites, according to a Pew study on the media: **73, 68, 66**
- Percentage of each who report blogging: **22, 13, 14**
- Percentage of 18- to 29-year-olds who use the Internet as a major news source: **71**
- Percentage of those over 65 who do: **18**

---

*Properly speaking, media is the plural of medium—usually defined as the way we convey something. We use the term, media—meaning mass communication—as a singular noun in keeping with the way the language is evolving.

blogs, Facebook, Tumblr, and more. It is the major information connection between citizens and government.

Every change in the media affects politics. The rise of radio, television, and the Internet each had a profound impact on American political culture. Fifty years ago, everyone heard the same newscast and took part in the same debate. Today, each position on the political spectrum tunes in to its own news source and links to its own network. A key question looms above the rising **new media**: Do all the new outlets enhance democracy? Diminish it? Or perhaps some of both?

Who are we? From the start of this book, we have seen that the United States is an immense, ongoing argument over political ideas. The media brings the people into political debates; it is the great link between leaders and citizens. The national media reflects America itself: raucous, fast changing, multilingual, multicultural, forceful, rich, loud, and lucrative. It communicates in many languages at home. It broadcasts America to the world.

New media: On-demand access to information and entertainment on digital devices that also features interactive participation with content. Arose in the late twentieth century.

American Media Today: Traditional Formats Are Declining

Media technology changes quickly, and each change remakes the connections between citizens and their leaders. The media affects the news we get, the arguments we hear, and the deliberations we engage in.

Where People Go for News

Our lead story is simple. Fifty years ago, three national networks and the daily paper delivered essentially the same news to a largely passive audience. Most households subscribed to one newspaper. Your grandparents' choices were simple: tune in or not. Today, new technologies give Americans a host of options that are shaking up both media and government. This story—rapid media change with major consequences for politics and democracy—is nothing new. It has marked media advances throughout American history. Figure 7.1 summarizes where people have been going for their news over the past ten years.

As you can see, television remains the top source of news for most Americans. However, the audience is declining; TV was the chief source of news for 82 percent of the public in 2002 and 55 percent by 2012. Newspapers are crashing. Radio hangs on; almost everyone listens (especially in the car).

The biggest change is the rise of the Internet, which seizes more of the media pie every year. New online technologies complicate the picture.

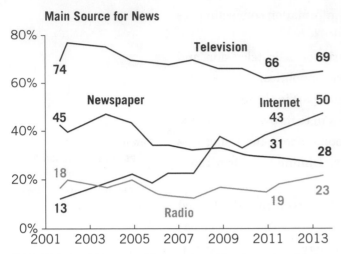

Main Source for News

Television 66 69
74
Newspaper
45 Internet 50
43
31 28
18
13 23
19
Radio
2001 2003 2005 2007 2009 2011 2013

● **FIGURE 7.1** *Reliable sources. The percentage of Americans who get their national and international news from each medium. (Pew Research Center)*

Two-thirds of U.S. adults get some news through a smartphone or tablet, and more than a third of eighteen- to twenty-four-year-olds turn to social-network sites like Facebook or Instagram as a primary news source. Every technology is losing ground to the Internet.

The velocity of change is even greater when we focus on different segments of the American audience. The Internet is already the main source of news among adults under thirty, soaring past television in 2010. A total of 71 percent of young adults (eighteen to twenty-nine years old) consider the Net their main news source. In contrast, not many people over sixty-five (just 18 percent) go online for their news. The media's future rests in the hands (or on the thumbs) of the young—and the young are online.

What do these changes mean for the media, for politics, and for democracy? We can learn more by focusing on developments in each of the major media.

Newspaper Decline

Newspapers have always been midwives to American democracy. The Federalist Papers (still the most important commentaries on our Constitution) first appeared as newspaper articles in the *New York Independent Journal*. George Washington's most famous communication, the Farewell Address, was actually a letter addressed to his "fellow citizens" and printed in the papers.

Mass media: Information and entertainment for broad popular audiences— including newspapers, radio, and television.

The First Mass Media. In the 1830s, newspapers became the first **mass media**— just when the vote expanded to include all white men. Papers cost one penny and reflected the raucous and often corrupt politics of the era. The *New York Herald* broke with the stodgy past, hired reporters to go out and dig up facts, and gave the readers just what they wanted—murder, fire, suicide, and crime. That disgusted the old elites but made the *Herald* the most widely read newspaper in the world.

Newspaper influence grew through the nineteenth century. The Spanish–American War, in 1898, is known as the first media-driven war because banner headlines blamed Spain for sinking an American battleship in Havana Harbor (there was no evidence of this) and helped bully the McKinley administration into the conflict. The papers developed comic strips to stretch their markets to the many immigrants who did not speak English well. By the turn of the century, there were more than 2,200 newspapers in the United States.

Even after the rise of radio and television, newspapers remained the major source for gathering and disseminating news, especially local news. Now, after more than two centuries at the center of the news media, the newspaper era is ending. The advertisers who guaranteed profits have migrated to the web; so

The power of the media, 1898. No one was sure exactly why the American battleship Maine exploded. An industrial accident remains likely. But the newspapers left no doubt that it was "Spanish treachery." Note the prominent mention of Assistant Secretary of the Navy, Theodore Roosevelt. He would become a hero during the war—and the nation's next president.

have readers. Today, more people read their news online than in print—and most of them read it for free.

Should We Worry?   There is much to celebrate about reading the news online. It is up to the minute and invites active readers who can open a story in (say) the *Wall Street Journal*, post a comment, click on a link connecting them to a *Huffington Post* report, and then surf over to YouTube for a clip from a TV network—or an eye-witness. The reader, not the editor, chooses the material. The Internet permits readers to respond, to share, to network, and to learn more.

Media analysts, however, see two problems. First, newspapers still do the basic reporting. Web-based outlets add opinions, background, links, and multiple perspectives, but it all begins with stories developed by reporters. If newspapers can't generate revenue, they won't survive. Where will we get the basic facts and stories? Will the reporting function migrate to another media institution?

Second, important stories may get lost. Newspapers always covered the "hot" topics (war, murder, and high school sports) along with less exciting civic issues (such as school board meetings or wetland controversies). Since it was all one package, the popular stories paid for the civics lessons. As newspapers downsize staff and try to sell their stories by the piece on the web, there may be no way to subsidize coverage on limited-interest (but very important) issues like education.[1]

● *Roosevelt used the new medium—radio—to speak directly to citizens in their homes. The result: the rise of the personal presidency. The change in the media helped introduce a change in our politics.*

Radio Holds Steady

The first commercial radio stations sprang up in the 1920s. President Franklin Roosevelt seized the new technology during the Great Depression of the 1930s and delivered a weekly radio address, known as the Fireside Chat. The talks were informal, as if the president were talking to his listeners right by their own firesides. Hearing Roosevelt's voice changed the relationship between Americans and their presidents. The people grew to expect a personal link. Indeed, political scientists link this development to the rise of the **personal presidency**.

The radio also gave new immediacy to wartime reports during World War II—and to baseball games. It accelerated the velocity of news and information. The medium made the nation, and the world, a smaller place.

The radio era lasted just thirty years. By the mid-1950s, television displaced it. However, the radio still has political consequences. Conservative talk radio arose in the late 1980s after the Reagan administration cleared the way (we'll discuss the government connection below). Rush Limbaugh—a talented, loquacious, pugnacious host—syndicated his show, and a stream of other conservatives followed him onto the airwaves. Limbaugh pioneered the argument that became a foundation for conservative talk: the rest of the media is biased, so you have to dial in here. Liberals tried to counter with their own talk shows, but their efforts foundered, perhaps because liberals are less likely to complain that the media is biased.

Television: From News to Infotainment

Television came onto the American scene in the 1950s and revolutionized both entertainment and politics. President John F. Kennedy sensed TV's power and gave the first live press conference in February 1961. An incredible 65 million people—one in three Americans—tuned in. The young, charismatic president was a natural TV performer and, once again, a new media technology intensified the link between the people and their president.

Personal presidency: The idea that the president has a personal link to the public. Made possible by twentieth-century media.

The Rise of Cable.   Two networks, CBS and NBC, monopolized the television news business during the 1960s–1970s. Interested Americans all watched the same version of the day's events, solemnly read during the evening news show by celebrated anchors.

Technology broke the monopoly. Cable stations came online in the 1980s and began to reach for small slices of the network audience. They lingered on the fringe of the media until 1991 when an upstart network, CNN, showed live video of allied rockets screaming into Baghdad, the capital of Iraq, at the start of the Gulf War. CNN introduced a new model: It reported news all day. It gathered footage from local stations around the country, which now had the technical capacity to produce their own videos; in exchange for the feeds, CNN shared its footage of breaking news with local stations. No more waiting until 6 p.m. for the national network news. A new format was born: the twenty-four-hour news cycle. Twenty years ago, White House staff, and the reporters who covered them, all relaxed when the news cycle ended around 5 p.m. Today, the cycle never ends.

In 1996, Rupert Murdoch launched Fox News, a network with a conservative slant. As Republican viewers headed for Fox, other cable networks (most notably MSNBC) moved to the left and developed shows with a liberal spin. Eventually, cable channels filled every niche along the political spectrum—Fox offerings like *Hannity* on the right, shows like *Hardball* with Chris Matthews in the center, and the *Rachel Maddow Show* and the *Colbert Report* on the left.

Infotainment.   As cable channels proliferated, the line between news and entertainment began to evaporate. Late-night talk shows got into the political act. Hosts gleefully lacerated the political losers of the day. Politicians responded by lining up to participate. A major threshold of the new era: Senator John McCain, the Republican nominee for president in 2008, announced his candidacy on the *Late Show with David Letterman*—with bandleader Paul Shaffer in pink shades blasting out "Hail to the Chief." In 2014, President Obama appeared with comedian Zach Galifianakis to encourage Americans to sign up for health-insurance exchanges after a glitch-filled rollout—an appearance that was widely credited with helping boost enrollment.

see for yourself 7.3

Go online to see Senator McCain's announcement. (Flash required)

Jon Stewart refined the formula by merging comedy, entertainment, political talk, and savvy media criticism on the *Daily Show*. Stewart himself pointed out the fading line between news and entertainment when he noted that his show airs on *Comedy Central* and the lead-in features puppets. When the Obama administration botched the rollout of its health care web site, the Secretary of Health and Human Services, who was responsible, rushed onto to the *Daily Show* to explain. Her terrible performance was widely cited for her resignation six months later.

When asked about their major source of news in a recent Pew poll, young viewers (eighteen to twenty-nine years old) were as likely to tap the *Daily Show* as the network news shows. The corporate setting helps blur the line between news, politics, and entertainment, a phenomenon now described as **infotainment**.

Amid this colorful scene, the network news steadily declines. In 2012 alone, the three network nightly news shows lost 418,000 viewers (2 percent).[2]

Infotainment: The blurred line between news and entertainment.

 The line between news and entertainment has blurred. Here, President Obama gamely sits for a comic interview with Zach Galifianakis in 2014—and helped encourage public enrollments in health exchanges, a key feature of the Affordable Care Act.

THE BOTTOM LINE

- Thirty years ago, a few outlets—three networks, the local newspaper—delivered roughly the same news. Americans had few choices about what news source to follow. Today, media outlets cater to every perspective—left, right, and center. Americans no longer share a single source of news.

- Traditional newspapers and networks still aim for objective reporting, but the effort is increasingly hard to sell. A pointed question now dogs producers and editors: Who will pay to gather hard news?

- New Internet sources, especially social media platforms like Twitter and Instagram, are taking their place—especially among young people. What will be the political effects of this change?

- In the past, the rise of new media—newspapers, radio, and television—changed the nature of news reporting and altered political institutions like the presidency.

◗ The Rise of the New Media

In 2012, Barack Obama skipped the traditional networks and newspapers and announced his re-election candidacy for president on a YouTube video. What lasting effects on the media sector will these latest technologies produce? Some observers predict a new era of citizen participation. Now everyone can be their own producer and reporter, conveying political events and ideas from a thousand different perspectives. Gloomier critics warn about eroding news coverage.

On the positive side, the Internet and social-media sites turn us all into potential news providers. Traditional news always awaited the arrival of a camera team. Now anyone can record an event on their phone, post it to Facebook or YouTube or Twitter (or all three), and watch it go viral. The political equilibrium changes when the public actually sees police officers beating a black motorist, for example.

Similarly, new technologies enable us to trace events that were much harder to track when communication was over (untapped) telephones. Today public officials' texts or e-mail trails can connect them to scandalous revelations. Early in 2014, top staffers to New Jersey governor and leading Republican presidential hopeful Chris Christie were caught deliberately causing massive traffic delays to punish a local mayor who refused to endorse Christie for re-election. E-mail threads led directly to scandal.

Even more dramatically, in 2013, an unknown information-technology specialist working for the National Security Agency released secret government documents that shocked the world and shook up American foreign policy. New media technology enabled Edward Snowden to publicize a vast stockpile of classified information.

Still, the new outlets primarily rely on old media sources, which they are choking off (see Figure 7.2). Yes, the new media generates important stories. But these topics—like almost every other story—became important when traditional media focused attention on them. Newspapers, networks, and cable channels still develop and spread most news. The list of the top fifteen websites includes all the same old players (see Table 7.1).

Search engines and web portals link largely to stories posted by traditional news sources—the *New York Times*, the *Washington Post*, CNN, and ABC. The worrisome part, for both mainstream media and citizens: the portals and search engines grab the revenue. The web relies on the same old news sources but avoids paying them. The people who gather the news—for old and new media alike—find it difficult to get paid for their services. As they cut their own costs, news coverage gets thinner and less reliable—and the old media's downward spiral affects most of the stories that people read on their laptops and cell phones.

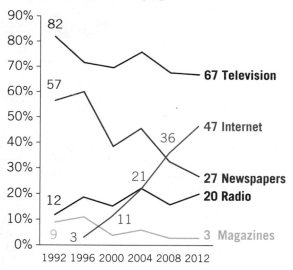

Internet Grows as Campaign News Source

● **FIGURE 7.2** *Campaign news sources: The Internet grows in importance, cable TV holds steady, and others decline in popularity as sources of campaign news. (Pew Research Center)*

THE BOTTOM LINE

● Emerging new media forms are sparking a revolution that is changing the way Americans produce and process news and political information.

● The new media's effects are only beginning to reverberate across our government and politics. Unclear is whether the benefits—everyone contributing to "the news" or increased transparency—outweigh the dangers of losing traditional reporting sources.

TABLE 7.1 Top Visited News Sites in 2010, Nielsen

RANK	DOMAIN	UNIQUE VISITORS
1	Yahoo! News Websites	125,000,000
2	Huffington Post	105,000,000
3	CNN	85,000,000
4	Google News	80,000,000
5	NYTimes.com	70,000,000
6	Fox News Digital Network	65,000,000
7	NBC News	63,000,000
8	Mail Online	53,000,000
9	washingtonpost.com	47,000,000
10	Wall Street Journal	40,000,000
11	The Guardian	38,000,000
12	ABC News	36,000,000
13	USA Today	35,000,000
14	BBC	34,000,000
15	LA Times	32,500,000

Source: Nielsen, Pew Research Center.

Selling Old Products via New Media

Once upon a time, if the folks who sold milk wanted to spread the word about their product, they ran an ad in the local paper. Since lots of people read the paper, the ad could be pretty boring and still reach a lot of eyes.

Today there are so many sources of news that it is difficult to grab attention. Imagine you are a dairy producer hoping to boost purchases of milk. Your advertising rep shows up with a new, attention-getting ad for one of milk's newly discovered health benefits. The agency has built a microsite called everythingidoiswrong.

org. To attract an audience, they've opted for crude comedy. The site pretends to advise men how to deal with their partner's PMS. The tagline: "Milk Can Help Reduce the Symptoms of PMS."

Do you green-light this, um, unconventional approach? The California Milk Processor Board faced exactly this decision—and decided to give the ad campaign a try. Site visitors were not amused, and they let the advertisers know it. "Wrong," texted one visitor to the web page. "Milk ad campaign blames PMS,

insults women." The Board, stung by the backlash, shut down the site and replaced it with an apology. The mainstream media picked up the story and spread it, further embarrassing the campaign's sponsor.

Moral: The crowded new media environment leads to strange antics designed to attract attention. But here's the positive side. The eyeballs can talk back. After just one day, the website disappeared because visitors told the milk people their idea of humor was offensive.[3]

● Is the Media Biased?

"What you have to do in order to earn the approval of the people in the media," declared Rush Limbaugh, is "to adopt their causes," such as global warming. "And it really helps if you take a position opposite me." Conservative media draws strength from a furious charge: the mainstream media is too liberal (see Figure 7.3).[4]

On the other side, liberals also charge the media with bias. In his book *What Liberal Media?* Eric Alterman complains that the news corps rarely challenges the rich, the powerful, or the status quo. The media breathlessly tracks the stock market but underplays stories about the rise of inequality. It ignores labor issues, child poverty, or homelessness. One of three Democrats believes the media is biased against them.[5]

Which is it? A powerful left-wing media out to destroy conservatives? Or timid reporters, editors, and producers, collectively bullied by the right?

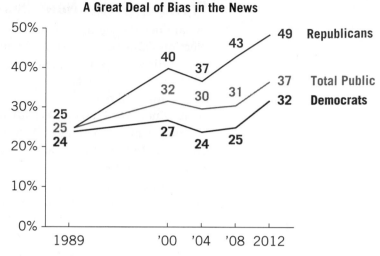

A Great Deal of Bias in the News

● **FIGURE 7.3** *Half of all Republicans and a third of Democrats believe the media is biased. The feeling has grown over the past 25 years—especially among Republicans. (Pew Research Center)*

Reporters Are Democrats

Conservatives are correct about the press corps' personal attitudes. Reporters in the mainstream media are more liberal than the country as a whole. Roughly 85 percent of the press corps calls itself liberal or moderate, compared to about 60 percent of the population. Although most reporters call themselves moderates (especially those in the local media, where the number runs well above 60 percent), very few are self-described conservatives. Moreover, the press corps tends to vote for Democratic presidential candidates.

However, dozens of studies about election campaigns fail to show a systematic bias toward Democratic candidates. Scholars have searched for bias in coverage, in statements, and in the kinds of stories that are aired. Some studies in some elections did find favoritism. Overall, however, the media does not lean either to Democrats or to Republicans during election campaigns.

There have been fewer studies of media bias outside of elections. Perhaps reporters' views creep into coverage of policy fights or presidential speeches, although there is no reliable evidence to suggest that. However, there is hard evidence of a much deeper bias that runs through the news media—the need to attract a larger audience. We suggest that the media is indeed biased, but not in the way either side imagines. The largest bias comes from the media's real purpose: making money. Media outlets print or say or film with an eye to drawing an audience.

Profits Drive the News Industry

What does the media actually sell? It is not news about government actors or election campaigns. Media sells its audience to advertisers. As a result, the prime directive is to expand the audience. When ratings rise, the business prospers; when they fall, networks replace anchors and newspapers cut staff. These financial realities give the news media a strong incentive to pitch its own politics near the views of its audience. For the large networks, that means the political center, where most Americans are comfortable. And, that's why both Left and Right complain about bias; the center *is* to the left of conservatives and to the right of liberals.

At the same time, each publication and each network seeks its own audience. More conservative communities usually get more conservative newspapers, and the current media is, as we have seen, divided into strong partisan niches.

In short, the market forces each news source toward the politics of its audience. That pressure, however, is just the start of the market's influence on the media. Other market biases include the search for drama, conflict, and scandal.

Drama Delivers Audiences

There's not much excitement in a school board meeting or a health care proposal. Miners trapped below the earth, on the other hand, pull people to their televisions and radios. A good drama must have a narrative arc with a beginning, middle, and end. It has a protagonist (the miners), pathos (anxious spouses), a villain (the coal company or the government regulators), drama (will they be rescued before they run out of air?), an ending (tired but jubilant miners hugging their families), and a take-home message (we need to worry about mine safety).

Local news gets much of its drama from crime. A classic rule of thumb guides the local TV news: "If it bleeds, it leads." Many good things may have happened that day, but the lead story features the most grisly event. The images are familiar to the point of cliché—a breathless reporter live on the scene, yellow tape blocking the area, grim-faced cops or firefighters in the background, weeping relatives in a daze, and perhaps a blank-faced perpetrator blinking into the camera.

The need for drama transforms election coverage as well. It rarely focuses on the issues, an audience turnoff. Instead, it is about the drama of two protagonists, their families, their strategies, their dirty tricks, and their blunders. Elections have a built-in narrative arc, again with all the familiar features: a *beginning* (the candidates throw their hats

● The rule for local news: If it bleeds, it leads.

into the ring), a *middle* (who is ahead? who had the best week?), a *conclusion* (someone wins), and a *take-home message* (the loser had a fatal flaw that other candidates should avoid).

Political debates—about the environment, government spending, education, or taxes—generally reflect the same pressure to build a narrative. Regardless of the issue, media coverage focuses on drama and conflict, heroes and villains, winners and losers.

Check out your favorite news website. Can you see the dramatic narrative that frames the lead story? Pundits criticize the news for lacking substance. However, as a student of political science, you have learned to examine the *institution* and its incentives. The media, seeking a large audience to serve to advertisers, covers whatever attracts most attention. Simply calling for serious coverage will not change the incentives in the media market.

● *President Clinton: "I did not have sexual relations with that woman."*

Sex and Scandal

Nothing attracts an audience like scandals—and the bigger the name involved, the bigger the media bonanza. President Bill Clinton's sexual involvement with a White House intern received enormous coverage. A scan of sixty-five newspapers revealed that they averaged more than a story a day for the entire year. During the coverage, CNN quadrupled its average rating. By the end of the year, 97 percent of the public could identify the president's alleged lover, while only 12 percent knew who was chief justice of the United States.[6]

The Skeptical Media

Other media biases have to do less with market and more with the profession of journalism. Two are especially powerful: skepticism and objectivity. Back in the early 1960s, Washington reporters were a small, white, male club with a code that winked at extramarital affairs in the White House or falling-down drunks serving in Congress. Then a series of events transformed the media's stance toward powerful men and women: the moral intensity of the civil rights movement, administration efforts to manipulate the press during the Vietnam War, and the **Watergate scandal** all made the old accommodations seem irresponsible. How could reporters go easy on segregationists or liars?

Watergate was especially significant in fostering skepticism. Reporters investigated a burglary of Democratic Party headquarters that led directly to the White House. President Nixon had secretly taped conversations in the Oval Office and, pursuing the case of the botched burglary, the Supreme Court forced the release of the tapes. Their content stunned Americans. Nixon had always seemed a bit sanctimonious. Now the public could hear him order aides to "stonewall" the Watergate investigations. Even more shocking, the presidential

see for yourself 7.4

President Clinton claims he did not have sex with that woman.

see for yourself 7.5

Go online to listen to two infamous denials: Richard Nixon declares he is not a crook.

Watergate scandal: A failed effort in 1972 by Republican operatives to break into Democratic Party headquarters in the Watergate office complex in Washington, D.C.; tapes revealed that President Nixon attempted to cover up the event—causing him to resign the presidency.

tapes bristled with ethnic slurs, anti-Semitism, and foul language. (The newspaper transcripts were full of the notation, "expletive deleted.")

Reporters redefined their roles. Rather than acting as chummy insiders, they became skeptics, aiming to pierce through official propaganda and find the hidden truth. Relations between press and politician turned adversarial. Each time the members of the press felt misled by an administration, their skepticism grew. For example, George W. Bush insisted that Iraq owned dangerous weapons that threatened the United States. (It did not.) Barack Obama promised Americans "if you like your health plan, you can keep it." (Not all could.) The reporter's gold standard became uncovering lies or bad behavior.

THE BOTTOM LINE

- Both conservatives and liberals complain of media bias. However, the media generally reflects the politics of its audience.

- The media's deepest bias comes from the need to win ratings and appeal to advertisers. That puts an emphasis on drama, scandal, and conflict—exacerbating partisan political divisions.

How Governments Shape the Media

We have seen how technology constantly changes the media. The media, in turn, changes politics. In this section, we examine how political rules shape the development of the media.

Democratic nations organize their media in three different ways: First, the government can fund the media. This **public ownership** model is familiar in many nations—but not the United States. Second, the government can *regulate* the media to ensure that it operates in the public interest. Third, the government can stand aside and let the *market* guide the media; the assumption in the market model is that private companies will give the people (and the advertisers) what they want.

Public ownership: A situation in which media outlets are run by the government and paid for by tax dollars.

The First Amendment Protects Print Media From Regulation

You have already encountered the primary political rule governing print media—the *First Amendment*: "Congress shall make no law . . . abridging the freedom of speech or of the press." As we saw in Chapter 4, the Supreme Court has been strict about forbidding government interference with the press. It is very difficult to censor news (known as prior restraint), to convict someone of slander or libel (spoken or written lies), to restrict pornography, or to forbid hate speech.

Market forces impose the limits that do exist. American newspapers, paid for by local advertisers, generally reflect local mores. They are tame compared with, for example, the English tabloids. The Internet, of course, operates in a different kind of market—unmoored to local communities and their values. The result is a much wilder format—so far, an almost unregulated media frontier.

Regulating Broadcasters

Radio and television fall into a separate category. They have been subject to government regulations from the start. As radio stations spread in the 1930s, their signals began to interfere with one another. In 1934 the Franklin Roosevelt administration created the Federal Communications Commission (FCC) to referee the industry. The agency began with a political philosophy: the airwaves belong to the public. The FCC would license stations on a given frequency—meaning no more overlapping signals—but in exchange, stations were required to be "socially responsible." When a station secured or renewed its license, it had to show that it operated in the public's interest. When television emerged, the FCC expanded its jurisdiction to include it.

In 1949, the FCC issued an important regulation, the **fairness doctrine**. The fairness doctrine required radio and TV stations to give equal time to each side of a public issue. The rule reflected the era's expectations: sober, nonpartisan coverage of news and politics. Although it was not strictly enforced,

Fairness doctrine:
Regulation that required media outlets to devote equal time to opposite perspectives.

TABLE 7.2 Public Television—Abroad and at Home

COUNTRY	DAILY AUDIENCE (BY NATION)	TAXES PAID FOR PUBLIC TV PER PERSON
Denmark	69%	$130
UK (BBC, Ch 4)	50%	$90 (BBC only)
Germany	40%	$130
France	30%	$51
Australia	19%	$34
Netherlands	35%	$50
Norway	32%	$133
Canada	9% (English speaking) 17% (French speaking)	$30
Japan	17%	$54
United States	**1.2%**	**$3.75***

*and even that $3.75 is extremely controversial in the United States.
Source: Benson and Powers, Public Media and Political Independence.[7]

the fairness doctrine led stations to shy away from political controversies altogether; that way they avoided the bother of achieving a balance.

In the 1980s, the Reagan administration challenged the entire idea of public responsibility enforced by regulatory agencies. It promoted a different political philosophy, viewing media as a private commodity rather than as a public good: end government regulations and let the consumers use the market to enforce what they value. The FCC repealed the fairness doctrine in 1983. The consequences were huge. Under the fairness doctrine, each talk show with a point of view would have to be balanced by another talk show from the opposite perspective. A station that broadcast conservatives like Rush Limbaugh would be required to air an equal amount of liberal programming. Repealing the rule opened the door to the media landscape we have today: a rich and raucous menu of news and politics that reaches across the political spectrum.

Protecting Competition

Consolidation: A media company grows, acquires other companies, and threatens to dominate the market.

The market model is based on competition. If one corporation captures too much of the market, might it diminish consumer choice? The question arose when corporations moved to control companies across different media markets—print, radio, and television. Some observers warned that a few companies might come to dominate—and stifle the marketplace of ideas. The top two radio companies, Clear Channel and CBS, control so many stations that they broadcast to a larger audience (263 million strong) than all twenty-four of the remaining radio networks combined. **Consolidation**, from this perspective, threatens free speech and fair debate.

Telecommunications Act of 1996: A major congressional overhaul of communications law that opened the door to far more competition by permitting companies to own outlets in multiple media markets—radio, television, magazines, etc.

Those who favor deregulation respond that today's media takes so many different forms, from radio stations to online news, blogs, and tweets, that stiff competition for consumer attention is inevitable. The **Telecommunications Act of 1996** reflected this second view and permitted many forms of cross-ownership. However, the debate about controlling media consolidation lingers on.

THE BOTTOM LINE

- Democratic nations organize their media in three ways: government ownership, regulation, and markets. The United States has relied on the latter two, regulation and markets.

- The First Amendment protects print media from most government regulation.

- Broadcast media in the United States was originally regulated by agencies like the FCC, which imposed the fairness doctrine—a reflection of a less partisan era.

- Deregulation, new technologies, and the rise of multiple media have created the spectrum of perspectives and views that mark American media today. This contributes to our partisan and conflicted politics.

● How the Media Shapes Politics

The media influences not just how we talk, but what we talk *about*. It sets the agenda and frames our politics. This section describes how.

● *If a story has a loud signal, all of the media will be talking about it, as these commentators are here, on* The View. *The stories everyone talks about are the news items that reach undecided voters.*

News Stories Reinforce Existing Beliefs

Imagine that you're a Republican with lots of Democratic friends. You come across a detailed news story that crushes one of their cherished beliefs. You send it to them with a snide comment—and what happens? Rather than changing their minds, the story simply reinforces what they believe. Researchers have discovered that new information rarely influences people who already have strongly held opinions. Instead, new information reinforces existing opinions regardless of the content of the story. You may find this conclusion surprising: news stories do not change the opinions of people who pay the most attention to the news.

However, news items can have an impact on people who have not already made up their minds. About a third of the public does not have a strong political view and is less likely to follow the news. But this group *is* open to influence by the media. Here is a paradox: The news media is most likely to influence the people who pay the least attention to it. Since this group does not follow politics and government very closely, only news stories with a "**loud signal**" are likely to reach them and influence their views. A loud signal means that a news story gets *broad media coverage* and delivers an *unambiguous message*.

Loud signal: Media stories with very broad coverage and an unambiguous message.

The Political Agenda

Media outlets may have limited influence on what politically savvy people think, but editors and reporters have enormous influence on what they think *about*. Editors and other media leaders listen to the American political din and pluck out one or two stories to headline and a dozen others for the second tier. Those become the topics that politicians address, Congress investigates, talk shows debate, and you discuss and tweet and blog. When an issue commands such attention, we say it is on the political agenda or **policy agenda**. And this is generally the first step to political action. If something you care about—homelessness, immorality, or animal cruelty—is not being discussed, it is unlikely that political leaders will pay attention to it. The first step to political action is to get your issue onto the national agenda.

The surest route onto the agenda is through the media. Setting the agenda is one of the most important influences the news media has on American politics. Politicians, think tanks, interest groups, citizens, and experts all try to influence the agenda. Sometimes they succeed; far more often they fail.

Policy agenda: The issues that the media covers, the public considers important, and politicians address. Setting the agenda is the first step in political action.

Large demonstrations in major American cities against the Iraq war in 2003 got scant mention. Ten years later, demonstrations against government spying caught the media's attention. As the news reverberated, the demonstrations multiplied and grew. The coverage kept the efforts to limit government data collection squarely on the national agenda. How does the media pick the issues it will emphasize? You already know the answer to that: drama, conflict, a narrative, heroes, villains, and a story that sells.

Priming the Public

The issues that rise onto the agenda and dominate the news affect public perceptions of candidates and officials. This influence is known as **priming**. For example, because the Republican Party is identified with smaller government, stories about government incompetence *prime* the public to see the world through Republican eyes. Stories about the plight of the elderly or the hardworking poor prime voters to think along Democratic Party lines.

Priming: Affecting voters' or poll respondents' perception of candidates or public officials by raising issues that are perceived to enhance or diminish the candidates.

Priming is a very subtle form of political bias, because media outlets do not need to explicitly favor one side or the other. Rather, they simply run stories on a particular topic—which plays to the strength (or weakness) of one party or one candidate. Candidates are evaluated by the kinds of issues that are featured in the news.

Racial images have an especially powerful priming effect. Certain programs— "welfare" or "food stamps"—tend to raise negative, highly radicalized associations. When Newt Gingrich, running for the Republican presidential nomination in 2012, termed Barack Obama "the food stamp president," he was widely accused of priming: He hoped to diminish his rival by simply raising the subject of welfare programs and, by implication, race and poverty.

Framing the Issue

Framing: The way an issue is defined—every issue has many possible frames, each with a slightly different tilt in describing the problem and highlighting solutions.

There are many ways to cover an issue, and each offers a slightly different perspective. When the media chooses a particular slant, we say it is **framing** the issue. For example, the Obama administration issued regulations that required employers to offer contraception as part of their health insurance coverage. Catholic organizations claimed that the ruling violated their religious beliefs. Then the battle over framing began. Republicans charged that the Obama administration was hostile to religion; the Democrats countered that the real Republican purpose was to attack contraception as part of a "war on women" designed to deny women legal access to birth control.

Often, media framing is invisible to the public because it simply reflects social conventions. The issue of equality was once framed as a problem concerning white men: Could they achieve the American dream in an industrial system devoted to profits? Later, mass

● Media framing battles are carried out on every front: social media like Twitter and Instagram, paid advertising in print and on the air, and humorous cartoons. Here, cartoonist Joe Heller weighs in on the gun control debate.

social movements rose up and reframed the issue as one that spoke directly to race, ethnicity, and gender.

In short, framing defines the nature of the problem, organizes potential solutions, and wipes out alternative policies. Media coverage plays a crucial role—often, *the* crucial role—in issue framing.

THE BOTTOM LINE

- News stories generally do not change minds that are already made up, but a story with a loud, clear signal can influence the undecided.

- The media plays a crucial role in setting the national agenda, priming voters to focus on issues that help or harm one side, and framing the way those issues are seen—and resolved.

The Media's Electoral Connection

Every aspect of the media's influence on politics is on full display during election campaigns. The usual emphasis on entertainment now places a particular focus on the horse race: Who is winning and why?

The Campaign as Drama

Media coverage has evolved and now devotes much less time to the candidate's speeches. In 1968, the average clip of a candidate speaking on the news, called a **sound bite**, went uninterrupted for over forty seconds. Today, the average clip has fallen to under eight seconds. After those eight seconds, the candidate's speech is simply backdrop for the anchor or the pundit. You might see the candidates gesture and move their lips, but those are just the backdrop for analysis, often centered on (you guessed it!) why the candidate is winning or losing.

Throughout the campaign, reporters' antennae are always up for gaffes and hints of scandal. When one appears, the entire media throngs after it. Every speech and each debate are carefully combed over for blunders. Effective campaigns develop rapid-response teams that can deal with whatever crisis gusts through the media on that day. George W. Bush dealt with allegations of cocaine use with a simple, firm answer: "When I was young and foolish, I was young and foolish." Newt Gingrich briefly vaulted to the top of the Republican pack in the 2012 primary when he turned a potential scandal (his second wife alleged that he asked her for an open marriage) into a raking assault on the media. "I think the destructive, vicious, negative nature of much of the news media," he said to roars of approval at one CNN debate, "makes it harder to govern this country, harder to attract decent people to run for public office, and I am appalled that you would begin a presidential debate on a topic like that." Gaffes and scandals are part of life on the campaign trail, and effective politicians learn how to blunt them—or even turn them to advantage.

see for yourself 7.6

Go online to see a long list of late-night political jokes.

Sound bite: A short clip of speech taken from a longer piece of audio. Often refers to a brief excerpt from a speech by a candidate or politician.

see for yourself 7.7

Go online to see Newt Gingrich deflect comments about his personal scandal.

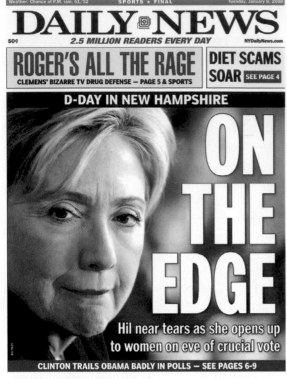

Weather: Chance of P.M. rain. 61/52   SPORTS ★ FINAL   Tuesday, January 8, 2008

DAILY●NEWS

2.5 MILLION READERS EVERY DAY

50¢   NYDailyNews.com

ROGER'S ALL THE RAGE
CLEMENS' BIZARRE TV DRUG DEFENSE — PAGE 5 & SPORTS

DIET SCAMS SOAR SEE PAGE 4

D-DAY IN NEW HAMPSHIRE

ON THE EDGE

Hil near tears as she opens up to women on eve of crucial vote

CLINTON TRAILS OBAMA BADLY IN POLLS — SEE PAGES 6-9

● *Are the rules different for women? When Hillary Clinton briefly choked up during the New Hampshire primary, the story echoed throughout the media. Originally cast as a cold-hearted shrew, she came from behind in the polls to win the New Hampshire primary.*

see for yourself 7.8

Go online to see Hillary Clinton's human response to a personal question.

see for yourself 7.9

Go online to see some of the most famous fear-driven advertise-ments—starting with the little girl and the atom bomb in 1964. (Flash required)

Candidate Profiles

Campaign coverage often features a powerful narrative. The media sketches a profile of each candidate—simplistic, exaggerated, and very hard to escape. That image then shapes future coverage. Once the portrait develops, it reverberates through the world of infotainment. Behavior that "fits" immediately gets airtime, reinforcing the narrative.

The media first pictured Barack Obama as cool—"no drama Obama"—and later "cold and aloof." The press played Mitt Romney as an out-of-touch rich guy; the *Washington Post* and the *Wall Street Journal* ran columns listing the "top ten Romney wealth gaffes," leading off with his quip that he appreciated American cars because his wife "drives a couple of Cadillacs."[8]

Narratives about woman candidates often fall into gender stereotypes. When asked about stereotypes that offend her, Michelle Obama points to the "angry black woman." Hillary Clinton has been cast as the grind, the shrew, the scold, the harpy, and the emasculator. Sarah Palin, the former vice-presidential candidate, was portrayed as a ditz, a diva, a hysteric, or a dim but charming beauty queen.

Campaigns spend extraordinary sums on advertising. Some ads have become classics, usually because of their wicked stings. The Democrats painted Republican Barry Goldwater in 1964 as an extremist, with a spot that featured a little girl plucking the petals off a daisy suddenly interrupted by an ominous countdown and a fiery mushroom cloud.

Political advertisements become especially effective if they seep into the news coverage and become part of the campaign narrative. That can amplify the signal enough to reach the voters in the middle who are not paying much attention. As in every other aspect of politics, the new media raise the prospect of great changes in campaigning. Social-media outlets like Facebook and Twitter give candidates a targeted way to circumvent the mass media and speak directly to supporters. Online messaging creates a sense of movement, of belonging. It offers a way to mobilize supporters behind a cause without relying on traditional media coverage. Ironically, the mainstream media eagerly reports on successful new media campaigns—amplifying that success by publicizing it.

THE BOTTOM LINE

● Media coverage of campaigns reflects the general patterns of the contemporary media. It emphasizes drama, conflict, and the horse race narrative.

● Campaigns attempt to influence the media or bypass it and speak directly to supporters. These efforts in turn become part of the media coverage.

● Conclusion: At the Crossroads of the Media World

The media reflects the United States—and broadcasts it to the world. American media has many critics. Conservatives blast the mainstream media's bias; liberals lament Fox News and Rush Limbaugh. We should remember, however, that the American broadcast media has always been a commercial enterprise. For better or for worse, whatever draws an audience survives and flourishes.

America's media reflects the nation and its people. The fifth-largest network in the United States is the Spanish-language Univision. Univision beats all the major networks on both Wednesday and Friday nights among young adults (eighteen- to thirty-four-year-olds, the demographic that advertisers most seek). In fact, the dozen Spanish-speaking networks boast a total of more than 260 affiliates. Together, they reach more local stations than any one of the major networks. Nor does the foreign-language media stop at Spanish. In San Francisco, Comcast offers 35 foreign-language channels, and the DISH satellite menu includes 100 foreign-language stations. Sixty million Americans (including one of your authors) have at least one parent born abroad, and the media reflects that reality.

What else does the media tell us about who we are? Here's another important indicator: the ten largest religious networks have 338 affiliates. The largest, the Worship Network, reaches an estimated 69.9 million households (by way of comparison, Fox reaches 112 million).

As we have seen, television in every demographic is being squeezed by the web and the new media. And, in this booming new category, it is America's young people who drive the change—pioneering new technologies, picking winners and losers among sites and applications. What had once appeared to be a great digital divide is now falling, as African American and Latino youth catch up. In forums like Twitter, they even nudge to the top of their demographic.

Pessimists lament the collapse of our national community. Every political side now has its own news shows; Americans don't just disagree about their values—they don't even hear or see the same reality. Mainstream newspapers and networks are losing money and, as a result, their capacity to collect the news is declining. The hard news media cut staff and lay off reporters. As the details about national and international events get sketchier, the void is filled by loud, ill-informed opinions. The entire news apparatus dashes after drama, conflict, and scandal. Important issues like education, the environment, and impartial analysis of the health care system are downplayed in this chase for audience where victory goes to the loudest or the most outrageous.

To pessimists, the new media only hastens the demise of the old reflective politics that permitted leaders to work together, forge compromises, and address our national problems. Today's media—fragmented, declining, sensationalist— exacerbates the conflicts in American politics.

In contrast, optimists see a thriving democracy where people are active and engaged. Debates in Washington may be long and loud, but that only reflects an energetic nation undergoing enormous change. As media outlets expand, people's choices grow richer. Today, the United States has a broad

DOES THE MEDIA ENHANCE DEMOCRACY?

Return to the question that opened this chapter. When you think about the American media, what do you see for the future of democracy and politics? Are you with the optimists or the pessimists?

Agree. A booming media enhances American democracy. Media offers new ways to process news, build networks, and interact with leaders. New Media—or clicktivism—works as a robust new form of political action.

Disagree. Media harms democracy. The Babel of voices hastens national decline by chasing sensation and fomenting conflict. New media in particular erodes our news-producing capacity, increases inequalities, and offers dark corners that incubate malice.

Unsure. Of course, the answer may lie somewhere in the middle, but keep the range of possibilities in mind as you monitor the media in the years ahead.

lineup of news, information, and analysis. Members of the traditional media try to present objective reports as best they can. Cable channels and radio stations get partisans excited about their ideas and their parties. And new media—Internet-based outlets like Twitter and Facebook—permits people, especially young people, to engage in political dialogue like never before. The media stirs up the best feature of American politics: broad participation and strong opinions, which leaders cannot help but hear.

All of these features add up to a nation at the crossroads of the media world. The United States consumes programs and programming in hundreds of languages. All that content offers one answer to our question, *Who are we?*: The United States is multinational and multicultural, bustling with changes and beaming its images to the world—through television, cinema, blogs, Instagram posts, and tweets.

CHAPTER SUMMARY

● The media links people to information about politics and the wider world. It includes television, radio, newspapers, the Internet, Facebook, Twitter, and more.

● Media technology changes rapidly, and each change reshapes the connections between citizens and their leaders—a crucial criterion for democracy. A big question, however, runs through this chapter: Does today's media strengthen American democracy or weaken it?

● News sources are changing. Newspapers, television, and radio are all declining. Online news is rising fast. It is the number-one source of news for people under thirty. The enormous number of news sources blurs the line between entertainment and news and report from across the political spectrum.

● The new social media changes news and information. On the upside, users are more active. They can choose, respond, report, comment, and share. Candidates and parties have new ways to connect. On the downside, online media are destroying the newspapers, which are still the most important way to develop and spread the news. The new media environment means that we as a society do not share the same news. It facilitates the spread of rumors.

● Yes, the media is biased. Reporters in the mainstream press are less conservative than the general population, but they do not seem to tilt election coverage. The deepest bias—across the entire news-media spectrum—comes from the media's purpose: They are businesses that need audiences to generate revenue. That means that the news emphasizes drama, conflict, and scandal.

● Media stories affect public opinion among people who do not have strong opinions. Since those people tend to pay less attention to the news, stories with strong signals (heavy coverage, a strong perspective) will change opinion.

● The media—and the stories it chooses to emphasize—helps set the political *agenda*, *prime* the electorate, and *frame* issues. This influence gives it considerable power over American politics.

● In many ways, the media reflects America. What we watch and hear tells us who we are.

KEY TERMS

Consolidation, 242
Fairness doctrine, 241
Framing, 244
Infotainment, 233
Loud signal, 243

Mass media, 230
New media, 229
Personal presidency, 232
Policy agenda, 243
Priming, 244

Public ownership, 240
Sound bite, 245
Telecommunications Act
   of 1996, 242
Watergate scandal, 239

STUDY QUESTIONS

1. Where do most Americans get their news? From local television, network television, newspapers, or the web?
2. What source do young Americans (eighteen to twenty-nine) rely on most for their news?
3. Name two problems most analysts see in the decline of the newspaper. Do you agree that these are problems? Why or why not?
4. How is the American media biased? Describe three of its biases.
5. How is the American media different from other nations?

6. Research a presidential candidate for 2016. What does she or he stand for? Now, design a campaign commercial for that candidate. Put them in the best possible light using visuals and voiceovers. Post your creation on YouTube.
7. Pick a story. Read the coverage in the *New York Times*. Now compare the coverage with two other sources: the BBC and Al Jazeera. Identify at least one difference in the way the other two outlets covered the story.

8

Campaigns and Elections

THE CAMPAIGN STAFF WAS FRANTIC. Two days before the presidential debate, their candidate, President Barack Obama, had done a full-scale dress rehearsal. And he was terrible. Long winded, pedantic, and boring. Two weeks earlier, Republican challenger Mitt Romney had routed the president in the first debate. Romney had been warm, quick, articulate—and presidential. Gallup reported that 72 percent of the public considered Romney the winner while just 20 percent gave the edge to Obama, the most lopsided tally for any presidential debate in history. The president's staff knew their poll numbers had taken a hit after the first debate. Another inept performance and they could lose the election.

What could they do? The campaign leaders huddled, screened videos of the practice sessions, and racked their brains for a strategy. This campaign would end up spending more than a billion dollars and now, they knew, it might all come down to ninety minutes on next Tuesday night. In the other camp, the Republicans were still surging, feeding on the momentum from the last debate. Mitt Romney's crowds had come alive. Money was beginning to pour in. The last debate had been a game changer and the next one could be their breakthrough.

Or perhaps none of it really mattered. "68," wrote political scientists John Sides and Lynn Vavreck. "That is how many moments were described as 'game-changers' in the 2012 presidential election." Almost none of them were. More fundamental factors—like the economy, war and peace, the media coverage, or the president's approval rating—determined the election outcome. Not the hyped-up, media-saturated, roller coaster campaign. This is a major question for political scientists: Do campaigns matter and if so, how much?[1]

In 2012, as in past elections, political scientists stepped up with econometric models designed to predict the results months before the first ballot was cast. How did they do? One political science journal listed the outcomes: six predicted Obama, four Romney. Four of the ten got within 1.5 percent of the actual vote count.[2] The models are powerful, and yet . . .

Campaigns do decide elections. This chapter will show you how and why. The long race for president involves a large number of candidates—fourteen

IN THIS CHAPTER, YOU WILL:

● Ask how democratic American elections are today.

● Discuss the influence of money in elections.

● Explore presidential and congressional campaigns.

● Identify the keys to a successful campaign for Congress.

● Consider campaign and election reforms.

● *Republican Mitt Romney makes his point. He easily won the first debate. The question for political science: How much did it really matter?*

Republicans participated in the primaries in 2012—and winnows them down until the United States has its president. Meanwhile, thousands of other races take place—from U.S. senators to judges to municipal drain inspectors. Elections make American government.

Who are we? A nation of elections. The Declaration of Independence focused on public representation more than any other topic. Two hundred thirty-nine years later, Americans vote more often and for more officers—on every level of government—than the people of most other nations. Through elections, Americans choose leaders, guiding philosophies, programs, policies, and the nation's attitude toward the rest of the world.

BY THE NUMBERS
Campaigns and Elections

- Number of people filing to run for president as Republican Party candidates in 2012: **167**
- Number filing as Democratic Party candidates: **83**
- Number filing as Jedi Party candidates: **1**
- Sequential rank of Iowa and New Hampshire in presidential primary season: **1, 2**
- Percentage of U.S. population that is white, 2010 census: **72.4**
- Percentage of Iowa's and New Hampshire's population that is white: **91.0, 98.3**
- Year of first election with universal white-male suffrage in most states: **1828**
- Year of first election when senators were chosen by the people in all states: **1914**
- Year in which women first voted in Wyoming: **1890**
- Year when women in all states could vote: **1920**
- Cost of 30-second commercial, New York's 3rd District (Lower Manhattan): **$450,000**
- Cost of 1,000 yard signs, North Dakota at-large House district: **$3,500**
- Percentage of Americans who support limiting House and Senate campaign spending, 2013: **79**
- Total votes cast, congressional elections, 2014: **83.3 million**
- Percentage of voting-age population who turned out: **36.6**
- Total votes cast, congressional elections, 1910: **31,244,017**
- Percentage of voting-age population who turned out: **44**
- Average number, since 1950, of House/Senate incumbents who lose in an election: **16**
- Number of House/Senate incumbents who lost in 2014: **16 House/4 Senate**
- Percentage of incumbent losers who typically join Washington lobbying firms: **33**

● How Democratic Are American Elections?

The Constitution leaves most election details to the states. For example, states choose the "**time, place, and manner**" for electing members of Congress. Right from the start, the Constitution produces fifty slightly different election systems. Wyoming refused to accept statehood unless women were granted the vote in 1890; in New York, women could not vote for another thirty years. Government by the people can be measured along multiple dimensions: How often do people vote? How many positions do they vote for? What role does money play in the process? The American electoral process is distinctive along each of these dimensions.

Time, place, and manner clause: The constitutional clause that delegates control of elections to the state governments.

Frequent and Fixed Elections

One way to hold public officials accountable is to require them to face the public frequently. The United States schedules elections for national office more often than most other democratic countries. With House members chosen every two years and presidents every four years, we troop to the polls at a record pace. Add in our regular state and local elections (for governor, mayor, state legislature, city council, and so on), and there is never a year in the United States without major statewide elections.

This tally only covers our general elections. Count all the primary contests, and the election calendar can stretch all the way from January to November—as

● *David Brat (right), an economics professor from Randolph-Macon College in Ashland, Virginia, rocked the political establishment when he defeated the number two Republican in the House, Majority Leader Eric Cantor (left). How did this happen? Low turnout meant only very intense voters showed up to the polls.*

in 2012, for example, when Iowa held its caucuses on January 3, and the process wasn't over until the people elected Barack Obama on November 6.

United States senators, however, face the voters only every six years; that's one of the *longest* elected terms in the world. You'll see more about the Founders' rationale for shorter House and longer Senate durations in office in Chapter 10.

All American national elections are on a fixed cycle, except when a sitting officeholder resigns or dies. On the first Tuesday after the first Monday in November of every even-numbered year, we elect all House members and a third of the Senate; every fourth year, we elect a president. Nothing—war, economic depression, terrorist attacks, or other major emergencies—has ever affected that schedule. This fixed calendar, along with the frequency of House and presidential elections, tilts the U.S. electoral system in a more democratic direction.

Do you see any drawbacks to this practice of frequent elections? Some analysts worry about the constant electoral preoccupation of politicians. All that campaigning consumes a great deal of public officials' time, as well as scarce resources (we'll get to the cost of elections in a few pages). Critics also worry that it is more difficult to focus on policy making when House members are constantly running for re-election. As a Canadian prime minister once remarked: "In your system, you guys campaign for 24 hours a day, every day for two years. You know, politics is one thing, but we have to run a government."[3]

520,000 Elected Officials

Not only are American elections unusually frequent compared to most countries, but the *number* of positions filled by elections is enormous. From presidents to municipal drain inspectors, Americans choose their public officials. And the roster of elected positions continues to expand. The United States was the first nation to choose its chief executive by popular election—even if the Founders hedged by adding the Electoral College. American judges were also the first to face the voters, more than a century ago. Today thirty-nine states elect judges. Most other countries would not dream of electing judges since they are meant to be impartial officials and select them by appointment. Instead, most nations appoint all judges.

To better grasp the number of elective offices, look at Table 8.1, which lists elected officials representing the residents of Iowa City, Iowa.

Count them up: There are fifty-eight elected officials for Iowa City alone. That number is one measure of democracy in action. Some argue, however, that this is *too much* democracy. From Anchorage, Alaska, to Zapata, Texas, there are more than 520,000 elective offices at the local, state, and national level. That's roughly 1 for every 420 Americans eligible to vote. Too many? What do you think?

TABLE 8.1 Who Do You Vote for in Iowa City?

NATIONAL OFFICIALS	
1 U.S. president	
2 U.S. senators from Iowa	
1 U.S. representative from Iowa's 2nd District	
STATE OFFICIALS	
1 Iowa governor	
1 Iowa lieutenant governor	1 Iowa secretary of state
1 Iowa attorney general	1 Iowa state treasurer
1 Iowa agriculture secretary	1 Iowa state auditor
1 Iowa state senator	1 Iowa state representative
COUNTY OFFICIALS	
1 county supervisor	1 county sheriff
1 county treasurer	1 county attorney
1 county auditor	1 county recorder
TOWNSHIP/CITY OFFICIALS (IOWA CITY IS BOTH A CITY AND A "TOWNSHIP")	
1 township clerk	
3 township trustees	
7 school board members	
4 education agency directors	
7 city council members (who in turn elect 1 member as Iowa City mayor)	
9 agriculture extension members	
1 soil and water conservation commissioner	
7 Iowa Supreme Court justices (appointed for one year by governor, then must win a public "retention election" every eight years)	

Financing Campaigns: The New Inequality?

In a democracy, all voters should have an equal say in selecting the winner. Legally, each registered American voter can show up at the polls only once per election. But there is growing concern about the ever-larger sums of money flowing through U.S. elections. Do big contributors have more influence over elections?

TOO MANY ELECTED POSITIONS?

| **Yes, there are too many elective positions.** The public is asked to vote too often. Few voters can learn about so many races. The U.S. should appoint more experts to handle the technical aspects of government. | **No, we need to encourage people to vote more often.** With U.S. voting rates so low, reducing the number of elected officials would be unhealthy for our democracy. Voting permits the people to hold their public officials directly to account. |

Too Much Money?   Candidates for national office (presidency and Congress) spent an estimated $6 billion on their campaigns in 2012, a new standard. The 2014 congressional elections also set a record for midterm spending, estimated at $3.7 billion. Both in overall cost and in per-candidate expense, American federal campaigns are by far the world's most expensive. Do we spend too much? Many critics say yes. Nonprofit organizations like Democracy 21 and the Sunlight Foundation devote their energies to reducing the costs of campaigns, saying that the ever-rising price tag violates norms of equal influence.

Figure 8.1 reports spending by candidates for the presidency, House, and Senate, as well as funds from political parties and from corporate and advocacy groups.

Polls consistently run up lopsided majorities for reducing the role of money in U.S. elections. Yet the Supreme Court's 2014 *McCutcheon v. FEC* ruling (more details below) allowed more funds to pour into campaigns and did not result in a major public outcry. Americans generally oppose the rising tide of campaign cash, but most do not see reducing campaign spending as a high priority.

Election Spending in Context.   The numbers sound huge, but let's consider election spending in context. The total amount spent on all congressional races (435 House and 34 Senate) in 2014 was less than half of what Americans paid for potato chips that same year and under a fifth of the estimated amount spent for online pornography.

Beyond the sheer cost, critiques of election spending raise further questions about

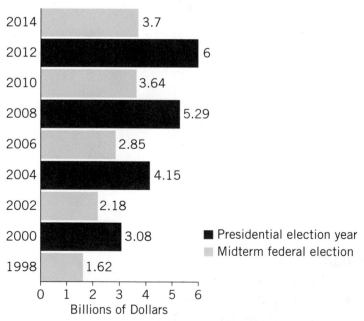

● **FIGURE 8.1** *The cost of national elections (inflation-adjusted dollars). Every federal election breaks the record for money spent. (Federal Election Commission and Opensecrets.org)*

democracy and fairness. Are America's wealthy—individuals, corporations, organized groups like labor unions—able to "buy" elections or at least gain unequal influence over outcomes? This concern is divided into two parts: first, that one political party unfairly stacks the deck in its direction; and second, that influence (exercised by individuals or corporations) is unevenly distributed in ways that add up to dangerous inequities.

Some groups of professionals, spurred by ideology or other partisan influences, contribute mainly to one party. For example, labor unions financially back Democrats (by a ten-to-one margin, in recent elections), and some industries—like oil and gas companies—largely support Republican candidates. But most business sectors split their donations about evenly between the two major parties. The biggest-spending group of corporate donors, finance/insurance/real estate (FIRE) companies, gave 50 percent of their donations in 2010 to Republican candidates for Congress and 46 percent to Democrats. (The remainder went to independent or third-party candidates.) Two years earlier, in 2008, those figures were essentially reversed: Democrats received slightly more than half of FIRE industry donations. Thus, conventional views that Wall Street only supports Republicans, who have long been seen as the party of high finance, are not historically true. Most corporations want a seat at the table in both parties.

The two major parties have also spent at roughly equal levels in recent elections. In 2012, Democratic candidates for president and Congress spent $1.52 billion, whereas Republican office-seekers spent $1.58 billion.

Looking beyond partisan balance, do some people or companies gain unfair advantages because of the large amounts of money they give to future officeholders? A tiny proportion of Americans provides most personal donations to candidates. In 2014, fewer than one in every two thousand Americans donated more than two hundred dollars to a political candidate. That relatively small group (about eighty-two thousand people) provided more than two-thirds of the total funds raised by candidates. Figures like this, argue campaign finance reform advocates, suggest that a handful of wealthy people wield outsized influence in politics through their financial contributions. Figure 8.2 summarizes the sources of the 2012 presidential campaign for Obama and Romney.

Major Donors: Easier to Give.   Shawn McCutcheon, a conservative Alabama businessman, donated large sums to political parties and candidates in 2010 and 2012—and wanted to give more. But campaign-finance laws limited the amount McCutcheon, or any individual, could spend. McCutcheon sued the Federal Election Commission, claiming that his constitutional right to donate money on behalf of his favored candidates and causes was violated. In 2014 the Supreme Court agreed with McCutcheon, effectively ending limits on the aggregate amount any person may donate.

Do individual donors have too much influence on American elections? Although some limits remain on donations (no one may contribute more

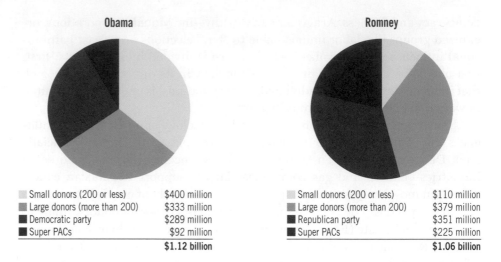

Obama

▨ Small donors (200 or less)	$400 million
▨ Large donors (more than 200)	$333 million
▨ Democratic party	$289 million
▨ Super PACs	$92 million
	$1.12 billion

Romney

▨ Small donors (200 or less)	$110 million
▨ Large donors (more than 200)	$379 million
▨ Republican party	$351 million
▨ Super PACs	$225 million
	$1.06 billion

● **FIGURE 8.2** *Sources of funds, by type of contributor, 2012 presidential campaign.* (The Washington Post)

Bundling: A form of fundraising in which an individual persuades others to donate large amounts that are then delivered together to a candidate or campaign.

Political Action Committee (PAC): An organization of at least fifty people, affiliated with an interest group, that is permitted to make contributions to candidates for federal office.

Super PACs: Organizations that are permitted to raise and spend unlimited amounts of money to promote a candidate or publicize a cause. However, they may not directly contribute to a candidate or coordinate with a campaign.

than $2,600 to any individual candidate), wealthy donors are legally able to deliver unlimited amounts of money to a presidential or congressional candidate they support. They do so through **bundling**: shorthand for the process of convincing dozens of colleagues and friends to donate at or near the maximum amount, then delivering all the checks. In 2012, the Obama and Romney campaigns each collected more than $100 million through bundlers. Each candidate had well over five hundred bundlers working on their behalf.

The small pool of individual donors—like McCutcheon—who contribute hundreds or thousands of dollars, as well as the even smaller group who bundle campaign checks, are joined in financing campaigns by various institutional donors. Many corporations and advocacy groups form **political action committees** (**PACs**) to make legal donations to candidates. PACs, which by law must comprise fifty or more contributors, may legally contribute higher dollar amounts than may individuals. In 2014, the limit on a PAC donation was five thousand dollars per candidate in a given election cycle. (Candidates often collect up to two times the limit from an individual or PAC, since they typically run in both a primary and a general election.[4])

New to presidential politics in 2012 were so-called **super PACs**, formally known as "independent expenditure-only committees." Created in 2010 after another Supreme Court ruling, super PACs are allowed to raise unlimited sums of money from virtually any source—business firms, unions, or individuals—and spend as much as they like to openly support or oppose political candidates. Unlike traditional PACs, super PACs cannot donate money directly to political candidates. They appeared to have considerable influence in the 2012 campaign. More than 1,300 super PACs were registered in 2012; they spent more than $609 million on presidential, congressional, and other candidates for office. Table 8.2 lists the biggest-spending super PACs during the 2012 election cycle.

TABLE 8.2 "Super PAC" Funds, 2012 National Elections

Super PACs that raised and spent more than $5 million during the 2012 campaign include:			
SUPER PAC	CANDIDATE	AFFILIATION	TOTAL $ RAISED
Restore Our Future	Supported Romney	Conservative	$96,700,000
American Crossroads		Conservative	$56,800,000
Winning Our Future	Supported Gingrich	Conservative	$23,907,272
Priorities USA Action	Supported Obama	Liberal	$35,600,000
Red, White & Blue	Supported Rick Santorum	Conservative	$8,346,179
Club for Growth Action		Conservative	$13,800,000
AFL-CIO Workers' Voices PAC		Liberal	$7,100,000
American Bridge 21st Century		Liberal	$8,600,000
Make Us Great Again	Supported Rick Perry	Conservative	$5,585,945
Congressional Leadership Fund		Conservative	$6,500,000
Sources: Center for Responsive Politics, Federal Election Commission (as of August 31, 2012).			

Another source of campaign-related funds are **527 groups**, which are forbidden from advocating directly on behalf of any candidate's election. They can accept and spend unlimited amounts for "issue advocacy." They may not explicitly support or oppose a candidate, but the ads they run can be indirectly supportive—or scathing. "Senator Jones is a tree killer who hates the environment" is an acceptable message a 527 group may broadcast; "Vote against Senator Jones" is not.

Presidential and congressional campaigns have been affected by 527 involvement. "Swift Boat Veterans for Truth," for example, spent more than $22 million on the 2004 election and managed to redefine Democratic senator John Kerry from a war hero to a traitor—a brutally effective advertising campaign that helped defeat Kerry.

PACs, bundlers, 527s, super PACs: In the 2012 presidential contest, outside groups spent an estimated $1.04 billion, supplementing the roughly $2 billion raised by the Obama and Romney campaigns. Each innovation raises a fresh round of questions about democracy and campaign spending. As the limits come off campaign spending, very wealthy individuals can keep a primary campaign going. Does this help or hurt democracy? Does contributing funds to a legislator "buy" anything valuable for donors? Should the system be changed to reduce the influence of monetary contributions? Or is spending money on campaigns a vital form of free speech? We'll come back to these questions at the end of this chapter.

527 groups: Organizations governed by Section 527 of the federal tax code; they are allowed to raise and spend unlimited amounts for "issue advocacy"—but are forbidden to coordinate their efforts with any candidate or campaign, and their ads cannot mention a candidate, favorably or unfavorably.

Critics raise a final point: Members of Congress spend a great deal of time and energy raising money. Many complain that "dialing for dollars" proves a major distraction from governing. (We will consider this problem in Chapter 10 when we study Congress.)

> **THE BOTTOM LINE**
>
> ● Are American elections truly democratic? Americans vote more often than the citizens of most democracies.
>
> ● Americans vote for more offices—from state judges to school board members—than the people in other democracies. Some critics suggest we vote on too many offices.
>
> ● The most familiar question about American democracy today fixes on the role of money in election campaigns. PACs, super PACs, and 527s have become fixtures in national elections. Recent court decisions have significantly expanded the ability of wealthy donors and outside groups to spend large sums in support of their preferred candidates, party, and causes.

● Presidential Campaigns and Elections

The presidency is the greatest electoral prize. Presidential candidates receive a crush of media and public attention. Front-runners attract large audiences wherever they go, and candidates become an instant campaign case study if they win their party's nomination. Small wonder that every four years so many political leaders catch "presidential fever" and declare their candidacy. Fourteen hopefuls considered themselves serious contenders for the 2012 Republican nomination, and candidates from both parties are already lining up to run in 2016.

Who Runs for President?

One-time candidate Morris "Mo" Udall, who ran in 1976, said afterward, "You have to be a little crazy to run for president." Along with the positive aspects (if you like attention, that is), seeking the presidency is expensive, privacy shredding, and exhausting. Yet in every campaign, dozens take up the challenge. Some are third-party hopefuls, representing various ideologies or causes. Norman Thomas ran under the Socialist Party banner

● *The 2016 presidential election campaign began soon after the votes were counted in 2012. Here Rand Paul departs the GOP Freedom Summit in April 2014, after wowing the delegates.*

a record six times from 1928 to 1948; Princess Christina Gerasimos Billings-Elias, who ran in 2008 and 2012, vowed to apologize for all past U.S. "wrongful actions."

Serious presidential candidates generally have experience as elected officials—and, in the past half-century, both parties always have nominated only candidates with one of three offices on their résumé—vice president, governor, or senator. Three points about successful candidates (see Table 8.3).

Senators usually lose. Barack Obama was the first in forty-eight years to win running from the Senate. Five senators ran and lost between 1964 and 2004.

Vice presidents have a better record than those in the other two offices. Seven sought the White House in the past fifty years; all won their party's nomination, and three went on to win the presidency.

Governors are the new winners. Before Jimmy Carter won in 1976, no governor had won the presidency since Franklin Roosevelt in 1932. In fact, only two governors had been elected in the entire twentieth century. Since 1976, however, four of our six presidents have come from governors' mansions. What changed? As we have seen again and again, after the upheaval of Vietnam, civil rights, and Watergate, Americans lost their confidence in Washington, D.C.,

TABLE 8.3 The President's Résumé

YEAR	WINNER	PREVIOUS POSITION	LOSER	PREVIOUS POSITION
1960	John Kennedy	Senator	Richard Nixon	Vice president (53–61)
1964	Lyndon Johnson	Vice president (1961–1963)	Barry Goldwater	Senator
1968	Richard Nixon	Vice president (1953–1961)	Hubert Humphrey	Vice president (1965–1969)
1972	Richard Nixon	Incumbent	George McGovern	Senator
1976	Jimmy Carter	Governor	Gerald Ford	Vice president/Incumbent
1980	Ronald Reagan	Governor	Jimmy Carter	Incumbent
1984	Ronald Reagan	Incumbent	Walter Mondale	Vice president (1977–1981)
1988	George H. W. Bush	Vice president (1981–1989)	Michael Dukakis	Governor
1992	Bill Clinton	Governor	George H. W. Bush	Incumbent
1996	Bill Clinton	Incumbent	Bob Dole	Senator
2000	George W. Bush	Governor	Al Gore	Vice president (1993–2001)
2004	George W. Bush	Incumbent	John Kerry	Senator
2008	Barack Obama	Senator	John McCain	Senator
2012	Barack Obama	Incumbent	Mitt Romney	Governor

and its insiders. Governors from both parties win by claiming they were successful state executives untainted by the mess in D.C.

No one else gets elected. Every election season, people from other positions toss their hats into the ring. There is almost always a member of the House and often a businessperson. They never win modern elections. The last president to come directly out of the House of Representatives? Andrew Jackson back in 1828. Businesspeople with no experience in elected office? None has ever won the presidency. It takes enormous political talent to run the contemporary gauntlet from primaries through the general election and into the White House. In the past sixty years, newcomers to the political process have not been able to negotiate it.

Presidential Campaigns Have Three Phases

Presidential campaigns involve distinct stages. First, the *nominating process*, in which each party chooses its contender, is often drawn out over years of campaigning followed by some six months of state-by-state primary elections. Second, the two major *party conventions* take place during late summer of an election year. Finally, the *general election* features the final battle for the White House and kicks off in earnest after the conventions. Each stage requires very different political strategies, played out amid the white-hot lights of national—and global—media coverage.

Winning the Nomination

The presidential nominating process seems to get more grueling every four years. For the 2016 election, media reports assessing which Republicans were likely to compete for their party's nomination began appearing on November 8, 2012—less than a day after Barack Obama was re-elected.[5]

Presidential candidates must master the nominating process's elaborate rules and primary-election calendar to have any hope of success. Complicating matters further, both the rules and the calendar change for every presidential election. Remember that each state determines its own primary-election calendar—carefully negotiated with the national parties. Every four years, states jockey to schedule their balloting near the front of the line. Holding a primary early in the process, before the nomination is decided, attracts attention—and gives the voters an important say in selecting the nominee. Back in 1992, the national party leaders scheduled multiple elections on a single date, known as **Super Tuesday**—hoping to keep the contest from dragging out too long; in 2012, that "Super" day was March 6, when eleven states held primaries or caucuses. By then twelve states—nearly a quarter of the total—had already voted.

Both parties require that a winning candidate amass a certain number of delegates, assigned proportionately based on state population. In 2016, for example, California will have 172 delegates; Maine and Rhode Island have just 19. Traditionally Republicans used a **winner-take-all** system, under which the winning candidate receives all the delegates for that state. Democrats, in contrast, have generally employed a system of **proportional representation**,

Super Tuesday: The date on the presidential primary calendar when multiple states hold primaries and caucuses.

Winner-take-all: The electoral system used in U.S. general presidential as well as many primary and other elections. The candidate receiving a simple majority (or, among multiple candidates, a plurality) receives all electoral votes or primary delegates. Sometimes called "first-past-the-post."

Proportional representation: The allocation of votes or delegates on the basis of the percentage of the vote received; contrasts with the winner-take-all system.

WHY IOWA AND NEW HAMPSHIRE?

Starting around two years before each presidential election, the nation's most powerful politicians and skilled campaign advisers start traveling to two small states. By tradition, Iowa's caucuses and New Hampshire's primary are the first two presidential contests held every four years—giving them an outsized influence in the process. If you win, or perform better than expected, in one or both, you're launched toward the nomination. If you do badly in both, your campaign is in trouble. These states are less populated and not very diverse: Iowa ranks thirtieth in population and is 91 percent white, and New Hampshire is forty-second in population and is 98 percent white. Should they continue to have such an important say in choosing a president?

Yes. Proponents answer that the small states test the candidates' ability at one-to-one meetings with small groups—a very different kind of test than the media campaigns that follow in large states.

No. Opponents point out that two unrepresentative states eliminate many candidates before any large state has even had a chance to vote.

allocating delegates based on the proportion of the vote a candidate wins. In 2012, most GOP primaries also shifted to proportional representation. Why? Party activists thought the previous nomination had been decided too soon—before their candidate had been fully tested. Sure enough, the new rules appeared to extend the contest.

Far fewer Americans turn out for primary than for general elections, and those who do tend to be more ideologically driven than the more middle-of-the-road fall electorate. Conventional political wisdom holds that candidates must therefore run more to the extreme—farther left for Democrats, farther right for Republicans—to capture the nomination and then move back to the middle for the fall election. Although this tendency may be overstated,[6] the end of primary season generally enables both nominees to reintroduce themselves—while their opponents will try to define them in a negative way (a job that is much easier with relatively unknown candidates).

● *Hillary Clinton, preparing to run for president again in 2016? In 2008 she came close to becoming the first woman to win a major-party nomination for president.*

● *Chicago—1968 Democratic Convention. Angry protests both in and outside the hall created an image of disarray and crisis. Democrats had won nine of the previous eleven presidential elections, but this convention symbolized the collapse of the old Democratic coalition. Republicans would take the White House in five of the next six elections.*

Electoral bounce: The spike in the polls that follows an event such as a party's national convention.

see for yourself 8.1

Go online to see excerpts from the 1960 Nixon–Kennedy debate.

Organizing the Convention

Political party conventions showcase the party's presidential nominee on a national stage; they also gather party insiders from across the United States for several days of meetings and celebration. Advocacy groups and corporate interests flock to the conventions as well: Everyone jockeys to be noticed by a potential future president and his or her closest advisers. When it works well, the convention can provide the nominee an **electoral bounce**, a boost in the polls that lasts from a few days to several weeks.

The General Election

Until the past decade, presidential nominees typically took a break for vacation after the conventions, held in July or early August, and resumed campaigning after Labor Day weekend (in early September). Since 2000, however, the campaigns have continued with virtually no pause. With just three months between convention and Election Day, every hour matters. Campaigns lose no opportunity to stage a media event, approve a Facebook post, criticize the opposing candidate, or meet with donors to gather more cash.

General elections usually feature two or three debates between the nominees, as well as a vice-presidential debate. These contests are among the most widely watched political events on the political calendar. Debates, like the party convention, might make a difference to the November outcome: A slip-up might turn off some wavering voters, whereas a strong performance can attract more support to a candidate's side.

The first televised presidential debate, held in 1960, featured Republican Richard Nixon (the sitting vice president) and Senator John F. Kennedy, the Democratic nominee. More than 70 million Americans tuned in—some two-thirds of the adult population at the time. Although listeners who heard the debate on the radio told pollsters that Nixon had won narrowly, on TV the charismatic Kennedy seemed the winner.

At each stage of the election, style can matter as much as substance. As we saw in the previous chapter, some critics blame the media for providing primarily "horse race" coverage, or paying attention only to which candidate is rising or falling in the polls.

Winning Presidential Elections

Along with the candidates themselves—their speeches, gaffes, debate performances, and responses to the many unexpected events on and off the campaign trail—a variety of factors help determine the winner. Some are under candidates' control, like raising sufficient funds to mount a worthy campaign; others are a matter of luck and circumstance.

Economic Outlook. Economic factors, like the unemployment rate, economic growth (or decline), and stock market trends, have a powerful place in many voters' minds. Bill Clinton's headquarters in 1992 featured a whiteboard displaying a reminder to campaign staffers: "The Economy, Stupid," as his opponent, President George H. W. Bush, found out the hard way when he lost the election.

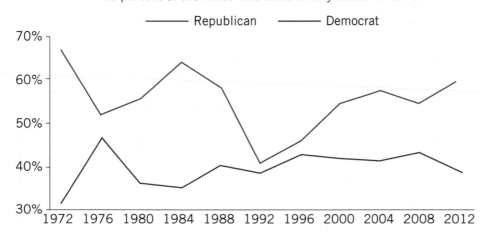
● *Kennedy and Nixon launch the televised campaign age, 1960.*

Demographics. Each party works to build a winning coalition, relying on its base of likely supporters and reaching out to undecided groups. In the 2012 fall campaign, Mitt Romney targeted white voters, a constituency that had not given a Democratic nominee more than 43 percent of the vote in thirty-five years (see Figure 8.3). Although Romney did not poll well among evangelicals, Tea Party faithful, and other conservative groups during the GOP primaries, he ended up winning a lopsided 59 percent of the white vote. Despite that, observers attributed the president's victory to what NBC news described as a "demographic time bomb": The white vote is a shrinking part of the electorate while President Obama ran up big margins in the fastest growing

No Democratic presidential candidate has won more than
43 percent of the white vote since Jimmy Carter in 1976.

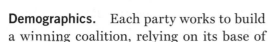

● **FIGURE 8.3** *Percentage of white vote won by major-party candidates, 1972–2012 ("Obama Performance with White Voters on Par with Other Democrats," NBC News).*

populations: Latinos (an estimated 71 percent supported the president), Asian Americans (73 percent), African Americans (93 percent), and young people eighteen to twenty-nine years old (60 percent voted for President Obama).

War and Foreign Policy.   Most Americans pay closer attention to domestic issues—especially those that touch their pocketbooks. Occasionally, foreign policy issues become pivotal, especially when the nation is at war. Barack Obama's campaign highlighted the president's decision to launch a daring raid that killed Osama bin Laden, mastermind of the 9/11 terrorist attacks. Democrats used the raid as an example of the candidate's toughness. Governor Romney tried to challenge this narrative, arguing that President Obama had not been tough enough on China, Iran, and Libyan terrorists and that he sowed confusion among allies by "apologizing for America."

Domestic Issues.   Every presidential candidate has a list of favorite programs and strategies. Bill Clinton talked about education, energy, Medicare, and Medicaid so often that his staff started calling his campaign E2M2. The candidate's issues are important, not because they will decide the election (highly unlikely), but because they set the agenda for the presidency. In 2012, Republicans extensively criticized "Obamacare," the health reform legislation that passed in 2010. In contrast, one staple of past presidential campaigns, opposition to gay marriage, played a minor role in the campaign despite President Obama's announcement of support in May 2012. Why? As we saw in Chapter 6, public opinion had turned on the issue.

The Campaign Organization.   One truism that every would-be president knows: It is essential to assemble a team of talented, loyal advisers capable of charting a plan for victory. Yet this obvious task can be immensely difficult in practice. Building a large, multistate organization—often from scratch—is an enormous job that tests every candidate's executive skill.[7]

Political scientist Samuel Popkin argues that a strong campaign chief of staff can be a decisive factor in whether campaigns thrive or founder.[8] Among other difference-making advisers in any modern presidential race: skilled communications professionals. Back in 1964, during the *Mad Men* era, Madison Avenue advertising executive Tony Schwartz created the "Daisy" ad for President Lyndon B. Johnson. Deployed against the lesser-known Senator Barry Goldwater, an Arizona Republican, the controversial ad helped create doubt about Goldwater's fitness for office.

There is no fail-safe recipe for winning a presidential election. They occur so rarely—the 2016 contest will only be the eighteenth since World War II—and involve such an immense array of influences that journalists, academics, and political professionals spend the next several years making sense of the outcome. Our ability to explain why one candidate or another won a race is exceeded in difficulty only by predicting that outcome in advance.

see for yourself 8.2

Go online to see the Obama campaign's political spot focusing on the killing of Osama bin Laden.

see for yourself 8.3

Go online to see the controversial "Daisy" political advertisement from the 1964 Johnson campaign.

- Presidential elections, despite their grueling intensity and duration, attract many aspirants every four years.

- Nearly all of the serious candidates are experienced politicians. Senators tend to run most frequently, but vice presidents and governors are the likeliest party nominees in recent decades. Since 1976, governors have won most often.

- The three phases of the campaign—nominating process, party conventions, and general election—require different political strategies.

- Election outcomes are influenced by many factors. Notable among them: economic performance, war and peace, domestic issues, advisers and organization, the coalition of supporters, and the candidate's own personality and performance. Add to this the role of accident and luck, and election outcomes are difficult to predict.

Congressional Campaigns and Elections

In contrast to the focus on two presidential candidates, congressional elections feature a colorful kaleidoscope of races across the country. Every two years, all 435 House districts hold an election, with an additional thirty-three or thirty-four Senate seats in play as well. The result is a political junkie's dream.

Candidates: Who Runs for Congress?

The 2014 congressional races featured, among other colorful characters, a rodeo clown, a filmmaker who alleges the government has covered up evidence of extraterrestrial life, and a live-action role-playing vampire. (None of that trio made it to Congress.)

Almost anyone can seek a seat in Congress. Convicted felons, although prohibited from voting in many states, can still run for Congress—and occasionally win. Apart from the age, citizenship, and residency requirements outlined in Table 8.4, there are virtually no limits on candidacy.

TABLE 8.4 Requirements for Running for Congress

Age	Successful House candidates must be at least twenty-five years old to take office; senators must be at least thirty.
Citizenship	House candidates must have been a U.S.citizen for at least seven years—nine for the Senate.
Residence	Candidates must live in the state, although not necessarily the House district, where they are seeking election.

● *Little-known Tea Party conservative Chris McDaniel forced six-term Senator Thad Cochran of Mississippi into a Republican primary runoff in June 2014 by attacking Cochran's long-time strength: bringing federal dollars to his state.*

Contending seriously for a seat in Congress is a different story. Winning an average House race costs more than $1.7 million; to make it to the Senate, you'll need on average $10.5 million. (These figures differ depending on district and state, of course.) Most successful candidates spend long hours on the phone raising money. The time required to mount a legitimate race requires freedom from the long working hours that most jobs demand. The personality traits that inspire candidates to run for Congress—self-confidence, leadership ability, interest in politics—increase as people move up the ladder of educational and economic success.

Even so, Congress is not a rich person's club. Most members are not from blue-collar backgrounds; however, in contrast to many democracies, congressional races attract relatively few top American business leaders, wealth holders, or celebrities. It's hard to imagine Mark Zuckerberg, Warren Buffett, or Oprah in Congress. The sociologist C. Wright Mills noted long ago that House and Senate races represent the "middle levels of power" in America. And when the famous or wealthy mount a run, they don't always win. Meg Whitman, then eBay's CEO, spent an eye-popping $175 million of her own money in a failed race for governor of California; wrestling CEO Linda McMahon spent $100 million on her two failed Senate races in 2010 and 2012. On the other hand, former "American Idol" star Clay Aiken won his 2014 race for Congress in North Carolina—following the sudden death of his Democratic primary challenger Keith Crisco.

Each time one party targets a Senate candidate, the other party matches it; the price tag for 2014 Senate races ran up to $97 million in Colorado, $114 million in North Carolina, and $85 million in Iowa. The results reflected what political scientists have long found: Money alone rarely swings Congressional elections.[9]

If neither money nor celebrity guarantees a seat, here's a more promising shortcut to Congress: be related to a member. Plenty of representatives and senators have followed relatives into office. Back in 2004, nearly a fifth of the forty-one new House members traced their family legacies to members of Congress or other high national office. Add in President Bush, re-elected that year; he was grandson of a senator, son of a president, and brother of a governor. The current Congress features more than two dozen such family ties. All these dynastic connections can lend Capitol Hill the air of a royal court—minus the powdered wigs. House Republican Rodney Frelinghuysen is the latest in a long line of Frelinghuysens, dating back to the 1790s, to represent north-central New Jersey. He comments: "You sort of get it in your blood."[10]

Despite the uptick in famous names, political amateurs still dominate the crop of House challengers today. Typically, about one in six nonincumbents running for the House is an elected official, usually from the state legislature; another 10 percent or so serve in nonelected government positions—often they are former Congressional staff. The remaining candidates—generally around three-quarters of the total—are new to government service. Senate candidates, because they run statewide, tend to be more experienced. Most are political veterans.

As for demographic considerations, women are on average just as likely as men to win elections to Congress—but fewer run. The parties are slower to recruit them as candidates, and women are less likely to seek election. One study shows that when a woman announces her intention to run, she is more likely to draw primary challengers than a man is.[11] Members of large minority groups (African Americans, Latinos, and Asian Americans) tend to run much less often than Caucasians, proportionate to population, but their ranks are rapidly growing (as we discussed in Chapter 5).

● *Left: Frederick Frelinghuysen, New Jersey delegate to the Continental Congress (1779) and later U.S. Senator (1793–1796). Right: Frederick's great, great, great, nephew, Rodney Frelinghuysen, has served in the U.S. House since 1995. He is the sixth Frelinghuysen to represent New Jersey in Congress.*

Talent and experience are vital in congressional races. Party leaders know that recruiting skilled candidates—more political background, better education—gives them a leg up in the contest between Democrats and Republicans for power in Congress. A candidate's background also has an impact on the quality of representation in Washington. How well Congress carries out its work depends on the political ability of its members.

The Power of Incumbency

If you talk to sitting members of Congress about re-election, you will see the worry wash over their faces. House and Senate officeholders face a more volatile American electorate than they did a quarter-century ago: voters are less predictable and harder to reach through traditional advertising. Now that virtually every utterance is digitally preserved, candidates have to be more careful about what they say. The popular senator George Allen of Virginia, cruising with a twenty-point lead in 2006 against little-known Democratic challenger James Webb, was caught on videotape at a campaign rally calling an Indian American Webb staffer "macaca," a slang racial insult. The clip ran everywhere from CNN to the *Colbert Report* to *Letterman*. Allen tried to deny it or laugh it off and eventually apologized, but he could not shake the media storm and wound up narrowly losing—dooming his presidential aspirations as well. Allen never recovered. In 2012 he again ran for the Senate, this time against former governor Tim Kaine. Outside groups poured $50 million into the election (the majority for Allen) but the Republican lost again.

Despite this more treacherous electoral environment, most incumbent House and Senate members fare well in their quest for reelection. Even in 2010, when Republicans won back the House in the largest Republican landslide since 1890, more than nine of every ten incumbents won another term. At first glance, this **incumbency advantage** is a mystery. As we will explore in Chapter 10, Americans overwhelmingly give Congress a thumbs-down. The 113th Congress (which took over in 2013) recorded the lowest approval ratings in modern history, sinking as low as 9 percent in one poll. Yet in 2014, incumbents running for re-election won 96 percent of the races in the House and 89 percent in the Senate (see Figure 8.4).

What explains these consistently high incumbent success rates? For one thing, members have become skilled at running *against* Congress. They position themselves as reasonable individuals fighting against a dysfunctional institution. And the way Congress operates—stalemate on the big issues, lots of little favors to constituents—makes the stance an easier sell. "I'm for expanding aid to needy children," say liberal members, "but I can't get it past the Republicans on Capitol Hill. Oh, and how about that new aquarium I funded?" GOP members have a similar story. Members are attentive to constituents, raise a great deal of money, and already have staff and name recognition. Most win re-election in a landslide.

Incumbency advantage: The tendency for members of Congress to win re-election in overwhelming numbers.

see for yourself 8.4

Go online to hear Senator George Allen's "macaca moment."

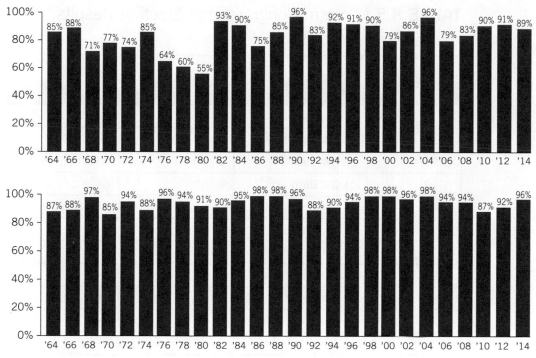

● **FIGURE 8.4** *Senate (top) and House (bottom) re-election rates, 1964–2014.*

Congressional Election Results

Along with incumbents' tendency to win reelection, congressional elections feature additional intriguing patterns. One of these concerns **midterm elections**, or those held in a nonpresidential year. In most elections the president's party loses Congressional seats. In the past twenty-four midterm elections (twelve each in the House and Senate), the president's party picked up seats in either chamber of Congress only four times—and only a few seats each time. In contrast, the president's party lost double-digit House seats eight of twelve times—including huge swings in 2010, 1994, and 1974 (sixty-three, fifty-four, and forty-eight seats, respectively). (See Table 8.5.)

Another intriguing pattern concerns America at war. Although we might expect voters to "rally around the flag" and support the president's party, in fact the opposition usually wins seats in the congressional election following a war's outbreak.

Redrawing the Lines: The Art of the Gerrymander

Membership of the House of Representatives has been fixed at 435 for more than a century. The American population keeps shifting, and after every ten-year census, U.S. House representatives also have to deal with **reapportionment**. First, the census determines which states have gained or lost population,

Midterm elections: National elections held between presidential elections, involving all seats in the House of Representatives, one-third of those in the Senate, thirty-six governors, and other positions.

Reapportionment: Reorganization of the boundaries of House districts, a process that follows the results of the U.S. census, taken every ten years. District lines are redrawn to ensure rough equality in the number of constituents represented by each House member.

TABLE 8.5 Midterm Congressional Election Results, 1970–2014

ELECTION YEAR	PRESIDENT	SEAT GAIN	
		HOUSE	SENATE
2014	Obama (D)	R+12**	R+4**
2010	Obama (D)	R+63	R+6
2006	GW Bush (R)	D+30	D+6
2002	GW Bush (R)	R+8*	R+2*
1998	Clinton (D)	D+5*	(No change)
1994	Clinton (D)	R+54	R+8
1990	GHW Bush (R)	D+8	D+1
1986	Reagan (R)	D+5	D+8
1982	Reagan (R)	D+26	(No change)
1978	Carter (D)	R+15	R+3
1974	Nixon (R)	D+48	D+3
1970	Nixon (R)	D+12	R+1*

*The president's party has won seats in a midterm election only four times in the past forty years.

**Projected as of November 6, 2014.

and House seats are reapportioned accordingly. In 2010, Texas gained four new seats, Florida gained two, and New York and Ohio each lost two. Each state has the job of redrawing the boundaries of the election districts in a process called redistricting. Sometimes two U.S. House representatives will find themselves running against one another when their districts are combined.

In a **gerrymander**, the party in control of the state legislature draws the lines to help itself. See Figure 8.5 for a hypothetical example of how it works in an imaginary state called PoliSciLand.

Today, with sophisticated information technology, state legislatures can carefully craft political boundaries. Two main techniques are "packing," or placing all the like-minded voters into one district, and "cracking," or spreading them out so that they form a minority in many districts. Our imaginary PoliSciLand, illustrated by Figure 8.5, cracked the Democratic district.

Gerrymander: Redrawing an election district in a way that gives the advantage to one party.

Nonpartisan Districting and Minority Representation

Some reformers would like to put the whole process of drawing electoral districts into the hands of a nonpartisan commission that would divide states into natural communities and not tilt to any political side. California passed a law to do just that after the 2010 census. State legislative districts were redrawn by

**PoliSciLand
Before**

Existing District Lines

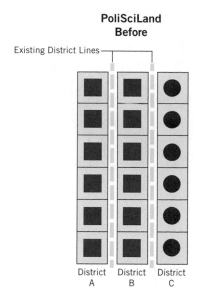

District A | District B | District C

Two districts are 100% Republican, one district is 100% Democrat. PoliSciLand sends two Republicans and one Democrat to Congress.

**PoliSciLand
After**

Redrawn District Lines

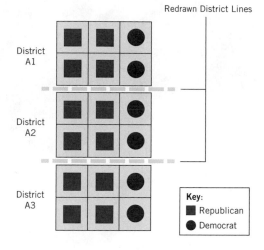

District A1

District A2

District A3

Key:
■ Republican
● Democrat

After redistricting, all three districts have a Republican majority of 66.6%. PoliSciLand sends three Republicans to Congress.

● **FIGURE 8.5** *How gerrymandering works. A hypothetical case of highly political redistricting.*

a "Citizens' Redistricting Commission" rather than by elected politicians, who naturally seek to protect their personal and partisan interests. The result was compact, contiguous districts faithful to existing geographic communities—and a lot of angry legislators at the state and U.S. House level, as they scrambled to figure out their new district lines. Ten other states have commissions that make some effort to draw nonpartisan lines. For the rest of the country, redistricting is left to the political process. Thus, the election contest usually begins in earnest—long before anyone starts running—when the state legislature sits down to draw the district.

After the 1990 census, some states used the process to enhance the number of black representatives. They created majority–minority districts packed with African American voters, and these districts proved very likely to send African American representatives to Congress. White Republicans strongly supported the effort because packing black Democratic voters into some districts left the surrounding areas more Republican. The overall effect was an increase in Republican representatives, alongside the expected increase in black legislators.

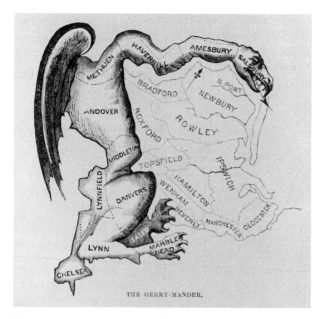

● *The original gerrymander: Massachusetts, 1812.*

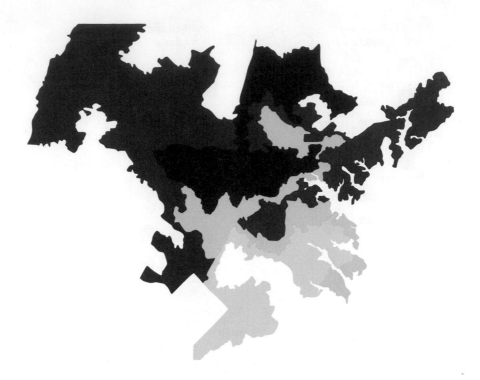

● **FIGURE 8.6** *Maryland's congressional districts, 2014.*

Caucus: A local meeting at which registered members of a political party meet to select delegates representing presidential candidates.

Was that a good deal for African American Democrats? The black congressional **caucus** continued to grow, from twenty-nine House members (in 1995) to forty-five after the 2014 election. In 1995, however, the Supreme Court ruled that race could not be the predominant factor in creating congressional districts, and this packing was halted.[12] Despite dire predictions, the minority delegations continued to grow.

THE BOTTOM LINE

- Every two years, all 435 House seats and a third of the Senate seats are up for election.

- Few restrictions govern who may run—and some candidates are true characters.

- House and Senate incumbents have powerful built-in advantages when running for re-election.

- The president's party generally loses House and Senate seats during the midterm election following the president's victory. Presidents who declare war also tend to see their party lose seats in the subsequent election.

- Decennial redistricting of House seats can result in some strangely shaped—and politically motivated—districts, known as gerrymanders. Redistricting tends to further increase the advantage of incumbency.

⬤ How to Run for Congress

Having mastered the broad outlines of U.S. national campaigns and elections, perhaps you are pondering your own race for a local position or even for Congress. How can you make that first run a successful one? Here we highlight four keys to winning a congressional election—*money*, *organization*, *strategy*, and *message*. Even if you are not planning to be a candidate, remember these as you watch House and Senate races shape up in coming months.

Key 1: Money

First and foremost, you will need funds to mount a legitimate challenge—up to $2 million in many House districts, and five or six times that if you are running for Senate. Where does all the money go? TV advertising, along with radio and print ads, takes a big chunk, followed by everything from staff salaries to yard signs. Unless you are wealthy (or married to a rich person), you are going to have to "dial for dollars." Your staff will prepare **call lists** for any downtime you might have, as you desperately seek to pack your war chest.

To boost your chances of winning and reduce the cost of campaigning, you may want to wait and run for an **open seat**—one with no incumbent running, because of a sitting member's retirement or death. Taking on an incumbent costs more each election cycle (see Figure 8.7).

Call list: A long list of potential donors whom candidates must phone.

Open seat: A seat in Congress without an incumbent running for reelection.

CAMPAIGN LINGO

• If you're running for Congress, you will want to know what your advisers are talking about. Here are a few insider terms from the campaign trail.

• **Robocall**: Automated phone call used to contact thousands of voters simultaneously; may feature a recorded message by the candidate or a popular party leader—or an attack on the opponent.

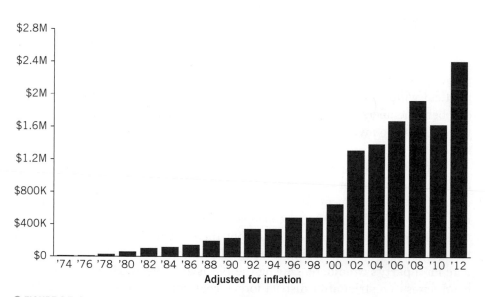

⬤ **FIGURE 8.7** *Cost of beating a House incumbent, 1974–2012. (Center for Responsive Politics)*

(continued)

CONTINUED

- **Advance team**: Campaign staffers who arrive at major event sites—for example, for a speech—a day or more ahead of time, to organize the site and build crowds.

- **Retail campaigning**: Attracting supporters or votes one by one, through door-to-door visits or small meetings. More efficient is *wholesale* campaigning, reaching hundreds or thousands at once through a speech or targeted advertisement—or robocall.

- **Text-to-donate**: Use of text messages to donate funds to a campaign. Currently banned by the Federal Election Commission, despite a strong push by industry professionals.

Key 2: Organization

You will also need a well-constructed team to run for Congress. Somebody has to recruit and train all those speechwriters and fundraisers, supportive community leaders, get-out-the-vote experts, and volunteer envelope stuffers. Until the advent of candidate-centered politics in the 1980s, parties took care of most of that work. The local Republican or Democratic organization provided the knowledge and manpower to mount a campaign. Today, challengers like you usually have to build your own organization from scratch. Yes, the parties get involved in a handful of high-profile races, pumping in funds where possible and providing occasional strategic advice. But most often the candidate and core supporters build an organization.

When Jon Corzine decided to mount a Senate race from his home state of New Jersey in 2000, he quickly realized that he needed "a different paradigm: I couldn't do this with a small team from the office."[13] Corzine, a former senior executive at the investment firm Goldman Sachs, took a straightforward approach to developing a good campaign organization: he bought one. Professional campaign specialists, deploying the sophisticated tools of modern elections, are not cheap.

There is a side benefit to the expense of assembling a talented campaign organization. Political insiders see hiring established pollsters, media experts, and so forth as the sign of a competitive campaign. Funders, recognizing a possible winner, will start directing more money your way. Although most new congressional candidates publicly decry the "professionalization" of campaign politics, they usually hire at least some established members of the Beltway insiders' club.

Key 3: Strategy

A fat bankroll and seasoned organization can't compensate for a common rookie-congressional-candidate mistake—the lack of a well-conceived campaign strategy. Uncertainty is a central fact in every election, given fast-shifting political winds, opponents' moves, and the power of unexpected events. Incumbent members tend to stick to the strategy that got them there last time; you will have to invent a strategy that plays well to your political and personal strengths.

Two elements of successful congressional campaign strategies are vital: building a coalition of supporters and connecting with voters. Every state or district includes "influentials," such as local business leaders, political activists, religious leaders, and spokespeople for identity groups. Strategically attracting some of them—and, presumably, their voting followers—is essential to victory. A coalition-building strategy also targets broader groups likely to vote for a party's candidate. During the 1980s and 1990s, House Republican candidates in district after district forged coalitions of conservative, middle-aged, white, Protestant, relatively affluent voters. By 2006, this reliable lineup had fragmented in many places, and Democrats won forty-seven of forty-eight contested House seats to retake control of the chamber. By 2010, the Republican coalition was back, now fueled by Tea Party activists and featuring a larger proportion of lower-income, disaffected white voters. Notice how fast the winds shift in contemporary electoral politics.

Candidates primarily contact voters through the media. Candidate strategies need to include plenty of high-profile events, such as speeches before substantial crowds and press conferences engaging new ideas for helping the district or state. All of these can attract reporters without cost to the candidate. If you cannot build crowds because of your low **name recognition**, you may resort to more creative approaches. For example, Democrats call on Bruce Springsteen, Republicans on Clint Eastwood.

Name recognition: An advantage possessed by a well-known political figure, a political celebrity.

Paid advertising is also a cornerstone of any successful strategy, but marketing a House or Senate candidate involves more than big-budget TV ads. Your campaign will need a smart social media strategy because outlets like Facebook and Twitter are inexpensive ways to reach large numbers of potential voters.

Another traditional approach will receive attention from your trusted strategists: **negative campaigning**. This usually involves strewing seeds of doubt in voters' minds about your opponent's policy positions, ethics, and character. Much as you may find this repugnant, without "going negative" you will have a hard climb to victory. Expect that the other side's opposition researchers will strive to portray you in the least flattering light possible. It is a lot easier to play offense than to defend against attacks, no matter how unfair.

Negative campaigning: Running for office by attacking the opponent. An unpopular tactic that is, nevertheless, very effective.

Key 4: Message

Meeting the voters, either virtually through technology or firsthand, is important. But they also need a reason to vote for you. Candidates with a clear, powerful rationale for why they are running can sometimes topple better-financed and more elaborately organized opponents.

In the relatively rare case that a first-time challenge like yours is victorious, what can you expect as a freshman member of Congress? (Yes, *freshman*: The term is the same as in high school or college, and the learning curve is surely as steep!) What comes next?

A *new campaign*, starting immediately. For House members, election looms just two years away. Senators have a more relaxing six years—but must run statewide, which in high-population or sprawling states is very time-consuming. Winning election to become a congressional "sophomore" can be especially difficult. The legendary House Speaker Sam Rayburn told each incoming House freshman class that "a member of Congress can be elected by accident, but seldom reelected by accident." Voters back home will watch a first-term member especially closely, as will his or her colleagues on Capitol Hill.

THE BOTTOM LINE

- To run successfully for Congress, follow a few vital steps: raise sufficient funds (then raise more), organize a talented and loyal team, develop a strategy that plays to your strengths, and hone your message.

- If you and your team do a splendid job and luck is on your side, you may be a first-time congressional victor; well done! Next up: starting all over again, with a new campaign.

● Conclusion: Reforming American Elections

Does the U.S. electoral system work? In this chapter we have highlighted a variety of concerns—from gerrymanders to incumbency rates to the influence of money in politics. Is it a problem that we keep sending the same representatives back to Congress, up to 98 percent of the time? Is it a problem that big spenders often win? Many reforms have been proposed to address problems like these.

Start with *gerrymanders*. We could end partisan battles over House districts and ask neutral panels to draw the lines—as California did after the 2010 census. Reformers praise the idea of moving away from bluntly partisan gerrymanders designed to pad the majority party.

Next comes *money*. Do we really want our legislators spending hours each day, every day, raising funds? Do we want them piling up so much cash that no one can afford to run against them? Although the system is highly unpopular, there is little agreement about how to change it. Many reformers call for publicly financed elections, where (as in most other advanced democracies) the government provides equal funding to each candidate and allows relatively small donations from the public, typically less than two hundred dollars. This would create a much more even playing field between incumbents and challengers. Several states—including Arizona, Connecticut, and Maine—have passed laws to enable public funding for congressional and other statewide elections, although court challenges have brought into question the constitutionality of these laws. Arizona's system, for example, was struck down by the Supreme Court in 2011 and is undergoing revisions.

We also saw concerns in this chapter that money buys donors unfair influence. Campaign finance reform polls well, but it also has strong critics. They argue that contributing to campaigns is a form of free speech. If a candidate excites you, why shouldn't you send money? This is the logic upheld by the Supreme Court in the *McCutcheon* case discussed earlier in this chapter.

The greatest disagreement rests on who can spend: Should we give large organizations—like corporations and labor unions—the same right to free speech as citizens? The Supreme Court in 2009 reaffirmed the argument that corporate or labor union contributions to campaigns are protected as a form of free speech. Another concern is that a single very wealthy individual can simply bankroll a candidate—as appeared to happen in the 2012 primaries. Congress has been reluctant to move boldly toward finance reform, with Republicans especially skeptical. The debate remains intense but the institutional barriers to finance reform—in both Congress and the courts— have gotten steeper.

Along with redistricting and campaign finance reform, some analysts have proposed *term limits*. The president is limited to two terms, as are many governors. Why not limit members of Congress to, say, twelve years of service? The problem with this reform is that good legislating takes skill. Term limits clear out legislators just when they have learned how to become effective.

Whether the system needs reform or not, campaigns and elections provide avenues to participation for the many groups in American society. Every system—and every change—creates a new configuration of winners and losers. Each generation of Americans decides whether to shake up the system of campaigns and elections—or to leave things in place. Every election brings new excitement, new voters, and new ideas into American politics. We hope that you get engaged with our electoral system—it is the one and only way to insure government by the people.

CHAPTER SUMMARY

● Elections—free, fair, competitive elections— define democracies. They give the people a say over who governs them.

● A key question in the chapter: Are American elections democratic enough?

● American electoral systems are unique because:

– The number of positions that we vote for is huge—more than 520,000.

– We vote often compared to other nations.

– Federal elections for the House of Representatives take place every even- numbered year.

– In some places, there are elections every single year.

● The Constitution puts the states in charge of running elections, instructing them to manage "the time, place, and manner."

● In the past sixty years, presidents have had one of just three jobs on their résumés: vice president, governor, or senator.

● The road to the White House passes through three stages: primaries, the convention, and the general election.

● The most familiar question about American democracy today involves the role of money in election campaigns. PACs, super PACs, and 527s have become fixtures in national elections.

● Econometric models have become fine predictors of which party will control the White House. They cannot predict primary winners and sometimes fall short at predicting very close elections or Electoral College results.

● The only constitutional limits to running for Congress are age, citizenship, and residency in the state.

● Winning a race for Congress takes money, organization, constituent service, name recognition, and a good knowledge of the district.

● Every ten years, the state legislatures redraw the congressional districts to keep up with changes in the population. The *gerrymander* is a district that is redrawn to help one party. Across time, some striking patterns have emerged in congressional elections: The president's party loses seats in the midterm, results have grown more volatile (with the party in power shifting often), and war spells trouble for the president's majority.

KEY TERMS

527 groups, 259
Bundling, 258
Call list, 275
Caucus, 274
Electoral bounce, 264
Gerrymander, 272
Incumbency advantage, 270

Midterm election, 271
Name recognition, 277
Negative campaigning, 277
Open seat, 275
Political action committee (PAC), 258
Proportional representation, 262

Reapportionment, 271
Super PACs, 258
Super Tuesday, 262
Time, place, and manner clause, 253
Winner-take-all, 262

STUDY QUESTIONS

1. Who decides about who can vote?

First describe what the Constitution says about the matter in the "time, place, and manner" clause.
Next, consider the role of constitutional amendments in the voting process.

2. Describe the American system of campaign finance. What are PACs? How about super PACs?

What influence on the system did the 2014 *McCutcheon v. FEC* Supreme Court decision have?
3. For further study: What is campaign finance reform? Make an argument for or against campaign finance reform. If possible, explain how recent research supports your argument.
4. Describe the three stages of the presidential campaign.

5. You have decided to run for Congress. What four things will your campaign need to be successful?

6. What is negative campaigning? Why do candidates rely on it so heavily?

7. For further study: If you were running for Congress, would you use negative campaign ads on your opponent? Why or why not?

8. Describe three reforms that have been suggested for campaigns and elections in the United States. Now, pick one and argue for or against it. Be sure to defend your position.

9

Interest Groups and Political Parties

YOU HAVE BEEN HIRED as a new congressional staffer—and today is your first day at work on Capitol Hill. (Congratulations!) You arrive during a wildly busy legislative season. The office is bustling, and nobody has time to get you oriented. In fact you barely know where you are assigned to sit . . . and now the legislative director has asked you to prepare a detailed analysis of a new bill on a topic that you have never heard of—by tomorrow morning.

Where to begin?

Quick, call the Congressional Research Service, the research arm of Congress. They're glad to help you out, they say—but it will take a few weeks. *Weeks*? You have hours, at best.

You feel like slinking out of the office before anyone notices and disappearing into a completely different career. Then salvation arrives on your desk, in the form of an elegantly bound, meticulously researched report on the bill. All the details you need are laid out clearly. You wonder whether to cry or laugh with relief. Who *wrote* this? You look around to thank your angel of an office-mate. Not here, your colleagues smile: over on **K Street**. An interest-group lobbyist sent it directly to you. As this chapter shows, that informative and timely report is at the heart of what interest groups do in Washington.

Interest groups and parties have become so central to American government that it is difficult to imagine our system without them. These organizations play a more active role in our government today than the Founders ever envisioned.

Who are we? A deeply partisan nation of too many lobbyists and special interests, many Americans lament. Or are we? Pause for a moment and consider: How many lobbying groups work in Washington on behalf of *your* interests? None, you say? In fact, like most Americans, you are represented by dozens of groups: advocates who push for clean air, safe food, open Internet access, and most everything else you care about. Your college or university probably has representatives who lobby to promote the school's concerns, at the state capital and in Congress. Your student fees or tuition may help pay for their work. The United States Student Association and the National Association of College Students lobby directly on behalf of undergraduates; they promote

IN THIS CHAPTER, YOU WILL:

⬤ Learn what interest groups do— and how they do it.

⬤ Reflect on whether interest groups wield too much power.

⬤ Learn about the role of political parties in governing America.

⬤ Explore the two-party U.S. system.

⬤ Investigate why people identify with one party (or why they don't).

⬤ Analyze a longstanding paradox: why Americans embrace parties and reject partisanship.

⬤ Reflect on whether the U.S. has grown too partisan—or not.

K Street: A major street in downtown Washington, D.C., that is home to the headquarters for many lobbying firms and advocacy groups—and thus synonymous with interest-group lobbying.

⬤ Lobbyists in action. Health care lobbyists pack the senate finance hearing room during a crucial committee debate on the Affordable Care Act.

policies like expanding college access and opposing cuts in federal student-loan programs. Yet lobbyists and the interest groups they represent consistently receive among the lowest approval ratings of any professionals, in or outside politics (Figure 9.1).

And political parties do not fare much better. *A political party is an organization with a public following, established to win elections, generally by promoting a set of principles.* Political parties organize American government around competing ideas. However, many Americans dislike the name-calling and disagreement—expressions of strong **partisanship**—that follows. Americans increasingly are disdainful of parties and partisanship: one survey found that nearly 90 percent of respondents identify "too much partisan infighting" as a chief obstacle to effective U.S. government.[1] Despite their declining reputation, parties are essential to American government. National elections, congressional

Partisanship: Taking the side of a party, or espousing a viewpoint that reflects a political party's principles or position on an issue. Often decried by those who wish the parties would work together.

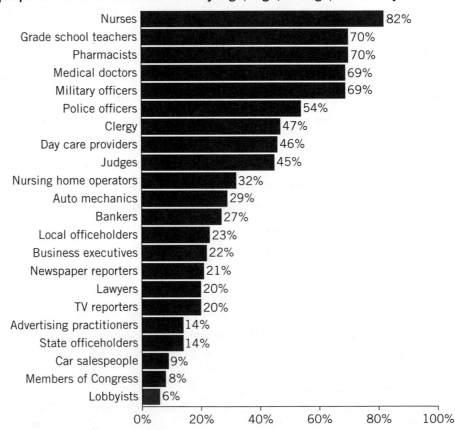

How would you rate the honesty and ethical standards of people in these different fields—very high, high, average, low or very low?

● **FIGURE 9.1** *Lobbyists—and members of Congress—rank at the bottom of Americans' approval ratings for various professions, just below car salespeople. (Gallup)*

BY THE NUMBERS
Interest Groups

- Number of lawyers active in Washington, D.C.: **73,500**
- Number of lobbyists who registered with Congress, 2013: **12,278**
- Percentage of registered lobbyists who serve only public interest clients: **33**
- Total spending reported by health care lobbying groups, 2013: **$480,463,898**
- Total spending on lobbyists reported by the city of Dallas, Texas, 2013: **$280,000**
- Number of groups registered to lobby on defense spending and related issues, 2013: **1,288**
- Number of groups registered to lobby on welfare issues, 2013: **58**
- Estimated percentage of former members of Congress who work as Washington lobbyists: **42**
- Total amount donated to "527" groups for issue advocacy, 2012 election: **$547,800,000**
- Estimated spending by "Super PAC" and other outside organizations, 2014 election: **$690 million**
- Total spent on lobbying, 2003–2013, AT&T Inc.: **$203,500,000**
- Number of former Defense Department officials registered as lobbyists, 2014: **495**

votes, policy decisions, judicial rulings, state government, and our own political opinions and beliefs are all stamped by party influence. In this chapter, we will explore the role that interest groups and parties each play in our democratic system.

● Interest Groups and Lobbying

A longtime U.S. House member from Texas named Kent Hance—who won his seat by beating future president George W. Bush—was fond of telling a story from his first race, for the Texas legislature. After one campaign speech in rural west Texas, an elderly woman told Hance he'd win her vote "if you promise me that you'll never talk to any of those lobbyists in Austin," the state capital.

"Ma'am," said Hance, "I sure wish I could promise you that, but I simply can't."

"Why not?" she said.

Safely assuming the woman was a Baptist, Hance replied: "Why, ma'am, if a religious issue came up for a vote, I wouldn't dream of taking a position until I had talked to the lobbyist for the Southern Baptist Convention"—the church's governing body.

"You mean," the astonished woman asked, "that our *church* hires a lobbyist?"

"Yes ma'am, it sure does," said Hance. "And a fine Christian gentleman he is, too."[2]

James Madison warns against interest groups—which he terms "factions"— in *Federalist* no. 10, calling them the "mortal diseases" that repeatedly killed off popular governments across the ages. Madison's innovative solution? *Increase* the number of interest groups. That way, no single group would become too powerful and interests would have to work together to accomplish anything. Increase the number of groups? That is one piece of advice the United States has certainly taken.

Concern about **special interests** has surged periodically since Madison published his famous warning. Jacksonian Democrats, Progressives, New Dealers, 1960s radicals: many of the reformers we saw in earlier chapters expressed a fear that a few select groups (usually big business) were getting fat off the rest of us. All the outcry, however, obscures the basic truth: Interest groups aren't just "them"—they're us.

Maybe you don't think of college wrestlers or clean-air activists or Baptists when you imagine interest-group lobbyists in action. We define **interest group** as an *organization whose goals include influencing government.*

At least two hundred thousand interest groups are active in American politics today. About three-quarters of those are public-advocacy or citizen groups; the remainder represent private (usually corporate) interests. The American Association of Retired People (AARP) is an example of an interest group. It represents nearly 40 million Americans and provides financial services, insurance products, discounts at hotels, and information to people aged fifty and over. It also hires lobbyists to influence the government.

What is a **lobbyist**? Put simply, a lobbyist contacts government officials on behalf of a particular cause or issue. Some lobbying professionals work full-time and are paid by clients to promote their views among lawmakers. Plenty of other people occasionally try to influence government—like college students who fan out across their state capital each year, asking legislators to oppose higher student fees or appropriate more funding for science labs. We reserve the term "lobbyist," however, for those who are hired to interact with public officials on a regular basis.

The AARP retains lobbyists to influence government on a wide range of issues affecting seniors, from

Special interest: A pejorative term, often used to designate an interest group whose aims or issue preferences one does not support.

Interest group: An organization whose goals include influencing government.

Lobbyist: A person who contacts government officials on behalf of a particular cause or issue.

● *American Farm Bureau Federation annual meeting. After farmers organized themselves and sought to influence government—for flood or drought relief, crop subsidies, and the like—they became a powerful interest group. Here Secretary of Agriculture Tom Vilsack dutifully appears at the Farm Bureau's annual meeting.*

Social Security benefits to disability insurance.[3] In 2006, when President Bush tried to add a new prescription-drug benefit to Medicare, Democrats thought they had the votes to block the legislation on Capitol Hill. Then AARP threw its weight behind the bill—and it passed.

Interest groups perform important functions for their members. Let's take a closer look at what those activities are.

What Private Interest Groups Do

Interest groups like the AARP and the American Farm Bureau Federation perform three main functions for their members. First, groups *inform members about political developments*. The American political system, like the nation it serves, is sprawling: every House member represents some seven hundred thousand people, and Congress considers hundreds of issues every year. Interest groups have become a primary link between the public and its government. Groups provide access through which members (such as animal rights activists or Future Business Leaders of America) learn details about Washington, D.C., or state or local governments. Most of us have little time to keep up with the huge range of policies, even those affecting our career or personal interests. That's where interest groups, who monitor topics that matter to their members, can help.

The channel of access runs two ways. A second main role interest groups play is to *communicate members' views to government officials*. These members can be corporate or other private actors, or they can be collections of Americans interested in a topic. Join a citizen group, and its Washington representatives will convey your opinions directly to public officials—across all three branches of the government.

Third, interest groups *mobilize the public*; that is, they get groups of people to act politically. Lobbyists create issue campaigns involving, along with detailed reports, TV ads, mailgram alerts, Facebook postings, and tweets that are meant to provoke action.

Many Americans care deeply about abortion policy, for example. They usually are not satisfied merely by voting every two or four years for candidates who share their position. Pro-life and pro-choice groups offer members frequent opportunities to *do something* on this issue of personal concern. Contributing funds, writing letters, joining protests, exchanging ideas with others of similar views, and even winning an occasional audience with policy makers: interest groups facilitate all these means of political participation.

When groups mobilize their members, they're often pushing *their own* specific angle, of course. A few years ago, the Food and Drug Administration proposed regulations to reduce teen smoking. Tobacco-company lobbyists mounted a big "education" campaign, aimed at both the public and the lawmakers—about the dangers of a giant, out-of-control federal bureaucracy meddling with people's freedom to smoke. Public health groups pushed right back with graphic advertisements showing the ravages of smoking—amputations, voice boxes, and death.

● Twenty interest groups join together in a "Rally of Unity" at the Georgia State House.

How well represented by lobbying groups are your specific political concerns? If you care about something that is already on the government agenda, groups are very likely promoting your view in Washington. More obscure topics—and less powerful interests—may be less likely to get a hearing. However, if you have strong opinions about a policy that seems to be overlooked, do not despair. American political history is full of "crackpots" who believed in supposedly outlandish causes—ending segregation, cleaning up polluted rivers, requiring airbags in cars, eliminating tobacco use in public places—that eventually won government approval.

● Two perspectives on tobacco policy. This cartoon caricatures government antismoking policy as an assault on freedom while real crimes go unnoticed. Tobacco companies have been active in supporting such images.

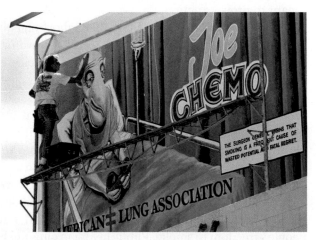

● Antismoking groups create stark images of their own: One recast "Joe Camel," the cartoon figure used to promote Camel cigarettes, as "Joe Chemo."

What Public Interest Groups Do

Lobbying groups can do a good job promoting your personal interests. But how well is the entire public represented in the interest-group system? Some **public interest lobbyists** aim to represent what they describe as Americans' collective interests, such as environmental protection or consumer product safety.

Advocates representing public interest groups must attract, and retain, enough supporters to promote their cause, whether that involves fighting global warming or reducing immigration or ensuring safer food. Most public interest organizations face the problem of free riders: Why would anyone join a membership group when they can leave the hard work to others and still enjoy the results?

Log on to the website of a public interest group you find appealing—Greenpeace or the National Rifle Association (NRA) or Habitat for Humanity, which builds homes for needy people around the globe. Alongside the rhetoric about global warming or the right to bear arms, you'll see quite a bit of swag available. Tote bags, organized trips to Yosemite, gun-safety videos, teddy bears, logo-adorned travel mugs—all free or discounted for joining. (Ironically, the NRA also offers its members accidental-death insurance.)

In political science terms, these **material benefits** are a key part of what membership groups provide. Such benefits help attract new members, whose dues provide part of the funds needed to keep the lights on and lobbyists on board. Others join because of **expressive benefits**: The group expresses values that its members share, such as social justice or individual freedom. Still other people may join an interest group for **solidary benefits**. Think of your own experience as a Girl Scout or fraternity member: It can feel very powerful to be part of the group. Interest-based organizations tap into that feeling, attracting and holding members based on shared social fellowship.

Public interest lobbyist: A representative of an organization that seeks to benefit the population at large, not a specific client or small collection of people.

Material benefits: Items distributed by public interest groups as incentives to sign up or remain a member.

Expressive benefits: Values or deeply held beliefs that inspire individuals to join a public interest group.

Solidary benefits: The feeling of shared commitment and purpose experienced by individuals who join a public interest group.

● *The wide world of interest groups: Retired members of the Portland Trail Blazers basketball team help build a house in an event sponsored by Habitat for Humanity. The new homeowners are in green shirts.*

Corporate firms or trade associations are subsidized by their sponsoring firms. Members of the American Petroleum Institute, for example, pay annual dues based on the size of their organization, starting at $1,525 and rising to tens of thousands of dollars. Public groups are partly supported by members, but their dues are much less, averaging around fifteen or twenty dollars. Larger donations might come from foundations, government grants, or wealthy individuals, who are called "angels" in the public interest-group world.

What Do Interest Groups Do for Democracy?

Pluralism: An open, participatory style of government in which many different interests are represented.

Whether our interest-group system represents all (or most) people is a red-hot debate, both among political scientists and across the public. Some, in a view called **pluralism**, hold that as long as the American political process is open to a wide range of different groups, then government policies will roughly correspond to public desires. No single set of interests dominates our system, pluralists insist, and all the different groups pushing and tugging allows the collective good to shine through. You might see this as a latter-day update of James Madison's argument in *Federalist* no. 10 that began this chapter: The answer to the problem of interest groups is—more interest groups.

Two less optimistic theories respond to the pluralists. First, *hyperpluralists* fear that there are so many interests and so many groups that the entire system is bogging down in stalemate. Any time a group proposes a new project—education reform, a new highway, privatizing Social Security, or promoting alternative energy forms like wind or solar—there are always other groups ready to oppose it because it costs too much or will harm the environment. Hyperpluralists fear gridlock, in short. The journalist Jonathan Rauch coined the term **demosclerosis** to describe the sheer number of lobbyists at work in Washington. *Demo* is the Greek root meaning "of the people" (think *democracy*). *Sclerosis*—well, we should all keep our arteries clear of dangerous sclerotic plaque and other hardening agents. Rauch, echoing the hyperpluralists, suggests that the American body politic is endangered by the sheer buildup of lobbyists.[4]

Demosclerosis: The collective effect of the sheer number of Washington lobbyists in slowing the process of American democratic policy making.

Others worry that the playing field is tipped too far toward the richest and most powerful interests. This **power elite theory** portrays a group of wealthy, influential Americans—mostly from the corporate sector—who mingle with one another regularly and thus are able to promote their shared ("class") aims in government. Most of the power elites live and work in cities other than Washington, D.C., so business lobbyists do the day-to-day work of influencing government on the elite's behalf.

Power elite theory: The view that a small handful of wealthy, influential Americans exercises extensive control over government decisions.

"Power elite" analysts look at events like the $125 billion U.S. government bailout of big banks in 2008–2009—using public tax dollars—and conclude that corporations get a special deal in American government. Nobody bailed out the more than 1 million property owners who lost their homes during the economic crisis, most of them because of the same subprime-mortgage crisis that devastated the banks. One recent analysis by three political scientists gave new life to the power-elite perspective. Washington lobbying, the researchers wrote, is dominated by business, which comprises 53 percent of interest groups and 72 percent of lobbying expenditures. In contrast, public-interest groups weigh in at about 5 percent of the funds spent on lobbying. And groups supporting less privileged people employ just 2 percent of the lobbyists in Washington. The results, this study suggests, reflect the conclusion of a famous political scientist back in 1960: This is a chorus that "sings with a decidedly upper class accent."[5]

Which view—pluralist, hyperpluralist, or power elite—is correct? Political scientists can't say for sure. It is difficult to tell whether big business or other powerful groups successfully turn policies in their direction on a regular basis. For every example like the bank bailout that affirms the power of elites in the American system, another story seems to suggest the opposite—that small business or retired people or environmental advocates prevail. The best guess: All three of these theories at times capture the truth.

THE BOTTOM LINE

- Interest groups, or organizations that seek to influence government, employ lobbyists to pursue benefits for their clients or membership.

- Groups serve members by communicating political information to them, analyzing and relating members' views to policy makers, and mobilizing people to act politically.

- A long debate among pluralist, hyperpluralist, and power elite theorists continues about whether the collective public is well represented by interest groups—and whether the neediest among us are represented.

Lobbying the Federal Branches of Government

The traditional model of Washington power brokers depicted a closed process dominated by **iron triangles**—tight, durable links among powerful interest groups, congressional committee chairs, and administration officials.

Consider one example: *farm subsidies.* For decades, many American farmers—growing crops from corn to tobacco—have received "price supports," or subsidies worth millions of dollars, from the U.S. government. Critics charge that this practice is a huge giveaway of taxpayer dollars. A big fight over farm policy in 2012–2014 led many to expect that farm subsidies would be cut sharply, but with minor tweaks, the system remains in place.

In some accounts, a classic iron triangle explains the staying power of farm subsidies. Congressional staffers on the agriculture committees in the House

Iron triangle: The cozy relationship in one issue area among interest-group lobbyists, congressional staffers, and executive-branch agencies.

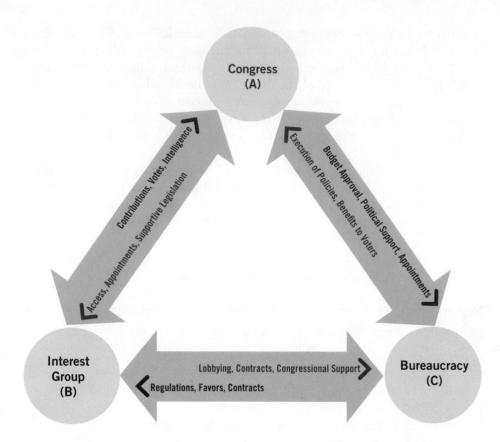

● **FIGURE 9.2** *Iron triangle. The classic image of interest group power features the close relationship among Congress, special interest groups, and federal government bureaucracy.*

and Senate (point A on Figure 9.2) developed close relationships with lobbyists for various farm groups (point B), who encouraged them to appropriate funds managed by Agriculture Department bureaucrats (point C). The lobbyists made sure to establish friendly connections with Department of Agriculture officials as well. But if executive-branch bureaucrats (C) balked at implementing subsidies, they might find their congressional appropriation cut the following year, so they usually kept the programs humming along. The combination of executive branch, legislative branch, and lobbyists—the iron triangle—was unstoppable.

Iron triangles proliferated around Washington into the 1960s, given the relatively closed environment of national policy making. The subsequent "advocacy explosion" initially brought more lobbyists in closer contact with Capitol Hill staffers, which ensured the triangles' survival for a while.

Although senior lobbying figures may have friends on both sides of the political aisle, nearly all Washington lobbyists are clearly identified as Republicans or Democrats. These connections between lobbyists and their preferred political party are best described as symbiotic. Washington actors often serve sequentially (and sometimes even simultaneously) as policy makers, lobbyists, and formal party officials—a phenomenon termed the **revolving door** that helped facilitate the rise of iron triangles.

Revolving door: The tendency of Washington's most seasoned lobbyists to move from government work (e.g., as a presidential advisor) to lobbying and back again.

Rise of the Issue Network

Over the past thirty years, however, iron triangles have given way to a very different image—of loose, open **issue networks**. More and more lobbyists representing more and more groups, in addition to growing numbers of congressional staffers, have broken apart the cozy triangles. Political scientist Mark Peterson charts a "radical change" during the 1980s, as triangles dissolved into a "far more diverse and open system" that featured "looser, less stable, less predictable, and more diverse patterns of interaction and decision."[6]

Figure 9.3 illustrates an example of an issue network, in telecommunications policy. Note how much more complicated than a simple triangle this network is. Welcome to the life of a Washington lobbyist today! To negotiate these networks—to faithfully represent members or to attract new clients—modern interest group representatives cannot count on a few reliable contacts, with a committee chair and a bureaucrat or two. Instead, they must constantly cultivate connections across Capitol Hill and in multiple executive departments and agencies.

Issue network: Shifting alliances of public and private interest groups, lawmakers, and other stakeholders all focused on the same policy area.

Intergovernmental and Reverse Lobbying

Public officials are not simply passive recipients of lobbying appeals: They also make those appeals themselves. Some engage in **intergovernmental lobbying**, pushing their counterparts in other branches to support their policy aims. When President Lyndon Johnson promoted a civil rights program in the mid-1960s, he made more than 150 telephone calls a day to members of the House

Intergovernmental lobbying: Attempts by public officials in one part of the government to influence their counterparts elsewhere—in another branch, or at a different (state or local) level.

Education
Teachers union, National PTA, Schools, Department of Education, Catholic Education Groups

Social Welfare
Liberal Groups, Community Based Organizations, Benton Foundation, ALA, Rural Health Clinics, RAC, AHA

Telecommunications
Local telephone companies, Long distance companies, USTA, COMPTEL, NCTA, FCC, USAC, NTIA, White House, Commerce Committees in Congress, CBO, CRS, Court, Department of Justice, FTC, Cellphone companies, VoIP providers, Lawyers, Lobbying firms

Conservative Groups
Heritage Foundation, PFF, CES, Cato Institute, National Taxpayers Union

High-tech Industry
Wireless Infrastructure Association (PCIA), Apple, IBM, Software Information Industry Association (SIIA), Gates Foundation

● **FIGURE 9.3** *Issue network. Today scholars generally see a more extensive network of actors influencing policy than the classic iron triangle. Here, the issue network that influences telecommunications policy. (Based on Kiyohara 2008; Berry and Wilcox 2007)*

and Senate, urging them to pass his legislative package. When mounting a full-blown effort on behalf of his goals, a president can be the most powerful lobbyist in Washington.

Reverse lobbying: Attempts by government officials to influence interest groups on behalf of their preferred policies.

Government officials also lobby interest groups, an activity termed **reverse lobbying**. Members of Congress and White House officials regularly reach out to groups aligned with their legislative efforts, coordinating efforts by lobbyists to promote their programs with the public and other lawmakers. These efforts can be controversial. In 2001, Vice President Dick Cheney headed an energy task force that included six cabinet members—plus oil, gas, coal, and other industry executives and lobbyists. They met privately (no names released, no public record of the discussions). Public interest groups sued, demanding a list of names. They charged that the administration had invited oil executives to come in and help shape energy policy to their own benefit: reverse lobbying run amok.

White House and congressional leaders alike regularly convene closed-door meetings of a wide range of affected interest groups before moving forward on a policy proposal. Hearing from the various sides can generate a broad scope of information and ideas and also may establish a compromise that wins enough support to push legislation through Congress.

● *Choosing a justice. Supreme Court nominee Elena Kagan arrives for her Senate hearings. The room is packed with lobbyists. Interest groups spent millions of dollars for or against her confirmation. In the end, Kagan was confirmed by a wide margin.*

Lobbying the Courts

Iron triangles and issue networks portray lobbyists engaging with the two elective branches, Congress and the presidency. What about the courts, which—as you will see in Chapter 13—have a major role in federal and state policy making? By law and custom, interest groups have almost no access to Supreme Court justices and very little connection to other federal (or senior state) judges. But interest groups still manage to weigh in on judicial decision-making, even without lobbying judges in person. They do so in three main ways.[7]

Lobbying on Judicial Confirmations. One way to shape court decisions is to influence the central players—to help determine who gets appointed as Supreme Court or federal judges in the first place. Each federal judge must be approved by the Senate. Today, every Supreme Court nomination immediately prompts a multi-million-dollar confirmation fight. Interest groups spend heavily on public campaigns to influence the presidents who choose judges and the senators who confirm—or block—a president's choice.

Filing Amicus Curiae ("Friend of Court") Briefs. Groups interested in a pending case are permitted to—and sometimes invited by a court to—write up legal memos, or "briefs," arguing their position on the case. Major cases attract dozens of such documents. In 2013, when the Supreme Court reviewed affirmative action, in a case involving the University of Texas, hundreds of groups and individuals filed seventy-three different amicus curiae briefs.

Sponsoring Litigation. It can be very expensive to take a case to court. Researching the relevant issues, paying the lawyers, and pursuing litigation through multiple appeals can cost millions of dollars. Interest groups often take up a legal cause, contributing both financial resources and expertise. When the Supreme Court agreed to review "establishment clause" rules about what counts as state sponsorship of religion—for example, whether government funds can go to Catholic schools or whether a state courthouse can post the Ten Commandments—interest groups like the American Civil Liberties Union (liberal) and the Federalist Society (conservative) provide substantial expertise and financing to the parties involved in the case.

THE BOTTOM LINE

- Lobbyists working in specific areas sometimes still form "iron triangles" with congressional staff and executive-branch officials.

- More fluid "issue networks," featuring lobbyists as central players, increasingly characterize today's complex policy-making environment.

- Lawmakers also lobby: they seek to persuade other public officials (intergovernmental lobbying) or secure assistance from interest groups (reverse lobbying).

- Interest groups also lobby the judicial branch by funding confirmation battles, filing amicus curiae briefs, and financing litigation.

● Interest Groups and Power

Critics of interest-group influence in U.S. politics charge that lobbyists are intimately involved in the details of policy making, writing bills and shaping legislative outcomes. How would we know if this is true—and if so, whether this represents an unsavory practice? Lacking hard evidence about interest groups' power—did this bill pass because lobbyists said it should or did it pass regardless of all their politicking?—we fall back on typical measures of what matters in national politics: *numbers* and *money*. Washington insiders gauge the status of a White House agency, or a special congressional committee, based partly on how many staff it has. Rising numbers of lobbyists might similarly suggest something about their sway in national policy making. If interest groups are spending a lot to influence lawmakers, their financial input may be a clue to the return their clients are getting on their investment.

Just how many lobbyists are there in Washington? Around twelve thousand professionals registered as congressional lobbyists in 2014, but that number represents a fraction—likely less than a quarter—of the total number of lobbyists on Capitol Hill. Lobbyists can avoid registering if they spend less than 20 percent of their work time on "lobbying activities," a term that is not well defined. (Although legal penalties apply to those failing to disclose lobbying work, not one criminal case has been filed under this law.) One researcher counts the number of lawyers active in Washington, on the assumption that most of them lobby the federal government as part of their work. The current figure: just under eighty thousand.[8]

Tens of thousands of lobbyists, all chasing members of Congress and their staffs as well as White House and executive-branch officials: Many commentators see these numbers as decisive evidence of interest group influence. When health reform was atop the national agenda during 2009–2010, one report calculated that six lobbyists were engaged on the issue for each member of the House and the Senate.[9] That's more than 3,200 lobbyists, all clamoring to be heard on a single topic.

Ultimately, if you measure the power of lobbyists by simple numbers, then this sector is certainly powerful. Do the rising numbers suggest overbearing power? Not necessarily. They mean only that interest-group lobbyists have become a central part of the operation of national, state, and local government.

Lobbyist Spending

Lobbyists rarely visit lawmakers just to offer a cheerful greeting. Interest groups big and small, from Wall Street financial interests to Michigan asparagus growers, spend an estimated $8 billion each year attempting to influence Washington policy making. This doesn't include spending on political campaigns, discussed later in this chapter.

This $8 billion figure is inexact. Official Senate and House records indicate that *registered* lobbyists reported spending nearly 3.5 billion on lobbying activities in 2014 (see Figure 9.4). As noted earlier, many of those seeking to influence Congress never bother to register. Analysts estimate that total spending is about twice the amount indicated in lobbying registrations.[10]

Clients of private groups and members of public groups together provide those billions of dollars, which are spent on lobbyists' salaries, research costs (remember that neatly bound report!), the expense of running a Washington office, travel, and so forth. Table 9.1 lists the top-spending lobbying clients for 2013. Note the various sectors represented: health care, oil/gas, telecommunications, military contractors, real estate, and American seniors. Most of these big spenders are corporate interests: Does that fuel the "power elite" view? Or is it merely a waste of money, given that business loses plenty of policy battles?

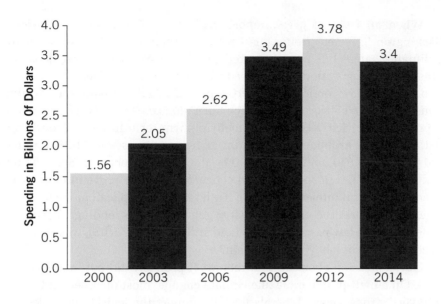

● **FIGURE 9.4** *Trends in spending by registered lobbyists, 2000–2014, in billions of dollars. (Center for Responsive Politics)*

TABLE 9.1 Biggest-Spending Lobbying Clients, 2013

LOBBYING CLIENT	TOTAL
U.S. Chamber of Commerce	$74,470,000
National Association of Realtors	$38,584,580
Blue Cross/Blue Shield	$22,510,280
Northrop Grumman	$20,590,000
National Cable & Telecommunications Association	$19,870,000
American Hospital Association	$19,143,813
Comcast Corporation	$18,810,000
American Medical Association	$18,160,000
Pharmaceutical Research & Manufacturers of America	$17,882,500
General Electric	$16,130,000
AT&T Inc.	$15,935,000
Google Inc.	$15,800,000
Boeing Co.	$15,230,000
National Association of Broadcasters	$14,450,000
Lockheed Martin	$14,436,226
Source: Center for Responsive Politics.	

When an issue of great importance to a group or industry arises in Washington, affected groups tend to boost their spending. In 2009–2010, a climate-change bill was promoted by President Obama and debated in Congress. The legislation aimed to reduce Americans' use of coal and oil. Sharp spending increases on lobbying were reported by oil companies, coal-mining industries, and electric utilities, which burn thousands of tons of coal each year to produce electricity. The largest lobbying firm for utilities, Edison Electric Institute, spent around $7 million on lobbying expenses in 2008, a number that jumped to $10.5 million in 2009—a 50 percent increase. Some analysts look at these hikes in spending and conclude that they prove interest groups' extensive political influence. But the truth is more complicated. We might ask, for example, what the energy industry got for all its spending. Although no climate-change law passed in 2010 (and still has not in 2015), was this lack of success a result of lobbying opposition?

Our conclusion about all that money: It probably did not influence many votes. On a high-profile issue like climate change, most members of Congress have very strong views: Liberals fiercely support the legislation (unless they think it does not go far enough); conservatives are equally strongly against it. You can predict most of the votes. What are the lobbyists spending funds on, then? They are supporting the members that agree with them or trying to "soften up" the few members who might be persuadable on this topic. If members need facts for the debate, lobbyists are there to provide background. That's why, in our story at this chapter's opening, that invaluable report landed on your desk.[11]

A clearer sign of lobbying heft may be an adjustment in a policy or specific bill. Energy companies, for example, successfully pushed to include an "offset program" in climate-change legislation that allowed them to invest in projects to remove carbon dioxide from the atmosphere if they were unable to meet reduced emissions targets. This technical policy change underlines an important truth: The more obscure the provision, the better the chances of winning it. The less the public is aware of a topic, the more room Congress has to deliver favors.

THE BOTTOM LINE

- Because of the difficulty of directly measuring interest group influence in government, researchers turn to metrics like number of lobbyists and the funds they spend on lobbying.

- Beginning in the mid-1960s, an advocacy explosion saw lobbyist numbers climb dramatically. Resources devoted to lobbying also rose sharply beginning in this period.

- Despite their extensive presence and billions of dollars in spending, lobbyists are not likely to change congressional minds on high-profile votes; their role is more akin to supporting the members already on their side. Votes on more obscure or highly technical topics may be easier for lobbyists to sway.

● Political Parties and U.S. Government

On January 26, 2010, the Senate voted on a bill to create a committee to propose government spending cuts that would be "fast-tracked." The bill started with broad support from both parties. But when it came time to vote, the Senate rejected the plan. To the amazement of most observers, eight Republicans who were listed on the bill as co-sponsors now voted against it. Why? Because the Democratic president, Barack Obama, had supported the legislation and his Republican opponents did not want to give him a "win" ahead of the midterm elections later that year. The final result? The Republicans won the largest midterm victory—picking up sixty-three seats in the House—in seventy-five years. After that, partisanship just intensified.[12] Stories like this one might tempt you to echo President George Washington: Do we really need parties? The answer is yes. The next section explains why.

What the Parties Do

Love them or hate them, political parties are an essential part of American government. They are responsible for five major jobs: championing ideas, selecting candidates, mobilizing voters, organizing postelection government activity, and integrating new voters into the political process.

Parties Champion Ideas. U.S. politics reverberates with ideas, and every candidate takes a position on scores of issues. How do voters keep all these candidates, issues, and ideas straight? In effect, parties create a brand that gives people an easy way to find political figures and ordinary fellow-citizens who roughly share their views. If you strongly support environmental activism, a path to citizenship for undocumented immigrants, robust social programs, a woman's right to choose, public radio, and high-speed rail, you are probably a Democrat. If, on the other hand, you care more about lowering taxes, reducing the size of government, rolling back regulations, supporting morality and traditional families, and outlawing abortion, you are probably a Republican. You prefer to mix and match from the lists? You're likely an independent who belongs to neither party. Each party has its language and symbols. Do people in a group raise their voices when they say "under God" in the Pledge of Allegiance? They're most often Republicans, participating in a conservative ritual.

Parties Select Candidates. Parties choose the candidates who will run for election. Republicans began with twelve contenders running for president in 2012 and voted, state by state, until they had selected Mitt Romney. The two major parties select candidates to run for office at every level of government—except local government, which as we will see often relies on **nonpartisan elections**.

Parties Mobilize the Voters. Party leaders work to get the people to vote for their candidates. The parties raise money, hire consultants, craft advertisements,

Nonpartisan election: An election where candidates run as individuals, without any party affiliation. Many towns and cities feature nonpartisan elections.

take polls, and organize phone banks. They have also become adept at suppressing the other side's votes through negative advertising.

Parties Organize Governing Activity After the Election.   Once the election is over, each party works to enact its signature programs. Leaders propose action, line up votes, and organize government activity in Congress, in presidential administrations, and in the state governments.

Political socialization:
Education about how the government works and which policies one should support; provided partly at school, partly by party officials and other national institutions.

Party system: The broad organization of U.S. politics, comprising the two main parties, the coalition of supporters backing each, the positions they take on major issues, and each party's electoral achievements.

Parties Help Integrate New Groups into the Political Process.   Parties are important agents of **political socialization**, transmitting basic lessons about politics and government (the details may differ, depending on the party). Party messages have attracted immigrants, young voters, evangelical Christians, high-tech entrepreneurs, and many more into the American polity. Parties provide crucial communication links between 320 million Americans, spread across a continent, and their elected leaders.

Political parties provide an efficient, effective solution to these five issues.[13] Is there anything especially distinctive about the American **party system**? Yes: The United States is unusual because it relies on just two major parties.

Two-Party America

In January 2015 all 435 members of the House of Representatives, 98 of 100 senators, and all 50 governors were either Democrats or Republicans. Why is the United States so resolutely devoted to the number "two" when it comes to party politics?

One reason for this two-party tradition draws on American ideas. As we saw in Chapter 1, Americans long ago embraced a set of national ideals. Each side of these great debates is typically associated with one of the two major parties.

Parties socialize new groups into politics. When evangelical Christians started getting involved in politics in the 1970s and 1980s, Republican leaders were there to show them the ropes. Here, President Ronald Reagan speaks to evangelical leaders.

Barack Obama supporters celebrate his presidential re-election in 2012. For the first time in history, African Americans voted at a higher rate than white voters.

For example, most Republicans see liberty as freedom from government; most Democrats fight for programs that will help free needy people from want. The two parties each rally around a classic definition of liberty—what we described as negative and positive liberty, respectively.

As you know by now, institutions invariably reinforce ideas. In this case, the winner-take-all electoral rules keep third parties out. A party that wins 20 percent of the national vote but doesn't actually win any states or districts is shut out in both Congress and the Electoral College. In contrast, most other democracies operate multiparty systems. Proportional representation systems give small parties a chance to compete.

The result is simple and dramatic: The rules push every group to join one of the two major parties. When candidates decide to break out of the two-party system, they are accused of being "spoilers"—attracting voters from the party that is more sympathetic to their cause and, as a result, throwing the election to the party that does not share their philosophy at all. This is precisely what happened in the 2000 presidential election. In Florida, Republican George Bush won 48.847 percent of the vote; Democrat Al Gore won 48.846 percent of the vote; and Green Party candidate Ralph Nader won 1.635 percent of the vote. Although Bush won by only 0.0001 percent, because our system is "winner take all" he commanded all of Florida's twenty-five Electoral College votes and won the presidency. What did disappointed Democrats say? Ralph Nader and the Green Party had drawn just enough liberals away from the Democrats to throw the election to the Republicans—who were far less sympathetic to Nader's causes. The Florida experience only reinforced a key institutional lesson: work within the two parties.

Additional institutional forces help keep the two main parties at the center of American politics. State laws determine who gets on the ballot, and they often make it very difficult for a minor-party candidate to be listed. In Florida, for example, after reforms in 2011 that *eased* restrictions, a third party still needs to collect more than 112,000 notarized signatures simply to list its candidate on a presidential-primary ballot—a high bar for a small party.

The advantage of America's two-party system is its predictablity and stability. In nations with many parties, each election is followed by negotiations among the parties trying to form a majority.

There are also disadvantages to two-party dominance in the United States.[14] For starters, it is less representative. In 2012, almost 30 percent of the voters in Massachusetts voted for Republican congressional candidates. Is it fair to end up with nine Massachusetts Democrats—and no Republicans—in Congress? Voters in Germany or Japan or other proportional representation systems generally have more choices for national or local office; people passionate about a cause—immigration, the environment, religion, free markets—often can find a party devoted to that cause. Perhaps you're wondering if we have ever made room for additional parties? That's easy to answer: No!

Third Parties in American Politics

Theodore "Teddy" Roosevelt is one of the most colorful figures in U.S. political history: a military hero who suffered from asthma, a big-game hunter who adopted an orphaned bear cub (giving rise to the familiar "Teddy Bear"). When Roosevelt came out of retirement to run as a Progressive Party candidate, he became the only third-party presidential candidate to come in second— but he still got clobbered by Woodrow Wilson, who won 435 electoral votes to Roosevelt's 88.

Table 9.2 lists all third-party presidential contestants who gained more than 5 percent of the popular vote or more than ten electoral votes since 1840. It's a short list, without a single candidate who came close to winning. And most third parties lasted just one term (or four years) at the national level. Roosevelt's Progressive Party, for example, elected some fifteen members to Congress and spearheaded important reforms but dissolved within four years. The "Tea Party," which has attracted considerable attention in American politics in recent years, is not in fact an organized national party, but a label that some local candidates adopt to signal their conservative views.

On the state level Minnesota marks one of the few third-party gubernatorial successes in modern American politics. Jesse Ventura, a former professional wrestler (known as "The Body"), rode his blend of outsized personality and blunt commonsense to the governor's mansion as a Reform Party candidate in 1998. In the last quarter-century, four other states have elected governors outside the major parties: Alaska (1990), Connecticut (1990), Rhode Island (2010),

TABLE 9.2 The Road to Nowhere: The Most Successful Third-Party Presidential Contenders, 1840–2012

ELECTION	THIRD-PARTY CANDIDATE(S), PARTY	PERCENTAGE OF POPULAR VOTE (NO. OF ELECTORAL VOTES)
1856	Millard Fillmore, American (Know-Nothing) Party	22% (8)
1860	John Bell, Constitutional Union Party	12.6% (39)
1892	James Weaver, People's Party	8.5% (22)
1912	Theodore Roosevelt, Progressive Party Eugene Debs, Socialist Party	27.4% (88) 6% (0)
1924	Robert LaFollette, Progressive Party	16.6% (13)
1948	Strom Thurmond, States' Rights (Dixiecrat) Party	2.4% (39)
1968	George Wallace, American Independent Party	13.5% (45)
1980	John Anderson, National Unity Party	6.6% (0)
1992	Ross Perot, United We Stand Party	18.9% (0)

● *Wrestler-turned-governor Jesse Ventura, a member of the Reform Party.*

and Maine (1994, 1998). All four winners were independents rather than representatives of third parties.

Despite this limited record of electoral success, minor parties are valuable contributors to American government. Third-party movements have often injected strong and controversial views into the major parties. They have fought for the abolition of slavery, the direct election of senators, votes for women, laws eliminating child labor, the prohibition of drinking, the income tax, limits on immigration, and smaller government. They often provide a vehicle for people to express alternative views. This helps dissidents get a hearing, expands civic engagement, and perhaps minimizes the potential of anger and violence that arise when people see their cause as ignored.[15] Third parties shake up a government system that can be resistant to change, as we shall see in the next section.

America's Party Systems: Origins and Change

Political parties are always evolving. Once in a while the entire party system changes—the winners, the losers, the ways the parties organize, and the issues they debate. In short, the party gets a makeover. We can identify at least six distinctive "party systems" stretching across American history.

Beginnings: First Party System (1789–1828). Political parties are as American as hot dogs or Chevrolets—and much older than either. After the Revolution, the battle over ratification featured pro-Constitution Federalists (who supported a stronger central government) and their Anti-Federalist opponents (who thought power should remain with the states and communities). Candidates for the first Congresses identified as either Federalists (strong national government) or Democratic-Republicans (states' rights and limited national power). The Federalists controlled the first three administrations. The immensely popular Washington ran unopposed in the first two presidential campaigns (even his opponents never criticized him directly—attacking those around him instead); John Adams, Washington's vice president, won the third election.

In 1800, Democratic-Republican candidate Thomas Jefferson won a bitter, razor-thin victory over President John Adams. This was the first time the

White House changed party hands. For the rest of the first-party period, the Democratic-Republicans dominated national politics, winning the next six presidential elections and dominating both chambers of Congress for twenty-four years.

The first party system set a durable pattern: two main parties contesting elections and building coalitions.

Rise: Second Party System (ca. 1828–1860). When Andrew Jackson won the presidency in 1828, some twenty thousand Democrats (many of them angling for government jobs) swarmed into Washington for his inauguration. Supreme Court Justice Joseph Story, watching the spectacle, spoke for many old-style gentry: "The reign of King Mob seemed triumphant."[16] What he was really seeing was the birth of modern party politics.

In just three decades, political parties had evolved into a form that we would recognize today. Party competition grew fierce; voting rights expanded to most males; enthusiastic party members threw themselves into politics. These hallmarks of America's second-party system remain the backbone of our party practices.

"The rise of the common man" came with significant downsides: It meant fewer rights for the small population of free blacks (90 percent of African Americans were still slaves). And, political connections—known as the spoils system—dictated the distribution of jobs at every level.

Party names changed along with the institutional shifts. The Federalists had vanished. Jefferson's old Democratic-Republicans split into two factions in the 1820s. Supporters of Andrew Jackson adopted the "Democratic" half, while a separate faction aligned with a brilliant young Kentucky politician, Henry Clay, called themselves "Whigs," a British term associated with opposition to tyranny—in this case, "King Andrew."

Both parties foundered on the question of slavery. Neither, however, could duck the issues. As the United States spread west, every new territory and state raised the same urgent question: Should slavery be permitted to spread? Factions formed within each party. In the early 1850s, the Whigs, who had attracted the strongest opponents of slavery, collapsed under the issue. Out of the Whigs' demise a new party system arose—and clarified the future of slavery in the United States.[17]

War and Reconstruction: Third Party System (1860–1896). Abraham Lincoln joined the Whig Party as soon as it was formed and remained a supporter until the party folded. He then helped form the new antislavery Republican Party, which strongly supported free labor (which today we call capitalism) and insisted that new western settlements should be free of slavery (free soil) since slavery's expansion would undermine the people's right to work for themselves (free labor). Lincoln won the presidential election of 1860; the southern states feared the end of slavery and the nation soon entered its terrible Civil War.

● *Reconstruction featured a hotly fought battle between the parties. While Republicans promoted images of new racial harmony and national economic health, Democrats warned of impending doom. This caricature was part of the racist campaign designed to show that the former slaves were not prepared for freedom—a false charge backed by violence that eventually helped defeat efforts at racial reconstruction.*

After the war, Republicans again drew on the party to help rebuild the nation. "Radical Republicans" promoted black rights, helping to boost many former slaves into Congress and statehouses under the Republican banner. Democrats, fighting back in the South, denounced Reconstruction's "excesses" and often resorted to violence and racist tactics that tried to limit the freedom of the former slaves to travel, to vote, or to seek employment.

Republicans dominated elections between 1864 and 1880. By the end of "Radical Republican" rule in 1877, each party had developed a strong regional identity. Democrats controlled the former Confederate states (which became known as the "Solid South" because they reliably voted Democratic), while the Republicans grew strongest in the Northeast and Midwest. Large numbers of European and Asian immigrants streamed into the cities during the 1870s and 1880s; city governments featured well-developed **party machines**—powerful political organizations. Managed by **party bosses**, the machines provided immigrants with such basic services as food, shelter, jobs, contacts, and a sense of belonging. In exchange, the party could count on a block of all-important votes, once immigrants became naturalized citizens. The machines grew notorious for bribery and corruption.

Reformers eventually cleaned up city politics (although the hardiest machines lasted well into the twentieth century) through a series of institutional reforms that included banishing the parties themselves from urban elections.

Party machine: A hierarchical arrangement of party workers, often organized in an urban area to help integrate immigrants and minority groups into the political system. Most active in the late nineteenth and early twentieth centuries.

Party boss: The senior figure in a party machine.

THE "BRAINS"
THAT ACHIEVED THE TAMMANY VICTORY AT THE ROCHESTER DEMOCRATIC CONVENTION.

● *A caricature of William M. "Boss" Tweed of New York City by popular cartoonist Thomas Nast—instead of brains he has a bag of money. Tweed epitomized the party bosses of the nineteenth and early twentieth centuries. Bosses organized urban populations, especially immigrant arrivals, gaining power rivaling that of mayors and governors—and often wielded it in corrupt fashion.*

Thus, today parties remain crucial on the national and state level, but many cities have nonpartisan elections. In fact, you can measure how strong the urban reformers have been in any city by checking whether the parties still operate in local elections.

Business and Reform: Fourth Party System (1896–1932).   At the end of the third party period, national elections had become very close. Suddenly, in 1896, the party system changed again and a renewed Republican Party, sometimes tagged the "millionaires' party" swept back into control. After President William McKinley was assassinated in 1901 his vice president, Theodore Roosevelt, stepped into the White House and challenged the "millionaires' club."

The leading debates of the fourth party system featured support for the status quo and business, on the one side, and pressures for political and economic equality (championed by the Progressive movement) on the other. Should women be granted the vote? Should the government regulate emerging corporate giants, like Standard Oil or the Central Pacific Railroad? Should judges be elected? On the state level, should the government regulate child labor? Should it limit the workday for men and women? Should it provide funds for the blind or the aged? To the Progressive reformers, led by Theodore Roosevelt, the answer was yes, yes, yes.

The 1920s were a boom time, marked by the dominance of business interests and rising new industries like advertising, automobiles, and electricity. Then the economy collapsed in 1929–1930, taking down the entire "fourth party system" as well.

Depression and New Deal: Fifth Party System (1933–1968). Another President Roosevelt, Teddy's distant cousin Franklin, helped define the fifth party system. The Great Depression (1929–1941) unhinged party politics, crippling a Republican Party associated with business interests and economic incompetence.

After three years of economic misery, FDR's uncompromising inaugural address swept in a new politics. Roosevelt frankly blamed the "unscrupulous money changers" and "self-seekers"—the old "millionaires' club"—for the nation's "dark days." Roosevelt's **New Deal** focused on jobs, infrastructure, government aid to the elderly (Social Security), temporary assistance for the needy (unemployment insurance and welfare), and new federal government agencies to manage it all. Roosevelt's Democratic Party reaped the electoral rewards, reshaping party coalitions.

The Democratic Party coalition included an unusual mix of interests. It had controlled the South since Reconstruction, when defeated Confederates rejected their Republican military conquerors. The big-city machines, with their ethnic supporters, also voted reliably Democratic (occasionally cheating at the ballot box to offset rural Republicans). To this reliable base, Roosevelt added labor unions (the Democrats sponsored legislation that permitted the movement to grow); farmers who saw agricultural prices rise during these years; and perhaps most surprising—African Americans.

● *The story of Jack and the Beanstalk with President Theodore Roosevelt, brandishing the sword of "public service," as Jack, confronting corrupt "giants" of Wall Street like banker J. P. Morgan.*

Roosevelt's employment programs, along with early efforts to reduce racial segregation, won many black voters to the Democratic Party for the first time. However, there was a tension within the base of the Democratic Party: Liberals, labor unions, and African Americans pressured the party to expand social programs and civil rights, while the Southern Democrats struggled to rein in social programs and supported segregation. Democrats kept the coalition together—and hung on to their southern majority—for another thirty years, but as they became known as the party of civil rights, white southern voters shifted to the "Grand Old Party" (GOP).

The Democrats dominated the fifth party system. As the Democrats embraced civil rights, however, southern Democrats turned into Republicans. As the Democratic coalition began to crumble, a new generation of Republicans promoted fresh ideas for America.

The Sixth Party System: The Parties at Equal Strength (1972–Present). Richard Nixon (1969–1973) and, later, Ronald Reagan (1981–1989) developed a "southern strategy" to win middle-class white votes. They emphasized small business,

New Deal: Broad series of economic programs and reforms introduced between 1933 and 1936 and associated with the Franklin Roosevelt administration.

limited government, and a more market-oriented vision. The Republican Party had always had a conservative wing, but now this wing rose to dominance. By 1981, Republican president Ronald Reagan had launched a direct assault on the fifth party system: Government is not the solution to our problems. Instead, said the rising Republican coalition, government is the source of the problem.

By the 1980s, the parties had lined up in their contemporary configuration. On economic and social issues alike, Democrats leaned left, Republicans right. Republicans had controlled the fourth party period and Democrats the fifth. The new party era introduces something new: Neither party is in control. Instead, very close elections swing party control back and forth. One result was to fuel growing partisanship.

THE BOTTOM LINE

- Political parties are an essential part of U.S. government, carrying out five major functions: championing ideas, selecting candidates, mobilizing voters, organizing postelection government activity, and integrating new voters into the political process.

- America's two-party style has endured for more than two hundred years, with Democrats and Republicans the main standard-bearers since 1856.

- Two main parties have always dominated U.S. party politics—and since 1856 it has been the same two parties, Republicans and Democrats. Election rules help explain this dominance, which is challenged periodically by third parties; none has ever managed to break through.

- We count at least six party systems since the U.S. founding. The latest, which began in 1969, is the period of very close elections.

● Party Identification . . . and Ideas

Americans have always had a love–hate relationship with parties. They are not even mentioned in the Constitution. George Washington despised them and, in his Farewell Address, warned against their "destructive," "frightful," and "fatal" consequences.[18] In a 2012 poll, for the first time ever, more people identified themselves as independents than as Democrats or Republicans (see Figure 9.5).

Yet many Americans feel strongly attached to their parties. That attachment is called **party identification**, and deeply affects how individuals view political events. In one study, individuals were asked forty-eight questions about their values. The difference between party members has soared from nine points (in 1997) to eighteen points (in 2012). Where do these differences come from? And exactly who is attached to each party?

Party identification: Strong attachment to one political party, often established at an early age.

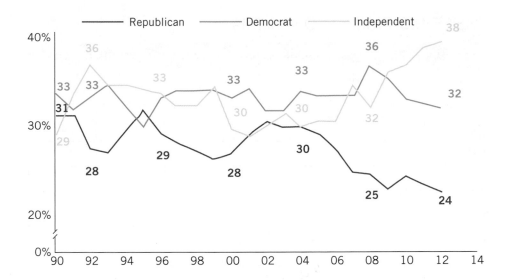

● **FIGURE 9.5** *Trends in party identification. Percentages represent annual totals based on all Pew Research surveys conducted in each calendar year. (Pew Research Center)*

Building Party Identification

Party loyalty often starts with family. Mark Losey, running for a U.S. House seat in 2006, told his Ohio audiences how he chose his party. As a child, he used to go walking on his grandfather's farm. "On one of those walks," recalled Losey, "I asked, 'Grandpa, are we Democrats or Republicans?' My Grandpa, who grew up on a farm during the height of the Great Depression, paused. 'Before Roosevelt became president, our family almost starved to death,' he replied. Grandpa Wren is still a Democrat. So am I."[19]

Of course, political views change. Senator Orrin Hatch, a Utah Republican, was raised a staunch Democrat. In college, recalls Hatch, "I learned that personal responsibility and a government closer to the people was supremely better for businesses and individuals than an intrusive federal government that led to personal dependency."[20] That shift in belief turned him into a Republican.

Party identification is also shaped by who you are. The Republican Party today is mostly white (87%). The Democratic Party, in contrast, is increasingly diverse; today it is 55 percent white, 24 percent black, 13 percent Hispanic, and 7 percent other (see Tables 9.3 and 9.4). The buzz in political science is about the demographics of the future. Figure 9.6 shows how the American electorate is growing dramatically less white. When Ronald Reagan whipped Jimmy Carter in 1980, the electorate was almost 90 percent white; by 2012 the white share of the electorate was down to 72 percent—and falling further.

Gender also distinguishes the parties. Republicans draw an equal number of men and women. Democratic voters and officeholders, on the other hand, tend to be women—by a 3–2 margin. In fact, the 2013–2014 Democratic House members represented a first for any congressional party: a minority of white males.[21]

TABLE 9.3 Profile of Democrats

	2000	2004	2008	2012
% of Democrats who are . . .				
White	64	61	59	55
Black	21	21	21	24
Hispanic	11	13	13	13
Other	4	5	6	7
Male	41	41	42	41
Female	59	59	58	59
Average age	47.0	47.6	46.9	47.7
Think of self as . . .				
Conservative	24	24	25	20
Moderate	41	42	37	38
Liberal	28	29	34	38

Source: Pew Research Center 2012 Values Survey.
Whites and blacks include only those who are not Hispanic; Hispanics are of any race.

TABLE 9.4 Profile of Republicans

	2000	2004	2008	2012
% of Republicans who are . . .				
White	88	87	87	87
Black	2	2	2	2
Hispanic	7	7	6	6
Other	2	3	4	4
Male	51	51	52	50
Female	49	49	48	50
Average age	45.5	46.8	48.2	49.7
Think of self as . . .				
Conservative	60	63	68	68
Moderate	29	29	26	26
Liberal	7	5	5	5

Source: Pew Research Center 2012 Values Survey.
Whites and blacks include only those who are not Hispanic; Hispanics are of any race.

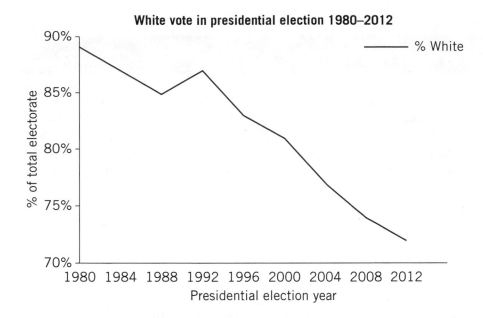

White vote in presidential election 1980–2012

% of total electorate (y-axis: 70%, 75%, 80%, 85%, 90%)

Presidential election year (x-axis: 1980 1984 1988 1992 1996 2000 2004 2008 2012)

—— % White

● **FIGURE 9.6** *One of the most important trends in American politics: the steady decline of the white vote. In recent elections the Republican vote remains just 13 percent nonwhite; the Democratic vote, in contrast, was 45 percent nonwhite. This chart demonstrates how important it is for the parties to broaden their appeal to nonwhite voters (CNN Opinion Research Poll, April 19, 2011).*

Other traits also make a difference, such as where you live (urbanites lean Democratic, suburbanites Republican); how much you make (high earners lean Republican, low Democratic). Even personality seems to matter. Recent studies suggest that people who exhibit more "openness" (eager to explore new experiences) and "agreeableness" (very social in outlook) are more likely to be strong Democrats. Those who measure high in "conscientiousness" (strong sense of duty, discipline, impulse control) and "emotional stability" (even-tempered) tend to be stronger supporters of the Republican Party.[22] Think about your own personality: Does it fit with this recent political science wisdom?

Another influence on party affinity is political context—put simply, what's happening in national politics when a voter forms attachments. Certain political moments can carry magic for a political party—John Kennedy's election seemed to do so in 1960 (for the Democrats) and Ronald Reagan (for the Republicans) in 1980. Will Barack Obama have the same effect and inspire millennials to become Democrats? Although political historians are always alert to a sea change, no mass shift in party identification has shown up for the past twenty-five years or so. Currently, around 33 percent of Americans list themselves as Democrats; the Republican figure is between 24 percent and 29 percent, depending on the poll. Recently one thing appears to be changing—the surge in independents, weary of both parties. Recent polls put them above 40 percent of registered voters. Why? One reason may be the intense conviction among the party faithful.

The Power of Party Attachment

Party identification shapes three key aspects of public involvement: voting/political participation, "filtering," and ideology.

PERSONALITY AND PARTY

Consider your own personality and party preference. Does recent political science research help predict your view—and the views of the people around you?	**Yes.** I believe that Democrats are more likely to seek new experiences and Republicans are more likely to emphasize duty and discipline.	**No.** I think there are different traits that explain party identification. (Please specify which traits you think matter most.)	**Interests, not personality.** I don't believe personality predicts politics. We are rational creatures pursuing our own self-interest regardless of personality.

Straight-ticket voter: One who votes for the same party for all offices on a ballot.

Split-ticket voter: One who votes for at least one candidate from each party, dividing his or her ballot between the two (or more) parties.

Base voters: Party members who tend to vote loyally for their party's candidates in most elections.

Voting/Participation.   Your Democratic or Republican party identity tends to be a very strong predictor of your voting habits. In 2012, for example, 92 percent of Democrats voted for Obama for president, while 93 percent of Republicans voted for Romney. Analysts measuring the strength of party attachment find that strong partisans tend to be very loyal **straight-ticket voters**, sticking with their party's candidates right down the ballot. Their opposite? **Split-ticket voters**, who make their choices candidate by candidate.

Voting rates are higher among those with strong party identification than among the rest of the public. The key to every election is turning out the party's **base voters**—those who are highly unlikely to vote for the other party—while winning over the independents. Conventional wisdom used to hold that independents were in the middle. Not anymore. Today, most lean strongly toward either the Democratic or Republican Party.

Filtering.   Party identification also plays a *filtering* role. *Filters choose what signals in the media environment people are liable to accept or reject.* As one political scientist writes, "people tend to *project* favorable characteristics and acceptable issue positions onto the candidates of the party they favor."[23] In a set of experiments, social scientists asked respondents to rate a generic series of political candidates ("Candidate A," "Candidate B," etc.), based on photos and fairly detailed personal and political biographies. Each of the candidates was sometimes described as a Democrat, sometimes as a Republican, and sometimes as an independent. The study found that self-identified Democrats (especially strong partisans) liked the candidates described as Democrats the best, and the same result occurred for Republicans: The candidate's policy positions, appearance, family background, and so forth were all far less important than the party label.

Ideology.   The parties take divergent views on issue after issue. This creates the polarization we described at the start of the chapter. Should we provide government support to people who can't take care of themselves? Democrats say yes (75 percent), Republicans say no (only 40 percent agree). Should we make every effort to improve the position of minorities, even if it means preferential treatment? A majority of Democrats say yes (52 percent) while just 12 percent of Republicans agree. Do you doubt the existence of God? Republicans are more likely to say no (92 percent) than Democrats (77 percent). On all these indicators, differences between the parties have more than doubled in the past fifteen years.[24]

Of course, even with the growing intensity of party ideology, no party is a monolith. Each includes multiple factions with different—sometimes very different—ideas. Balancing among these various factions is among the toughest jobs a party leader faces.

Organizing the Parties

The work of parties is carried out by three different groups: the party organization, the party in government, and the party in the electorate. Let's take a closer look.

The Party Bureaucracy.   The central organization for both parties is a national committee—the Republican National Committee (RNC) and the Democratic National Committee (DNC). These committees raise funds for the party, coordinate election strategies, decide which local races to fund, organize a national convention every four years, and prepare the **party platform**—the party's statement of purpose and its position on issues. If you are a candidate for a prominent office—from senator to mayor—your success may rest in large part on your ability to persuade the party organization to contribute funds to your campaign.

The committees also issue and enforce the party's rules for primary elections, from the presidential level downward. Important members of the DNC and RNC include the state party chairs and vice chairs, who typically are the most faithful activists in each party.

Party organizational leaders rarely have much of a public profile. Can you name the official chairs of the Democratic or Republican Party? Even most political scientists flunk that question (Debbie Wasserman and Reince Priebus respectively). These officials may be unknown, but they are important: they coordinate the party's image, message, and actions across fifty states.

Party in Government.   The **party in government** gets the recognition. These are the government officials in each party, and include elected leaders, appointed officers, individuals running for political office, and their staffs. The party in government struggles to enact the policies they support—and to stop their rivals from enacting theirs.

There is a constant struggle for influence within each party in government. Presidents usually command their own party—although members of the party may challenge them if the administration's policies grow unpopular. There is constant jockeying to become the face of the party that does not control the

Party platform: The written statement of a party's core convictions and issue priorities. Generally revised every four years, in time for the national party convention.

Party in government: The portion of a political party's organization that comprises elected officials and candidates for office.

● *Republican Party organizers in Congress. The eight-member House Republican leadership team, including whips.*

White House. Congressional leaders, governors, and presidential candidates all vie to put their own stamp on the party.

Party in the Electorate.   What is left after the party organization and office-holders? We are! Each party's followers make up the **party in the electorate**.

Party in the electorate: The largest (and least organized) component of a political party, drawn from the public at large: registered members and regular supporters.

The parties are enormous: roughly 72 million Democrats and 55 million Republicans, with another highly prized 40 million citizens registered as independents. Recently the public has begun to drift from joining a party to registering as independents—although this effect is more pronounced in opinion polls than in actual registrations.

The Big Tent.   The media generally focuses on the best-known party names. Political parties thrive, however, when all their elements—the organization, the officeholders, and the public supporters—work together. That means sharing the same message, getting enthused about shared principles, and embracing the party symbols—right down to the bumper stickers.

American federalism makes unanimity difficult. Local officials run the party in each state. Democrats in a conservative state like Alabama often have more in common with many Republicans in their own state than they do with liberal Democrats in San Francisco or New York. The same is true, of course, for the more liberal Republicans in New York or Massachusetts.

The party organizations always make tactical calculations: Do they put their resources in a few swing states that they have a good chance of winning

● *Party in the electorate. The Republican faithful gather in Tampa, Florida, in 2012 and cheer their nominee.*

in the next election cycle? Or should they spread their resources across many states—even supporting candidates who are long shots—with the hope of slowly building up their party in places where it does not often win?

Federalism pushes each of the two major parties to adopt a "big tent" spread themselves wide, embrace followers of divergent views, and hope any resultant ideological muddle doesn't turn off too many party members. However, many party members reject the big-tent approach and insist on sticking to their political principles, which can make for tumultuous politics within each party.

THE BOTTOM LINE

● A substantial majority of voting-age Americans identify strongly with one of the two major parties. Others declare themselves independents.

● Our powerful sense of party identification is a result of many factors, including parental influence, political context, and even personality type.

● Party identification in turn helps shape our voting patterns, the ways we filter political information, and our bedrock ideas about politics and government.

● Each party includes three groups: the party organization, the party in government, and the party in the electorate.

Party Competition . . . and Partisanship

Parties began to lose their influence over politics and government in the mid-1960s. Interest groups muscled in on party territory, mobilized voters, and shaped issue positions. Americans began to identify with movements and organizations—civil rights, environmentalism, the right to life, libertarianism. The parties floundered in response. By the 1970s and 1980s, political observers were publishing books like *The Party's Over* and *The Decline of American Political Parties*.[25] The central role of parties in organizing elections also slipped, with the rise of the "candidate-centered election" that we encountered in the preceding chapter.

Parties Rise Again

Even as political science analysts declared the death of parties, however, their revival was beginning. During the 1980s, changing congressional rules shifted power from committee chairs back to party leadership, strengthening the parties in Congress. A huge influx of money into politics further revitalized party organizations, buoyed by the widespread adoption of political action committees (PACs) in the 1980s, "527" committees in the 2000s, and super PACs in the 2010s. The DNC and RNC, along with the congressional campaign organizations, became the chief recipients of campaign funds—and directed them in turn to candidates, who became more dependent on the parties as a result.

The parties also became ideologically purer. Each party was now organized around a clear set of ideas and principles. Each side could concentrate on defeating its foes—rather than on negotiating the differences within its own ranks.

Competition and Partisanship Intensifies

Today the two parties are thriving, contesting very close national elections. The three presidential elections between 1996 and 2004 featured the closest trio of successive races since the 1880s. Close contests and party turnover, in this sixth party system, have increased with the rise of partisanship (see Table 9.5).

In the past, partisan differences on Capitol Hill were blurred by factions within each party. Democrats were so bitterly divided that they could barely hold a **party caucus** during the 1950s–1960s. Today those differences within the parties have almost disappeared. Party factions remain, as we saw earlier, but party members are far less diverse in their views. The strongest divisions are now between the two parties. By 2010, the most left-leaning Republican in the U.S. Senate was to the right (in terms of voting record) of the most rightward Senate Democrat. For the first time, ideological conflict in both House and Senate breaks down perfectly along party lines. This partisan divide makes the political contest—over ideas, programs, and even the meaning of America—louder and angrier than it has been in more than a century. No matter where you look, partisanship within government is rising. It is also increasing among the public.[26] It is not clear who influences whom. Are partisan officials fanning the flames of party difference among Americans? Or do activists within each

Party caucus: A meeting of all House or Senate members of one or the other main party, usually to discuss political and policy strategies.

TABLE 9.5 Party Control of U.S. National Institutions Since 2000

		PARTY IN CONGRESSIONAL MAJORITY (SIZE OF MAJORITY)	
ELECTION YEAR	CONTROL OF PRESIDENCY	SENATE	HOUSE
		Eight changes of control in eight elections is an unusual level of turnover.	
2000	R (Bush)	50-50 (later +1 D)*	R (9 seats)
2002	R (Bush)	R (2 seats)**	R (24 seats)
2004	R (Bush)	R (10 seats)	R (29 seats)
2006	R (Bush)	D (2 seats)	D (37 seats)
2008	D (Obama)	D (19/20 seats)	D (79 seats)
2010	D (Obama)	D (6 seats)	R (49 seats)
2012	D (Obama)	D (10 seats)	R (34 seats)
2014	D (Obama)	R (8 seats)***	R (57 seats)***

*After May 2001, when Senator Jeffords switched parties, Democrats controlled the Senate.
**Red indicates that party control switched after that year's election.
***Projection as of November 6, 2014.

party push their leaders to take stronger positions against the opposition? Or perhaps have media outlets like Fox News and MSNBC, catering respectively to conservatives and liberals, driven us into our party corners? The answer is probably yes to all three questions.

Political scientists and pundits alike wonder whether the rise in partisan differences is dangerous, and whether it significantly impairs governance. Public opinion surveys repeatedly report Americans' dismay at partisan disagreement, even while we fan the flames of party polarization. What is it that Americans are so worried about?

First, the argument goes, party divisions lead to gridlock—a slowdown in government's ability to get things done. Second, bitter partisanship, as one commentary put it, "breeds bad public policy."[27] Third, a toxic partisan climate is said to drive more public officials away from government service, because less-partisan members of Congress retire early in the face of incivility and relentless conflict. And fourth, it leads to disenchantment among the public.

Is partisanship really generating these types of bad government outcomes? Some political scientists break with popular wisdom and argue that the fears of partisan breakdown are exaggerated: American government—replete with checks, balances, and federalism—was designed to move incrementally. Delay

PARTISANSHIP

Should we be trying to diminish partisanship?	**Yes, partisanship is harmful.** Partisanship leads to paralysis. Worse, it is turning people off from politics, and that will create problems for us in the long run.	**No, partisanship is healthy.** The problems of partisanship originate with strong ideas and close elections. The arguments are useful and part of the democratic process. We should encourage intense views and strong arguments—that's what introduces bold new ideas.	Some partisanship is useful but today the parties are taking disagreement too far.

Divided government: Periods during which at least one house of Congress is controlled by a party different from the one occupying the White House.

is part of the normal process. **Divided government** (when at least one house of Congress is controlled by a party different from that occupying the White House) has always been loud, divisive—and unexpectedly productive.[28]

There are two sides to the argument about whether rising partisanship is harming American government. Which strikes you as most persuasive? As the debates go on, social scientists—like the general public—tilt increasingly toward the pessimistic perspective.[29]

THE BOTTOM LINE

- After declining thirty to forty years ago, the main political parties are now both thriving—and highly competitive. Recent national elections have featured narrow margins of victory in presidential races and frequent shifts in party control.

- This competition has helped fuel a rise in partisan differences, evident among both national policy makers and the U.S. public.

- Most Americans—and many social scientists—believe that partisanship is affecting the quality of American government. The intensity of the conflict, they believe, will weaken our institutions.

⬤ Conclusion: A Political System Ripe for Reform?

Calls for reforming the U.S. political system are as old as the system itself. Today, many people call for new laws that regulate interest groups and reduce partisanship. Here are some of the most commonly voiced proposals. As always, we invite your own ideas.

1. Regulating Lobbyists

How might we better tap the potential benefits of interest group activity while minimizing the dangers? Many have advocated regulating lobbyists. What are lobbyists forbidden to do in pursuit of their policy goals? For a long time, the answer was "not much." Until 1946, there were no real limits on lobbying action, although out-and-out bribery—clearly exchanging votes for money or other favors—was prohibited. That year, Congress passed the **Federal Regulation of Lobbying Act**, which required lobbyists seeking influence in the House or Senate to:

Federal Regulation of Lobbying Act: The initial U.S. statute spelling out requirements on lobbyists active in Congress, passed in 1946.

- *Register with Congress.* An office was opened in the Capitol—today registration is online—for lobbyists to fill out forms (first annually and eventually every three months) listing all clients on whose behalf they sought to influence Congress.

- *Report the amount and sources of income derived from lobbying Congress.* This line-by-line list is supposed to include all of a lobbyist's clients and how much each paid, but some lobbyists exploit the rules to keep some of their clients out of sight.

Notice the absence of any restrictions on lobbying activity. In theory, a lobbyist could accept a large sum from one client and pass those funds on to a member of Congress as a "gift." The 1946 law merely required interest group representatives to identify both themselves and the source/amounts of their payments for lobbying.

What Do You Think?

ASSESSING THE INFLUENCE OF LOBBYISTS

We have discussed numbers and money as indicators of the power of interest groups in American government. In what other ways might we determine the extent of their influence? Count up the meetings between lobbyists and legislators? Trace the complicated connections between campaign donations from an interest group and a Congress member's vote on specific legislation? Scholars have been working for years to answer this question—and are still trying. Can you imagine any other ways to better assess lobbyists' influence in American policy making?

Gift ban: A regulation that eliminates (or sharply reduces the dollar amount of) gifts from interest groups to lawmakers.

Tighter restrictions on gift giving were imposed in 1995, following public clamor about presents, meals, and travel "junkets" for Congress members, paid for by interest groups. The House banned virtually all gifts. On the Senate side, inexpensive items like T-shirts and other trinkets were still allowed—up to a value of fifty dollars per year for any senator from a given lobbyist. This **gift ban** law was designed to make it more difficult to "buy" favors from a member of Congress.

Loopholes in the 1995 law swiftly appeared. The House prohibition on lobbyists' buying meals for congressional members or their staff was clarified to cover only meals consumed while sitting down, presumably at a restaurant. "Finger food," such as hors d'oeuvres eaten standing up at parties, was a legitimate expense—enabling lobbyists to continue attending or even sponsoring fundraising events for congressional members. Lobbyists could also pay for a meal with lawmakers as long as the member or staffer was a "personal friend." Imagine how many new friendships were born after that ruling!

Stories like the "finger food exception" inspired a fresh round of popular outrage, sparking Congress to revisit interest-group lobbying reform. Congress has closed many of the loopholes in the gift ban and barred senators from lobbying their former colleagues for two years after leaving the Senate.

Perhaps the best counter to the influence of lobbyists in Washington is public engagement—getting involved. The proliferation of groups on all sides of an issue has tended to mean that if one sector (like business) gains the upper hand in Washington, the pendulum will eventually swing to the other side, and other sectors (like public interest groups) win a string of policy victories.

2. Reduce Partisanship in Government

Reformers promoting this approach sometimes call for a "postpartisan" American politics. Ideas include limiting negative campaigning (unfortunately, this is hard to do, because negative campaigning works), reducing the role of outside advocacy groups in campaigns (attempts to do so have been struck down by the Supreme Court), and adopting public financing (implemented in a few places, but without notable reduction in partisan polarization).

A new alternative is a growing list of organizations, supported by moderates in business and government, that try to reward politicians in the middle. "No Labels" is one such organization, seeking to promote middle-of-the-road solutions; Olympia's List, organized by former Maine Republican Senator Olympia Snowe, is the most prominent group championing the moderates' cause.

So far, the attempts at unity have been swamped by disagreements. Neither governors nor governed have shown much inclination to change their practice of decrying partisanship while fiercely embracing their party and its ideas.

Here is a slightly different way to think about parties and partisanship. Consider the rich history of party politics in America that we have traced across six party systems. Those 225 years have often seen a spirit that the Greeks called *agonistic*—a willingness to disagree with your adversaries while acknowledging their views as legitimate. This spirit means engaging wholeheartedly in a process of debate. In a democracy, successful political ideas must not just be rationally sound. We must also contest them, and we do this through party competition.

After all, the United States has always been a nation based on ideas—and intense disagreements about what they mean. The important goal is that as many citizens as possible all join in. The greatest dangers come, not from strongly held views but from apathy among the citizens. That, in the long run, might be the greatest risk of our charged partisan times.

CHAPTER SUMMARY

● Interest-group lobbying has long been a vital feature of U.S. government and politics. Interest groups are deeply engaged in all parts of our policy-making system, and groups have sprung up to represent virtually every imaginable professional, personal, and identity-based interest, providing their members with information about federal policies and conveying those members' concerns to Washington.

● Public anxiety about lobbying centers on interest groups' reputed power to affect policy making. Groups spend billions of dollars each year to advance their views, and they swarm over Washington in vast numbers. Although critics insist that lobbyist influence to shape government outcomes is extensive, political science research has not turned up much definitive evidence.

● Lobbyists are active in all three branches of government; in each, they both seek and provide information—the currency of politics. They also work on (and help finance) political campaigns and are closely intertwined with leadership of both Republican and Democratic Parties.

● America's two-party style has endured for over two hundred years, with Democrats and Republicans its main standard-bearers since 1856.

● The foundational American ideas and the organization of our elections help explain the dominance of the two parties. Third parties arise periodically, but none has ever managed to break through and seriously challenge two-party rule.

● The system of two parties—and the contest between them—regularly shifts as new party systems arise. Each change in party system means a different coalition of voters making up each party and in the ideas that inspire those voters.

● A substantial majority of voting-age Americans identifies strongly with one of the two major parties, though a growing number declare themselves independents. The powerful sense of party identification is a result of many factors, including parental influence, political context, and even personality type.

● Party identification in turn helps shape our voting patterns, the way we filter political information, and our bedrock ideas about politics and government.

● Each major party must work to unite under one "big tent" their key figures and followers. These include the *party in government* (elected politicians, their staffs, and affiliated political professionals);

the *party organization* (party chairs, the national committees, and the state party leaders); and the *party in the electorate* (the millions of people who identify with the party).

● Most Americans—and many social scientists—believe that partisanship is affecting the quality of American government. The intensity of the conflict, they warn, will weaken our institutions.

KEY TERMS

Base voters, 312
Demosclerosis, 290
Divided government, 318
Expressive benefits, 289
Federal Regulation of
    Lobbying Act, 319
Gift ban, 320
Interest group, 286
Intergovernmental lobbying, 293
Iron triangle, 291
Issue network, 293
K Street, 283

Lobbyist, 286
Material benefits, 289
New Deal, 307
Nonpartisan election, 299
Partisanship, 284
Party boss, 305
Party caucus, 316
Party identification, 308
Party in government, 313
Party in the electorate, 314
Party machine, 305
Party platform, 313

Party system, 300
Pluralism, 290
Political socialization, 300
Power elite theory, 290
Public interest lobbyist, 289
Reverse lobbying, 294
Revolving door, 292
Solidary benefits, 289
Special interest, 286
Split-ticket voter, 312
Straight-ticket voter, 312

STUDY QUESTIONS

1. Name the three main theories about the effects of interest groups (pluralism, for example, is one). Describe each, reflecting on which strikes you as most persuasive.
2. Describe the traditional iron triangle. Explain the issue network that has now replaced it in large part.
3. Describe the three ways that interest groups try to affect Supreme Court decisions.
4. One of the most important elements of lobbying success is gathering information. Explain how and why.

5. Think of the interest group that represents you the best. Is it a group that works on a specific issue, like gun control or lower taxes? Or one representing a specific "identity" group, like women or Latinos or LGBT people? Or a geographically based organization, concerned with the interests of Texans or New Englanders or Mountain States residents? Or, to take still another example, is the group organized around a partisan or ideological perspective, from libertarian to progressive? Why is that group your preferred representative?

6. What are the two main reasons American politics is usually limited to two political parties?

7. What is proportional representation? In your opinion, should we adopt it in the U.S.?

8. Describe four functions that parties serve in the American electoral process.

9. What are the three separate parts of the party organization? Explain what each part is responsible for.

10. What is party identification? Name three factors that influence party identification.

10

Congress

PASSING LEGISLATION through the U.S. Congress is remarkably difficult. Consider the long and winding road that confronted health care reform, also known as Obamacare—and the fireworks that followed in the years since it passed.

Action kicked off in the House of Representatives in March 2009. Over four months, three different House committees produced two different bills. The Speaker of the House, Nancy Pelosi (D-CA)—the first woman Speaker in American history—worked to combine elements of both bills into a single "Affordable Health Care for America Act." Pelosi and her top lieutenants spent the summer and early fall meeting one by one with different **congressional caucuses** in the House: conservative Blue Dogs, the liberal Progressive Caucus, the Congressional Black Caucus, the Hispanic Caucus, abortion opponents, and others. Each wanted to add to or subtract from the bill. All kinds of hot issues came up. While the members negotiated, all kinds of interest groups lined up to lobby the Speaker's team. After months of dealing, the House version of the bill emerged.

The health reform bill then went to the House Rules Committee, which sets the rules that guide the debate whenever a measure goes to the full House of Representatives for a vote. By now it was late October—and after seven feverish months of activity the legislation had still not reached the House **floor**. On Saturday, November 7, the legislation squeaked through by a vote of 220–215 as the clock moved toward midnight. The House proceedings were the easier part of the process.

The Senate (with one hundred members) also began deliberating in March 2009. Two committees produced two *more* bills—making five different versions so far, each one topping a thousand pages. After major debate, negotiating, and compromise, an exhausted Senate voted yes at 7:15 a.m. on December 24. Senate Majority Leader Harry Reid was so tired he mistakenly voted nay and—as everyone laughed—he sheepishly changed his vote. All forty Republicans voted against the bill.

Since the House and Senate had passed different versions of the law, leaders in each chamber began appointing members to a **conference committee** to iron

Congressional caucus: A group of House or Senate members that convene regularly to discuss common interests; they may share demographic characteristics, geography, or issue concerns.

Floor: The full chamber, either in the House of Representatives or in the Senate. A bill "goes to the floor" for the final debate and vote.

● *Congress has often been divided. But when members refused to fund the government and shut it down, in October 2013, some political scientists concluded that this had become "the broken branch."*

Conference committee:
A temporary collection of House and Senate members, appointed to work out a compromise version of legislation that passed both chambers in different forms.

out the differences. Several weeks of complicated parliamentary maneuvering resulted in the passage of the Affordable Care Act (ACA) in late March 2010.

The ACA traversed a familiar legislative path. Nearly every significant law faces multiple stages, each featuring a fresh set of obstacles that can derail a bill. This is, to put it mildly, an excruciatingly difficult way to pass legislation.

Meanwhile, the passage of the new law spurred public opposition, and an energized Republican party won control of the House in the 2010 midterm election. The eager new Republican majority voted to repeal Obamacare; since the Senate—still in Democratic hands—refused to go along, nothing happened. By March 2014, the Republican House had voted to repeal the health law fifty times.

In September 2013, opponents of the ACA saw a new opportunity. House Republicans voted to fund the government only if the Obama administration delayed putting crucial sections of the health law into effect. On October 1, the start of the new fiscal year, the government shut down. From Yellowstone Park to the National Institutes of Health (which funds biomedical research), all non-essential government services came to a halt.

As public criticism grew, the Republican leadership compromised on a measure that passed the House with all the Democrats and 87 (of 231) Republicans

---

BY THE NUMBERS
Congress

- Percentage of Americans who approved of Congress in 2010, 2012 and 2014: **11, 8, 9**
- Percentage of House members reelected in 2010: **85**
- Percentage of House members reelected in 2012: **90**
- Percentage of House members who won in a landslide (by more than 20 points): **70**
- Number of African Americans in the Senate, 1950: **0**
- Number of African Americans in the Senate, 2014: **2**
- Number of African Americans who have ever served a full term in the Senate: **3**
- Number of women in the House of Representatives, 1949: **7**
- Percentage of those women who were Republicans, 1949: **57**
- Number of women in the House of Representatives, 2014: **83***
- Percentage of those women who were Republicans, 2014: **27***
- Percentage of women in European legislatures (average): **35**
- House Speaker John Boehner's annual salary: **$230,000**
- Estimated annual lobbying salary earned by ex-House Speaker Bob Livingston: **$1,200,000**

*Projected as of November 6, 2014.

voting for it. "We fought the good fight, we just didn't win," said House Speaker John Boehner. The government reopened but the partisan tensions did not subside. The two branches, each controlled by one party, rarely cooperated. Soon observers began to notice something dramatic: This 113th Congress passed fewer laws than any Congress in history. Partly as a result, many analysts now dub Congress—especially the Senate, with its archaic filibuster rules—the "broken branch" of American government.[1]

Who are we? A vibrant people that are suspicious of government. Congress builds that suspicion right into its governing process: It is very difficult to introduce important changes. This raises the key question about Congress: Is it indeed "the broken branch of government"? Or does it reflect the spirit of the American nation by slowing the government down and ensuring that it does less? Keep these two different views in mind as we explore Congress.

Introducing Congress

The Constitution put Congress at the center of American government. The document's first and longest article provides a detailed account of legislative organization and authority (see Table 10.1).

TABLE 10.1 Constitutional Powers of Congress

From Article 1, Section 8 (unless otherwise noted).*
Financial. Power to raise revenue through taxes and borrowing, to pay national debts and "provide for the common defense and general welfare"; regulate trade and commerce among the American states and with other countries.
Legal. Establish U.S. citizenship laws. Regulate bankruptcy laws, issue U.S. money, and punish counterfeiters. Establish a patent system ("to promote the progress of science and useful arts"). Fix national weights/measures standards. Enact laws subject to presidential approval.
Institutional. Organize judicial and executive branches; establish postal system (Article 2, Section 2). Set up and control the national capital—since 1797, in Washington, D.C. Admit new states and exercise control over U.S. territories (Article 3, Section 3).
National defense. Declare war and regulate rules for prisoners of war. Raise and fund U.S. Army, Navy, and other defense forces.
*Additional congressional powers are provided by constitutional amendment. For example, the Thirteenth (1865), Fourteenth (1868), and Fifteenth (1870) Amendments authorize Congress to enforce African Americans' civil rights, as you read in Chapter 5.

This is a formidable set of powers. For most of American history, Congress ruled. When Senator Warren Harding won the presidential election of 1920, one of his old Senate buddies told him to "sign whatever bills the Senate sends you . . . and don't send bills for the Senate to pass."[2] By the middle of the twentieth century, however, Congress had become increasingly deferential to the White House, especially in foreign affairs. Today, the nation looks first to the president to manage the economy, deploy troops, address crises, and pursue policy objectives.

Still, Congress remains near the center of American government. As President Obama discovered during the health care debate, presidents may command more public attention, but they need cooperation from the House and Senate to advance their policies. Moreover, Congress' importance extends far beyond the vital responsibility of lawmaking. As much as any other actor or institution in U.S. government, it is Congress that answers the question, *Who are we?*

Two Houses, Different Styles

Congress reflects two faces of the American people in its basic makeup. Like most other national legislatures, Congress is bicameral—comprising "two houses." The *House of Representatives* is the larger chamber and includes 435 members, divided among the states based on population size, along with six nonvoting delegates from Washington, D.C., Puerto Rico, American Samoa, Guam, and other U.S. territories. All 441 House members serve two-year terms and each represents a district of around seven hundred thousand people.

The House is organized around a relatively clear set of rules and procedures. The majority party wields centralized control, through a powerful leadership team. In the **114th Congress** (which holds office between 2015 and 2017), Republicans are in the majority; this permits the GOP leader, Speaker of the House Boehner, to control what issues reach the floor, and frequently to get them passed.

The smaller Senate is made up of one hundred members, two from each U.S. state, each elected for a six-year term. The Democrats lost the Senate in 2014.

In its organization, the Senate reflects Americans' liberty-loving, individualistic side. Back in the nineteenth century, an old truism (sometimes attributed to Mark Twain) declared "every senator a little king"; the old quip still resonates today.[3] Each woman and man in the Senate possesses a remarkable degree of autonomy, especially compared to the average House member. Any senator—even the most junior—is able to halt the entire body's consideration of a bill merely by placing a **legislative hold** on it.

Let's consider a typical example. Before the U.S. military can promote an officer, the Senate must vote its approval. Normally this is a routine formality. In 2003, however, Senator Larry Craig (R-ID) quietly put a hold on all Air Force promotions. No Air Force officer could advance to the rank of major, colonel,

114th Congress: The Congress elected in 2014. The first Congress met in 1789–1790. Each Congress is elected for a two-year session and numbered consecutively.

Legislative hold: An informal way for a senator to object to a bill or other measure reaching the Senate floor. The action effectively halts Senate proceedings on that issue, sometimes for weeks or longer.

lieutenant general, or anything else. The Senate tabled—put aside—every proposed promotion. What had upset Senator Craig? The Air Force had promised to station some planes in Idaho, and Craig charged that they had reneged on their promise. So he did what any senator is permitted to do—bring the Senate to a halt with a one-man veto.[4]

Popular American culture, in films such as *Mr. Smith Goes to Washington* or the *West Wing* TV episode featuring a noble **filibuster**—"democracy's finest show"—celebrates the lone senator standing up bravely for justice. But much of the time these stands involve narrow-minded issues, like Senator Craig's.

The two congressional chambers present a familiar contrast in the United States. Americans, we saw in Chapter 1, embrace direct democracy—and the centralized House can move swiftly on national legislative priorities. Americans also fear government power and seek stability: enter the independent senators, slowing legislation down with filibusters and holds. Legend has it that Thomas Jefferson, who had been in Paris during the Constitutional Convention, asked George Washington why the Constitution established two chambers in Congress. "Why," responded Washington, "do you pour your tea into the saucer?" "To cool it," replied Jefferson. "Just so," returned Washington, "we pour House legislation into the senatorial saucer to cool it." Whether or not the exchange actually took place, it neatly captures the contrast between House and Senate.[5] The key question for us now is whether the Senate is too good at this task—cooling legislation. Do we need a more nimble and responsive government in the twenty-first century? Or is the senatorial function—slowing things down—more important than ever?

The House and Senate Have Some Unique Roles

The Constitution also gives each branch some unique authority. All budget measures must originate in the House. Now that the Senate is also directly

see for yourself 10.1

Go online to see Senator Smith's noble filibuster celebrating the lone brave voice.

Filibuster: Rule unique to the U.S. Senate that allows any senator to hold the floor indefinitely and thereby delay a vote on a bill to which they object. Ended only when sixty senators vote for cloture.

What Do You Think?

SENATE FILIBUSTERS

Should senators be allowed to hold up legislative initiatives indefinitely or until their opposition can round up sixty votes to stop their stalling action? What do you think?

Yes. Filibusters ensure independence and protect minority rights. Slowing government down is a good idea.

No. The sixty-vote rule makes a mockery of simple majority rule and causes gridlock, slowing policy making to a crawl. It is time to rewrite Senate rules and end the filibuster.

Not Sure? You may want to ponder this question as you read the rest of the chapter.

elected by the people, however, this rule has become less important. The House also has the power to impeach public officials—including the president—for "high crimes and misdemeanors." After the House impeaches (or indicts) an officeholder, the Senate holds a trial and decides whether to remove him or her. For its part, the Senate has exclusive authority over two important matters. The president negotiates treaties with other countries, but the Senate must approve by two-thirds majority. Sixty-seven votes is a very high bar in today's politics, and, as we will see in the next chapter, presidents have found some creative ways around it.

The Senate also has sole power to review presidential appointments—the Constitution calls it "advice and consent." Each nominee for the Supreme Court, for example, goes before the Senate Judiciary Committee and then must win confirmation from the full Senate.

THE BOTTOM LINE

- Congressional powers, as granted under the Constitution, are extensive and very clearly defined.

- America's Congress is bicameral: The House has 435 members (plus 6 nonvoting members) who are elected every two years. The 100 senators serve six-year terms.

- The two houses of Congress reflect different national priorities. Populists appreciate the responsive House; advocates of stability embrace the more deliberate Senate, where rules like the filibuster make it more difficult to pass legislation.

◆ Congressional Representation

Members of Congress represent their constituents in multiple ways. They live in the same state or district—which is known as *geographic* representation. They share views about the political issues—or *substantive* representation. Another angle is *descriptive* representation—which measures the extent to which they look like the people they represent in terms of race, ethnicity, gender, age, national origin, and so on. Geographic representation is required—members must live in their state or district. However, citizens often have to choose between descriptive representation (she is the same gender, race, ethnicity, and/or religion as I am) and substantive representation (she does not look like me but believes what I believe).[6]

Trustees and Delegates

Each member of Congress—in fact, every representative in any organization—faces the same conundrum: Do what you think is right? Or, do what your constituents want?

Do the Right Thing. On the one hand, representatives owe us their best judgment. They sit in the House or Senate, with considerably more information than their constituents. Just like your doctor or your lawyer, your House and Senate members' job is to pursue what is best for you. And, if you disagree with the result, you can always vote for their opponent. This perspective is known as the *trustee* view of representation.

On a lot of issues, members of Congress must rely on their best judgment or that of their staff: Constituents have no strongly held views, or express "doorstep opinions," as we saw in Chapter 6. Most people care little whether their senators voted to approve the president's choice for deputy undersecretary of commerce.

Do What the People Want. Another view holds that true representation involves House or Senate members faithfully following popular preferences. A lot of choices before Congress have to do with basic values. You do not need more information to know how you feel about the right to own guns or whether health care is a universal human right. A legislator, according to this view, should take his voting instructions directly from his constituents. This is the *delegate* view of representation.

Political scientists recognize that the rules help tilt individuals one way or another (here is the institutional perspective again). When the constitutional framers required members of the House to run every two years, they favored the delegate view: Pay close attention to the people, or you will be out of a job. The Senate has six years between elections; the rules practically instruct them to be trustees, to act as they think best.

What ultimately makes for good representation? The theoretical answer is simple: *Representatives effectively pursue their constituents' substantive interests.* The trick comes in figuring out what those interests are and promoting them through the complicated legislative process. Eventually, at election time, the people will judge whether their members of Congress effectively pursued their interests. To political scientists, this is how a well-operating representative system works.

This theorizing barely registers on the radar screens of most members of the House and Senate. They come to Congress with a clear perspective that informs nearly all of their important votes. They rarely stay up late at night pondering what stand to take on gun rights or on national health insurance. The answers are part of their basic philosophy, forged years before they arrived in Congress. Most politicians do not pander—at least not on large, visible issues. They know what they believe and—despite popular wisdom—they rarely say merely what they think their audience wants to hear.[7] However, a great outcry from the constituency over an issue will often back a member off. It is always safer to do nothing—and blame the other members.

TWO VIEWS OF REPRESENTATION

The trustee and the delegate views are both legitimate ways to represent people. Do what you think best—or do what the people tell you to do. On every issue, each representative must decide how to weigh these two key factors. Take a moment and ask yourself how you would act as a member of the Senate or House.

Delegate. I am more apt to be a delegate and take my voting instructions directly from my constituents.

Trustee. I am more inclined to be a trustee and simply do what I believe to be the right thing on behalf of my constituents.

Unsure. Maybe the choice is not so black and white. Perhaps the answer depends on the issue. If you take this middle ground, think about the kinds of issues that would make you a delegate or a trustee.

THE BOTTOM LINE

- Members of the House and Senate represent Americans in multiple ways. These include:

  - *Geographic representation*: The election rules say members must live in the state or district.

  - *Descriptive representation*: Does the assembly look like the people?

  - *Substantive representation*: Do members of Congress effectively pursue constituent interests?

- Along with these different styles of representation, members can act as delegates or trustees. Representatives can faithfully follow what the people want or do as their political experience, instincts, and core principles dictate.

● Elections: Getting to Congress— and Staying There

How do members of Congress spend their days? From occasional glimpses of C-SPAN you might imagine Congress as a sustained feast of debates, but members of the House and the Senate spend relatively little time in floor sessions. Table 10.2 displays the typical workweek of a member of the House, taken from a survey. Not a lot of time left for quietly contemplating the major issues of the day, is there?

Congressional Elections

Congress spends a great deal of time campaigning. House members face the voters every two years—more frequently than most other national legislatures around the world. Even senators, with a more comfortable six years between races, must keep their campaign operation—especially fundraising—humming along. Note, in Table 10.2, that the members spend as much time raising money as they do on committee meetings or floor action. Does this constant pressure to attract donations and remind voters of their virtues turn off members of Congress or potential candidates? Most of them stay in office a long time. And when a seat in either chamber opens because of retirement or death, the list of eager office seekers from both parties is almost always a long one.

It was always clear at the Constitutional Convention that the United States would have an elected national legislature. But a major dispute involved the extent of popular participation in choosing members of Congress. Recall the original compromise: House members would be elected directly, whereas senators were to be insulated from the whims of public opinion and chosen by state legislatures.

As western states joined the Union, their legislatures turned the Senate elections over to the people (the westerners also gave women the vote); the entire nation began voting for senators in 1913 when the Seventeenth Amendment was ratified. Did the state legislatures pick more elevated senators than the people (as the constitutional framers expected)? Not necessarily. In the very first congressional elections, for example, Virginia's legislature passed over James Madison for the Senate; the people of his district had better sense and elected him to the House, where he immediately pushed through the Bill of Rights (discussed in Chapter 2).

TABLE 10.2 Division of Time of a Member of the House

Meeting with staff (mostly in Washington)	19%
Meeting with constituents (mostly in district)	19%
Ceremonial events (some in district, some in D.C.)	15%
Fundraising calls/meetings	8%
Committee meetings (hearings, member meetings)	8%
Floor action (votes, debates, morning business)	7%
Office work (e-mail, reading, legislative drafting)	7%
Informal talks (with colleagues, lobbyists, media)	6%
Caucus meetings (all-party or subgroup gatherings)	5%
Other (miscellaneous)	5%
Source: Congressional Management Foundation, Life in Congress: The Member Perspective (Washington, D.C.: 2013): 10–14.	

Reapportionment:
Reorganization of the boundaries of House districts, a process that follows the results of the U.S. census, taken every ten years. District lines are redrawn to ensure rough equality in the number of constituents represented by each House member.

Another important influence on U.S. House elections is **reapportionment**. Every ten years the U.S. census determines which states have gained or lost population, and since each district is the same size, House seats are reapportioned accordingly. In 2010, Texas gained four new seats, Florida gained two, and New York and Ohio each lost two. The new districts are drawn by the state legislature, and, as we saw in Chapter 8, fierce political battles surround the way the lines are drawn. Savvy political observers pay special attention to elections for the state legislatures in a census year (the next one is 2020), since the majority party in the state legislature often skews the districts in its own favor—advantaging either Democrats or Republicans in the effort to control Congress. Once the redistricting is completed (often after a further battle in the courts initiated by the party that lost out in the state legislature), another round of competition begins: House elections.

Home Styles: Back in the District

New members of Congress—and most of the long-serving representatives and senators, for that matter—spend a lot of time back in their district or state. Often they are literally returning home—to families who have decided to stay in San Francisco or St. Louis or Scranton, Pennsylvania, rather than making the move to Washington. Most members leave Washington on Thursday evenings and only return on Monday evening or even Tuesday morning, unless House or Senate votes are scheduled on a Friday or Monday.

Back in their constituency, members are kept hopping. District staff, dedicated 24/7 to making sure that the folks at home know all the benefits their representative or senator is providing, line up events for them to attend every morning, afternoon, and evening. Members spend this time meeting with constituents, giving talks about Washington issues (and hearing plenty of advice about how to do things better), cutting ribbons on new ballparks or office buildings or schools, visiting with local party leaders and elected officials, and raising funds for their next election.

Why do the members insist on rushing home each week? Because it helps them win re-election. That is an ever-present concern for most members. In fact, when political scientists build models to explain and predict congressional behavior, they often assume that re-election is a member's primary goal. We consider this an exaggeration. Many members are genuinely pursuing their political ideals. But there is no denying that the pressure for re-election dominates congressional behavior.

THE BOTTOM LINE

• Members of Congress are always running for office. Fundraising takes a particularly important amount of time and attention.

• Members pay special attention to their home style: Most go back to the constituency every week—compressing normal congressional business into Tuesday through Thursday.

• Congress has become an institution of strangers who do not know one another. Most members focus most intensely on re-election.

Congress at Work

When members of the House and Senate do gather in Washington, they have a staggering to-do list: managing the nation's legislative business, investigating executive-branch activities, staging public hearings about everything from auto safety to U.S. aid to Zimbabwe, and, of course, raising money. How—and where—do they accomplish all that work?

The City on the Hill

The huge Capitol building is perched on an actual hill; its majestic marble dome dominates the Washington skyline. Traditionally, no building in the District of Columbia except the Washington Monument may be taller. The Capitol building is also the heart of a small "city within a city." Six grand office buildings house the members and their staff; the newer buildings feature offices the size of basketball courts. Three ornate structures house the Library of Congress, which has mushroomed from Thomas Jefferson's personal book collection to the largest library in the world.

Inhabitants of this "city" include the 535 members of Congress, along with more than 25,000 staff members, who range from well-paid senior policy experts to summer interns; the Capitol police force, 250 members strong; and the U.S. poet laureate, a Congress-appointed position whose occupant receives a beautiful office in the Library of Congress. And don't forget the 75,000 or so lobbyists. It all adds up to a very busy place.

How much are members paid? As of 2014, the rate is $174,000 for House and Senate members (frozen since 2009). That is more than four times what the average American makes (see Table 10.3). Leaders earn a slightly higher salary; House Speaker Boehner is the best paid, at $223,500. Constituents frequently complain that congressional salaries are too high. Note, however, that comparable leaders in other areas—from business to academia—make much higher salaries. If your primary professional aim is to make money, running for Congress is not your best bet.

The congressional staff members are a major presence in this company town. Until 1893, most members of the House had no staff support and senators were allotted one part-time staffer (beginning in 1891), paid six dollars per day. Congress's professionalization meant a steady increase in assistants, researchers, committee experts, legal counsel, and the like. By the 1990s, the congressional staffs leveled off at around twenty-seven thousand total members.

Each House and Senate member has a chief of staff, a legislative director, a press secretary, a scheduler, and a host of others, including legislative correspondents (LCs) who handle the huge volume of constituent requests that pour into each member's office. Many graduates take entry positions (like the LC), since there are generally opportunities to move up quickly. Legislative staffs are dominated by young men and women often right out of college.

In addition, each summer thousands of college students descend on Capitol Hill to work, usually without pay. One of us worked as a congressional intern.

TABLE 10.3 Average Annual Salaries by Profession

CEO, top 500 company	$12.9 million
NBA player	$5.6 million
NFL player	$1.9 million
U.S. president	$400,000
Four-year university president/chancellor	$385,909
Physician, ophthalmology	$250,500
Senior U.S. executive-branch official	$196,700
Member of Congress	**$174,000**
Pharmacist	$106,000
Personal financial advisor	$90,900
IT professional	$80,500
Social worker	$54,220
Plumber	$48,700

Note: All figures are as of 2012.

Source: Data from Bureau of Labor Statistics and U.S. Office of Personnel Management.

It is not glamorous activity, but congressional offices hum with excitement and offer a ringside seat on one of the most fascinating institutions in the world.

New staffers arriving on the Hill soon hear the most common question: not "*What do you do?*" but "*Who are you with?*" Working for a congressional leader, a committee chair, or a nationally known figure can catapult even new staffers up the Washington pecking order. Many staff members feel a rush when an important bill they helped craft passes, or when they prepare their boss to succeed on a major news show, or when they simply watch their member meet with the president.

Capitol Hill life runs on a unique rhythm. Congress usually remains in session from the beginning of January through early August; members return after Labor Day and rush to finish for the year in early October during election (or even-numbered) years—since they are anxious to focus on their campaigns. In nonelection years, the session lasts longer—this chapter opened with a discussion of the 2009 session, which lasted until December 24. When in session, the Hill buzzes with action Tuesday through Thursday. Staffers work late into the night, while lobbyists and media swarm around the Capitol.

Like any company town, Capitol Hill generates insider slang. Some expressions catch on in the wider world; others remained confined to the Hill. For example, the idea that members can ride a popular president's *coattails* in

● *Congressional staff at work. Staff members (standing) brief their House members before the start of a Budget Committee hearing.*

office was a term coined on the House floor in 1848 by Congressman Abraham Lincoln.

Members of Congress know that they stand in the vortex of history. Every move—like the deep bow made by clerks carrying House bills to the Senate and vice versa—reflects a legacy that may stretch as far back as the Virginia House of Burgesses in 1619. In fact, new members of Congress make a candlelight visit to that historical site as part of their orientation.

Minnows and Whales: Congressional Leadership

When Lyndon Johnson (D-TX) served as Senate majority leader in the 1950s, he divided colleagues into two camps: "whales," who could enact landmark legislation, and "minnows," who dutifully followed others. Most whales are chairs of important committees or part of the formal leadership structure.

The House and Senate feature very different leadership styles. The smaller, more collegial Senate—where any member can request a hold and bring the entire body to a halt—usually requires patient, consensus-minded leadership. Majority leaders do not so much lead as manage Senate procedures, cajoling and pleading proud senators to move legislation along. The larger House, run on majoritarian principles, permits much tighter central control from the Speaker and other top leaders.

House Leadership

Democrats and Republicans each choose a party leader from their ranks. When a new Congress opens after an election (in January of odd-numbered years), the majority party votes its leader to the top post in Congress, the Speaker of the House. In 2010, the Republicans captured the House and John Boehner (R-OH) replaced Nancy Pelosi as Speaker. The Speaker serves as the public face of the House. He or she is simultaneously an administrative officer, a political spokesman, and a party leader.

As chief administrative officers of the House, Speakers preside over the chamber on special occasions (for example, when a president delivers the State of the Union message to Congress). They rule on procedural issues, choose members for committees, assign legislation to committees, and "maintain order and civility"—although civility is sometimes difficult to maintain.

As political leaders, Speakers set the House's agenda, determining which bills are considered and when. They negotiate with the Senate and executive branch. And they help manage the Rules Committee, which, as we saw at the start of the chapter, guides the floor action for all legislation. Speakers sometimes work with Rules to invent ways to hold the majority together on important votes. In 1981, for example, Speaker Tip O'Neill, a colorful Massachusetts Democrat, worried that House Democrats would feel pressured to support measures backed by the very popular new president, Ronald Reagan. O'Neill came up with a new rule, the **King of the Hill**. It permitted Democrats to vote for amendments that Reagan favored and—at the same time—alternative amendments preferred by O'Neill and the Democrats. The last vote is the King of the Hill—the vote that counts.

The House majority leader is the second in command. He or she acts as the majority party's floor manager, negotiator, and spokesperson. The majority

King of the Hill rule: A special rule governing floor consideration of a bill. A series of amendments on the same topic may all win majority approval, but only the last amendment receiving a majority vote—the "king of the hill"—is incorporated into the bill.

● *Outgoing Speaker Nancy Pelosi (D-CA) passes the gavel to new Speaker John Boehner (R-OH), who is momentarily overcome with emotion.*

leader also serves as the Speaker's eyes and ears, tracking party members' actions and preferences.

The number-three position is the majority-party whip. The *whip*, currently Kevin McCarthy (R-CA), is responsible for party discipline—ensuring that Republicans vote the way the leadership wants them to. The term whip comes from the British Parliament, which long ago borrowed the term from fox hunting, where the "whipper-in" was responsible for keeping the pack of hounds together—and yes, those fox hunters did the job by cracking whips. The majority whip leads a team of nine deputy whips, each responsible for members from a different region.

The minority generally has the same leadership structure, with one big difference: no Speaker. The top Democrat in the 113th Congress, minority leader (and former Speaker) Nancy Pelosi, is joined by the minority whip, Steny Hoyer of Maryland, in trying to thwart the Republican majority.

House whips have a challenging time persuading their proud, talented colleagues to vote the way they want them to. They do a lot of arm twisting and deal cutting—and they have to be creative. Back in the 1970s, minority whip Leslie Arends (R-IL) needed one more GOP vote to win an important agriculture bill. One Ohio Republican, knowing the bill was unpopular with his constituents, simply flew home. When Arends discovered his crucial vote was missing, he called an Ohio radio station and persuaded the DJ to announce, every fifteen minutes: "If anybody spies Representative Jones, who should be representing us in Washington but isn't, tell him he's supposed to be in Washington tomorrow for an important vote." Jones flew back the next morning and sheepishly voted with his fellow Republicans.

Senate Leadership

When you think about the Senate, take all the difficulties involved in managing the House—and quadruple them. Senate rules like the filibuster and the hold give each individual a great deal of autonomy—recall how one senator scuttled an entire section of the health reform bill. The Senate leadership must turn to personal skills, especially an ability to negotiate with colleagues.

The senators elect a majority leader—currently Mitch McConnell (R-KY). However, the Senate leader does not even formally preside over the chamber. The Constitution gives that job to the vice president. In practice, vice presidents rarely show up in the Senate—appearing mainly for very important votes (the VP can break a tie) and on ceremonial occasions. Similarly, the **president pro tempore** (currently Patrick Leahy, D-VT) has presiding authority at certain formal occasions. Otherwise, every senator presides in turn over the body, serving rotating half-hour stints. A staff member stands by the presiding member's side, helping him or her negotiate the complex rules.

Senate whips from both majority and minority parties serve the same functions as in the House—although they command much less power to demand party discipline, again because of the Senate's individualistic ways. This difficulty extends right up to the majority leader. It is hard to set the Senate's agenda or command floor action, for example, in a context of unlimited debate and

President pro tempore: Majority-party senator with the longest Senate service.

amendments, with the constant threat that any one senator will place a hold on legislation or mount a filibuster. The best that majority leaders and their team can muster is to influence which policies will be considered on the Senate floor and in what order—although that is usually done in consultation with the minority leader. If the minority leader indicates that an item will be subject to a filibuster or a hold, the majority leader normally passes over it and moves to the next item on the agenda.

Committee chairs, although important figures in the House and Senate, do not serve as part of the formal leadership team. Chairs are appointed by leaders in each chamber, rather than elected by a majority of members—although traditional norms of seniority often mean that the longest-serving committee member from the majority party becomes chair.

Committees: Workhorses of Congress

The regular duties of congressional lawmaking play out mainly in committees. As instruments of policy making, House and Senate committees are center stage; party leaders or presidents sometimes struggle to overcome their decisive influence. George W. Bush learned the hard way after winning a second term in 2004, when he presented Congress with legislation to partly privatize Social Security. Congressional Republicans dutifully introduced the president's bill; it soon disappeared into a maze of committee consideration, where it quietly died within a year. Barack Obama had the same experience with environmental regulation and gun control.

The Enduring Power of Committees

Table 10.4 lists the types of committees, which have not changed in more than a century. The committee system is yet another way American government separates powers. It means that Congress winds up with multiple centers of

TABLE 10.4 Congressional Committee Types

• *Standing committees*: Permanent bodies, with fixed jurisdiction. (Table 10.5 lists them all.) House and Senate standing committees vary widely in prestige: The oldest are traditionally the most influential, although some newer ones (like Intelligence, created after 9/11 in both chambers) deal with significant topics. Standing committees are further divided into multiple *subcommittees*, organized around areas of expertise.
• *Select committees*: Created to investigate a particular issue; these exist for a defined period of time. Also called *special committees*. A select committee to investigate the causes of 9/11 was convened from 2002 to 2003, for example.
• *Joint committees*: Made up of both House and Senate members, organized to address topics of continuing importance. Can remain in place for decades; the Joint Committee on Taxation has existed since 1971, for example. *Conference committees*, introduced earlier in this chapter, are temporary joint committees.

authority; the process is slower and harder for the public (and the media) to follow. But the division of labor allows an institution—with distracted, busy members—to accomplish more. By dividing their labor, Congress is able to dispatch more than ten thousand items of business each year.

The standing committees (see Table 10.5) provide a main avenue to get favored services, or "pork," home to the district. Members on the Appropriations Committee—which decides how U.S. funds are spent—are known as

TABLE 10.5 House and Senate Permanent Committees, 113th Congress

U.S. HOUSE COMMITTEES	U.S. SENATE COMMITTEES
Agriculture	Aging (Special)
Appropriations	Agriculture, Nutrition, and Forestry
Armed Services	Appropriations
Budget	Armed Services
Education and Labor	Banking, Housing, and Urban Affairs
Energy and Commerce	Budget
Financial Services	Commerce, Science, and Transportation
Foreign Affairs	Energy and Natural Resources
Homeland Security	Ethics (Select)
House Administration	Environment and Public Works
Intelligence (Permanent Select)	Finance
Judiciary	Foreign Relations
Natural Resources	Health, Education, Labor, and Pensions
Oversight and Government Reform	Homeland Security and Governmental Affairs
Rules	Indian Affairs
Science and Technology	Intelligence (Permanent Select)
Small Business	Judiciary
Standards of Official Conduct	Rules and Administration
Transportation and Infrastructure	Small Business and Entrepreneurship
Veterans' Affairs	Veterans' Affairs
Ways and Means	

"cardinals," like the ruling cadre in the Vatican. Other members approach them, hat in hand, to request **earmarks** in the form of items in appropriations bills: a dam in this district, funds for highway construction in that one. Appropriations members saw their power diminished in 2012, after the 112th Congress's decision to outlaw earmarks took effect; within a year, however, Congress began to find creative ways to fund the practice.

The committee system makes Congress far more efficient. But there is also a harsher reality. The committee system fragments Congress into small fiefdoms, hides action from public view, makes it relatively easy to do little favors for well-placed constituents (a tax break or a phone call to back off a pesky regulator), and makes it extremely difficult to pass major legislation or to address large national problems.

The organization of Congress raises, once again, the dilemmas of American democracy: Is the system biased toward the powerful? Does the bias against action frustrate the popular will or simply reflect the American wariness of government (or both)? What do you think?

Leadership and Assignments

House Republicans gathered late in the 1999 session to celebrate another year in the majority, with several representatives rising in humorous spirit to toast Speaker Denny Hastert (R-IL), who'd replaced disgraced Speaker Newt Gingrich earlier that year. Together they sang in rhyme:

> I love Speaker Hastert, his heart is so warm;
> And if I love him he'll do me no harm.
> So I won't sass the Speaker, not one little bitty . . .
> And then I'll wind up on a major committee.

Congress members' idea of fun may be a little different from yours. An important truth lies beneath the hilarity, though. The Speaker assigns members (and chairs) to each committee—a vital decision, given all the power committees wield. Over in the Senate, the decision involves more give-and-take but ultimately rests in the majority leader's hands. Minority party assignments are recommended by minority leaders in both chambers.

Members compete fiercely for assignment to the most influential committees. Once they are on a committee, representatives and senators often stay for many years—gaining power and influence and aspiring to become chair. Members also seek to join committees that reflect the concerns of their district. When Representative David Price (D-NC) joined Congress after an upset victory in 1993, he requested committee assignments not because of his intellectual interests—although, as a political science professor, he had plenty of those. Instead, Price judged the House Banking (now Financial Services) Committee to be vital to North Carolina and his district in particular, because of all the banks and other financial centers in the area.[8]

Skilled committee chairs are able to broaden the jurisdiction of their committee by claiming pieces of bills that are referred to many different committees. President Clinton's health-reform proposal went to ten different House and Senate committees in 1994. Each committee has its own process. It can bury the bill, change it completely, or report a modified version. Often, multiple committees produce different bills.

Jurisdictional squabbles can erupt into battles for influence between committees when their responsibilities overlap. The House and the Senate each have different committees for Homeland Security, for Intelligence, and for Foreign Affairs. Sometimes they all hold hearings on the same issue; and, since legislation is assigned to every committee that has jurisdiction over the topic, overlapping authority means multiple committees wrestling to shape the same legislation.

THE BOTTOM LINE

- Congress is a like a small city. Its citizens include the 535 members of Congress, 25,000 staff, and an army of lobbyists. The city includes its own amenities, traditions, and slang.

- Congressional leadership in the House includes a Speaker, majority and minority leaders, and ten whips. Successful leaders in the House impose discipline on their party members. The Senate allows far more individual action. Party leaders and whips have fewer institutional tools with which to impose discipline.

- Congressional committees are the workhorses of Congress. They have proved efficient and adaptable over the years. However, the committee system also fragments Congress, hides action from public view, advantages well-placed constituents looking for individual favors, and makes it difficult to pass major legislation.

Legislative Policymaking

As the Affordable Care Act's convoluted passage testifies, congressional lawmaking can be boiled down to five words: *Complex process. Difficult to win.* The past ten years (or, as you now know to call it, the past five sessions of Congress) saw an average of 4,239 bills submitted each year. How many made it all the way through the process? An average of 4.2 percent.

Americans complain about the nation's failure to face up to global warming. Or our broken public education system. Or our inability to ban abortion, regulate handguns, or reduce the federal budget deficit. Pundits explain these failures by invoking "American attitudes" or "American culture" or "powerful lobbyists." Here's a more accurate explanation: Congressional rules make it very hard to do any of these things—even when a majority of legislators (and of the nation) are in support. Let's find out why by taking a close look at the procedure.

President Obama delivers the 2014 State of the Union address. The House chamber is packed with Members of Congress, Supreme Court justices, Cabinet members, and distinguished guests—including First Lady Michelle Obama.

see for yourself 10.2

Go online to view an example of a congressional bill, its description, supporters, and status.

Drafting a Bill

Anyone can petition Congress to consider a bill, but only members of the House and Senate have the right to introduce one. Every piece of legislation needs at least one primary sponsor, whose name is publicly inscribed on the first page. Major bills are often referred to by the sponsors' names, with some creative exceptions (see Table 10.6).

Bills can feature any number of cosponsors, or members who agree to have their names listed as supporters. The main sponsors usually try to sign on many members, especially powerful ones like committee chairs, as cosponsors. A loose rule of thumb: The more cosponsors a bill has, the higher the likelihood of passage.

TABLE 10.6 Examples of Creative Legislative Titles

• "Greener America Act" (2007): Protect West Virginia coal industry against stronger environmental regulations.
• "Pass a Budget Now Act" (2012): Cut congressional pay for each day that a budget resolution (overview of spending/revenue targets for the coming year) fails to pass.
• "Personal Responsibility in Consumption Act" (2006): Immunize fast-food companies against lawsuits by obese consumers.
• "What Really Happened Act" (2002): Require instant TV replay in all major sports.
Note: None of these passed.

Anything can be introduced as legislation—no matter how far out of the box. Congressman Ron Paul (R-TX) once introduced a bill mandating that the Treasury buy a one-inch-wide strip of land stretching down the middle of the United States from Canada to Mexico. All goods or people crossing that line would be charged a toll, declared Representative Paul, eliminating the need for any other taxes or government fees. The bill has not made it out of committee—at least not yet.

The sponsors rarely write the legislation themselves. Some bills include language taken from state legislation or even foreign governments. Congress members "borrow" legislative language from each other, adapting colleagues' bills for their own use. Most serious bills go to the experts at the Congressional Research Service for drafting help. Bill drafters also consult with outside experts, including executive-branch officials, lobbyists, and academics. And members especially enjoy copying themselves: It's something of a ritual in many congressional offices, as a new year begins, to dust off and reintroduce bills that failed in the previous session.

There is a great art to bill drafting. Writing legislation necessitates major political choices. How much money should we ask for in spending bills? How far can we push changes to current laws? Do we dare test existing constitutional limits in this legislation? Many bills include bargaining chips—provisions the sponsors are willing to give up to win their most desired aims. Legislation to reduce average elementary school class size might also feature a sentence promising healthier lunches in all public schools. When the serious bargaining starts on Capitol Hill, that section may quietly be dropped. Drafters must also be aware that if the law passes, it may very well end up involved in litigation—which puts a premium on clarity and precision.

Once the bill is drafted and the cosponsors have signed on, it is ready for the next step: submission.

Submitting the Bill

The more traditional Senate typically introduces bills as the legislative day opens, around noon on Tuesdays, Wednesdays, and Thursdays. Let's take a peek inside the chamber.

The presiding officer taps his or her gavel, bringing the stir of conversation to a halt. Members pause as the Senate chaplain recites a prayer. A swirling bustle breaks out as the chaplain concludes. Routine administrative motions (like approving records of the previous day's proceedings) are followed by morning-hour statements—short speeches that celebrate home-state achievements. A constituent is turning one hundred years old or a softball team has won the state title.

Watch carefully: a senator snaps her fingers. A page (usually a high school student, specially trained for this role) dashes down the aisle, takes the senator's document, and places it in a flat wooden tray beside the bill clerk. The clerk writes a number on the first page (bills are numbered serially, starting each session with S.1), notes the senator's suggestion for committee referral, and places it in a tray. That night it is printed. A bill has been born!

The House is less ritualized, in keeping with its democratic spirit—but bill introduction continues an old-fashioned practice. Representatives carry proposed bills themselves, down to the rostrum. They hand their legislation to the clerk or drop it in a mahogany box, called the "hopper." From there, bills are delivered to the Speaker's office, where they are assigned a number—starting each session with H.R. 1—and referred to committee.

Committee Action

As we have seen, committees are the congressional workhorses. The House leadership normally assigns the proposal to committees with authority (or jurisdiction) over the area affected by the proposed legislation—recall that the health care bill went to five different committees. Once they get a bill, the committees perform four major tasks.

Committee hearing: The primary means by which committees collect and analyze information as legislative policy making gets under way. Hearings usually feature witnesses providing oral testimony, along with questioning of the witnesses by members of Congress.

1. Committees Hold Hearings on Policy Topics. Witnesses submit written testimony (for staff members and reporters to read); unless they are really important, they are limited to a five-minute presentation before the committee. When they begin, a little green light goes on; at the four-minute mark, a yellow light goes on. At five minutes, a red light blinks. Nervous rookies stop mid-sentence; veterans ignore the lights and talk serenely on—until the chair bangs the gavel.

The staff carefully puts together a list of who is testifying at each **committee hearing**. Witnesses generally include White House officials and cabinet heads—each of whose testimony has to be cleared with the Office of Management and Budget (introduced in the next chapter as "the agency that says no"). At many hearings, officials try to stick to their authorized script while critical Congress members pummel them.

Celebrities are popular witnesses, attracting media attention to what might otherwise be a low-profile event. Angelina Jolie has appeared five times on international aid issues; Alexis Ohanian, cofounder of the social networking site Reddit, testified in 2012 against a bill to curb online piracy; Michael Crichton, the science fiction writer, explained a few years ago that global warming was pure fiction. More often, witnesses include interest group lobbyists, think tank experts, academics, and pollsters reporting public opinion on the issues.

Hearings can also get tough. When the CEOs of three big U.S. automakers went to Congress in 2008 for a bailout, their trouble began when Representative Sherman (D-CA) needled them about flying to Washington on corporate jets while claiming that their companies faced bankruptcy.

● Celebrity congressional witnesses include . . . Elmo! The Muppet "testifies," with the help of Rep. Duncan Hunter (R-CA). Elmo urged the House Education Appropriations subcommittee to fund school music programs.

Rep. SHERMAN:	I'm going to ask the three executives here to raise their hand if they flew here commercial.
Mr. MULALLY [Ford CEO], **Mr. WAGONER [GM],** **Mr. NARDELLI [Chrysler]:**	(No response.)
Rep. SHERMAN:	Second, I'm going ask you to raise your hand if you're planning to sell your [private] jet . . . and fly back commercial.
Messrs. MULALLY, **WAGONER,** **NARDELLI:**	(No response.)
Rep. SHERMAN:	Let the record show no hands went up.
Rep. ACKERMAN:	It's almost like seeing a guy show up at the soup kitchen in high-hat and tuxedo. . . . I mean, couldn't you all have downgraded to first class or jet-pooled or something to get here?

Other members asked the CEOs if they would give up their hefty compensation packages and work for one dollar a year. Nardelli, the Chrysler chairman, declined with a muttered "I'm good." The CEOs learned their lesson: When they next testified before Congress, they rode to Washington in cars manufactured by their company.

2. Committees Prepare Legislation for Floor Consideration.
They are the primary source of policy development in Congress. Members and committee staff, drawing on their collective knowledge, assess and revise a bill.

Major rewrites of bills occur in **committee markup sessions**, when the committee gathers to work through the legislation's language, line by line. The result, called a "chairman's mark," is hot property among lobbyists, public advocates, and other interested parties; it contains many of the details that will become law if the legislation wins approval.

Following markup, the committee holds a vote on whether to report a bill to the full House or Senate. When the Senate Finance Committee considered economic stimulus legislation in 2009, it voted down more than one hundred amendments before passing the bill on party lines, 13–10. All that work is in just one Senate committee—and remember that at least one other committee (and usually more) is negotiating another version of the same legislation.

Committee votes are pivotal moments in a bill's career, as important as roll-call votes on the floor. If a bill is voted down in committee—not reported, in Congress-speak—it is usually dead. Those voted up by a narrow margin probably face tough sledding on the floor and the Speaker may decide never to bring it up for a vote—the bill dies even though it won a majority vote in committee.

3. Committees Also Kill Legislation.
Of the more than four thousand bills referred to the forty House and Senate standing committees each year, about one in eight sees any action at all. Well into modern times, bills

Committee markup session: A gathering of a full committee to draft the final version of a bill before the committee votes on it. Markups open to the public are often standing-room only.

were often quietly deleted in committee, without any public acknowledgment of how members voted. A key reform of the 1970s required all committees to keep full records of important votes.

4. Committees Exercise Oversight.   Congress monitors the executive branch, making sure cabinet departments and agencies perform their roles properly. Oversight can be high-stakes activity: Oversight hearings investigate scandals, review major issues like the attacks on the American mission in Benghazi, Libya, that left four dead, and evaluate presidential appointees. Committees also continue to monitor the programs that they have passed.

Floor Action

A successful bill makes it through committee markup (where it is amended, but remains recognizable) and is approved by one or more committees. Next stop: the House or Senate floor. Once it gets here, your measure's chance of becoming law has increased dramatically. Of bills that make it to the floor, more than half are enacted. But legislation may take a long time to get there—leaders rarely call up a bill until they know they have the votes to win.

Floor procedures in the House and Senate are very different from one another. After a Senate committee approves a bill, it is placed on the "business calendar," from which it will be called up for consideration on a timing schedule worked out by the majority and minority leaders. Only bills that receive **unanimous consent**—agreement by all senators—can be brought to the floor. One nay and the bill is put on hold.

In the House, the majority-party leaders exert more control over what issues make it to the floor. They may have to start by rewriting the legislation—sometimes because multiple committees have passed different chairman's marks and cannot come to agreement among themselves. Other times, the Speaker, majority leader, and fellow leaders must rewrite a bill to get the measure through.

Once it confirms the language of the bill, the House Rules Committee issues a directive about what type and how many amendments it will permit. The membership of the Rules Committee is usually stacked to favor the majority party, and the committee chair works closely with the Speaker to ensure that floor action will follow the leadership's wishes. The Senate, in contrast, allows virtually unlimited consideration on the floor; amendments of all kinds just keep on coming.

In both chambers, once bills make it to the calendar, they can get stuck there—for an entire session, in some cases. A logjam of legislation may be the reason. Or it might be the result of coordination issues between House and Senate, given the requirement that legislation has to move through both chambers. Bills also may be bottled up in the Senate because of the "unanimous consent" requirement. Achieving 100 percent agreement to allow a bill to come up for a vote often involves elaborate negotiations.

Unanimous consent:
A Senate requirement, applied to most of that body's business, that all senators agree before an action can proceed.

Eventually the calendar clears, and a bill's moment for floor consideration arrives. Often advocates hope their measure will be taken up in the House and Senate roughly at the same time, although plenty of legislation makes it only to one or the other chamber during a session—another form of death sentence. A bill to prohibit any taxpayer funding for abortion, another that capped government spending, and fifty efforts to repeal the Affordable Care Act all sailed through the House during the 113th Congress—and vanished when the Senate failed to act.

In both chambers, floor action on legislation follows the same broad procedures.

First, a bill is assigned a floor manager—usually the legislation's main sponsor, but on big issues the chair of the committee or subcommittee that reported the bill takes up this role. The manager handles amendments as they come up and controls the time for debate. Majority and minority party members each have a certain number of hours and minutes to discuss the legislation.

Then the political maneuvers really start. In both House and Senate, floor action involves amendments, procedural moves, eventually a final vote—and a lot of talk along the way. Members rarely change any votes with their eloquence. But floor speeches are not empty oratory. The real audience for much of the speechmaking is the constituency back home eager to see their representatives fight for (or against) an issue.

The rules in the House permit leaders to introduce creative strategies to get their legislation through. Earlier we saw the King of the Hill rule worked out by Speaker O'Neill with Rules Committee Democrats in 1981.

Senate leaders, far from inventing new rules, are more likely to breathe a sigh of relief after steering a bill past the potential member "holds" and simply getting it to the floor. There, a related danger lurks: the filibuster. A senator may halt all activity by refusing to yield the floor and the only way to stop him or her is through a **cloture vote,** which requires the approval of three-fifths of the Senate—sixty votes.

Filibusters used to be rare events. Between 1927 and 1960, there were only eighteen efforts to break a filibuster (or cloture filings); not a single one succeeded in *invoking cloture* or stopping the filibuster and permitting a vote on the issue. As you can see in Figure 10.1, the effort to "invoke cloture" became more common in the 1970s (which averaged thirty-two filibusters every two-year session) and became a familiar tactic in the 1990s (averaging seventy-two a session). Both Democrats and Republicans, when in the minority, resorted to the filibuster to stop action or exact concessions.

In the past three sessions, sixty votes has effectively become the new Senate threshold for passing legislation. The 113th Congress (2013–2014) broke the record for cloture votes with six months still left to go in its term (see Figure 10.1).

Once amendments are voted down or adopted, the time for speeches has expired, and the leadership reckons it has a winning majority, it's time for a

Cloture vote: The Senate's only approved method for halting a filibuster or lifting a legislative hold. If sixty senators—three-fifths of the body, changed in 1975 from the original two-thirds—vote for cloture, the measure can proceed to a vote.

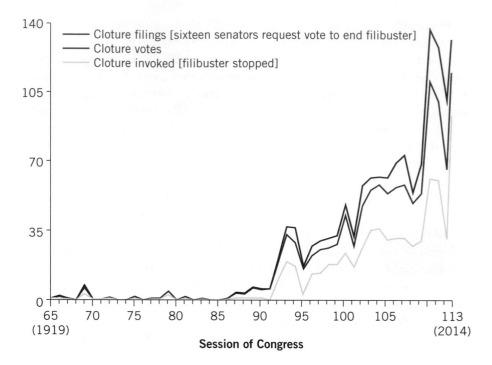

● **FIGURE 10.1** *Cloture votes are votes to end a filibuster. When they are successful, cloture is invoked and the filibuster ends. Notice how they used to be rare events. The 113th Congress (2013–2014) broke the all-time record for cloture votes (which is one way to measure the number of filibusters) with six months still to go in its term (U.S. Senate).*

Voice vote: A congressional vote in which the presiding officer asks those for and against to say "yea" or "nay," respectively, and announces the result. No record is kept of House or Senate members voting on each side.

Roll-call vote:
A congressional vote in which all members' votes are recorded, either by roll call (Senate) or electronically (House).

final floor vote. On uncontroversial matters, a **voice vote** of all members is sufficient. But several dozen votes each session are judged important enough to require a **roll-call vote**. In the Senate, a clerk still calls the roll, alphabetically scrolling through senators by last name, with each responding "yea" or "nay" (or "present," if they wish to abstain). Because the much-larger House would take hours to proceed in this way, roll calls are done electronically. Representatives use a card about the size of a credit or ATM card that they plug into kiosks located around the House chamber.

Roll-call votes on major bills are among the most important public acts a member of Congress performs. These votes attract a great deal of attention, from constituents, lobbyists, potential opponents, and media alike.

Conference Committee

Legislation must pass the Senate and House in identical form to be ready for presidential signature. If different versions of a bill pass—and technically a single comma, in a five-hundred-page bill, counts as a "difference"—a conference committee must reconcile them. These special sessions, made up of lawmakers from both chambers, provide a golden opportunity for disgruntled members or attentive lobbyists to revisit a bill. Interested parties who failed to get a favorite item included during committee or floor action now have another chance. As the final stop on the congressional lawmaking train, conference committees can turn into a political circus.

● *Conference committee in action. With staffers at the ready and media recording every utterance (and lobbyists crowded in the halls outside), a Senate–House conference committee works to resolve differences on a bill.*

House–Senate conferences, if successful, yield a single version of a bill. Each chamber then has an "up-or-down" floor vote—no further amendments permitted. Opponents in the Senate may launch another filibuster hoping to win over new members who object to the compromises made with the House. If the majority beats the filibuster in the Senate and a majority of both houses votes in favor, the bill has passed Congress.

Presidential Action: Separated Powers, Once More

Even after all that, the bill has still another hurdle. No bill becomes law until the president signs it. On important issues, the signing ceremony often takes place in the White House Rose Garden. Presidents sign multiple copies of the bill, handing out pens to the original sponsors and other high-ranking congressional members in attendance.

Presidents can also **veto** legislation. Here's yet another place a bill can falter. If the president says no, Congress has one more shot at passing the legislation. It's a high bar, however. To deny or override a veto, both chambers need a two-thirds majority: At least 67 senators and 291 members of the House have to say no to the president. Only in this way can a bill become law without a presidential signature.

We will cover more details about veto practices in the next chapter, on the presidency. Fortunately for most legislative advocates, presidential opposition is rare: George W. Bush vetoed just twelve bills during his eight years as president, and Barack Obama was even more sparing, vetoing only two bills during his first six years in office.

Veto: The constitutional procedure by which a president can prevent enactment of Congress-passed legislation.

THE
BOTTOM
LINE

- Transforming a policy idea into a federal law is highly complex—but the power of an officially sanctioned law inspires the introduction of thousands of bills in Congress each year.

- Bills often have creative titles and multiple authors inside and outside Congress—but only a member may introduce a bill.

- Congressional committees are the central actors in legislative policy making, holding hearings and marking up (or deleting) bills to prepare them for floor action.

- Floor procedures are another intricate part of the process. Once passed by House and Senate, legislation may still face a conference committee, a presidential veto, or both.

◗ Why Is Congress So Unpopular?

Congress, the "people's branch," might be expected to win the most public approval among our three national governing institutions. Yet it is by far the least-popular branch. For a half-century, polls have reported the popularity of Congress, the sitting president, and the Supreme Court, along with other institutions. Since the 1970s, Congress has come in last in virtually every survey—often by a great margin. Today, Congress is less popular than at any time in modern history and less popular than most other political figures and institutions—including the Internal Revenue Service, witches, zombies, and hipsters.[9] (Figure 10.2 compares today's Congress with other unpopular institutions.)

Constituents tend to like their own representatives and senators, who receive far higher approval numbers and are reelected at very high rates. We vote for our own members of Congress—yet despise the institution they serve in. Why? Based on opinion surveys and other research, here is what we know: The public dislikes partisan fighting and gridlock. Let's look more carefully at each complaint.

Partisan Polarization in Congress

Congress has exhibited partisan differences since its origins. Strong party disputes, fueled by the regional contention that ultimately sparked civil war, led many senators and representatives to carry swords, pistols, or Bowie knives while in the Capitol. Following a rousing antislavery speech by Senator Charles Sumner of Massachusetts in 1856, a Southern House member, Preston Brooks, slipped onto the Senate floor and beat Sumner unconscious with a cane. Sumner was unable to resume his Senate duties for nearly three years.

Subsequent combat in the House or Senate was mostly—but not entirely—limited to rhetorical, rather than physical, disagreement. Partisanship rose largely after 1990 because the Republicans were challenging the Democrats for control of the House for the first time in almost forty years.[10]

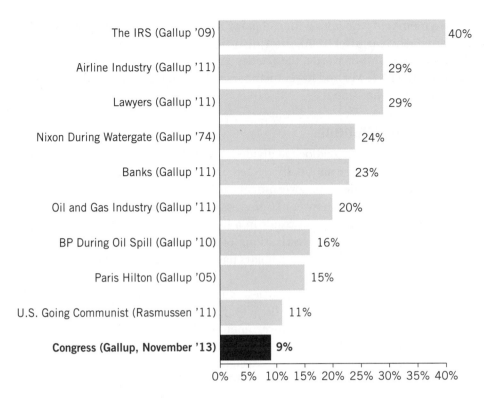

The IRS (Gallup '09)	40%
Airline Industry (Gallup '11)	29%
Lawyers (Gallup '11)	29%
Nixon During Watergate (Gallup '74)	24%
Banks (Gallup '11)	23%
Oil and Gas Industry (Gallup '11)	20%
BP During Oil Spill (Gallup '10)	16%
Paris Hilton (Gallup '05)	15%
U.S. Going Communist (Rasmussen '11)	11%
Congress (Gallup, November '13)	**9%**

0% 5% 10% 15% 20% 25% 30% 35% 40%

● **FIGURE 10.2** *Public approval of Congress compared to other institutions. Note that the congressional approval rating is only at 9%—it would fall as low as 7% in 2014 (Gallup).*

SOUTHERN CHIVALRY — ARGUMENT VERSUS CLUB'S.

● *Congressional partisanship, Civil War–era style. South Carolina Congressman Andrew Brooks beat abolitionist Senator Charles Sumner till he was bloody and unconscious. Both men became heroes in their region as a result.*

Political scientist Barbara Sinclair has shown that the proportion of House votes in which a majority of Democrats voted against a majority of Republicans increased by more than 50 percent during the 1990s and early 2000s.[11] By another measure, party cohesion—the proportion of each party's House or

Senate members who vote with the party majority—remained at or above 90 percent each year after 1990, after historically varying from the mid-60s to the low 80s. In other words, the parties in Congress were digging in against each other, with fewer and fewer members willing to look for middle ground or vote with the other side.

Divided Government

A source of legislative gridlock is divided government, when each party holds at least one of the three nationally elected branches: the presidency, the House, or the Senate. Include state governments and the courts and the gridlock gets even worse. One or both houses of Congress led by a party opposed to the president, the argument goes, will result in a legislative standoff—as well as more aggressive congressional investigations of the White House. The argument makes intuitive sense, but some scholars have gone counter to the conventional wisdom.

Political scientists David Mayhew and Keith Krehbiel have separately shown that divided government is actually no less productive of legislative achievements than is unified government—when the presidency and both houses of Congress are in the same party hands.[12]

Many other political scientists disagree. Sarah Binder, a scholar at the Brookings Institution, questions the results. Divided government, she argues, leads directly to stalemate. Others argue that, whatever the historical record, the recent polarization has brought "the virtual disappearance of regular order in Congress."[13]

The conclusion is simply that careful scholars disagree. However, the endless battle over the Obama health reform—still raging five years after the legislation passed—has even the optimists thinking twice about Congress' ability to solve its conflicts—one way or the other.

As you observe Congress in the future, keep both perspectives in mind. Watch to see if, after all the dramatics and the finger pointing, the two sides quietly agree on legislation—especially toward the end of the sessions. If so, it reflects the optimists: divided we govern. If not, you'll know the pessimists made the right prediction and Congress has proven to be "the broken branch."

THE BOTTOM LINE

- Congress has grown more partisan. The parties themselves are more ideologically consistent. This makes for sharper conflict, but it also gives people clearer choices.

- Does divided government lead to more gridlock? Political scientists disagree. Some argue that it does not; "Divided we govern," they insist. Others argue that recent developments—the growing ideological purity of the parties, the regular use of the filibuster—signal that divided government now means an inability to solve America's problems.

IS A PARTISAN CONGRESS A GOOD THING?

Should Congress seek more cross-party agreement? The answer might not be so obvious—especially if you view politics in terms of principles and high ideas, not merely the pursuit of self-interest. The modern "partisan" Congress features a significant ideological divide between conservative Republicans and progressive Democrats. Partisanship is the way members pursue the things they believe in and try to persuade the public of their perspectives. What do you think?

Yes, a partisan Congress is a good thing. It permits the public to choose between different political philosophies. The two parties represent different visions of America. That's better than two parties that basically say the same things.

No, Congress has gotten too partisan. The parties may disagree with one another, but they do not reflect most Americans. Most people are moderates who do not feel well represented by the strong party views on either side.

It Depends. The context matters. For example, in times of economic suffering, people should put aside their political philosophy (whether pro- or antigovernment) and legislate relief.

● Conclusion: Congress and the Challenge of Governing

The story of this chapter can be summed up like this: Congress, as an institution, does some important things very well—and others not very well at all. Representatives and senators look after the American public, as individuals, remarkably well. Direct constituent service, at home in the district and state, is often superb. That's why re-election rates are so high.

But as our individual needs have become better supported, solving the big societal problems—immigration, health care, government spending, inequality, global warming, an attractive business climate—has suffered. By any measure, Americans' collective concerns are at least as important as our personal aims. The great question we have asked throughout this chapter is whether the U.S. Congress has lost its ability to do the big collective things well or whether it still muddles through precisely as the constitutional framers intended.

In the past, Congress has certainly proven capable of remarkable collective achievements. Medicare and Social Security, to take two of the largest congressional programs, have cut the rate of poverty among elderly Americans by more than half and provided seniors with perhaps the most generous health benefits across the globe.

Genuine democratic, popular government can be chaotic, muddled, and sometimes repugnant. But it is essential. Our national legislative branch, our representatives in Congress, must continue to fulfill their democratic duties—and be rewarded by the public for doing so—if we are to approach the goal of living in freedom together.

CHAPTER SUMMARY

● America's Congress is bicameral: The House of Representatives has 435 members elected every two years; in the Senate, 100 Senators serve six-year terms.

● The two chambers of Congress reflect different national priorities. Populists appreciate the responsive House; advocates of stability embrace the more deliberate Senate.

● Members of the House and Senate represent Americans in multiple ways. These include:

- *Geographic representation*: The election rules say members must live in the state or district.

- *Descriptive representation*: Does the assembly look like the people?

- *Substantive representation*: Do members of Congress effectively pursue constituent interests?

● Members of Congress are always running for office. Fundraising takes a particularly important amount of time and attention. Members pay special attention to their home style: Most go back to the constituency every week—compressing normal congressional business into Tuesday through Thursday.

● Congressional leadership in the House includes a Speaker, majority and minority leaders, and ten whips. Successful leaders in the House impose discipline on their party members. In the Senate, party leaders and whips have fewer institutional tools with which to impose discipline.

● Congressional committees are the workhorses of Congress. They have proved efficient and adaptable over the years. However, the committee system also fragments Congress, hides action from public view, advantages well-placed constituents looking for individual favors, and makes it difficult to pass major legislation.

● Floor procedures are another intricate part of the process. Once passed by House and Senate, legislation may still face a conference committee, a presidential veto, or both.

● Congress has grown more partisan. The parties themselves are more ideologically consistent. This makes for sharper conflict, but it also gives people clearer choices.

KEY TERMS

114th Congress, 328
Cloture vote, 349
Committee hearing, 346
Committee markup session, 347
Conference committee, 326
Congressional caucus, 325

Earmark, 342
Filibuster, 329
Floor, 325
King of the Hill rule, 338
Legislative hold, 328
President pro tempore, 339

Reapportionment, 334
Roll-call vote, 350
Unanimous consent, 348
Veto, 351
Voice vote, 350

STUDY QUESTIONS

1. Discuss the following reforms:

   A. There should be public financing for all congressional elections, even if it means raising taxes.
   B. The Senate filibuster should be abolished.
   C. There should be more limits on lobbyists.

2. How did Congress lose so much power to the president? Are there ways to get some of that power back? Should power be more balanced between the two branches?

3. Why is Congress so partisan? Can you think of ways to reduce partisanship? Are there any advantages to drawing strong partisan lines between Republicans and Democrats?

4. Should it be easier to pass laws through Congress than it is currently? What, if any, benefits do all the checking and balancing provide?

5. Why is Congress so unpopular with the American people? In your view, does Congress deserve its low approval ratings?

The Presidency

GEORGE WASHINGTON, the first president of the United States, faced a problem. He had to find a way to persuade thirteen independent-minded states to think of themselves as one unified nation. Washington decided to foster unity by touring the new country—a grueling journey in the 1790s. He set out with assistants, slaves, horses, and dogs. As the party approached each town, the president mounted a great white steed and cantered handsomely into the cheering throngs, his favorite greyhound trotting at his side. Washington named the dog Cornwallis, after the British general who surrendered to end the Revolutionary War. Poor Cornwallis the greyhound died while touring the southern states, but his name reminded the people that they were part of a proud and independent nation. Everywhere Washington went, the people greeted their president with ringing bells, cheers, songs, speeches, parades, and flags. The crowds felt, at least for a day, like Americans.[1]

Who are we? Each president offers a different answer. Washington may be our greatest president, not because of his domestic programs or foreign policies—critics were scathing about both. Instead, Washington embodied the new nation. He championed American ideals, spoke to national aspirations, introduced new ideas, and personified the nation's sense of identity—both to Americans and to the world. All presidents do the same—some more successfully than others. Each offers a different answer to the question, Who are we?

The president's role is difficult partly because Americans rarely agree about who we are. The United States are often the *Un*-United States. Washington took slaves on his unity tour. Didn't slavery violate the new nation's ideals? Many Americans knew that it did.

More than 225 years after Washington's tour, the Barack Obama administration confronted an outcry over a new kind of war: drone strikes. Drones are sophisticated unmanned aircraft. Personnel sit in dark, air-conditioned rooms around the United States and pilot the aircraft as they streak across the skies of Afghanistan, Pakistan, Iraq, or Yemen at 230 miles an hour. The drones upload vivid images and—when the operators get approval from the chain of command—they fire hellfire missiles or laser-guided bombs at targets halfway

IN THIS CHAPTER, YOU WILL:

● See how the Constitution defines the presidency.

● Focus on presidential power.

● Learn what presidents do.

● Reflect on presidential popularity—and greatness.

● Consider the personal side of the office.

● Tour the Executive Office of the President and meet the team around a president.

● *The president has many advisers but has to make the tough decisions alone. Here, President Obama prepares his remarks to the nation about the raid on bin Laden's compound in Pakistan.*

around the globe. The drones killed more than 2,300 people between 2009 and early 2014.

Is the program effective in the fight against terrorism? Leaders hotly debated that question in the summer of 2014. On the one hand, drone attacks have decimated terrorist organizations—killing 58 known leaders and almost 2,000 foot soldiers. Osama Bin Laden, who planned the 9/11 attacks, wrote a memo warning about the toll the drone strikes were taking—before he himself was captured and killed by Navy Seals. On the other hand, by 2014 drones had killed at least 250 civilians—perhaps many more—sparking fury at the United States, especially in Pakistan. Stories of drones swooping out of the sky and massacring a wedding party or schoolchildren or other innocents inflamed anti-American sentiment. Some Americans—both conservatives and liberals—were arguing that the attacks ended up recruiting more terrorists than they killed.

The drone program demonstrates the extensive power of the modern presidency. Today, the American executive can approve the death of an enemy on the other side of the world. The power and reach of the office raise the same question the delegates debated at the Constitutional Convention. How much authority should the president have?

Washington's tour and Obama's drone program illustrate three essential features about the American president:

The president personifies America. More than any other individual, presidents tell us who we are—and what we are becoming.

The president injects new ideas into American politics. Our discussion of Congress emphasized the institutional rules of the game; the presidency puts more focus on individuals and ideas.

The president has enormous powers—at least on paper. That authority, and how presidents use it, raises a fundamental question: Is the president too powerful for a democratic republic? Or is the office too weak to do what Americans demand of it? Perhaps the same president can be both too strong and too weak at different points. Keep this question about presidential power in mind as you read the chapter.

BY THE NUMBERS
The Presidency

- Number of presidents in the past 100 years: **18**
- Number of Democratic presidents in the past 100 years: **8**
- Length, in months, of the shortest presidency (William Henry Harrison): **1**
- Length, in months, of the longest presidency (Franklin D. Roosevelt): **145**
- Number of years by which Franklin D. Roosevelt's lifespan was shorter than that of the average person at the time: **12.4**
- Number of presidents younger than Barack Obama when they were elected: **2**
- Election year of last president without a college education (Harry S. Truman): **1948**
- Election year of last president with no formal schooling (Andrew Johnson): **1865**
- Birth year of first president to be born in a hospital (Jimmy Carter): **1924**
- Year in which first woman (Victoria Woodhull) ran for president: **1872**
- Year in which women could first vote for president nationwide: **1920**
- Number of presidents who lost the popular vote but still won the election: **4** (John Quincy Adams, Rutherford B. Hayes, Benjamin Harrison, George W. Bush)
- Number of presidents who were sons, nephews, or cousins of prior presidents: **4** (John Q. Adams, Benjamin Harrison, Franklin D. Roosevelt, George W. Bush)
- Percent average winning margin in the popular vote in the past 20 elections: **9.8**
- Percent average winning margin in the Electoral College vote: **52.2**
- Highest presidential approval ratings (percent) ever recorded by Gallup (for Harry Truman, George H. W. Bush, and George W. Bush, respectively): **91, 89, 89**
- Lowest approval ratings recorded by Gallup at end of a full term (for Harry Truman, Jimmy Carter, and George W. Bush, respectively): **31, 34, 34**
- Highest approval ratings at end of a full term (for Bill Clinton, Ronald Reagan, and Dwight Eisenhower, respectively): **66, 63, 59**
- Estimated proportion of presidents who had affairs: **1 in 3**
- Number of presidents to hold a patent: **1** (Abraham Lincoln, for an invention to free boats trapped on a sandbar)

◗ Defining the Presidency

A time traveler from the nineteenth century would easily recognize today's Senate or the Supreme Court. However, the modern White House would stun her. The presidency is the branch of the federal government that has changed the most.

One hundred fifty years ago Americans could walk right in the front door of the White House and greet the president. In 1829, during President Andrew Jackson's inauguration, supporters mobbed the mansion and forced the president to climb out a window for his own safety; aides filled tubs with whiskey and orange juice on the lawn to lure the crowds outside.

Today there are no more mobs in the White House. The presidency is a different institution. Presidents have redefined their roles and renegotiated their powers. To this day, each president has the opportunity to reshape the office. One reason the presidency is so fluid lies in the job description. By now, you know where to look for that: the Constitution.

Defined by Controversy

The Constitutional Convention faced three tough questions when it defined the presidency. First, *should the United States even have a president?* Traditional republics feared executive power. The founders feared the English king as too powerful; but they worried that the state governments did not have enough executive power and were too feeble to govern effectively.

The job of the Constitutional Convention was to find a happy medium. In the end, they selected a single president and established simple qualifications for the post: a natural-born citizen at least thirty-five years old who had lived in the United States for fourteen years.

Second, *how long should the president serve?* Delegates debated many options: four, six, seven, eight, eleven, and fifteen years as well as a life long term before settling on four years; in 1945, the Twenty-Second Amendment limited presidents to two terms.

Third, *how should the United States choose its president?* This was the toughest question of all. Delegates believed that the public could not be trusted, the state legislatures were too self-interested, and Congress would become too powerful if given the task. They finally settled on a roundabout method, the Electoral College, which you encountered in Chapter 8: the states each get electoral votes equal to their congressional delegation. Political scientists still debate the merits of the Electoral College because it distorts the popular vote— and has put the loser in the White House four times.

The President's Powers

Article 2 of the Constitution, which defines the presidency, seems puzzling at first glance. Article 1 meticulously defines everything Congress is empowered to do: The instructions run for fifty-two paragraphs. In contrast, Article 2 says very little about who the president is and what the president does, devoting

TABLE 11.1 The President's Powers Are Balanced by Congress

The president is commander in chief of the army, navy, and state militias. But Congress has the power to declare war, set the military budget, and make the rules governing the military.
The president can grant pardons and reprieves for offenses against the United States.
The president can make treaties (with the approval of two-thirds of the Senate), appoint ambassadors (with the advice and consent of the Senate), and select Supreme Court justices and other officers (again, with Senate approval).
The Constitution also authorizes presidents to solicit the opinions of his officers (the cabinet members) and requires presidents to report on the state of the Union.

only thirteen paragraphs to the office. This vague constitutional mandate is one reason why the office keeps evolving.

The Constitution is especially concise when it gets to the heart of the presidency: the powers and duties of the chief executive. It grants the president a limited number of **expressed powers**, or explicit grants of authority. Most are carefully balanced by corresponding congressional powers. Table 11.1 summarizes this balance.

The president draws real authority from a simple phrase at the end of the section: "take care that the laws be faithfully executed." Congress votes on legislation and then sends it to the executive branch to put into effect. In other words, Congress grants **delegated powers** to the president. For example, Congress passes legislation that aims to improve hospital care. It delegates power to the executive branch, which issues a detailed rule saying that hospitals will receive lower federal payments if patients develop infections after surgery.

Modern presidents claim a third source of authority: **inherent powers of the presidency**. These are not specified in the Constitution or delegated by legislation, but are implicit in the vague Article 2 phrase "The executive power shall be vested in a president." During crises, presidents have often seized new "inherent" powers. During the Civil War, for example, President Lincoln took a series of unprecedented military actions with no clear legal basis. He imposed censorship, ordered a naval blockade, and issued orders while Congress was not in session. When ISIS, an organization of radical Islamists, won victories in Iran and Syria, President Obama exercised inherent powers to launch an air campaign in both nations. Did he need Congressional approval? The administration said it did not. Presidents claim inherent powers; the Supreme Court then weighs whether they have overstepped the constitutional boundaries of their authority.

The result is a very fluid definition of presidential power. Presidents define their roles, negotiating the limits of the office through their actions at home and abroad. Crises generally expand the presidential role. More than any other institution, the presidency is a constant work in progress. The arc of presidential

Expressed powers: Powers the Constitution explicitly grants to the president.

Delegated powers: Powers that Congress passes on to the president.

Inherent powers of the presidency: Powers assumed by presidents, often during crisis, on the basis of the constitutional phrase "The executive power shall be vested in the president."

history begins with a modest constitutional grant of power that has grown enormously through the years.

This discussion brings us back to the question we posed at the start of the chapter: Has the president become too powerful? We turn to that question in the next section.

THE BOTTOM LINE

- Presidents serve a four-year term and can run for re-election once.

- They are elected indirectly, via the Electoral College.

- The president has three kinds of powers: *expressed* in the Constitution, *delegated* by Congress, and *inherent* in the role of chief executive.

- In theory, Congress passes laws and the president executes them. In reality, presidents constantly negotiate the limits of their power—which often expands during crises.

Is the President Too Powerful?

The constitutional framers wrestled with the same issue we debate today: *power*. How much authority do presidents need to protect the nation and get things done? How much power goes so far as to violate the idea of limited government?

An Imperial Presidency?

During George Washington's national tour, a few Americans fretted about his nine stallions, gold-trimmed saddles, personal attendants, and all that adulation. Washington, they whispered, was acting more like a king than the president of a homespun republic. They were articulating a constant American theme: The president has grown too mighty. Flash forward two centuries. Today, the president travels with a cast of hundreds: lawyers, secretaries, cooks, speechwriters, baggage handlers, doctors, aides, snipers, bomb-sniffing dogs, and armored cars. When President Clinton visited China, it took thirty-six jumbo jets (each holding 145 tons of cargo) to carry the presidential team and all its baggage. When the second President Bush visited England, the imperial trappings of the presidential entourage (five hundred members strong) reportedly shocked the Queen.[2]

Presidents have constantly redefined the authority of their office—setting off the critics who charge that they have gone too far. The second president, John Adams, did not have to worry about cheering crowds. Critics mocked the chubby second president as "His Rotundity." Adams attracted so little attention that he regularly swam naked in the Potomac River (until a woman reporter allegedly spied him, sat on his clothes, and demanded an interview). Even Adams, however, aroused widespread fears about executive power when he signed the Alien and Sedition Acts, which gave the executive broad powers to deport "dangerous aliens" and punish "false, scandalous, and malicious" speech. The president seemed to be trampling the First Amendment by silencing criticism.

Arthur Schlesinger Jr., a celebrated historian, warned of an **imperial presidency**. Very powerful presidents, he feared, become like emperors: They run roughshod over Congress, issue secret decisions, unilaterally deploy force around the world, and burst past the checks and balances limiting presidential power. Critics worry that imperial features have become part of the presidency itself. Many critics have leveled this charge at President Obama. Republicans organized their 2014 midterm-elections strategy in part around criticism that White House overreach had created another imperial presidency.[3]

At issue are two vital principles: We need a president who is strong enough to lead the country and face our problems. But if presidents become too strong, we lose our republican form of government. This is a deep paradox in American politics: *We need powerful leaders; we fear powerful leaders.*

Imperial presidency: A characterization of the American presidency that suggests it is demonstrating imperial traits and that the republic is morphing into an empire.

A Weak Office?

At the same time, the presidency can also seem very weak. Every modern president has complained about his inability to get basic goals accomplished. Congress, courts, the opposing political party, the media, interest groups, and bad luck can all humble a president. In the past half-century, only three (of ten) presidents completed two full terms. What kind of "imperial" presidency is that?

Presidents can seem weakest when they wrestle with domestic issues. Even under the best of circumstances, as we saw in the previous chapter, it is difficult to get major legislation through Congress. The president nominally runs the executive branch, but the bureaucracy is immense and often difficult to control.

For a case study in the weak presidency, take Jimmy Carter. Congressional relations turned frosty early in his term, when Carter unexpectedly vetoed a spending bill. Congress was stung at the abrupt rejection. Carter's major legislative proposals quickly ran into trouble on Capitol Hill. Then the economy turned bad. Interest rates spiraled toward 20 percent and unemployment topped 10 percent. Gas prices also soared, forcing customers in some regions to wait in long lines at gas stations.

● Gas lines. A case study in a troubled presidency: An international energy crisis led to long lines at gas stations during the Jimmy Carter years. Presidents take the blame for many events they cannot control—like this one.

Carter did not seem to have an answer to all the woes besetting the nation. A mischievous editor at the *Boston Globe* captured one reaction to Carter's speech when he designed a mock headline, "Mush from the Wimp." By mistake, the headline ran in the first edition.[4] A few months later, militant Iranian students took fifty-three Americans hostage at the U.S. embassy in Tehran and held them for 444 days. A weak president seemed to be completely overwhelmed by events all around him.

Back and forth goes the debate. Is the president getting too powerful and breaking free from popular control? Or is the president not up to the job of governing a superpower? To answer this question, let's take a closer look at just what presidents do.

THE BOTTOM LINE

- Americans want a powerful president; Americans fear a powerful president.

- The executive branch has grown far stronger over time, especially when it comes to foreign policy.

- At the same time, presidential power is limited, especially when it comes to solving domestic problems.

What Presidents Do

Over time, presidents have taken on many jobs. Some are described in the Constitution. Others arise organically during national crises. Presidents seized still others as they jockeyed for political advantage. By now, the president has accumulated an extraordinary number of hats (and helmets). More than most other American political actors, presidents can—given the right circumstances—be "agents of change."[5] In this section we will review the many things the president does—starting with commanding the armed forces.

Commander in Chief

The Constitution lays it out simply: "The president shall be the Commander-in-Chief of the Army and Navy of the United States and the militia of the several states, when called into the actual service of the United States." Congress declares war and presidents manage it.

For many years, the United States had a small standing army and called men and women to service in wartime. The size of the army jumped thirty-eight-fold during the Civil War and thirty-six times during World War I. After each war, the army quickly demobilized. This approach reflected classical theory. In great republics like Athens and Rome, citizens took up arms when enemies loomed and then returned home when the crisis had passed—just as

● **FIGURE 11.1** *The military and how it grew, 1820–2011. Traditionally, the United States called soldiers to war and then demobilized after the war. However, troop levels never went back down to prewar levels. The United States began to play a global role after the Spanish–American War. (Historical Statistics/ Statistical Abstracts)*

George Washington had done during the American Revolution. Peacetime armies were, according to the traditional perspective, a recipe for empire or monarchy.

This tradition changed after World War II, when the United States faced off against the Soviet Union in the so-called Cold War. An army of around 250,000 (after World War I) grew into a force of more than 2 million and spread across the globe. Back in 1835, Tocqueville mused that the Constitution gave the president "almost royal prerogatives which he has no occasion to use." Now the occasion had arrived, and the president's power grew.

Today, America's active-duty force numbers 1.3 million, with another 850,000 in reserve (see Figure 11.1). To save costs, Congress has reduced the reserve forces by a third—with steeper cuts planned in the years ahead. Many military experts decry the steep reductions but the public, perhaps weary from years of war in Iraq and Afghanistan, have barely reacted (only about one in four call for a larger military).

Even with the cuts, the defense budget runs more than $620 billion (in 2014)—not including the Department of Veterans Affairs, Homeland Security, intelligence agencies, and other related efforts. The military operates 750 installations that span the globe. In short, the commander in chief oversees the world's largest fighting force. That role, by itself, makes the president one of the most powerful individuals in the world.

Meanwhile, checks on the commander in chief have faded. The Constitution authorizes Congress to declare wars, but since the nuclear age dawned in 1945, presidents have rarely waited for Congress to act. Facing the doomsday threat

● *A uniformed officer with "the football"—a briefcase that contains launch codes for the nuclear arsenal. The football is always a few feet away from the president.*

of nuclear missiles, military response time is measured in minutes—too fast for congressional deliberation.

In an effort to regain some of its authority, Congress passed the War Powers Act in 1973, requiring congressional approval after troops had been deployed for sixty days. That is a far weaker check than the constitutional power to declare war. It concedes the president's authority to unilaterally deploy troops; Congress does not get its say until American men and women are already in combat—when it is very difficult to vote no. Moreover, presidents have been contemptuous of the War Powers Act.

In Libya, American forces demolished Muammar Gaddafi's air defense system. That helped turned the tide in favor of the rebels. But, after doing the job, the United States turned control of the skies over to its allies. Congress demanded that the administration seek Congressional approval under the War Powers Act. The Obama administration refused, arguing that the United States had no ground forces in combat—although the United States had significant forces providing aerial surveillance and other operations. The Gaddafi regime fell before the dispute could be resolved.

Presidential powers have always waxed during wartime. Two developments since then have further increased the president's military authority: America's powerful military machine, always poised for deployment, and the perception of perpetual threat—first from the communists and then from terrorists. However, when wars drag on and become unpopular, such as the recent wars in Iraq and Afghanistan, the president's powers seem to fade: Congress holds hearings and threatens military budgets; public approval ratings decline; protests spring up.

Presidents are deeply engaged by their military role. They start each day with a security briefing that reviews all the dangers stirring around the world; they have a large national security staff; and—the great symbol of our nuclear age—they are never more than a few feet away from "the football."

If you see the president in person, or a wide-angle shot on television, you will glimpse a military officer standing about twenty feet away and clutching a medium-size black briefcase, known as "the football." What's in the bag? The answer is classified, but over the years the public has learned that it is a mobile communications center locked into the American nuclear arsenal. Every minute of every day the American president is steps away from a kit that would enable him or her to launch an attack that could obliterate any nation from the face of the Earth.

Top Diplomat

The Constitution gives presidents the lead role in foreign affairs. Presidents and their international advisers set an overall framework for the U.S. role in the world. Some administrations emphasize international alliances; they work closely with foreign powers and build multinational institutions. Others prefer to go it alone—they ignore the United Nations and are reluctant to sign treaties for fear that they will bind the United States to foreign governments.

Foreign policy issues bombard each president. Should the United States take the lead on global warming or reject international agreements in favor of bulking up domestic manufacturing? Should we press foreign governments on social justice issues (like the right to unionize without facing violence) when negotiating trade agreements? Should we try to broker peace in the Middle East? Respond to aggression like Vladimir Putin's in Ukraine in 2014? Should we intervene in the Syrian civil war? Go back into Iraq to stop the threat posed by radical Islamists? What should be done about rogue states with nuclear weapons? Presidents and their team constantly meet, discuss, threaten, and negotiate with nations near and far.

Foreign diplomacy is not just about trouble spots. The State Department manages 305 embassies, consulates, and diplomatic missions around the world. Presidents must hash out American relations with nearly 200 nations that range from "special friends" to distant allies to avowed enemies. Intricate questions arise about how to approach each country: Should the president shake hands with our nation's enemies? Every smile or snub sends a diplomatic message. A president sets the tone and the policy for all these relationships.

Foreign policy crises differ vastly from everyday domestic politics. Passing laws is a long, complicated process full of compromise and constraint. During international crises—hostage situations, terror attacks, the outbreak of wars—all eyes turn toward the president and his team.

The First Legislator

The Constitution includes presidents in the legislative process. It authorizes them to *recommend measures* for Congress's "consideration," report to Congress *information on the state of the Union*, and *veto legislation* they oppose.

Recommending Measures. Until modern times, presidents generally avoided legislative affairs. In 1840, William Henry Harrison devoted his inaugural address—the longest in history—to denouncing the insatiable love of power creeping into the presidency. He pledged to honor congressional authority by avoiding legislative involvement. Dwight Eisenhower (1953–1961) was the last president to try and leave legislation to Congress. His cabinet officers complained, and before long

● How to back down without backing down? President Obama seemed to commit himself to American intervention in Syria when he accused the Assad regime of crossing a red line by using poison gas on his own people. Later, intelligence reports suggested that rebels might have deployed the gas. The administration's response? Rather than back down it simply announced it would ask Congress for approval—knowing full well that Congress was too divided to approve an attack.

Eisenhower was recommending measures—and blasting Congress when they failed to approve his proposals.

Today presidential candidates define the legislative agenda long before they arrive in office. As the 2016 election begins to shape up, click on candidate websites for proposals to deal with issue after issue: economic policy, health care, education, energy, budgets, taxes . . . and the list will go on. In our fast-paced media environment, silence on any topic invites criticism. At every news conference and debate, candidates joust over their proposals. Listen carefully: Amid all the talk lie a handful of issues that a candidate is passionate about. Presidents-elect generally try to advance these once in office. For President George W. Bush, it was tax cuts, education reform, and privatizing Social Security. President Barack Obama emphasized economic improvement, health reform, and global warming. Each president arrives in office with a few legislative priorities. However, they are inevitably enmeshed in many others. Campaign promises require attention. Top advisers lobby for their favorite programs. And unexpected issues constantly spring up and require presidential attention.

State of the Union.   The Constitution invites the chief executive to report on the state of the Union "from time to time." Today the SOTU address, as insiders term it, is an annual event, delivered with great fanfare before Congress, Supreme Court justices, official Washington, and a national television audience. The SOTU address is also the annual focal point of the cabinet members and other White House officials, who compete to get their favorite programs mentioned in the message. All submit their proposed ideas months in advance, and the president's staff picks the winners (or substitutes its own favorites).

The president declares his legislative program for the year in the speech. What you hear is a long and often dull list of programs: For the president's team, however, each little bullet point is a triumph for one person or department and a defeat for all those pushing programs that failed to make the cut.

Following the SOTU address, each issue undergoes a second round of debates within the administration: Does it really fit our budget? Can we make

● The State of the Union address: one of the great pageants on the Washington calendar—and a great victory for the agencies that get their programs mentioned.

it work smoothly? Did Congress cheer or yawn when the boss rolled it out? What was the public reaction? Most policies have friends and enemies in the administration—and if you get your favorite program, I may not get mine. The process is a polite version of a knife fight. Proposals that survive go up to Capitol Hill, where they face the long, complicated congressional process we described in the last chapter.

Presidential "Batting Average."   Only members of Congress can formally propose a law, so presidents rely on supporters in each chamber to submit their bills. The White House has a congressional liaison team to negotiate and cut deals. Generally hidden from public view, the liaison is a key role in the modern presidency. No matter how talented a liaison might be, frustration inevitably sets in. To the executive branch, legislators seem overly parochial as they focus on their states and districts. Still, most presidents quickly learn the same lesson: work closely with Congress. Managing relations with House and Senate members is one of the most important presidential skills.

We can measure each president's legislative success—generally referred to as the batting average (see Table 11.2). There are many different ways to keep score: all the bills the president endorses, the most important bills, or bills that the other party opposes. You can see that when the same party controls the White House and Congress, known as unified government, the batting average is much higher—usually around .800. When the opposition party controls Congress (divided government), the average usually falls below .500. Some political scientists have argued that divided government makes for a more effective legislative process. But notice how divided governments (the red lines) have been yielding less agreement in recent years. President Obama enjoyed the highest batting average in the past seventy-five years with a Democratic Congress and the second lowest when he faced a divided Congress.

Veto.   When Congress passes a law, presidents have the authority to sign or **veto** (*veto* means "I forbid," in Latin). A veto blocks the legislation unless two-thirds of both chambers vote to **override** it, a very high bar to achieve. Presidents have ten days to return the legislation to Congress with a message explaining why they have rejected it. If the president does nothing, the bill becomes law in ten days.

The veto is a formidable weapon. In the past eighty years presidents have rejected more than 1,400 bills. Congress managed to override just sixty times: a congressional "batting average" of 4 percent. Recently the veto has become a more partisan weapon, as conflict between the parties has escalated. Franklin D. Roosevelt, Harry Truman, and Jimmy Carter all flourished the veto pen against a Congress controlled by their own party; in their first two years the three presidents struck down seventy-three, seventy-four, and nineteen bills, respectively. In contrast, the most recent presidents—Clinton, Bush, and Obama—*combined* for a total of two vetoes against their own party majorities in their

Veto power: The presidential power to block an act of Congress by refusing to sign it.

Override: The process by which Congress can overcome a presidential veto with a two-thirds vote in both chambers.

TABLE 11.2 Presidential Batting Average

Measuring the proportion of congressional bills on which the president took a position that passed.

PRESIDENT	PARTY	YEARS IN OFFICE	CONGRESSIONAL CONTROL	PERCENT OF CONGRESSIONAL VOTES SUPPORTING PRESIDENT'S POSITION
Dwight Eisenhower	R	1953–1954	Republicans control Congress	86.0%
Dwight Eisenhower	R	1955–1960	Democrats control Congress	67.7%
John F. Kennedy	D	1961–1963	Democrats control Congress	84.6%
Lyndon Johnson	D	1963–1969	Democrats control Congress	82.2%
Richard Nixon	R	1969–1974	Democrats control Congress	64.3%
Gerald Ford	R	1974–1977	Democrats control Congress	58.3%
Jimmy Carter	D	1977–1981	Democrats control Congress	76.6%
Ronald Reagan	R	1981–1986	Mixed control (R Senate, D House)	67.4%
Ronald Reagan	R	1987–1989	Democrats control Congress	45.4%
George H. W. Bush	R	1989–1993	Democrats control Congress	51.8%
Bill Clinton	D	1993–1994	Democrats control Congress	86.3%
Bill Clinton	D	1995–2000	Republicans control Congress	48.1%
George W. Bush	R	2001–2006	Republicans control Congress	80.9%
George W. Bush	R	2007–2008	Democrats control Congress	43.0%
Barack Obama	D	2009–2010	Democrats control Congress	92.0%
Barack Obama	D	2011–2013	Mixed control (D Senate, R House)	52.8%

▬ President's party controls Congress
▬ Opposition party controls Congress
▬ Congress split

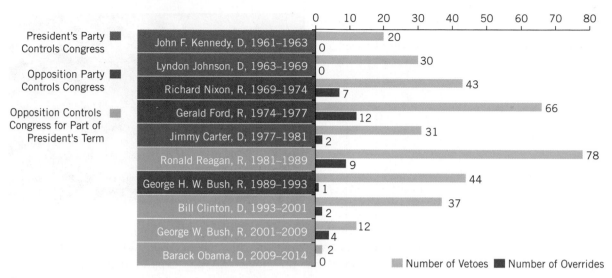

● **FIGURE 11.2** *Presidential vetoes and overrides. Note that vetoes were far more common 50 years ago, even when the same party controlled Congress and the White House; Congress rarely manages to override a presidential veto (United States Senate, "Summary of Bills Vetoed, 1789–Present").*

first two years (see Figure 11.2). Barack Obama vetoed only two bills in his first six years in office—you have to go back to 1822 (James Monroe) to find fewer vetoes.

A president's veto rarely comes as a surprise. As Congress works on a law, the president's congressional liaisons are ever-present. Administration officials may threaten a veto to shape the legislation in favorable ways. When negotiations get especially intense, the president can also go public and threaten Congress. Congressional leaders in turn can threaten to bury a bill the president wants or openly defy a president to veto popular bills. After all the back-and-forth, presidents have developed yet another strategy: They can voice their displeasure while signing bills into law.

Signing Statements.   Bill signing has become a great Washington ritual, especially for popular legislation. Congressional sponsors flank the president, who has a big pile of pens to hand out to the program's key supporters while cameras capture the smiling moment.

In recent decades, presidents increasingly issue **signing statements** as they are signing a bill into law. These statements may offer their administration's interpretation of the law—one sometimes at odds with Congress's expressed ideas. President George W. Bush, reflecting his strong view of the unitary executive, used signing statements to challenge, limit, or reject an estimated 1,200 sections of congressional bills—roughly twice as many challenges as all previous presidents combined. Late in the Bush presidency, the American Bar Association condemned the practice as an undue expansion of federal authority.[6] President Obama, like most Democrats, criticized the signing statements. Once he was in office, however, he continued the practice, although he had only issued a total of twenty-seven statements as of spring 2014. Unless the

Signing statements: Written declarations commenting on the bill that is signed into law.

● President Obama signs the Violence against Women Act, March 2013.

Supreme Court rules on the matter, this may become another example of the pattern: Presidents redefine their own office and expand its powers.

Chief Bureaucrat

The Constitution gives the president the power to appoint the men and women of the executive branch of government, subject to confirmation by the Senate. President Washington took the top officers of the major departments and organized them into a cabinet to advise him. The original cabinet included four officers: the secretaries of war, treasury, and state and the attorney general. By 1800 the executive branch included two hundred officeholders.[7]

Today, the executive branch includes fifteen departments and 2.7 million employees—or more than 4 million, counting active-duty military. Presidents appoint some four thousand **political appointees** who direct the executive agencies; the rest of the staff are **civil servants** who remain from one administration to the next. We will explore these officials and their agencies in the next chapter, on the executive bureaucracy.

As chief executive, presidents wield powers that do not need to go through Congress. They can sign **executive orders**, with the force of law, setting guidelines for federal agencies. Contemporary administrations issue thirty to forty executive orders a year. Some are simply instructions for operating the executive branch: setting up a new council or office, for example. Others involve controversial decisions. They can be issued with fanfare or executed secretly. Recent executive orders have declared wilderness areas off-limits to snowmobiles (Clinton, rewritten by Bush); introduced new guidelines for interrogating enemy combatants (Bush, rewritten by Obama); required government preparations for the impact of climate change (Obama); blocked companies from trading with Cuba or Iran (Bush, Obama); and regulated the use of stem cells in federally funded research (Bush introduced limits; Obama rescinded them).

The George W. Bush administration relied on executive orders to prosecute its war on terror. It made new rules on wiretaps, detention of enemy combatants, and trials by military tribunals. Barack Obama used them for more technical

Political appointees: Top officials in the executive agencies appointed by the president.

Civil servants: Members of the permanent executive-branch bureaucracy who are employed on the basis of competitive exams and keep their positions regardless of the presidential administration.

Executive order: A presidential declaration, with the force of law, that issues instructions to the executive branch without any requirement for congressional action or approval.

purposes until the Republicans took control of the House in 2011. The Obama team, then blocked in Congress, began to make policy through executive orders. For example, when Congress voted down the Dream Act, which offered a path to citizenship for some undocumented aliens, President Obama issued an executive order designed to stop deportation (and allow work permits) for young, undocumented men and women who had been brought to the United States as children—one provision in an act that Congress had refused to pass. The administration has been blunt: If partisan gridlock blocks important action, the executive will use other tools. Some observers worry that in the process, Congress is slowly losing authority while presidents—from both parties—use a traditional form of executive authority to expand the scope and authority of their office.

Economist in Chief

Economic authority is one power the Constitution definitely does *not* grant the president. The power of the purse—taxing, spending, borrowing, and regulating commerce—is all in congressional hands. However, during the Great Depression of the 1930s, the Roosevelt administration seized responsibility for putting the nation back to work, launching one recovery program after another. "Take a method and try it," insisted Roosevelt. "If that fails, try another. . . . Above all try something."[8]

The idea soon took root: The president was responsible for a smooth-running economy. The year after Roosevelt died, Congress legislated the Council of Economic Advisers to help presidents oversee the economy. Today, the president and a host of advisors monitor economic conditions. White House economists vet every plan and proposal for its impact on American prosperity. Every new administration crowds more economists into its ranks. When Obama won re-election in 2012, among his first moves was to announce the revamped White House economic team—stocked with both formal and informal advisors. Presidential popularity and the party's chances of holding onto the office in the next election are heavily influenced by economic conditions.

The Head of State

Most nations have a ceremonial head of state who stands above partisan politics and represents the nation. The queen of England, the emperor of Japan, and the president of Israel all play this nonpolitical role while their prime ministers make the policies that govern their countries. Citizens of the British Isles do not need to check their political affiliation when they sing "God Save the Queen"—she represents them across the political spectrum. In contrast, the presidents of the United States play both roles. They stand for the nation even while they represent one party in political debate.

Presidents spend a lot of time in their ceremonial role. They throw out the first pitch during the World Series, spare a turkey every Thanksgiving, light the White House Christmas tree, smash a bottle of champagne across the bow of a

President as Head of State. President Bill Clinton and first lady Hillary Clinton wear traditional kente cloth. They are waving to thousands of cheering Ghanaians. With them is then president of Ghana, Jerry Rawlings.

new aircraft carrier, congratulate national heroes, host championship sports teams, and embody America every time the Marine Corps Band plays "Hail to the Chief." When presidents travel abroad they represent all Americans, not just their party or their supporters.

Party Leader

George Washington repeatedly warned the country against political parties and the strife they brought. However, by his second term, rival parties were not so quietly emerging. As suffrage spread beyond landowning gentlemen, parties grew into the largest political organizations in America. They created yet another role for the president: party leader.

This role sharpens the tension we described in the last section. There is a fine line between leading the nation (and standing for everyone) and leading the Democrats (which means defeating Republicans). The tension becomes acute during war. As the Cold War developed, Senator Arthur Vandenberg (R-MI) famously declared that party "politics stop at the water's edge"—the nation had to be united to defeat communism. That idea, never fully honored, collapsed in the debate over Vietnam. Almost everything the president does, home and abroad, is now part of the great American political debate.

Ronald Reagan hosted a reception at the White House to celebrate Democratic legislators who had switched allegiance to his Republican party.

Bill Clinton astonished everyone at his prowess—rivals called it shamelessness—at raising money for Democratic candidates; Republicans charged that the president rewarded big donors with a night in the Lincoln Bedroom. When George W. Bush took over, Democrats complained that the president was using the war on terror to defeat Democrats and build a permanent Republican majority. Republicans, in turn, accused Barack Obama of leaking classified information about the death of Osama bin Laden for political gain. Each side accuses the other of taking politics to unprecedented extremes.

President Obama took office determined to dial down the party conflict. He offered Republicans important positions in his administration, like secretary of defense; he tried a bipartisan Super Bowl party; and he negotiated long and hard to win over at least a couple of Senate Republicans to his health plan. The efforts failed. When Democrats began calling the Republicans "the Party of No," the Republicans defiantly responded that they were the party of "Hell No!" Voters rewarded the sentiment in 2010 with a midterm Republican landslide.

Can anything tamp down the partisan conflict? Yes: The secret ingredient is fear. When a president grows very popular, opponents will often go along out of fear that the voters might punish them if they do not. Presidents who get more votes in a district than a House member of Congress, or more votes in the state than a senator, can be very persuasive—as long as their poll numbers remain high.

The Bully Pulpit: Introducing Ideas

President Theodore Roosevelt was bursting with ideas, opinions, exhortations, and warnings. He called the presidency itself a "bully pulpit" (today we might say "awesome platform"). Roosevelt knew that an active president has the country's ear, an opening to introduce and promote new ideas.

Most presidencies are marked by a few big ideas. In his inaugural, John F. Kennedy called the nation to public service. "Ask not what your country can do for you," said Kennedy. "Ask what you can do for your country." Ronald Reagan championed a very different idea when he called government the source of our national problems; individuals pursuing the American dream and trying to get rich were, he declared, the real source of national vitality. Successful presidents arrive in office with powerful ideas—and persuade the public to embrace new visions of our political life.

More than any political office in America, the presidency rises and falls on ideas. "The power of the presidency," as one scholar famously put it, "is the power to persuade."[9]

● *Theodore Roosevelt called the presidency a "bully pulpit." No other office is more effective for introducing new ideas. Here, TR takes full advantage of his pulpit.*

The Impossible Job

How can anyone juggle so many different presidential roles? The honest answer is that no one can. Even great presidents cannot handle all their jobs well all of the time. Still, this is what we demand of our presidents.

Each presidential role requires different strengths and skills. No person will have them all. However, the bully pulpit can help. Bold ideas bring together the many threads of this huge task. They make a presidency coherent. Without that, presidents may seem overwhelmed by the job, skittering from one task to another without a broader sense of purpose and vision.

Finally, note one theme that has run through every role: Presidential authority has grown in every aspect of the office. The president's many roles are one more way to measure the swelling power and importance of the office. That brings us back again to the central paradox of the executive: The presidency grows ever more powerful, yet the role has grown so large that no one person can perform every aspect of it well.

THE BOTTOM LINE

- The president wears many hats and helmets. Some are specified in the Constitution. Others have developed over time.

- Presidential roles include commander in chief, top diplomat, first legislator, head bureaucrat, economist in chief, head of state, and party leader. Presidents are also uniquely situated to introduce new ideas—tying together these many different roles.

- The president's authority has grown in every one of these roles. At the same time, it is difficult to do so many different things effectively.

● Presidential Leadership: Success and Failure in the Oval Office

Presidents try to manage perceptions of their performance. They address the public, use (and bypass) the media, schedule eye-catching events, and rely on polls to hone their message. How do we know if they have succeeded? We'll examine three different measures: polls, historical rankings, and the great cycles of political time.

Managing the Public

Going public: Directly addressing the public to win support for oneself or one's ideas.

As the only nationally elected official (excepting the vice president, who is elected as a package with the president), presidents develop a relationship to the people, which they cultivate by **going public**—directly addressing citizens to win support. Each new form of media—radio, television, Twitter/Facebook—shifts the way presidents go public.

Presidents "go public" primarily through the media. Each effort—from the town hall meeting with a small group to the speech in front of thousands—is designed to control the spin that filters out through newscasts, talk shows, and Twitter feeds.

Images are often more important than words. Presidents hug disaster victims, play basketball with the troops, or wave to cheering throngs holding American flags in a foreign nation. The image can turn negative in an instant. President Johnson playfully lifted his beagle by the ears in front of the press (cruel!). President Ford slipped and fell in public (clumsy!). President George H. W. Bush threw up at a state dinner in Japan (you can imagine!). In a complicated world, a single picture can distill popular perception. Images have an impact—positive or negative—when they seem to reveal the president's true strengths or weakness. The key point is simple: *Presidents constantly try to manage their image in the public eye.*[10]

see for yourself 11.1

Go online to see President Ford's unfortunate stumble. (Flash required)

However, the velocity of the news cycle means that most efforts only linger a few hours before they are displaced by the next story. A generation ago, an important presidential address might dominate the news for several days. Now, the sheer volume of information flowing through the media means that only the most important events will command attention for long. The president's message now requires constant repetition, amplification, and—to grip viewers—a touch of novelty and drama.

The White House runs a sophisticated polling operation that guides its outreach efforts. The president's daily schedule frequently includes briefings from the administration's pollster. An administration's goals don't change, but the language and the pitch are heavily poll tested in the constant search for the most effective way to communicate to the public.[11]

Approval Ratings

Every week, another wave of polls report how Americans view the president's performance. These are used widely, inside and beyond Washington, as a rough barometer of the administration's success. Any one poll can be misleading (as we saw in Chapter 6), but if you eliminate the outliers—the occasional polls that are much higher and lower than the others—and scan the rest, you'll have a snapshot of the administration's ratings that are reverberating through the media and around Washington.

● *Lyndon Johnson lifting his beagle by the ears. The president was trying for a lighthearted moment but quickly felt the backlash from outraged pet lovers.*

RANKING THE PRESIDENT

Table 8.3 (page 384) lists presidential rankings by historians, political scientists, and statistical experts. Time for you to weigh in. Where, in your considered opinion, does President Obama rate alongside the previous forty-three presidents to hold the office?

Among the Greats.	**In the Middle.**	**Near the Bottom.**
Obama entered the presidency during a time of grave economic difficulty and, steering the nation to safer financial shores, pushed through landmark health reform act (which eluded other presidents, Democrats and Republicans alike, for nearly 100 years), took executive action on clean air, and brought a successful close two wars (in Iraq and Afghanistan), which qualifies him among the very best presidents in U.S. history.	Obama's important achievements, noted at left, are balanced by his frequent inability to advance his agenda. Yes, he faced a staunch opposition party—but the most successful presidents are able to overcome opponents and move their ideas and agenda forward.	The Obama administration has produced one failure after another: an expensive and intrusive health reform law, an economy that has stayed stuck in neutral for too many years, and an incoherent and weak foreign policy that has led to the rise of antidemocratic forces. History will judge him poorly.

A president riding high in the polls finds governing easier. The press corps and Washington insiders are slightly more deferential. Members of Congress watch the president's popularity in their own states and districts; when presidents are popular, members think twice about opposing them. As the president's approval sinks, criticism rises. Congressional allies back away. Press coverage turns sour. The late-night talk shows serve up mockery.

All administrations run through polling cycles; no president stays above 50 percent approval for an entire term. Average out differences across administrations and roughly the same pattern generally emerges: high approval scores at the start, usually above 60 percent; a slow decline that bottoms out midway through the second year; a gradual ascent and peak toward the end of the fourth year (see Figures 11.3 and 11.4). With luck, it rises above 50 percent in time for re-election. Each individual administration offers its own unique variations—with general economic performance especially affecting the general approval level.[12]

Dramatic events create spikes in approval (or disapproval). The two highest ratings on record boosted George H. W. Bush after a quick, dramatic victory in the first Gulf War, as well as his son George W. Bush after he responded to terrorist attacks on the World Trade Center in September 2001 by standing defiantly on the rubble with a bullhorn, surrounded by cheering firefighters

see for yourself 11.2

Go online to see President George W. Bush's dramatic bullhorn speech at Ground Zero.

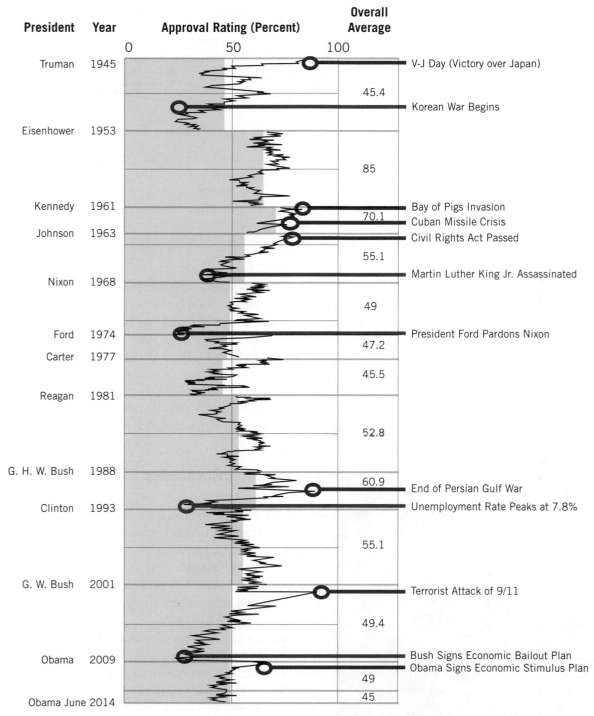

President	Year	Approval Rating (Percent)	Overall Average	
Truman	1945			V-J Day (Victory over Japan)
			45.4	
				Korean War Begins
Eisenhower	1953			
			85	
Kennedy	1961			Bay of Pigs Invasion
			70.1	Cuban Missile Crisis
Johnson	1963			Civil Rights Act Passed
			55.1	
Nixon	1968			Martin Luther King Jr. Assassinated
			49	
Ford	1974			President Ford Pardons Nixon
			47.2	
Carter	1977			
			45.5	
Reagan	1981			
			52.8	
G. H. W. Bush	1988			
			60.9	End of Persian Gulf War
Clinton	1993			Unemployment Rate Peaks at 7.8%
			55.1	
G. W. Bush	2001			Terrorist Attack of 9/11
			49.4	
Obama	2009			Bush Signs Economic Bailout Plan
				Obama Signs Economic Stimulus Plan
			49	
Obama June 2014			45	

● **FIGURE 11.3** *Presidential job approval. Every administration goes through polling cycles—rising and falling in public esteem. Note how approval ratings are affected by important events and political decisions. (Gallup)*

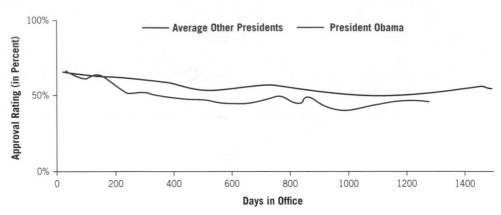

● **FIGURE 11.4** *Presidential job approval. This graph compares Obama's first 1,400-plus days in office to the average for other presidents. The line between approval and disapproval is shown across the middle of the graph. (Gallup)*

and cleanup crews. Each Bush peaked at 89 percent approval rating in Gallup polls. Such spikes in popularity are usually temporary. A year after his military triumph, George H. W. Bush's approval rating had fallen below 40 percent and he lost his re-election campaign. The younger Bush narrowly won re-election but ended his time in office tied for the lowest ratings after a full term. President Obama went from a high of 69% in his first month to 40% by the fall of 2014 according to Gallup Polls.

Polls offer immediate public feedback, but they do not reflect an administration's historical importance or long-term success. For that we can turn to a different kind of poll.

● *George W. Bush visits the scene of the 9/11 terrorist attack. The dramatic days following the attack drove President Bush's approval ratings to one of the highest levels ever recorded by Gallup.*

Presidential Greatness

Back in 1948, historian Arthur Schlesinger Sr. asked a panel of historians to rank the presidents. Their choice for the top three: Abraham Lincoln, George Washington, and Franklin D. Roosevelt.

Poll followed presidential poll—we list five different versions in Table 11.3. In each, a different panel of historians and political scientists ranks the presidents in order from great to failed.

Liberals and conservatives rarely disagree about how the presidents rank. Ronald Reagan is an exception, although his ratings from left-leaning scholars have climbed in recent polls. Such agreement returns us to the question: What makes a great president?

There are plenty of answers. President Harry Truman said that all the great presidents were especially decisive. Political scientists Marc Landy and Sidney Milkis suggest that great presidents redefine

TABLE 11.3 Rating the Presidents

Here are the results of five independent polls by historians and political scientists (you can find dozens of them). Historian Arthur Schlesinger polled historians in 1948; his son, Arthur Schlesinger Jr., repeated the exercise with historians and political scientists in 1996; the *Wall Street Journal* did a "balanced poll" of both liberals and conservatives—note that liberals and conservatives do not disagree very much on the presidential rankings; Sienna College polled 750 professors in 2010; and Nate Silver applied his statistical wizardry to the rankings question in 2013.

	SCHLESINGER (1948)	SCHLESINGER JR. (1996)	*WSJ* (2005)	SIENNA (2010)	SILVER (2013)
George Washington	2	2	1	4	3
John Adams	9	11	13	17	16
Thomas Jefferson	5	4	4	5	5
James Madison	14	17	17	6	15
James Monroe	12	15	18	7	14
John Q. Adams	11	18	25	19	20
Andrew Jackson	6	5	10	14	13
Martin Van Buren	15	21	27	23	31
William H. Harrison	—	—	—	35	40
John Tyler	22	32	35	37	36
James K. Polk	10	9	9	12	11
Zachary Taylor	25	29	35	33	33
Millard Fillmore	24	31	36	38	37
Franklin Pierce	27	33	38	40	42
James Buchanan	26	38	40	42	43
Abraham Lincoln	1	1	2	3	1
Andrew Johnson	19	37	37	43	39
Ulysses Grant	28	24	29	26	23
Rutherford Hayes	13	23	24	31	32
James Garfield	—	—	—	27	30
Chester Arthur	17	26	26	25	28
Grover Cleveland	8	13	12	20	21
Benjamin Harrison	21	19	30	34	34

(Continued)

TABLE 11.3 Rating the Presidents (*Continued*)

	SCHLESINGER (1948)	SCHLESINGER JR. (1996)	*WSJ* (2005)	SIENNA (2010)	SILVER (2013)
William McKinley	18	16	14	21	19
Theodore Roosevelt	7	6	5	2	4
William H. Taft	16	22	20	24	25
Woodrow Wilson	4	7	11	8	7
Warren Harding	29	39	39	41	41
Calvin Coolidge	23	30	23	29	27
Herbert Hoover	20	35	31	36	35
Franklin D. Roosevelt	3	3	3	1	2
Harry Truman	—	8	7	9	6
Dwight D. Eisenhower	—	10	8	10	8
John F. Kennedy	—	12	15	11	9
Lyndon B. Johnson	—	14	18	16	12
Richard Nixon	—	36	32	30	29
Gerald Ford	—	28	28	28	24
Jimmy Carter	—	27	34	32	26
Ronald Reagan	—	25	6	18	10
George H. W. Bush	—	24	21	22	22
Bill Clinton	—	20	22	13	18
George W. Bush	—	—	—	39	38
Barack Obama	—	—	—	—	17

the presidency. Our view is that great presidents redefine America; they reshape the way the nation sees itself.[13] Or, to put it slightly differently, *great presidents tell us who we are*. Their definitions of America resonate with the public and endure over time.

Greatness in Context: The Rise and Fall of Political Orders

Presidents are by no means masters of their destiny. The times make the presidents as much as they make the times. Individual presidents fit into national cycles of politics and power. Presidential scholar Stephen Skowronek describes each presidency as part of a great historical pageant: the rise and fall of **political orders**. A political order is a set of ideas, institutions, and coalitions that dominate an era.[14] On Skowronek's telling, orders rise and fall in three steps. Every president fits somewhere in the cycle.

Step 1: A New Order Rises.   Outstanding leaders take over the presidency and shake up the political system. An Abraham Lincoln, Franklin D. Roosevelt, or Ronald Reagan introduces a fresh philosophy of government. He leads a political party with new allies and new ideas into power. The public responds enthusiastically to this bold break with old political ways.

Step 2: The Order Refreshed.   Every governing coalition eventually grows tired. The great president who boldly articulated its themes is gone. Many of the original goals are won. New problems arise that have nothing to do with the philosophy that fired up the party in the first place. The ideas begin to look out of date; the great coalition begins to unravel. In fortunate times, a new leader will come along and infuse the party with a fresh variation of the old philosophy, renewing the aging order.

Step 3: The Old Order Crumbles.   No order lasts forever. Over time, the party finds its ideas increasingly irrelevant. The old order feels outdated, a political dinosaur.

Every president comes to Washington with fresh hope and promise. Political historians look back and see that they operate within a cycle. Some (Lincoln, Roosevelt, Reagan) take office as the head of a new coalition with fresh ideas. Others come to Washington at the end of an era (Herbert Hoover, Jimmy Carter). They face a far more difficult governing challenge. To some extent, the rankings we saw above reflect each president's place in political time.

THE BOTTOM LINE

- Presidents try to manage public perceptions of the job they are doing. They get immediate feedback from polling. A president's place in history, however, usually does not emerge right away.

- Great presidents change the way Americans see themselves. They change what government does. They forge a new answer to the question, *Who are we?*

- Individual presidents don't completely control their own destiny. They operate in the historical cycle of political orders.

● The President's Team: A Tour of the White House

When Herbert Hoover moved into the Oval Office in 1929, he presided over a presidential staff of four administrative assistants plus thirty-six typists, clerks, and messengers. That was it. No speechwriter, no press secretary, no congressional liaison; no chief of staff, no drug czar, no budget director. Today, the presidency is more than a person or an idea or a party. It is a bureaucracy staffed by thousands of people.

The Political Solar System: Presidential Appointments

Every time a new president is elected, thousands of people hope for a job. College professors who've always dreamed of government service, college students who worked on the campaign, business executives looking for a plum on their résumé, and supporters who believe the president-elect will make America a better place: all want to work for the new administration.

To get a job in a presidential administration, do not start by being modest. You must campaign: One executive angling to be a senior Treasury Department official a few years back tasked four subordinates to do nothing but promote his name to the administration's transition team in charge of selecting top appointees (yes, he got the job).

This section highlights those officials working directly for the president. A crucial opening point: Power is always measured by proximity to the president. The executive branch is like the solar system, with the president as the sun and everyone else rotating around him. A trump card in any Washington, D.C., conversation is "When I was talking to the president . . . " Most people who work for the president are in an orbit somewhere past Pluto: They never get any face time. Let us look at some who do.

The Vice President

Traditionally, the vice president's primary job was to stand in the wings in case the president died. That awful transition has happened eight times in American history, four times by murder. Almost one in five presidents came to office after the death of his predecessor. There were at least four more close calls: Assassins fired point-blank at Andrew Jackson (the gun jammed), Franklin D. Roosevelt (the shooter missed the president and killed the mayor of Chicago), Gerald Ford (a bystander grabbed the gunwoman's arm, diverting the shot), and Ronald Reagan (the bullet lodged less than an inch from his heart).

In addition to standing by in case of catastrophe, vice presidents preside over the Senate and cast a vote in case of a tie. There is not much power in presiding; it is more like being a parliamentarian than a majority leader, and the vice president only appears in the Senate chambers on special occasions.

Otherwise, a vice president's responsibilities are entirely up to the president. For a long time, the role was meager. Senator Daniel Webster rejected the vice-presidential nomination in 1848 with an acid comment: "I do not choose to be buried until I am really dead." Bad move: Webster would have become the thirteenth president when Zachary Taylor died in the White House. Franklin D. Roosevelt's first vice president, John Nance Garner, offered the most famous assessment of the post when he said the job was "not worth a pitcher of warm piss."

The weak vice presidency continued well into the twentieth century. Harry Truman had barely met with President Roosevelt when FDR's death in 1945 catapulted him into the Oval Office. "Boys," he said when he met the press the next day, "if you ever pray, pray for me now." In 1960, reporters asked President Eisenhower what ideas Vice President Nixon, who was running to succeed him, had contributed. "If you give me a week," quipped the president nastily, "I might think of one."

The vice presidency became an important office during the Carter administration (1977–1981). From Carter through Obama, five of the past seven presidents were Washington outsiders who had never held a federal job; every newcomer chose a longtime federal government insider as his vice president, relying on him as advisor, confidant, and envoy. Slowly but surely, vice presidents gathered the emblems of power: a seat at cabinet meetings (1950s), an office in the White House (1970s), a vice-presidential jet (Air Force 2, in the 1970s), a growing staff, and—perhaps most important in status-obsessed Washington— regular meetings with the president.

In recent years, vice presidents are put in charge of major administration efforts: Dick Cheney's office effectively managed the war on terror for President Bush, and Joe Biden has been a major voice on foreign policy for Barack Obama.

● Joe Biden: a garrulous, upbeat, blue-collar Democrat spent 36 years in the Senate representing Delaware before becoming vice president. At first he was a crucial link between the White House and the Republicans in the Senate. Like many recent vice presidents, his influence waned in the administration's final years.

Even with these changes, vice presidents' power and influence still depend on the president.

The Cabinet

Members of the cabinet have two primary roles: They run executive-branch departments, and they meet to discuss policy with the president in cabinet meetings. Once the cabinet served as a president's governing team. As we saw earlier, Washington's initial cabinet had four members. By Abraham Lincoln's time, there were seven. Today the cabinet has grown to fifteen members; add the vice president and other important officers on the president's staff, and meetings are too large to serve as a real decision-making body.

We discuss the cabinet, and the hundreds of thousands of federal bureaucrats who work under cabinet secretaries in the executive agencies, in the next chapter. Today, cabinet meetings have become largely ceremonial occasions.

In most administrations, a handful of cabinet officers rise above the rest and shape administration policy. Political scientists call them the "inner cabinet": the secretaries of State, Defense, Treasury, and Justice—precisely the quartet in Washington's original cabinet. Most other cabinet secretaries operate far from the centers of power. Departments like Transportation and Energy have vital roles to play. But, unless they have personal connections or unusual responsibilities, they are rarely part of a president's inner circle.

Cabinet secretaries often come to see issues from the perspective of their own bureaucracy rather than the administration or the party. After all, they are surrounded by tens of thousands of employees who do a lot of work with limited resources and look to the secretary to champion their causes. Richard Nixon's close adviser John Ehrlichman groused that the administration chose

● President Obama runs a cabinet meeting. As you can see, today's cabinet has become too large to make important decisions.

solid, budget-cutting conservatives to run the cabinet departments—and then watched their appointees run off and "marry the natives." They abandoned the administration's priorities, complained Ehrlichman, and began to think like their subordinates about the importance of their agency's work.

Presidents must manage the tension between senior cabinet officials and the circle of presidential advisors in the White House. At one cabinet meeting during the Carter years, the secretary of Housing and Urban Development summed up her frustration by blurting out: "We can move government forward by putting phones in the White House staff offices and then using them." Translation: No one in the White House even returns my phone calls. The president's inner circle (and the power of proximity) had shifted from the cabinet to the White House staff.[15]

The tension grows intense when a Cabinet agency gets involved in a media storm. Kathleen Sebelius, the Secretary of Health and Human Services (2009–2014), was widely blamed for the botched roll-out of the Affordable Care Act—the website crashed, making it impossible to shop for health insurance. To make matters worse, the secretary went on the *Daily Show* to explain and got roasted. "If you're a Democrat and you've lost Jon Stewart," commented one critic after the secretary's deer in the headlights performance, "you have a problem." Secretary Sebelius soon resigned.[16]

The Executive Office of the President

In modern times, influence over the president has leaked steadily into the **Executive Office of the President** (EOP), made up of agencies that help a president manage his daily activities. These administrators and advisors surround the chief executive. President Franklin D. Roosevelt organized the EOP in 1939; it now has about 1,800 employees. Many are experts who stay on from one administration to the next. Presidents who have been most adamant about expanding the EOP are conservatives frustrated that the cabinet agencies did not pursue their values. Richard Nixon created or revamped four of the EOP offices, and Ronald Reagan added three more. Today every president—left, right, or center—relies on them.

In the EOP, a familiar clash gets especially intense. On one hand, most EOP employees are experts on specific issues—drug policy, health care, or the budget. On the other, they have to serve each president's political philosophy (not to mention re-election prospects). Slowly the balance between these goals has tipped toward politics.[17] Let's visit the most important offices in the EOP.

The Office of Management and Budget (OMB).   This is the most powerful agency in the executive branch—known (not very fondly) as "the agency that says no." The OMB uses its authority over the federal budget to manage the entire executive branch. During the Reagan administration, the agency acquired its most powerful weapon—**central clearance**: the power to review and "clear" (or OK) anything a member of the administration says or does in public. All members, from the secretary of defense to an analyst in the Small Business Bureau, must

Executive Office of the President (EOP): The agencies that help the president manage daily activities.

Central clearance: The OMB's authority to review and "clear" (or okay) anything a member of the administration says or does in public.

submit every speech they make, opinion piece they write, congressional testimony they deliver, and policy they propose to OMB for its approval. Until they get OMB's nod, they may not say or publish a word.

The OMB vets every administration proposal. When Congress passes a bill, OMB coordinates various White House officials' recommendations about signing or vetoing the legislation. Officials at the OMB often get the last word as well. Imagine how frustrating it is for energetic new secretaries to take over their departments, only to learn they must clear all their formal statements and policy proposals with the budget office.

Notice a slow change in our political process over the past thirty years or so: *the economic perspective rules*. While the long-standing tension between experts (crunching numbers) and political appointees (pushing the president's agenda and big ideas) continues, the entire system tilts toward and empowers the economic perspective.

Before the Nixon administration organized the OMB (in 1971), fiscal control was much looser. President Lyndon Johnson famously low-balled his economic estimates. One day, instructing a young senator from Massachusetts named Ted Kennedy, Johnson warned him not to let economic projections slow up his favorite bills and illustrated the point with Medicare. "The fools [at the Bureau of the Budget] had to go projecting [Medicare] down the road five or six years, and when you project it the first year it runs $900 million."[18] Those anticipated costs, complained LBJ, cost him votes in Congress; he advised the new senator to stop economists from interfering with important proposals. Today, OMB requires cost–benefit analyses for all White House policy moves. The era of simply suppressing cost estimates is long past. Still, the future is never certain and every savvy political operator knows plenty of ways to massage the numbers.

The Council of Economic Advisers.   Meet another clutch of economists. The council and its chair keep an eye on the whole economy, private as well as public. This office does economic analysis for the president: unemployment predictions, productivity measurements, economic forecasts, and all the rest.

The National Security Council (NSC).   The NSC brings together the powerful officers who make national security policy: secretaries of state, defense, intelligence, and treasury (economists again); the chair of the Joint Chiefs of Staff; and others that the president selects. The national security advisor directs the council and must work for consensus across all the different perspectives and formidable personalities: diplomatic, military, and economic. In some administrations, the national security advisor is as influential as the secretaries of state or defense. Empowering the NSC has tightened White House control over foreign policy.

The Offices in the Executive Office of the President.   Table 11.4 illustrates the offices in the Executive Office of the President. The list reflects the hats and

TABLE 11.4 Offices in the Executive Office of the President

OFFICE	EMPLOYEES	YEAR ORGANIZED	ORGANIZED BY
White House Office	406	1939	F. D. Roosevelt
Office of the Vice President	24	1972	Nixon
Office of Management and Budget	521	1921/1971	Harding/Nixon
Office of Administration	212	1977	Carter
Council of Economic Advisers	28	1946	Truman
Council on Environmental Quality	22	1969	Nixon
Domestic Policy Council	25	1985	Reagan
Executive Residence	95 (full-time)	—	—
National Security Staff	54	1947	Truman
Office of National Drug Control Policy	102	1988	Reagan
Office of Science and Technology Policy	28	1976	Ford
Office of the U.S. Trade Representative	212	1963	Kennedy
Homeland Security Council	16	2001	G. W. Bush

helmets that the president wears. Organizing a new EOP office is one way for administrations to signal the things they consider most important. Nixon added the Council on Environmental Quality and George W. Bush an office for his Faith-Based Initiatives. Obama's latest contribution, housed in the White House Office: an Office of Digital Strategy.

The Heart of Power: The White House Office

Our tour ends at the heart of power. The White House Office is part of the Executive Office of the President, but it also stands apart. This group of four hundred or so advisors, aides, and associates work directly for the president, most of them in the West Wing. At the center sits the **Chief of Staff**, the president's gatekeeper, traffic cop, and coordinator. Other important offices include speechwriters, White House counsel (the president's official lawyer), and the legislative affairs team.

Chief of Staff: The individual responsible for managing the president's office.

Until President Obama, the two parties organized their White House Offices very differently from one another. Franklin D. Roosevelt set a mixed example for future Democrats: creative chaos. Roosevelt surrounded himself with gifted intellectuals, gave them overlapping tasks, and let them freelance from issue to issue. In theory, bold ideas would flow from an office full of talented, loosely organized thinkers. Many Democratic administrations tried to mimic Roosevelt. John Kennedy valued broad-minded intellectuals and encouraged

SPEAK LIKE A WEST WING INSIDER

Want to learn to talk like a member of the White House staff? Start practicing now. Casually toss off something like: "I'm given to understand that WHO is the real force in the EOP." Those are two indecipherable acronyms (the more the better) and, of course, the passive voice: You don't want to risk revealing your sources!

them to weigh in on any subject. So did Bill Clinton; early in his administration, staffers would jump in and out of meetings and conversations regardless of their assigned tasks. The bull sessions went on deep into the night.

In contrast, Republicans like clearly defining organization and tasks. You'll find no vague or dotted lines on their personnel tables. The Republicans usually model their organization on the military or traditional business: Crisp lines of authority go from the president to the Chief of Staff. Everyone has a clearly defined role.

Democrats often dismiss their rivals' style as unimaginative, stifling, and conformist. Republicans answer that good organization avoids confusion and error and that the Democrats are disorganized and undisciplined. Each style has advantages and drawbacks.

In either style, the Chief of Staff makes the White House run. He or she directs traffic through the president's office, oversees the schedule, sums up the decisions that are made, and follows up to see that those decisions are understood and implemented. The office requires a strong, talented, smooth, competent administrator familiar with the levers of power. Occasionally, a president will try to act as his own Chief of Staff (Jimmy Carter) or bring in a political neophyte (Bill Clinton); when that happens, chaos generally follows. The other extreme is equally dangerous. If the Chief of Staff seems arrogant, aloof, or rude, the White House loses support and cooperation.

The White House staff is like a little village, full of odd folkways and habits that reflect the way the president wishes to run the country. For example, Ronald Reagan put special emphasis on his speechwriting team; they spent hours watching his past speeches to learn his rhythms and his way of thinking. The president reworked their draft speeches with great care. Reagan's successor, George H. W. Bush, thought the president should speak more plainly and rejected all the attention on crafting speeches. He demonstrated the new order by stripping the speechwriting team of its White House Mess (dining hall) privileges. The village recognized a major demotion.

When a new president comes to town, attention focuses on his cabinet selections. The wise observer knows to track more subtle appointments to the White House Office. After all, no matter how brilliant the secretary of labor or how experienced the secretary of HHS, they will have to rely on unseen advisors in the White House to convey their ideas, programs, and problems to the president.

Officials located farther from the West Wing—like cabinet secretaries, in their giant departments scattered around Washington—can seem desperate in seeking presidential attention. Cabinet meetings can be a circus, with every member anxious to get a minute alone with the president. But busy presidents are deft at vanishing. The route to influence—the path to "yes" on any program—runs through the White House Office staff.

Unlike the high-ranking members of the cabinet agencies, most EOP staffers are not subject to Senate confirmation. They are elected by no one, overseen only by the Chief of Staff, and often have regular access to the president's ear.

TOO MANY PRESIDENTIAL AIDES?

The Executive Office of the President (EOP) now houses more than 1,800 staff members, from economic and foreign policy advisers to communications specialists and "chiefs of protocol," who organize White House state dinners and other functions. All answer directly to the president and his top aides; most do not even require Senate confirmation. By comparison, President Lincoln had four personal assistants, and when Franklin D. Roosevelt took office eighty-two years ago, he had a staff of thirty-six. Does the modern presidency require such a large staff?

Yes, absolutely.	Not sure.	No—start staff cuts immediately.
Given the office's immense range of responsibilities, presidents need reliable, trustworthy experts and assistants to analyze intelligence and economic data, to assess overseas threats, and to help manage public perceptions of the president. In fact, it's surprising there isn't more support (Congress, after all, has more than 20,000 staffers).	The huge array of presidential staff reportedly work incredibly hard, and the White House certainly has a plateful of duties. But if past presidents got by with far fewer staff, perhaps we've gone too far and could reduce this EOP army?	Modern technology could make the presidency far more efficient. If CEOs can run major companies with far fewer staff reporting to their office, and other sectors— like the military—are able to function with far fewer personnel, so could the White House.

Should the president's advisors, rather than the experienced cabinet secretaries confirmed by the Senate, run the executive branch? Again, we confront the fundamental question: power and control versus democracy and enhanced accountability. Perhaps the twenty-four-hour media cycle forces presidents to keep power and expertise right at their fingertips. Perhaps granting authority to White House staff makes the whole federal leviathan more responsive to the will of the people. Most democracies are, ultimately, ruled by experts. American government is run in part by men and women with a sharp eye on winning the next election.

One final feature of the White House staff strikes most newcomers: Its members are young—much younger than the staff running other governments, large corporations, universities, or major nonprofit organizations. Cabinet secretaries with years of experience often complain that their access to the president is governed by young people in their twenties and thirties.

The First Spouse

One team in the White House Office does not fit any traditional political category: the office of the president's spouse. Traditionally, the "First Lady" role was simply that of hostess. Eleanor Roosevelt broke the traditional mold and

"For gosh sakes, here comes Mrs. Roosevelt!"

pioneered a new role, the First Lady as activist. Eleanor was a powerful liberal activist, a popular symbol of the New Deal, and a forceful advocate for Franklin and his policies. In effect, she became a one-woman campaign for liberal social policy. A *New Yorker* cartoon captures the First Lady's spirit of tirelessly campaigning for social and labor reform. Deep underground, two sooty coal miners stop their labors as one remarks with surprise: "For gosh sakes, here comes Mrs. Roosevelt!"

Few First Ladies were as active or committed as Eleanor Roosevelt, but she set a pattern of policy engagement that her successors have followed. Lady Bird Johnson chose "beautification" of American cities and highways. Nancy Reagan became a spokesperson for the war on drugs. Mrs. Reagan was the first to achieve that mark of status, an office in the West Wing. Bill Clinton assigned his wife, Hillary, the signature policy initiative of his presidency, national health care reform. In fall 1993, Hillary Clinton's virtuoso performance in a series of congressional hearings appeared to signal success for national health insurance. The legislation failed, but Mrs. Clinton went on to her own successful political career—and established a new ceiling for First Ladies' contribution to presidential action.

By the time Michelle Obama came to the office, expectations were high. Here was a charismatic First Lady with a Harvard law degree and a successful career independent of her husband. With some fanfare, Mrs. Obama focused on childhood obesity, a prominent policy issue. She is honorary chair of President Obama's signature White House Council for Community Solutions, and she plays a very visible role as "First Mother"—an emblem of the American family. Political scientists—especially those interested in gender and power—have begun to pay particular attention to the role of the First Spouse.

THE BOTTOM LINE

- Each president directs a massive organization—the executive branch of the federal government.

- Cabinet secretaries manage the great bureaucracies of the executive branch of government but only a few have influence in the White House.

- Over time, executive-branch policy making has migrated from the cabinet to the Executive Office of the Presidency—the network of offices that help the president manage the government.

- The president's innermost circle is the White House Office. These close advisors—often relatively young—include the Chief of Staff, speechwriters, legislative liaison, and the office of the First Lady.

● Conclusion: The Most Powerful Office on Earth?

President Obama took office with soaring hopes. He was a symbol of American aspiration: After centuries of racial struggle, the United States had elected an African American leader. Like all presidents, Obama put a new set of ideas, proposals, and priorities before the American people.

Obama traveled around the world—London, Ankara, Port of Spain, Moscow, Accra, Cairo—drawing a sharp line with his predecessor. "We must embrace a new era of engagement based on . . . mutual respect," Obama told the United Nations.[19] The United States would no longer act unilaterally, without regard for other nations' views. Ten months after his inauguration he was awarded the Nobel Peace Prize—a sign of how world leaders cheered a pivot away from the go-it-alone American attitude.

The new president shifted America's policy making. The issues he cared about became those in the news and before Congress: health care reform, college loans, education, and clean air. Obama removed American troops from Iraq and expanded the number in Afghanistan, while setting a definite withdrawal date—all controversial actions. The Oval Office reverberates with power and responsibility.

From another angle, it is full of limitations, checks, and balances. The economy remained weak—and sapped President Obama's popularity. Congress rejected some of his signature reforms. It blocked him from closing the military prison at Guantánamo. He won health care reform—an extraordinary

see for yourself 11.3

Go online to see Obama's 2009 address to the United Nations.

● *Senior officials watch with President Obama and Vice President Biden as the Navy SEALs raid Osama bin Laden's compound.*

achievement—but five years later had still not persuaded the public of its merits, to the great advantage of the Republicans who had been united against it. In 2010, Obama's Democratic Party lost its House majority in the party's largest midterm defeat in a century. The most powerful office on earth was hemmed in by checks and balances.

The Obama record raises, once again, the fundamental question about the presidency. It is a far more powerful office than it was a century ago. Has it grown too powerful for a republic? Or, on the other side, is it too hobbled to carry out the mandate of the public? Or, perhaps it is most accurate to say that the same president can be too powerful or too weak, depending on the issue, the circumstances, and the incumbent.

Now President Obama has just two years remaining in his presidency, and after the 2014 midterm elections he faces Republican control of both chambers in Congress. Into its final years in office, the Obama Administration raises the perennial question: Is the president too powerful? Or not powerful enough?

Who are we? The president offers us an answer—actually, several different answers. Americans seek a powerful, confident figure at the government's center. At the same time, we fear strong executives and hem them in through a labyrinth of checks and balances. We want our collective democratic voice ringing in the ears of our national leaders—but also want our security protected in ways that may require secrecy and fast, decisive choices. We are a people that demands small government—yet complains when every need isn't speedily met by the executive branch. We are a complicated, diverse, paradoxical people—like the presidency that reflects and serves us.

CHAPTER SUMMARY

● *The president personifies America.* More than any individual, the president tells us who we are—and what we are becoming.

● *The president injects new ideas into American politics.* Our discussion of Congress emphasized the institution, the rules of the game; the presidency puts more focus on individuals and ideas.

● The president has three kinds of powers: those expressed in the Constitution, those delegated by Congress, and those inherent in the role of chief executive.

● The executive branch has grown far more powerful over time, especially when it comes to foreign policy.

● The office of the president constantly raises the same fundamental question: *Is the president too powerful for a democratic republic? Or, on the other hand, is the office too weak to do what Americans demand of it?* Or, perhaps, the president is both too strong and too weak at the same time.

● The president wears many hats and helmets. The presidential roles include commander in chief, top diplomat, first legislator, head bureaucrat, economist in chief, head of state, and party leader. The president's authority has grown in every one of these many roles. At the same time, it is difficult to do so many different things effectively.

● Presidents try to manage public perceptions of the job they are doing by going public and getting feedback from polls.

● Over time, executive-branch policy has flowed from the cabinet secretaries to the Executive Office of the Presidency—the network of offices that help the president manage the government.

● The president's innermost circle is the White House Office. These close advisors—often relatively young—include the Chief of Staff, speechwriters, legislative liaison, and the office of the First Lady.

KEY TERMS

Central clearance, 389

Chief of Staff, 391

Civil servants, 374

Delegated powers, 363

Executive Office of the President
(EOP), 389

Executive order, 374

Expressed powers, 363

Going public, 378

Imperial presidency, 365

Inherent powers of the
presidency, 363

Override, 371

Political appointees, 374

Signing statements, 373

Veto power, 371

STUDY QUESTIONS

1. Some people have suggested changing the president's term to one seven-year term without the possibility of re-election. What do you think? How would that shift the incentives that currently face a first-term president?

2. Why is the Constitution so much more vague about presidential than congressional powers? What problems—and benefits—does that ambiguity create?

3. What do you think: Is the president too strong? Or too weak? Defend your opinion.

4. Name seven different roles the president plays. Which do you consider the most important right now? How well do you think the president is carrying out this role today?

5. How well do you think President Obama "goes public"—appealing to the American public to support his policies? Do *you* respond positively to his speeches and legislative requests?

6. Should presidents care about their approval ratings from the American public? Why or why not?

7. Explain the role of the OMB. What does this agency do? What perspective was it designed to bring to the policy debates?

8. Describe the role of a First Lady. Despite getting involved in policies, First Ladies are often more popular than the presidents. Why do you think that is so?

Bureaucracy

IN *THE PERFECT STORM*, actor George Clooney plays a real-life fishing boat captain who ignores U.S. Weather Service warnings and heads his boat into impossibly high seas—and death for all the men aboard. Another captain, Linda Greenlaw, obeys the alert, steams for shore, and saves her crew. Five years later, Clooney wrote, directed, and starred in *Good Night, and Good Luck*, which tells the story of Senator Joseph McCarthy's search for communists allegedly working in the U.S. State Department. A counsel for the U.S. Army, Joseph Welch, along with CBS anchor Edward R. Murrow, helped expose McCarthy's witch hunt. And, in the 2014 feature *The Monuments Men*, Clooney plays the head of a special American task force dedicated to recovering works of art stolen by the Nazis during World War II. Each of these George Clooney films highlights the work of government bureaucrats.

The National Ocean and Atmospheric Administration (NOAA)—part of the Department of Commerce—issued those weather bulletins in *The Perfect Storm*. With a budget of about $5.5 billion, NOAA provides detailed weather predictions across the globe. The U.S. Coast Guard—part of the Department of Homeland Security—performed a daring rescue of a family aboard a sailboat that had strayed into the same storm. Senator McCarthy caused an uproar in the State Department—today, an agency with nineteen thousand employees staffing 305 embassies and consulates around the world. He was eventually humiliated on national television by a lawyer working for the largest bureaucracy in America, the U.S. Army. Although the "monuments men" receive a dose of Hollywood glamour, the intelligence they rely on to track and recover priceless cultural treasures originated in the Departments of State, Treasury, Justice, and Defense (which today has twelve separate intelligence agencies spread across the four military branches) as well as the Central Intelligence Agency (CIA) and the Federal Bureau of Investigation (FBI).

One of Hollywood's leading men regularly celebrates the good works of government bureaucracy. Surprising? Of course it is. Most Americans hold a very low opinion of the federal government. In some polls, only 19 percent of the public "trust the government to do what is right always or most of the time," according to

IN THIS CHAPTER, YOU WILL:

● Learn how the bureaucracy developed, how it is meant to work—and why programs and processes sometimes fail.

● See how federal agencies do their job.

● Examine the different kinds of agencies that comprise the public service.

● Consider who—if anyone—controls the bureaucracy.

● Review possible reforms.

● *George Clooney, as seen in the film* The Monuments Men. *Clooney seems to like making movies with connections to government bureaucracy.*

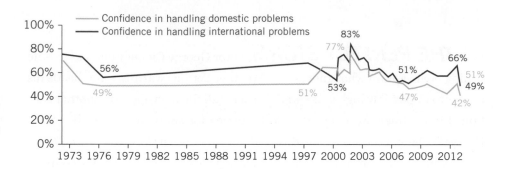

● **FIGURE 12.1** *How much of the time do you think you can trust government in Washington to do what is right? Notice how trust peaked after the 9/11 attacks. Today more than half of Americans take a negative view. (Gallup)*

Gallup polls.[1] Politicians often campaign for office against the faceless bureaucracy in Washington, now at "the point where it feels it is infallible, omnipotent, and can impose its will at its discretion," as a Michigan candidate for the U.S. House said in 2014.[2] Republican candidates promise to cut whole agencies—although they rarely do so when they win office; Democrats join right in and promise to shrink government programs "that do not work"—as President Obama put it in his first inaugural address. And, if you look, it is not hard to find examples of hapless bureaucracies doing foolish things.

This chapter tells a different story about the federal bureaucracy—one that you might not expect. Bureaucrats, despite their terrible reputation, perform valuable, even life-saving services. The bureaucracy is what makes government run.

The criticism of generic bureaucrats generally melts away when pollsters ask about specific agencies. For example, 75 percent of the public give high marks to the Centers for Disease Control, and nearly as many (73 percent) approve of the space-explorer team at NASA.[3] The bureaucrats look a lot better when we focus on what they actually do.

Who are we? In many ways, the government bureaucracy is us. U.S. national departments and agencies employ 2.7 million civilians (and more than 4 million men and women if you include active duty military). State and local governments employ 19 million more Americans. These numbers add up to more than 23 million people on government payrolls. Moreover, the federal bureaucracy is the part of American government that most resembles the population it serves. Congress is overwhelmingly white, male, and middle aged (Chapter 10); the White House staff is mostly white and young (Chapter 11). But the 2.7 million people who make up the U.S. civilian bureaucracy are as diverse as the nation (see Figure 12.2).

Does its diversity make the bureaucracy more democratic? Not necessarily. One of the great management challenges posed by every national bureaucracy is

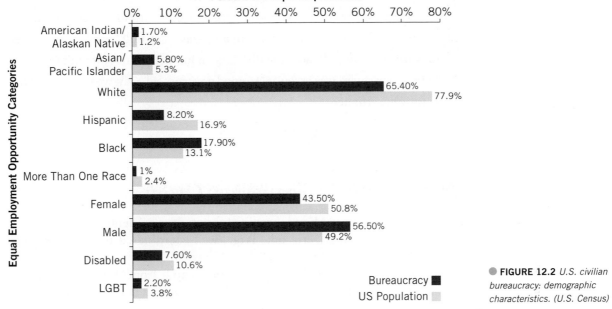

Percent of People Represented

FIGURE 12.2 *U.S. civilian bureaucracy: demographic characteristics. (U.S. Census)*

BY THE NUMBERS

The Bureaucracy

- Number of cabinet departments, U.S. executive branch, 2014: **15**
- Number of agencies/independent commissions, 2014: **493**
- Number of agencies during the George Washington administration (1789): **4**
- Number of agencies during the Theodore Roosevelt administration (1905): **7**
- Number of ministries (like cabinet departments), Japanese government, 2001: **20**
- Number since 2002, following extensive Japanese government restructuring: **12**
- Total federal bureaucracy workforce: **4.4 million**
- Percentage of that total who work for the military: **41**
- "Hidden workforce" of federal contractors and grantees: **as many as 8 million**
- Number of women, in U.S. history, who have headed cabinet-level departments: **29**
- Number of those named since 1975: **26**
- Total cabinet secretary positions filled since the end of World War II (1945): **255**
- Miles of hallways in the largest U.S. federal building, the Pentagon: **17.5**
- Average salary of a civil servant, 2014: **$79,314**
- Maximum annual salary earned by a civil servant (GS-15, top of scale), 2014: **$130,810**
- Number of GS categories, which specify earnings ranges within each category: **15**
- Average number of layers of upper management in large U.S. cabinet departments: **64**

how to synchronize it with the people's will. The same question we raised in the last chapter—does presidential power threaten popular rule?—returns in this chapter in a slightly different form: Can a bureaucracy of 2.7 million unelected federal workers govern democratically? It is an important and difficult question. The federal bureaucracy is essential to good government. Can we make it fit with democratic governance?

How the Bureaucracy Grew

Predicting storms near Miami, keeping tabs on developments in Ukraine, and tracking terrorists in Nigeria take large, well-coordinated bureaucracies—as NOAA, the State Department, and the CIA are intended to be. In this section, we will look at where the U.S. bureaucracy came from, how bureaucracies should be organized, and some of the problems that can make them fall short.

Before the Bureaucracy

Spoils system: Government jobs given out as political favors.

Universalistic politics: Government by universal rules, impartially applied.

In the nineteenth century, U.S. government jobs were political prizes. Men got their posts—as officers in the army, postmasters in rural towns, or tax collectors in the ports—because they helped politicians win elections. When George Washington Plunkitt, a colorful New York politician, decided to enter politics, he went to the local boss with what he called a marketable commodity: votes. He got his start in politics by delivering the votes of all his friends and neighbors.[4]

As you can imagine, this system was inefficient, unfair, and corrupt. Senator William Marcy, another New Yorker, gave the system its name when he declared, "To the victor belong the spoils." After he made his comment, giving jobs to political friends became known as the **spoils system**.

Reformers fought for years to break this corruption. Jobs, they believed, should be distributed on the basis of merit, not political connections. These good-government advocates championed what we now call **universalistic politics:** a government of impartial rules that apply equally to everyone. That ideal was the basis for bureaucratic government in the United States.

A great political battle erupted between reformers and defenders of the spoils

● *James Garfield is assassinated in the Baltimore train station by a frustrated job seeker. Although it was the act of a madman, reformers blamed the spoils system and used the tragedy to introduce the civil service.*

system. In 1883, a crazed office seeker assassinated President James Garfield. Suddenly, the reformers had a martyr for their cause. The spoils system, they said, had caused the president's assassination. Popular outcry pushed a reluctant Congress to pass the **Pendleton Civil Service Act**, which required the federal government to hire well-qualified individuals, who must take exams to qualify for their posts. It was the first step toward building the bureaucracy that runs the government today.

Reformers fighting for a more efficient government had a big advantage: There were jobs that needed doing. As the society and economy grew more complex, the spoils system (which too often attracted the lazy and incompetent) failed to answer the nation's needs. Five important national needs pushed the United States toward a more efficient—and more bureaucratic—government.

War. Each time the United States mobilized for war, the government grew. Matters of life and death could not depend on political hacks; each military effort spurred a new search for competent administrators and new bureaus and offices. After each war, government maintained some of the new jobs it had taken on. The number of civilian employees doubled during World War I and tripled during World War II. World War II, more than any other force in American history, created the large national bureaucracy we have today.[5]

Morality. Nineteenth-century observers often noted that the United States had an underdeveloped government. They usually added that the government was very active in regulating morality. Enforcing moral rules required the creation of increasingly sophisticated agencies. For example, the effort to outlaw

Pendleton Civil Service Act: The law that shifted American government toward a merit-based public service.

"Your Honor, this woman gave birth to a naked child!"

● *Moral reformer Anthony Comstock and his quest to stamp out any signs of smut. His effort helped build a sophisticated postal bureaucracy.*

all liquor (under Prohibition, which lasted from 1920 to 1933) created a powerful new law enforcement agency in the Department of the Treasury.[6]

Economics. Over time, the federal government took over responsibility for economic performance. This created many new government offices—commissions designed to regulate business (starting in the 1887 with efforts to manage the giant railroads), the Federal Reserve to stabilize banking (created in 1913 after a series of financial panics), and a host of new offices and agencies after the Great Depression (in the 1930s).

Geography. The United States spread rapidly across the continent. Keeping the far-flung nation together led to a more sophisticated postal service (including, briefly, the famous Pony Express); new forms of transportation; the distribution of public lands to homesteaders; and endless military actions against Native Americans.

Race. The issue of slavery and civil rights constantly engaged the federal government—leading, most dramatically, to the Civil War and the Reconstruction-era occupation of southern lands by the federal army. Likewise, shifting immigration policies, often based on ethnicity (think of the Chinese Exclusion Act of the 1880s, for example), required a huge network of federal officials who determined who would be permitted to settle in the United States.

Each of these forces—war, morality, economics, geography, and racial questions—pushed the United States toward more efficient national bureaus and agencies. The Pendleton Act of 1883 laid the cornerstone for the civil service; by 1900 (after the Spanish–American War), the United States had an emerging national bureaucracy; and by 1946 (after World War II) the country had developed the bureaucracy that governs America to this day.

The Bureaucratic Model

What is a bureaucracy supposed to look like? The German sociologist and political economist Max Weber (1864–1920) reduced it to five characteristics that, in theory, mark all modern bureaucracies—including the American civil service. Let's consider these one at a time. And, remember, this is the way the bureaucracy is *supposed* to operate—not the way it always does.[7]

Hierarchy. All bureaucracies have a clear chain of command. Each individual reports to the person above her all the way up to the president—or the queen, or the pope, or the chancellor of the university. Every individual along the chain has well-defined superiors and subordinates. Weber noted that the desire to move up the ladder makes most individuals sensitive to their superior's orders. In this way, the efforts of thousands of people can be coordinated.

Figure 12.3 shows the hierarchy of the U.S. Department of Energy, starting with the cabinet secretary and moving down through an elaborate subset of assistants, deputies, and associate administrators. This chart lists only the top

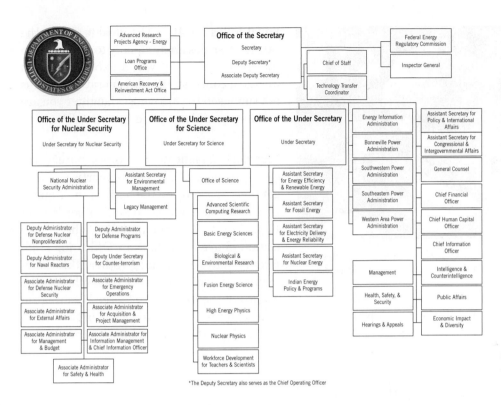

● **FIGURE 12.3** *Organizational chart for the Department of Energy. (Department of Energy)*

forty-eight positions—more than fifteen thousand men and women work in the agency (and another eighty thousand or more work under contracts with the Department of Energy). The principle of hierarchy allows leaders to coordinate the work of all their subordinates.

Division of Labor.   Bureaucracies divide complex tasks and assign each piece to an individual or a group. Members of the agencies become experts at their own specialized tasks. The hierarchy coordinates all the specialists into a smoothly working operation. For example, the division of labor permits the State Department to have specialists in each region of the globe, each language, and each country.

Fixed Routines.   Rather than making things up as they go along, bureaucrats are expected to follow well-specified codes of conduct called Standard Operating Procedures (SOPs).

Have you ever applied for food stamps or unemployment compensation? If you do, you'll face forms, details, and visits to different offices. This is bureaucratic routine in action, designed to treat everybody the same way. If you've been stopped for speeding, you'll ruefully recall the ritual that police officers follow, from requesting your license and registration to checking your plates for outstanding warrants. That's a fixed routine, too, and each step has a purpose.

● *Diego Mariaca seeks to qualify for the DREAM Act. The executive order offered legal status to some undocumented people—but required a confusing welter of bureaucratic forms.*

Equal Rules for All.   The ideal is always the same: The rules apply equally to everyone. In the spoils system, it was all about who you knew. In contrast, the bureaucratic official is not supposed to care whose daughter you are or what special story you have to tell.

Technical Qualifications.   Since bureaucracies operate on the basis of expertise, people get their jobs only on the basis of their qualifications. For example, take another look at Figure 12.3. Near the middle of the organization chart you'll find an Office for High Energy Physics (among other things, it maintains accelerators for research into the origins of the universe). George Washington Plunkitt got his job by rounding up votes for the Democratic Party of New York; in contrast, the High Energy Physics staff got their jobs thanks to their scientific expertise.

Bureaucratic Pathologies

These five characteristics look good on paper. However, the real world can work entirely differently.

Early in 2010, news reports revealed that eight-year-old Mikey Hicks, an ordinary American boy with no ties to terrorism, was stopped, searched, and interrogated every time he and his family boarded a plane. The Transportation Security Authority (TSA) explained that his name was on the agency's no-fly list (because a real suspect had a similar name). Despite his family's complaints, it took the TSA months to remove Mikey from the list. And, while the TSA agents were grilling Mikey, a *real* terrorist, Umar Farouk Abdulmutallab, boarded a Northwest Airlines flight and unsuccessfully tried to blow it up. No one asked him any questions, even though two months earlier his father, a prominent businessperson, had reported that his son was training at an Al Qaeda camp for terrorists in Yemen.

Why do these errors happen? Because every feature of the ideal bureaucracy has its potential downside. The problems that develop are known as **bureaucratic pathologies**. Familiar pathologies include the following:

Bureaucratic pathologies: The problems that tend to develop in bureaucratic systems.

- **Rote.** Rote involves slavishly following old standardized routines despite new developments. The failure to adjust (with the excuse of "I'm just doing my job") can lead to problems, even tragedies. When members of an organization get too used to following standard procedures, they avoid responsibility—and potential blame—by hiding behind their assigned routines.

- **Imperialism.** Bureaucracies compete just like private companies. They want bigger budgets and better staffs. This status seeking can lead them to grow too big and engage in turf wars.

- **Turf war.** Agencies often find that they are doing overlapping jobs. This replication leads to tensions about who is responsible for what. For example, there are at least nineteen intelligence agencies in the federal government. Agencies like the FBI and CIA that view each other as competitors may fail to share information.

- **Lack of coordination.** Even agencies that are good at doing their own jobs often have few mechanisms for cooperating with other agencies. That's because their routines are internal to the agency and don't apply to other organizations. If the agencies are imperialistic or fighting a turf war, the problem can become acute.

- **Clientelism.** Sometimes an agency develops routines (SOPs) that favor some constituents over others. For example, if the Department of Agriculture sends out complicated forms to qualify for loans, they will favor agricultural corporations (which have bookkeepers and secretaries) over small family farms where there is little time for fifty-page forms. The bias may not be explicit, but it is built into the routines. And, since the favored clients—the big farms—don't complain, the routine continues.

● *A threat to national security? Mikey Hicks was subjected to intense questioning every time he flew—thanks to a glitch in the no-fly list. Bureaucratic pathologies—such as an inability to break routines—are an exaggerated form of exactly what make bureaucracies effective. Call it too much of a good thing.*

What was the problem for Mikey? Primarily, the problem of rote. Once his name was on the watch list, the agency kept running through its routine and questioning him. Because the agency would be in serious trouble if it removed a real terrorist, the routine for removing names is slower, with more checkpoints and approvals, than the routine for adding a name. Why did the real terrorist slip through? Here, the problem lay in different security agencies that competed over turf and failed to coordinate. Umar Farouk Abdulmutallab's father contacted one agency, which failed to pass the information to another.

In popular culture, the story of bureaucratic pathology often completely eclipses every other aspect of the subject. This is a mistake. We could not run the military, deliver the mail, operate an airport, process Social Security checks, or predict the weather without bureaucratic agencies. The key question for all governments—for all organizations, including your college or university—is this: How do we produce the benefits of bureaucracy while minimizing the pathologies?

The Democratic Dilemma

Bureaucracies have an inherently difficult fit with democracy. Democracy works from the bottom up. Citizens express their opinions about what the government should do. Congress and the presidency are essentially democratic institutions because each claims its authority directly from the people.

In contrast, bureaucracy runs on expertise. The deputy secretary of Civilian Radioactive Waste Management in the Energy Department relies on highly specialized knowledge regarding radioactive waste. The security agencies handle classified information about potential terrorists. NOAA specialists monitor scientific weather data. None of these jobs involves public sentiment or popular votes about technical matters.

The difference between elected office and bureaucratic posts creates a clash of cultures. Democracy flows up from the people. Bureaucracy, when it runs properly, operates on the basis of specialized information, often organized top-down. The enduring challenge for American government is how to manage the tension between these two polarities.

Before we think about democratic controls on the bureaucracy, let's take a more detailed look at what bureaucrats actually do.

THE BOTTOM LINE

- Before the rise of the bureaucracy, government jobs were distributed as spoils, or political rewards. Reformers challenged this system and eventually built a national bureaucracy.

- The ideal bureaucracy has five characteristics: hierarchy, division of labor, fixed routines, equal rules for all, and technical expertise.

- Bureaucracies are prone to pathologies like hewing too closely to a routine, fighting over turf, favoring some clients over others, and refusing to coordinate. These are all exaggerations of the very features that make bureaucracies efficient.

- Because they rely on specialized expertise and information, bureaucracies pose a dilemma for democratic governance.

What Bureaucracies Do

After Congress passes a law or the president issues an executive order, the bureaucracy puts it into effect. This step involves making many judgments, since inevitably there are gaps in the law. Sometimes Congress sidesteps difficult questions to avoid a conflict—or an unpopular decision; sometimes the laws are vague because they were written in a hurry or amended at the last minute; and sometimes legislation involves technical details that Congress simply leaves to the bureaucratic experts. There are two steps to the bureaucratic process of putting a law into practice: rule making and implementation.

Rule Making

Rule making showcases classic bureaucratic principles in action: a fixed process with multiple steps always carried out in the same way (see Figure 12.4). First, the agency studies the law and proposes a "rule" that spells out how the new program will operate; the details must make clear to the thousands of businesses and individuals exactly what they are required to do. For example, in 2014 a rule was issued requiring fast-food restaurants to list on their menu board the calories of an item, right next to its price.

Sounds simple, right? It is not. What restaurants must post calorie labels? Does the rule apply to hot dog carts? Pretzel stands? Soup kitchens for people without homes? How large should they make their labels? If the font is not specified,

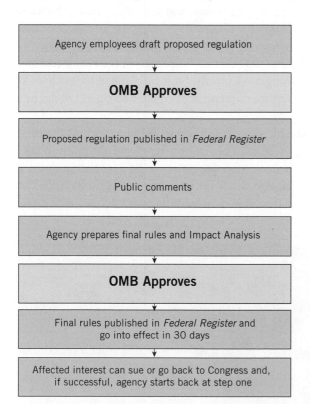

● **FIGURE 12.4** *Rule making in practice. Government rule making showcases classic bureaucratic principles in action: a fixed process with multiple steps always carried out in the same way. (Office of Management and Budget)*

some companies might be tempted to list the calories in tiny numbers that no one will notice. It is the bureaucracy's job to spell out those kinds of details.

After the agency has devised the rule, it sends the rule to the Office of Management and Budget (OMB) for approval. (You know from our tour of the White House in the last chapter that OMB has the power of central clearance—it gets a chance to say "no" to almost anything.) After OMB gives its okay, the agency publishes the **proposed rule** in a document called the *Federal Register*, the daily journal of the federal government. Anybody who is interested can comment. Who reads the *Federal Register*? In theory, any citizen can read it online or at a library. In practice, most people don't know it exists, while lobbyists and lawyers pore over it as if it were the latest hot novel. The day we wrote this chapter, for example, the *Federal Register* included proposed rules on air quality (from the Environmental Protection Agency) and a final rule regulating fish harvest limits off the northeastern coast of the United States (from the National Oceanographic and Atmospheric Administration). You can be sure that lawyers and lobbyists for manufacturing companies with high pollution emission rates and fishing fleets will be bombarding the agencies with comments and questions (which are also published in the *Federal Register*). Environmental and consumer groups also take part. As you might guess, the actual details of the proposed rule and the comments are extremely technical.

The agency reviews all the public comments, makes changes, and proposes a **final rule**, along with an analysis of the likely impact of the new rule. Back it goes to the OMB, which has thirty days to review the final rule. Then, the final rule is published in the *Federal Register*. Thirty days later, the regulation goes into effect. The final rule is not necessarily the end of the process. An individual citizen, group, or corporate firm that does not agree with the result can sue the agency for misinterpreting Congress's intent. Or it can appeal to its allies in Congress and try to get the legislators to criticize the rule and push the agency to restart the process.

In practice, lobbyists for the industry negotiate with the agency as the proposed and final rules are being written. They offer advice and threaten to sue. The experts in the agency push back and decide when to call the industry's bluff. Consumer groups often get into the action as well, trying to balance the views of the industry. Once in a while, this debate spills over into the public eye,

Proposed rule: A draft of administrative regulations published in the *Federal Register* for the purpose of gathering comments from interested parties.

Final rule: The rule that specifies how a program will actually operate.

see for yourself 12.1

Go online to view a video about the history and operation of the *Federal Register*.

● *What goes on the label? Today, that's a controversial issue.*

when a rule taps into a broader controversy. In summer 2014, the Environmental Protection Agency issued a draft rule proposing caps on carbon emissions, in an attempt to curb the greenhouse gases that contribute to global warming. Coal producers were furious, seeing it as a direct attack on their livelihood, and the ensuing firestorm had an impact on midterm elections to Congress in coal-producing states like West Virginia.

Apart from occasional flash points (like the Environmental Protection Agency and carbon emissions), rule making involves a very narrow slice of American life (like fish harvests) that takes place every day, far from the public eye. Congress gets plenty of media coverage when it considers legislation. But negotiations over how laws will work usually take place in the shadows, where only the most informed experts understand what is going on.

Implementation

After the rules are in place, bureaucracies have to implement the new policies. The fish have to be inspected or polluting chemicals regulated.

Implementation is the last step in a long process: The president proposed the law; then Congress passed it, the courts upheld it, and the bureaucratic agency published draft rules, gathered comments, and published final rules in the *Federal Register*. Although the process ends up in bureaucratic hands, bureaucrats are active at every stage in the process. For example, they often propose programs; they help write the legislation (after all, they are experts on the topic); and they testify before congressional committees that are considering the law.

Sometimes executive bureaucrats develop close alliances with members of Congress as well as with interest group lobbyists. A specialist in the Environmental Protection Agency might spend years working with "green" members of Congress, as well as environmental groups and the industries that are most affected by the regulations. As another example, the Bureau of Alcohol, Tobacco, Firearms, and Explosives works closely with gun makers and members of Congress who care about guns. Some criticize these arrangements as too cozy (recall iron triangles). In any case, you should recognize that the bureaucracy is not walled off from other actors in government. It is part of the process all along the way.

THE BOTTOM LINE

- Once a law is passed or an executive order is signed, the program goes to the bureaucracy to be put into effect.

- Bureaucrats propose rules, publish them in the *Federal Register*, gather comments, rewrite the rules, and publish the final version. The law or executive order is now in effect.

- At every step of the process, lawyers and lobbyists interact with the bureaucracy; this interaction is politics for experts far from the political limelight.

- Top bureaucratic officials often take part in every step of the political process—from proposing legislation to putting it into effect.

How the Bureaucracy Is Organized

Each presidential administration names the heads of the government bureaucracy—about four thousand people known as political appointees. The Senate must approve these men and women, including cabinet secretaries, their assistants and deputies, the ambassadors to countries around the world, and other top figures. Their role is to steer their agencies in the direction charted by the president—and the voters.

Civil servants: Members of the permanent executive-branch bureaucracy who are employed on the basis of competitive exams and keep their positions regardless of the presidential administration.

Under these four thousand appointees toil some 2.7 million **civil servants** who work at their jobs regardless of which party is in the White House. Imagine the tensions when a new political appointee (often a campaign official) arrives eagerly touting the new president's philosophy to an office of career officials. Those long-serving bureaucrats usually have more expertise than the political appointee who has just been named as their boss. The civil servants know that before long (on average, a bit more than three years) the eager new appointee will move on, to be replaced by another. The civil servants are acutely aware of the rules, regulations, and SOPs that guide their agency. They literally tell their new bosses what they can do, how they should do it, and the many things that they might want to do but that could land them in trouble because they fall outside the rules, clash with another agency's mission, or raise a sore point with a powerful member of congress.

Over the years, civil servants have built up a vocabulary of their own, often caricatured as "bureaucratese"—the cautious, cover-your-backside language of experts with lifetime appointments who are tasked with providing $3 trillion worth of federal services every year.

The federal government's organizational chart includes four different kinds of agencies: cabinet departments, autonomous bureaus, independent regulatory agencies, and the bureaucracy's service organizations. Let's take a closer look.

The Cabinet Departments

President George Washington's cabinet had just four departments: State, Treasury, War (now called Defense, which sounds a little less aggressive), and the Office of the Attorney General (later called the Justice Department). Over time, presidents added new departments till the cabinet reached its current size—fifteen departments. Table 12.1 lists each department, the year it was founded, and how large it is today. Note how the military dominates the government's personnel count. The Department of Defense houses more than 2.4 million employees, including the men and women in uniform, and manages facilities that take up 30 million acres around the world; no other organization in the United States comes close. If we add the second two largest cabinet agencies—veterans, which takes care of retired military personnel (235,000 employees),

TABLE 12.1 U.S. Executive Bureaucracy: How the Bureaucracy Grew

CABINET DEPARTMENT	FOUNDING	CURRENT EMPLOYEES
State	1789	41,577
Treasury	1789	112,461
Defense	1789	758,465 civilians; 1.4 million uniformed military
Justice	1789	117,380
Interior	1849	68,813
Agriculture	1862	97,213
Commerce	1903	44,238
Labor	1913	17,785
Health & Human Services (originally "Health, Education and Welfare")	1953	74,017
Housing & Urban Development	1965	8,536
Transportation	1966	57,036
Energy	1977	15,529
Education	1979	4,201
Veterans Affairs	1989	323,208
Homeland Security	2002	194,558
ADDITIONAL FEDERAL AGENCIES (NONCABINET)		
Social Security Administration		64,539
Environmental Protection Agency		17,740
NASA		17,922
General Services Administration		12,383
Other independent agencies		68,547
U.S. Postal Service (a semi-independent federal agency since 1971)		595,783
Executive Office of the President (detailed in Chapter 11)		1,852
Total federal service		2,713,783
Estimated number of federal contractors and grantees		Between 7.5 million and 10 million (depending on who's counting and how)

Source: U.S. Office of Personnel Management, "Employment and Trends," January 2013.

A 2014 Cabinet meeting in the White House. Each member has a plaque affixed to the back of their chair, specifying the agency and the year it was founded.

and Homeland Security (191,000)—America's defense establishment is larger than the rest of the government combined.

New secretaries face the fundamental problem of managing a large bureaucracy that they know very little about. Cabinet secretaries are accomplished individuals, but they are unlikely to have much experience with the many facets of their departments. For example, Obama's first secretary of the Department of Homeland Security, Janet Napolitano, had been governor of Arizona. On the one hand, she was familiar with some homeland-security issues, like those surrounding immigration; on the other hand, she probably did not know much about the Office of Cybersecurity, the Coast Guard, or the Animal and Plant Inspection Service—all bureaus under her direction. Almost all secretaries face the same problem. And, with a new administration in town, a huge to-do list of policy goals awaits each new executive.

The Rotating Bureaucracy. The turnover at the top rung of the U.S. bureaucracy is unique. No other democracy works in this way—nor does any other major institution. No private company, nonprofit organization, or university routinely asks thousands of outsiders to take over for an average of three or so years and then expects them to step aside and make way for a new crop of leaders. Meanwhile, the political appointees scrambling to catch up are in charge of a huge bureaucratic leviathan. Thousands of civil servants toil away at the agency's tasks, working from one administration to the next.

Management consultants would run screaming from the room if you suggested setting up a business in this way. Here, we cannot look to the Constitution because it does not mention cabinet departments, much less an entire bureaucracy. Many political scientists, however, think the bureaucracy does work. The civil service does its job, often quite well. And the political leadership, for all the problems of the transition, comes to the job with a definite philosophy, based on a president's central ideas.

Pairing a suitable philosophy with skilled political leadership can make a real difference in an agency's management. An example is the Federal Emergency Management Agency (FEMA), which responds to natural disasters. President Bill Clinton named a talented FEMA director, James Lee Witt, with emergency-management experience. With Clinton's support, Witt transformed the agency into a decentralized, authority-sharing outfit with a very proactive approach. When floods hit the Midwest in 1993, the new FEMA won widespread applause for its swift, well-organized assistance. People might despise federal bureaucrats, but Witt and his FEMA team drew high praise at the time.

When the George W. Bush administration came to office, FEMA was on its list of target agencies. From a conservative perspective, FEMA had become *too* proactive. Republican members of Congress charged that the agency had bought out homeowners to avert disaster the next time the river flooded. Wasn't that a kind of big government welfare program? The Bush administration restored the old FEMA policies—and installed an inexperienced (but politically connected) campaign donor, Michael Brown, as director.

In this case, the changes led to political disaster. In part because of the restoration of a rules-bound, elaborately hierarchical structure and in part because of Brown's inexperience as a leader, FEMA responded feebly to Hurricane Katrina, a massive storm that flooded New Orleans in 2005. The tragedy played out in real time as the media depicted widespread desperation: more than 1,800 people lost their lives in the storms and subsequent flooding—and no federal response in sight. Director Brown lost his job, and President Bush's popularity ratings tumbled.

President Obama, learning from his predecessors, appointed an experienced, well-regarded FEMA director, W. Craig

● *FEMA success: Midwest floods, 1993 (top). FEMA failure: Hurricane Katrina, 2005 (bottom).*

Fugate. The agency received high marks when another devastating storm, Hurricane Sandy, hit the East Coast in 2012. "Officials and experts praising FEMA for its response to Hurricane Sandy," read a representative headline in the *Washington Post*.[8]

Along with the value of savvy leadership, the FEMA example illustrates another important point about the federal bureaucracy. Calling for smaller government sounds promising on the campaign trail. However, each nook and cranny of the sprawling government establishment has a job to do; almost all deliver services that some people rely on. That responsibility makes cutting government agencies difficult in actual practice.

Other Agencies

Most of the federal bureaucracy—about 1.7 million civilians—work in the cabinet departments. There are three other categories of federal workers, however, and each offers a different twist to the life of the bureaucracy.

Executive Agencies.   Independent executive agencies have more focused jobs than the cabinet departments. The Social Security Administration, for example, is responsible for running the Social Security program, which provides pensions for Americans over sixty-five. The Environmental Protection Agency is entirely focused on the difficult job of overseeing the environment. In contrast, the Interior Department (a cabinet agency) has responsibilities that include—among many other things—supervising Indian affairs, national parks, geological surveys, oceans and energy, and surface mining.

The roughly one hundred independent executive agencies perform a wide range of jobs: among them, they land astronauts on the moon (NASA), send Americans around the world to perform service projects (the Peace Corps), gather intelligence (CIA), manage the banking system (the Federal Reserve), monitor elections (the Federal Election Commission), and investigate violations of civil rights in the workplace (Equal Employment Opportunities Commission).

The U.S. Postal Service became a cabinet agency in 1792. Some 180 years later, in 1971, the post office became an independent agency of the U.S. federal government—operating without direct federal subsidy. The Postal Service has just under 500,000 employees (down from nearly 800,000 in 1999) and 250,000 vehicles; it is the second-largest federal bureaucracy after the Defense Department.

Independent Regulatory Commissions.   Another kind of bureau emerged to regulate business. The first one set the organizational template. In the 1880s, farmers and small business complained bitterly that they were at the mercy of the railroads, which could make or break them with their arbitrary freight rates. The farmers pleaded for government controls. However, reformers faced a problem. The railroad owners were so wealthy and powerful that they dominated the state legislatures and Congress. How could consumers be protected

TABLE 12.2 Independent Regulatory Commissions (listed in order of creation)

INDEPENDENT REGULATORY COMMISSION	YEAR CREATED	SHUT DOWN
Interstate Commerce Commission	1887	1995
Federal Trade Commission	1914	—
Federal Communications Commission	1928	—
Federal Power (later Federal Energy Regulatory) Commission	1930	—
Securities and Exchange Commission	1935	—
National Labor Relations Board	1935	—
Civil Aeronautics Board	1940	1985
Atomic Energy (later Nuclear Regulatory) Commission	1954	—
Federal Maritime Commission	1961	—
Equal Employment Opportunity Commission	1965	—
Consumer Product Safety Commission	1972	—
Federal Election Commission	1975	—

against these powerful "robber barons"? Reformers organized a regulatory agency, the Interstate Commerce Commission (ICC), that would operate independently from Congress and the White House. Reformers hoped that the agency's independence would permit it to regulate industry—free from corrupting lobbyists and politics. Table 12.2 lists all the independent regulatory commissions that eventually followed the ICC.

All independent regulatory commissions have the authority to issue regulations, enforce laws, and settle disputes—essentially combining legislative, executive, and judicial powers in one agency. A set of commissioners, nominated by the president and confirmed by the Senate, runs the agency for a fixed term that does not overlap with the president's term—still another way to minimize political influence. The hope, beginning with the ICC, was that modern management methods rather than politics would guide regulatory policy.

You likely recognize the reformers' naivete: independent agencies were no less political than any other branch of government. As we saw when we examined the rule-making process, regulating an industry inevitably involves plenty of back-and-forth negotiations between regulators and the industry. Each proposed rule draws comments, criticism, and threats of litigation. Moreover, to understand an industry well enough to monitor its activities, regulators generally need some expertise about the industry. Commissioners are frequently drawn from the ranks of the regulated industry. Ironically, the effort to keep the regulatory commissions independent of Congress and the White House has left them more susceptible to industry influence. For decades, critics have

HISTORY REPEATS ITSELF. — THE ROBBER BARONS OF THE MIDDLE AGES, AND THE ROBBER BARONS OF TO-DAY.

● The nineteenth century railroad barons were among the "robber barons"—mocked in this cartoon for squeezing farmers, workers, and businessmen as mercilessly as the barons of the middle ages.

charged that the independent regulatory agencies are "captured" or "acquired" by the industry and simply do its bidding.

There is no escaping the politics that pervade the independent regulatory agencies. Still, the **"regulatory capture"** argument is often overstated. Consumer groups also lobby, provide information, and sue. Moreover, government civil servants often work hard to achieve the goals of their agency.

Regulatory capture: The theory that industries dominate the agencies that regulate them.

In the past thirty years, a new generation of reformers has come up with a solution to regulatory capture: deregulation—that is, abolishing the agencies altogether and letting free market competition protect consumers. The original ICC was dismantled in 1995. The Civil Aeronautics Board, another regulatory commission, which protected the airline industry by limiting competition, was abolished in 1985, leading, directly or indirectly, to all kinds of consequences, good and bad—frequent-flier programs, fewer airlines, huge fluctuations in fares, and inedible (or nonexistent) food.

Deregulation brings us full circle. Once, farmers and small business pleaded for relief from predatory markets. Now, a new generation of reformers offers a solution to problems with the regulatory agencies: return to the markets.

An Army of Their Own. A small support army maintains and services the massive office buildings housing the executive branch. Imagine supplying 2.7 million workers; imagine the job of hiring, paying, reviewing, promoting, and sometimes firing all those workers. These details require still another type of institution in the U.S. bureaucracy: independent **central service agencies**, most notably the Office of Personnel Management (OPM) and the General Services Administration (GSA).

Central service agencies: The organizations that supply and staff the federal government.

Do you want to work for the U.S. government, as a civil servant? OPM manages the giant "USAJobs" website, listing hundreds of thousands of federal bureaucracy job openings each year. Once you apply for your position, your application will be read and screened by OPM staff. When you are hired, your employment materials (pay level, vacation-time details, health benefits) will come from them. And, when you are ready to leave government service, you'll talk to OPM about the government pension you may have accumulated.

While you are working for the government, GSA manages all the details of maintenance and supply. Your building just got painted? GSA did the work—or hired and supervised the company who did it under contract. Do you need a shipment of forest fire–fighting helicopters (for the National Park Service) or a more sophisticated smartphone (at the OMB)? GSA is your one-stop shopping spot.

Private Contractors. One final category of government workers does not work for the government at all. They work for private companies that provide goods and services under contract to the government. **Private contractors** now perform many of the jobs that once were handled directly by government employees. For example, the military increasingly relies on private firms to provide meals, transportation, security services, and even commando teams. For the first time in American history, there were more private contractors (about 200,000) than uniformed military personnel (about 190,000) in the war zones in both Iraq (2003–2012) and Afghanistan (2001–present). Beyond war, private companies provide a full range of government services, including homeland security, international diplomacy, prison management, and garbage collection.

Why contract out government services? There are three reasons: First, private companies, foundations, and nongovernmental organizations often have special skills and resources they can bring to a job. Second, they lobby hard for the business. And, third, Americans critical of the bureaucracy often assert that private companies can do a better and cheaper job.

The truth is that sometimes private contractors can do a better job than the public sector; at other times they charge more for inferior services.

Private contractors: Private companies that contract to provide goods and services for the government.

● *Private contractors, like Blackwater Worldwide, provided military services in Iraq and Afghanistan. Here, a private contractor is part of the security detail for L. Paul Bremmer, who oversaw the American operation in Iraq.*

Recognizing that private contracting in government is here to stay, the key to making it work is ensuring that government officials maintain careful oversight of the work that is done for hire.[9]

Executive-branch agencies and commissions all face leadership challenges similar to those faced by the cabinet departments. The appointment process is cumbersome and complicated by politics. New appointees scramble to learn the bureaucratic ropes, even as the to-do list piles ever higher. And the administrative team takes longer to get into place.

How can the nation's agencies operate effectively when their leaders are on the way in and just learning the ropes or are on the way out and operating as lame ducks? For an answer, we need to confront the complicated question of just who is in charge of the American bureaucracy.

THE BOTTOM LINE

- The federal bureaucracy includes five different types of agencies. The fifteen cabinet departments, forming the largest group, employ roughly 1.8 million civilians.

- The president appoints a small number of executives; the rest are members of the permanent civil service. The cabinet has grown far more diverse in the past twenty-five years.

- The cabinet and other appointed executives provide political direction; the civil servants provide expertise and continuity.

- Among the many challenges to a smoothly functioning system is the time—more than a year—that it takes a new administration to get its leadership team in place.

- The government includes four other kinds of bureaucracies: executive agencies focus on one type of issue like environmental quality; independent regulatory commissions oversee specific industries; central service agencies staff and supply the entire bureaucracy; and private contractors are licensed to provide goods and services for the government. Different kinds of agencies face different kinds of political problems and challenges.

● Who Controls the Federal Bureaucracy?

Controlling 2.7 million civilian bureaucrats, 1.6 million military personal, and an unknown number of private contractors (one reliable estimate pegs it at 10 million) is a daunting leadership responsibility—and a giant management headache. It is also crucial for democracy. Self-rule requires mastering the bureaucracy. But who is in charge?

The People

In a democracy, the federal government must, ultimately, respond to the people. Most executive departments trumpet something like *"We Serve the People"* on their websites. However, real popular control faces the problem we have discussed throughout this chapter: Much of what the bureaucracy does is too technical for direct public engagement.

How does the IRS figure tax penalties for S corporations wrongly electing to amortize anticipated losses with write-downs? What is the maximum engineering pendular sway ratio on truss-style bridges? Does the chemical compound bisphenol A, widely used in plastics, leach into bottled drinking water—and, if it does, how dangerous is it to public health? Americans do not have the time or the knowledge to develop opinions about such matters. We need someone else to act on our behalf.

The President

In theory, the president controls the bureaucracy. The Constitution is clear on this issue: "the executive Power shall be vested in a President of the United States of America." The president is the bureaucrat in chief. The form of bureaucratic control that follows from this declaration is known as **overhead democracy**: The people elect presidents who, through their appointees, control the bureaucracy from the top.

Overhead democracy: A system by which the people elect the presidents, who, through their appointees, control the bureaucracy from the top.

In practice, most presidents are frustrated in their efforts to manage the millions of men and women under their command. Harry Truman put it famously when he commented on his successor, General Dwight D. Eisenhower. "He'll sit here and he'll say 'Do this!' and 'Do that!' *And nothing will happen.* Poor Ike, it won't be a bit like the army. He'll find it very frustrating."[10]

When presidents appoint the directors of the executive branch, they quickly discover that the bureaucracy has its own preferences, processes, and routines. Before long, many appointed officials begin to see the world through the eyes of their agencies—rather than from the perspective of the White House. President Richard Nixon, a Republican, bluntly expressed his frustration: Nixon believed that many of the career civil servants were simply Democrats waiting for the next liberal administration. "If we don't get rid of these people," Nixon wrote, "they will sit back on their well-paid asses and wait for the next election to bring back their old bosses."[11] Of course the whole point of a neutral civil service is that the president cannot easily "get rid of those people."

Congress

Although bureaucrats "belong" to the executive branch, the legislative branch wields a surprising amount of authority. Congress shapes the bureaucracy through four powers.

- *Funding.* Most important, Congress funds nearly all executive-branch programs, since it determines the federal budget. If Congress doesn't like a bureaucratic proposal, or if some agency head falls out of favor with a powerful subcommittee, that program or department may find its budget slashed by congressional appropriators.

- *Oversight.* Congress has oversight power to supervise the executive branch, including both White House and federal bureaucratic operations. Policing department and agency actions is normally a routine operation—making sure that funds are properly expended or programs achieve their stated goals. But Congress can extend its oversight authority into major investigations of executive-branch actions. The mere mention of oversight hearings is a major threat to the bureaucracy.

- *Authorization.* Of course, Congress passes all laws and often has to reauthorize them after a specified number of years. Although we have seen that recent administrations have increasingly relied on executive orders, Congress wields the power to amend programs or even deny their reauthorization.

- *Reorganization.* Finally, Congress can change the structure and nature of executive-branch organizations. In the wake of the September 11, 2001, attacks, President George W. Bush called for creation of the Department of Homeland Security. Three years later, Congress finally approved his request—but added many rules about things like employee pay and unionization rules.

These four sources of power add up to extensive congressional influence. Agency heads and cabinet secretaries are often more responsive to Congress—with its power of the purse and oversight authority—than to the president. Bureaucratic leaders regularly lobby Congress for additional funding or authority. They also frequently complain, however, about congressional "micromanagement."

Political scientists have recently focused on a theoretical way of looking at the relationship between Congress and the bureaucracy. **Principal-agent theory** analyzes problems that develop when a principal (in this case, Congress) hires an agent (the bureaucracy) to do a job. The problem arises when the agent has much more information than the principal. How do you control a bureaucracy when there is "information asymmetry"—that is, when they know a lot more than you do? The answer: Make sure their interests are the same as yours. Many scholars now suggest that, although Congress cannot possibly oversee everything the bureaucracy does, the power of its weapons—especially funding and oversight—leads bureaucratic officials, by and large, to try and conform to congressional wishes. Put differently, the fear of being hauled before a congressional panel—and threatened with loss of funding—is enough to make the bureaucrats worry about congressional intent and desires.

Congressional power is also circumscribed, of course. The power to shape or influence is still a far cry from the power to command or control. Presidents and congressional leaders sometimes clash over who controls the bureaucracy. Meanwhile, another powerful set of players—interest groups—quietly exert influence as well.

Principal-agent theory: Analyses of how policy makers (principals) can control actors who work for them (agents) but have far more information.

Interest Groups

Interest groups closely engage bureaucrats as they administer the laws. As we saw earlier (in Chapter 9) lobbying groups comment extensively on proposed rules. They offer information about the needs and capacity of the affected industry. As bureaucrats finalize the rules and implement the program, they often engage the industry, whose cooperation may be necessary to make the program work smoothly. Officials in the bureaucracy, the trade groups, and consumer alliances often share expertise and interests. Over time, they can develop close relations, which make lobbyists influential in the day-to-day operations of the executive agencies. Interest groups—often fighting among themselves—can also complain, report back to Congress, or sue. The result is another set of influences on bureaucrats in action.

Bureaucratic Autonomy

Partly because they have so many would-be masters, bureaucrats wind up with considerable autonomy in how they do their work. Many of these civil servants have strong views about their fields—protecting the environment, enforcing the civil rights laws, or keeping the homeland safe. They also have an interest in increasing their own autonomy—applying their best judgment to the problems they face.

Some federal bureaucrats themselves call attention to abuses within their department or agency. It happens enough that there even is a term for a worker—public or private—who reports corruption or fraud: **whistle-blower**. In many cases, permanent civil servants blow the whistle on fraudulent or misbehaving political appointees higher up in the department or agency. In 2014, for example, dozens of whistle-blowers in the Veterans Administration (VA), which provides health care to retired U.S. soldiers, reported fraudulent practices such as mistreatment of patients and falsified medical records to improve performance reviews. The ensuing scandal forced the VA secretary, Eric Shinseki (a former top Army general), to resign.

Whistle-blower: A federal worker who reports corruption or fraud.

Street-level bureaucrats: Government officials who deal directly with the public.

This search for autonomy is especially true for government officials who deal directly with the public. These **street-level bureaucrats** are administrators at the bottom of the government organization who interact with the public—welfare officers, police, teachers, or poultry-plant inspectors. General policies are formulated in the higher administration, but it is the street-level bureaucrats who actually run the programs, constantly using their own judgments. The police officer may write you a speeding ticket—or let you off with a warning.[12]

● *A street-level bureaucrat in action! A local official in the Modesto California Health Department, part of the Women, Infants, and Children program, measures the growth of a young client.*

Consider a more complicated case. The Women, Infants, and Children program provides vouchers for meals to low-income families with children. On the national level, Congress debates the funding and the administration determines the rules for eligibility. On the local level, the street-level bureaucrats constantly make judgment calls about exactly how strictly to apply the rules. For example: This woman makes too much money on paper, but her ex-husband is not paying his child support. That woman was ill and missed the application deadline—do you give her the EBT card anyway (for buying food)? This family has broken the rules again and again but if you cut them off the program the children will suffer. Street-level bureaucrats have enormous influence in deciding just how strictly to apply the rules. Program beneficiaries quickly learn about the power of the bureaucrats they see again and again.

Moreover, at the street level, every program has its own tone. Some programs (like Social Security) treat their beneficiaries with respect; others (like Temporary Assistance for Needy Families) take a more disciplinary stance.[13]

Democracy Revisited

Many agents—the president, Congress, and interest groups—exert some control over the bureaucracy. Each does so on behalf of others: The White House tries to speak for the public, Congress for voters in a state or district, and interest groups on behalf of clients who might range from a business sector to the environmental or civil rights community. Bureaucrats try to maximize their own discretion to do what they think is best. Do all these clashing forces add up to democratic control?

The answer is yes and no. At times, these different forms of democratic control offer a rough form of popular oversight. Administrations that focus on delivering services can have considerable success; presidents who seek to change the direction of federal policy can, if they stick to it, have some success; congressional oversight often improves responsiveness. But all the levers for democratic control are blunt instruments. They take hard work, constant attention, and considerable luck. In the next section, we examine three reform proposals that might improve the odds for popular control.

THE BOTTOM LINE

- In a democracy, the public must ultimately control the government bureaucracy. The question is how.

- Different actors exert some control on the bureaucracy: the president (who names the leaders), Congress (through funding and oversight), and interest groups.

- Bureaucrats still operate with considerable autonomy—they make their own judgments.

Reforming the Bureaucracy

The bureaucracy's reputation for being expensive, slow moving, and scandal-ridden has attracted a long history of reform efforts. Let's consider three popular proposals.

Open Up the System

The public's faith in government tumbled in the late 1960s and the early 1970s, after an unpopular war in Vietnam, civil rights unrest, and President Nixon's shocking behavior during the Watergate scandal. One response was a concerted attempt to make the executive bureaucracy more transparent. Sunshine laws require public hearings and citizen input; they open up bureaucratic debates to public view. The **Freedom of Information Act** extends citizen access to agency and department deliberations. Any individual or news organization may file a Freedom of Information Act request to see an unreleased government document (the legislation created a new verb, "to FOIA" a document). Today, every federal agency has its own website that tries to explain just what it is doing.

The trend within the bureaucracy generally favored openness—until the 9/11 terrorist attacks. Government agencies began restricting all kinds of material as potentially helpful to terrorists. Audits later concluded that more than a quarter of the twenty-five thousand documents removed from public access after 9/11 were incorrectly classified as secret.

Especially after a mid-level National Security Agency (NSA) employee named Edward Snowden downloaded thousands of classified documents and began releasing them to media outlets in 2013, this debate continues. Advocates, often citing NSA revelations of illegal spying on U.S. allies and our own citizens, push for more access. Many government agencies have genuine security concerns. Others resent the time and effort it takes to ensure sunshine. And many simply want to protect themselves from criticism.

Freedom of Information Act:
A 1966 law that facilitates full or partial disclosure of government information and documents.

Reinventing Government

During the 1980s and 1990s, some bureaucratic reformers began to stress responsiveness. Departments should treat the public as "customers" and make their services more efficient and user-friendly. Early in the Clinton administration, Vice President Al Gore took charge of a sweeping "Reinventing Government" project—designed to cut bureaucratic delays, increase efficiency, reduce costs, decentralize management, and empower employees to make decisions.[14] The efforts continued into President George W. Bush's administration with a special emphasis on *deregulation*—leaving businesses and private citizens freer to look after themselves.

Some success stories emerged. In fact, many of the measures of bureaucratic effectiveness that were developed under the "Reinventing Government" project remain in place today.

SHOULD WE PRIVATIZE MORE GOVERNMENT FUNCTIONS?

Although benefits of privatization are still debated, research in this area suggests that competitive contracting can save money and boost quality. However, using private contractors poses its own problems, including the need for careful oversight. Do you think we should privatize more government functions?

Yes. Because private companies are driven by the profit motive, they will work hard to succeed. They bring expertise to the area. They can adjust to changing conditions more quickly than can slow-moving government bureaucracies. And as long as public officials insist on competitive bids and monitor the job the company is doing, the result will be more efficient services.

No. The profit motive means that private companies are more interested in making money for investors than performing a public service well. Moreover, it is often difficult to monitor the work of private contractors; doing so requires skill and resources from public-sector agencies—and the public will pay for both the work and the monitors. Finally, private companies go in and out of business all the time, whereas public services—from military support to school bus drivers—need to be reliable.

Unsure. Do you need more information? We'll return to this question in Chapter 14.

Privatization

If the bureaucracy seems slow and inefficient, perhaps private companies can do the job more efficiently. As we have discussed, one powerful trend in government has been outsourcing public services to private firms. For-profit companies collect garbage, manage prisons, protect the homeland, cook for the troops, and launch commando raids abroad.

The movement for privatizing federal (and many state) programs took flight in the 1970s and received a boost from President Reagan in the 1980s. His administration turned some forty thousand government jobs over to private contractors, for reported savings of more than $600 million dollars. As we noted above, as many as 10 million private contractors—there is no accurate count—are working for the federal (or state or local) government today.

Private firms often can do the job for less. But the savings are at least partly offset by the need for government supervision. What happens when private managers—worrying, as they must, about the bottom line—cut corners or violate rules? For example, the Blackwater Corporation did many indispensable jobs for the U.S. military in Iraq. They also created multiple headaches. Poorly trained operators who killed Iraqi civilians created waves of protests—critics charged the company with 195 shooting incidents. The firm also experienced chronic cost overruns. As criticism grew, the company quietly changed its name to "Xe" and then changed its name again to "Academi."

Private providers can also walk away from their government services when they are no longer making a profit—or when they go out of business. In New York City, Mayor Rudolph Giuliani (1992–2001) privatized many school bus services. When the private company that had won the contract defaulted, the city had to scramble to find buses and prepare drivers in time for the start of the school year—paying a premium for the last-minute services.

The benefits of privatization are still debated, like the other reforms we've discussed here. Research in this area suggests that *competitive contracting* (requiring more than one bid from outside contractors who want to provide government services) can save money and boost quality. However, the most important calculation, often overlooked by reformers, is factoring in a way for government officials to supervise the private contractor. Careful oversight is a critical dimension of making privatization work.

An employee of Immigration and Customs Enforcement's Stewart Detention Center in Lumpkin, Georgia, waiting for the front gate to be opened. The detention center is operated on contract by Nashville-based Corrections Corporation of America.

THE BOTTOM LINE

- Critics of the bureaucracy focus on cost, inertia, and public mistrust.

- Solutions include sunshine reforms, reinventing government to make it more constituent-friendly, and privatizing some of its functions.

● Conclusion: The Real Solution Lies with You

President Kennedy came to office amid a burst of idealism and declared, "Ask not what your country can do for you—ask what you can do for your country." Inspired by the young president, the early civil rights movement, and the general optimism of the era, many college graduates streamed into public

Wanted! A few good bureaucrats!

service. Today, fewer Americans are attracted to government service. Can this trend change? What would draw *you* into government?

The ultimate answer to the problems of bureaucracy, we believe, lies in the interest and commitment from a new generation. We are deeply concerned that men and women like you and your classmates—a well-educated group interested in political science—will bypass government altogether.

Indeed, politicians from both parties take shots at the bureaucrats. They freeze pay, downsize departments, and disparage millions of individuals. However, a closer look suggests that the bureaucracy performs many jobs we need and value—from predicting the weather to defending the United States. Ultimately, our government—our democracy—is only as good as the bureaucracy that puts public policy into effect. And this brings us back to you and your generation's commitment to public service and what public officials can do to foster it.

CHAPTER SUMMARY

● Within the executive branch, the U.S. federal bureaucracy does a vast amount of work in governing—and more closely resembles the nation's population than any other segment of our national government. However, Americans express deep ambivalence about our bureaucracy, generally rating it very low in opinion polls.

● The American bureaucracy was established in reaction to the spoils system (1828–1901).

● In theory, bureaucracies operate with five characteristics: hierarchy, division of labor, fixed routines, equal rules for all, and technical qualifications.

● Bureaucrats perform a wide range of functions—from managing the nation's defense and national economy to organizing and providing food stamps and tax cuts. The bureaucracy is specifically charged

with implementing the laws passed by Congress and signed by the president. This typically involves an administrative rule-making process as well as actual delivery of services and carrying out of programs.

● Since the 1930s, the federal bureaucracy has grown to more than 4 million employees—roughly two-thirds civilian and a third military. It is not readily apparent who is in charge of managing the bureaucracy. Many different players have a role, including the public, the president, Congress, and interest groups. Even with—or perhaps because of—all those masters, bureaucrats have considerable discretion in how they carry out their work. This freedom can lead to serious tensions between Americans' democratic ideals of representative accountability, and an unelected, often *un*accountable workforce of civil servants.

● Reform efforts include enhancing transparency of bureaucratic practices, reinventing government to improve responsiveness and reduce layers of management, and privatizing government services.

KEY TERMS

Bureaucratic pathologies, 406	Overhead democracy, 421	Regulatory capture, 418
Central service agencies, 418	Pendleton Civil Service Act, 403	Spoils system, 402
Civil servants, 412	Principal-agent theory, 422	Street-level bureaucrats, 423
Final rule, 410	Private contractors, 419	Universalistic politics, 402
Freedom of Information Act, 425	Proposed rule, 410	Whistle-blower, 423

STUDY QUESTIONS

1. Look back at the Department of Energy's (DOE's) organizational chart on p. 405 of this chapter. If you were in charge of the DOE, how strict would you be about adhering to this chart? Would you allow wiggle room, in the name of creativity and innovation? Or would reporting authority go up the channels described here to ensure that the rules are faithfully followed?

2. Is the U.S. federal bureaucracy too large? Do we need 6.5 million people working for the government—in addition to several million more or so hired under federal contracts? If you'd like to see it smaller, where should we start cutting workers?

3. Who *should* run the bureaucracy, in your informed view? Do bureaucrats have too much discretion in how they perform their duties? What are the respective merits of a "street-level" or "top-down" management style? And should presidents (or Congress, or interest groups, etc.) have more authority than they currently wield to exert their will on the bureaucracy?

4. Let's say you have just learned about some unsavory doings in your bureaucratic agency or department. Do you blow the whistle—report the problem? Or do you keep quiet? What would affect your decision?

5. Based on what you now know about the U.S. bureaucracy, should we mount a major push for reform? What type(s) of reforms would be most useful? Or are the various parts of the bureaucracy working pretty well the way they are?

13

The Judicial Branch

TERRI SCHIAVO, a twenty-six-year-old woman, collapsed in her home in St. Petersburg, Florida, went into a coma, and then lingered in what her doctor called "a persistent vegetative state." She exhibited no brain activity and was kept alive by a feeding tube. After eight years, her husband, Michael, decided to remove the tube and allow Terri to die. He filed a petition with the court requesting permission to remove the feeding tube; her parents went to court to stop the removal—and the political frenzy began. Politicians, disability rights groups, pro-life organizations, and the national media all leapt into action, issuing moral judgments, medical opinions, and political threats. William Frist, the Senate majority leader and a former heart surgeon, declared that he saw "signs of life" in a videotape of Terri. Demonstrations and counter-demonstrations raged outside the courthouse.

The Florida legislature passed "Terri's Law," signed by Governor Jeb Bush, which ordered the hospice to reinsert the feeding tube. The U.S. Congress passed its own bill authorizing Terri's parents to go to federal court and claim that her federal rights had been violated. President George W. Bush flew to Washington from his Texas ranch and, with maximum media exposure, signed the legislation. Amid all the intense activity, however, it soon became clear that Terri Schiavo's fate was entirely in the hands of the courts.

After almost three years, in February 2000, a local Florida court ruled that the tube could be removed, and in April 2000 the state **appellate court** upheld the ruling. Four years of legal maneuvers followed, but both state and federal courts upheld the decision to remove the tube. Various Florida courts also struck down "Terri's Law" and other legislative efforts to stop the courts from permitting the tube removal; an appellate court and finally the Supreme Court backed up the decision by repeatedly refusing to hear the case. Finally, in March 2005—after almost seven years of legal wrangling—the Supreme Court refused to intervene one last time, Terri Schiavo's feeding tubes were removed, and she died.

By the end of the fight, all sides were focused on the judicial system. "I'm glad the courts are in charge of this, not Congress or [Florida governor] Jeb

IN THIS CHAPTER, YOU WILL:

► Consider how the law reflects the American people—and our national culture.

► Learn how the judicial system operates.

► Examine the courts' role in American politics.

► Explore the inner workings of the Supreme Court.

► Reflect on how judges decide cases.

► Review landmark judicial cases.

Appellate courts: The system of federal justices, organized into district courts and circuit courts, who hear appeals from lower courts, culminating in the Supreme Court.

Bush," one Florida resident told a reporter.[1] A protester outside Terri's hospice clutched a sign that expressed the opposite view: "Hey Judge," his poster read. "Who Made You God?"

Alexander Hamilton predicted that the judiciary "will always be the least dangerous" and "the weakest" branch of government because, he reasoned, it has "no influence" over "the sword" (the president controls the army) or "the purse" (Congress is in charge of the budget).[2] Yet, as the Schiavo case illustrates, the U.S. judiciary has accumulated sweeping powers—including the ability to overrule state legislatures, Congress, governors, and even presidents. The courts have the authority to strike down laws, rules, or regulations that violate the Constitution—as the courts interpret it.

We have seen in earlier chapters the great reach and power of the Supreme Court—for example, when it struck down compromises and protected slavery (in *Dred Scott*, 1857); when it cracked the entire edifice of segregation (*Brown v. Board of Education*, 1954); and when it swept away a state network of laws prohibiting abortion (*Roe v. Wade*, 1973). More recently, the Supreme Court decisively stopped the vote counting in the disputed 2000 election—making George W. Bush president (*Bush v. Gore*); rejected bipartisan efforts to limit money flowing into American elections (*Citizens United* followed by *McCutcheon v. Federal Election Commission*); upheld the signal achievement of the Obama administration, the Affordable Care Act (*National Federation of Independent Business v. Sebelius*); and then ruled that a privately held corporation could refuse to provide contraception under the Affordable Care Act on the basis of religious beliefs (*Hobby Lobby*). The last four cases were all the more controversial because each was decided by a single vote, 5–4.

At least on the surface, judicial authority can seem breathtaking. Unelected officials with lifetime appointments wield the power to overrule the long, hard, democratic process of forging legislation. The Founders believed that the more political branches of government—the president and Congress— needed the courts to check them. Has that check now grown too powerful? Has it grown too political? These are the questions that guide our examination of the courts.

Who are we? We are a nation founded on the world's oldest constitution, which directly or indirectly governs almost every aspect of our collective life. "Without the Constitution, there would be no America," observes one historian.[3]

The courts ultimately rule on how the Constitution applies to the problems we face. Small wonder that the United States is—and always has been—a nation of courts, lawyers, and people ready to sue.

We will begin with the basics. What does the court system look like? How does it make decisions? How did it amass so much power over our politics, our government, and our daily lives? The answer starts with the basic character of the American people: *who we are.*

BY THE NUMBERS
The U.S. Judiciary

- Original number of Supreme Court justices: **5**
- Largest number of justices (1863–1866): **10**
- Number of Supreme Court justices appointed, 1882–1910: **18**
- Number of Supreme Court justices appointed, 1982–2010: **9**
- Number of years John Marshall was chief justice of the United States: **34**
- Number of years served by his successor, Roger Taney: **28**
- Number of chief justices in American history: **16**
- Number since 1953: **4**
- Number of U.S. presidents since 1953: **11**
- Total number of Catholic justices on Supreme Court, 1789–1910: **3**
- Number of Catholic justices currently serving on Supreme Court: **6**
- Total number of cases heard by Supreme Court, 1987–1988 term: **155**
- Total number of cases heard by Supreme Court, 2011–2012 term: **69**
- Vacancies on the Supreme Court during Eisenhower presidency (1953–1960): **5**
- Vacancies on the Supreme Court during Carter presidency (1977–1980): **0**
- Salary, federal district court judge, 2010: **$169,300**
- Average salary, first-year associate, New York City law firm, 2010: **$163,000**
- Supreme Court chief justice salary: **$223,500**
- Supreme Court associate justice salary: **$213,900**
- Median annual income for all lawyers: **$112,000**
- Average salary, NBA player, 2010: **$5,600,000**
- Charge for filing a civil case (anyone can do so) in federal district court: **$350**
- Estimated number of Americans who served on juries, 2012: **344,500**
- Total fine charged in jury trial to Minnesota woman for illegal downloads, 2009: **$1,900,000**
- Total number of songs she illegally downloaded: **24**

● Who Are We? A Nation of Laws . . . and Lawyers

The United States relies on courts to resolve more matters than most nations. The result is a deeply legalistic political culture.

Embracing the Law—and Lawsuits

Litigation: The conduct of a lawsuit.

Lawsuits, or **litigation**, are a near-constant feature of American public life. The annual U.S. criminal caseload includes 35–40 million cases filed in state courts. Traffic violations add another 55 million cases to the total. Federal courts open 361,000 new cases a year (note that federal cases equal about 1 percent of the volume in state courts). And another 1.6 million cases enter bankruptcy courts. Add all of these up and the United States approaches 100 million legal actions a year. And that's before we get to all the cases heard in specialized federal courts.

Courts are the primary sites for settling both private and public disputes. Advocacy groups, private citizens, and corporations go to court as a "first-strike" option. Litigation is an essential part of the rule-making process (discussed in the previous chapter). Business competition spills into the courts. Most other industrial nations rely more on **mediation** in noncriminal cases; citizens are also more likely to defer to civil servants. In contrast, Americans sue. Only a few other nations–most notably, Great Britain and Denmark—have as many suits per capita as the United States does.

Mediation: A way of resolving disputes without going to court, in which a third party (the mediator) helps two or more sides negotiate a settlement.

Declining Trust

Traditionally, lawyers and courts enjoyed high prestige. Tocqueville described lawyers as democracy's natural aristocrats and noted that the American people trusted them. Not anymore.

Today, law, lawyers, and the legal system all face shrinking reputations. The Supreme Court recently received its lowest approval ratings ever recorded in June 2014 (see Figure 13.1). Even when the judiciary's prestige ebbs, it still generally ranks roughly the same as the president and towers over Congress— which was down to 9% approval in 2014.

Courts in American Culture

Images of law and lawyers run through American culture, with the image alternating between heroism and cynicism. On the one side, in *To Kill a Mockingbird*, Gregory Peck's Atticus Finch wins the African American community's respect when he passionately defends a black man unjustly accused of rape: "In our courts all men are created equal," he proclaims at the film's climax. "That's no ideal to me. That is a living, working reality." The book and movie's racial idealism reflected the idealism of the early 1960s. Julia Roberts played another

Do you approve or disapprove of the way the Supreme Court is handling its job?

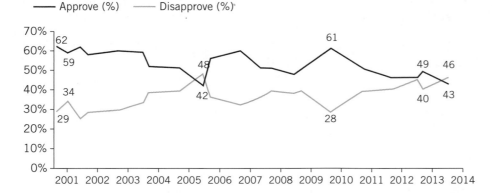

—— Approve (%)   —— Disapprove (%)

● **FIGURE 13.1** *The Supreme Court declines in public esteem. After the 2000 Bush v. Gore decision, Democrats gave the court low rankings, but Republicans didn't. Today, skepticism is rising among Democrats, Republicans, and independents alike. Recent polls put the Court's approval rate below 50% (Gallup, shown here), with some falling as low as 28% (Rasmussen).*

legal heroine, the real-life Erin Brockovich, a clerk without any legal training whose indefatigable work led to a major environmental suit against Pacific Gas and Electric for contaminating the water supply of Hinkley, California. Still other examples of movie heroes before the bar include Tom Cruise, exposing fraud as he cross-examines a colonel played by Jack Nicholson in *A Few Good Men*, and even Marisa Tomei's comic heroine winning the day on the stand in *My Cousin Vinny*. Images of law as a kind of crusade—for racial justice, environmental protection, or personal honor—reflect and reinforce cultural images of political idealism.

● *Images of law are everywhere in popular culture. Here, Marisa Tomei saves the day in* My Cousin Vinny.

● Organizing the Judicial Branch

The Constitution offers detailed instruction for Congress (Article 1) and vague rules for the executive branch (article 2). The judiciary gets the least attention of all. The Constitution vests judicial power in the Supreme Court, without specifying the number of justices, and empowers Congress to design the rest of our federal court system. This section examines how the courts are organized.

Divided We Rule

By now you know the story: When Americans see government power, they divide it. Two chambers of Congress, with layers of committees and subcommittees; an executive branch split into departments, agencies, commissions, and White House offices; and a federalist system of national, state, and city officials all co-operating, competing, and overlapping. Court powers are also divided.

Most other nations feature a single, unitary system of courts. In contrast, the United States exhibits *judicial federalism*. Both federal and state court systems are further divided into three layers, as Figure 13.2 displays: Lower courts conduct trials; appellate courts hear appeals; and a supreme court in both state and federal systems renders a final verdict. The national Supreme Court is the ultimate arbiter for all cases. However, millions of cases are filed each year; the Supreme Court only reviews around seven thousand lower-court cases and, in recent years, accepts and hears eighty or fewer. That leaves a great deal of authority in the lower ranks of the judiciary.

State and Local Courts

Local trial and state appeals courts are the workhorses of the judiciary, handling most of the nontraffic cases in the United States each year. State courts are responsible for all cases that arise under state law; they rule on everything from antitrust disputes to murder cases and from medical malpractice to marijuana possession. States organize their judicial system in their own way—so there is considerable variation around the nation.

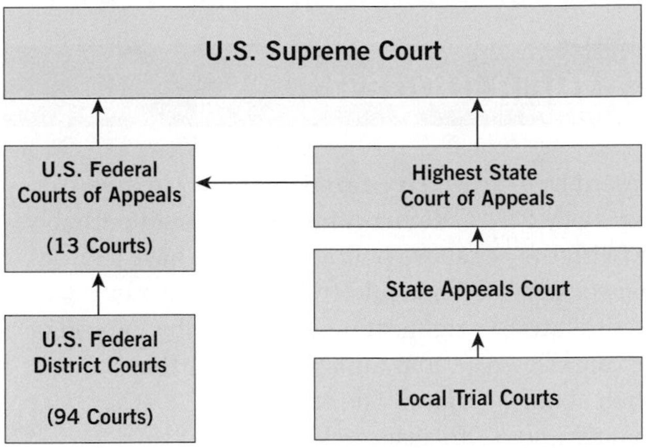

● **FIGURE 13.2** *Organization of the U.S. federal courts system.*

The first stop in most cases is a state trial court; appeals usually are handled in state appellate courts. In high-profile cases, appeals from state courts may be heard by the U.S. Supreme Court. Many landmark cases originate—and sometimes reach settlement—in state courts. The 2012 decision to uphold the "Obamacare" health reform law began as a state decision, as did the Terri Schiavo case that opened this chapter. However, very few of the millions of state cases ever reach a federal judge—as these cases did.

Judicial Selection

Do you think you might like to become a state judge? There are surprisingly few formal criteria for selection. You may not even need a law degree: Twenty-two states require no formal training before judges start hearing cases. Most judges first make their name as lawyers, although many come from government or academic positions. If you plan to lobby a governor to ensure your judicial appointment, make sure you pick the right state: Only seventeen states authorize their governor to select judges, and two leave selection to the state legislature. Most states (thirty-one) elect judges. Judges' terms range, depending on the state, from two to fourteen years, and these are usually renewable.

The idea of electing judges is controversial. After all, the courts are meant to be above partisan politics, protecting rights and weighing evidence separate from political pressures. Elections, say the critics, undermine the courts' ability to stand up to a majority intent on denying the rights of the minority. Moreover, campaign contributions could lead to bias and even corruption on the state benches. Former Supreme Court justice Sandra Day O'Connor has been an especially vocal critic of the political pressures that encroach on elected judges; she calls the campaigns "tawdry and embarrassing."[4] Still, the United States is the land of five hundred thousand elected officials. The American

What Do You Think?

HOW SHOULD STATES SELECT THEIR JUDGES?

Which of these three arguments about judicial selection in the states seems most persuasive to you?

Let the people vote. The people are the best guardians of their own welfare. Let them decide who should be their justices. No matter how courts are organized, it is naive to think that politics can be kept out of the equation. Today, 75 percent of the public thinks that justices sometimes let their own political views influence their rulings (see Figure 13.5). Since politics is inevitable, the public should have a direct voice in judicial selection.

Appointment by a governor. A state governor (with the advice and consent of the state senate) will have valuable information about the candidates and can keep better track of which justice is doing a good job. With selection by public officials, the problems of campaigning and raising funds (with their possible corruption) will not filter into the courts.

Merit committees. Courts must be above politics. They must defend the rights of minorities and unpopular views. The only way to ensure such fairness is to let impartial merit commissions make the selection. The commission's nominees can then be voted up or down by the legislature.

Unsure. You will probably have a stronger opinion by the end of the chapter.

● Judicial elections: emblem of democracy—or path to corruption?

ideal—government by the people—leads many states to insist that judges stand directly accountable to the public. Voters tend to agree: In 2010, Nevada's voters decisively rejected a referendum that would have ended judicial elections (57 percent voted no).

Federal Courts

Federal courts hear three kinds of cases. First, they handle crimes that violate federal laws, issues that involve federal treaties, or cases touching on the Constitution. Examples range from the dramatic to the mundane: terrorism, immigration, organized crime, civil rights, patents, insider trading, or flag burning. Second, they decide disputes that spill across state lines—for example, interstate drug trafficking or conflicts between parties in different states (with at least $75,000 in dispute). Finally, after state courts have ruled on a case, the parties can appeal to federal courts.

Most federal cases begin in one of the ninety-four **district courts**, which house just under seven hundred judges. Every state has at least one district court, and the larger states (like California and Texas) have as many as four. District courts determine the facts of the case (did John Smith try to blow up a federal building?), they build a record detailing the evidence, and they then apply the law to reach a ruling. Cases at this level are heard by a single district judge.

District court judges, like all federal judges, are appointed by the president, subject to "advice and consent" review by the Senate, and hold their office for life. Until recently, the Senate routinely approved nearly all judicial appointments, sometimes with very little scrutiny. In today's hyperpartisan Congress, however, the opposition party generally challenges judicial nominations—slowing them down in the hopes that their party will take the presidency and fill the empty seats. By the Obama administration's fourth year, a full 9 percent of the federal bench was vacant, creating an alarming backlog of cases. The Democratic majority in the Senate broke the logjam in 2013 by forbidding filibusters for lower court nominations (although not for Supreme Court nominations).

Above the ninety-four district courts are thirteen federal appellate courts, known as **circuit courts**. A party that loses in district court can appeal to this next level. Three circuit court judges hear each case, usually to determine whether the district court made the correct ruling. They rule on the basis of the record established on the lower level: There is no jury and no cross-examination. Some 180 judges serve these circuit courts, collectively ruling on nearly seventy thousand cases in a typical year. Like district courts, the circuit courts are organized geographically and referred to by their number: Figure 13.3 displays the current organization. Cases from Florida—like the Terri Schiavo case—go to the Eleventh Circuit Court of Appeals, which is based in Atlanta. Some kinds of cases (like those involving patents or international trade) go directly to a court known as the U.S. Court of Appeals for the Federal Circuit.

Sometimes multiple versions of a case reach different district and circuit courts. Cases challenging the Affordable Care Act as unconstitutional were filed in forty state courts across the United States. Nineteen different district courts considered the matter. On the next level, seven circuit courts eventually accepted appeals. Of these, one—the Eleventh Circuit's ruling that the individual mandate to buy insurance was unconstitutional—was ultimately heard by the Supreme Court, which issued the definitive ruling, overturning the Eleventh Circuit's ruling on the mandate. Other cases have a more difficult time making it into federal court: for example, four different federal courts—two district, one circuit, and the Supreme Court—refused to hear an appeal

District courts: The first level of federal courts, which actually try the cases. Each decision is based not on a statute but on previous judicial decisions.

Circuit courts (U.S. Court of Appeals): The second stage of federal courts, which review the trial record of cases decided in district court to ensure they were settled properly.

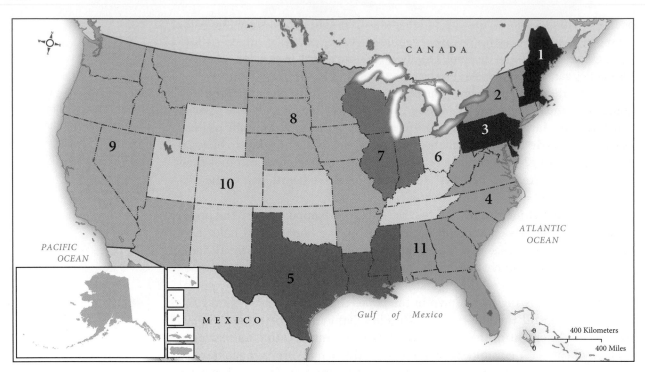

● **FIGURE 13.3** *A map of the federal circuit courts. (Federal Judicial Center)*

to the Florida Supreme Court's decision to allow removal of Terri Schiavo's feeding tube.

Specialized Courts

The federal judiciary also includes a set of specialized courts, each covering a specific subject. These include military justice, tax disputes, and bankruptcy. In recent years bankruptcy claims have risen to more than 1.5 million annually. Shortly after 9/11, the federal government established a new secret court, the Foreign Intelligence Surveillance Court, to rule on federal government requests to conduct electronic surveillance of suspected spies.

Judges on all these courts are appointed by the president and are subject to Senate confirmation. Unlike other federal judges, however, they do not serve for life. Bankruptcy judges, for example, serve renewable fourteen-year terms; federal magistrates, who handle certain types of civil trials, are appointed to renewable eight-year terms.

The U.S. military runs its own separate court system, addressing breaches of justice by members of the armed forces. These courts have been a source of controversy in recent years, after President George W. Bush called for military tribunals to try defendants charged with terrorism against the United States, many of them held as "enemy combatants" in Guantánamo Bay, Abu Ghraib, or other detention centers around the globe. The Obama administration first suspended the military trials; but after Congress resisted moving the trials to civilian courts, the administration reinstated the tribunals with some changes in their rules. In rare cases, tribunals are permitted under the Constitution. The last large-scale use of military tribunals occurred after World War II, to try Nazi war criminals.

Together, these specialized courts, ranging from bankruptcy to military, constitute something of a "third judiciary" alongside state and federal courts. Periodically, critics advance proposals for a new type of special court, usually to deal with some technical area of law they believe regular citizen juries cannot handle adequately. The latest proposals focus on medical malpractice, where multimillion-dollar damage suits turn on ambiguous "medical errors." Overall, specialized courts provide a further example of the complexity characterizing the divided, fragmented U.S. judicial branch—as Figure 13.4 vividly demonstrates.

Diversity in the Federal Judiciary

Do federal judges reflect America's population? No. Roughly one out of four judges are women, and more than 80 percent are white. Eleven percent of federal judges are African American (compared to 12.2 percent of the population),

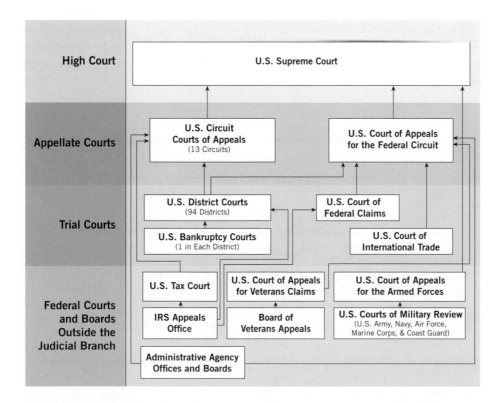

● **FIGURE 13.4** *Special courts within the federal system. A more detailed snapshot of the federal system illustrates that it is, in reality, far more complicated than the simple tripartite system of district, circuit, and supreme courts.*

IDENTITY ON THE BENCH

As Justice Sotomayor's comment (below) suggests, a person's life experience can deeply inform his or her judgment about politics, culture, and other matters.	**Agree**. Every person inevitably brings his or her life experience to important decisions and justices are no different. That's why diversity on the bench is so important.	**Disagree**. Judges should rule on the basis of law. Their background is irrelevant and should not cloud sound legal judgment based on the laws and the facts of the case.

7 percent are Hispanic (compared to 16.3 percent), and only 1 percent are Asian American (compared to 4.7 percent). Does it make a difference if the judge presiding over a federal case is female, or Latino?

Supreme Court Justice Sonia Sotomayor suggested that it did, ten years before she was appointed to the Court. "I would hope that a wise Latina woman," Sotomayor said, "with the richness of her experience would more often than not reach a better conclusion than a white male who hasn't lived that life." In other words, personal experience will inform judicial decisions. The comment provided cause for reflection—and also raised controversy. Former House Speaker Newt Gingrich claimed that a white male judge making a similar claim on behalf of white men would be forced to resign.[5]

THE BOTTOM LINE

- State courts handle the vast majority of cases. Although each state's judiciary system is distinctive, all are divided into three levels: trial courts, appeals courts, and a state supreme court. A majority of U.S. states elect their judges.

- Federal courts rule on cases involving constitutional questions, federal laws, and federal treaties. They are divided into ninety-four district courts, eleven appeals courts, and the Supreme Court.

- Federal justices are selected by the president and confirmed by the Senate, and they hold their position for life. Party polarization in Congress has created a serious problem of unfilled judgeships.

- Numerous additional federal courts handle everything from bankruptcy to military matters.

The Court's Role

Alexander Hamilton's assurance that the judiciary would play a minor role in American government did not last long. John Marshall, the longest-serving chief justice in U.S. history—he held the office from January 1801 to July 1835—helped establish the U.S. courts as unusually powerful. How did Marshall do it?

Judicial Review

The breakthrough came in the landmark case *Marbury v. Madison*. Marshall asserted that the Supreme Court has the authority to overrule any act of Congress that violates the Constitution.

The case arose after John Adams lost the 1800 election and, during his last hours as president, made "midnight appointments" that installed his supporters in judicial positions. The new president, Thomas Jefferson, came to office with very different political views and vehemently opposed the last-minute appointments. Jefferson directed his secretary of state, James Madison, to destroy the appointment letters—including one naming William Marbury as justice of the peace for the District of Columbia. The Judiciary Act of 1789, which established the position, referred some cases (involving writs of mandamus—or direct

● *John Marshall denied Marbury's suit and, in the process, asserted the power of the Supreme Court to strike down acts of Congress when they violated the Constitution.*

orders to government officials) directly to the Supreme Court. Marbury duly petitioned the Court to order Madison to deliver his commission. This action constituted a high-stakes early test of the Court's authority.

Marshall and his fellow justices faced a trap. On the one hand, if the Court ruled in favor of Marbury, the recently elected President Jefferson might very well ignore the Court—and diminish its importance in the new federal government. On the other hand, Marshall did not wish simply to accept President Jefferson's defiance. Marshall found an ingenious way around the dilemma—and vastly expanded the role of the Court in the process.

Led by Marshall, a unanimous Court ruled that Congress, in drafting the Judiciary Act of 1789, had erred in granting the Supreme Court the direct authority (or "original jurisdiction") to decide the question. The Constitution implied that the Supreme Court should rule on such cases only on appeal from the lower courts. However, the Constitution was silent on what would happen if Congress passed a law that clashed with the Constitution. Marshall filled in the blank with a dramatic move: "It is emphatically the province and duty" of the Court, wrote Marshall, to judge "if a law be in opposition to the Constitution." With that, Marshall established the court system's mighty power of **judicial review**—although that authority is never mentioned in the Constitution itself.

Judicial review: The Court's authority to strike down acts that violate the Constitution and to interpret what the Constitution means.

The Court decided the case by striking down section 13 of the Judiciary Act of 1789—the section that referred writs of mandamus directly to the Supreme Court. Since that was the basis of Marbury's petition, the Court ruled that it had no constitutional authority to force the administration to deliver the petition. President Jefferson opposed Marshall's clever move; he vigorously denounced the "despotism" and "oligarchy" by which unelected officials "usurp[ed]" control of the Constitution from elected ones. But what could Jefferson do? In asserting the Court's power, Marshall had sided with the president and denied Marbury his petition. By apparently relinquishing power, Marshall permanently strengthened the federal judiciary.[6]

Marshall deftly addressed a basic issue in American government, with profound implications that reverberate in the present day. When there is doubt about what the Constitution holds or implies, the Supreme Court makes the call.[7]

Activism versus Restraint

The Supreme Court was slow to wield the power it had asserted. It did not overrule another act of Congress for fifty-four years, until the *Dred Scott* decision struck down the Missouri Compromise and declared that black people were "so far inferior that they had no rights which the white man was bound to respect." That decision brought the issue of slavery to a boil in 1857—and established a pattern: Many of the most intense disputes in American politics wind up decided in court.

Recently the judiciary has stepped up the pace with which it overrules Congress. In the 150 years following *Marbury*, it struck down just twenty-two federal laws; in the twenty-one years between 1990 and 2014, it struck down forty-four acts of Congress, including laws designed to ban or limit flag burning, guns near school yards, child pornography, violence against women, barriers to voting, and same-sex marriage.

Today, the Supreme Court is embroiled in many intense debates: May the United States hold "enemy combatants" at Guantánamo Bay without charge or trial? May Congress limit campaign contributions? Is the right to bear arms so fundamental that it may not be curtailed by state or local governments? Does the right of privacy forbid states from banning abortions? Each of these questions was removed from the court of public opinion, or the jurisdiction of elected officials, and settled by the Supreme Court—generally by a 5–4 vote.

The Supreme Court also reviews state and local statutes. This power required far less subtle maneuvering to establish. The Constitution's "supremacy clause" declares that "this Constitution and the laws of the United States . . . shall be the supreme Law of the Land" (article 6). The Judiciary Act of 1789, which established the federal court system (yes, the same act that created William Marbury's position), granted the Court the authority to enforce the supremacy clause and to strike down state laws that clash with the Constitution or with federal statutes. The judiciary has been more active on this level, striking down state actions at about six times the rate it overturns federal laws. Over time, federal courts have declared more than one thousand state and local laws unconstitutional. Many landmark cases struck down state laws that established segregation, outlawed abortion, or established school prayer.

The rising pace of judicial action overturning legislation leads to an enduring question: How energetic should courts be in reviewing cases? **Judicial activists** take a vigorous approach to reviewing the other branches of government; the courts must be vigilant in protecting rights. Between the 1950s and the 1970s, liberal activists were in the Supreme Court majority. The Court struck down segregation, forbade school prayer, and found a right to privacy in the penumbra (or shadow) of the Constitution.

Judicial restraint holds, on the contrary, that the courts should overturn the elected branches of government reluctantly and as a last resort. The terms— *activism* and *restraint*—are easily politicized. Conservatives bitterly attacked liberal judicial activism; as the courts turned conservative, however, liberals began to criticize activist judges for being eager to overrule the will of the people's representatives.

The idea of activism is, in many ways, similar to the discussion in Chapter 2 about how to read the Constitution. Is it a living and evolving document, as the pragmatists believe? Or should we insist on going back and reconstructing the original meaning, as originalists think we should do? The difference between these positions is less stark than it might appear. The Constitution can be ambiguous; it often requires a nimble analysis to apply it to a contemporary case.

Judicial activism:
A vigorous or active approach to reviewing the other branches of government.

Judicial restraint:
Reluctance to interfere with elected branches, only doing so as a last resort.

The Judicial Process

The judiciary's role goes far beyond weighing constitutionality. Legal cases constantly raise the question of how a law should be applied in a specific dispute. The court has the job of determining legislative intent. We saw this in the last chapter, in the case of the bureaucratic rule-making process. If the lobbyists do not like the new regulations for inspecting poultry slaughterhouses, they can go to court and claim that the regulatory agency has mistaken what Congress intended when it authorized those inspections. Ultimately, the court has to rule on what Congress meant to do—perhaps in the distant past. Because lawsuits are a regular feature of policy making, federal courts stay very busy interpreting the intent of the other branches.

Often there is no legislative record or executive action to settle a case. The American colonists introduced an English system known as **common law**. Common law (also known as *case law*) is a system of law developed by judges in deciding cases over the centuries. Since legal judgments should be consistent from case to case, each time a court settles a case it sets a **precedent** that will guide similar cases in the future. Over the years, the common law offers a rich legal heritage to guide judges in settling disputes. In countries without a common law tradition, like France, judges may not rule unless there is a statute or regulation to guide them.

American courts handle two different kinds of cases. **Civil law** handles cases between two parties. William Marbury sues James Madison for his commission; a young man sues his Catholic diocese because a priest molested him; a major corporation sues a local pizza chain for borrowing its corporate logo. **Criminal law** involves cases where someone is charged with doing something prohibited by the government.

The party who complains—Marbury, the man who was molested, or the government coming down on an alleged criminal—is called the **plaintiff**; the party that is sued is the **defendant**. In court cases, the plaintiff is listed first and the defendant second; thus, the case is called *Marbury* (the plaintiff) *versus Madison* (the secretary of state who did not deliver the commission).

Too Much Power?

Keep in mind the key question about the Court: Should nine unelected, lifetime appointees wield this much power in a twenty-first-century democracy?

Both our litigious society and the range of judicial authority—from judicial review to common law—give the courts the power to shape American policy. In other nations, the elected branches make vital decisions about environmental protection, gun rights, immigration rules, and other urgent questions. In the United States, courts are major players in resolving these issues . . . and other issues in almost every policy realm.

American courts profoundly shape American politics. Are they the guarantors of American constitutional rights? Or an outmoded throwback to an

Common law: A system of law developed by judges in deciding cases over the centuries.

Precedent: Judicial decisions that offer a guide to similar cases in the future.

Civil law: Cases that involve disputes between two parties.

Criminal law: Cases in which someone is charged with breaking the law.

Plaintiff: The party that brings the action in a lawsuit.

Defendant: The party that is sued in a court case.

earlier, more elitist, age? You can get a better sense below when we look behind the scenes at the inner workings of the Supreme Court.

Or Still the "Least Dangerous" Branch?

Although the courts are undeniably powerful, every institution faces limits. The courts operate with four different kinds of restraints.

First, the federal courts have *no electoral base*. Their prestige and mystique are balanced by a lack of democratic authority. This has made some past courts careful about confronting elected officials. For example, the Supreme Court delayed the ruling in *Brown v. Board of Education* (striking down segregated schools) for almost two years while the justices struggled to reach unanimity. Chief Justice Earl Warren felt that such an important case—challenging segregation laws across many states—should have the backing of all nine members.

Second, courts have relatively *limited resources* compared to other units of government. A typical senator commands more than fifty staff members and has elaborate research enterprises at his or her beck and call. The Congressional Research Service and Government Accountability Office houses hundreds of experts devoted to reporting in detail on any question a member might raise. In contrast, most federal judges have only two or three clerks—young staffers, usually fresh from law school with little judicial experience—who serve them for less than a year. Supreme Court justices, whose decisions can shape the course of government and policy making for generations, have at most four clerks, who are always new at the job.

The courts command small budgets. The Supreme Court operates on an annual budget of around $70 million a year. The entire federal judiciary—thirteen circuit courts, ninety-four district courts, and the Supreme Court—receives less than $6 billion. That is about the same budget as the National Oceanographic and Atmospheric Administration, the federal weather service.

Third, courts are by definition *reactive decision makers*. Executive-branch agencies or legislators can tackle problems and devise solutions. Courts await disputes; cases must come to them. True, most major issues do wind up before the courts—but, unlike the other branches, they do not define the problem or shape the question that is being disputed.

Finally, the courts must rely on other branches for *enforcement*. The Court rules. Other actors—in and out of government—implement the decision. The Supreme Court could strike down school desegregation; it could not, however, enforce the decision, which was blocked for years by intransigent state and local officials (until the civil rights protests finally moved Congress to pass the Civil Rights Act). President Andrew Jackson made the point dramatically. When the Supreme Court struck down a Georgia law governing relations with the Cherokees, he reputedly said, of the chief justice: "John Marshall has made his decision, now let him enforce it."[8]

- Chief Justice John Marshall asserted the court's authority to review acts of Congress for their fit with the Constitution in *Marbury v. Madison*. The Judiciary Act of 1789 authorized the Court to review state laws.

- Historically the Court has not often struck down acts of Congress, but it began to do so at a quicker pace beginning in the 1990s.

- There are two general approaches toward defining the courts' role in government: *activists* believe in a vigorous judiciary scrutinizing the other branches; judicial *restraint* holds that courts should intervene rarely and reluctantly.

- The vital overarching question remains the same one that Chief Justice Marshall and President Jefferson crossed swords over more than two centuries ago: Is the Court acting in ways that are indispensable for democracy? Or in ways that threaten it?

◗ The Supreme Court and How It Operates

Tucked away at the top of the majestic marble Supreme Court building on East Capitol Street, among all the justices' offices and conference rooms and libraries lined with leather law books, is . . . a small basketball court. Known as the "highest court in the land," the court is used exclusively by Supreme Court insiders: the justices' clerks, both current and former; a few staff members; and occasionally one of the justices joins a game. We can imagine the basketball court as symbolic of the Supreme Court itself: exclusive, little known, and open to a tiny membership on a lifetime basis. The basketball court is open for play except when the Court is hearing oral arguments.

● *A formal portrait of the Supreme Court. Standing, from left: Sotomayor, Breyer, Alito, Kagan. Seated: Thomas, Scalia, Roberts, Kennedy, Ginsburg.*

Hearing Cases

The Supreme Court is in session for approximately nine months each year, by tradition opening on the first Monday in October. The justices are generally out of public view, except when the Court meets to hear *oral arguments*—the presentation of a case that the Court has agreed to review.

Supreme Court oral arguments do not resemble the courtroom scenes on TV. Rather than dramatic arguments by lawyers to juries or fierce cross-examination of witnesses, the Supreme Court features justices as the sole audience: No jury is present, and no witnesses are called. Any case that the Supreme Court agrees to hear has already been thoroughly aired by at least one lower court, except in rare instances. Normally, cases are heard in one hour, and each side's lawyer—called "counsel" in Court-speak (whether it is one lawyer or many)—is granted thirty minutes to make his or her best argument. The justices usually interrupt the presenting lawyer almost immediately with questions, some supportive and others combative. They may also deliver minispeeches of their own; no lawyer ever dares interrupt a Supreme Court justice, even if the lawyer's thirty minutes is slipping away.

Before the hearing, the parties submit written briefs spelling out the details of their argument. Other interested parties may submit their own briefs, endorsing the side they favor. The outside contributions are known as **amicus curiae** (Latin for "friend of the court") briefs.

Are oral arguments important? Perhaps not. Justice Clarence Thomas told one interviewer that they influence his colleagues "in five or ten percent of the cases, maybe, and I'm being generous there." What matters far more are the written briefs that the counsel submit.

Selecting Cases: Formal Requirements

How do the justices decide which cases to hear? Losing parties in lower courts are permitted, depending on the nature of the case, to file a petition with the Supreme Court—stating the facts of the case and setting out detailed arguments as to why the Court should hear the case. The petitions are split up among the justices and their clerks; on selected Fridays the justices meet to choose the cases they will hear. At least four judges have to vote to hear a case for it to make it to the Supreme Court; that requirement is known as the **rule of four**.

When the justices agree to hear a case, the Supreme Court issues a *writ of certiorari* (legal-speak for "to be informed") demanding the official record from the lower court that heard the case. Roughly eight thousand petitions are filed with the Supreme Court each year, and some eighty are accepted—barely 1 percent. How do cases make it into that elite group? That remains one of the great mysteries of American government. The Court never gives any formal explanation for why it decided to grant certiorari to this case and not that one.

see for yourself 13.1

Go online to listen to oral arguments on the Obama health care plan.

see for yourself 13.2

Go online to hear additional oral arguments for the Obama health care plan.

Amicus curiae: A brief submitted by a person or group that is not a direct party to the case.

Rule of four: The requirement that at least four Supreme Court judges must agree to hear a case before it comes before the Court.

Formally, a case must meet three conditions before it is even eligible for the Supreme Court—or any other court, because these requirements apply at all judicial levels. The case must involve a *legitimate controversy*—that is, an actual dispute between two parties. Supreme Court justices do not deal with hypothetical matters; no court offers "advisory opinions."

Second, the parties bringing a case must have *standing*: They must prove an actual harm (or imminent harm) to receive a hearing. Merely being distressed or concerned about a far-off environmental disaster's effect is not enough to bring a lawsuit, for example; you must prove that the oil spill or pollutant is directly affecting your livelihood (or your health or your property).

Finally, if the Court's proceedings will no longer affect the issue at hand, it is considered *moot*—irrelevant—and the case is thrown out. A famous example occurred in *Roe v. Wade*, where a federal district court dismissed the case as moot because the plaintiff, "Jane Roe" (real name: Norma McCorvey), had already delivered her child. The Supreme Court rejected this view, noting that the typical length of legal appeals processes meant that pregnancies would usually conclude too soon for a court decision to be reached.

Selecting Cases: Informal Factors

Thousands of cases each year meet the standards—controversy, standing, and mootness. Informally, we can identify three additional factors that help predict whether a case is more or less likely to be accepted by the Court.

First, the Supreme Court is more inclined to hear a case when two lower courts decide the legal question differently (usually two federal courts, but sometimes federal and state). Different rulings in similar cases require some resolution.

Second, justices are inclined to grant certiorari to cases in which a lower-court decision conflicts with an existing Supreme Court ruling. In 1989, the Court ruled in *Penry v. Lynaugh* that a death sentence was sometimes permissible for criminals under the age of eighteen. More than a decade later, the Missouri Supreme Court declared that the death penalty for nonadults was "cruel and unusual punishment," citing a recent Supreme Court ruling that struck down capital punishment for mentally disabled people. The Supreme Court agreed and, in *Roper v. Simmons*, reversed its 1989 decision.

Third, the Supreme Court is more likely to look favorably on cases that have significance beyond the two parties involved.

For the cases that the Court agrees to hear, oral arguments generally run from early October through late April. The Court then issues decisions in all cases that it heard during the session, usually on Monday mornings in May and June. Those Mondays are very exciting—and, for those involved in a case's outcome, very anxious—occasions. No one knows when the Court will hand down a decision in a given case, nor is there a set time period in which the justices must reach a decision. However, the Court generally decides all the cases it has heard during a term before the summer recess begins.

Conference Sessions and Written Decisions

What do the justices do when they are not on the bench, hearing oral arguments? Justices keep busy writing opinions (usually with substantial assistance from their clerks, who prepare drafts and discuss details with their boss); deciding which cases to hear in the future; and reading briefs for upcoming oral arguments. And, most intriguing of all, the justices meet in conference.

Supreme Court conferences are closed to everyone except the justices—even their clerks are not allowed in. Justices sit around a conference table; by tradition, the most junior justice (currently Elena Kagan, the most recent appointee to the Court) sits nearest the door, opening it only to allow a staff member to wheel in carts piled with materials for the next case under consideration. The Supreme Court's most significant collective decisions take place in conference.

Justices discuss the cases recently heard in oral argument, indicating their voting preferences, and the chief justice assigns the job of writing the **majority opinion** in each decided case. This is the official statement of the Court. Any justice who wishes to can issue a **concurrent opinion**, explaining why he or she voted in favor of the majority outcome—different justices come to the same opinion for different reasons. Justices who disagree about the outcome write a **dissent** indicating why they voted against the majority. Some dissents become celebrated after the fact—or form the basis for future rethinking of the issues by the Court.

Majority opinion: The official statement of the court.

Concurrent opinion: A statement that agrees with the majority opinion.

Dissent: A statement on behalf of the justices who voted in the minority.

Supreme Court Clerks

Supreme Court clerks assist the justices. These recent law school graduates, usually in their twenties, exercise a remarkable amount of influence. They help the justices write opinions and reach decisions in the cases before the Court; the clerks also perform initial screening of the thousands of certiorari petitions that reach the Court each year.

Although the process is kept strictly private, it is clear that clerks reject many of the petitions, choosing a smaller set of a few hundred potential cases for the justices' consideration. Remember: These cases can shape American government in powerful ways. And often a small group of unelected young people significantly influence whether a case will reach the Court.

Interested in expressing your civic passions—and exercising real political influence—by serving as a Supreme Court clerk? It's a tough position to win: Of the more than one thousand applicants each year, only three dozen or so will achieve this post. After completing your JD, you would generally serve one year in a lower-court clerkship—for a district court judge or in a state supreme court. During that year, you would apply to a specific Supreme Court justice's chambers—many aspirants apply to all nine to maximize their chances of being selected.

Should you receive the congratulatory call, you'll join one of the most exclusive clubs in American government. Supreme Court clerks who elect to stay in public service often go on to be lawyers themselves or professors at top law schools. If you decide instead to go into private practice, you'll be hot property: "court clerk bonuses" to sign with a law firm competing for your talents can be as high as $250,000.

Confirmation Battles

Given the lifetime tenure and the immense influence often wielded by the Supreme Court justices, one of the most significant moments on the American political calendar is the appointment of a new justice. Confirmation hearings have become unusually heated, with strong partisanship apparent both in Senate Judiciary Committee hearings on a nominee and among a wide range of interested groups across the U.S. population.

Until recently, most of those decisions were relatively uncontroversial. The two most senior members of the Court, Justices Scalia and Kennedy, were both confirmed unanimously (see Table 13.1). The politics changed dramatically in 1987, when President Ronald Reagan nominated Robert Bork to the Court. Bork certainly seemed qualified: He was a national authority on antitrust law; he had served under President Nixon as solicitor general, representing the U.S. government in cases before the Supreme Court; and he had been acting attorney general and a circuit court judge. However, he was a no-apologies conservative who would replace Justice Lewis Powell, a moderate "swing vote." Liberal groups mobilized to oppose the nomination; Democratic senators, led by Ted Kennedy, criticized what they called "Robert Bork's America." After twelve days of hearings, the Senate defeated the nomination, 58–42. What surprised observers was the swift rise of organized opposition based not on the candidate's qualification, but on his judicial philosophy. Conservatives coined a new word to describe the phenomenon: *Borking*. They have returned the favor. Every judicial appointment now faces a partisan nomination fight: packed hearings, demonstrations (pro and con), intense media coverage, and public opinion polls serving up regular updates on how the nominee fares in the public view.

President Obama selected the most recent nominee, Elena Kagan, when ninety-year-old justice John Paul Stevens decided to retire after thirty-five years on the Court. During Kagan's confirmation hearings, Republican members of Senate Judiciary Committee pushed her to take a strong stand on controversial issues such as the right to abortion or permissibility of torture of suspected terrorists. Kagan had criticized previous Court nominees for ducking substantive questions; now she discovered the wisdom of that strategy for herself. She was confirmed by a fairly comfortable margin, 63–37, but Republicans voted 36–5 against her.

● *Supreme Court nominee Robert Bork testifying at his confirmation hearing. His nomination was a watershed in the politicization of the Court. Before Judge Bork, the major question was competence; now, the question became the political direction of the Court.*

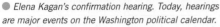
● *Elena Kagan's confirmation hearing. Today, hearings are major events on the Washington political calendar.*

● *To Bork: To turn down a competent nominee for political reasons.*

The party battles over each nominee reflect the new stakes that surround the Supreme Court. The Court is closely divided, lining up 5–4 on a wide range of social and political issues. A single vote makes the difference on a host of issues: the right to privacy and abortion, gun control, the rights of criminals, campaign finance, health care reform, the rights of terrorism suspects, and the list goes on. Small wonder that the debates over each new justice get so heated—especially when a moderate swing vote is up for replacement. "The least dangerous branch" was not designed to be in the eye of the political hurricane.

THE BOTTOM LINE

- The Supreme Court generally hears cases on the basis of petitions requesting a review of lower-court decisions. Four justices must vote to hear a case before it becomes part of the 1 percent that come before the Court.

- To be heard in federal court, a case must meet criteria involving controversy, standing, and mootness. Other factors that make it more likely that the case will be heard include the scope of the question, a clash between lower courts, the justices' own interests, and requests from the solicitor general.

- Cases involve oral arguments, written briefs, and conferences with only the justices present. The chief justice assigns a majority opinion; others write concurring or dissenting opinions for the record.

- Confirmation to the federal bench—and especially to the Supreme Court—was once a polite affair that largely involved questions of competence. Today, confirmations are some of the most politically charged dates on the political calendar. This discord raises an important question: How does the charged politics that surrounds the Court affect its own workings—and its standing with the public?

TABLE 13.1 Supreme Court Nominations and Confirmations

Nomination votes have gotten closer. Before the Bork appointment, qualified justices were easily confirmed. Note that both Kennedy (a moderate) and Scalia (a conservative) won unanimously. After Bork, unanimous votes disappeared and the hearings have gotten more contentious. Debates become especially heated when a swing vote is up for replacement. It is much easier to replace a liberal with a liberal or a conservative with a conservative.

JUDGE	APPOINTED BY (PRESIDENT)	SELECTED FROM	YEAR	SENATE VOTE		PUBLIC OPINION*		
				YES	NO	YES	NO	NO OPINION
Elena Kagan	Obama	U.S. Solicitor General	2010	63	37	44	34	22
Sonia Sotomayor	Obama	U.S. Court of Appeals	2009	68	31	56	36	9
Samuel Alito	G. W. Bush	U.S. Court of Appeals	2006	58	42	54	30	16
John Roberts	G. W. Bush	U.S. Court of Appeals	2005	78	22	60	26	14
Stephen Breyer	Clinton	U.S. Court of Appeals	1994	87	9	—	—	—
Ruth Bader Ginsburg	Clinton	U.S. Court of Appeals	1993	96	3	53	14	33
Clarence Thomas	G. H. W. Bush	U.S. Court of Appeals	1991	52	48	58	30	12
Robert Bork	Reagan	U.S. Court of Appeals	1987	42	58	38	35	26
Anthony Kennedy	Reagan	U.S. Court of Appeals	1988	97	0	—	—	—
Antonin Scalia	Reagan	U.S. Court of Appeals	1986	98	0	—	—	—

*Results of Gallup Poll, when available.

⬤ Judicial Decision Making and Reform

How do judges reach their decisions in a case? Social scientists emphasize four different perspectives.

The Role of Law

In theory, justices decide cases on the basis of the legal facts as laid out in the documents submitted. They read the law, consider the intent of those who framed the law, and place it in the context of the Constitution.

According to long-established principle, justices generally abide by previously decided cases. This is known as **stare decisis** (literally, "stand by the things decided"). Occasionally (but rarely), the Supreme Court concludes that the precedents were wrongly decided and overrules a past decision. In general, however, legal theory suggests that the Supreme Court rules on the facts, guided by precedent. As Chief Justice John Roberts put it at his confirmation hearing, "Judges are like umpires. Umpires don't make the rules; they apply them . . . My job is to call balls and strikes."[9]

The umpire metaphor is appealing. However, legal cases are often ambiguous. Applying the Constitution, 235 or more years later, is rarely simple or straightforward. Political scientists who analyze Supreme Court decisions have found another perspective with a good deal of analytic power.

> **Stare decisis:** Deciding cases on the basis of previous rulings or precedents.

Ideology and Partisanship

Ideology provides another guide to the judicial mind. Political scientists have generally found that the justices' beliefs are the most powerful predictor of how they will vote, especially on the difficult cases. Some studies look at the party identification of the justices, others at their ideology prior to confirmation, and still others at the views of the presidents who appointed them. No matter how ideology is measured, one study after another suggests a strong relationship between the justices' beliefs and their votes. In brief, we can predict the justices' votes, over time, with considerable accuracy, based on their political orientation.[10]

Ideology appears to go hand in hand with the judicial philosophy we discussed above. *Pragmatists* (who see a living, changing Constitution) will approach cases differently from *originalists* (who believe we must interpret the document's text literally). Likewise, activists might be quicker to strike down acts of Congress, state laws, and court precedents. Conservatives charged liberal justices with being overly activist during the Warren Court (1953–1969); today, liberals repeat the complaint about conservative justices. Ultimately, simple political perspective—liberal versus conservative—is one of the most effective ways of explaining how justices rule.

The current Court breaks relatively evenly along the partisan divide: Four members are conservative—and, according to one study, rank among the six most consistently conservative voters in the past fifty years. They are Chief Justice Roberts and Associate Justices Scalia, Thomas, and Alito, all of whom vote conservative more than 70 percent of the time. Justice Anthony Kennedy tends to vote conservative but provides a swing vote for liberals about one-third of the time. Four justices (Ginsburg, Breyer, Sotomayor, and Kagan) vote liberal between 60 and 70 percent of the time.[11] In recent years, justices have begun to read their dissenting opinions aloud, an unusual move designed to attract public attention to their dissatisfaction—which they often express in strong terms.[12]

To be sure, the ideological model has its limits and by no means explains all votes. In 2013–2014, 64% of the cases brought before the Court were decided

Politics in the Courtroom?

Do you think the Supreme Court justices usually decide their cases based on legal analysis without regard to politics and ideology, or do you think they sometimes let their own ideological views influence their decisions?

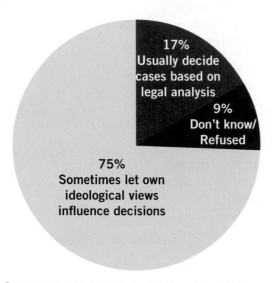

17%
Usually decide cases based on legal analysis

9%
Don't know/ Refused

75%
Sometimes let own ideological views influence decisions

● **FIGURE 13.5** *Most think justices' ideology plays a role in decision making. Scholarly analysis generally backs up this popular opinion (Kaiser Family Foundation).*

unanimously (up from 49% in the previous session). Ideology does not usually play a role in criminal justice cases or in many technical cases.

Collegiality and Peer Pressure

Collegiality, or more bluntly *peer pressure*, is a third factor that shapes decisions. Supreme Court justices (in fact, all federal court judges) spend a lot of time together, hearing cases and discussing their decisions. They exert some influence on one another's outlook and decision making. Persuasion is a regular feature of Court discussions; according to the few insider reports available, as well as academic analysis, justices appear to change positions in many cases based on legal arguments and personal appeals of colleagues. They may also change their votes for strategic reasons—trading votes in different cases.[13]

Another angle on the idea of "peer pressure" arises from the larger legal community. A few hundred people—law professors, law students, legal bloggers, congressional members, committee staff on the House and Senate Judiciary Committees, interest group activists—make up the attentive audience for most judicial decisions. The audience's judgment about a specific judicial opinion can be laudatory or scathing.

Institutional Concerns

Finally, justices sometimes appear to think about the interests of the Court as an institution. They spend many years on the bench and are aware of the outside forces that might affect the standing of the Court—public opinion, a hostile Congress, or a skeptical executive. We saw a prime example in the early years of our nation with *Marbury v. Madison*. Marshall was thinking about the role and standing of his institution as he crafted his complicated opinion. Some recent studies underscore the importance of this perspective.[14]

Many analysts used this factor to explain Chief Justice John Roberts's dramatic vote to uphold the Obama administration's health care law. At stake was the most important achievement of the Democratic Obama administration; each party was taking its case, for and against the law, before the voters. Perhaps Roberts feared that the prestige of the Court would continue declining if it came to be seen as overly partisan—precisely what the polls were saying the public believed (see Figure 13.5). Whether or not institutional concerns swung this case, it is one factor in explaining decisions over time.

- Four different perspectives help explain how justices make their decisions.

- First, we should pay attention to their own explanation: they follow precedent and the facts of the case.

- Political scientists are more likely to find that ideology is the best predictor in the long run. Recently, the public has also taken this view. It poses a dilemma for American governance: An institution designed to be above politics is increasingly seen as essentially political. That perception has helped turn confirmation hearings volatile.

- Two final factors also play a role: collegiality and institutional protection.

Nineteen Cases You Should Know

The history of American court cases includes a long list of famous—and occasionally infamous—decisions, from *Marbury v. Madison* forward. Some you have encountered in other parts of this book. All are part of American *jurisprudence*, or the study of law. Here we list nineteen cases that every student of American government ought to be familiar with, organized chronologically.

1. *Marbury v. Madison* (1803)

Without Marshall's momentous decision, we might not have judicial review—or courts so deeply engaged in U.S. government and policy making. You read about this one earlier in this chapter.

2. *McCulloch v. Maryland* (1819)

James William McCulloch was an obscure clerk who worked for the Baltimore branch of the National Bank of the United States. The state of Maryland levied an annual tax on all banks "not chartered by the state" of Maryland; at the time the National Bank was the only one. On behalf of the bank, McCulloch refused to pay the Maryland tax and sued. The Maryland Supreme Court ruled against McCulloch, arguing that the Constitution said nothing about establishing a bank—the national bank was unconstitutional in the first place.

Taking a loose interpretation of the Constitution (rather than a strict construction that would have limited Congress to doing only what was explicitly allowed), Chief Justice Marshall upheld the constitutionality of the bank. Marshall argued that Congress had every right to establish a national bank under the Constitution's necessary and proper clause (which authorizes Congress to do anything that is "necessary and proper" for "carrying into execution" the powers it was granted).

Furthermore, declared the Court, Maryland was forbidden to tax the national bank. "The power to tax," declared Marshall for the unanimous majority, "involves the power to destroy."[15] The states had no such power over federal institutions since the collective American citizenry had established a national government with the Constitution's ratification. The Court's action affirmed the federal government's superiority to state governments in all specific instances named by the Constitution; this decision marked a significant advance toward American nationhood.

3. *Dartmouth College v. Woodward* (1819)

In one of the classic speeches before the Supreme Court, future Senate leader Daniel Webster delivered a ringing address on behalf of his alma mater, Dartmouth College. New Hampshire's legislature had sought to extend control over the college, effectively converting it from a private to a public institution. King George had originally issued the charter for the school. The Court now ruled that the state had to respect the charter as a private contract. At the heart of the case, Marshall defined contracts as transactions involving private property rights (rather than "political relations between the government and its citizens"). The Court extended contract rights to private corporations, providing a foundation for free enterprise as we know it today.

4. *Dred Scott v. Sandford* (1857)

As tensions mounted over the spread of slavery into the West, Chief Justice Roger Taney inserted the Supreme Court squarely into the middle of the debate. The Court ruled that Dred Scott, a Missouri slave who was taken to a free state, did not have standing: Slaves did not have the rights of free citizens to file lawsuits.

Taney continued further still, in passages that are shocking to read today: Blacks, he insisted, were "beings of an inferior order and altogether unfit to

● Chief Justice Roger Taney, who served on the Court from 1836 to 1864, authored the Dred Scott decision—often described as the worst decision in Court history.

● Dred Scott, a slave, sued for his own freedom and that of his two daughters, arguing that he had been taken to Illinois and the Wisconsin Territory, both free areas. The Court rejected his bid for freedom, 7–2.

associate with the white race." They were not and could never become U.S. citizens. The Court went on to rule that Congress did not have the power to prohibit slavery in the western territories.[16] Many constitutional historians choose *Dred Scott* as the worst Supreme Court decision in American history. (For more details, see Chapter 5.)

5. *Santa Clara Co. v. Southern Pacific Railroad* (1886)

Santa Clara Co. v. Southern Pacific Railroad was a boring tax case, decided unanimously without much notice—but it reverberates through our politics today. California had forbidden corporations from deducting their debts from their taxable property. The Court ruled that California had acted improperly, because corporations should be treated as persons and afforded the Fourteenth Amendment right of equal protection. The case established a precedent—later expanded—that enhanced the power of corporations. By 1938 Justice Hugo Black would complain that the Fourteenth Amendment had been written "to protect weak and helpless human beings," not to "remove corporations in any fashion from the control of state governments." A decade later, Justice William O. Douglas added: "The *Santa Clara* case becomes one of the most momentous of all our decisions. . . . Corporations were now armed with constitutional prerogatives." The bottom line: *Santa Clara* set a precedent that, with time, gave corporations all the legal benefits of individual citizens.

see for yourself 13.3

Go online to see a discussion of the *Plessy* case.

6. *Plessy v. Ferguson* (1896)

In 1890, a Louisiana statute required that railroads maintain separate cars for black and white ticket holders. Homer Plessy deliberately challenged the law by refusing to move to the "colored car" on an East Louisiana Railroad train. The case eventually reached the Supreme Court, where Plessy's lawyers argued that the segregation violated his Fourteenth Amendment rights. (Remember that the Fourteenth Amendment guaranteed to all Americans "equal protection under the law.") The Court rejected Plessy's argument and upheld Louisiana's law, cementing the infamous doctrine of "separate but equal" for nearly sixty years (until *Brown v. Board of Education*). The decision permitted racial segregation, and in the next ten years the Jim Crow system went firmly into place with the Supreme Court's blessing. After the decision was handed down, Homer Plessy pled guilty to the violation and paid a twenty-five-dollar fine. (For more detail, see Chapter 5.)

● *Keith Plessy and Phoebe Ferguson, descendants of the two men named in the famous case, have become friends and formed a foundation to promote new and innovative ways to study civil rights. As their own experience testifies, the battle for civil rights is passed on from generation to generation. Now, it is in your hands.*

7. *Lochner v. New York* (1905)

The rise of mass industry and manufacturing in the late nineteenth century bred strong demands for worker protection. Several states passed laws limiting working hours and banning child labor. New York State's worker protections, passed in 1897, included a "Bakeshop Act" that prohibited anyone from working more than ten hours a day, or sixty hours a week, in a bakery.

Joseph Lochner, a bakery owner in Utica, was fined for requiring employees to exceed the sixty-hour weekly limit. He took his case to court, insisting that the Fourteenth Amendment protected his right to establish free contracts with his workers, independent of state influence.

Two New York courts denied Lochner's appeals. In a 7–2 ruling, the Supreme Court reversed the New York decisions, holding that the Bakeshop Act was an invalid exercise of the state's power. The decision ushered in a thirty-year **Lochner era**, during which courts repeatedly struck down state economic and labor regulations, including minimum-wage laws, in the name of individual economic liberty. Governments could not interfere with the private right to contract by introducing worker protections.

8. *Muller v. Oregon* (1908)

Oregon limited the number of hours women could work. Whereas Lochner ruled that the state could not regulate men's hours, this case found that women were different from men. The Court ruled that "the difference between the sexes does . . . justify a different rule respecting a restriction of the hours of labor." It went on to say that the concern about "healthy mothers" justified the state intervention.

Louis Brandeis defended the law with an innovative strategy. He disposed of the legal arguments in two pages and then compiled page after page of data—health statistics, medical evidence, the experience of other nations. From that time forward, this kind of statistical brief—brimming with data—would be known as "a Brandeis brief."

The case is particularly important for gender readings of the law. Yes, women won labor protections, but note how: The decision rested on the idea that a woman was different from a man and, more to the point, that her role as child bearer and mother was more important than her role as worker.

9. *Schenck v. United States* (1919)

Charles Schenck, the secretary of the U.S. Socialist Party, printed and distributed leaflets expressing opposition to a U.S. military draft in World War I. Schenck was convicted under the Espionage Act of aiding the enemy during wartime. Insisting that he was exercising his First Amendment free speech rights, Schenck took his appeal to the Supreme Court.

For the first time, the Court formally marked out boundaries around protected speech: Words presenting a "clear and present danger" were legitimate subjects of legislative prohibitions. The **clear and present danger** test guided

---

Lochner era: A period from 1905 to 1937, when the Supreme Court struck down laws (like worker protection or minimum wage) that were thought to infringe on economic liberty or the right to contract.

Clear and present danger: Court doctrine that permits restrictions of free speech if officials believe that the speech will lead to prohibited action like violence or terrorism.

● *Lawyer Louis Brandeis, later a Supreme Court justice, relied on social science data to win* Muller v. Oregon. *To this day we call an argument that emphasizes social science research rather than legal argument a "Brandeis brief."*

the court for fifty years—it was rewritten in 1969. Recall that a "test" is a general principle designed to guide future court decisions on a topic. (For more detail, see Chapter 4.)

10. *National Labor Relations Board v. Jones and Laughlin Steel Corporation* (1937)

Jones and Laughlin was the nation's fourth-largest manufacturer of steel—an industry that had aggressively opposed unions. The company fired ten workers who tried to unionize and was sued by the labor board for violating the Wagner Act (of 1935), which protected the right to unionize. The company responded that the Wagner Act violated the Constitution. The lower courts both agreed that precedent was on the company's side.

In a 5–4 decision, Chief Justice Charles Evans Hughes reversed the lower-court decisions and held that Congress had the power, under interstate commerce, to regulate the company's treatment of its workers. This decision broadly expanded congressional power to regulate economic matters. It meant that the Court—by a one-vote margin—would accept New Deal legislation. We can understand the enormous scope of this new ruling when, three decades later, Congress used its authority over interstate commerce to outlaw segregation in hotels and restaurants (with the Civil Rights Act of 1964, discussed in Chapter 5).

Along with another case, *West Coast Hotel Company v. Parrish* (also decided 5–4 in 1937), the courts now permitted legislatures to regulate relations between business and workers. The cases meant the end of the "Lochner era." Today, conservative judicial activists are eager to roll back congressional use of the interstate commerce power. Some even call for a return of the Lochner era.

Strict scrutiny: The tendency to strike down as unconstitutional any legislation that singles out race or ethnicity unless the government has a compelling interest in such legislation.

11. *Korematsu v. United States* (1944)

During World War II, President Roosevelt's executive order forced Japanese Americans out of their homes and into hastily constructed internment camps. Fred Korematsu, a California native, was arrested for defying the order. The Court ruled 6–3 that the need to defend against espionage during wartime justified the order—and its violation of equal protection. The case was one of the first to use the **strict scrutiny** of government actions: The Court is primed to strike down any law that singles out a race or ethnicity unless there is a very strong reason for doing so (see Chapter 5 for discussion). In this case, the Court ruled, the government's action met the standards of strict scrutiny.

The case was always infamous for its mistreatment of Japanese Americans. In 1983, a federal district court in California used the new information to vacate (or void) Korematsu's conviction.

● *Fred Korematsu refused to enter a Japanese internment camp. Today his lifelong fight on behalf of civil liberties is commemorated by the "Fred Korematsu Day of Civil Liberties and the Constitution."*

12. *Brown v. Board of Education* (1954)

This landmark decision, decided unanimously, declared that segregating schools for black and white children violated the equal protection clause of the

Fourteenth Amendment. As Supreme Court Justice Earl Warren put it, "separate schools are inherently unequal." The decision boosted the civil rights movement and led the way to an end to legal segregation. It overturned *Plessy v. Ferguson*, described above. (For more details, see Chapter 5.)

13. *Mapp v. Ohio* (1961)

Cleveland police received a tip in 1959 that local resident Dollree Mapp was harboring a suspected bombing fugitive, and they swarmed her house without a search warrant. The police found no fugitive—but did find obscene material, at the time legally forbidden in Ohio. Mapp was arrested and convicted. She appealed. The Supreme Court reversed her conviction and, drawing on the Fourth Amendment (prohibiting unreasonable searches and seizures), devised the "exclusionary rule"—illegally obtained evidence cannot be admitted in a criminal trial. The Court extended this federal rule to cover state cases (incorporating part of the Fourth Amendment) and ruled that, since the evidence against Mapp was obtained without a search warrant, she could go free. The conservative majority on the Roberts Court has recently rolled back the exclusionary rule, and there is some speculation that it may be abolished altogether. (For more details, see Chapter 4.)

14. *Gideon v. Wainwright* (1963)

Perhaps you've read *Gideon's Trumpet*. If so, you'll never forget the story of Clarence Gideon, accused (unjustly, as it eventually was proved) of a minor theft from a Florida pool hall. Lacking funds to hire a defense attorney, Gideon represented himself at his trial—relatively common practice into the early 1960s. He was swiftly convicted, but he appealed his sentence based on the state's failure to provide a competent defense lawyer.

The Supreme Court held that Gideon was wrongly convicted and ordered a new trial. The *Gideon* legacy: Anyone charged with a serious criminal offense has the right to an attorney. Moreover, the state must provide a lawyer to any defendant unable to afford legal counsel. *Gideon* was the first in a series of landmark judicial decisions upholding the rights of defendants in criminal proceedings, including the so-called *Miranda rights* to counsel during police questioning. Recently, the Court has strengthened the right to counsel, holding that it applies to plea bargain cases where a defendant is offered a deal: plead guilty, avoid a trial, and receive a lighter sentence. (For more details, see Chapter 4.)

15. *Lemon v. Kurtzman* (1971)

Religion is another constitutionally guaranteed freedom attracting frequent judicial attention: Recall from Chapter 4 that the First Amendment both guarantees the *free exercise* of religion to every person and forbids the *establishment* of religion. It erects what Thomas Jefferson termed a "wall of separation" between church and state.

In *Lemon v. Kurtzman*, the court created a three-prong test for judging whether government action violated the first amendment by "establishing" a religion. The law could not create "excessive government entanglement" in religious affairs; it must not inhibit religious practice; and the law must have a secular purpose. Any law that violates any of these tests is unconstitutional.

The court has been growing more permissive about allowing religious practices. For example, in *Town of Greece v. Galloway* (2014) the court ruled (5–4) that the town's practice of starting its monthly meetings with a prayer did not violate the establishment clause. Despite the new, more permissive orientation, the court has repeatedly refused to strike down the Lemon test. (For more detail, see Chapter 4.)

16. *Roe v. Wade* (1973)

The *Roe v. Wade* decision, written by Justice Harry Blackmun, struck down a Texas statute outlawing abortion—and expanded the personal right to privacy under the Constitution. (For more detail, see Chapter 4.)

17. *United States v. Nixon* (1974)

This case revolved around the Watergate break-in and the white-hot political debate that ensued. President Nixon refused to turn over audiotapes of White House conversations, along with other requested materials, to the special prosecutor investigating Watergate, on the ground of "executive privilege," a sweeping claim of presidential immunity. Chief Justice Warren Burger (appointed by Nixon five years before) upheld the doctrine of executive privilege

● *The politics of abortion inflame passions, mobilize demonstrations, and shape American politics. For more than 40 years, the judiciary has been the central arena for this conflict.*

but concluded that presidents could not invoke it in criminal cases to withhold evidence. Nixon acquiesced—and resigned as president a month later.

18. *Bush v. Gore* (2000)

see for yourself 13.4

Go online to listen to the Supreme Court oral argument for *Bush v. Gore* (2000).

High drama surrounded a recount of some of Florida's disputed ballots in the 2000 presidential election, stretching well past the November 7 election. On December 8, Florida's supreme court ordered a manual recount of ballots; George W. Bush's lawyers, fearing this would result in an advantage for Vice President Gore, appealed the decision to the U.S. Supreme Court. The Court, acting with unusual speed because of the urgency of the issue—a presidential election hung in the balance—halted the recount the very next day. Three days later, Chief Justice Rehnquist handed down a 5–4 ruling that no constitutionally valid recount could be completed by Florida's December 12 deadline. As a result, George Bush won Florida's twenty-five electoral votes and, with them, the presidential election.

19. *National Federation of Independent Business v. Sebelius* (2012)

This blockbuster decision took on two controversial features of the Obama administration health reform law. The ACA required all Americans to buy health insurance or face a fine (paid with their income taxes); it also expanded Medicaid, a joint federal and state program, to cover all Americans under sixty-five who were poor or near poor (the federal government would pay 90 percent of the costs).

Can the federal government require individuals to carry health insurance? Proponents said yes: Congress has the power to regulate interstate commerce (see case number 10, above, *NLRB v. Jones and Laughlin*). Chief Justice Roberts and the four conservative justices ruled that Congress does *not* have the power under interstate commerce to require that people buy health insurance. Then, very dramatically, the chief justice broke with the conservatives and ruled that Congress does have the power to tax—and this is a tax. The Obama reform was upheld. However, Roberts got Supreme Court watchers buzzing. Remember, conservatives have long wanted to curtail the congressional use of interstate commerce. Was Roberts handing conservative jurisprudence a victory—perhaps a return to the Lochner era that conservatives have been calling for—even while upholding the Obama health care law? Time will tell.

In the other part of the case, the Court ruled 7–2 that Congress could not change the rules of the Medicaid program and require states to expand their Medicaid program. It could only offer the funds and encourage the states to participate. Was this, wondered analysts, a new rollback of the federal government's power over federalism? Again, time will tell. The true scope of a case like this often takes years to reveal itself.

NAME ANOTHER LANDMARK CASE

Why didn't we take our list to a nice round number? To leave room for your choice. Think about the many cases we have already discussed in this book. Then pick one that you would add to the list: What would it be?

Hint: Some cases that are frequently seen as landmark cases include *United States v. Windsor,* which struck down the Defense of Marriage Act that sought to limit marriage to heterosexual couples (Chapter 6), *Citizens United* (striking down campaign finance legislation, discussed in Chapter 8), *Miranda* (the right to remain silent, Chapter 4), *Tinker* (student free speech, Chapter 4), *Bakke* (affirmative action, Chapter 5), *Arizona v. United States* (on state authority over immigration control, Chapter 3) . . . now it is your turn. Choose a case, add it to the list, and explain why you consider it a landmark.

The Nineteen Cases—And the Power of the Court

This list illustrates the wide range of questions addressed in U.S. federal courts. These cases also illustrate the formidable reach of the judiciary over American politics and government.

Many of these cases were very controversial when decided—and some remain disputed today. Such controversy repeatedly raises the question we have asked throughout the chapter: Does the Supreme Court (and do courts in general) overstep democratic boundaries when ruling on such momentous political matters? How deferential should they be to the people's representatives? Each case introduces a different kind of judgment call—not just on the substance of the case but also on the scope of the Court's authority.

Conclusion: Democracy and the Courts

The debates about the judiciary's proper influence in a democracy will continue. We have seen in this chapter that U.S. courts wield an unusual amount of influence—far more than courts in most other nations, perhaps too much in a modern democratic society. We have also seen that there are clear limits to judicial power—from the reactive nature of the judicial process to the courts' reliance on others to implement decisions. Perhaps expanding resources and imposing term limits would modernize the courts and enhance their ability to serve American government by doing what they do at their best: faithfully reflecting—and consistently enforcing—the constitutional rules that guide our public life.

Reforms can only go so far. The powerful role of the courts in a democracy will always be vexing for a simple reason: The courts are designed to serve as a check, ultimately, on "We the People." The courts, when they are acting properly, stop the people and their representatives from violating the Constitution or from harming minority rights. However, as the steady parade of 5–4 decisions discussed in this chapter indicates, what exactly the Constitution means is often a highly controversial matter. As a result, the courts always face a delicate balance between enforcing the Constitution (as a majority on the Court sees it) and deferring to democracy (and the majority of the country).

CHAPTER SUMMARY

● The judiciary has a central place in U.S. government and politics—as well as in our legalistic national culture.

● Americans express uneasiness about their judicial system, despite their faith in the rule of law. This dichotomy leads to a complex dynamic: respect for judges and their rulings on the one hand and concerns that the legal system is biased and too costly on the other.

● Compared to other advanced democratic nations, U.S. courts possess a great deal of influence over our politics and government. This is primarily because of the power of judicial review, asserted long ago by Chief Justice John Marshall. Once again, Americans found a way to separate and fragment power—continuing the work begun in the Constitution.

● Alongside their uncommon influence, courts are hemmed in by restrictions like limited resources, stare decisis requirements, and their lack of an electoral base (at the federal level).

● The judiciary has affected a vast range of areas through its Constitution-interpreting authority, from religion and race to economic regulations and even presidential election outcomes. This impact is evident through a set of landmark cases—each of which typically arouses great controversy, leading to renewed calls for limits on judicial activism. Originalist and pragmatist schools have very different views of what constitutes such "activism."

● The Supreme Court marks the pinnacle of judicial—and constitutional—authority in the United States. Its operations, often carried out behind closed doors, are the subject of fascinated speculation: How do nine justices decide? The leading theories: They follow the rule of law; they are guided by their ideology; they are moved by peer pressure; and they are concerned about the institution of the courts.

KEY TERMS

Amicus curiae, 449

Appellate courts, 431

Circuit courts (U.S. Court of Appeals), 439

Civil law, 446

Clear and present danger, 460

Common law, 446

Concurrent opinion, 451

Criminal law, 446

Defendant, 446

Dissent, 451

District courts, 439

Judicial activism, 445

Judicial restraint, 445

Judicial review, 444

Litigation, 434

Lochner era, 460

Majority opinion, 451

Mediation, 434

Plaintiff, 446

Precedent, 446

Rule of four, 449

Stare decisis, 455

Strict scrutiny, 461

STUDY QUESTIONS

1. Should the judiciary have less power in American government and politics? How would you propose to restrain judicial authority in practice?

2. The Supreme Court is currently 33 percent women, around the same proportion as women in other federal courts (district and circuit). Does that seem unjustly low to you, given that women make up nearly 52 percent of the U.S. population? What about the fact that none of the nine justices is Protestant in a country that is around 51 percent Protestant? Should we care about the religious preferences of Supreme Court justices?

3. Do Supreme Court clerks—and other federal judges' clerks—have too much influence, given their relatively young ages? Should they serve for longer than one year, given the importance of the work they do?

4. Should we mandate more transparency for judicial operations? Televise Supreme Court oral arguments, for example? Require that Court conferences be transcribed and publicized? Are there any benefits to the secrecy that characterizes the federal judiciary?

5. Should the federal judiciary be the last line of defense in protecting Americans' constitutional rights and liberties? Why or why not? And if not, what other institution or group of people should have this responsibility? Be specific: How would another actor or group protect rights and liberties better than federal judges, and ultimately the Supreme Court, do today?

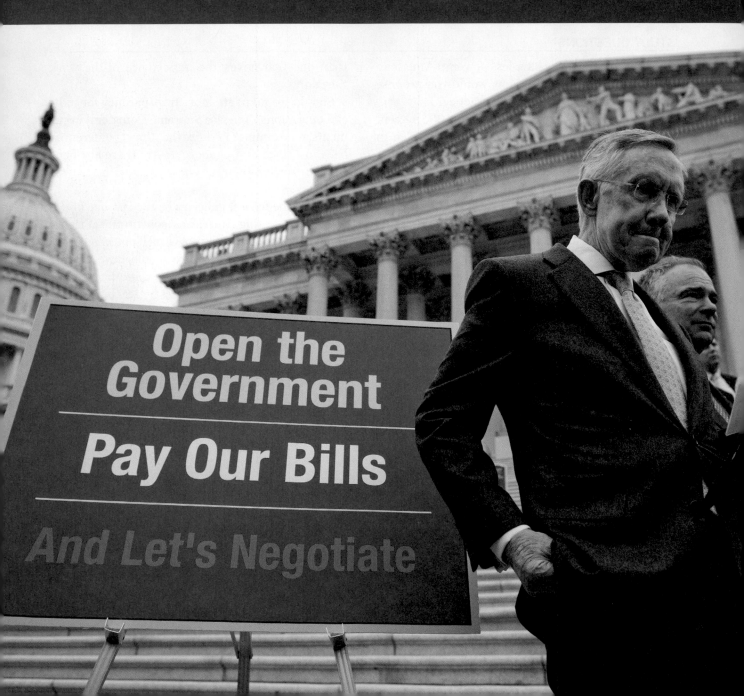

14 Domestic and Foreign Policy

OCTOBER 1, 2013, dawned warm and bright in Washington, D.C. Morning traffic was much lighter than usual: federal government workers playing hooky on a beautiful day? Not exactly. With Congress unable to agree on a budget plan for the new fiscal year (which runs from October 1 through September 30 in the United States), the government officially shut down.

The shutdown did not close all federal government doors: Essential functions like national defense and sending Social Security checks continued. But monuments like the Lincoln Memorial and all national parks were closed, health care research and monitoring at the Centers for Disease Control and National Institutes of Health were halted, and weather tracking—on which millions of people rely for information about everything from possible flight delays to fishing conditions—ceased, along with hundreds of other government activities. An estimated $24 billion of economic activity was lost because of the shutdown, which lasted until October 18, when an increasingly disgusted public outcry forced a compromise.

In the high-stakes debates that led to the shutdown, the White House and Congress were debating not just a number for the federal budget but also *what government should do*. In other words, they were debating public policy. Exchanges like these about policy decisions have far-reaching implications, affecting tens of millions of Americans and many more millions around the world. Policy debates also return to this book's familiar chapter-opening question: *Who are we*?

Perhaps Americans are best described in terms of the policies we enact—and those that we reject or abandon. Why do we seize privately owned land to protect spotted owls and flying squirrels? Provide hefty government subsidies to farmers growing corn, dairy, and beef but virtually none to growers of fruits and vegetables? Imprison one in nine young black men? Closely regulate sex but not violence in movies? These and thousands of other policy decisions contribute to the kaleidoscopic portrait of who we are.

All the actors introduced in this book—interest groups, Congress, the media, executive-branch officials, the courts, and more—come together to make public policy. Here we will look at domestic and foreign policy making.

IN THIS CHAPTER, YOU WILL:

● Trace the stages by which proposed solutions to problems become public policies.

● Review the history of U.S. social policy, with special attention to "entitlement" programs.

● Assess what counts as good policy, including claims for both fairness and economic efficiency.

● Learn how fiscal and monetary policy, the federal budget process, drives much of our domestic policy making.

● Learn the three goals of American foreign policy: security, prosperity, and spreading American values.

● See who makes foreign policy and how.

● Take a bird's-eye view of American foreign policy in the past one hundred years.

● *The 2013 government shutdown brought much public policy making—and visits to national parks and monuments—to a halt.*

BY THE NUMBERS
U.S. Public Policy

- Number of policy proposals (congressional bills and resolutions) introduced, 113th Congress (January 2013 to June 2014): **8,501**
- Number of laws passed, 113th Congress (through June 2014): **104**
- Number of laws passed, 110th Congress (January 2007 to January 2009): **460**
- Number of laws passed, 80th Congress (January 1947 to January 1949; labeled the "Do-Nothing Congress" by President Truman): **906**
- Average number of new federal regulations introduced each year, 2009–2014: **7,800**
- Total number of federal agencies, departments, and boards engaged in rule making, 2014: **269**
- Percentage of proposed federal rules required by OMB to include cost–benefit analysis, 2011–2014: **94**
- Number of the past 13 U.S. presidents who gave their policy program a name (e.g., "New Deal," "Fair Deal," or "Great Society"): **11**
- Initial election year of the two who did not (George W. Bush, Barack Obama): **2000, 2008**
- Fiscal year 2015 U.S. federal budget deficit (estimated): **$492,000,000,000**
- Spending on Social Security, Medicare, and Medicaid in FY 2015: **$1,879,800,000,000**
- Percentage reduction in the deficit if Congress cut all nondefense discretionary spending: **2.1**
- Number of U.S. schools offering a master's degree in public policy and administration, 1990: **97**
- Number offering this degree in 2013: **296**

● Public Policymaking in Five (Not-So-Easy) Stages

Policies often take the form of laws, but they can also be regulations, presidential executive orders, funding formulas (determining who gets how much), established norms, or action plans. Think of an issue you care about: clean drinking water, infant mortality, or protection against terrorist acts. All these, like every political issue reaching government officials' attention, play out through public policy making—whether in controlling waterborne pollutants, encouraging prenatal care and mandating safe infant delivery rooms, or devising effective antiterrorism efforts.

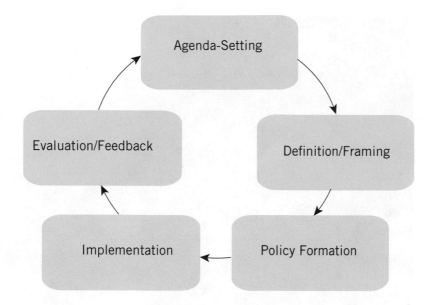

● **FIGURE 14.1** *The five stages of domestic policy making.*

Recall the seven basic American political ideas we explored in Chapter 1. For example, consider *limited government* or *self-rule*: both are at stake whenever we launch new domestic programs that expand federal government authority. At the same time, Americans' sense of *equality* is embedded in a whole range of policies, from affirmative action to welfare rules requiring recipients to find work within a certain time period.

Achieving policy responses is an elaborate process, involving five stages. Figure 14.1 displays the stages graphically. We will organize our trip through the public policy system by exploring each of these in turn.

1. Agenda Setting

Policy making doesn't begin in earnest until public officials recognize that something is a problem worthy of government attention. President Obama, arriving in office in 2009, identified nuclear power as a promising "clean" alternative to coal and oil—two finite energy sources that give off air pollution when burned. Nuclear power developers planned new construction across the United States; they won early encouragement in the form of tax incentives and relaxed regulatory restrictions. Then, in spring 2011, a **focusing event** changed Americans' minds about nuclear power. A massive tidal wave, the result of an earthquake off the Japanese coast, hit a nuclear plant in Fukushima, Japan. Safety mechanisms failed, part of the plant melted down, and a radioactive leak affected water, land, and air for miles around. The disaster quickly made nuclear plant safety a high-level agenda item for American policy makers. Government support for new nuclear construction disappeared and regulators' scrutiny sharpened, halting expansion plans.

Focusing event: A major happening, often of crisis or disaster proportions, that attracts widespread media attention to an issue.

● *Focusing event: a tragic accident in Japan. The nuclear plant in Fukushima, Japan, burns after a partial meltdown following a giant tsunami. The tragedy caused U.S. public approval for nuclear power to plummet, affecting President Obama's proposals to expand American nuclear energy production.*

2. Framing

In translating agenda items into proposed policy solutions, questions arise. What are the root causes of the problem? How bad a problem *is* this? How should public officials respond, if at all? Most agenda issues involve such questions of framing; the answers are far from obvious, and they can differ greatly depending on who is making the argument.

Let's consider an example from education policy. As Table 14.1 displays, American secondary school students lag behind counterparts from many other advanced countries in science, math, and reading tests. Parents, teachers, and businesses all agreed: scores had to improve. That goal merely placed the issue on the agenda. Then disputes about defining, or framing, the problem began. Was it that American kids were poorly prepared for the tests compared to children in other countries? Or that many U.S. classrooms were overcrowded, with too few teachers to provide pupils with personalized instruction?

On and on the discussion raged—retracing familiar paths. Federal government officials had no formal say in education policy until the mid-1960s, when Congress established an extensive program of national funding through the Elementary and Secondary Education Act. The U.S. Department of Education was created later still, in 1979. Champions of local control of education have fought to limit federal activity ever since. In the 2012 presidential primary, Republican candidates unanimously insisted that the Department of Education was a big part of the problem. To them, it had to be restructured—or shut down altogether. Progressives and moderate Democrats instead insisted that national education officials had to step in to reduce inequities in school financing, so that

TABLE 14.1 Framing School Education Policies: Poor U.S. Student Performance

Top ten countries and the United States in overall scores for reading, math, and science in 2012*					
READING	OECD AVERAGE SCORE: 496	MATH	AVG. 494	SCIENCE	AVG. 501
1. Shanghai-China	570	Shanghai-China	613	Shanghai-China	580
2. Hong Kong	545	Singapore	573	Hong Kong	555
3. Singapore	542	Hong Kong	561	Singapore	551
4. Japan	538	Taiwan	560	Japan	547
5. South Korea	536	South Korea	555	Finland	545
6. Finland	524	China-Macao	538	Estonia	541
7. Canada	523	Japan	536	South Korea	538
8. Taiwan	523	Liechtenstein	535	Vietnam	528
9. Ireland	523	Switzerland	531	Poland	526
10. Poland	518	Netherlands	523	Liechtenstein, Canada (tie)	525
24. United States	**498**	**36. United States**	**481**	**28. United States**	**497**

Testing is done every three years.
Source: Organization of Economic Cooperation and Development (OECD), "PISA 2012 Results in Focus." OECD, 2013.

the richest districts in a state—able to provide more resources—do not leave schoolchildren in lower-income areas far behind.

These different ways of "framing" issues, also called problem definition, have big consequences: They help determine which policy responses the government considers. As issues are framed and reframed, policy actors translate their preferred solutions into law, propelling policy making to a third stage.

3. Policy Formation

After a problem reaches the policy agenda, and after struggles to define it settle into one or two primary frames, proposed solutions must be evaluated—and adopted or discarded. This process of policy formation is again sprawling and complicated. Members of Congress and, often, state and local legislators engage in drafting bills, holding hearings, and hammering out compromises in committee meetings and floor debates. Executive-branch experts weigh in, all the way up to the president if the issue is sufficiently high-profile. Advocacy groups and industry lobbyists swarm around lawmakers, judicial rulings reshape the policy debate, and media experts opine through print, broadcast, the blogosphere, and Twitter.

AND THE LITTLE PIG WITH THE HIGHER MATH & VERBAL LIVED HAPPILY EVER AFTER. THE OTHER TWO WERE SWALLOWED UP BY THE WOLF.

● *Educational reform: the lighter side. Programs like Head Start, No Child Left Behind, and Race to the Top respond to education policy makers' worries about U.S. students' performance—which can be exaggerated, as this cartoon suggests.*

Analyzing Policy, *Ex Ante*. Competing ideas, rhetorical displays, deft procedural moves, power plays: These features underpin policy formation in every society, as they have for hundreds of years. Recently, more technical work has also become vital to policy success. Policy analysis involves constructing scientific measures of a proposed policy's costs and benefits *ex ante*—before it passes and goes into effect. Such assessment efforts are a central feature of contemporary policy making in the United States and other advanced industrial nations.

A relatively straightforward approach to analyzing a proposed policy involves **cost-effectiveness** studies. Here, analysts compare several policy alternatives that deliver the same overall benefit. Thus they can measure which one does so at the *lowest cost*.

Cost effectiveness: The projected costs of a proposed policy, as revealed by a relatively simple study.

Not many policy decisions are that straightforward, however, especially when they reach the national agenda. In 2008, a commission appointed by then-president Bush recommended a hike in the federal gasoline tax, both to pay for highway maintenance and to reduce Americans' oil consumption. Since 1993, the national gas tax has remained at 18.4 cents per gallon, after slowly rising over the preceding sixty years from a penny per gallon. To illuminate the likely effects of this policy shift—and to help estimate the range of an ideal tax increase—experts performed a **cost-benefit analysis**. The first step in a cost–benefit analysis is to list all the expected costs of a policy proposal, as well as the benefits. For the gas tax, researchers identified two primary categories of cost and five main areas of benefit. The results are summarized in Table 14.2.

Cost–benefit analysis: A more complex study of the projected costs and benefits associated with a proposed policy.

Researchers then "monetize," or assign dollar values to, these costs and benefits, using elaborate mathematical formulas. In the gas tax example, combining several policy-analysis models for simplicity's sake, estimates were that the *costs* of a higher tax averaged 75 cents per gallon, but the predicted *benefits* were considerably higher, as Table 14.3 shows.

Thus, according to cost–benefit analysis, national gas taxes could be raised by just more than a dollar per gallon. From the perspective of economic effectiveness, society would be better off as a whole.

From Cost–Benefit Analysis to Politics. Cost–benefit and other *ex ante* evaluations are widely used in policy making, with significant impact on both legislative

TABLE 14.2 Gas Tax Costs/Benefits

GAS TAX COSTS
• Direct cost of the tax to drivers (those in rural areas, and with lower incomes, are hardest hit)
• Higher price of services dependent on transportation, like shipping goods by truck
GAS TAX BENEFITS
• Reduced urban air pollution (thereby improving public health)
• Reduced CO_2 emissions (slowing the pace of climate change)
• Reduced U.S. dependence on imported oil
• Diminished traffic congestion (saving drivers' time)
• Reduced traffic accidents (because people drive less or switch to mass transit)

TABLE 14.3 Cost–Benefit Valuation of a Proposed Gas Tax

COSTS OF GAS TAX	VALUE*	BENEFITS OF GAS TAX	VALUE*
• Direct cost to drivers	$0.23	• Public health (air pollution)	$0.40
• Transportation services	$0.52	• Climate (CO_2 emissions)	$0.11
		• Reduced oil imports	$0.12
		• Time saved (less traffic)	$0.58
		• Reduced accidents	$0.55
Total	**$0.75**		**$1.76**

*Values are estimated per gallon of gas.
Source: Authors' calculation, combining several existing models.

votes and judicial decisions. They alone, however, do not determine policy. In the gas tax example, lawmakers from both parties recognized that a hefty tax hike would arouse furious opposition. Instead, some congressional Democrats proposed a phased-in sequence of higher gas taxes, rising incrementally from 18.4 cents to 40 cents per gallon by 2014. As midterm elections approached, however, Democrats, fearing the electoral penalty of any tax increase they advocated, quietly abandoned the plan. Political considerations can trump even a clearly positive policy analysis.

If the swirling legislative and executive-branch preferences align just right and the cost–benefit analysis comes out positive, a figurative **policy window** opens.[1] Might a new policy be launched? There is no guarantee of success, especially at the national level. Policy windows rarely stay open for long.

Policy window: A figurative description of the opportunity—often brief, measured in days or weeks rather than years—to pass a bill in Congress or a state legislature.

4. Policy Implementation

When a new law does make it onto the books, policy making passes to the implementation stage, primarily handled by the executive bureaucracy, which labors mostly out of public view. Does this shift in visibility mean that the work of policy implementation is less politicized? Many American political thinkers and actors have thought so, dating back at least to Woodrow Wilson, who as a political scientist in 1887 described bureaucratic activity as "a technical science." Wilson insisted that "administrative questions are not political questions."[2]

As Wilson learned upon becoming president thirty years later, implementing public policy is in fact a highly political event. Implementation involves two main steps that attract intense interest and political fighting: working out the specifics of the law, primarily through the rulemaking process, as we have seen in Chapter 12, and then delivering the government services or enforcing the new regulations. Governments can deliver services through a top-down or bottom-up process.

● *Tainted food and top-down policy response. When the Food and Drug Administration receives reports about possibly tainted food products, the agency, along with the Department of Agriculture, spearheads a national top-down response.*

Top-Down Delivery. Once the final rule setting out a policy's details has been reviewed and published, it is time to provide the benefits or regulations that the law was designed to achieve. As the American national government stepped up its level of domestic policy activity following World War II, delivery of public services was established as a "top-down" process. They saw cabinet secretaries and agency heads as firmly in charge of the process. Lower-level bureaucrats and "policy clients" (the people government was serving) were mainly concerned with *compliance*, or doing what they were told to do.

Many policy planners still promote this top-down model of delivering government benefits and services. It can work when a policy is relatively simple, with clear, well-specified goals that are not difficult to meet. Imagine a national ban on sales of a food found to be tainted by potentially fatal bacteria, for example. A high-ranking figure, like the secretary of agriculture or head of the Food and Drug Administration, issues a public warning. Government inspectors then ensure that the dangerous product is removed from grocery shelves, law-enforcement officials investigate the cause of the outbreak, and prosecutions may follow. The public's role is simple: avoid the tainted product. The policy aim is clear, as are the lines of authority.

Bottom-Up Delivery. For complicated policies, "bottom-up" provision of public services or regulations can be more effective than top-down efforts to command and control outcomes. Bottom-up service delivery starts with **street-level bureaucrats**. Examples include the social worker who calls on needy families to make sure their food stamps have arrived; the IRS agent who checks to confirm that your charitable claims are all legitimate donations; or the air-traffic controller who brings your flight in for a safe landing.

All these policy providers and regulators work directly with the public, and they can exercise discretion in making decisions. Certainly a hierarchy is still in place, with cabinet secretaries and agency heads at the top. But when street-level officials are allowed a measure of autonomy, or at least some input into decision making, government services are often delivered more efficiently and regulations are put in place with less disruption. Sometimes, these street-level actors may even ignore superiors' orders and do what they consider best, based on experience.

THE HARVEST

A series of conflicting legal, congressional and state legislative decisions on medicinal marijuana illustrate the complexity of many policy issues—making top-down delivery of public services difficult to carry out.

5. Policy Evaluation and Feedback

Once implemented, it is still essential to confirm whether a new benefit or regulation actually works. This is the stage of policy evaluation. Does a school-lunch program need tweaking in practice because its benefits are not reaching many kids? Should we abandon an ineffective government effort to reduce tax cheating and try something else? Nearly every policy of significance, once adopted, "feeds back" into the policy process, shaping public agendas. Sometimes that feedback process creates new policy problems in turn. In short, policy making never really ends.

Policy Feedback. New policies, once implemented, do not just play out in a vacuum. They in turn shape and constrain future policy making, as a growing body of political science research shows. Scholars term this process "policy feedback."

A program that distributes benefits will attract loyal supporters, who push for its extension. Lawmakers seeking to reform or cancel the program (perhaps based on an *ex post* evaluation) can find their efforts thwarted by these grateful recipients. More subtly, as a policy is rolled out, actors of various types will adapt to the policy, making it difficult to change. Bureaucrats get organized to administer a benefit; businesses rework their economic forecasts to account for a new regulatory framework. The political scientist Paul Pierson describes

Path dependence: The tendency of policy makers to follow established routines in thinking about or acting on a specific topic.

these tendencies as **path dependence**: Once a policy is established, possibilities for reform or change are constrained by the "path" it has followed through implementation and service delivery.[3]

A classic example of a policy with powerful feedback effects is Social Security, passed in 1935. By introducing a language of "entitlement," the designers of Social Security achieved far-reaching effects. Senior citizens feel that they have earned their right to receive old-age government benefits. Millions of Americans to this day organize their investment decisions and retirement planning around the path created by Social Security. This view makes it virtually untouchable by policy makers, even as the program has grown into a $750 billion behemoth.

THE BOTTOM LINE

- U.S. policy making may be described in terms of five stages. Policies do not proceed neatly from one to the next, but the "stages" idea is a useful way of distinguishing among different actions carried out by policy officials.

- The first of these is agenda setting, whereby concerns receiving widespread attention become policy issues.

- A second stage is problem definition and framing, featuring debates about how to describe an issue and which solutions are most viable.

- A third stage is policy formation, a process of legislative and executive activity to develop the policy idea in concrete terms.

- A fourth stage is policy implementation, marked by rule making and service delivery.

- The fifth stage includes evaluation and policy feedback, steps that help determine whether a policy works—and that often start the debate all over again.

● U.S. Social Policy

Public policy comes in many forms, as the various examples above attest. *Fiscal policy* has to do with matters of finance, like monetary supply and taxes; we will address fiscal matters later in this chapter, when we look at federal budgeting. *Foreign policy* covers topics like wars and defense, diplomacy, and trade agreements. Most other issues are grouped together as *social policy*, having to do with people's individual or group well-being. Health, housing, education, employment, criminal justice, child welfare, and old-age security: all these vital areas make up social policy. Also under this heading are controversial topics like abortion, gay marriage, and recreational drug use.

Compared to industrialized western European countries, most of which developed modern social policies in the late nineteenth century, the United States was slow to adopt these at a national level. Old-age insurance, for example, was provided in Germany as far back as 1883 and in Great Britain in 1911. Yet not until the mid-1930s and Franklin Roosevelt's New Deal was a similar policy (Social Security) established here. Many advanced democracies enacted universal health insurance starting in the 1880s; the United States still does not guarantee health care to all its citizens. Americans' embrace of individualism along with a federalist structure that provides a patchwork of benefits through state and local officials, helps explain the distinctive (and slow) growth of social policy making in the United States. So do our fragmented institutions—the organization of government (especially Congress)—which stymie reforms even when the public votes for them.

From colonial days onward, "poor relief" offered support for needy Americans, inspired by both religious tenets and laws inherited from Elizabethan England. Benefits were limited, however—and came with a price. People on relief sometimes faced the loss of their personal property and the right to vote. The able-bodied unemployed were often forced to work or were jailed, although laws varied from state to state. Even with all these conditions, until the Civil War, poor relief was the largest single budget item in most American towns and cities.[4] And the term was still used well into the twentieth century, especially during the Great Depression.

The Great Depression starting in 1929 helped lead to more extensive federal social policies, many arising from Franklin Roosevelt's New Deal. Among the numerous social programs run or financed by the U.S. government today, let us look at three of the longest lived and most extensive.

Old-Age Insurance: Social Security

Since its 1935 enactment, Social Security has provided Americans sixty-five and older—provided they have lived in the United States at least five years—with a monthly living stipend. The minimum age was recently raised to sixty-six, and Congress has discussed increasing it by another year or two. Social Security payments vary with income: A worker who retires making $65,000 a year would currently receive around $1,630 per month. The original act also created an unemployment insurance program (more on that below), paid benefits to disabled workers and their families, and offered financial assistance to low-income families with children. Financing comes from a payroll tax on all eligible workers, today as in the original act.

● *The first Social Security check. Ida May Fuller, the first recipient (in 1940) of a monthly retirement Social Security check, for $22.54.*

As initially passed, the Social Security Act excluded a wide range of occupations from the program, primarily limiting benefits (and payroll-tax contributions) to white males. In subsequent years, such jobs as teachers, nurses, domestic helpers, librarians, and agricultural laborers were added to the act's coverage, effectively creating the first universal social policy in American history. Although the program began small—only fifty-three thousand beneficiaries in 1937, the first full year of implementation, who together received a little more than $1.2 million in benefits—it grew rapidly. In 2014, Social Security paid some $863 billion to more than 59 million workers supported by payroll taxes from more than 165 million employees. At nearly 5 percent of the nation's **gross domestic product** (GDP), Social Security is the largest single federal government program.

Although the old-age benefits provided by Social Security have helped lift many seniors out of poverty, for decades alarms have been sounded about financially supporting the program. Those concerns grow more urgent today, as Social Security moves inexorably toward a $1 trillion annual cost—as the huge "baby boomer" generation increasingly receives benefits. A major debate turns on the gravity of the problem. Many moderates and conservatives argue that Social Security poses a dangerous economic risk. Many liberals accuse the conservatives of exaggerating the threat and argue that relatively small adjustments (increasing the retirement age, raising taxes, limiting benefits) will fix the problem. Once again: a debate over problem definition. Whether or not the problem is grave, however, the system is extremely difficult to reform and changes are routinely rejected. Social Security's sacrosanct status has given rise to a colorful metaphor, borrowed from electrified train lines: touch the "third rail" surging with electricity, and you will receive a fatal shock. Politicians refer to Social Security as the "third rail of American politics": propose major changes, and electoral penalties will swiftly follow.

Gross domestic product:
The value of all the goods and services produced in a nation over a year.

Unemployment Benefits

As the Great Depression stretched into the 1930s, some 34 million Americans (more than a quarter of the 122 million population) lived in households with no full-time wage earner. Across the United States, unemployment rates reached shocking levels, topping out at 80 percent of able-bodied adults in Toledo, Ohio, for example. In 1932, Wisconsin became the first state to provide cash assistance to temporarily jobless residents. Three years later, the Social Security Act included a provision for joint federal–state unemployment benefits, funded like old-age insurance through a payroll tax on employees. States administer the program, with federal oversight and funding assistance.

During the recent major recession, unemployment levels rose from less than 4 percent in 2008 to more than 10 percent in 2009. A federal supplement to laid-off workers extended eligibility for unemployment benefits to ninety-nine weeks, up from the twenty-six weeks that most states provide. Costs soared accordingly, and Republicans sought to scale back the extra federal assistance.

With unemployment rates dipping only slowly through summer 2012, job creation—and the cost of benefits for unemployed workers—was a central issue in the presidential and congressional elections. Similar concerns arose during the 2014 midterms and will also be on the agenda as the 2016 presidential contest progresses.

Health and Disability: Medicare/Medicaid

In the early 1960s America ranked as the wealthiest nation in the world, but barely half of the nation's seniors had health insurance. Even with Social Security, an estimated third of those over sixty-five lived in poverty, in significant part because of the cost of health care.

Lyndon Johnson, fresh from a landslide election victory in 1964, promoted health insurance coverage for all Americans over sixty-five as part of his Great Society plan. Critics fought hard against the proposed new social benefit. Johnson's Republican opponent in that election, Arizona senator Barry Goldwater, tapped into a long-lived American vein of disapproval for handouts: "Having given our pensioners their medical care in kind, why not food baskets, why not public housing accommodations, why not vacation resorts, why not a ration of cigarettes for those who smoke and of beer for those who drink?"[5]

After some fancy footwork in Congress, Medicare was passed in 1965, as an amendment to the Social Security Act. As with old-age and unemployment benefits, Medicare was financed through a payroll tax on all employees. And like Social Security, the program grew rapidly after it was implemented in 1966. Today some 49 million Americans receive Medicare benefits; by the late 2020s the program is expected to serve nearly 80 million people, as the last of the baby boomer generation (born between 1945 and 1964) retire. The program's costs currently exceed $500 billion each year and are projected to grow to nearly $750 billion by 2030.

Paying this giant tab became more difficult after 2006, when a new Congress-authorized prescription-drug benefit for seniors went into effect. Rising health care costs put constant pressure on this popular program.

As the battle over Medicare raged in 1965, a companion measure to provide health insurance to disabled and low-income people, dubbed "Medicaid," was quietly passed. Each state was encouraged (but not required) to establish a Medicaid program of its own; Arizona was the last state to sign on, in 1982. Over time, a variety of additional benefits were added to Medicaid, including dental and nursing home coverage.

Distinctive among these large American entitlement programs, Medicaid was established as a "means-tested" program, with benefits provided only to those below a certain income level—which varies by state. In Texas, the cut off in 2013 was $5,884 for a family of four while in Connecticut it was $44,980. The Affordable Care Act (ACA) initially included a requirement that all states provide Medicaid funding to everyone whose income is below 133 percent of the **federal poverty line**—about $31,000 for a family of four. The Supreme Court's historic 2012 decision to uphold the ACA as constitutional also repudiated

Federal poverty line: The annually specified level of income (separately calculated for individuals and families) below which people are considered to live in poverty, becoming eligible for certain federal benefits. In 2014, the poverty line was set at $23,850 for a family of four.

SHOULD WE REFORM SOCIAL SECURITY AND MEDICARE?

Social Security and Medicare are perhaps the two most fiercely defended U.S. government programs. At any hint of a cut in either, senior citizens respond vehemently, as do the House and Senate members who represent them. Are you braver than most American elected officials? Are you willing to tackle cutting Social Security and Medicare (and, while you're at it, Medicaid)?

Yes, reform Social Security and Medicare programs. The budget savings of even minor adjustments—such as raising the eligibility age—would be immense.

No, leave Social Security and Medicare intact. The political fallout would certainly be furious, but so would the impact on the lives of seniors. Suggesting such reforms could also have long-term political consequences because the opposing party would sound the alarm immediately.
Besides, we are a rich nation and can afford to be generous to our seniors.

Unsure. To better understand the situation, think through the reasons that seniors (like your grandparents or other over-sixty-five people you may know) would be upset to have the rules of the game changed as they come to expect health coverage and an older-age pension. Can you think of any ways to strenthen these programs with lesser consequences for older Americans?

Entitlement program: A government benefit program whose recipients are *entitled* by law to receive payments. Social Security, Medicare, and Medicaid are the three largest.

the universal Medicaid funding requirement. Instead, each state is allowed to decide whether it will adopt the 133 percent standard.

Like Social Security and Medicare, Medicaid has grown rapidly, both in the number of people it serves and in the associated expense. In 2013, more than 51 million Americans received some Medicaid coverage, at a cost of more than $275 billion. And over the first half of 2014, ACA enrollment saw more than 5 million additional Americans sign up for Medicaid.

Figure 14.2 displays projected costs for Social Security, Medicaid, and Medicare in the years ahead, measured as a percentage of the expected U.S. GDP. Taken together, these **entitlement programs** will require some very tough choices about spending on other programs and about tax rates to raise the revenue required to fund them.

Policy makers across Washington and the nation's universities and think tanks devote years of study to these giant social programs, raising various possibilities for "bending the cost curve"—in other words, reducing their drain on the federal budget. On the plus side, the growth of American social policies like these has greatly reduced the number of people—especially seniors and children, arguably our most vulnerable citizens—living in dire need. Balancing those needs against the budget consequences of continued program growth is among the most important policy challenges facing the country in coming years.

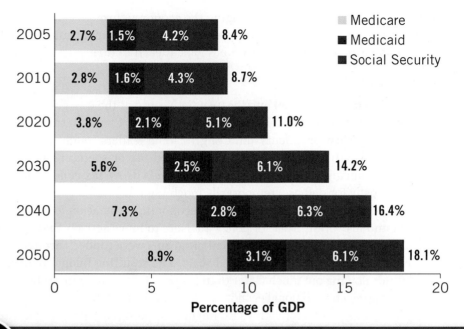

● **FIGURE 14.2** *Spending on the three big entitlement programs totals a little under 9% of U.S. GDP. That figure is projected to double over the next 30-plus years. That, in turn, puts significant pressure on actors to devise viable reforms. (Congressional Budget Office)*

THE BOTTOM LINE

- Social policy making in the United States is typically more controversial and features less expansive coverage than social policies in other advanced industrial nations.

- Wars, along with severe economic downturns, have been major sources of expansions in American social policies across U.S. history.

- Three large social programs—old-age insurance, or Social Security; unemployment insurance; and health/disability benefits, or Medicare and Medicaid—are especially significant in U.S. politics and government.

● Economic Policymaking, I: Fiscal and Monetary Policy

People judge their governments first and foremost on their economic performance. Despite scandalous affairs as well as domestic and foreign policy disappointments, Bill Clinton's presidency is widely considered a success: The economy roared ahead during his time in office. On the other hand, Clinton's predecessor, George H. W. Bush, enjoyed the highest popularity rating in modern history after the first Gulf War (1990–1991). Barely a year later, an economic downturn battered Bush's public-opinion ratings and left him a one-term president.

Economic policy is carried out in two primary ways. Government decisions about taxing and spending—generally managed through the budget process

Fiscal policy: Taxing and spending policies carried out by government, generally in an effort to affect national economic development.

Monetary policy: Actions of central banks, in the United States culminating in the Federal Reserve, designed primarily to maximize employment and moderate inflation.

below—is termed **fiscal policy**. Managing the economy through central banks' control of the money supply, directly affecting unemployment and inflation rates, is known as **monetary policy**. Let's look at each in turn.

Fiscal Policy

Across the nineteenth and well into the twentieth century, the U.S. government's fiscal policy can best be described as "laissez-faire," a French term meaning "leave it alone." Most presidents and Congressional leaders sought to balance the (relatively small) federal budget, with limited tax or spending authority. That changed during wartime, when military needs drove tax collections and spending (mostly for defense) temporarily much higher.

During the Great Depression, national economic devastation led Franklin Roosevelt and his "brain trust" of policy advisors to more actively manage the levers of fiscal policy. Immense New Deal programs were funded through government spending at an unprecedented scale. The resulting budget deficits—federal funds flowing out much faster than tax revenues coming in—reflected a Keynesian approach to national economic policy, named for the early twentieth-century British economist John Maynard Keynes. Wielding considerable influence over British thinking about fiscal policy, Keynes recommended "pump-priming" during economic downturns: pouring government funds into a faltering economy and cutting taxes, giving consumers and businesses confidence enough to start spending and hiring again.

Following close on the Depression came World War II, which resulted in another round of major fiscal engagement. Spending rates ran so high that, at the height of the war in 1943, the federal deficit reached an all-time high of 30 percent of GDP. After the war, American policy makers brimming with confidence about their ability to manage the economy adopted active taxing and spending policies as a routine national practice. Since then, through conservative and liberal presidents and through Democratic and Republican control of Congress, fiscal policy has continued to serve as a means of securing the general welfare of the American public.

The parties do differ on which fiscal levers to pull, of course. Facing an economic downturn, Democrats are more likely to favor expanded spending. Republicans generally prefer tax cuts, criticizing their counterparts as "tax and spend liberals." Yet reducing taxes still involves government use of fiscal policy.

Although fiscal policy making may sound straightforward—or even boring—few policy areas are more important—or controversial. Early in 2013, for example, the nation was riveted by the spectacle of an approaching "fiscal cliff"—a failure by Congress and the White House to agree on specific tax cuts and spending reductions that would prevent the United States from paying its debt. The threat of a global economic meltdown loomed as a budget deadline approached. The crisis was averted, but chalk up another dramatic political showdown in the realm of fiscal policy.

Monetary Policy

Following the collapse of the venerable investment bank Lehman Brothers in fall 2008, with other giant financial institutions tottering, the U.S. government leapt into action. Surprisingly, the main actors were not presidents or Congressional leaders, but rather more obscure figures like Ben Bernanke, the Federal Reserve chairman; Henry Paulson, the Treasury Secretary; and Timothy Geithner, chair of the Federal Reserve Bank of New York. (Geithner went on to become Treasury Secretary a few months later, as the Obama administration took over the reins of national government.) And the economic tools they applied had nothing to do with increasing (or cutting) taxes or spending: instead the conversation was about liquidity and the national money supply.[6]

These experts were deploying monetary policy in response to the gravest financial crisis in seventy-five years. Manipulation of the national money supply and of interest rates, which in turn affect employment and inflation rates as well as expectations about economic performance, is at the heart of this approach. Although the White House and Congress are the chief institutional architects of fiscal policy, monetary shifts are carried out by central bankers: In the United States, the main actor is the Federal Reserve system, comprising a headquarters building in Washington, D.C., along with twelve bank branches around the country. The current Federal Reserve (or "Fed," in Washington-speak) director is Janet Yellen.

Put simply, the Federal Reserve has several tools—such as buying Treasury securities and setting required dollar reserve levels that banks are required to hold. These tools allow the Fed to influence interest rates. The Fed reduces interest rates to stimulate economic growth because businesses are able to borrow money more easily to expand production and hiring or invest in research and development; similarly, individuals can borrow at lower interest

● *A relatively obscure trio of monetary-policy experts—Timothy Geithner, Ben Bernanke (pictured on the right), and Henry Paulson (on the left)—were central actors in attempting to stave off global financial disaster in fall 2008.*

rates to buy new homes or consumer goods. If, however, the economic demand is growing too fast, the Fed raises interest rates to reduce inflationary pressures that raise prices and result in an economic slowdown.

Think of the Federal Reserve as performing an essential balancing act—enabling growth when the economy slows, but easing inflation as the economy heats up. And during crisis times—like 2008, as we saw above, and also after the September 11 terrorist attacks and a stock-market plunge in 1987—the Fed is often the strongest means of sustaining our national economy through its monetary policy decisions.

● Economic Policymaking, II: The Federal Budget Process

"It's a good policy idea, but we just don't have the budget room to pursue it." Variations on that phrase have been repeated countless times in Washington in recent years, as American policy making has become more oriented around the budget. This bottom-line focus owes primarily to the U.S. **federal budget deficit**—the gap between how much our national government spends and how much we take in through taxes and fees. The deficit for 2014 is projected at $492 billion, down from 2009's record high of $1.3 trillion, or 8.5 percent of our GDP.

Federal deficits have remained stubbornly persistent for three main reasons. First, our most expensive trio of entitlement programs—Social Security, Medicare, and Medicaid—continue to grow rapidly (see Figure 14.3). Together they now cost an annual $1.9 trillion, roughly half the entire U.S. budget. Second, U.S. conflicts in Iraq and Afghanistan have also rung up a high cost. Although spending totals are disputed, they exceeded $400 billion each year (driving total defense spending near the trillion dollar mark) until troops began departing in 2011.[7] Third, federal revenues declined after large tax cuts were enacted in 2001, a trend accelerated by the economic crisis beginning in September 2008, as both corporate and individual income shrank.

Can the historic deficits of recent years be reversed, and is such an effort even desirable? To tackle budget reform, it is essential first to grasp the basics of how national government budgeting works. As we will see, much of American domestic policy making is organized around our budget process.

Budget politics, like U.S. policy making more generally, progresses more or less in stages, as described in Figure 14.4.

More often than not in recent years, Congress fails to pass an omnibus bill, leaving some areas unfunded as the new fiscal year opens. In that case, the president asks Congress to pass a **continuing resolution** (CR), which keeps the dollars flowing—usually at the just-ended fiscal year's rate—for a specified period, usually two weeks or a month. In some years, Congress is forced to pass

Federal budget deficit: The gap between revenues received by the national government (primarily through individual income and corporate taxes) and spending on all public programs.

Continuing resolution: A Congress-approved act required when no national budget has been passed before the start of a new fiscal year. This extends spending at current levels for a prescribed period of time.

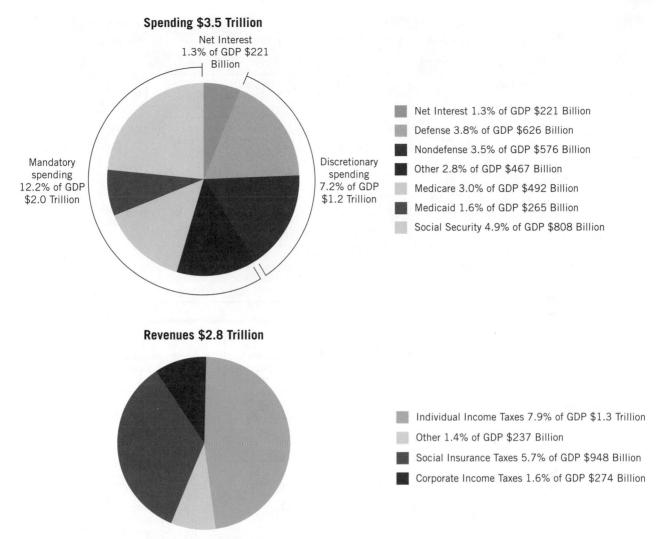

Spending $3.5 Trillion

Net Interest
1.3% of GDP $221
Billion

Discretionary
spending
7.2% of GDP
$1.2 Trillion

Mandatory
spending
12.2% of GDP
$2.0 Trillion

Net Interest 1.3% of GDP $221 Billion

Defense 3.8% of GDP $626 Billion

Nondefense 3.5% of GDP $576 Billion

Other 2.8% of GDP $467 Billion

Medicare 3.0% of GDP $492 Billion

Medicaid 1.6% of GDP $265 Billion

Social Security 4.9% of GDP $808 Billion

Revenues $2.8 Trillion

Individual Income Taxes 7.9% of GDP $1.3 Trillion

Other 1.4% of GDP $237 Billion

Social Insurance Taxes 5.7% of GDP $948 Billion

Corporate Income Taxes 1.6% of GDP $274 Billion

● **FIGURE 14.3** *Snapshot of the U.S. federal budget. A broad overview of main spending and revenue categories in the U.S. national budget. Notice the large share of spending going to "entitlements"—Social Security, Medicare, and Medicaid. The difference between spending and revenues (around $700 billion, for the 2014 fiscal year) constitutes the federal budget deficit (Congressional Budget Office).*

CR after CR. Otherwise, the government officially runs out of spending authority for discretionary programs and shuts down—as happened in 2013, described at the opening of this chapter.

All big decisions are affected by the budget, because every government action has significant financial implications. And because most budget decisions have winners and losers—more money for my program means less for yours—this is one of the most politically charged aspects of policy making. Who gets what, when, and how? In the United States, we make those decisions in significant part through our budget process.

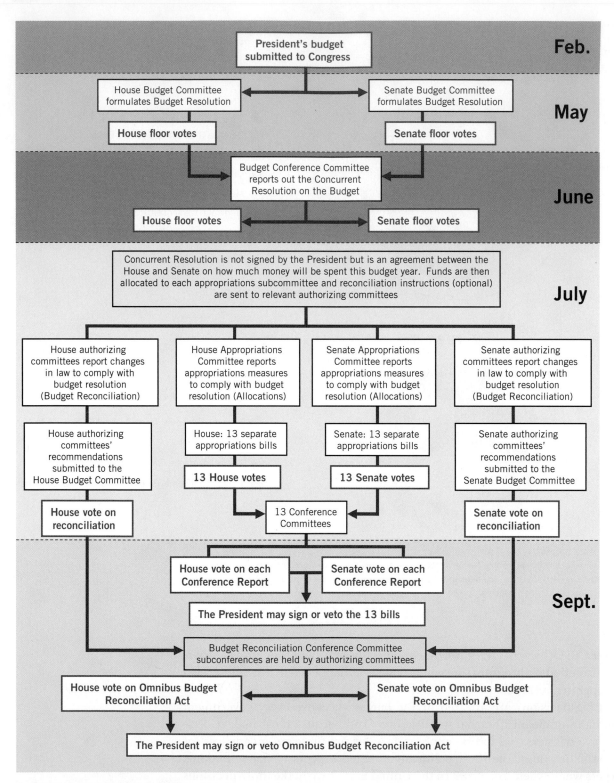

● **FIGURE 14.4** *U.S. federal budget process (House Budget Committee).*

- The U.S. budget process, when on schedule, runs from early February through October 1 and encompasses a presidential proposal, concurrent budget resolution, and appropriations bills.

- In practice the process rarely runs on time, and various "fixes" like omnibus bills and continuing resolutions have been invented to keep the budget system functioning.

- Although the details can be obscure, budget battles in Washington are almost always among the most dramatic features of U.S. policy making because of the high stakes that are involved.

American Foreign Policy Goals

September 11, 2012. Things were quiet around the American consulate in Benghazi, Libya—"Not even an ant was moving," reported a guard. Then, as night fell, some 150 men—their faces covered—came screaming into the American compound. They fired rocket-propelled grenades, mortars, and heavy machine guns mounted on trucks. The seven Americans in the building retreated into a safe haven and called for help as the militants, stymied by a heavy steel grate, poured diesel fuel around the building and lit it up. Eventually Libyan security forces drove off the attackers and a crowd of men tried to rescue the popular American ambassador, J. Christopher Stevens. They rushed him to a hospital where he was declared dead of smoke inhalation. By the time the attacks were over, four Americans were dead. Libyan mobs, demanding "justice for Chris," retaliated against the militants, burned their headquarters—and, along with government troops, soon routed them from the city.

Benghazi grew into a hot political issue. Republicans accused the administration of leaving American diplomats unprotected, of being slow to react to the attack, and of covering up its fatal incompetence by pretending that the attack was all just a protest that got out of hand. Democrats shot back: Republicans in Congress had left state department employees vulnerable by refusing to fund needed security upgrades. The debate goes to the hardest question in politics: What did our fellow Americans die for?

Foreign policy defines American relations with external nations, groups, and problems. It focuses on how the United States pursues its goals around the world. Foreign policy involves countless small decisions—like negotiating the trading rules with Korea or Brazil, and the biggest decisions of our lifetimes—like sending forces to Libya or dropping an atomic bomb on Hiroshima. American foreign policies have changed the world. They have also boomeranged back home and changed the United States.

● *Is global warming a security threat? Here, a polar bear family clings to a vanishing ice floe.*

Three goals guide foreign policy—security, prosperity, and the spread of American values. These goals often clash with one another: Pursuing one sometimes means sacrificing another. As we describe each goal, think about which seems most important to you.

American Foreign Policy Goal No. 1: Security

First, the United States must defend itself. *Security means protecting important national values from external threats.* But American policy makers must decide what constitutes an external threat. Should we focus on terrorists? China's rising military power? Russian incursions into Ukraine? Or is economic decline the biggest danger? Or perhaps the greatest danger comes from global warming or the limits on natural resources? Different threats require different strategies.

The Military. Every administration, Democratic and Republican, seeks security through a powerful military. The United States vastly outspends every other nation on its armed forces. The Department of Homeland Security, intelligence agencies, and the Veterans Administration add more than $200 billion to the total.

A large military comes with a very high price tag (see Figure 14.5). The costs include higher taxes, larger deficits, and a more powerful central government. Why spend so much more than other nations? Because U.S. military strategy is based on the theory of **primacy**: The United States can best protect its security by maintaining an unrivaled military force.

Primacy: The doctrine asserting that the United States should maintain an unrivaled military.

Soft Power. The military is only one aspect of American national security. In addition to the military, or *hard power*, the United States also deploys *soft power*. **Soft power** focuses on the cultures and values that people in other nations find appealing. More than 690,000 foreign students attend American universities—with the largest numbers coming from China, India, South Korea, Canada, and Japan.[8] The United States is the top tourist destination in the world. Packed stadiums from Barcelona, Spain, to Brisbane, Australia, shout out the words at Bruce Springsteen concerts. American music, movies, and television are everywhere—indeed, some foreign critics accuse the United States of "cultural imperialism." For better or for worse, you can find McDonald's, Coke, Starbucks, and Apple stores in every corner of the world. Sharing these cultural experiences forms bonds among people, which create a different kind of security. Soft power, writes political scientist Joseph Nye, is "the means to success in world politics."[9]

Soft power: Influence a nation exerts by attracting others through culture and commerce; a contrast to persuasion through force of money.

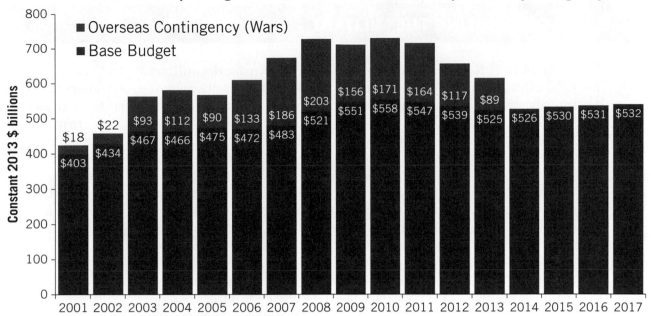

US Defense Spending Trends (billions of $; Defense Department spending only)

■ Overseas Contingency (Wars)
■ Base Budget

Constant 2013 $ billions

Year	Overseas Contingency	Base Budget
2001	$18	$403
2002	$22	$434
2003	$93	$467
2004	$112	$466
2005	$90	$475
2006	$133	$472
2007	$186	$483
2008	$203	$521
2009	$156	$551
2010	$171	$558
2011	$164	$547
2012	$117	$539
2013	$89	$525
2014		$526
2015		$530
2016		$531
2017		$532

● **FIGURE 14.5** *Military spending peaked in 2010 (when the U.S. spending accounted for 47% of the world's military spending). The figure has declined as the wars in Iraq and Afghanistan end (Center for Media and Democracy).*

● *Soft power: American lattes are welcome where the military is not. Here, Starbucks in the heart of the Forbidden City, the imperial palace in Beijing, China.*

DOWNSIZING THE MILITARY

Let's return to the $700 billion question. Should we downsize the American military? Keep it large—or grow it even more? It is time for *you* to advise the president. Which option would you choose?

No, do not downsize the military. In a dangerous world, the United States needs a very strong military. Remaining much stronger than any other nation is the best way to keep the United States safe. It also permits us to protect other democratic nations—and people rebelling against tyranny. The entire world would be worse off if the United States could not respond to crises around the world. The high price tag is the price of freedom.

Yes, downsize the military. We put too much emphasis on the military. We cannot afford to spend so much more than the rest of the world. That drains resources from other national priorities; it makes taxes too high and government too large. Besides, military intervention creates its own problems because, despite our best intentions, people resent the intrusion into their nations. We should rely much more on diplomacy and soft power.

Unsure. In Washington, there is always an alternative to making a decision: create a bipartisan commission to do a thorough study and report back in six months.

Foreign Aid and National Security.   The United States is the largest foreign aid donor in the world. Many Americans believe we spend too much. The reality is that we spend less than 1 percent (less than half of 1 percent if we take out military aid) of our gross national income. Is this too little—or too much?

Many liberals think that assisting other nations is an important path to security. It builds goodwill and helps lift nations out of the poverty that breeds extremists. Many conservatives counter that each nation should take care of itself. Providing funds will only make other nations reliant on us. Moreover, they argue, foreign aid often flies straight into the pockets of the rich and the powerful. The argument goes on, but the reality is that foreign aid forms a tiny part of the U.S. budget.

American Foreign Policy Goal No. 2: Prosperity

The second goal of foreign policy is to ensure prosperity. A nation's power ultimately rests not on its armies but on its economic engine.

Today, the U.S. economy is the largest in the world—it makes up more than a fifth of the entire global economy. Will the United States retain its economic power? Or is it a declining economic power?

At first glance, the United States certainly does not look like a country on the skids. It accounts for almost twice as much economic production as China, more than four times as much as Germany, and more than 163 other nations *combined* (see Figure 14.6). Every nation uses American dollars for trade, and English has become the language of international affairs.

A. Nation's GDP as percentage of world total, 2013

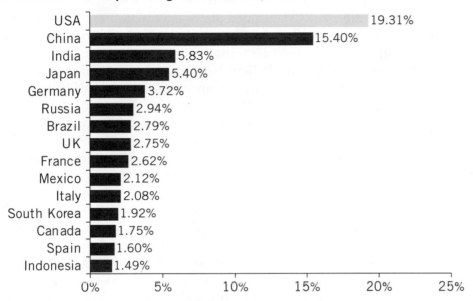

B. Selected GDP growth rates, 2013

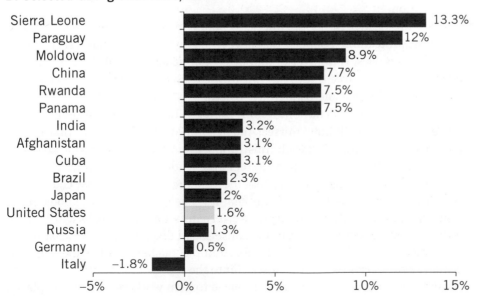

● **FIGURE 14.6** *The world's 15 largest economies. A: Note that despite the talk of economic decline, the United States is still the largest economy—although China is catching up fast. (A half-century ago, the United States had nearly 40% of world economic production.) B: For years the United States has been growing more slowly than emerging economies in China, India, and many developing countries. In 2013, the United States grew at around the average rate of other developed nations (International Monetary Fund/The World Bank Group).*

Although the U.S. economy remains by far the largest, China is rapidly catching up. Look at economic performance over a recent five-year period and the winners and losers look very different (see Figure 14.6). America's growth ranked tenth among the world's fifteen largest economies. China grew more than nine times faster, Brazil five times faster, and Canada and Germany both 25 percent faster. In little more than a decade, China vaulted ahead of Japan and now has an economy almost half the size of the United States'. If that trend continues (a very big if), the United States will soon have a genuine economic rival with a large and dynamic economy.

Another possible risk: The United States buys more from other nations than it sells to them. This imbalance, known as a **trade deficit**, has existed every year since 1975. Is it a problem that Americans import more than they export? Economists differ. Most believe that the nation cannot continue buying more from other nations than it sells to them without this eventually threatening the economy.

Which is it? A nation in decline or an entrepreneurial dynamo setting the pace for the world? You can keep your own score in the years ahead by watching just one measure of world power: the size of the American economy relative to the rest of the world.

Free Trade.   American economic policy champions **free trade**—*the idea that goods and services should move across international boundaries without government interference*. Until the twentieth century, most governments tried to protect their own industries. They slapped tariffs on foreign goods—special taxes that made imports more expensive than local products. Governments also boosted local business with subsidies and tax breaks. This favoritism is called **protectionism**, because it is designed to protect local business from foreign competition.

For the past fifty years, American policy makers have worked to break down the protectionist policies that have kept American goods and services out of other countries. A quarter of all our economic activity involves imports or exports. In theory, free trade helps businesses and consumers in every country, since it offers more choices and lower prices.

In 1994, the international community established the **World Trade Organization**, which now oversees the negotiations and the rules that reduce barriers to free trade. Every administration, every team of economic advisors, and almost every policy textbook agree: Free trade makes everyone better off. However, many citizens fiercely oppose the idea. Free trade faces four challenges.

First, critics of free trade charge that it is cheaper to produce goods in nations that pollute, outlaw unions, and reject safety standards. Jobs will move to those nations. Second, free markets cause social displacement, at least in the short run. Free trade in agriculture, for example, pushes small farmers in poor nations like Nigeria off their farms and into the slums of megacities like Lagos. Most nations have not put policies in place to help workers who are displaced

Trade deficit: The deficit arising when a nation imports (or buys) more goods from foreign nations than it exports (or sells) to them.

Free trade: Goods and services moving across international boundaries without government interference.

Protectionism: Effort to protect local business from foreign competition.

World Trade Organization: An international organization that oversees efforts to open markets and promote free trade.

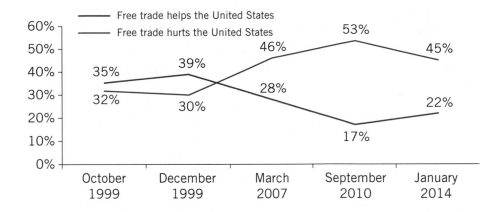

by international competition. Third, as international markets have opened, they have grown volatile. Fourth, American leaders champion free trade only until they run into powerful interests. When government helps American farmers, it violates the rules of free trade—that the government itself is championing. Today, both Democratic and Republican administrations champion free trade despite growing public hostility to the idea (see Figure 14.7).

Energy.   Foreign policy makers keep a close eye on energy supplies. The United States consumes more than 20 million barrels of oil a day, a quarter of the world total. Disruptions in the supply would crash the economy. In the past twenty years, the United States has fought three major wars in the Mideast—which has an estimated 60 percent of the world's oil reserves.

However, the energy story is rapidly changing. Today, the United States and Canada produce almost 60 percent of the nation's supply. As reliance on foreign energy diminishes, a major issue for American foreign policy—the struggle to insure a reliable supply of energy—fades as an issue.

Economic Weapons.   Economic weapons sometimes disrupt free trade. American officials use economic relations as carrots to reward other nations or as sticks to punish them—for attacking another country, trying to build nuclear weapons, or repressing their own citizens. Economic sanctions include the following:

- A boycott, or refusing to buy goods or services from a country.

- An economic embargo, or restricting the flow of trade into a country. Sometimes the navy or the air force enforces the embargo.

- Divestment or refusing to invest in another country. Even local governments and private actors can use this strategy; for example, during South Africa's brutal apartheid regime, many American cities and universities refused to hold any stocks or bonds originating in that country.

- Freezing assets, or seizing the bank accounts and other finances that foreign nationals have invested here. This especially targets elites by stripping them of their foreign bank accounts.
- Finally, withholding foreign aid—if the country is receiving any.

Applying these economic sanctions is never easy, because it requires building an international coalition. If other countries refuse to go along, the United States simply loses a market for its own goods without applying any real pressure. Economic weapons can also hurt ordinary people long before they touch the rich and powerful.

Foreign Policy Goal No. 3: Spreading American Ideals

Most people believe that every nation's foreign policy goal can be described simply: blunt self-interest. However, explaining American action only in terms of power or prosperity misses something important.

In the very first inaugural address, in 1789, President George Washington declared that the new nation had a special mission: "The sacred fire of liberty and the destiny of the republican model of government are . . . entrusted to the hands of the American people." This, he told his countrymen, might even be liberty's best and final chance.[10] From the very start, American leaders believed that the United States had a special role in the world—to champion liberty. American leaders often justify foreign policy action in terms of promoting values such as liberty and democracy.

The belief that the United States plays a special role in world affairs is known as **American exceptionalism**. Is the nation really exceptional? Many Americans believe it is "a nation like no other," as former Speaker of the House Newt Gringrich put it, with a "sacred commitment" to our founding principles. Foreign observers warn, however, that a belief in exceptionalism can be dangerous. It can lead Americans to reduce complicated reality into a simple clash of good and evil.

American Exceptionalism: The view that the United States is unique, marked by a distinct set of ideas such as equality, self-rule, and limited government.

Critics fear American society is increasingly unequal, marked by less opportunity and a growing gulf between rich and poor. The United States seems, to many observers, more fixed on hard-knuckle economic competition and amassing great wealth than on a genuine belief that all people are equal.

Nevertheless, more immigrants crowd into the United States than into any other nation. Even in countries that are skeptical of America's intentions, people stand in long lines to sign up for the lottery that—if they are very lucky—will grant them a visa. If the United States is a nation in decline, then why are so many people fighting to move here? And what other nations are so wide open that the son of a man from Kenya, like Barack Obama, could end up in the White House?

In short, American values play a crucial role in guiding American foreign policy. The key questions are whether they are still vital or beginning to fade and whether they can inspire people around the world or whether, in the last analysis, American leaders simply cloak self interest in the language of rights and freedom.

THE BOTTOM LINE

- The first goal of American foreign policy is security.

- To pursue security, the United States deploys a large military and maintains a policy of primacy—the idea that no military power should rival ours.

- Additional security tools include diplomacy, soft (or cultural) power, and foreign aid.

- Every one of these strategies has strengths and weaknesses and must be deployed carefully.

- The second goal of foreign policy is to protect prosperity. Economic strength is the ultimate source of power on the world stage.

- Today, the U.S. economy is the largest in the world, but will the United States maintain its economic strength relative to other nations?

- American economic policy has been guided by pursuit of free trade—the dropping of barriers to international commerce.

- The United States tries to spread its own values, of democracy and freedom. This is a rare goal for a nation's foreign policy.

◗ Who Makes Foreign Policy?

What is misleading about the following newspaper headlines?

- "The United States Warns Syria about Attacks on Protesters"
- "The United States Seeks Closer Ties to Brazil"
- "Iran Threatens Saudi Arabia"

They all describe nations as if they were *unitary actors*, or individuals with minds of their own. Every chapter in this book has told a different story. The United States constructs politics out of many perspectives, interests, institutions, and arguments. So does every other nation. Foreign policy emerges out of negotiation. Let's now look at the major players with a seat at the table when American foreign policy is made.

Congress

The Constitution carefully balances responsibility for foreign policy between Congress and the president. Congress has the power to declare war, to budget the military, and to ratify treaties. These responsibilities worked fine in a slower world. In the early nineteenth century, the Americans defeated the English in the Battle of New Orleans because word had not filtered back across the Atlantic that a peace treaty had already ended the War of 1812.

Today, the response time can be measured in minutes rather than weeks or months. As the decision clock sped up, defense—and, more generally, foreign policy—shifted away from Congress and to the White House. Congress has not declared war since 1941 despite major wars in Korea (where thirty-six thousand Americans died), Vietnam (another fifty-eight thousand), the Persian Gulf, the Balkans, Afghanistan, and Iraq. Congress is divided, slow, uneasy about taking risks, focused on domestic issues, and always running for re-election. For all these reasons, it has let control of foreign policy slip to the executive branch.

In 1973 Congress tried to reassert some control by passing the **War Powers Act**, which requires presidents to get congressional permission for military action after the troops are in the field for sixty days. Presidents generally ask Congress for support before they commit troops. And, when wars drag on and grow unpopular, Congress asserts itself: It holds hearings, rallies opposition, and squeezes the budget.

The Constitution requires the Senate to ratify international treaties with a two-thirds vote—a high bar in our partisan era. To get around the requirement, presidents sign *executive agreements* with other nations; these have the same legal effect as formal treaties but do not require the two-thirds vote. *Legislative-executive agreements* pass with a simple majority, like any other legislation. A *sole executive agreement* is simply signed by the president without any congressional approval at all.

The Constitution also makes Congress responsible for confirming top foreign policy appointments. Partisan politics has hampered this process. A year into the Obama administration, 170 administration positions were still bottled up in Congress.

In short, Congress has evolved from a partner to a kind of check on executive foreign policy making. The executive branch crafts the policies. It then must win over Congress for funding, legislation, confirmations, and cooperation. In effect, Congress pushes back when presidential policies become unpopular.

War Powers Act: Legislation passed in 1973 to increase congressional involvement in undeclared wars. It requires Congress to approve military action undertaken by the president in no more than sixty days.

The President

The president commands the military, negotiates treaties, rallies Americans during crises, and oversees relations with more than two hundred nations. Each administration defines America's stance toward the world. The presidents and their team decide whether, when, where, and how to intervene around the globe. They balance foreign policy with domestic priorities and political calculations.

Recent administrations have demonstrated the enormous power inherent in the president's foreign policy role. Ironically, modern presidents have more authority and less experience. Early presidents all had a rich foreign policy background. With just one exception, recent presidents have arrived in the White House with no foreign policy experience at all (see Table 14.4).

The State Department

The State Department, the first cabinet agency established under the Constitution, is responsible for managing diplomatic relations with more than two

TABLE 14.4 The Presidents' Foreign Policy Experience

The first six presidents had extensive foreign policy experience. Of the six most recent presidents, only one, George H. W. Bush, had any foreign policy experience at all.

	SECRETARY OF STATE	OTHER DIPLOMATIC OR CABINET POST	CHIEF U.S. REPRESENTATIVE TO GREAT BRITAIN	CHIEF U.S. REPRESENTATIVE TO OTHER MAJOR POWER	COMMANDED U.S. FORCES IN WAR
FIRST SIX PRESIDENTS					
George Washington					X
John Adams		X	X	X	
Thomas Jefferson	X	X		X	
James Madison	X				
James Monroe	X	X	X	X	
John Quincy Adams	X	X	X	X	
MOST RECENT PRESIDENTS					
Jimmy Carter					
Ronald Reagan					
George H. W. Bush		X		X	
Bill Clinton					
George W. Bush					
Barack Obama					

Source: Adapted from Walter Russell Mead, Special Providence: American Foreign Policy and How It Changed the World *(New York: Random House, 2002), 13.*

hundred nations. State is responsible for negotiating treaties, distributing foreign assistance, and managing daily contact with other nations. The men who died in the Benghazi attack were state department officials and their security personnel.

The Department of Defense

The Department of Defense (DOD) manages the military. It is the largest organization in government and the biggest employer in the United States. The

DOD is responsible for more than 2 million military personnel and seven hundred thousand civilian employees—all led by the secretary of defense, who is always a civilian. The department is housed in a huge five-sided office building known as the Pentagon.

Not surprisingly, defense officials see the world very differently than the State Department. The DOD makes military calculations, toting up risks and threats, assets and strategy.

Intelligence

The United States has a large and complicated intelligence community. More than fifteen different agencies and offices gather information from around the world. The best known is the Central Intelligence Agency, which is responsible for foreign intelligence. However, the Departments of State, Defense, Energy, and the Treasury all have their own foreign intelligence operations, as do the military branches. The Federal Bureau of Investigation is responsible for domestic intelligence, which often has to be coordinated with information from abroad.

In theory, each intelligence office and agency monitors a different spectrum of threats. In reality, they have overlapping jurisdictions and act as rivals (yes, a familiar theme in the foreign policy bureaucracy). They are slow to share information or communicate. In 2004, after hearings into the 9/11 terrorist attacks exposed the chaos, Congress created a director of national intelligence charged with bringing order to American intelligence. Did they impose coordination or simply inject one more voice into the contest? Answer: both.

The National Security Council

The National Security Council is part of the Executive Office of the President. It brings the most important foreign policy officers together to advise the president. The council includes the president and the vice president, along with the secretaries of state, defense, and homeland security. It also includes the director of national intelligence, the head of the Joint Chiefs of Staff (the top military officer), and others that the president may name. This is one of the most high-powered groups in a city of high-powered groups. Very different perspectives and personalities come together to hammer out major foreign policy decisions.

Success or Fragmentation?

The results of these many agencies and offices, legislators, and groups—all pulling and hauling and scrambling for influence—are typical of American government. It is chaotic, messy, unpredictable, open—and often democratic. Yet there is always the foreign policy difference: At the end of the process, the president can make a decision and break the stalemate—deploy the navy, issue a warning, embrace a foreign leader. And, despite the messy process, U.S. foreign policy has been relatively successful through much of the nation's history. The United States emerged victorious and more powerful than ever from World War I, World War II, and the Cold War.

- Although we often talk about nations as if they had a single interest, many different individuals and institutions shape foreign policy.

- Congress and the presidents were originally foreign policy partners. Today, the president takes the lead and Congress offers a check.

- The most important executive agencies in foreign policy making are the State Department, the Defense Department, and the National Security Council.

◗ Grand Strategies over Time

Every administration develops a foreign policy strategy by answering three key questions. Should the United States engage the world or withdraw from it? Do we go it alone or work with others? Which foreign policy goals and values are most important?

Grand strategy: An overarching vision that defines and guides a nation's foreign policy.

American leaders create an overall framework to meet the challenges of the time. Their **grand strategy** includes everything from a military doctrine to ways of seeing and interpreting the world. The United States has adopted four different grand strategies over the past century. Once the strategy is in place it can be very difficult to change—until a dramatic event breaks up the old order.

World War I and Isolationism (1918–1939)

George Washington warned his countrymen to stay clear of foreign politics. "The great rule of conduct for us, in regard to foreign nations, is . . . to have . . . as little *political* connection as possible." The United States should limit itself to commerce. We can promote our values simply by building an ideal society that other nations would admire and want to imitate.[11]

Many Americans still hold this view, now known as **isolationism**—the desire to avoid interfering in other nations' affairs. The United States is strong and secure. It can best remain that way by staying home and looking after its own interests.

In contrast, most contemporary foreign policy analysts are **internationalists**. They believe that America's interests are best protected by actively engaging the world's. America must protect shipping

An isolationist poster from just before World War II. The view is blunt: going to war threatens American liberty. The attitude vanished when the United States was attacked at Pearl Harbor. However, today, the sentiment has returned.

Isolationism: The doctrine that a nation should not interfere in other nations' affairs and should avoid all foreign commitments and alliances.

Internationalism: The belief that national interests are best served by actively engaging and working with other nations around the world.

lanes from Somali pirates, hunt down terrorists wherever they lurk, oppose Iran's effort to build a nuclear bomb, protect Asia from an unpredictable North Korea, defend Israel from hostile nations, intervene to stop genocide in Northern Iraq, and the list goes on. This perspective insists that withdrawing from world affairs will allow problems to fester, enemies to multiply, and people to suffer.

Many people believe that the United States traditionally practiced isolationism. This is a myth. Right from the start, the United States exerted its muscle around the world. It battled the French navy in 1798, just ten years after the Constitution went into effect. It fought the Barbary Wars on the north coast of Africa beginning in 1801. (If you are familiar with the Marine Corps anthem, its "shores of Tripoli" refers to the Barbary Wars.) American forces entered Mexico ("the halls of Montezuma") five times between 1836 and 1848 before declaring all-out war.

World War I was horrific. The fighting bogged down into trenches in eastern France, and hundreds of thousands of men died moving the line back and forth a few miles. In the years following World War I, American grand strategy was simple. The United States would intervene only when its own interests were threatened. The United States sent ships and troops around the world—to Russia (during and after the Bolshevik Revolution), Mexico, Panama, Turkey, China, and many other places. It almost always acted independently and minded its own interests.

For all the action, however, the United States maintained a small standing army until the end of World War II. Then, locked in a Cold War with the Soviet Union, the country built an army ready to deploy anywhere around the globe at a moment's notice. The sheer size and sophistication of the military pushes the United States away from isolationism.

Institutions tilt politics: The sheer size and sophistication of the American military pushes the nation away from isolationism. Here, U.S. soldiers from the 234th infantry travel to Afghanistan.

World War II, the Cold War, and Multilateralism (1942–1989)

Although the United States was rarely isolationist, through most of its history it acted alone. President Washington broke the alliance with France that had helped win the Revolutionary War, and America did not enter another peacetime alliance for the next 150 years. This perspective is known as **unilateralism**: American foreign policy should be independent and self-sufficient. Unilateralists oppose treaties with foreign nations or international organizations because they tie America down.

When World War II began in 1939, many Americans wanted nothing to do with another foreign war. "America first," they said. This position changed in December 1941, when Japan attacked the navy base at Pearl Harbor, sank eleven ships, and killed 2,400 men. On that day, the era of standing alone ended.

After World War II, American policy changed. **Multilateralism** means operating together with other nations to pursue common goals. Less than four years later, large swaths of Europe and Asia lay in rubble. A mind-numbing 50 million people were dead (the chilling estimates vary from 38 to 70 million). When the war ended, in September 1945, the only rival to the United States was the Soviet Union, whose armies occupied the nations of central Europe. Many observers warned that the Soviets were poised to extend their control. If anyone was going to lead the free world against the Soviet Union, it had to be the United States. The period from 1945 to 1991 is known as the Cold War.

The Truman administration decided to accept the Soviets' current sphere of influence but to oppose every effort to expand it, a policy known as **containment** (see Figure 14.8). The crucial test came in February 1947. The Democratic administration asked a Republican Congress to pour funds into Greece and Turkey to stop them from turning to communism. Legend has it that the chair of the Foreign Relations Committee, Senator Arthur Vandenberg (R-MI), promised to support Truman but gave him a word of advice about rallying the nation: "You are going to have to scare the hell out of the American people."[12] This Truman proceeded to do in a famous speech before Congress.

While the United States retained economic and military primacy, it joined with other nations in **multilateral organizations** dedicated to opposing communism and spreading democracy and capitalism. It broke with its own past to help establish multiple organizations: the United Nations (formed in 1945), the Organization of American States (1948), the North Atlantic Treaty Organization (1949), and the Southeast Asia Treaty Organization (1954).

Fighting communism back during the Cold War required concerted action. Today, only international cooperation can defeat terrorism, reverse climate change, secure prosperity, keep the oil flowing, end starvation, stop ethnic killing, resist global pandemics, stop the international traffic in drugs and sex, and end violence against women.

Unilateralism: A doctrine that holds that the United States should act independently of other nations. It should decide what is best for itself—not in coordination with partners and allies.

Multilateralism: A doctrine that emphasizes operating together with other nations to pursue common goals.

Containment: American Cold War strategy designed to stop the spread of communism.

Multilateral Organization: International organization of three or more nations organized around a common goal.

● **FIGURE 14.8** *Europe during the Cold War. For 50 years, American foreign policy, operating with its allies (through the North Atlantic Treaty Organization) focused on containing the Soviet Union in its sphere.*

see for yourself 14.1

Go online to see footage of the joyous destruction of the Berlin Wall in 1989.

The New World Order (1989–2003)

Around the world, people gaped at the incredible television footage in November 1989. Germans were clambering onto the Berlin Wall and ripping it apart. For almost thirty years, the Wall—running through Berlin and separating communist and democratic Germany—had been the symbol of the Cold War. Communist guards had shot people trying to leap to freedom. President John Kennedy had looked out at the Wall and declared, "All free [people], wherever they may live, are citizens of Berlin." Ronald Reagan had stood on the same spot and challenged the Soviet leader, "Mr. Gorbachev, tear down this wall." Now the East German guards stood awkwardly by, uncertain what to do, as the delirious mob hammered the Wall to pieces. Within two years, the entire Soviet empire collapsed. The framework that had guided American foreign policy for more than fifty years was suddenly irrelevant. What next? President George H. W.

One of history's turning points: Jubilant Berliners climb the Berlin Wall as communism collapses. Suddenly, American foreign policy makers needed an entirely new grand strategy.

Bush proclaimed "a new world order." He touted an active, multilateral march toward free markets and democracy. With the collapse of communism, Americans hoped for a safer, more prosperous, and more democratic world. That all changed after the terrorist attacks of September 11, 2001.

The War on Terror (Began 2001)

The 9/11 attacks killed almost three thousand people. The attacks shut down American institutions from coast to coast—financial markets in New York, Disney World in Florida, the great arch in St. Louis, and air travel across American airspace (for five days). In the stunned aftermath, the George W. Bush administration constructed a formidable new foreign policy framework. To define the attacks as a crime would have brought in the American justice system. Instead, the administration declared them an act of war and responded with a "war on terror." That choice changed America's role in the world.

President George W. Bush returned American foreign policy to a forceful unilateralism. It was the first administration to do so in sixty years. The **Bush Doctrine**, a grand strategy forged after 9/11, held that the United States would not permit nations to harbor terrorists and that the United States would launch **preemptive** and unilateral military action against such nations—regardless of whether other nations or international organizations supported the action.

During the Cold War, the United States operated on the theory of *deterrence*: build a military so overpowering—including nuclear weapons—that other nations will be afraid to attack. Deterrence is aimed at other governments. However, the strategy does not work with extremists who are willing to

Bush Doctrine: An international strategy that aggressively pursued terrorists and the nations that harbored them through unilateral and preemptive military action.

Preemptive action: Military action that responds to threats before they happen—as opposed to responding to the aggression of others.

sacrifice their lives for a cause. The war on terror targeted terrorists, nations that harbored terrorists, and any organizations that assisted terrorists.

War in Afghanistan.

American leaders quickly traced the 9/11 attacks to Al Qaeda. The terrorist network had found sanctuary in Afghanistan, a nation ruled by the **Taliban**, a fundamentalist Islamic group. The United States organized antigovernment militias in Afghanistan and helped them swiftly overthrow the Taliban government. Most American allies, as well as many nations in the region, supported the campaign. After the quick victory over the Taliban government, American and Afghani forces tried to capture or kill Al Qaeda leaders—some took shelter next door in Pakistan. After more than ten years of fighting, funding, and diplomacy, Al Qaeda in Afghanistan is a shadow of its former self and most of its leaders are dead. However, Al Qaeda has spread to other countries, most notably Yemen, Somalia, and Iraq. Meanwhile, the United States continues its struggle to pacify the Taliban and promote democracy in Afghanistan.

Taliban: A fundamentalist Islamic sect that took control of Afghanistan in 1996 and gave shelter to the Al Qaeda terrorist network.

War in Iraq.

The Bush administration followed the strike against Afghanistan with a fateful decision to topple Saddam Hussein in Iraq. Officials argued that Saddam had "weapons of mass destruction," such as atomic weapons or poison gas. Since he was a sworn enemy of the United States, he might turn those weapons over to terrorists. Neoconservatives believed the United States should act more vigorously around the world. The war in Iraq was the first big test of their approach. The United States, they believed, should deploy its unrivaled power to depose a dictator, free a people, and wipe out another potential state sponsor of terrorism.

There was, however, a problem. Iraq had not actually attacked the United States. This would be America's first preemptive war. To complicate matters, UN inspectors were already in Iraq, looking for weapons of mass destruction. Although they had followed every lead from U.S. intelligence, they found none.

The United States launched its attack on Saddam Hussein's government in March 2003. The military easily toppled the dictator, but Iraq burst into violence. Religious sects and tribes attacked one another; some turned their guns and explosives on the United States. The death toll rose among both American troops and Iraqi civilians. Iraqi society teetered on the edge of chaos. After a decade, the United States withdrew its forces, but Iraq remains an unstable nation racked by sectarian tensions.

Terrorist Threats Today.

In tackling terrorist threats, conventional means of warfare, such as invading another country, prove less effective than policing measures—gathering intelligence and punishing criminal behavior. Yet, the United States has struggled to implement such methods. As we've seen, intelligence agencies within the United States do not always cooperate. Preventing terrorist attacks often involves cooperating with intelligence services abroad—a further complication. Since the United States cannot extradite terrorists from areas where they have proliferated, the government has resorted to extraordinary actions that have raised humanitarian concerns. Controversial actions include *extraordinary rendition*, snatching suspects off the street and whisking them away to a foreign prison. Some of these "ghost prisoners" later reappeared in public and proclaimed their innocence. Although the Obama administration scaled back the secret programs and outlawed "harsh interrogation techniques" such as waterboarding, it never formally rejected the practice of extraordinary rendition.

The United States has also carried out assassinations of terrorists around the globe. In September 2011, the Obama administration authorized a missile strike that killed Anwar al-Awlaki, an American-born cleric living in Yemen who was accused of plotting terrorist attacks on the United States. Is that kind of killing justified? The answer takes us back to the Constitution itself, which requires every criminal to receive a fair trial. In a war, however, nations kill their enemies. Was Awlaki an enemy in a war? Or, a full decade after 9/11, was it time to consider Awlaki a murder suspect who deserved a trial?

Another especially pressing issue is the spread of nuclear weapons. Five nations openly possess them (the United States, England, France, Russia, and

What Do You Think?

TERRORISTS AND THE RULE OF LAW

From the start of this chapter, we have described the debate between two foreign policy goals: bolstering security and projecting American values. That tension has taken a new form in recent times. Which of the following policies would you choose in pursuing the war on terror in the future?

Hunt down terrorists. The United States has no choice but to chase after terrorists with every weapon at its disposal. Terrorists are evil and kill innocent people. We must interrogate terrorism suspects using any method that can elicit information, hunt down those who plan to do us harm, and attack nations that harbor terrorists before they can attack civilian populations around the world. A strong emphasis on national security is the only way to keep the United States—and the world—safe.

Let the law prevail. America has always stood for the rule of law. Permanent security lies not in hunting terrorists but in inspiring people around the world with the power of our ideas—democracy, equality, and equal protection under the law. We proclaim our view of justice to the world when we give even our worst enemies a fair trial. The war on terror undermines our Constitution, subverts our values, and makes us weaker.

Unsure. Maybe the truth lies in between these choices. Perhaps you can design your own policy somewhere between these positions.

China). Four others are thought to have developed them (India, Pakistan, North Korea, and Israel). A small number of foreign policy experts argue that the spread of the weapons make wars less likely since either side can annihilate the other.[13] Most observers believe the opposite: As nuclear weapons spread to less stable nations, they are more likely to be used and to fall into the hands of extremist groups. American foreign policy must work around the globe to avoid the nightmare scenario of nuclear catastrophe.

The Obama administration has struggled to pivot away from the war on terror and establish a new grand strategy. This has proved difficult. As we have seen so often, institutions—once established—are hard to undo. The key question confronting Americans remains: What sort of grand strategy should the nation pursue now?

THE BOTTOM LINE

- The United States forged four grand strategies in the twentieth century.

- It stood alone and acted unilaterally (1918–1939), it led the democratic nations in multilateral coalitions during the Cold War (1945–1991), it debated a new world order after the Cold War (1991–2001), and it launched a war on terror.

- The Obama administration called for a move away from the war on terror but found that difficult to do. The administration scaled back many of the Bush administration policies (forbidding torture, overseeing extraordinary rendition, quietly dropping the phrase "the war on terror" itself); nevertheless, it has kept the basic institutional framework of the war on terror in place.

Conclusion: Policy Matters

As you go about your day today, on campus or off, take a moment to notice all the different ways you encounter the policy system. Notice the "USDA Organic" label on your breakfast cereal or yogurt container, along with all those government-mandated nutrition facts. Hopping in your car or on your bike? The cost of any gas you buy, the condition of the roads you travel on, the street signs you navigate by: all those are the result of policy decisions, often hard-fought ones. Federal agencies license and manage the electromagnetic spectrum that you use to communicate by smartphone or watch TV, regulate the safety of the gym where you work out, and inspect (plus, moving to the state/local level, charge tax on) the food you buy. Headed to class? Policy decisions determined the subsidy supporting you and rates you pay on any student loans you hold, and if you attend a public university, they may have some say over the curriculum you study.

These are just a few of the ways in which public policy helps shape your daily experience. We return once more to a theme throughout this book: As a member of this vast but often surprisingly accessible democracy, you have the ability (and now, we hope, enhanced knowledge) to shape those policy decisions in turn. May you find a fulfilling role in the great continuing American experiment: government by the people.

CHAPTER SUMMARY

● Public policy making inevitably involves choices: Should we reduce the interest rate on student-loan repayments? Launch a manned mission to Mars? Ban automatic weapons in the wake of a tragic shooting? Understanding those choices is the essence of politics and government in America.

● Five stages mark the process of devising domestic policies. These are not a recipe or blueprint for action, but most policy achievements pass through all these.

– *Agenda setting* describes the transformation of an idea into a policy issue, as public attention expands.

– Once a topic is on the agenda, it must be *defined*—What is this issue about?—and *framed*: How lawmakers and public talk about an agenda item often determines whether it will move forward or gather dust.

– A third stage, *policy formation*, involves the legislative and executive activities that translate talk into concrete statutory language.

– Once a policy has been passed into law, it must be *implemented*, involving rule making and then delivery of public services.

– Finally, policies are *evaluated*; once implemented, they create a *feedback* process that affects future policy making in that area.

● The largest U.S. policy programs, in terms of spending and numbers of people served, are social policies like Social Security, Medicare, Medicaid, and unemployment insurance.

● Heightened attention to fiscal and monetary policy, combined with harder economic times, has elevated the importance of budgeting in American politics and government.

● Foreign policy explores how the United States engages the world. Ultimately it raises the deepest question about the nation. Is it the richest and most powerful nation, ready to lead the world? Or is it a declining superpower?

● The three goals of American foreign policy are security, prosperity, and spreading American values. These three goals sometimes conflict.

● The United States spends as much on its military as the rest of the world combined. Primacy suggests that it should act with unparalleled power.

● The United States is responsible for almost a quarter of the world economy and more than two and half times as much as its nearest rival, China. But China's growth rate in recent years has been more than eight times higher.

● U.S. economic policy has revolved around free trade—reducing barriers to trade between nations. Lately, free trade has met resistance.

● Congress originally shared foreign policy with the executive branch, but today prime responsibility has shifted to the executive. However, foreign policy is best understood in the light of domestic policy, as the outcome of many agencies and groups pushing for their own interests and advantage.

● Twentieth-century grand strategies included isolationism (1918–1939), World War II, the Cold War, and internationalism (1942–1989), the search for a new world order (1991–2003), and the war on terror (since 2003).

KEY TERMS

American Exceptionalism, 496

Bush Doctrine, 505

Containment, 503

Continuing resolution, 486

Cost–benefit analysis, 474

Cost effectiveness, 474

Entitlement program, 482

Federal budget deficit, 486

Federal poverty line, 481

Fiscal policy, 484

Focusing event, 471

Free trade, 494

Grand strategy, 501

Gross domestic product, 480

Internationalism, 502

Isolationism, 502

Monetary policy, 484

Multilateral organization, 503

Multilateralism, 503

Path dependence, 478

Policy window, 475

Preemptive action, 505

Primacy, 490

Protectionism, 494

Soft power, 490

Taliban, 506

Trade deficit, 494

Unilateralism, 503

War Powers Act, 498

World Trade Organization, 494

STUDY QUESTIONS

1. What is "public policy"? Why is it so important to the work of government?

2. How do items get on the policy agenda?

3. Think of an issue you care about. How is it currently *framed* in national discussions about the issue? Would you frame it differently—and if so, how?

4. Why does policy formation—translating a topic from "good idea" into a bill ready for a congressional vote—take so long?

5. Why are our largest entitlement programs—Social Security, Medicare, and Medicaid—so expensive?

6. Given a choice, would you emphasize managing the economy through fiscal policy (taxing and spending) or monetary policy (managed by banks, especially the Federal Reserve)? Defend your choice.

7. Why does Congress have to pass continuing resolutions at the end of most budget years?

8. Name the three foreign policy goals that the United States pursues. Discuss the relative importance of each goal. If you had to stress one, which would it be?

9. What do you consider the most important threat to American security? Would it be a traditional threat like foreign enemies or a more common problem like global warming? Explain your thinking.

10. What is free trade?

11. Define isolationism and internationalism. Pick one perspective and defend it.

12. Define unilateralism and multilateralism. Which position makes more sense to you? Explain why.

13. What four grand strategies did the United States pursue in the twentieth century? Describe each one.

14. If you had to design a grand strategy for today, what would you emphasize?

APPENDIX I

The Declaration of Independence

When in the course of human events, it becomes necessary for one people to dissolve the political bands which have connected them with another, and to assume, among the powers of the earth, the separate and equal station to which the Laws of Nature and of Nature's God entitle them, a decent respect to the opinions of mankind requires that they should declare the causes which impel them to the separation.

We hold these truths to be self-evident, that all men are created equal, that they are endowed by their Creator with certain unalienable Rights, that among these are life, liberty and the pursuit of happiness. That to secure these rights, governments are instituted among men, deriving their just powers from the consent of the governed; that whenever any form of government becomes destructive of these ends, it is the right of the people to alter or to abolish it, and to institute new Government, laying its foundation on such principles and organizing its powers in such form, as to them shall seem most likely to effect their safety and happiness. Prudence, indeed, will dictate that Governments long established should not be changed for light and transient causes; and, accordingly, all experience hath shown, that mankind are more disposed to suffer, while evils are sufferable, than to right themselves by abolishing the forms to which they are accustomed. But when a long train of abuses and usurpations, pursuing invariably the same object evinces a design to reduce them under absolute despotism, it is their right, it is their duty, to throw off such government, and to provide new guards for their future security. Such has been the patient sufferance of these colonies; and such is now the necessity which constrains them to alter their former systems of government. The history of the present King of Great Britain is a history of repeated injuries and usurpations, all having in direct object the establishment of an absolute tyranny over these States. To prove this, let facts be submitted to a candid world:

He has refused his assent to laws, the most wholesome and necessary for the public good.

He has forbidden his governors to pass laws of immediate and pressing importance, unless suspended in their operation till his assent should be obtained; and, when so suspended, he has utterly neglected to attend to them.

He has refused to pass other laws for the accommodation of large districts of people, unless those people would relinquish the right of representation in the legislature, a right inestimable to them and formidable to tyrants only.

He has called together legislative bodies at places unusual, uncomfortable, and distant from the depository of their public records, for the sole purpose of fatiguing them into compliance with his measures.

He has dissolved representative houses repeatedly, for opposing with manly firmness his invasions on the rights of the people.

He has refused for a long time, after such dissolutions, to cause others to be elected; whereby the legislative powers, incapable of annihilation, have returned to the People at large for their exercise; the State remaining in the mean time exposed to all the dangers of invasion from without, and convulsions within.

He has endeavored to prevent the population of these States; for that purpose obstructing the laws for naturalization of foreigners; refusing to pass others to encourage their migrations hither, and raising the conditions of new appropriations of lands.

He has obstructed the administration of justice, by refusing his assent to laws for establishing judiciary powers.

He has made judges dependent on his will alone, for the tenure of their offices, and the amount and payment of their salaries.

He has erected a multitude of new offices, and sent hither swarms of officers to harass our people, and eat out their substance.

He has kept among us, in times of peace, standing armies without the consent of our legislatures.

He has affected to render the Military independent of, and superior to, the civil power.

He has combined with others to subject us to a jurisdiction foreign to our constitution and unacknowledged by our laws; giving his assent to their acts of pretended legislation:

For quartering large bodies of armed troops among us;

For protecting them, by a mock trial, from punishment for any murders which they should commit on the inhabitants of these States;

For cutting off our trade with all parts of the world;

For imposing taxes on us without our Consent;

For depriving us, in many cases, of the benefits of Trial by Jury;

For transporting us beyond Seas to be tried for pretended offences;

For abolishing the free System of English Laws in a neighbouring Province, establishing therein an Arbitrary government, and enlarging its Boundaries so as to render it at once an example and fit instrument for introducing the same absolute rule into these colonies;

For taking away our charters, abolishing our most valuable laws, and altering fundamentally the forms of our governments;

For suspending our own legislatures, and declaring themselves invested with power to legislate for us in all cases whatsoever.

He has abdicated government here, by declaring us out of his protection and waging war against us.

He has plundered our seas, ravaged our coasts, burnt our towns, and destroyed the lives of our people.

He is at this time transporting large armies of foreign mercenaries to complete the works of death, desolation and tyranny, already begun with circumstances of cruelty and perfidy scarcely paralleled in the most barbarous ages, and totally unworthy the head of a civilized nation.

He has constrained our fellow citizens taken captive on the high seas to bear arms against their country, to become the executioners of their friends and brethren, or to fall themselves by their hands.

He has excited domestic insurrections amongst us, and has endeavored to bring on the inhabitants of our frontiers, the merciless Indian savages, whose known rule of warfare, is an undistinguished destruction of all ages, sexes and conditions.

In every stage of these oppressions we have petitioned for redress in the most humble terms; our repeated petitions have been answered only by repeated injury. A prince whose character is thus marked by every act which may define a tyrant, is unfit to be the ruler of a free people.

Nor have we been wanting in attentions to our British brethren. We have warned them from time to time of attempts by their legislature to extend an unwarrantable jurisdiction over us. We have reminded them of the circumstances of our emigration and settlement here. We have appealed to their native justice and magnanimity, and we have conjured them by the ties of our common kindred to disavow these usurpations, which, would inevitably interrupt our connections and correspondence. They, too, have been deaf to the voice of justice and of consanguinity. We must, therefore, acquiesce in the necessity, which denounces our separation, and hold them, as we hold the rest of mankind, enemies in war, in peace friends.

We, therefore, the representatives of the United States of America, in general Congress, assembled, appealing to the Supreme Judge of the world for the rectitude of our intentions, do, in the name, and by the authority of the good people of these colonies, solemnly publish and declare, that these united colonies are, and of right ought to be free and independent states; that they are absolved from all allegiance to the British Crown, and that all political connection between them and the state of Great Britain, is and ought to be totally dissolved; and that, as free and independent states, they have full power to levy war, conclude peace, contract alliances, establish commerce, and to do all other acts and things which independent states may of right do. And for the support of this declaration, with a firm reliance on the protection of Divine Providence, we mutually pledge to each other our lives, our fortunes and our sacred honor.

The Constitution of the United States of America

We the People of the United States, in Order to form a more perfect Union, establish Justice, insure domestic Tranquility, provide for the common defence, promote the general Welfare, and secure the Blessings of Liberty to ourselves and our Posterity, do ordain and establish this Constitution for the United States of America.

Article I
Section 1

All legislative Powers herein granted shall be vested in a Congress of the United States, which shall consist of a Senate and House of Representatives.

Section 2

The House of Representatives shall be composed of Members chosen every second Year by the People of the several States, and the Electors in each State shall have the Qualifications requisite for Electors of the most numerous Branch of the State Legislature.

No Person shall be a Representative who shall not have attained to the Age of twenty five Years, and been seven Years a Citizen of the United States, and who shall not, when elected, be an Inhabitant of that State in which he shall be chosen.

Representatives [and direct Taxes]* shall be apportioned among the several States [which may be included within this Union, according to their respective Numbers, which shall be determined by adding to the whole Number of free Persons, including those bound to Service for a Term of Years, and excluding Indians not taxed, three fifths of all other Persons].** The actual Enumeration shall be made within three Years -after the first Meeting of the Congress of the United States, and within every subsequent Term of ten Years, in such Manner as they shall by Law direct. The Number of Representatives shall not exceed one for every thirty Thousand, but each State shall have at Least one Representative; and until such enumeration shall be made, the State of New Hampshire shall be entitled to choose three, Massachusetts eight, Rhode-Island and Providence Plantations one, Connecticut five, New York six, New Jersey four, Pennsylvania eight, Delaware one, Maryland six, Virginia ten, North Carolina five, South Carolina five, and Georgia three.

---

*Modified by the Sixteenth Amendment.
**Negated by the Fourteenth Amendment.

When vacancies happen in the Representation from any State, the Executive Authority thereof shall issue Writs of Election to fill such Vacancies.

The House of Representatives shall choose their Speaker and other Officers; and shall have the sole Power of Impeachment.

Section 3

The Senate of the United States shall be composed of two Senators from each State, chosen [by the Legislature thereof]* for six Years; and each Senator shall have one Vote.

Immediately after they shall be assembled in Consequence of the first Election, they shall be divided as equally as may be into three Classes. The Seats of the Senators of the first Class shall be vacated at the Expiration of the second Year, of the second Class at the Expiration of the fourth Year, and of the third Class at the Expiration of the sixth Year, so that one third may be chosen every second Year, [and if Vacancies happen by Resignation, or otherwise, during the Recess of the Legislature of any State, the Executive thereof may make temporary Appointments until the next Meeting of the Legislature, which shall then fill such Vacancies].**

No Person shall be a Senator who shall not have attained to the Age of thirty Years, and been nine Years a Citizen of the United States, and who shall not, when elected, be an Inhabitant of that State for which he shall be chosen.

The Vice President of the United States shall be President of the Senate, but shall have no Vote, unless they be equally divided.

The Senate shall choose their other Officers, and also a President pro tempore, in the Absence of the Vice President, or when he shall exercise the Office of President of the United States.

The Senate shall have the sole Power to try all Impeachments. When sitting for that Purpose, they shall be on Oath or Affirmation. When the President of the United States is tried, the Chief Justice shall preside: And no Person shall be convicted without the Concurrence of two thirds of the Members present.

Judgment in Cases of Impeachment shall not extend further than to removal from Office, and disqualification to hold and enjoy any Office of honor, Trust or Profit under the United States: but the Party convicted shall nevertheless be liable and subject to Indictment, Trial, Judgment and Punishment, according to Law.

Section 4

The Times, Places and Manner of holding Elections for Senators and Representatives, shall be prescribed in each State by the Legislature thereof;

---

*Changed by the Seventeenth Amendment.
** Modified by the Seventeenth Amendment.

but the Congress may at any time by Law make or alter such Regulations, except as to the Places of chusing Senators.

[The Congress shall assemble at least once in every Year, and such Meeting shall be on the first Monday in December, unless they shall by Law appoint a different Day.]*

Section 5

Each House shall be the Judge of the Elections, Returns and Qualifications of its own Members, and a Majority of each shall constitute a Quorum to do Business; but a smaller Number may adjourn from day to day, and may be authorized to compel the Attendance of absent Members, in such Manner, and under such Penalties as each House may provide.

Each House may determine the Rules of its Proceedings, punish its Members for disorderly Behaviour, and, with the Concurrence of two thirds, expel a Member.

Each House shall keep a Journal of its Proceedings, and from time to time publish the same, excepting such Parts as may in their Judgment require Secrecy; and the Yeas and Nays of the Members of either House on any question shall, at the Desire of one fifth of those Present, be entered on the Journal.

Neither House, during the Session of Congress, shall, without the Consent of the other, adjourn for more than three days, nor to any other Place than that in which the two Houses shall be sitting.

Section 6

The Senators and Representatives shall receive a Compensation for their Services, to be ascertained by Law, and paid out of the Treasury of the United States. They shall in all Cases, except Treason, Felony and Breach of the Peace, be privileged from Arrest during their Attendance at the Session of their respective Houses, and in going to and returning from the same; and for any Speech or Debate in either House, they shall not be questioned in any other Place.

No Senator or Representative shall, during the Time for which he was elected, be appointed to any civil Office under the Authority of the United States, which shall have been created, or the Emoluments whereof shall have been increased during such time; and no Person holding any Office under the United States, shall be a Member of either House during his Continuance in Office.

Section 7

All Bills for raising Revenue shall originate in the House of Representatives; but the Senate may propose or concur with Amendments as on other Bills.

---

*Changed to January 3 by the Twentieth Amendment.

Every Bill which shall have passed the House of Representatives and the Senate, shall, before it become a Law, be presented to the President of the United States: If he approve he shall sign it, but if not he shall return it, with his Objections to that House in which it shall have originated, who shall enter the Objections at large on their Journal, and proceed to reconsider it. If after such Reconsideration two thirds of that House shall agree to pass the Bill, it shall be sent, together with the Objections, to the other House, by which it shall likewise be reconsidered, and if approved by two thirds of that House, it shall become a Law. But in all such Cases the Votes of both Houses shall be determined by yeas and Nays, and the Names of the Persons voting for and against the Bill shall be entered on the Journal of each House respectively. If any Bill shall not be returned by the President within ten Days (Sundays excepted) after it shall have been presented to him, the Same shall be a Law, in like Manner as if he had signed it, unless the Congress by their Adjournment prevent its Return, in which Case it shall not be a Law.

Every Order, Resolution, or Vote to which the Concurrence of the Senate and House of Representatives may be necessary (except on a question of Adjournment) shall be presented to the President of the United States; and before the Same shall take Effect, shall be approved by him, or being disapproved by him, shall be repassed by two thirds of the Senate and House of Representatives, according to the Rules and Limitations prescribed in the Case of a Bill.

Section 8

The Congress shall have Power

To lay and collect Taxes, Duties, Imposts and Excises, to pay the Debts and provide for the common Defence and general Welfare of the United States; but all Duties, Imposts and Excises shall be uniform throughout the United States;

To borrow Money on the credit of the United States;

To regulate Commerce with foreign Nations, and among the several States, and with the Indian Tribes;

To establish an uniform Rule of Naturalization, and uniform Laws on the subject of Bankruptcies throughout the United States;

To coin Money, regulate the Value thereof, and of foreign Coin, and fix the Standard of Weights and Measures;

To provide for the Punishment of counterfeiting the Securities and current Coin of the United States;

To establish Post Offices and post Roads;

To promote the Progress of Science and useful Arts, by securing for limited Times to Authors and Inventors the exclusive Right to their respective Writings and Discoveries;

To constitute Tribunals inferior to the supreme Court;

To define and punish Piracies and Felonies committed on the high Seas, and Offences against the Law of Nations;

To declare War, grant Letters of Marque and Reprisal, and make Rules concerning Captures on Land and Water;

To raise and support Armies, but no Appropriation of Money to that Use shall be for a longer Term than two Years;

To provide and maintain a Navy;

To make Rules for the Government and Regulation of the land and naval Forces;

To provide for calling forth the Militia to execute the Laws of the Union, suppress Insurrections and repel Invasions;

To provide for organizing, arming, and disciplining the Militia, and for governing such Part of them as may be employed in the Service of the United States, reserving to the States respectively, the Appointment of the Officers, and the Authority of training the Militia according to the discipline prescribed by Congress;

To exercise exclusive Legislation in all Cases whatsoever, over such District (not exceeding ten Miles square) as may, by Cession of particular States, and the Acceptance of Congress, become the Seat of the Government of the United States, and to exercise like Authority over all Places purchased by the Consent of the Legislature of the State in which the Same shall be, for the Erection of Forts, Magazines, Arsenals, dock-Yards, and other needful Buildings;—And

To make all Laws which shall be necessary and proper for carrying into Execution the foregoing Powers, and all other Powers vested by this Constitution in the Government of the United States, or in any Department or Officer thereof.

Section 9

The Migration or Importation of such Persons as any of the States now existing shall think proper to admit, shall not be prohibited by the Congress prior to the Year one thousand eight hundred and eight, but a Tax or duty may be imposed on such Importation, not exceeding ten dollars for each Person.

The Privilege of the Writ of Habeas Corpus shall not be suspended, unless when in Cases of Rebellion or Invasion the public Safety may require it.

No Bill of Attainder or ex post facto Law shall be passed.

[No Capitation, or other direct, Tax shall be laid, unless in Proportion to the Census or enumeration herein before directed to be taken.]*

No Tax or Duty shall be laid on Articles exported from any State.

No Preference shall be given by any Regulation of Commerce or Revenue to the Ports of one State over those of another; nor shall Vessels bound to, or from, one State, be obliged to enter, clear, or pay Duties in another.

No Money shall be drawn from the Treasury, but in Consequence of Appropriations made by Law; and a regular Statement and Account of the Receipts and Expenditures of all public Money shall be published from time to time.

No Title of Nobility shall be granted by the United States: And no Person holding any Office of Profit or Trust under them, shall, without the

*Modified by the Sixteenth Amendment.

Consent of the Congress, accept of any present, Emolument, Office, or Title, of any kind whatever, from any King, Prince, or foreign State.

Section 10

No State shall enter into any Treaty, Alliance, or Confederation; grant Letters of Marque and Reprisal; coin Money; emit Bills of Credit; make any Thing but gold and silver Coin a Tender in Payment of Debts; pass any Bill of Attainder, ex post facto Law, or Law impairing the Obligation of Contracts, or grant any Title of Nobility.

No State shall, without the Consent of the Congress, lay any Imposts or Duties on Imports or Exports, except what may be absolutely necessary for executing it's inspection Laws: and the net Produce of all Duties and Imposts, laid by any State on Imports or Exports, shall be for the Use of the Treasury of the United States; and all such Laws shall be subject to the Revision and Control of the Congress.

No State shall, without the Consent of Congress, lay any Duty of Tonnage, keep Troops, or Ships of War in time of Peace, enter into any Agreement or Compact with another State, or with a foreign Power, or engage in War, unless actually invaded, or in such imminent Danger as will not admit of delay.

Article II
Section 1

The executive Power shall be vested in a President of the United States of America. He shall hold his Office during the Term of four Years, and, together with the Vice President, chosen for the same Term, be elected, as follows:

Each State shall appoint, in such Manner as the Legislature thereof may direct, a Number of Electors, equal to the whole Number of Senators and Representatives to which the State may be entitled in the Congress: but no Senator or Representative, or Person holding an Office of Trust or Profit under the United States, shall be appointed an Elector.

[The Electors shall meet in their respective States, and vote by Ballot for two Persons, of whom one at least shall not be an Inhabitant of the same State with themselves. And they shall make a List of all the Persons voted for, and of the Number of Votes for each; which List they shall sign and certify, and transmit sealed to the Seat of the Government of the United States, directed to the President of the Senate. The President of the Senate shall, in the Presence of the Senate and House of Representatives, open all the Certificates, and the Votes shall then be counted. The Person having the greatest Number of Votes shall be the President, if such Number be a Majority of the whole Number of Electors appointed; and if there be more than one who have such Majority, and have an equal Number of Votes, then the House of Representatives shall immediately choose by Ballot one of them for President; and if no Person have a Majority, then from the five highest on the List the said House shall in like Manner choose the President. But in choosing the President, the Votes shall be taken by States, the Representation from each State having one Vote; a quorum for this purpose shall consist of a Member or Members from two thirds of the States, and a Majority of all the States shall be necessary to a Choice. In every Case, after the Choice of the President, the Person having the greatest Number of Votes of the Electors shall be the Vice President. But if there should remain two or more who have equal Votes, the Senate shall choose from them by Ballot the Vice President.]*

The Congress may determine the Time of choosing the Electors, and the Day on which they shall give their Votes; which Day shall be the same throughout the United States.

No Person except a natural born Citizen, or a Citizen of the United States, at the time of the Adoption of this Constitution, shall be eligible to the Office of President; neither shall any Person be eligible to that Office who shall not have attained to the Age of thirty five Years, and been fourteen Years a Resident within the United States.

In Case of the Removal of the President from Office, or of his Death, Resignation, or Inability to discharge the Powers and Duties of the said Office, the Same shall devolve on the Vice President, and the Congress may by Law provide for the Case of Removal, Death, Resignation or Inability, both of the President and Vice President, declaring what Officer shall then act as President, and such Officer shall act accordingly, until the Disability be removed, or a President shall be elected.

The President shall, at stated Times, receive for his Services, a Compensation, which shall neither be increased nor diminished during the Period for which he shall have been elected, and he shall not receive within that Period any other Emolument from the United States, or any of them.

Before he enter on the Execution of his Office, he shall take the following Oath or Affirmation:—"I do solemnly swear (or affirm) that I will faithfully execute the Office of President of the United States, and will to the best of my Ability, preserve, protect and defend the Constitution of the United States."

Section 2

The President shall be Commander in Chief of the Army and Navy of the United States, and of the Militia of the several States, when called into the actual Service of the United States; he may require the Opinion, in writing, of the principal Officer in each of the executive Departments, upon any Subject relating to the Duties of their respective Offices, and he shall have Power to grant Reprieves and Pardons for Offences against the United States, except in Cases of Impeachment.

He shall have Power, by and with the Advice and Consent of the Senate, to make Treaties, provided two thirds of the Senators present concur; and he shall nominate, and by and with the Advice and Consent of the Senate,

---

*Changed by the Twelfth and Twentieth Amendments.

shall appoint Ambassadors, other public Ministers and Consuls, Judges of the supreme Court, and all other Officers of the United States, whose Appointments are not herein otherwise provided for, and which shall be established by Law: but the Congress may by Law vest the Appointment of such inferior Officers, as they think proper, in the President alone, in the Courts of Law, or in the Heads of Departments.

The President shall have Power to fill up all Vacancies that may happen during the Recess of the Senate, by granting Commissions which shall expire at the End of their next Session.

Section 3

He shall from time to time give to the Congress Information of the State of the Union, and recommend to their Consideration such Measures as he shall judge necessary and expedient; he may, on extraordinary Occasions, convene both Houses, or either of them, and in Case of Disagreement between them, with Respect to the Time of Adjournment, he may adjourn them to such Time as he shall think proper; he shall receive Ambassadors and other public Ministers; he shall take Care that the Laws be faithfully executed, and shall Commission all the Officers of the United States.

Section 4

The President, Vice President and all civil Officers of the United States, shall be removed from Office on Impeachment for, and Conviction of, Treason, Bribery, or other high Crimes and Misdemeanors.

Article III
Section 1

The judicial Power of the United States shall be vested in one supreme Court, and in such inferior Courts as the Congress may from time to time ordain and establish. The Judges, both of the supreme and inferior Courts, shall hold their Offices during good Behaviour, and shall, at stated Times, receive for their Services a Compensation, which shall not be diminished during their Continuance in Office.

Section 2

The judicial Power shall extend to all Cases, in Law and Equity, arising under this Constitution, the Laws of the United States, and Treaties made, or which shall be made, under their Authority;—to all Cases affecting Ambassadors, other public Ministers and Consuls;—to all Cases of admiralty and maritime Jurisdiction;—to Controversies to which the United States shall be a Party;—to Controversies between two or more States;— [between a State and Citizens of another State];—between Citizens of different States;—between Citizens of the same State claiming Lands under

Grants of different States, [and between a State,] or the Citizens thereof, [and foreign States, Citizens or Subjects].*

In all Cases affecting Ambassadors, other public Ministers and Consuls, and those in which a State shall be Party, the supreme Court shall have original Jurisdiction. In all the other Cases before mentioned, the supreme Court shall have appellate Jurisdiction, both as to Law and Fact, with such Exceptions, and under such Regulations as the Congress shall make.

The Trial of all Crimes, except in Cases of Impeachment, shall be by Jury; and such Trial shall be held in the State where the said Crimes shall have been committed; but when not committed within any State, the Trial shall be at such Place or Places as the Congress may by Law have directed.

Section 3

Treason against the United States, shall consist only in levying War against them, or in adhering to their Enemies, giving them Aid and Comfort. No Person shall be convicted of Treason unless on the Testimony of two Witnesses to the same overt Act, or on Confession in open Court.

The Congress shall have Power to declare the Punishment of Treason, but no Attainder of Treason shall work Corruption of Blood, or Forfeiture except during the Life of the Person attainted.

Article IV
Section 1

Full Faith and Credit shall be given in each State to the public Acts, Records, and judicial Proceedings of every other State. And the Congress may by general Laws prescribe the Manner in which such Acts, Records and Proceedings shall be proved, and the Effect thereof.

Section 2

The Citizens of each State shall be entitled to all Privileges and Immunities of Citizens in the several States.

A Person charged in any State with Treason, Felony, or other Crime, who shall flee from Justice, and be found in another State, shall on Demand of the executive Authority of the State from which he fled, be delivered up, to be removed to the State having Jurisdiction of the Crime.

[No Person held to Service or Labour in one State, under the Laws thereof, escaping into another, shall, in Consequence of any Law or Regulation therein, be discharged from such Service or Labour, but shall be delivered up on Claim of the Party to whom such Service or Labour may be due.]**

---

*Altered by the Twelfth Amendment.
**Repealed by the Thirteenth Amendment.

Section 3

New States may be admitted by the Congress into this Union; but no new State shall be formed or erected within the Jurisdiction of any other State; nor any State be formed by the Junction of two or more States, or Parts of States, without the Consent of the Legislatures of the States concerned as well as of the Congress.

The Congress shall have Power to dispose of and make all needful Rules and Regulations respecting the Territory or other Property belonging to the United States; and nothing in this Constitution shall be so construed as to Prejudice any Claims of the United States, or of any particular State.

Section 4

The United States shall guarantee to every State in this Union a Republican Form of Government, and shall protect each of them against Invasion; and on Application of the Legislature, or of the Executive (when the Legislature cannot be convened), against domestic Violence.

Article V

The Congress, whenever two thirds of both Houses shall deem it necessary, shall propose Amendments to this Constitution, or, on the Application of the Legislatures of two thirds of the several States, shall call a Convention for proposing Amendments, which, in either Case, shall be valid to all Intents and Purposes, as Part of this Constitution, when ratified by the Legislatures of three fourths of the several States, or by Conventions in three fourths thereof, as the one or the other Mode of Ratification may be proposed by the Congress; Provided that no Amendment which may be made prior to the Year One thousand eight hundred and eight shall in any Manner affect the first and fourth Clauses in the Ninth Section of the first Article; and that no State, without its Consent, shall be deprived of its equal Suffrage in the Senate.

Article VI

All Debts contracted and Engagements entered into, before the Adoption of this Constitution, shall be as valid against the United States under this Constitution, as under the Confederation.

This Constitution, and the Laws of the United States which shall be made in Pursuance thereof; and all Treaties made, or which shall be made, under the Authority of the United States, shall be the supreme Law of the Land; and the Judges in every State shall be bound thereby, any Thing in the Constitution or Laws of any State to the Contrary notwithstanding.

The Senators and Representatives before mentioned, and the Members of the several State Legislatures, and all executive and judicial Officers, both of the United States and of the several States, shall be bound by Oath or Affirmation, to support this Constitution; but no religious Test shall ever be required as a Qualification to any Office or public Trust under the United States.

Article VII

The Ratification of the Conventions of nine States, shall be sufficient for the Establishment of this Constitution between the States so ratifying the Same.

The Word, "the," being interlined between the seventh and eighth Lines of the first Page, the Word "Thirty" being partly written on an Erazure in the fifteenth Line of the first Page, The Words "is tried" being interlined between the thirty second and thirty third Lines of the first Page and the Word "the" being interlined between the forty third and forty fourth Lines of the second Page.

Attest William Jackson Secretary

Done in Convention by the Unanimous Consent of the States present the Seventeenth Day of September in the Year of our Lord one thousand seven hundred and Eighty seven and of the Independence of the United States of America the Twelfth In witness whereof We have hereunto subscribed our Names,

G°. WASHINGTON
Presidt and deputy from Virginia

Delaware
Geo: Read
Gunning Bedford jun
John Dickinson
Richard Bassett
Jaco: Broom

Maryland
James McHenry
Dan of St Thos. Jenifer
Danl. Carroll

Virginia
John Blair
James Madison Jr.

North Carolina
Wm. Blount
Richd. Dobbs Spaight
Hu Williamson

South Carolina
J. Rutledge
Charles Cotesworth
    Pinckney
Charles Pinckney
Pierce Butler

Georgia
William Few
Abr Baldwin

New Hampshire
John Langdon
Nicholas Gilman

Massachusetts
Nathaniel Gorham
Rufus King

Connecticut
Wm. Saml. Johnson
Roger Sherman

New York
Alexander Hamilton

New Jersey
Wil: Livingston
David Brearley
Wm. Paterson
Jona: Dayton

Pennsylvania
B Franklin
Thomas Mifflin
Robt. Morris
Geo. Clymer
Thos. FitzSimons
Jared Ingersoll
James Wilson
Gouv Morris

Articles

In addition to, and Amendment of the Constitution of the United States of America, proposed by Congress, and ratified by the Legislatures of the several States, pursuant to the fifth Article of the original Constitution.

(The first ten amendments to the U.S. Constitution were ratified December 15, 1791, and form what is known as the "Bill of Rights.")

Amendment I

Congress shall make no law respecting an establishment of religion, or prohibiting the free exercise thereof; or abridging the freedom of speech, or of the press; or the right of the people peaceably to assemble, and to petition the Government for a redress of grievances.

Amendment II

A well regulated Militia, being necessary to the security of a free State, the right of the people to keep and bear Arms, shall not be infringed.

Amendment III

No Soldier shall, in time of peace be quartered in any house, without the consent of the Owner, nor in time of war, but in a manner to be prescribed by law.

Amendment IV

The right of the people to be secure in their persons, houses, papers, and effects, against unreasonable searches and seizures, shall not be violated, and no Warrants shall issue, but upon probable cause, supported by Oath or affirmation, and particularly describing the place to be searched, and the persons or things to be seized.

Amendment V

No person shall be held to answer for a capital, or otherwise infamous crime, unless on a presentment or indictment of a Grand Jury, except in cases arising in the land or naval forces, or in the Militia, when in actual service in time of War or public danger; nor shall any person be subject for the same offence to be twice put in jeopardy of life or limb; nor shall be compelled in any criminal case to be a witness against himself, nor be deprived of life, liberty, or property, without due process of law; nor shall private property be taken for public use, without just compensation.

Amendment VI

In all criminal prosecutions, the accused shall enjoy the right to a speedy and public trial, by an impartial jury of the State and district wherein the crime shall have been committed, which district shall have been previously ascertained by law, and to be informed of the nature and cause of the accusation; to be confronted with the witnesses against him; to have compulsory process for obtaining witnesses in his favor, and to have the Assistance of Counsel for his defence.

Amendment VII

In Suits at common law, where the value in controversy shall exceed twenty dollars, the right of trial by jury shall be preserved, and no fact tried by a jury, shall be otherwise re-examined in any Court of the United States, than according to the rules of the common law.

Amendment VIII

Excessive bail shall not be required, nor excessive fines imposed, nor cruel and unusual punishments inflicted.

Amendment IX

The enumeration in the Constitution, of certain rights, shall not be construed to deny or disparage others retained by the people.

Amendment X

The powers not delegated to the United States by the Constitution, nor prohibited by it to the States, are reserved to the States respectively, or to the people.

Amendment XI

Passed by Congress March 4, 1794. Ratified February 7, 1795.

Note: Article III, Section 2, of the Constitution was modified by Amendment XI.

The Judicial power of the United States shall not be construed to extend to any suit in law or equity, commenced or prosecuted against one of the United States by Citizens of another State, or by Citizens or Subjects of any Foreign State.

Amendment XII

Passed by Congress December 9, 1803. Ratified June 15, 1804.

Note: A portion of Article II, Section 1, of the Constitution was superseded by the Twelfth Amendment.

The Electors shall meet in their respective states and vote by ballot for President and Vice-President, one of whom, at least, shall not be an inhabitant of the same state with themselves; they shall name in their ballots the person voted for as President, and in distinct ballots the person voted for as Vice-President, and they shall make distinct lists of all persons voted for as President, and of all persons voted for as Vice-President, and of the number of votes for each, which lists they shall sign and certify, and transmit sealed to the seat of the government of the United States, directed to the President of the Senate;—the President of the Senate shall, in the presence of the Senate and House of Representatives, open all the certificates and the votes shall then be counted;—The person having the greatest number of votes for President, shall be the President, if such number be a majority of the whole number of Electors appointed; and if no person have such majority, then from the persons having the highest numbers not exceeding three on the list of those voted for as President, the House of Representatives shall choose immediately, by ballot, the President. But in choosing the President, the votes shall be taken by states, the representation from each state having one vote; a quorum for this purpose shall consist of a member or members from two-thirds of the states, and a majority of all the states shall be necessary to a choice. [And if the House of Representatives shall not choose a President whenever the right of choice shall devolve upon them, before the fourth day of March next following, then the Vice-President shall act as President, as in case of the death or other constitutional disability of the President.—]* The person having the greatest number of votes as Vice-President, shall be the Vice-President, if such number be a majority of the whole number of Electors appointed, and if no person have a majority, then from the two highest numbers on the list, the Senate shall choose the Vice-President; a quorum for the purpose shall consist of two-thirds of the whole number of Senators, and a majority of the whole number shall be necessary to a choice. But no person constitutionally ineligible to the office of President shall be eligible to that of Vice-President of the United States.

Amendment XIII

Passed by Congress January 31, 1865. Ratified December 6, 1865.

   Note: A portion of Article IV, Section 2, of the Constitution was superseded by the Thirteenth Amendment.

Section 1

Neither slavery nor involuntary servitude, except as a punishment for crime whereof the party shall have been duly convicted, shall exist within the United States, or any place subject to their jurisdiction.

Section 2

Congress shall have power to enforce this article by appropriate legislation.

Amendment XIV

Passed by Congress June 13, 1866. Ratified July 9, 1868.

   Note: Article I, Section 2, of the Constitution was modified by Section 2 of the Fourteenth Amendment.

Section 1

All persons born or naturalized in the United States, and subject to the jurisdiction thereof, are citizens of the United States and of the State wherein they reside. No State shall make or enforce any law which shall abridge the

---

*Superseded by Section 3 of the Twentieth Amendment.

privileges or immunities of citizens of the United States; nor shall any State deprive any person of life, liberty, or property, without due process of law; nor deny to any person within its jurisdiction the equal protection of the laws.

Section 2

Representatives shall be apportioned among the several States according to their respective numbers, counting the whole number of persons in each State, excluding Indians not taxed. But when the right to vote at any election for the choice of electors for President and Vice-President of the United States, Representatives in Congress, the Executive and Judicial officers of a State, or the members of the Legislature thereof, is denied to any of the male inhabitants of such State, being twenty-one years of age,* and citizens of the United States, or in any way abridged, except for participation in rebellion, or other crime, the basis of representation therein shall be reduced in the proportion which the number of such male citizens shall bear to the whole number of male citizens twenty-one years of age in such State.

Section 3

No person shall be a Senator or Representative in Congress, or elector of President and Vice-President, or hold any office, civil or military, under the United States, or under any State, who, having previously taken an oath, as a member of Congress, or as an officer of the United States, or as a member of any State legislature, or as an executive or judicial officer of any State, to support the Constitution of the United States, shall have engaged in insurrection or rebellion against the same, or given aid or comfort to the enemies thereof. But Congress may by a vote of two-thirds of each House, remove such disability.

Section 4

The validity of the public debt of the United States, authorized by law, including debts incurred for payment of pensions and bounties for services in suppressing insurrection or rebellion, shall not be questioned. But neither the United States nor any State shall assume or pay any debt or obligation incurred in aid of insurrection or rebellion against the United States, or any claim for the loss or emancipation of any slave; but all such debts, obligations and claims shall be held illegal and void.

Section 5

The Congress shall have the power to enforce, by appropriate legislation, the provisions of this article.

---

*Changed by Section 1 of the Twenty-sixth Amendment.

Amendment XV

Passed by Congress February 26, 1869. Ratified February 3, 1870.

Section 1

The right of citizens of the United States to vote shall not be denied or abridged by the United States or by any State on account of race, color, or previous condition of servitude.

Section 2

The Congress shall have the power to enforce this article by appropriate legislation.

Amendment XVI

Passed by Congress July 2, 1909. Ratified February 3, 1913.

Note: Article I, Section 9, of the Constitution was modified by Amendment XVI.

The Congress shall have power to lay and collect taxes on incomes, from whatever source derived, without apportionment among the several States, and without regard to any census or enumeration.

Amendment XVII

Passed by Congress May 13, 1912. Ratified April 8, 1913.

Note: Article I, Section 3, of the Constitution was modified by the Seventeenth Amendment.

The Senate of the United States shall be composed of two Senators from each State, elected by the people thereof, for six years; and each Senator shall have one vote. The electors in each State shall have the qualifications requisite for electors of the most numerous branch of the State legislatures.

When vacancies happen in the representation of any State in the Senate, the executive authority of such State shall issue writs of election to fill such vacancies: Provided, That the legislature of any State may empower the executive thereof to make temporary appointments until the people fill the vacancies by election as the legislature may direct.

This amendment shall not be so construed as to affect the election or term of any Senator chosen before it becomes valid as part of the Constitution.

Amendment XVIII

Passed by Congress December 18, 1917. Ratified January 16, 1919. Repealed by Amendment XXI.

Section 1

After one year from the ratification of this article the manufacture, sale, or transportation of intoxicating liquors within, the importation thereof into, or the exportation thereof from the United States and all territory subject to the jurisdiction thereof for beverage purposes is hereby prohibited.

Section 2

The Congress and the several States shall have concurrent power to enforce this article by appropriate legislation.

Section 3

This article shall be inoperative unless it shall have been ratified as an amendment to the Constitution by the legislatures of the several States, as provided in the Constitution, within seven years from the date of the submission hereof to the States by the Congress.

Amendment XIX

Passed by Congress June 4, 1919. Ratified August 18, 1920.

The right of citizens of the United States to vote shall not be denied or abridged by the United States or by any State on account of sex.

Congress shall have power to enforce this article by appropriate legislation.

Amendment XX

Passed by Congress March 2, 1932. Ratified January 23, 1933.

Note: Article I, Section 4, of the Constitution was modified by Section 2 of this amendment. In addition, a portion of the Twelfth Amendment was superseded by Section 3.

Section 1

The terms of the President and the Vice President shall end at noon on the 20th day of January, and the terms of Senators and Representatives at noon on the 3d day of January, of the years in which such terms would have ended if this article had not been ratified; and the terms of their successors shall then begin.

Section 2

The Congress shall assemble at least once in every year, and such meeting shall begin at noon on the 3d day of January, unless they shall by law appoint a different day.

Section 3

If, at the time fixed for the beginning of the term of the President, the President elect shall have died, the Vice President elect shall become President. If a President shall not have been chosen before the time fixed for the beginning of his term, or if the President elect shall have failed to qualify, then the Vice President elect shall act as President until a President shall have qualified; and the Congress may by law provide for the case wherein neither a President elect nor a Vice President shall have qualified, declaring who shall then act as President, or the manner in which one who is to act shall be selected, and such person shall act accordingly until a President or Vice President shall have qualified.

Section 4

The Congress may by law provide for the case of the death of any of the persons from whom the House of Representatives may choose a President whenever the right of choice shall have devolved upon them, and for the case of the death of any of the persons from whom the Senate may choose a Vice President whenever the right of choice shall have devolved upon them.

Section 5

Sections 1 and 2 shall take effect on the 15th day of October following the ratification of this article.

Section 6

This article shall be inoperative unless it shall have been ratified as an amendment to the Constitution by the legislatures of three-fourths of the several States within seven years from the date of its submission.

Amendment XXI

Passed by Congress February 20, 1933. Ratified December 5, 1933.

Section 1

The eighteenth article of amendment to the Constitution of the United States is hereby repealed.

Section 2

The transportation or importation into any State, Territory, or Possession of the United States for delivery or use therein of intoxicating liquors, in violation of the laws thereof, is hereby prohibited.

Section 3

This article shall be inoperative unless it shall have been ratified as an amendment to the Constitution by conventions in the several States, as provided in the Constitution, within seven years from the date of the submission hereof to the States by the Congress.

Amendment XXII

Passed by Congress March 21, 1947. Ratified February 27, 1951.

Section 1

No person shall be elected to the office of the President more than twice, and no person who has held the office of President, or acted as President, for more than two years of a term to which some other person was elected

President shall be elected to the office of President more than once. But this Article shall not apply to any person holding the office of President when this Article was proposed by Congress, and shall not prevent any person who may be holding the office of President, or acting as President, during the term within which this Article becomes operative from holding the office of President or acting as President during the remainder of such term.

Section 2

This article shall be inoperative unless it shall have been ratified as an amendment to the Constitution by the legislatures of three-fourths of the several States within seven years from the date of its submission to the States by the Congress.

Amendment XXIII

Passed by Congress June 16, 1960. Ratified March 29, 1961.

Section 1

The District constituting the seat of Government of the United States shall appoint in such manner as Congress may direct:

A number of electors of President and Vice President equal to the whole number of Senators and Representatives in Congress to which the District would be entitled if it were a State, but in no event more than the least populous State; they shall be in addition to those appointed by the States, but they shall be considered, for the purposes of the election of President and Vice President, to be electors appointed by a State; and they shall meet in the District and perform such duties as provided by the twelfth article of amendment.

Section 2

The Congress shall have power to enforce this article by appropriate legislation.

Amendment XXIV

Passed by Congress August 27, 1962. Ratified January 23, 1964.

Section 1

The right of citizens of the United States to vote in any primary or other election for President or Vice President, for electors for President or Vice President, or for Senator or Representative in Congress, shall not be denied or abridged by the United States or any State by reason of failure to pay poll tax or other tax.

Section 2

The Congress shall have power to enforce this article by appropriate legislation.

Amendment XXV

Passed by Congress July 6, 1965. Ratified February 10, 1967.

Note: Article II, Section 1, of the Constitution was affected by the Twenty-Fifth Amendment.

Section 1

In case of the removal of the President from office or of his death or resignation, the Vice President shall become President.

Section 2

Whenever there is a vacancy in the office of the Vice President, the President shall nominate a Vice President who shall take office upon confirmation by a majority vote of both Houses of Congress.

Section 3

Whenever the President transmits to the President pro tempore of the Senate and the Speaker of the House of Representatives his written declaration that he is unable to discharge the powers and duties of his office, and until he transmits to them a written declaration to the contrary, such powers and duties shall be discharged by the Vice President as Acting President.

Section 4

Whenever the Vice President and a majority of either the principal officers of the executive departments or of such other body as Congress may by law provide, transmit to the President pro tempore of the Senate and the Speaker of the House of Representatives their written declaration that the President is unable to discharge the powers and duties of his office, the Vice President shall immediately assume the powers and duties of the office as Acting President.

Thereafter, when the President transmits to the President pro tempore of the Senate and the Speaker of the House of Representatives his written declaration that no inability exists, he shall resume the powers and duties of his office unless the Vice President and a majority of either the principal officers of the executive department or of such other body as Congress may by law provide, transmit within four days to the President pro tempore of the Senate and the Speaker of the House of Representatives their written declaration that the President is unable to discharge the powers and duties of his office. Thereupon Congress shall decide the issue, assembling within forty-eight hours for that purpose if not in session. If the Congress, within twenty-one days after receipt of the latter written declaration, or, if Congress is not in session, within twenty-one days after Congress is required to assemble, determines by two-thirds vote of both Houses that the President is unable to discharge the powers and duties of his office, the Vice President shall continue to discharge the same as Acting President; otherwise, the President shall resume the powers and duties of his office.

Amendment XXVI

Passed by Congress March 23, 1971. Ratified July 1, 1971.

Note: Amendment XIV, Section 2, of the Constitution was modified by Section 1 of the Twenty-Sixth Amendment.

Section 1

The right of citizens of the United States, who are eighteen years of age or older, to vote shall not be denied or abridged by the United States or by any State on account of age.

Section 2

The Congress shall have power to enforce this article by appropriate legislation.

Amendment XXVII

Originally proposed Sept. 25, 1789. Ratified May 7, 1992.

No law, varying the compensation for the services of the Senators and Representatives, shall take effect, until an election of representatives shall have intervened.

APPENDIX III

The Federalist Papers 1, 10, and 51

By Alexander Hamilton, James Madison, John Jay

The debate over ratifying the Constitution in 1787–1788 was very close, especially in New York. To persuade the people of the state, Hamilton, Madison, and Jay wrote eighty-five newspaper essays arguing for ratification. Three of the most influential, reproduced here, are Federalist Papers 1, 10, and 51.

FEDERALIST No. 1

General Introduction

For the *Independent Journal*. Saturday, October 27, 1787

HAMILTON

To the People of the State of New York:

AFTER an unequivocal experience of the inefficacy of the subsisting federal government, you are called upon to deliberate on a new Constitution for the United States of America. The subject speaks its own importance; comprehending in its consequences nothing less than the existence of the UNION, the safety and welfare of the parts of which it is composed, the fate of an empire in many respects the most interesting in the world. It has been frequently remarked that it seems to have been reserved to the people of this country, by their conduct and example, to decide the important question, whether societies of men are really capable or not of establishing good government from reflection and choice, or whether they are forever destined to depend for their political constitutions on accident and force. If there be any truth in the remark, the crisis at which we are arrived may with propriety be regarded as the era in which that decision is to be made; and a wrong election of the part we shall act may, in this view, deserve to be considered as the general misfortune of mankind.

This idea will add the inducements of philanthropy to those of patriotism, to heighten the solicitude which all considerate and good men must feel for the event. Happy will it be if our choice should be directed by a judicious estimate of our true interests, unperplexed and unbiased by considerations not connected with the public good. But this is a thing more ardently to be wished than seriously to be expected. The plan offered to our deliberations affects too many particular interests, innovates upon too many local institutions, not to involve in its discussion a variety of objects foreign to its merits, and of views, passions and prejudices little favorable to the discovery of truth.

Among the most formidable of the obstacles which the new Constitution will have to encounter may readily be distinguished the obvious interest of a certain class of men in every State to resist all changes which may hazard a diminution of the power, emolument, and consequence of the offices they hold under the State establishments; and the perverted ambition of another class of men, who will either hope to aggrandize themselves by the confusions of their country, or will flatter themselves with fairer prospects of elevation from the subdivision of the empire into several partial confederacies than from its union under one government.

It is not, however, my design to dwell upon observations of this nature. I am well aware that it would be disingenuous to resolve indiscriminately the opposition of any set of men (merely because their situations might subject them to suspicion) into interested or ambitious views. Candor will oblige us to admit that even such men may be actuated by upright intentions; and it cannot be doubted that much of the opposition which has made its appearance, or may hereafter make its appearance, will spring from sources, blameless at least, if not respectable—the honest errors of minds led astray by preconceived jealousies and fears. So numerous indeed and so powerful are the causes which serve to give a false bias to the judgment, that we, upon many occasions, see wise and good men on the wrong as well as on the right side of questions of the first magnitude to society. This circumstance, if duly attended to, would furnish a lesson of moderation to those who are ever so much persuaded of their being in the right in any controversy. And a further reason for caution, in this respect, might be drawn from the reflection that we are not always sure that those who advocate the truth are influenced by purer principles than their antagonists. Ambition, avarice, personal animosity, party opposition, and many other motives not more laudable than these, are apt to operate as well upon those who support as those who oppose the right side of a question. Were there not even these inducements to moderation, nothing could be more ill-judged than that intolerant spirit which has, at all times, characterized political parties. For in politics, as in religion, it is equally absurd to aim at making proselytes by fire and sword. Heresies in either can rarely be cured by persecution.

And yet, however just these sentiments will be allowed to be, we have already sufficient indications that it will happen in this as in all former cases of great national discussion. A torrent of angry and malignant passions will be let loose. To judge from the conduct of the opposite parties, we shall be led to conclude that they will mutually hope to evince the justness of their opinions, and to increase the number of their converts by the loudness of their declamations and the bitterness of their invectives. An enlightened zeal for the energy and efficiency of government will be stigmatized as the offspring of a temper fond of despotic power and hostile to the principles of liberty. An over-scrupulous jealousy of danger to the rights of the people, which is more commonly the fault of the head than of the heart, will be represented as mere pretense and artifice, the stale bait for popularity at the expense of the public good. It will be forgotten, on the one hand, that jealousy is the usual concomitant of love, and that the noble enthusiasm of liberty is apt to be infected with a spirit of narrow and illiberal distrust. On the other hand, it will be equally forgotten that the vigor of government is essential to the security of liberty; that, in the contemplation of a sound and well-informed judgment, their interest can never be separated; and that a dangerous ambition more often lurks behind the specious mask of zeal for the rights of the people than under the forbidden appearance of zeal for the firmness and efficiency of government. History will teach us that the former has been found a much more certain road to the introduction of despotism than the latter, and that of those men who have overturned the liberties of republics, the greatest number have begun their career by paying an obsequious court to the people; commencing demagogues, and ending tyrants.

In the course of the preceding observations, I have had an eye, my fellow-citizens, to putting you upon your guard against all attempts, from whatever quarter, to influence your decision in a matter of the utmost moment to your welfare, by any impressions other than those which may result from the evidence of truth. You will, no doubt, at the same time, have collected from the general scope of them, that they proceed from a source not unfriendly to the new Constitution. Yes, my countrymen, I own to you that, after having given it an attentive consideration, I am clearly of opinion it is your interest to adopt it. I am convinced that this is the safest course for your liberty, your dignity, and your happiness. I affect not reserves which I do not feel. I will not amuse you with an appearance of deliberation when I have decided. I frankly acknowledge to you my convictions, and I will freely lay before you the reasons on which they are founded. The consciousness of good intentions disdains ambiguity. I shall not, however, multiply professions on this head. My motives must remain in the depository of my own breast. My arguments will be open to all, and may be judged of by all. They shall at least be offered in a spirit which will not disgrace the cause of truth.

I propose, in a series of papers, to discuss the following interesting particulars:

THE UTILITY OF THE UNION TO YOUR POLITICAL PROSPERITY THE INSUFFICIENCY OF THE PRESENT CONFEDERATION TO PRESERVE THAT UNION THE NECESSITY OF A GOVERNMENT AT LEAST EQUALLY ENERGETIC WITH THE ONE PROPOSED, TO THE ATTAINMENT OF THIS OBJECT THE CONFORMITY OF THE PROPOSED CONSTITUTION TO THE TRUE PRINCIPLES OF REPUBLICAN GOVERNMENT ITS ANALOGY TO YOUR OWN STATE CONSTITUTION and lastly, THE ADDITIONAL SECURITY WHICH ITS ADOPTION WILL AFFORD TO THE PRESERVATION OF THAT SPECIES OF GOVERNMENT, TO LIBERTY, AND TO PROPERTY.

In the progress of this discussion I shall endeavor to give a satisfactory answer to all the objections which shall have made their appearance, that may seem to have any claim to your attention.

It may perhaps be thought superfluous to offer arguments to prove the utility of the UNION, a point, no doubt, deeply engraved on the hearts of the great body of the people in every State, and one, which it may be imagined, has no adversaries. But the fact is, that we already hear it whispered in the private circles of those who oppose the new Constitution, that the thirteen States are of too great extent for any general system, and that we must of necessity resort to separate confederacies of distinct portions of the whole. This doctrine will, in all probability, be gradually propagated, till it has votaries enough to countenance an open avowal of it. For nothing can be more evident, to those who are able to take an enlarged view of the subject, than the alternative of an adoption of the new Constitution or a dismemberment of the Union. It will therefore be of use to begin by examining the advantages of that Union, the certain evils, and the probable dangers, to which every State will be exposed from its dissolution. This shall accordingly constitute the subject of my next address.

PUBLIUS

FEDERALIST No. 10
The Same Subject Continued (The Union as a Safeguard Against Domestic Faction and Insurrection)
From the *Daily Advertiser*. Thursday, November 22, 1787.

MADISON

To the People of the State of New York:

AMONG the numerous advantages promised by a well constructed Union, none deserves to be more accurately developed than its tendency to break and control the violence of faction. The friend of popular governments never finds himself so much alarmed for their character and fate, as when he contemplates their propensity to this dangerous vice. He will not fail, therefore, to set a due value on any plan which, without violating the principles to which he is attached, provides a proper cure for it. The instability, injustice, and confusion introduced into the public councils, have, in truth, been the mortal diseases under which popular governments have everywhere perished; as they continue to be the favorite and fruitful topics from which the adversaries to liberty derive their most specious declamations. The valuable improvements made by the American constitutions on the popular models, both ancient and modern, cannot certainly be too much admired; but it would be an unwarrantable partiality, to contend that they have as effectually obviated the danger on this side, as was wished and expected. Complaints are everywhere heard from our most considerate and virtuous citizens, equally the friends of public and private faith, and of public and personal liberty, that our governments are too unstable, that the public good is disregarded in the conflicts of rival parties, and that measures are too often decided, not according to the rules of justice and the rights of the minor party, but by the superior force of an interested and overbearing majority. However anxiously we may wish that these complaints had no foundation, the evidence, of known facts will not permit us to deny that they are in some degree true. It will be found, indeed, on a candid review of our situation, that some of the distresses under which we labor have been erroneously charged on the operation of our governments; but it will be found, at the same time, that other causes will not alone account for many of our heaviest misfortunes; and, particularly, for that prevailing and increasing distrust of public engagements, and alarm for private rights, which are echoed from one end of the continent to the other. These must be chiefly, if not wholly, effects of the unsteadiness and injustice with which a factious spirit has tainted our public administrations.

By a faction, I understand a number of citizens, whether amounting to a majority or a minority of the whole, who are united and actuated by some common impulse of passion, or of interest, adversed to the rights of other citizens, or to the permanent and aggregate interests of the community.

There are two methods of curing the mischiefs of faction: the one, by removing its causes; the other, by controlling its effects.

There are again two methods of removing the causes of faction: the one, by destroying the liberty which is essential to its existence; the other, by giving to every citizen the same opinions, the same passions, and the same interests.

It could never be more truly said than of the first remedy, that it was worse than the disease. Liberty is to faction what air is to fire, an aliment without which it instantly expires. But it could not be less folly to abolish liberty, which is essential to political life, because it nourishes faction, than it would be to wish the annihilation of air, which is essential to animal life, because it imparts to fire its destructive agency.

The second expedient is as impracticable as the first would be unwise. As long as the reason of man continues fallible, and he is at liberty to exercise it, different opinions will be formed. As long as the connection subsists between his reason and his self-love, his opinions and his passions will have a reciprocal influence on each other; and the former will be objects to which the latter will attach themselves. The diversity in the faculties of men, from which the rights of property originate, is not less an insuperable obstacle to a uniformity of interests. The protection of these faculties is the first object of government. From the protection of different and unequal faculties of acquiring property, the possession of different degrees and kinds of property immediately results; and from the influence of these on the sentiments and views of the respective proprietors, ensues a division of the society into different interests and parties.

The latent causes of faction are thus sown in the nature of man; and we see them everywhere brought into different degrees of activity, according to the different circumstances of civil society. A zeal for different opinions concerning religion, concerning government, and many other points, as well of speculation as of practice; an attachment to different leaders ambitiously contending for pre-eminence and power; or to persons of other descriptions whose fortunes have been interesting to the human passions, have, in turn, divided mankind into parties, inflamed them with mutual animosity, and rendered them much more disposed to vex and oppress each other than to co-operate for their common good. So strong is this propensity of mankind to fall into mutual animosities, that where no substantial occasion presents itself, the most frivolous and fanciful distinctions have been sufficient to kindle their unfriendly passions and excite their most violent conflicts. But the most common and durable source of factions has been the various and unequal distribution of property. Those who hold and those who are without property have ever formed distinct interests in society. Those who are creditors, and those who are debtors, fall under a like discrimination. A landed interest, a manufacturing interest, a mercantile interest, a moneyed interest, with many lesser interests, grow up of necessity in civilized nations, and divide them into different classes, actuated by different sentiments and views. The regulation of these various and interfering interests forms the principal task of modern legislation, and involves the spirit of party and faction in the necessary and ordinary operations of the government.

No man is allowed to be a judge in his own cause, because his interest would certainly bias his judgment, and, not improbably, corrupt his integrity. With equal, nay with greater reason, a body of men are unfit to be both judges and parties at the same time; yet what are many of the most important acts of legislation, but so many judicial determinations, not indeed concerning the rights of single persons, but concerning the rights of large bodies of citizens? And what are the different classes of legislators but advocates and parties to the causes which they determine? Is a law proposed concerning private debts? It is a question to which the creditors are parties on one side and the debtors on the other. Justice ought to hold the balance between them. Yet the parties are, and must be, themselves the judges; and the most numerous party, or, in other words, the most powerful faction must be expected to prevail. Shall domestic manufactures be encouraged, and in what degree, by restrictions on foreign manufactures? are questions which would be differently decided by the landed and the manufacturing classes, and probably by neither with a sole regard to justice and the public good. The apportionment of taxes on the various descriptions of property is an act which seems to require the most exact impartiality; yet there is, perhaps,

no legislative act in which greater opportunity and temptation are given to a predominant party to trample on the rules of justice. Every shilling with which they overburden the inferior number, is a shilling saved to their own pockets.

It is in vain to say that enlightened statesmen will be able to adjust these clashing interests, and render them all subservient to the public good. Enlightened statesmen will not always be at the helm. Nor, in many cases, can such an adjustment be made at all without taking into view indirect and remote considerations, which will rarely prevail over the immediate interest which one party may find in disregarding the rights of another or the good of the whole.

The inference to which we are brought is, that the CAUSES of faction cannot be removed, and that relief is only to be sought in the means of controlling its EFFECTS.

If a faction consists of less than a majority, relief is supplied by the republican principle, which enables the majority to defeat its sinister views by regular vote. It may clog the administration, it may convulse the society; but it will be unable to execute and mask its violence under the forms of the Constitution. When a majority is included in a faction, the form of popular government, on the other hand, enables it to sacrifice to its ruling passion or interest both the public good and the rights of other citizens. To secure the public good and private rights against the danger of such a faction, and at the same time to preserve the spirit and the form of popular government, is then the great object to which our inquiries are directed. Let me add that it is the great desideratum by which this form of government can be rescued from the opprobrium under which it has so long labored, and be recommended to the esteem and adoption of mankind.

By what means is this object attainable? Evidently by one of two only. Either the existence of the same passion or interest in a majority at the same time must be prevented, or the majority, having such coexistent passion or interest, must be rendered, by their number and local situation, unable to concert and carry into effect schemes of oppression. If the impulse and the opportunity be suffered to coincide, we well know that neither moral nor religious motives can be relied on as an adequate control. They are not found to be such on the injustice and violence of individuals, and lose their efficacy in proportion to the number combined together, that is, in proportion as their efficacy becomes needful.

From this view of the subject it may be concluded that a pure democracy, by which I mean a society consisting of a small number of citizens, who assemble and administer the government in person, can admit of no cure for the mischiefs of faction. A common passion or interest will, in almost every case, be felt by a majority of the whole; a communication and concert result from the form of government itself; and there is nothing to check the inducements to sacrifice the weaker party or an obnoxious individual. Hence it is that such democracies have ever been spectacles of turbulence and contention; have ever been found incompatible with personal security or the rights of property; and have in general been as short in their lives as they have been violent in their deaths. Theoretic politicians, who have patronized this species of government, have erroneously supposed that by reducing mankind to a perfect equality in their political rights, they would, at the same time, be perfectly equalized and assimilated in their possessions, their opinions, and their passions.

A republic, by which I mean a government in which the scheme of representation takes place, opens a different prospect, and promises the cure for which we are seeking. Let us examine the points in which it varies from pure democracy, and we shall comprehend both the nature of the cure and the efficacy which it must derive from the Union.

The two great points of difference between a democracy and a republic are: first, the delegation of the government, in the latter, to a small number of citizens elected by the rest; secondly, the greater number of citizens, and greater sphere of country, over which the latter may be extended.

The effect of the first difference is, on the one hand, to refine and enlarge the public views, by passing them through the medium of a chosen body of citizens, whose wisdom may best discern the true interest of their country, and whose patriotism and love of justice will be least likely to sacrifice it to temporary or partial considerations. Under such a regulation, it may well happen that the public voice, pronounced by the representatives of the people, will be more consonant to the public good than if pronounced by the people themselves, convened for the purpose. On the other hand, the effect may be inverted. Men of factious tempers, of local prejudices, or of sinister designs, may, by intrigue, by corruption, or by other means, first obtain the suffrages, and then betray the interests, of the people. The question resulting is, whether small or extensive republics are more favorable to the election of proper guardians of the public weal; and it is clearly decided in favor of the latter by two obvious considerations:

In the first place, it is to be remarked that, however small the republic may be, the representatives must be raised to a certain number, in order to guard against the cabals of a few; and that, however large it may be, they must be limited to a certain number, in order to guard against the confusion of a multitude. Hence, the number of representatives in the two cases not being in proportion to that of the two constituents, and being proportionally greater in the small republic, it follows that, if the proportion of fit characters be not less in the large than in the small republic, the former will present a greater option, and consequently a greater probability of a fit choice.

In the next place, as each representative will be chosen by a greater number of citizens in the large than in the small republic, it will be more difficult for unworthy candidates to practice with success the vicious arts by which elections are too often carried; and the suffrages of the people being more free, will be more likely to centre in men who possess the most attractive merit and the most diffusive and established characters.

It must be confessed that in this, as in most other cases, there is a mean, on both sides of which inconveniences will be found to lie. By enlarging too much the number of electors, you render the representatives too little acquainted with all their local circumstances and lesser interests; as by reducing it too much, you render him unduly attached to these, and too little fit to comprehend and pursue great and national objects. The federal Constitution forms a happy combination in this respect; the great and aggregate interests being referred to the national, the local and particular to the State legislatures.

The other point of difference is, the greater number of citizens and extent of territory which may be brought within the compass of republican than of democratic government; and it is this circumstance principally which renders factious combinations less to be dreaded in the former than in the latter. The smaller the society, the fewer probably will be the distinct parties and interests composing it; the fewer the distinct parties and interests, the more frequently will a majority be found of the same party; and the smaller the number of individuals composing a majority, and the smaller the compass within which they are placed, the more easily will they concert and execute their plans of oppression. Extend the sphere, and you take in a greater variety of parties and interests; you make it less probable that a majority of the whole will have a common motive to invade the rights of other citizens; or if such a common motive exists, it will be more difficult for all who feel it to discover their own strength, and to act in unison with each other. Besides other impediments, it may be remarked that, where there is a consciousness of unjust or dishonorable purposes, communication is always checked by distrust in proportion to the number whose concurrence is necessary.

Hence, it clearly appears, that the same advantage which a republic has over a democracy, in controlling the effects of faction, is enjoyed by a large over a small republic,—is enjoyed by the Union over the States composing it. Does the advantage consist in the substitution of representatives whose enlightened views and virtuous sentiments render them superior to local prejudices and schemes of injustice? It will not be denied that the representation of the Union will be most likely to possess these requisite endowments. Does it consist in the greater security afforded by a greater variety of parties, against the event of any one party being able to outnumber and oppress the rest? In an equal degree does the increased variety of parties comprised within the Union, increase this security. Does it, in fine, consist in the greater obstacles opposed to the concert and accomplishment of the secret wishes of an unjust and interested majority? Here, again, the extent of the Union gives it the most palpable advantage.

The influence of factious leaders may kindle a flame within their particular States, but will be unable to spread a general conflagration through the other States. A religious scct may degenerate into a political faction in a part of the Confederacy; but the variety of sects dispersed over the entire face of it must secure the national councils against any danger from that source. A rage for paper money, for an abolition of debts, for an equal division of property, or for any other improper or wicked project, will be less apt to pervade the whole body of the Union than a particular member of it; in the same proportion as such a malady is more likely to taint a particular county or district, than an entire State.

In the extent and proper structure of the Union, therefore, we behold a republican remedy for the diseases most incident to republican government. And according to the degree of pleasure and pride we feel in being republicans, ought to be our zeal in cherishing the spirit and supporting the character of Federalists.

PUBLIUS

FEDERALIST No. 51
The Structure of the Government Must Furnish the Proper Checks and Balances Between the Different Departments.
For the *Independent Journal*. Wednesday, February 6, 1788.

MADISON
To the People of the State of New York:

TO WHAT expedient, then, shall we finally resort, for maintaining in practice the necessary partition of power among the several departments, as laid down in the Constitution? The only answer that can be given is, that as all these exterior provisions are found to be inadequate, the defect must be supplied, by so contriving the interior structure of the government as that its several constituent parts may, by their mutual relations, be the means of keeping each other in their proper places. Without presuming to undertake a full development of this important idea, I will hazard a few general observations, which may perhaps place it in a clearer light, and enable us to form a more correct judgment of the principles and structure of the government planned by the convention.

In order to lay a due foundation for that separate and distinct exercise of the different powers of government, which to a certain extent is admitted on all hands to be essential to the preservation of liberty, it is evident that each department should have a will of its own; and consequently should be so constituted that the members of each should have as little agency as possible in the appointment of the members of the others. Were this principle rigorously adhered to, it would require that all the appointments for the supreme executive, legislative, and judiciary magistracies should be drawn from the same fountain of authority, the people, through channels having no communication whatever with one another. Perhaps such a plan of constructing the several departments would be less difficult in practice than it may in contemplation appear. Some difficulties, however, and some additional expense would attend the execution of it. Some deviations, therefore, from the principle must be admitted. In the constitution of the judiciary department in particular, it might be inexpedient to insist rigorously on the principle: first, because peculiar qualifications being essential in the members, the primary consideration ought to be to select that mode of choice which best secures these qualifications; secondly, because the permanent tenure by which the appointments are held in that department, must soon destroy all sense of dependence on the authority conferring them.

It is equally evident, that the members of each department should be as little dependent as possible on those of the others, for the emoluments annexed to their offices. Were the executive magistrate, or the judges, not independent of the legislature in this particular, their independence in every other would be merely nominal.

But the great security against a gradual concentration of the several powers in the same department, consists in giving to those who administer each department the necessary constitutional means and personal motives to resist encroachments of the others. The provision for defense must in this, as in all other cases, be made commensurate to the danger of attack. Ambition must be made to counteract ambition. The interest of the man must be connected with the constitutional rights of the place. It may be a reflection on human nature, that such devices should be necessary to control the abuses of government. But what is government itself, but the greatest of all reflections on human nature? If men were angels, no government would be necessary. If angels were to govern men, neither external nor internal controls on government would be necessary. In framing a government which is to be administered by men over men, the great difficulty lies in this: you must first enable the government to control the governed; and in the next place oblige it to control itself.

A dependence on the people is, no doubt, the primary control on the government; but experience has taught mankind the necessity of auxiliary precautions.

This policy of supplying, by opposite and rival interests, the defect of better motives, might be traced through the whole system of human affairs, private as well as public. We see it particularly displayed in all the subordinate distributions of power, where the constant aim is to divide and arrange the several offices in such a manner as that each may be a check on the other—that the private interest of every individual may be a sentinel over the public rights. These inventions of prudence cannot be less requisite in the distribution of the supreme powers of the State.

But it is not possible to give to each department an equal power of self-defense. In republican government, the legislative authority necessarily predominates. The remedy for this inconveniency is to divide the legislature into different branches; and to render them, by different modes of election and different principles of action, as little connected with each other as the nature of their common functions and their common dependence on the society will admit. It may even be necessary to guard against dangerous encroachments by still further precautions. As the weight of the legislative authority requires that it should be thus divided, the weakness of the executive may require, on the other hand, that it should be fortified. An absolute negative on the legislature appears, at first view, to be the natural defense with which the executive magistrate should be armed. But perhaps it would be neither altogether safe nor alone sufficient. On ordinary occasions it might not be exerted with the requisite firmness, and on extraordinary occasions it might be perfidiously abused. May not this defect of an absolute negative be supplied by some qualified connection between this weaker department and the weaker branch of the stronger department, by which the latter may be led to support the constitutional rights of the former, without being too much detached from the rights of its own department?

If the principles on which these observations are founded be just, as I persuade myself they are, and they be applied as a criterion to the several State constitutions, and to the federal Constitution it will be found that if the latter does not perfectly correspond with them, the former are infinitely less able to bear such a test.

There are, moreover, two considerations particularly applicable to the federal system of America, which place that system in a very interesting point of view.

First. In a single republic, all the power surrendered by the people is submitted to the administration of a single government; and the usurpations are guarded against by a division of the government into distinct and separate departments. In the compound republic of America, the power surrendered by the people is first divided between two distinct governments, and then the portion allotted to each subdivided among distinct and separate departments. Hence a double security arises to the rights of the people. The different governments will control each other, at the same time that each will be controlled by itself.

Second. It is of great importance in a republic not only to guard the society against the oppression of its rulers, but to guard one part of the society against the injustice of the other part. Different interests necessarily exist in different classes of citizens. If a majority be united by a common interest, the rights of the minority will be insecure. There are but two methods of providing against this evil: the one by creating a will in the community independent of the majority—that is, of the society itself; the other, by comprehending in the society so many separate descriptions of citizens as will render an unjust combination of a majority of the whole very improbable, if not impracticable. The first method prevails in all governments possessing an hereditary or self-appointed authority. This, at best, is but a precarious security; because a power independent of the society may as well espouse the unjust views of the major, as the rightful interests of the minor party, and may possibly be turned against both parties. The second method will be exemplified in the federal republic of the United States. Whilst all authority in it will be derived from and dependent on the society, the society itself will be broken into so many parts, interests, and classes of citizens, that the rights of individuals, or of the minority, will be in little danger from interested combinations of the majority. In a free government the security for civil rights must be the same as that for religious rights. It consists in the one case in the multiplicity of interests, and in the other in the multiplicity of sects. The degree of security in both cases will depend on the number of interests and sects; and this may be presumed to depend on the extent of country and number of people comprehended under the same government. This view of the subject must particularly recommend a proper federal system to all the sincere and considerate friends of republican government, since it shows that in exact proportion as the territory of the Union may be formed into more circumscribed Confederacies, or States oppressive combinations of a majority will be facilitated: the best security, under the republican forms, for the rights of every class of citizens, will be diminished: and consequently the stability and independence of some member of the government, the only other security, must be proportionately increased. Justice is the end of government. It is the end of civil society. It ever has been and ever will be pursued until it be obtained, or until liberty be lost in the pursuit. In a society under the forms of which the stronger faction can readily unite and oppress the weaker, anarchy may as truly be said to reign as in a state of nature, where the weaker individual is not secured against the violence of the stronger;

and as, in the latter state, even the stronger individuals are prompted, by the uncertainty of their condition, to submit to a government which may protect the weak as well as themselves; so, in the former state, will the more powerful factions or parties be gradually induced, by a like motive, to wish for a government which will protect all parties, the weaker as well as the more powerful. It can be little doubted that if the State of Rhode Island was separated from the Confederacy and left to itself, the insecurity of rights under the popular form of government within such narrow limits would be displayed by such reiterated oppressions of factious majorities that some power altogether independent of the people would soon be called for by the voice of the very factions whose misrule had proved the necessity of it. In the extended republic of the United States, and among the great variety of interests, parties, and sects which it embraces, a coalition of a majority of the whole society could seldom take place on any other principles than those of justice and the general good; whilst there being thus less danger to a minor from the will of a major party, there must be less pretext, also, to provide for the security of the former, by introducing into the government a will not dependent on the latter, or, in other words, a will independent of the society itself. It is no less certain than it is important, notwithstanding the contrary opinions which have been entertained, that the larger the society, provided it lie within a practical sphere, the more duly capable it will be of self-government. And happily for the REPUBLICAN CAUSE, the practicable sphere may be carried to a very great extent, by a judicious modification and mixture of the FEDERAL PRINCIPLE.

PUBLIUS

APPENDIX IV

Presidential Elections, Congressional Control, 1789–2012

KEY: Party abbreviations: Dem = Democrat **| DemRep** = Democratic Republican **| Fed** = Federalist
IndRep = Independent Republican **| NatRep** = National Republican **| Rep** = Republican

Election Year	Presidential Candidates	Political Party	Electoral Vote	Percentage of Popular Vote	Control of Congress	
					House	Senate
1789	**George Washington** John Adams Others	None -- --	69 32 35	No Popular Vote	Fed	Fed
1792	**George Washington** John Adams Others	None -- --	132 77 55	No Popular Vote	DemRep	Fed
1796	John Adams Thomas Jefferson Thomas Pinckney Aaron Burr Others	Fed DemRep Fed DemRep --	71 68 59 30 48	No Popular Vote	Fed	Fed
1800	**Thomas Jefferson** Aaron Burr John Adams C. C. Pinkney	DemRep DemRep Fed Fed	73 73 65 64	No Popular Vote	DemRep	DemRep
1804	**Thomas Jefferson** C. C. Pinkney	DemRep Fed	162 14	No Popular Vote	DemRep	DemRep
1808	**James Madison** C. C. Pinkney	DemRep Fed	122 47	No Popular Vote	DemRep	DemRep
1812	**James Madison** De Witt Clinton	DemRep Fed	128 89	No Popular Vote	DemRep	DemRep
1816	**James Monroe** Rufus King	DemRep Fed	231 34	No Popular Vote	DemRep	DemRep
1820	**James Monroe** John Q Adams	DemRep IndRep	231 1	No Popular Vote	DemRep	DemRep
1824	**John Quincy Adams*** Andrew Jackson Henry Clay W. Crawford	DemRep DemRep DemRep DemRep	84 99 37 41	30.5 43.1 13.2 13.1	Pro Adams Pro Jackson (at midterm)	Pro Jackson
1828	**Andrew Jackson** John Q. Adams	Dem NatRep	178 83	56.0 44.0	Pro Jackson	Pro Jackson
1832	**Andrew Jackson** Henry Clay	Dem NatRep	219 49	55.0 42.0	Pro Jackson	Opposition Pro Jackson
1836	**Martin Van Buren** William H. Harrison	Dem Whig	170 73	50.9 36.7	Dem	Dem

* Lost the popular vote, won the Electoral College and became president
** Died in office

Election Year	Presidential Candidates	Political Party	Electoral Vote	Percentage of Popular Vote	Control of Congress	
					House	Senate
1840	William H Harrison**	Whig	234	53.1	Whig	Whig
	Martin Van Buren	Dem	60	46.9	Dem (at midterm)	
1844	James K. Polk	Dem	170	49.6	Dem	Dem
	Henry Clay	Whig	105	48.1	Whig (at midterm)	
	James Birney	Liberty (Abolition)	0	2.3		
1848	Zachary Taylor**	Whig	163	47.4	Dem	Dem
	Lewis Cass	Dem	127	42.5		
	Martin Van Buren	Free Soil	0	10.0		
1852	Franklin Pierce	Dem	254	50.9	Dem	Dem
	Winfield Scott	Whig	42	44.1	Opposition (at midterm)	
1856	James Buchanan	Dem	174	45.4	Dem	Dem
	John Fremont	Rep	114	33.0	Rep (at midterm)	
	Millard Fillmore	American (Know Nothing)	8	21.6		
1860	Abraham Lincoln	Rep	180	39.8	Rep	Rep
	Stephen Douglas	Dem	12	29.5		
	John Breckinridge	Dem	72	18.1		
	John Bell	Constitutional Union	79	12.6		
1864	Abraham Lincoln**	Rep	212	55.0	Rep	Rep
	George McClellan	Dem	21	45.0		
1868	Ulysses Grant	Rep	214	52.7	Rep	Rep
	Horatio Seymour	Dem	80	47.3		
1872	Ulysses Grant	Rep	286	55.6	Rep	Rep
	Horace Greeley	Dem	66	43.9	Dem (at midterm)	
1876	Rutherford Hayes*	Rep	185	48.0	Rep	Rep
	Samuel Tilden	Dem	184	51.0	Dem	Dem (at midterm)
1880	James Garfield**	Rep	214	48.3	Rep	Rep
	Winfield Hancock	Dem	155	48.2	Dem (at midterm)	
	James Weaver	Greenback-Labor	0	3.4		
1884	Grover Cleveland	Dem	219	48.5	Dem	Rep
	James Blaine	Rep	182	48.2		
	Benjamin Butler	Greenback-labor		11.8		
1888	Benjamin Harrison*	Rep	233	47.8	Rep	Rep
	Grover Cleveland	Dem	168	48.6	Dem (at midterm)	Rep
1892	Grover Cleveland	Dem	277	46.0	Dem	Dem
	Benjamin Harrison	Rep	145	43.0	Rep (at midterm)	Rep (at midterm)
	James Weaver	People's (Populist)	22	8.5		
1896	William McKinley	Rep	271	51.0	Rep	Rep
	William J. Bryan	Dem	176	45.5		
1900	William McKinley**	Rep	292	51.7	Rep	Rep
	William J. Bryan	Dem	155	45.5		
1904	Theodore Roosevelt	Rep	336	56.4	Rep	Rep
	Alton Parker	Dem	140	37.6		

* Lost the popular vote, won the Electoral College and became president

** Died in office

Election Year	Presidential Candidates	Political Party	Electoral Vote	Percentage of Popular Vote	Control of Congress	
					House	Senate
1908	**William H. Taft**	Rep	321	51.6	Rep	Rep
	William J. Bryan	Dem	162	43.1		Dem
1912	Woodrow Wilson	Dem	435	41.8	Dem	Dem
	Theodore Roosevelt	Progressive	88	27.4		
	William H. Taft	Rep	8	23.2		
	Eugene Debs	Socialist	0	6.0		
1916	Woodrow Wilson	Dem	277	49.2	Rep	Dem
	Charles Hughes	Rep	254	46.1		
1920	**Warren Harding**	Rep	404	60.0	Rep	Rep
	James Cox	Dem	60	34.6		
1924	**Calvin Coolidge**	Rep	382	54.1	Rep	Rep
	John Davis	Dem	136	28.8		
	Robert La Follette	Progressive	13	16.6		
1928	**Herbert Hoover**	Rep	444	58.2	Rep	Rep
	Alfred Smith	Dem	87	40.8	Dem (at midterm)	
1932	Franklin Roosevelt	Dem	472	57.3	Dem	Dem
	Herbert Hoover	Rep	59	39.6		
1936	Franklin Roosevelt	Dem	523	60.8	Dem	Dem
	Alfred Landon	Rep	8	36.4		
1940	Franklin Roosevelt	Dem	449	54.7	Dem	Dem
	Wendell Wilkie	Rep	82	44.8		
1944	Franklin Roosevelt**	Dem	432	52.8	Dem	Dem
	Thomas Dewey	Rep	99	44.5	Rep (at midterm)	Rep (at midterm)
1948	Harry Truman	Dem	303	49.5	Dem	Dem
	Thomas Dewey	Rep	189	45.1		
	Strom Thurmond	States Rights	39	2.4		
1952	Dwight Eisenhower	Rep	442	55.2	Rep	Rep
	Adlai Stevenson	Dem	89	44.5	Dem (at midterm)	Dem (at midterm)
1956	**Dwight Eisenhower**	Rep	457	57.4	Dem	Dem
	Adlai Stevenson	Dem	73	42.0		
1960	John F. Kennedy**	Dem	303	49.9	Dem	Dem
	Richard Nixon	Rep	219	49.6		
1964	Lyndon Johnson	Dem	486	61.1	Dem	Dem
	Barry Goldwater	Rep	52	38.5		
1968	**Richard Nixon**	Rep	301	43.4	Dem	Dem
	Hubert Humphrey	Dem	191	42.7		
	George Wallace	American	41	13.5		
1972	**Richard Nixon**	Rep	521	61.3	Dem	Dem
	George McGovern	Dem	17	37.3		
1976	Jimmy Carter	Dem	297	50.1	Dem	Dem
	Gerald Ford	Rep	240	48.0		
1980	**Ronald Reagan**	Rep	489	51.0	Dem	Rep
	Jimmy Carter	Dem	49	41.0		
	John Anderson			6.6		
1984	**Ronald Reagan**	Rep	525	58.8	Dem	Rep
	Walter Mondale	Dem	13	41.0		Dem (at midterm)

* Lost the popular vote, won the Electoral College and became president
** Died in office

Election Year	Presidential Candidates	Political Party	Electoral Vote	Percentage of Popular Vote	Control of Congress	
					House	Senate
1988	**George H. W. Bush**	Rep	426	53.4	Dem	Dem
	Michael Dukakis	Dem	111	46.0		
1992	**Bill Clinton**	Dem	370	43.0	Dem	Dem
	George H. W. Bush	Rep	168	37.4		
	Ross Perot	--	0	18.9	Rep (at midterm)	Rep (at midterm)
1996	**Bill Clinton**	Dem	379	49.2	Rep	Rep
	Robert Dole	Rep	159	40.7		
	Ross Perot	Reform	0	8.4		
2000	**George W. Bush***	Rep	271	47.8	Rep	Rep
	Al Gore	Dem	266	48.4		
	Ralph Nader	Green	0	2.7		
2004	**George W. Bush**	Rep	286	50.7	Rep	Rep
	John Kerry	Dem	251	48.2	Dem (at midterm)	Dem (at midterm)
2008	Barack Obama	Dem	365	52.8	Dem	Dem
	John McCain	Rep	173	45.6	Rep (at midterm)	
2012	Barack Obama	Dem	332	50.5	Rep	Dem
	Mitt Romney	Rep	206	47.9		

* Lost the popular vote, won the Electoral College and became president

** Died in office

Glossary

114th Congress: The Congress elected in 2014. The first Congress met in 1789–1790. Each Congress is elected for a two-year session and numbered consecutively.

527 groups: Organizations governed by Section 527 of the federal tax code; they are allowed to raise and spend unlimited amounts for "issue advocacy"—but are forbidden to coordinate their efforts with any candidate or campaign, and their ads cannot mention a candidate, favorably or unfavorably.

1963 March on Washington: A massive rally for civil rights highlighted by Martin Luther King's "I Have a Dream" speech.

Abolition: A nineteenth-century movement demanding an immediate and unconditional end to slavery.

Accommodation: The principle that government does not violate the establishment clause as long as it does not confer an advantage to some religions over others. (See "strict separation.")

Affirmative action: Direct, positive steps to recruit members of previously underrepresented groups into schools, colleges, and jobs; sometimes involves setting aside positions (known as quotas).

American exceptionalism: The view that the United States is unique, marked by a distinct set of ideas such as equality, self-rule, and limited government.

Amicus curiae: A brief submitted by a person or group that is not a direct party to the case.

Appellate courts: The system of federal justices, organized into district courts and circuit courts, who hear appeals from lower courts, culminating in the Supreme Court.

Approval rating: A measure of public support for a political figure or institution.

Bandwagon effect: When people join a cause because it seems popular or support a candidate who is leading in the polls.

Base voters: Party members who tend to vote loyally for their party's candidates in most elections.

Bicameral: Having two legislative houses or chambers—like the House and the Senate.

The Bill of Rights: The first ten amendments to the Constitution, listing the rights guaranteed to every citizen.

Black power: A slogan that emphasized pride in black heritage and the construction of black institutions to nurture black interests. It often implied racial separation in reaction to white racism.

Block grants: National government funding provided to state and local governments, with relatively few restrictions or requirements on spending.

Boomerang effect: The discrepancy between candidates' high poll ratings and election performance, caused by supporters' assumption that an easy win means they need not turn out.

Brown v. Board of Education: The landmark Supreme Court case that struck down segregated schools as unconstitutional.

Bundling: A form of fundraising in which an individual persuades others to donate large amounts that are then delivered together to a candidate or campaign.

Bureaucratic pathologies: The problems that tend to develop in bureaucratic systems.

Bush Doctrine: An international strategy that aggressively pursued terrorists and the nations that harbored them through unilateral and preemptive military action.

Call list: A long list of potential donors whom candidates must phone.

Caucus: A local meeting at which registered members of a political party meet to select delegates representing presidential candidates.

Central clearance: The OMB's authority to review and "clear" (or okay) anything a member of the administration says or does in public.

Central service agencies: The organizations that supply and staff the federal government.

Chicanismo: A defiant movement expressing pride in Latino origins and culture in the face of discrimination.

Chief of Staff: The individual responsible for managing the president's office.

Circuit courts (U.S. Court of Appeals): The second stage of federal courts, which review the trial record of cases decided in district court to ensure they were settled properly.

Civic voluntarism: Citizen participation in public life without government incentives or coercion (speaking at a town meeting versus paying taxes, for example).

Civil law: Cases that involve disputes between two parties.

Civil liberties: The limits on government so that people can freely exercise their rights.

Civil rights: The freedom to participate in the full life of the community—to vote, use public facilities, and exercise equal economic opportunity.

Civil Rights Act of 1964: Landmark legislation that forbade discrimination on the basis of race, sex, religion, or national origin.

Civil servants: Members of the permanent executive-branch bureaucracy who are employed on the basis of competitive exams and keep their positions regardless of the presidential administration.

Class action: A lawsuit filed on behalf of an entire category of individuals, such as all people in public housing in a state, or all the female managers of a large company.

Classical republicanism: A democratic ideal, rooted in ancient Greece and Rome, that requires citizens to participate directly in public affairs, seek the public interest, shun private gains, and defer to natural leaders.

Clear and present danger: Court doctrine that permits restrictions of free speech if officials believe that the speech will lead to prohibited action like violence or terrorism.

Clicktivism: Democracy enhanced through the click of a mouse.

Cloture vote: The Senate's only approved method for halting a filibuster or lifting a legislative hold. If sixty senators—three-fifths of the body, changed in 1975 from the original two-thirds—vote for cloture, the measure can proceed to a vote.

Committee hearing: The primary means by which committees collect and analyze information as legislative policy making gets under way. Hearings usually feature witnesses providing oral testimony, along with questioning of the witnesses by members of Congress.

Committee markup session: A gathering of a full committee to draft the final version of a bill before the committee votes on it. Markups open to the public are often standing-room only.

Common law: A system of law developed by judges in deciding cases over the centuries.

Compact: A mutual agreement that provides for joint action to achieve defined goals.

Compromise of 1850: A complicated compromise over slavery that permitted territories to vote on whether they would be slave or free. It also included a fugitive slave law forcing northerners to return black men and women into bondage and permitted California to enter the Union as a free state.

Concurrent opinion: A statement that agrees with the majority opinion.

Concurrent powers: Governmental authority shared by national and state governments, such as the power to tax residents.

Confederation: A group of independent states or nations that yield some of their powers to a national government, although each state retains a degree of sovereign authority.

Conference committee: A temporary collection of House and Senate members, appointed to work out a compromise version of legislation that passed both chambers in different forms.

Congressional caucus: A group of House or Senate members that convene regularly to discuss common interests; they may share demographic characteristics, geography, or issue concerns.

Conservatives: Americans who believe in reduced government spending, personal responsibility, traditional moral values, and a strong national defense. Also known as *right* or *right-wing*.

Consolidation: A media company grows, acquires other companies, and threatens to dominate the market.

Containment: American Cold War strategy designed to stop the spread of communism.

Continuing resolution: A Congress-approved act required when no national budget has been passed before the start of a new fiscal year. This extends spending at current levels for a prescribed period of time.

Cooperative (or marble cake) federalism: Mingled governing authority, with functions overlapping across national and state governments.

Cost–benefit analysis: A more complex study of the projected costs and benefits associated with a proposed policy.

Cost effectiveness: The projected costs of a proposed policy, as revealed by a relatively simple study.

Covenant: A compact invoking religious or moral authority.

Criminal law: Cases in which someone is charged with breaking the law.

De facto discrimination: More subtle forms of discrimination that exist without a legal basis.

Defendant: The party that is sued in a court case.

De jure discrimination: Discrimination established by laws.

Delegated powers: Powers that Congress passes on to the president.

Delegate representation: When representatives follow expressed wishes of the voters.

Democracy: A government in which citizens rule directly and make government decisions for themselves.

Demographic group: People sharing specific factors: for example, age, ethnicity/race, religion, or country of origin.

Demosclerosis: The collective effect of the sheer number of Washington lobbyists in slowing the process of American democratic policy making.

Devolution: The transfer of authority from national to state or local government level.

Diffusion: The spreading of policy ideas from one city or state to others; a process typical of U.S. federalism.

Din: Shorthand for the sheer volume of information and noise generated by online sources; can be a disincentive to participate politically.

Disproportionate impact: The effect some policies have of discriminating, even if discrimination is not consciously intended.

Dissent: A statement on behalf of the justices who voted in the minority.

District courts: The first level of federal courts, which actually try the cases. Each decision is based not on a statute but on previous judicial decisions.

Divided government: Periods during which at least one house of Congress is controlled by a party different from the one occupying the White House.

Domestic dependent nation: Special status that grants local sovereignty to tribal nations but does not grant them full sovereignty equivalent to independent nations.

Double jeopardy: The principle that an individual cannot be tried twice for the same offense.

Dred Scott v. Sandford: A landmark Supreme Court decision holding that black men could not be citizens under the Constitution of the United States. It created a national uproar.

Dual (or layer cake) federalism: Clear division of governing authority between national and state governments.

Earmark: A legislative item, usually included in spending ("appropriations") bills, that directs Congress to fund a particular item in one House district or senator's state.

Economic equality: A situation where there are only small differences in wealth between citizens.

Electoral activities: Public engagement in the form of voting, running for office, volunteering on a campaign, or otherwise participating in elections.

Electoral bounce: The spike in the polls that follows an event such as a party's national convention.

Electoral College: The system established by the Constitution to elect the president; each state has a group of electors (equal in size to that of its congressional delegation in the House and the Senate); the public in each state votes for electors who then vote for the president.

Emancipation Proclamation: An executive order issued by President Abraham Lincoln that declared the slaves in all rebel states free.

Entitlement program: A government benefit program whose recipients are *entitled* by law to receive payments. Social Security, Medicare, and Medicaid are the three largest.

Equal Employment Opportunity Commission (EEOC): Federal law enforcement agency charged with monitoring compliance to the Civil Rights Act.

Equality: All citizens enjoy the same privileges, status, and rights before the laws.

Equal opportunity: The idea that every American has an equal chance to win economic success.

Equal outcome: The idea that citizens should have roughly equal economic circumstances.

Equal protection of the laws: The landmark phrase in the Fourteenth Amendment that requires equal treatment for all citizens.

Equal Rights Amendment: An amendment, originally drafted by Alice Paul in 1923, passed by Congress in 1972, and ratified by thirty-five states, that declared: "Equality of rights . . . shall not be denied or abridged . . . on account of sex."

Establishment clause: In the First Amendment, the principle that government may not establish an official religion.

Exclusionary rule: The ruling that evidence obtained in an illegal search may not be introduced in a trial.

Executive Office of the President (EOP): The agencies that help the president manage daily activities.

Executive order: A presidential declaration, with the force of law, that issues instructions to the executive branch without any requirement for congressional action or approval.

Expressed powers: Powers the Constitution explicitly grants to the president.

Expressive benefits: Values or deeply held beliefs that inspire individuals to join a public interest group.

Fairness doctrine: Regulation that required media outlets to devote equal time to opposite perspectives.

Federal budget deficit: The gap between revenues received by the national government (primarily through individual income and corporate taxes) and spending on all public programs.

Federalism: Power divided between national and state government. Each has its own independent authority and its own duties.

Federal poverty line: The annually specified level of income (separately calculated for individuals and families) below which people are considered to live in poverty, becoming eligible for certain federal benefits. In 2012, the poverty line was set at $23,050 for a family of four.

Federal Regulation of Lobbying Act: The initial U.S. statute spelling out requirements on lobbyists active in Congress, passed in 1946.

Fighting words: Expression inherently likely to provoke violent reaction and not necessarily protected by the First Amendment.

Final rule: The rule that specifies how a program will actually operate.

First Continental Congress: A convention of delegates, from twelve of the thirteen colonies, that met in 1774.

Fiscal policy: Taxing and spending policies carried out by government, generally in an effort to affect national economic development.

Floor: The full chamber, either in the House of Representatives or in the Senate. A bill "goes to the floor" for the final debate and vote.

Focusing event: A major happening, often of crisis or disaster proportions, that attracts widespread media attention to an issue.

Framing effects: The influence, on the respondent, of how a polling question is asked; changes in wording can significantly alter many people's answers.

Freedom: The ability to pursue one's own desires without interference from others.

Freedom of Information Act: A 1966 law that facilitates full or partial disclosure of government information and documents.

Freedom Riders: Black and white activists who rode buses together to protest segregation on interstate bus lines.

Free exercise clause: In the First Amendment, the principle that government may not interfere in religious practice.

Free trade: Goods and services moving across international boundaries without government interference.

Full faith and credit clause: The constitutional requirement (in Article 4, Section 1) that each state recognize and uphold laws passed by any other state.

Gender gap: Patterned differences in political opinions between women and men.

Gerrymander: Redrawing an election district in a way that gives the advantage to one party.

Gift ban: A regulation that eliminates (or sharply reduces the dollar amount of) gifts from interest groups to lawmakers.

Going public: Directly addressing the public to win support for oneself or one's ideas.

Grand jury: A jury that does not decide on guilt or innocence but only on whether there is enough evidence for the case to go to trial.

Grand strategy: An overarching vision that defines and guides a nation's foreign policy.

Granted powers: National government powers set out explicitly in the Constitution.

Grants-in-aid: National government funding provided to state and local governments, along with specific instructions about how the funds may be used.

Great Migration: The vast movement of African Americans from the rural South to the urban North between 1920 and 1950.

Gross domestic product: The value of all the goods and services produced in a nation over a year.

Groupthink: The tendency among a small group of decision makers to converge on a shared set of views; can limit creative thinking or solutions to policy problems.

Hate crime: Crime stemming from prejudice based on someone's personal characteristics, such as race, ethnicity, religion, or sexual orientation.

Hate speech: Hostile statements based on someone's personal characteristics, such as race, ethnicity, religion, or sexual orientation.

Imperial presidency: A characterization of the American presidency that suggests it is demonstrating imperial traits and that the republic is morphing into an empire.

Incorporation: The process by which the Supreme Court declares that a right in the Bill of Rights also applies to state governments.

Incumbency advantage: The tendency for members of Congress to win re-election in overwhelming numbers.

Indentured servant: A colonial American settler contracted to work for a fixed period (usually three to seven years) in exchange for food, shelter, and transportation to the New World.

Individualism: The idea that individuals, not the society, are responsible for their own well-being.

Infotainment: The blurred line between news and entertainment.

Inherent powers: National government powers implied by, but not specifically named in, the Constitution.

Inherent powers of the presidency: Powers assumed by presidents, often during crisis, on the basis of the constitutional phrase "The executive power shall be vested in the president."

Institutions: The organizations, norms, and rules that structure government and public actions.

Internationalism: The belief that national interests are best served by actively engaging and working with other nations around the world.

Interest group: An organization whose goals include influencing government.

Intergovernmental lobbying: Attempts by public officials in one part of the government to influence their counterparts elsewhere—in another branch, or at a different (state or local) level.

Iron triangle: The cozy relationship in one issue area among interest-group lobbyists, congressional staffers, and executive-branch agencies.

Isolationism: The doctrine that a nation should not interfere in other nations' affairs and should avoid all foreign commitments and alliances.

Issue advocacy: Organized effort to advance (or block) a proposed public policy change.

Issue framing: The way an issue is defined—every issue has many possible frames, each with a slightly different tilt in describing the problem and highlighting solutions.

Issue network: Shifting alliances of public and private interest groups, lawmakers, and other stakeholders all focused on the same policy area.

Jim Crow: The system of racial segregation in the U.S. South that lasted from 1890 to 1965.

Judicial activism: A vigorous or active approach to reviewing the other branches of government.

Judicial restraint: Reluctance to interfere with elected branches, only doing so as a last resort.

Judicial review: The Court's authority to strike down acts that violate the Constitution and to interpret what the Constitution means.

King of the Hill rule: A special rule governing floor consideration of a bill. A series of amendments on the same topic may all win majority approval, but only the last amendment receiving a majority vote—the "king of the hill"—is incorporated into the bill.

K Street: A major street in downtown Washington, DC, that is home to the headquarters for many lobbying firms and advocacy groups—and thus synonymous with interest-group lobbying.

Laws of coverture: An outmoded legal tradition holding that a woman's rights and duties all operate through her husband.

Legislative hold: An informal way for a senator to object to a bill or other measure reaching the Senate floor. The action effectively halts Senate proceedings on that issue, sometimes for weeks or longer.

Liberals: Americans who value cultural diversity, government programs for the needy, public intervention in the economy, and individuals' right to a lifestyle based on their own social and moral positions. Also known as *left* or *left-wing*.

Libertarians: People who believe in minimal government: specifically, that public officials' only role should be defending borders, prosecuting crime, and protecting private property.

Likely voters: Persons identified as probable voters in an upcoming election. Often preferred by polling organizations, but difficult to specify with great accuracy.

Literacy test: A requirement that voters be literate; in reality, a way to restrict black suffrage.

Litigation: The conduct of a lawsuit.

Lobbyist: A person who contacts government officials on behalf of a particular cause or issue.

Lochner era: A period from 1905 to 1937, when the Supreme Court struck down laws (like worker protection or minimum wage) that were thought to infringe on economic liberty or the right to contract.

Loud signal: Media stories with very broad coverage and an unambiguous message.

Majority opinion: The official statement of the court.

Mandate: Political authority claimed by an election winner as reflecting the approval of the people.

Margin of sampling error: The degree of inaccuracy in any poll, arising from the fact that surveys involve a *sample* of respondents from a population, rather than every member.

Mass media: Information and entertainment for broad popular audiences—including newspapers, radio, and television.

Material benefits: Items distributed by public interest groups as incentives to sign up or remain a member.

Median: A statistical term for the number in the middle or the case that has an equal number of examples above and below it.

Mediation: A way of resolving disputes without going to court, in which a third party (the mediator) helps two or more sides negotiate a settlement.

Mercantilism: An economic theory according to which government controls foreign trade to maintain prosperity and security.

Midterm elections: National elections held between presidential elections, involving all seats in the House of Representatives, one-third of those in the Senate, thirty-six governors, and other positions.

Miranda warnings: A set of rights that police officers are required to inform suspects of, including the right to remain silent.

Missouri Compromise: An agreement to open southern territories west of the Mississippi to slavery while closing northern territories to slavery.

Monetary policy: Actions of central banks, in the United States culminating in the Federal Reserve, designed primarily to maximize employment and moderate inflation.

Motor voter law: Passed in 1993, this act enables prospective voters to register when they receive their driver's license.

Multilateralism: A doctrine that emphasizes operating together with other nations to pursue common goals.

Multilateral organization: International organization of three or more nations organized around a common goal.

Name recognition: An advantage possessed by a well-known political figure, a political celebrity.

National Association for the Advancement of Colored People, or NAACP: A civil rights organization formed in 1906 and dedicated to racial equality.

National Organization for Women (NOW): An organization formed to take action for women's equality.

Necessary and proper clause: The constitutional declaration (in Article 1, Section 8) that defines Congress's authority to exercise the "necessary and proper" powers to carry out its designated functions.

Negative campaigning: Running for office by attacking the opponent. An unpopular tactic that is, nevertheless, very effective.

Negative liberty: Freedom from constraints or the interference of others.

New Deal: Broad series of economic programs and reforms introduced between 1933 and 1936 and associated with the Franklin Roosevelt administration.

New Federalism: A version of cooperative federalism, but with stronger emphasis on state and local government activity versus national government.

New Jersey Plan: Put forward at the convention by the small states, it left most government authority with the state governments.

New media: On-demand access to information and entertainment on digital devices that also features interactive participation with content. Arose in the late twentieth century.

Nonpartisan election: An election where candidates run as individuals, without any party affiliation. Many towns and cities feature nonpartisan elections.

Open seat: A seat in Congress without an incumbent running for re-election.

Originalism: A principle of legal interpretation that relies on the original meaning of those who wrote the Constitution.

Overhead democracy: A system by which the people elect the presidents, who, through their appointees, control the bureaucracy from the top.

Override: The process by which Congress can overcome a presidential veto with a two-thirds vote in both chambers.

Path dependence: The tendency of policy makers to follow established routines in thinking about or acting on a specific topic.

Paradox of voting: For most individuals, the cost of voting (acquiring necessary information, traveling to polling site, and waiting in line) outweighs the apparent benefits. Economic theory would predict very low voter turnout, given this analysis.

Partisanship: Taking the side of a party, or espousing a viewpoint that reflects a political party's principles or position on an issue. Often decried by those who wish the parties would work together.

Party boss: The senior figure in a party machine.

Party caucus: A meeting of all House or Senate members of one or the other main party, usually to discuss political and policy strategies.

Party identification: Strong attachment to one political party, often established at an early age.

Party in government: The portion of a political party's organization that comprises elected officials and candidates for office.

Party in the electorate: The largest (and least organized) component of a political party, drawn from the public at large: registered members and regular supporters.

Party machine: A hierarchical arrangement of party workers, often organized in an urban area to help integrate immigrants and minority groups into the political system. Most active in the late nineteenth and early twentieth centuries.

Party platform: The written statement of a party's core convictions and issue priorities. Generally revised every four years, in time for the national party convention.

Party system: The broad organization of U.S. politics, comprising the two main parties, the coalition of supporters backing each, the positions they take on major issues, and each party's electoral achievements.

Pendleton Civil Service Act: The law that shifted American government toward a merit-based public service.

Personal presidency: The idea that the president has a personal link to the public. Made possible by twentieth-century media.

Plaintiff: The party that brings the action in a lawsuit.

Plessy v. Ferguson: An 1896 Supreme Court case that permitted racial segregation.

Pluralism: An open, participatory style of government in which many different interests are represented.

Policy agenda: The issues that the media covers, the public considers important, and politicians address. Setting the agenda is the first step in political action.

Policy window: A figurative description of the opportunity—often brief, measured in days or weeks rather than years—to pass a bill in Congress or a state legislature.

Political Action Committee (PAC): An organization of at least fifty people, affiliated with an interest group, that is permitted to make contributions to candidates for federal office.

Political appointees: Top officials in the executive agencies appointed by the president.

Political culture: The orientation of citizens of a state toward politics.

Political elites: Individuals who control significant wealth, status, power, or visibility and who, consequently, have significant influence over public debates.

Political equality: All citizens have the same political rights and opportunities.

Political mobilization: Efforts to encourage people to engage in the public sphere: to vote for a particular candidate (and donate money, work on the campaign, etc.) or to get involved in specific issues.

Political socialization: Education about how the government works and which policies one should support; provided partly at school, partly by party officials and other national institutions.

Political voice: Exercising one's public rights, often through speaking out in protest or in favor of some policy change.

Positive liberty: The freedom and ability to pursue one's goals.

Power elite theory: The view that a small handful of wealthy, influential Americans exercises extensive control over government decisions.

Pragmatism: A principle of legal interpretation based on the idea that the Constitution evolves and that it must be put in the context of contemporary realities.

Precedent: Judicial decisions that offer a guide to similar cases in the future.

Preemptive action: Military action that responds to threats before they happen—as opposed to responding to the aggression of others.

President pro tempore: Majority-party senator with the longest Senate service.

Primacy: The doctrine asserting that the United States should maintain an unrivaled military.

Priming: Affecting voters' or poll respondents' perception of candidates or public officials by raising issues that are perceived to enhance or diminish the candidates.

Principal agent theory: Analyses of how policy makers (principals) can control actors who work for them (agents) but have far more information.

Prior restraint: Legal effort to stop speech before it occurs—in effect, censorship.

Private contractors: Private companies that contract to provide goods and services for the government.

Proportional representation: The allocation of votes or delegates on the basis of the percentage of the vote received; contrasts with the winner-take-all system.

Proposed rule: A draft of administrative regulations published in the *Federal Register* for the purpose of gathering comments from interested parties.

Protectionism: Effort to protect local business from foreign competition.

Public interest lobbyist: A representative of an organization that seeks to benefit the population at large, not a specific client or small collection of people.

Public ownership: A situation in which media outlets are run by the government and paid for by tax dollars.

Push poll: A form of negative campaigning that masquerades as a regular opinion survey. Usually conducted by a campaign or allied group; features strongly critical or unflattering information about an opponent.

Racial profiling: A law enforcement practice of singling out people on the basis of physical features such as race or ethnicity.

Rational choice theory: An approach to political behavior that views individuals as rational, decisive actors who know their political interests and seek to act on them.

Reapportionment: Reorganization of the boundaries of House districts, a process that follows the results of the U.S. census, taken every ten years. District lines are redrawn to ensure rough equality in the number of constituents represented by each House member.

Reconstruction: The failed effort, pursued by Northerners and Southerners, to rebuild the South and establish racial equality after the Civil War.

Reframe the issue: To redefine the popular perception of an issue; to show it in a new light with a new set of costs or benefits.

Regulatory capture: The theory that industries dominate the agencies that regulate them.

Republic: A government in which citizens rule indirectly and make government decisions through their elected representatives.

Reserved powers: The constitutional guarantee (in the Tenth Amendment) that the states retain government authority not explicitly granted to the national government.

Response bias: The tendency of poll respondents to misstate their views, frequently to avoid "shameful" opinions like sexism or racism.

Reverse lobbying: Attempts by government officials to influence interest groups on behalf of their preferred policies.

Revolving door: The tendency of Washington's most seasoned lobbyists to move from government work (e.g., as a presidential advisor) to lobbying and back again.

Roll-call vote: A congressional vote in which all members' votes are recorded, either by roll call (Senate) or electronically (House).

Rule of four: The requirement that at least four Supreme Court judges must agree to hear a case before it comes before the Court.

Sampling frame: A designated group of people from whom a set of poll respondents is randomly selected.

School busing: An effort to integrate public schools by mixing students from different neighborhoods.

Second Continental Congress: A convention of delegates from the thirteen colonies that became the acting national government for the duration of the Revolutionary War.

Section 504: An obscure provision in an obscure rehabilitation act that required all institutions that received federal funds to accommodate people with disabilities.

Selective incorporation: Extending protections from the Bill of Rights to the state governments, one right at a time.

Self-rule: The idea that legitimate government flows from the people.

Seneca Falls Convention: A convention dedicated to women's rights held in July 1848.

Signing statements: Written declarations commenting on the bill that is signed into law.

Social capital: Relations between people that build closer ties of trust and civic engagement, yielding productive benefits for the larger society.

Social democracy: A government in which citizens are responsible for one another's well-being and use government policy to ensure that all are comfortably cared for.

Social equality: All individuals enjoy the same status in society.

Soft power: Influence a nation exerts by attracting others through culture and commerce; a contrast to persuasion through force of money.

Solidary benefits: The feeling of shared commitment and purpose experienced by individuals who join a public interest group.

Sound bite: A short clip of speech taken from a longer piece of audio. Often refers to a brief excerpt from a speech by a candidate or politician.

Special interest: A pejorative term, often used to designate an interest group whose aims or issue preferences one does not support.

Split-ticket voter: One who votes for at least one candidate from each party, dividing his or her ballot between the two (or more) parties.

Spoils system: Government jobs given out as political favors.

Stare decisis: Deciding cases on the basis of previous rulings or precedents.

Straight-ticket voter: One who votes for the same party for all offices on a ballot.

Street-level bureaucrats: Government officials who deal directly with the public.

Strict scrutiny: The tendency to strike down as unconstitutional any legislation that singles out race or ethnicity, unless the government has a compelling interest in such legislation.

Strict separation: The strict principles articulated in the Lemon test for judging whether a law establishes a religion. (See "accommodation.")

Super PACs: Organizations that are permitted to raise and spend unlimited amounts of money to promote a candidate or publicize a cause. However, they may not directly contribute to a candidate or coordinate with a campaign.

Super Tuesday: The date on the presidential primary calendar when multiple states hold primaries and caucuses.

Supremacy clause: The constitutional declaration (in Article 6, Section 2) that the national government's authority prevails over any conflicting state or local government's claims.

Survey research: Systematic study of a defined population, analyzing a representative sample's views to draw inferences about the larger public's views. Also termed *opinion poll*.

Symbolic expression: An act, rather than actual speech, used to demonstrate a point of view.

Taliban: A fundamentalist Islamic sect that took control of Afghanistan in 1996 and gave shelter to the Al Qaeda terrorist network.

Telecommunications Act of 1996: A major congressional overhaul of communications law that opened the door to far more competition by permitting companies to own outlets in multiple media markets—radio, television, magazines, etc.

Time, place, and manner clause: The constitutional clause that delegates control of elections to the state governments.

Trade deficit: The deficit arising when a nation imports (or buys) more goods from foreign nations than it exports (or sells) to them.

Trustee representation: Representatives do what they regard as the best interest of the voters—independent of what the voters want.

Unanimous consent: A Senate requirement, applied to most of that body's business, that all senators agree before an action can proceed.

Underdog effect: Sympathy for a candidate behind in the polls, contributing to a higher-than-predicted vote total—and sometimes a surprise election victory.

Unfunded mandate: An obligation imposed on state or local government officials by federal legislation, without sufficient federal funding support to cover the costs.

Unicameral: Having a single legislative house or chamber.

Unilateralism: A doctrine that holds that the United States should act independently of other nations. It should decide what is best for itself—not in coordination with partners and allies.

Unitary government: A national polity governed as a single unit, with the central government exercising all or most political authority.

United Farm Workers: An influential union representing migrant farm workers in the West.

Universalistic politics: Government by universal rules, impartially applied.

USA Patriot Act: Legislation that sought to enhance national security, passed in the aftermath of the September 11, 2001, attacks.

Veto: The constitutional procedure by which a president can prevent enactment of Congress-passed legislation.

Veto power: The presidential power to block an act of Congress by refusing to sign it.

Virginia Plan: Madison's plan, embraced by Constitutional Convention delegates from larger states; strengthened the national government relative to state governments.

Voice vote: A congressional vote in which the presiding officer asks those for and against to say "yea" or "nay," respectively, and announces the result. No record is kept of House or Senate members voting on each side.

Voter turnout: A measure of what proportion of eligible voters actually cast a legitimate ballot in a given election.

War Powers Act: Legislation passed in 1973 to increase congressional involvement in undeclared wars. It requires Congress to approve military action undertaken by the president in no more than sixty days.

Watergate scandal: A failed effort in 1972 by Republican operatives to break into Democratic Party headquarters in the Watergate office complex in Washington, DC; tapes revealed that President Nixon attempted to cover up the event—causing him to resign the presidency.

Whistle-blower: A federal worker who reports corruption or fraud.

Winner-take-all: The electoral system used in U.S. general presidential as well as many primary and other elections. The candidate receiving a simple majority (or, among multiple candidates, a plurality) receives all electoral votes or primary delegates. Sometimes called "first-past-the-post."

World Trade Organization: An international organization that oversees efforts to open markets and promote free trade.

Notes

Chapter 1 Ideas That Shape American Politics

1. Russell A. Burgos, "An N of One: A Political Scientist in Operation Iraqi Freedom," *Perspectives on Politics* 2, no. 3 (2004): 551–56.
2. Harold D. Lasswell, *Politics: Who Gets What, When, and How*, rev. ed. (New York: Peter Smith Books, 1990).
3. CNN/ORC poll, conducted July 18–20, 2014. Results at http://bit.ly/1r74Rew (last accessed September 6, 2014).
4. Simon Schama, *Rough Crossings: Britain, the Slaves, and the American Revolution* (New York: HarperCollins, 2006).
5. Isaiah Berlin, "Two Concepts of Liberty," reprinted in Berlin, *Liberty*, ed. Henry Hardy (Oxford: Oxford University Press, 2002), 166–217.
6. Samuel Huntington, *American Politics: The Promise of Disharmony* (Cambridge, MA: Harvard University Press, 1983); Rogers Smith, *Civic Ideals: Conflicting Visions of Citizenship in U.S. History* (New Haven, CT: Yale University Press, 1997).
7. Quoted in James A. Morone, *The Democratic Wish: Popular Participation and the Limits of American Government* (New Haven, CT: Yale University Press, 1998), 54.
8. Thomas Jefferson, "Response to the Citizens of Albemarle," February 12, 1790; First Inaugural Address, March 4, 1801. Jefferson's first inaugural is the best summary of what we now call Jeffersonian Democracy.
9. James Madison, Federalist no. 10. The quote is from Roger Sherman recorded in Madison's "Notes of Debates," in Winston Solberg, ed., *The Federal Convention and the Formation of the Union* (Indianapolis, IN: Bobbs Merrill, 1958), 84–85.
10. Michael Kammen, *People of Paradox* (New York: Knopf, 1972), 31.
11. Thomas Jefferson, "Response to the Citizens of Albemarle," Feb. 12, 1790. In Jefferson, *Writings*, ed. Merrill D. Peterson (New York: Library of America, 2011), 451.
12. John Kingdon, *America the Unusual* (New York: St. Martin's Press, 1999), 1.
13. Martin Luther King Jr., Speech at Ohio Northern University, Jan. 11, 1968. At http://www.onu.edu/node/28513 (last accessed September 5, 2014).
14. Milton Friedman, *Capitalism and Freedom* (Chicago: University of Chicago Press, 1962).
15. Bruce Stokes, "Public Attitudes Toward the Next Social Contract?" (Pew Research Center, 2013). At http://pewrsr.ch/1kRi61F (last accessed September 5, 2014).
16. The original statement of this theory is by Louis Hartz, *The Liberal Tradition in America* (New York: Harcourt, Brace, and World, 1955).
17. Franklin quotes from Poor Richard's Almanac; can be found at http://www.ushistory.org/franklin/quotable/.
18. James Truslow Adams, *The Epic of America* (New York: Taylor & Francis, 1938). Available from Google Books at http://books.google.com/books/about/The_Epic_of_America.html?id=-VMVAAAAIAAJ/.
19. Quoted in Jennifer Hochschild, *Facing Up to the American Dream* (Princeton, NJ: Princeton University Press, 1995), vi, 18.
20. Gordon Wood, *The Radicalism of the American Revolution* (New York: Knopf, 1992), 369.
21. Timothy Noah, *The Great Divergence: America's Growing Inequality Crisis and What We Can Do About It* (New York: Bloomsbury Press, 2012).
22. FDR and LBJ quoted in James Morone, *Hellfire Nation* (New Haven, CT: Yale University Press, 2004), 347, 427.
23. Tocqueville, *Democracy in America*, 1:9.
24. Hugh Brogan, *Alexis de Tocqueville: A Life* (New Haven, CT: Yale University Press, 2007), 352.
25. David Leonhardt and Kevin Quealy, "U.S. Middle Class No Longer World's Richest," *New York Times*, April 23, 2014, A1.
26. See Robert Putnam and David Campbell, *American Grace: How Religion Divides and Unites Us* (New York: Simon & Schuster, 2010).
27. Eileen W. Lindner, ed., *Yearbook of American & Canadian Churches* (National Council of Churches, 2013).
28. Pew Research, Religion and Public Life Project, "Religious Landscape Survey" (accessed March 15, 2014).
29. Pew Charitable Trusts, "Millennials in Adulthood," March 2014, 13.
30. Madison, in Federalist no. 10.
31. For a robust institutional perspective, see Sven Steinmo and Jon Watts, "It's the Institutions, Stupid! Why Comprehensive Health Insurance Always Fails in America," *Journal of Health Politics, Policy, and Law* 20, no. 2 (2003): 329–72; Theda Skocpol, *Protecting Soldiers and Mothers: The Political Origins of Social Policy in the United States* (Cambridge, MA: Harvard University Press, 1995), chap. 1; or Karen Orren and Stephen Skowronek, *The Search for American Political Development* (New York: Cambridge University Press, 2004).

Chapter 2 The Constitution

1. Taylor Branch, *Parting the Waters: America in the King Years 1954–63* (New York: Simon & Schuster, 1989).
2. Robert Middlekauff, *The Glorious Cause* (New York: Oxford University Press, 1982), 74.

3. Bernard Bailyn et al., *The Great Republic: A History of the American People*, (Boston: Little, Brown, 1977), 1: 256.

4. Middlekauff, *The Glorious Cause*, 223–28, quoted at 226.

5. Rogan Kersh, *Dreams of a More Perfect Union* (Ithaca, NY: Cornell University Press, 2001), 60–67.

6. Quoted in Gordon Wood, *Empire of Liberty* (New York: Oxford University Press, 2009), 14.

7. Richard Beeman, *Plain, Honest Men: The Making of the American Constitution* (New York: Random House, 2009), 3–7.

8. Beeman, *Plain, Honest Men*, 12.

9. Leonard Richards, *Shays's Rebellion: The American Revolution's Final Battle* (Philadelphia: University of Pennsylvania Press, 2002).

10. Beeman, 84.

11. "Madison's Notes," 81.

12. *Ibid.*

13. *Ibid.*, 122 ["swallowed up"]; David Brian Robertson, *The Constitution and America's Destiny* (New York: Cambridge University Press, 2005), 139.

14. Robertson, *The Constitution and America's Destiny*, 140.

15. John Dickinson, "Notes for a Speech." *Supplement to Max Farrand's The Records of the Federal Convention of 1787*. Ed. James H. Hutson. (New Haven: Yale University Press, 1987), 158.

16. Beeman, *Plain, Honest Men*, 333.

17. *Ibid.*, 349.

18. Herbert Storing, *What the Anti-Federalists Were For: The Political Writings of the Opponents of the Constitution* (Chicago: University of Chicago Press, 1981).

19. Thomas Jefferson, "Letter to Samuel Kercheval," July 12, 1816. In *The Works of Thomas Jefferson,* ed. Paul Leicester Ford (New York: G.P. Putnam's Sons, 1905), vol. 12, 13–14.

20. Robert Dahl, *How Democratic Is the American Constitution?* (2nd ed. New Haven, CT: Yale University Press, 2003).

Chapter 3 Federalism and Nationalism

1. Polling from Pew Center for People and the Press; polls of state and local government, April 2013; *idem.*, national government, October 2013.

2. David Brian Robertson, *Federalism and the Making of America* (New York: Routledge, 2012).

3. From Justice Brandeis's dissenting opinion in *New State Ice Co. v. Liebmann*, 285 U.S. 262, 311 (1932).

4. Theda Skocpol, *Protecting Soldiers and Mothers*, 9.

5. James Buchanan and Gordon Tullock, *The Calculus of Consent* (Ann Arbor: University of Michigan Press, 1962), 144.

6. William Berry, Richard Fording, and Russell Hanson, "Reassessing the Race to the Bottom in State Welfare Policy," *Journal of Politics* 65, no. 2 (2003): 327–49.

7. James Morone, *Hellfire Nation: The Politics of Sin in American History* (New Haven, CT: Yale University Press, 2003), part 3.

8. Dirksen, quoted in Richard P. Nathan, "Updating Theories of American Federalism," in *Intergovernmental Management for the Twenty-First Century.* Timothy Conlan and Paul Posner, eds. (Washington, DC: Brookings Institution Press, 2008), 15.

9. Quoted in Robert Dreyfuss, "Grover Norquist: 'Field Marshal' of the Bush Plan," *The Nation,* May 14, 2001.

10. 17 U.S. 316 (1819).

11. Benedict Anderson, *Imagined Communities: Reflection on the Origin and Spread of Nationalism*, 2nd ed. (New York: Verso, 2006).

12. Robert J. Taylor, et al., eds., *Papers of John Adams*, Robert J. Taylor, et al., eds. (Cambridge, MA: Harvard University Press, 1980), III: 141.

13. For the classic description of 19th century community activity, see Alexis de Tocqueville, *Democracy in America* (New York: Harper, 2006)

Chapter 4 Civil Liberties

1. Tom Topousis and Joe Mollica, "New Yorkers Wage Jihad versus WTC Mosque," *New York Post*, May 26, 2010, http:// www .nypost.com / p/news/ local/ manhattan/ nyers _wage_ jihad_ vs_ wtc_mosque_ UgJiOBY EhrSO w4Q6hpvb QLN/.

2. CNN/Opinion Research, August 11, 2010 (New Yorkers); *Time/CNN*, August 19, 2010 (all Americans). http://www.foxnews .com/ opinion/2010/08/17/ kt-mcfarland-ground- zero-mosque-god- september- obama-imam-feisal/.

3. *Schenck v. United States*, 249 U.S. 47 (1919).

4. "Islamic Center Opens Its Doors near Ground Zero," *Associated Press*, September 22, 2011. http://www.usatoday.com/ news/nation/story/2011-09-22/ new-york-city-mosque/ 50506728/1/.

5. *Barron v. Baltimore*, 32 U.S. 243 (1833).

6. *The Slaughter-House Cases*, 83 U.S. 36 (1873).

7. *Palko v. Connecticut*, 302 U.S. 319, (1937).

8. If you're interested in reading more on any of the cases we discuss, see Corey Brettschneider, ed., *Constitutional Law and American Democracy: Cases and Readings* (New York: Wolters Kluwer, 2012).

9. The cases were *Stenberg v. Carhart*, 2000, and *Gonzales v. Carhart*, 2007.

10. Thomas Jefferson, "Letter to the Danbury Baptist Association," January 1, 1802.

11. *Everson v. Board of Education*, 330 U.S. 1 (1947).

12. *Engel v. Vitale*, 370 U.S. 421 (1962).

13. In *Good News Club v. Milford Central School*, 533 U.S. 98 (2001), the Court ruled 6–3 in favor of the club.

14. Employment Division, *Department of Human Resources of Oregon v. Smith*, 494 U.S. 872 (1990).

15. The decision that explicitly adopted a preferred position for free speech was *Brandenburg v. Ohio*, 395 U.S. 444 (1969), discussed later in this section.

16. *Gitlow v. New York*, 268 U.S. 652 (1925). Gitlow, the socialist author of a left-wing manifesto, was convicted, but in the process the courts incorporated free speech.

17. *Brandenburg v. Ohio*, 395 U.S. 444 (1969). For a fine discussion, see Harold Sullivan, *Civil Rights and Liberties* (Upper Saddle River, NJ: Pearson Prentice Hall, 2005), chap. 2.

18. *Virginia v. Black*, 538 U.S. 343 (2003).

19. *Texas v. Johnson*, 109 S. Ct. 2544 (1989).

20. *Chaplinsky v. New Hampshire*, 315 U.S. 568 (1942).

21. *Tinker v. Des Moines Independent Community School District*, 393 U.S. 503 (1969).

22. *Bethel School District No. 403 v. Fraser*, 478 U.S. 675 (1986), and *Hazelwood School District v. Kuhlmeier*, 484 U.S 260 (1988).

23. *New York Times Company v. United States*, 403 U.S. 713 (1971).

24. Bob Egleko, "S.F. Judge Dissolves His Wikileaks Injunction," *San Francisco Chronicle*, March 1, 2008. http://www.sfgate.com/ bayarea/article/S-F -judge-dissolves-his -Wikileaks-injunction-3226168.php/.

25. Joseph Story, *Commentaries on the Constitution of the United States*, Vol. III (Boston: Hilliard, Gray, 1833), 746; Charlton Heston in *Chicago Tribune*, "Charlton Heston Rips Media," Sept. 12, 1997.

26. *District of Columbia v. Heller*, 554 U.S. 570 (2008).

27. *Olmstead v. United States*, 277 U.S. 438 (1928).

28. *United States v. Leon*, 468 U.S. 897 (1984).

29. *Herring v. United States*, 555 U.S. 135 (2009).

30. *Olmstead v. United States*, 277 U.S. 438 (1928); *Katz v. United States*, 389 U.S. 347 (1967).

31. *Kentucky v. King*, 131 U.S. 865 (2011).

32. Glenn Harlan Reynolds, "Ham Sandwich Nation: Due Process when Everything is a Crime, *Columbia Law Review*. Vol. 113 (July 8, 2013): 102–108.

33. Linda Monk, *The Words We Live By: Your Annotated Guide to the Constitution* (New York: Hyperion, 2003), 165.

34. *Illinois v. Perkins*, 496 U.S. 292 (1990); *New York v. Quarles*, 467 U.S. 649 (1984); *Harris v. New York*, 401 U.S. 222 (1970).

35. Anthony Lewis, *Gideon's Trumpet* (New York: Vintage, 1989).

36. *Missouri v. Frye*, 132 U.S. 55 (2012).

37. John Eligon, "State Law to Cap Public Defenders' Caseloads, but Only in the City," *New York Times*, April 5, 2009, http://www .nytimes.com/2009/04/06/ nyregion/06defenders.html/.

38. Frank Baumgartner, Suzanna De Boef, and Amber Boydstun, *The Decline of the Death Penalty and the Discovery of Innocence* (New York: Cambridge University Press, 2008).

39. Editorial, *New York Times*, Sunday, May 22, 2011, 7.

Chapter 5 The Struggle for Civil Rights

1. *The Autobiography of Malcolm X: As Told to Alex Haley* (New York: Random House, 1964), 43; Richard Wright, *Native Son* [Playing black]; James Morone, *Hellfire Nation: The Politics of Sin in American History* (New Haven, CT: Yale University Press, 2003), 441 [Airline Pilots].

2. Samuel Huntington, *American Politics: The Promise of Disharmony* (Cambridge, MA: Harvard University Press, 1981).

3. Rogers Smith, *Civic Ideals: Conflicting Visions of Citizenship in U.S. History* (New Haven, CT: Yale University Press, 1999).

4. *Pierce v. Society of Sisters*, 268 U.S. 510 (1925); *Romer v. Evans*, 517 U.S. 620 (1996).

5. W. E. B. DuBois, *The Souls of Black Folk* (New York: New American Library, 1982), 220.

6. Garry Wills, *Lincoln at Gettysburg* (New York: Simon & Schuster, 1992).

7. *The Civil Rights Cases*, 109 U.S. 3 (1883).

8. *Plessy v. Ferguson*, 163 U.S. 537 (1896).

9. Peggy Pascoe, *What Comes Naturally: Miscegenation Law and the Making of Race in America* (New York: Oxford University Press, 2008).

10. Daniel P. Franklin, *Politics and Film: The Political Culture of Film in the United States* (Lanham, MD.: Rowman and Littlefield, 2006).

11. *Smith v. Allright*, 21 U.S. 649, (1944).

12. *Morgan v. Virginia*, 328 U.S. 373 (1946) [bus lines]; *Sweatt v. Painter* 339 U.S. 629 (1950) [law school]; *McLaurin v. Oklahoma* 339 U.S. 637 (1950).

13. *Heart of Atlanta Motel Inc. v. United States*, 379 U.S. 241 (1964); *Katzenbach v. McClung*, 379 U.S. 294 (1964).

14. *Sheet Metal Workers v. EEOC*, 478 U.S. 421 (1986).

15. *Adarand Construction v. Peña*, 515 U.S. 299 (1995).

16. *University of California v. Bakke*, 438 U.S. 265 (1978).

17. Leo Kanowitz, *Women and the Law* (Albuquerque: University of New Mexico Press, 1971), 36.

18. Abby Kelly Foster, quoted in *Hellfire Nation*, 166.

19. Sheryl Gay Stolberg, "Obama Signs Equal Pay Legislation," *New York Times*, January 1, 2009.

20. Pew Hispanic Center, reported in Erin Rosa, "Pew: Latino Incarceration Rates Increase, Legal Confidence Wanes," *Colorado Independent*, April 7, 2009.

21. Heather Silber Mohamed, "Immigration, Protests, and the Politics of Latino/a Identity" (PhD diss., Brown University, 2012).

22. Rogers Smith, *Civic Ideals*, 361.

23. Tocqueville, *Democracy in America*, I: 323–24.

24. Pekka Hamalainen, *The Comanche Empire* (New Haven, CT: Yale University Press, 2008).

25. *Bowers v. Hardwick*, 478 U.S. 186 (1986); *Lawrence v. Texas*, 539 U.S. 558 (2003).

Chapter 6 Public Opinion and Political Participation

1. Drew Desilver, *Partisan Polarization, in Congress and Among Public, Is Greater Than Ever*. Pew Research Center, July

17, 2013. http://www.pewresearch .org/ fact-tank/2013/ 07/17/partisan-polarization-in-congress-and-among-public-is-greater-than-ever/.

2. Morris Fiorina, Samuel Abrams, and Jeremy Pope, *Culture War: The Myth of a Polarized America.* (New York: Longman, 2004).

3. John Zaller, *The Nature and Origins of Mass Opinion* (New York: Cambridge UniversityPress, 1992).

4. Pew Research Center for People and the Press, *Methodology: Questionnaire Design*, 2014-03-24, http://people-press.netcampaign .com/methodology/questionnaire/.

5. Walter Lippmann, *Public Opinion* (New York: Harcourt, Brace, 1922). On the movement to govern through technical expertise, see James A. Morone, *The Democratic Wish: Popular Participation and the Limits of American Government* (New Haven, CT: Yale University Press, 1998), chap. 3.

6. Michael S. Lewis-Beck, William G. Jacoby, Helmut Norpoth, and Herbert F. Weisberg, The American Voter Revisited (Ann Arbor: University of Michigan Press, 2008); Rick Shenkman, Just How Stupid Are We? Facing the Truth About the American Voter (New York: Basic Books, 2008).

7. James Surowiecki, *The Wisdom of Crowds* (New York: Doubleday, 2004), xii.

8. John F. Harris, *The Survivor: Bill Clinton in the White House* (New York: Random House, 2005), 331.

9. Harris, *The Survivor*, 159.

10. Lawrence R. Jacobs and Robert Y. Shapiro, *Politicians Don't Pander: Political Manipulation and the Loss of Democratic Responsiveness* (Chicago: University of Chicago Press, 2000).

11. Tocqueville, *Democracy in America*, 1: 189–95.

12. Larry M. Bartells, *Unequal Democracy: The Political Economy of the New Gilded Age* (Princeton, NJ: Princeton University Press, 2008).

13. Benjamin I. Page, Larry M. Bartels, and Jason Seawright, "Democracy and the Policy Preferences of Wealthy Americans,"

Paper delivered at the Annual Meeting of the American Political Science Association, 2011.

14. Donald P. Green and Alan S. Gerber, *Get Out the Vote: How to Increase Voter Turnout*, 2nd ed. (Washington, DC: Brookings Institution Press, 2008).

15. James H. Fowler, Laura A. Baker, and Christopher T. Dawes, "Genetic Variation in Political Participation," *American Political Science Review* 102, no. 2 (2008): 233–48.

16. Suzanne Mettler, *Soldiers to Citizens: The G.I. Bill and the Making of the Greatest Generation* (New York: Oxford University Press, 2005).

17. Doug McAdam, *Political Process and the Development of Black Insurgency, 1930–1970*, 2nd ed. (Chicago: University of Chicago Press, 1999).

18. John D. Griffin and Michael Keane, "Descriptive Representation and the Composition of African American Turnout," *American Journal of Political Science* 50, no. 4 (2006): 998–1012.

19. E. J. Dionne, *Why Americans Hate Politics: The Death of the Democratic Process* (New York: Simon & Schuster, 1991).

20. John Kenneth Galbraith, *The Culture of Contentment* (New York: Mariner Books, 1993).

21. Ron Fournier, "The Outsiders: How Can Millennials Change Washington If They Hate It?" *The Atlantic*, August 2013.

22. Clay Shirky, "The Political Power of Social Media: Technology, the Public Sphere, and Political Change," *Foreign Affairs* 90, no. 1 (January/February 2011).

23. See Matthew Hindman, *The Myth of Digital Democracy* (Princeton, NJ: Princeton University Press, 2009).

24. See Saul Levmore and Martha C. Nussbaum, eds., *The Offensive Internet* (Cambridge, MA: Harvard University Press, 2010).

Chapter 7 The Media

1. Albert Ibarguen, John S. and James L. Knight Foundation,

Senate Commerce, Science and Transportation Subcommittee on Communications, Technology and the Internet, May 6, 2009.

2. Darrell West, *The Next Wave: Using Digital Technology to Further Social and Political Innovation* (Washington, DC: Brookings Institution, 2011), 149.

3. Stuart Elliott, "Milk Campaign Ended Amid Social Media Firestorm," *New York Times*, July 21, 2011.

4. Doris Graber, *Mass Media and American Politics*, 8th ed. (Washington, DC: CQ Press, 2010), 203.

5. Eric Alterman, *What Liberal Bias? The Truth about Bias and the News* (New York: Basic, 2003).

6. Graber, *Mass Media and American Politics*, 266.

7. European media are increasingly overseen by the European Union, which creates different rules for three different sectors: public media, run by national governments (often the largest); commercial media; and fledgling community media. See Josef Trappel, Werner A. Meier, Leen d'Haenens, Jeanette Steemers, and Barbara Thomass, eds., *Media in Europe Today* (Chicago: Intellect, 2011).

8. The quotations are from a phrase used by Obama's campaign; Jay Leno on McCain; a bumper sticker criticizing Bush; and Robert Frank, "Romney's Top Ten Wealth Gaffes," *Wall Street Journal*, February 28, 2012.

Chapter 8 Campaigns and Elections

1. John Heilemann and Mark Halpern: *Double Down: Game Change 2012* (New York: Penguin, 2013); John Sides and Lynn Vavreck, *The Gamble: Choice and Chance in the 2012 Presidential Election* (Princeton, NJ: Princeton University Press, 2013).

2. Symposium: Forecasting the 2012 American National Elections. *PS Political Science and Politics*. October, 2012, Table 2, 612.

3. David Shribman, "In Canada, the Lean Season," *Boston Globe*, May 23, 1997.

4. Stephen J. Wayne, *The Road to the White House: 2012* (New York: Cengage, 2011).

5. Niall Stanage, "Speculation Begins Early on 2016 Presidential Race," *The Hill*, November 8, 2012.

6. See John Sides and Lynn Vavreck, "On the Representativeness of Primary Electorates," Paper presented at "Political Representation: Fifty Years after Miller and Stokes" conference, Vanderbilt University, March 1–2, 2013.

7. *Game Change*, 177–96.

8. Samuel Popkin, *The Candidate: What It Takes to Win—And Hold—The White House* (New York: Oxford University Press, 2012).

9. Nathan Burroughs, "The 'Money Primary' and Political Inequality in Congressional Elections," SSRN Working Paper, 2013.

10. Lacey Jackson-Matsushima, "New Jersey's Frelinghuysen Has Politics in His Blood," *FB Magazine*, July 21, 2011, http://www.financial-buzz.com/news/new-jerseys-frelinghuysen-has-politics-in-his-blood----blogger---lacey-jackson-matsushima/.

11. Jennifer L. Lawless and Richard L. Fox, *It Takes a Candidate: Why Women Don't Run for Office* (New York: Cambridge University Press, 2005).

12. *Shaw v. Reno*, 509 U.S. 630 (1993).

13. David Beiler, "Jon Corzine and the Power of Money," *Campaigns & Elections* 22:2 (2001), 22–23.

Chapter 9 Interest Groups and Political Parties

1. Mark Murray, "Poll: American Public Fed Up with Washington," NBC News, January 26, 2010, http://on.msnbc.com/oo7Tix/ (accessed July 21, 2011).

2. Paul S. Herrnson, Ronald G. Shaiko, and Clyde Wilcox, *The Interest Group Connection* (Chatham, NJ: Chatham House, 1998), 20.

3. For more on how AARP (and other membership groups) wield influence, see Peter Murray, "The Secret of Scale," *Stanford Social Innovation Review* (Fall 2013).

4. Jonathan Rauch, *Demosclerosis: The Silent Killer of American Government* (New York: Crown, 1994).

5. Kay Lehman Schlozman, Sidney Verba, and Henry Brady, *The Unheavenly Chorus: Unequal Political Voice and the Broken Promise of American Democracy* (Princeton, NJ: Princeton University Press, 2012) Chap. 1; E. Schnattschneider, *The Semi-Sovereign People: A Realist View of Democracy in America* (New York: Holt, Rinehart and Wilson, 1960), 35.

6. Mark Peterson, "Congress in the 1990s: From Iron Triangles to Policy Networks," in James Morone and Gary Belkin, eds., *The Politics of Health Care Reform* (Durham, NC: Duke University Press, 1994), 108, 127.

7. Quoted in Jack L. Walker Jr., *Mobilizing Interest Groups in America: Patrons, Professions, and Social Movements* (Ann Arbor: University of Michigan Press, 1991), 157.

8. Erin Delmore and Marisa M. Kashino, "How Many Lobbyists Are There?" *Washingtonian*, December 1, 2009 (at http://bit.ly/Tdmmb3/).

9. Jonathan D. Salant and Lizzie O'Leary, "Six Lobbyists per Lawmaker Work on Health Overhaul," *Bloomberg News*, August 14, 2009.

10. See Lee Fang, "Where Have All the Lobbyists Gone?" *The Nation*, March 17, 2014.

11. See Rogan Kersh, "Ten Myths About Health Lobbyists," in James A. Morone and Daniel C. Ehlke, eds., *Health Politics and Policy*, 5th ed. (Stamford, CT: Cengage, 2014).

12. Thomas Mann and Norman Ornstein, *It's Even Worse Than It Looks: How the American Constitutional System Collided with the New Politics of Extremism* (New York: Basic Books, 2012), Introduction.

13. John H. Aldrich, *Why Parties? The Origin and Transformation of Political Parties in America* (Chicago: University of Chicago Press, 1995).

14. See especially Teresa Amato, *Grand Illusion: The Myth of Voter Choice in a Two-Party Tyranny* (New York: New Press, 2009).

15. J. David Gillespie, *Challengers to Duopoly: Why Third Parties Matter in Two-Party American Politics* (Columbia: University of South Carolina Press, 2012).

16. R. Kent Newmeyer, *Supreme Court Justice Joseph Story: Statesman of the Old Republic* (Chapel Hill: University of North Carolina Press, 1985), 158.

17. Daniel Walker Howe, *What Hath God Wrought: The Transformation of America, 1815–1848* (New York: Oxford University Press, 2007).

18. Washington's text, and an informed commentary, is in Matthew Spalding and Patrick J. Garrity, *A Sacred Union of Citizens: George Washington's Farewell Address and the American Character* (Lanham, MD: Rowman & Littlefield, 1998).

19. Mark Losey, "Why I Am a Democrat," *Democratic Underground*, http://bit.ly/ oHsB2C (accessed July 24, 2011).

20. Orrin Hatch, "Why I Am a Republican," *Ripon Forum* 41, no. 6 (2008): 8.

21. See Katherine Tate, *Concordance* (Ann Arbor: The University of Michigan Press) 2014.

22. Alan S. Gerber et al., "Personality and Political Attitudes: Relationships Across Issue Domains and Political Contexts," *American Political Science Review* 104, no. 1 (2010): 11–133.

23. Marjorie Randon Hershey, *Party Politics in America*, 14th ed. (New York: Longman, 2010), 107.

24. Data from Pew Research Center for the People and the Press, "Partisan Polarization Surges in Bush and Obama Years," June 4, 201. http://www.people-press.org/2012/06/04/partisan-polarization-surges-in-bush-obama-years/.

25. David S. Broder, *The Party's Over: The Failure of Politics in America* (New York: Harper & Row, 1972); Martin P. Wattenberg, *The Decline of American Political Parties, 1952–1980* (Cambridge, MA: Harvard University Press, 1985).

26. John H. Aldrich and Melanie Freeze, "Political Participation, Polarization, and Public Opinion," in Paul M. Sniderman and Benjamin Highton, eds., *Facing the Challenge of Democracy: Explorations in the Analysis of Public Opinion and Political Participation* (Princeton, NJ: Princeton University Press, 2011).

27. Nancy Roman, "Bitter Fruits of Partisanship," *Baltimore Sun*, October 19, 2005.

28. David R. Mayhew, *Divided We Govern: Party Control, Investigations, and Lawmaking, 1946–2002*, 2nd ed. (New Haven, CT: Yale University Press, 2005).

29. Alan Abramowitz, *The Disappearing Center: Engaged Citizens, Polarization and American Democracy* (New Haven, CT: Yale University Press, 2010).

Chapter 10 Congress

1. Thomas E. Mann and Norman J. Ornstein, *The Broken Branch: How Congress Is Failing America and How to Get It Back on Track* (New York: Oxford University Press, 2006).

2. Robert A. Caro, *Master of the Senate: The Years of Lyndon Johnson* (New York: Knopf, 2002), 52.

3. For more along this line, see Mark Twain and Charles Dudley Warner, *The Gilded Age* (New York: Oxford University Press, 1996).

4. Barbara Sinclair, "The New World of U.S. Senators," in Lawrence Dodd and Bruce Oppenheimer, eds., *Congress Reconsidered*, 8th ed. (Washington, DC: CQ Press, 2009), 8.

5. Caro, *Master of the Senate*, 9.

6. Jane Mansbridge, "Rethinking Representation," *American Political Science Review* 97, no. 4 (2003): 515–528.

7. Lawrence R. Jacobs and Robert Y. Shapiro, *Politicians Don't Pander: Political Manipulation and the Loss of Democratic Responsiveness* (Chicago: University of Chicago Press, 2000).

8. Linda Greenhouse, "David E. Price; Professor in Congress Is Doing Homework on Theory and Reality," *New York Times*, February 11, 1988.

9. Public Policy Polling, "Congress Losing Out to Zombies, Wall Street, and . . . Hipsters." October 8, 2013. http://www.publicpolicypolling.com/ main/2013/10/congress-losing- out-to-zombies-wall-street-andhipsters.html/.

10. Juliet Eilperin, *Fight Club Politics: How Partisanship Is Poisoning the House of Representatives* (Lanham, MD: Rowman & Littlefield, 2007), 13.

11. Barbara Sinclair, *Unorthodox Lawmaking: New Legislative Procedures in the U.S. Congress*, 3rd ed. (Washington, DC: CQ Press, 2007), 71.

12. David R. Mayhew, *Divided We Govern: Party Control, Lawmaking, and Investigations, 1946–2002*, 2nd ed. (New Haven, CT: Yale University Press, 2005); Keith Krehbiel, *Pivotal Politics: A Theory of U.S. Lawmaking* (Chicago: University of Chicago Press, 1998).

13. Sarah Binder, *Stalemate: Causes and Consequences of Legislative Gridlock* (Washington, DC: Brookings Institution Press, 2003); Thomas Mann and Norman Ornstein, *It's Even Worse Than It Looks* (New York: Basic Books, 2012), 110.

Chapter 11 The Presidency

1. Joseph Ellis, *His Excellency: George Washington* (New York: Random House, 2004), 194–95.

2. Paul Harris, Kamal Ahmed, and Martin Bright, "Seeing Eye to Eye," *The Observer*, November 16, 2003, 1.

3. Ashley Parker, "'Imperial Presidency' Becomes a Rallying Cry for Republicans," March 31, 2014.

4. Kirk Scharfenberg, "Now It Can Be Told: The Story behind Campaign '82's Favorite Insult," *Boston Globe*, November 6, 1982.

5. See Daniel Galvin, "Presidents as Agents of Change," *Presidential Studies Quarterly* 44, no. 1 (2014), 95–119.

6. See Kevin Evans, "Challenging Law: Presidential Signing Statements and the Maintenance of Executive Power," *Congress and the Presidency* 38, no. 1 (2011). Electronic copy available at http://ssrn.com/abstract=1464334/.

7. Leonard White, *The Federalists* (New York: Macmillan, 1942).

8. For a description, see James Morone, *The Democratic Wish* (New Haven, CT: Yale University Press, 1998), 131.

9. Richard Neustadt, *Presidential Power and the Modern Presidents*, rev. ed. (New York: Free Press, 1991).

10. Samuel Kernel, *Going Public* (Washington, DC: CQ Press, 2007).

11. Lawrence R. Jacobs and Robert Y. Shapiro, *Politicians Don't Pander: Political Manipulation and the Loss of Democratic Responsiveness* (Chicago: University of Chicago Press, 2000).

12. Barbara Hinckley, *Follow the Leader: Opinion Polls and the Modern President* (New York: Basic Books, 1992).

13. Marc Landy and Sidney Milkis, *Presidential Greatness* (University Press of Kansas, 2001).

14. Stephen Skowronek, The Politics Presidents Make: Leadership from John Adams to Bill Clinton (Cambridge, MA: Harvard University Press, 1997).

15. Joseph Califano, *Governing America: An Insider's Report from the White House and the Cabinet* (New York: Simon & Schuster, 1981), 431, and personal interview with the authors, June 15, 2006.

16. Kevin Drum, "The Problem with Jon Stewart's Obamacare Interview," *Mother Jones* October 8, 2013. http://www.motherjones.com/ kevin-drum/2013/ 10/ jon-stewart-roasts- kathleen-sebelius-call-her-liar/.

17. For a fine description, see Matthew Dickinson, "The Executive Office of the President: The Paradox of Politicization," in Joel Aberbach and Mark Peterson, eds.,

The Executive Branch (New York: Oxford University Press, 2005).
18. Johnson quoted in Blumenthal and Morone, *Heart of Power*, 8.
19. President Barack Obama, "Address to the UN General Assembly," September 23, 2009.

Chapter 12 Bureaucracy

1. Gallup, "Trust In Government." http://www.gallup.com/poll/5392/trust-government.aspx/ (last accessed May 20, 2014).
2. Peter Konetchy for Congress (Michigan's Fourth District), at https://www.peterkonetchy.com/ (last accessed May 19, 2014).
3. Pew Research Center, "Trust in Government Nears Record Low, but Most Federal Agencies Regarded Favorably." http://bit.ly/SpJVEs/ (last accessed May 20, 2014).
4. William Riordon, *Plunkitt of Tammany Hall: A Series of Very Plain Talks on Very Practical Politics* (New York: Penguin, 1995).
5. James Sparrow, *Warfare State: World War II Americans and the Age of Big Government* (New York: Oxford University Press, 2012).
6. See Daniel Carpenter, *The Forging of Bureaucratic Autonomy: Reputations, Networks, and Policy Innovation in Executive Agencies* (Princeton, NJ: Princeton University Press, 2001); and James Morone, *Hellfire Nation: The Politics of Sin in American History* (New Haven, CT: Yale University Press, 2003).
7. Max Weber, "Bureaucracy," in H. H. Gerth and C. Wright Mills, eds., *From Max Weber: Essays in Sociology* (New York: Oxford, 1946), 196–98.
8. Steve Vogel, "Officials and Experts Praising FEMA for Its Response to Hurricane Sandy." *Washington Post*, November 1, 2012, A1.
9. Allison Stranger, *One Nation Under Contract: The Outsourcing of American Power and the Future of Foreign Policy* (New Haven, CT: Yale University Press, 2011).
10. Truman quoted in Richard Neustadt, *Presidential Power* (New York: Free Press, 1990), 10.

11. *RN: Memoirs of Richard Nixon* (New York: Simon & Schuster, 1990), 352.
12. Michael Lipsky, *Street-Level Bureaucracy: Dilemmas of the Individual in Public Services* (New York: Russell Sage, 1980).
13. Joe Soss, *Unwanted Claims: The Politics of Participation in the U.S. Welfare System* (Ann Arbor: University of Michigan Press, 2000).
14. Al Gore, *Common Sense Government: Works Better and Costs Less* (New York: Random House, 1995).

Chapter 13 The Judicial Branch

1. "Outside Terri Schiavo Hospice, A Crowd Waits," *Orlando Sentinel*, March 27, 2005.
2. Alexander Hamilton, Federalist no. 78.
3. John Murrin, "A Roof without Walls: The Dilemma of American National Identity," in Richard R. Beeman, Stephen Botein, and Edward Carlos Carter, eds., *Beyond Confederation: Origins of the Constitution and American Identity* (Chapel Hill: University of North Carolina Press, 1987).
4. John Schwartz, "Effort Begun to End Voting for Judges," *New York Times*, December 23, 2009.
5. Charlie Savage, "A Judge's View of Judging Is on the Record," *New York Times*, May 14, 2009.
6. Thomas Jefferson, "Letter to Justice Spencer Roane on the Limits of Judicial Review," in Thomas Jefferson, *Writings* (New York: Library of America, 1984), 1425–28.
7. Eleventh U.S. Circuit Court of Appeals, Docket No. 05-00530-CV-T-27-TBM (March 25, 2005), 14.
8. The case was *Worcester v. Georgia*, 1832.
9. Justice John Roberts, *Testimony before the Senate Judiciary Committee*, September 12, 2005.
10. Lee Epstein, Jeffrey A. Segal, Harold J. Spaeth, and Thomas G. Walker, *Supreme Court Compendium*, 4th ed. (Washington, DC: CQ Press, 2006).

11. Epstein et al., *Supreme Court Compendium*.
12. Adam Liptak, "In a Polarized Court, Getting the Last Word," *New York Times*, March 8, 2010.
13. Forrest Maltzman, James Spriggs, and Paul Wahlbeck, *Crafting Law on the Supreme Court: The Collegial Game* (New York: Cambridge University Press, 2000).
14. Thomas Keck, "Party, Policy, or Duty: Why Does the Supreme Court Invalidate Federal Statutes?" *American Political Science Review* 101, no. 2 (May 2007): 321 ff.
15. *McCulloch v. Maryland*, 17 U.S. (4 Wheat.) 316 (1819).
16. *Dred Scott v. Sandford*, 60 U.S. 393 (1857).

Chapter 14 Domestic and Foreign Policy

1. Deborah Stone, *Policy Paradox: The Art of Political Decision Making*, 3rd ed. (New York: Norton, 2011).
2. Woodrow Wilson, "The Study of Administration," *Political Science Quarterly* 2, no. 2 (1887): 197–222.
3. Paul Pierson, "When Effect Becomes Cause: Policy Feedback and Political Change," *World Politics* 45, no. 4 (1993): 595–628; for a recent overview of policy feedback and path dependence, see Daniel Béland, "Reconsidering Policy Feedback: How Policies Affect Politics," *Administration and Society* 42, no. 5 (2010): 568–90.
4. Walter I. Trattner, *From Poor Law to Welfare State*, 6th ed. (New York: Free Press, 1998).
5. American Medical Association, "Goldwater–Johnson: Remarks," *Washington News* 189, no. 3 (July 20, 1964): 3.
6. For a good insider's recap of the crisis and monetary-policy responses, see Timothy F. Geithner, *Stress Test: Reflections on Financial Crises* (New York: Random House, 2014), 258–387.
7. The most detailed accounting comes from Brown University's "Costs of War" study, at http://costsofwar.org/.

8. "The Open Doors Report on International Education Exchange," Institute of International Education, 2010. http://www.iie.org/en/Research-and-Publications/Open-Doors/.

9. Joseph Nye, *Soft Power: The Means to Success in World Politics* (New York: Public Affairs Books, 2004).

10. George Washington, Inaugural Address, New York City, April 30, 1789. You can find it here: http://www.bartleby.com/124/pres13.html/.

11. George Washington, Farewell Address: "To the People of the United States," September 19, 1796.

12. Robert Mann, *A Grand Delusion: America's Descent into Vietnam* (New York: Basic Books, 2002), 24.

13. Ken Waltz, "Why Iran Should Get the Bomb." *Foreign Affairs,* July/August 2012; John Mearsheimer, "Here We Go Again," *New York Times,* May 17, 1998, section 4, 17.

Credits

Photos

About the Authors
p. xv: Gabby Salazar; p. xiv: WFU/Ken Bennett

Preface
p. xvi: Joe Amon, The Denver Post

Chapter 1
p. 2: AP Photo/Jerome Delay; p. 6: © Bettmann/CORBIS; p. 10: © Bettmann/CORBIS; p. 12: http://www.saturdayeveningpostcovers.com/frame/60937/; © SEPS. All Rights Reserved; p. 18: AP Photo/Doug Mills; p. 21: © Bettmann/CORBIS; p. 23: Photo by MPI/Getty Images; p. 30: AP Photo/Lynne Sladky; p. 30: JustASC/Shutterstock.com Copyright © 2003–2012 Shutterstock Images LLC; p. 35: DOONESBURY © 2011 G. B. Trudeau. Reprinted with permission of UNIVERSAL UCLICK. All rights reserved

Chapter 2
p. 42: Time & Life Pictures/Getty Images; p. 42: Records of the Continental and Confederation Congresses and the Constitutional Convention, 1774–1789, Record Group 360; p. 46: National Archives; p. 68: Signing of the Mayflower Compact Edward Percy Moran (1862–1935 American) © SuperStock/SuperStock; p. 50: Image copyright © The Metropolitan Museum of Art. Image source: Art Resource, NY; p. 54: The Art Archive at Art Resource, NY; p. 56: The Granger Collection, NYC—All rights reserved; p. 58: Courtesy of the Saint Louis Art Museum/The County Election; Saint Louis Art Museum, Gift of Bank of America 45:2001; p. 62: Commissioned by Delaware, Pennsylvania, and New Jersey State Societies Daughters of the American Revolution Independence National Historical Park Collection, 1987; p. 68: Leap of the Fugitive Slave/Brown, William Wells, 1814?–1884—Author. Courtesy Library of Congress; p. 76: Getty Images; p. 80: AP Photo/Norm Shafer

Chapter 3
p. 85: AP Photo/Haraz N. Ghanbari; p. 87: Copyright Brooks Kraft/Corbis/APImages; p. 91: New York Times/Trip Gabirel; p. 92: AP Photo/Mike Groll; p. 97: Copyright Bettmann/Corbis/AP Images; p. 99: "In Two Words, Yes and No." A 1949 Herblock Cartoon, copyright by The Herb Block Foundation; p. 102: Jason Reed/Reuters; p. 108: p. 135: *Fourth of July Celebration in Centre Square, Philadelphia in 1819* (engraving), Krimmel; p. 109: *The First American Macadam Road* by Carl Rakeman (1823). Federal Highway Administration, United States Department of Transportation

Chapter 4
p. 112: AP Photo/David Goldman, File; p. 120: AP Photo/Doug Mills; p. 121: AP Photo/David J. Phillip; p. 122: © Lee Snider/Photo Images/Corbis; p. 125: AP Photo/Javier Galeano; p. 128: AP Photo/Al Maglio; p. 129: Mark Peterson/Redux/eyevine; p. 132: © Tribune Media Services, Inc. All Rights Reserved. Reprinted with permission; p. 140: Copyright Bettmann/Corbis/AP Images

Chapter 5
p. 146: David E. Klutho/Getty; p. 150: © Bettmann/CORBIS; p. 151: Bill Clark/Getty; p. 152: The Granger Collection, NYC—All rights reserved; p. 156: Courtesy Art.com; p. 158: Copyright Bettmann/Corbis/AP Images; p. 159: Copyright Bettmann/Corbis/AP Images; p. 161: Copyright Bettmann/Corbis/AP Images; p. 161: AP Photo/str; p. 163: Declan Haun/Getty; p. 172: Pan-American Unity: The Plastification of the Creative Power of the Northern Mechanism by Union with the Plastic Tradition of the South, 1940 (fresco), Rivera, Diego (1886–1957)/City College of San Francisco, California, USA/Photo © 1985 The Detroit Institute of Arts/The Bridgeman Art Library; p. 173: Photo courtesy Stanford Libraries; p. 175: AP Photo/Matt Rourke; p. 180: Copyright Bettmann/Corbis/AP Images

Chapter 6
p. 188: Getty/The Washington Post/Contributor; p. 200: Cartoonstock/Baloo -Rex May-; p. 200: 04-07-10 © Pamela Cowart-Rickman Copyright © 2012 iStockphoto LP; p. 207: Reuters/Jeff Haynes; p. 208: AP Photo/Office of Rep. Gabrielle Giffords; p. 208: © The Gallery Collection/Corbis; p. 213: AP

Gallup retains all rights of republication; p. 9: Created by OUP based on data from usgovernmentspending.com; p. 26: Created by OUP based on data from the OECD; p. 26: Christopher Chantrill, usgovernmentspending.com

Chapter 2
p. 49: Helen Hornbeck Tanner, Atlas of Great Lakes Indian History (Norman, Univ. of OK Press, 1987)

Chapter 3
p. 89: Pew Research Center for the People and the Press

Chapter 4
p. 137: Created by OUP based on data from Computed from Justice Policy Institute and the and U.S. Bureau of Justice; p. 141: Created by OUP based on data from CEPR/ICPS; p. 153: Created by OUP based on data from the Pew Research Center

Chapter 5
p. 166: Created by OUP based on data from the U.S. Census Bureau; p. 169: Created by OUP based on data from the U.S. Census Bureau; p. 169: Created by OUP based on data from the Pew Center on the States; p. 175: Created by OUP based on data from the U.S. Census Bureau; p. 177: Created by OUP based on data from the U.S. Census Bureau; p. 178: Created by OUP based on data from the U.S. Census Bureau; p. 181: Created by OUP based on data from the U.S. Census Bureau and the Pew Research Center

Chapter 6
p. 194: Created by OUP based on data from Edison Research, Associated Press, and CNN; p. 195: Created by OUP based on data from the Pew Center on the States; p. 196: Created by OUP based on data from the Inter-Parliamentary Union; p. 207: Created by OUP based on data from the U.S. Census Bureau; p. 208: Created by OUP based on data from the U.S. Census Bureau; p. 211: Created by OUP based on data from the U.S. Census Bureau; p. 212: Created by OUP based on data from the U.S. Census Bureau and the Pew Research Center

Chapter 7
p. 235: Created by OUP based on data from the Pew Research Center; p. 237: Created by OUP based on data from the Brookings Institution, 2009 Survey of Millennials

Chapter 8
p. 256: Created by OUP based on data from the Federal Election Commission and opensecrets.org; p. 258: Created by OUP based on data from opensecrets.org

Chapter 9
p. 297: Created by OUP based on data from the Center for Responsive Politics; p. 309: Created by OUP based on data from the Pew Research Center 2012 Values Survey

Chapter 10
p. 350: Created by OUP based on data from the Federal Election Commission and opensecrets.org; p. 353: Created by OUP based on data from opensecrets.org

Chapter 11
p. 367: Created by OUP based on data from the Pew Research Center 2012 Values Survey; p. 381: Created by OUP based on data from the Pew Research Center 2012 Values Survey; p. 382: Created by OUP based on data from Gallup

Chapter 12
p. 405: U.S. Department of Energy Created by OUP based on data from the U.S. Senate; p. 409: Created by OUP based on data from the Office of Management and Budget

Chapter 13
p. 435: Created by OUP based on data from Gallup; p. 456: Created by OUP based on data from the Administrative Office of the U.S. Courts/Federal Judiciary

Chapter 14
p. 483: Created by OUP based on data from the Congressional Budget Office; p. 493: Created by OUP based on data from the World Bank Group

Index

Note: *f* refers to figure and *t* refers to table. Page numbers in italics refer to photographs or illustrations.

presidential election victory
(1800), 303–4
presidential greatness ranking,
383t
on secrecy in republic, 56
as slave-owner, 52
Jehovah's Witnesses, 121, 144
jeopardy, double, 117t, 138–39
Jim Crow laws, 156, 158, 165, 186,
217, 459
jobs, of presidency, 366–78
Johns, Barbara, 42, 43
Johnson, Andrew, 383t
Johnson, Gregory Lee, 129
Johnson, Lyndon Baines ("LBJ"),
379f, 381f, 384t
Jones, Terry, 113
judges
decision making, 454–57
diversity, 441–42
selection, 437–38
judicial activism, 445
Judicial Branch, 430–67. See also
federal courts; state courts;
Supreme Court
checks and balances, 63–64,
64f, 67, 81
federalism in, 103–5, 104t
introduction, 431–33
lawyers, 434–36
By the Numbers, 433
organization of, 436–42
separation of powers, 63–64, 64f
summary of ideas, 466–67
Terri Schiavo case, 431–32, 437,
439, 440
judicial federalism, 436
judicial restraint, 445
judicial review, 444
Juneau-Douglas High School, 130

Kagan, Elena, 294f, 448f, 451, 452,
453f, 454t, 455
Kennedy, John F., 261t, 381f, 384t
Kennedy, Ted, 390, 452
Kerry, John, 193f, 200, 259, 261t
King, Martin Luther, Jr., 21, 24,
158, 161, 209
King, Rodney, 139
Kingdon, John, 20
King of the Hill rule, 338, 349
King Philip's War, 179
Klopfer v. North Carolina, 117t
Korematsu, Fred, 461, 461f
Korematsu v. U.S., 461
Krehbiel, Keith, 354
K Street, 283
Ku Klux Klan, 128–29, 155

"land of the free," 11
language controversy, Latinos,
174–75
Late Show with David
Letterman, 233
Latinos (Hispanics), 172–77.
See also immigration
caucus, 176, 325
as CEOs of Fortune 500
companies, 178t
Chicanismo, 173
countries of origin, 175f
discrimination challenges,
172–73
immigration politics, 85, 151f,
173–74
language controversy, 174–75
political mobilization of, 175–77
in poverty, 166f, 181f
protests (1960s), 173
race and ethnicity
(1970–2060), 9f
United Farm Workers, 173
voter turnout, 213f
Lau v. Nichols, 174–75
Law of the Land, 60, 71, 76, 95, 445
Lawrence, John Geddes, 121f
Lawrence v. Texas, 120–21, 121f
laws. See specific laws
laws of coverture, 168
lawsuits. See litigation
lawyers, 434–36
layer cake federalism. See dual
federalism
LBJ. See Johnson, Lyndon Baines
leadership
House, 337–39
presidency, 378–85
Senate, 339–40
LeBron, James, 30f
Ledbetter, Lilly, 170, 187
left-wing. See liberals
legislative hold, 328–29
legislative policy making, 343–52.
See also public policy
making
Lemon test, 123, 124, 125, 144,
145, 463
Lemon v. Kurtzman, 123, 462–63
lesbian, gay, bisexual, and
transgender (LGBT)
communities, 183, 184, 186.
See also same-sex relations
Letter from Birmingham Jail, 209
Letterman, David, 233, 270
LGBT. See lesbian, gay, bisexual,
and transgender
communities

libel, 133, 240
liberals, 17–18
libertarians, 12
liberty. See freedom
life, liberty, and pursuit of
happiness, 10, 41, 52, 82, 147
life expectancy, 167t, 181f
likely voters, 197, 204
Lilly Ledbetter Law, 170, 187
Limbaugh, Rush, 237
limited government. See also
American ideas
defined, 40
described, 16–20
libertarians, 12
limits on government action, 18
origins of, 17
paradox of, 17–18
self-rule versus, 19–20
Lincoln, Abraham. See also
Civil War
Cabinet members, 388
on Civil War and slavery, 66
coattails term, 336
Emancipation Proclamation,
154, 157
Gettysburg Address, 154, 222
"government of the people, by
the people, for the
people," 16, 154, 157, 222
military actions, during Civil
War, 363
Pan-American Unity mural, 172f
presidency (1860), 153–54, 304
presidential aides, 393
presidential greatness ranking,
382, 383t
Lippman, Walter, 201
literacy tests, 155, 162, 216
Literary Digest, 197
litigation (lawsuits), 434, 436, 446
Little, Malcolm (Malcolm X), 147
Little Rock, Central High School,
159, 159f
lobbying, 285–98. See also interest
groups
conclusion, 319–21
courts, 294–95
defined, 286
demosclerosis, 290
federal branches of
government, 291–95
Federal Regulation of Lobbying
Act (1946), 319
gift ban on, 320
intergovernmental, 102,
293–94, 295
public interest, 289